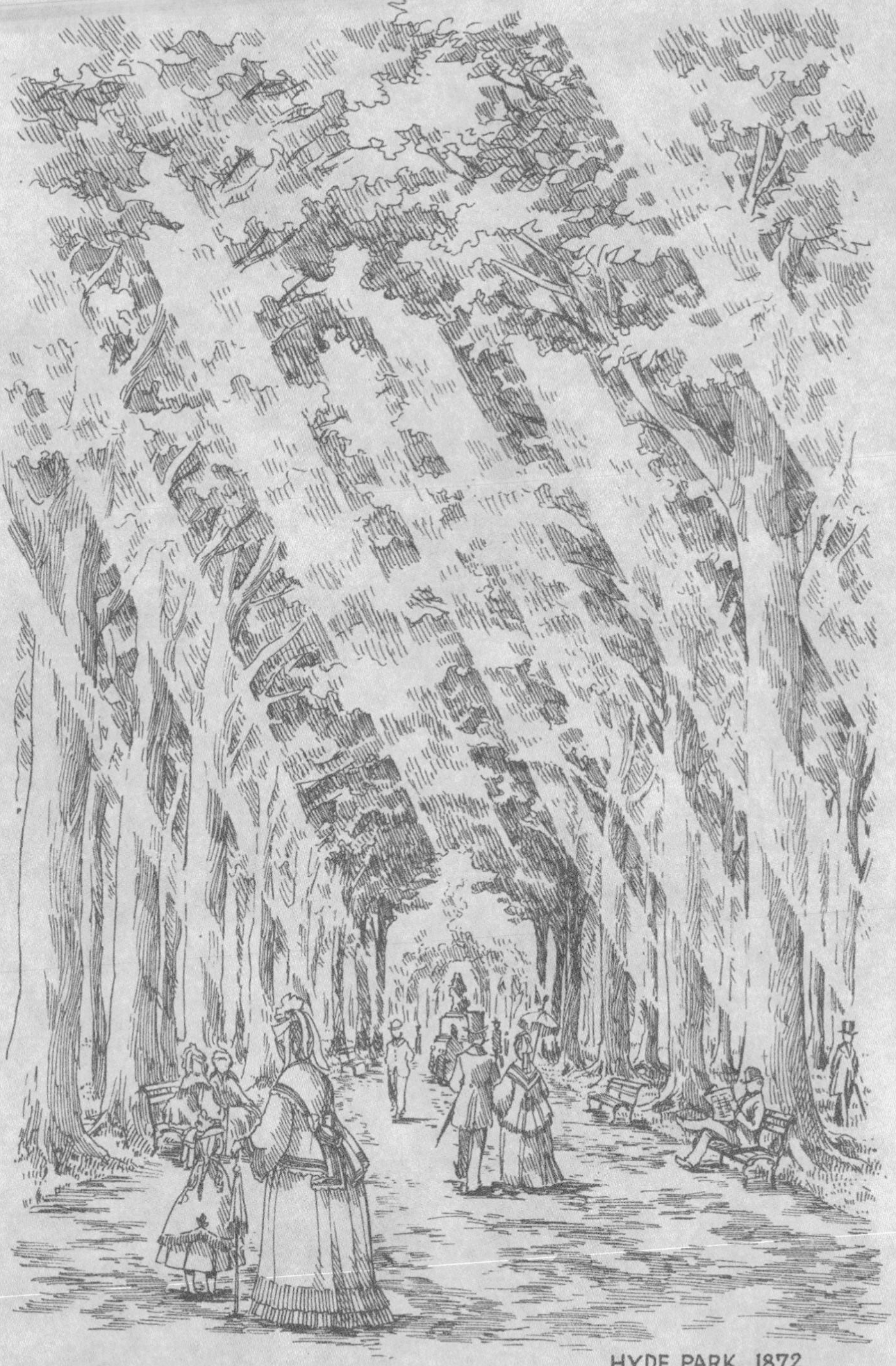
HYDE PARK 1872

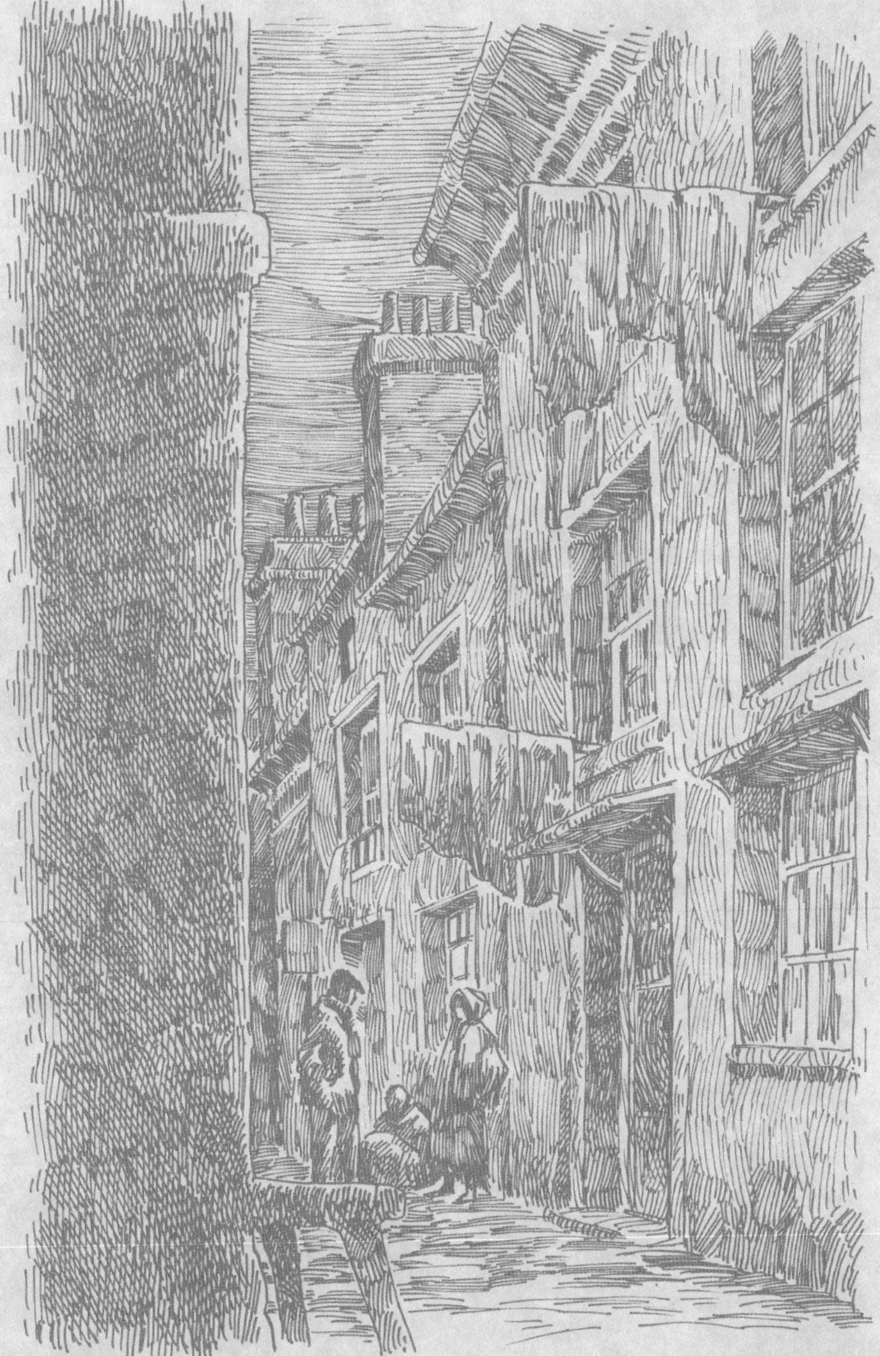

WHITE CHAPEL 1895

Emma

3

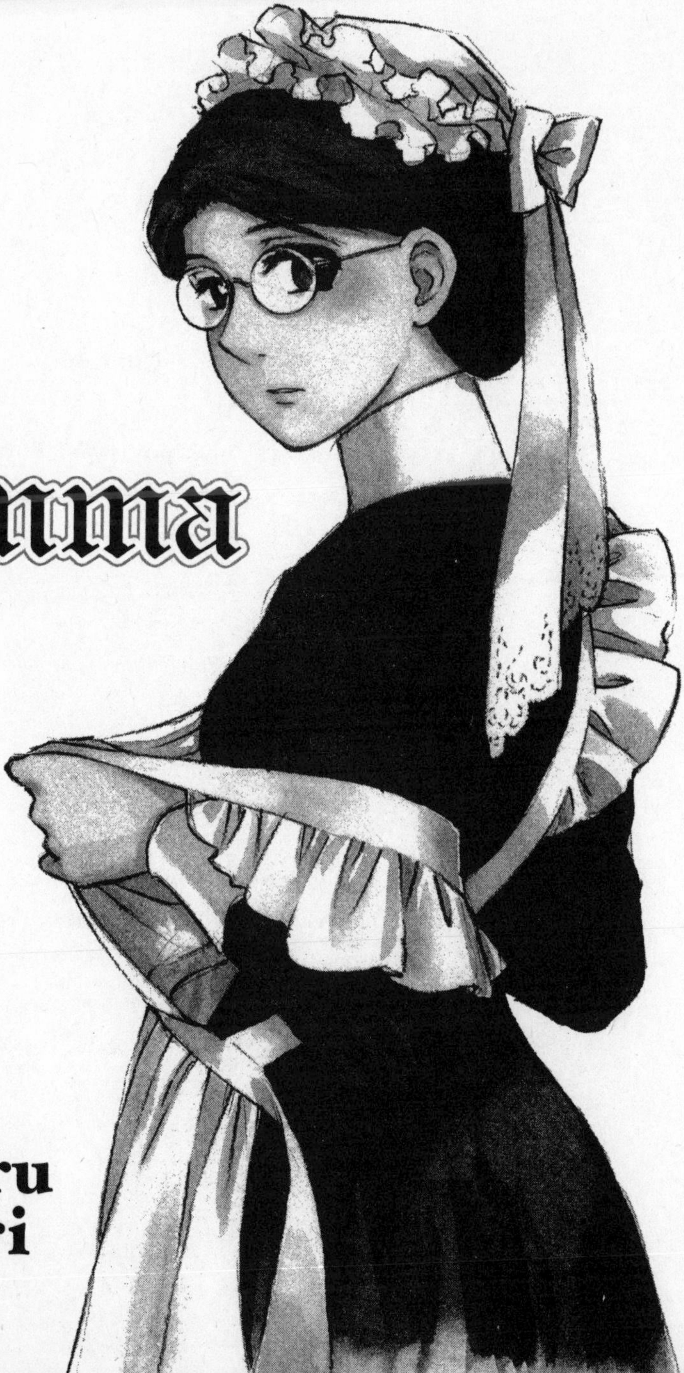

Kaoru
Mori

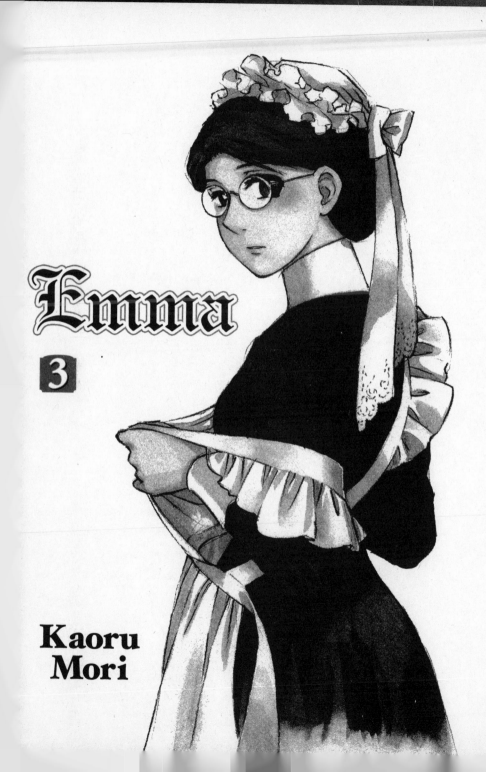

-Contents-

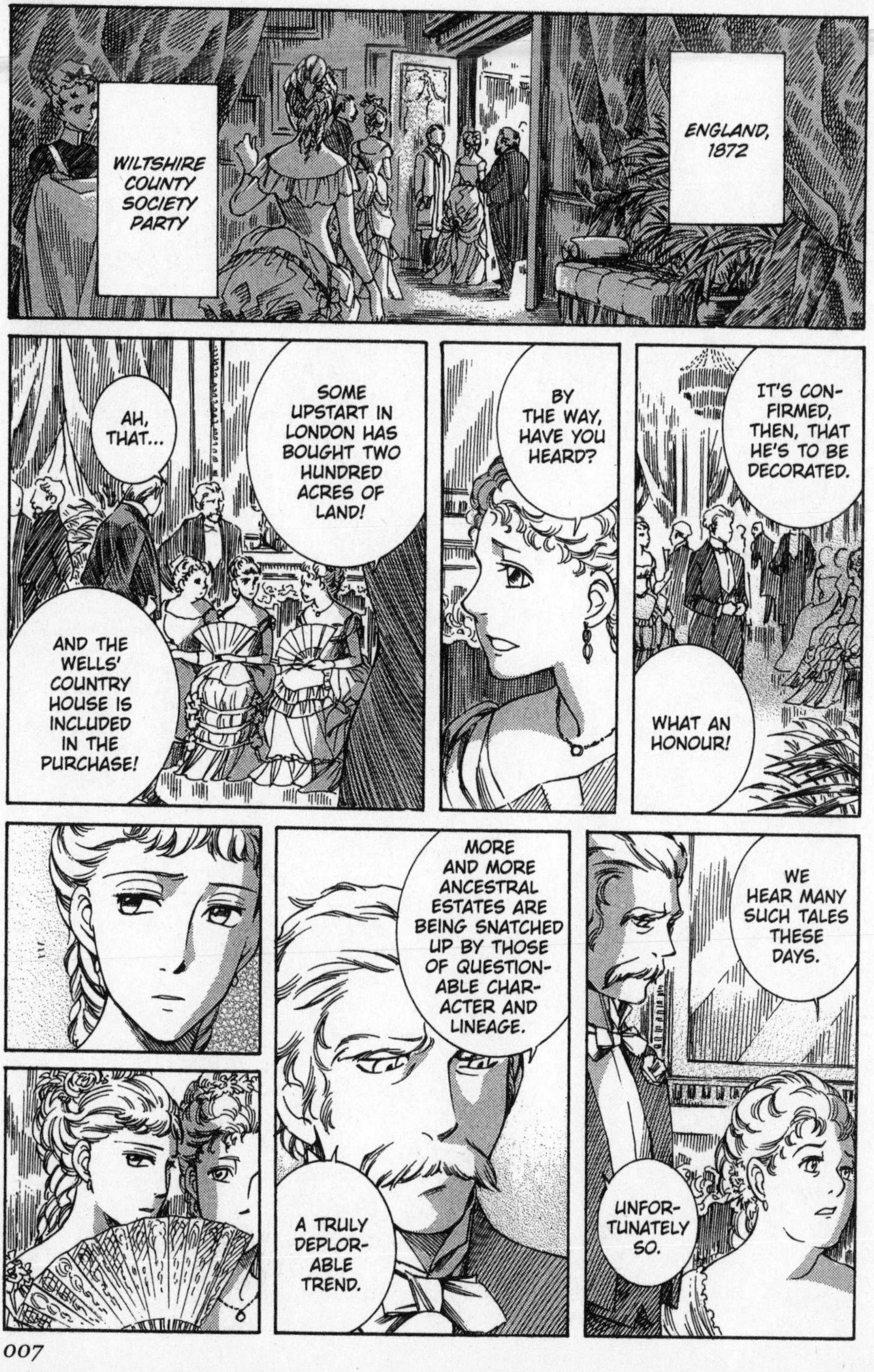
ENGLAND, 1872
WILTSHIRE COUNTY SOCIETY PARTY
IT'S CONFIRMED, THEN, THAT HE'S TO BE DECORATED.
WHAT AN HONOUR!
BY THE WAY, HAVE YOU HEARD?
SOME UPSTART IN LONDON HAS BOUGHT TWO HUNDRED ACRES OF LAND!
AH, THAT...
AND THE WELLS' COUNTRY HOUSE IS INCLUDED IN THE PURCHASE!
WE HEAR MANY SUCH TALES THESE DAYS.
UNFORTUNATELY SO.
MORE AND MORE ANCESTRAL ESTATES ARE BEING SNATCHED UP BY THOSE OF QUESTIONABLE CHARACTER AND LINEAGE.
A TRULY DEPLORABLE TREND.

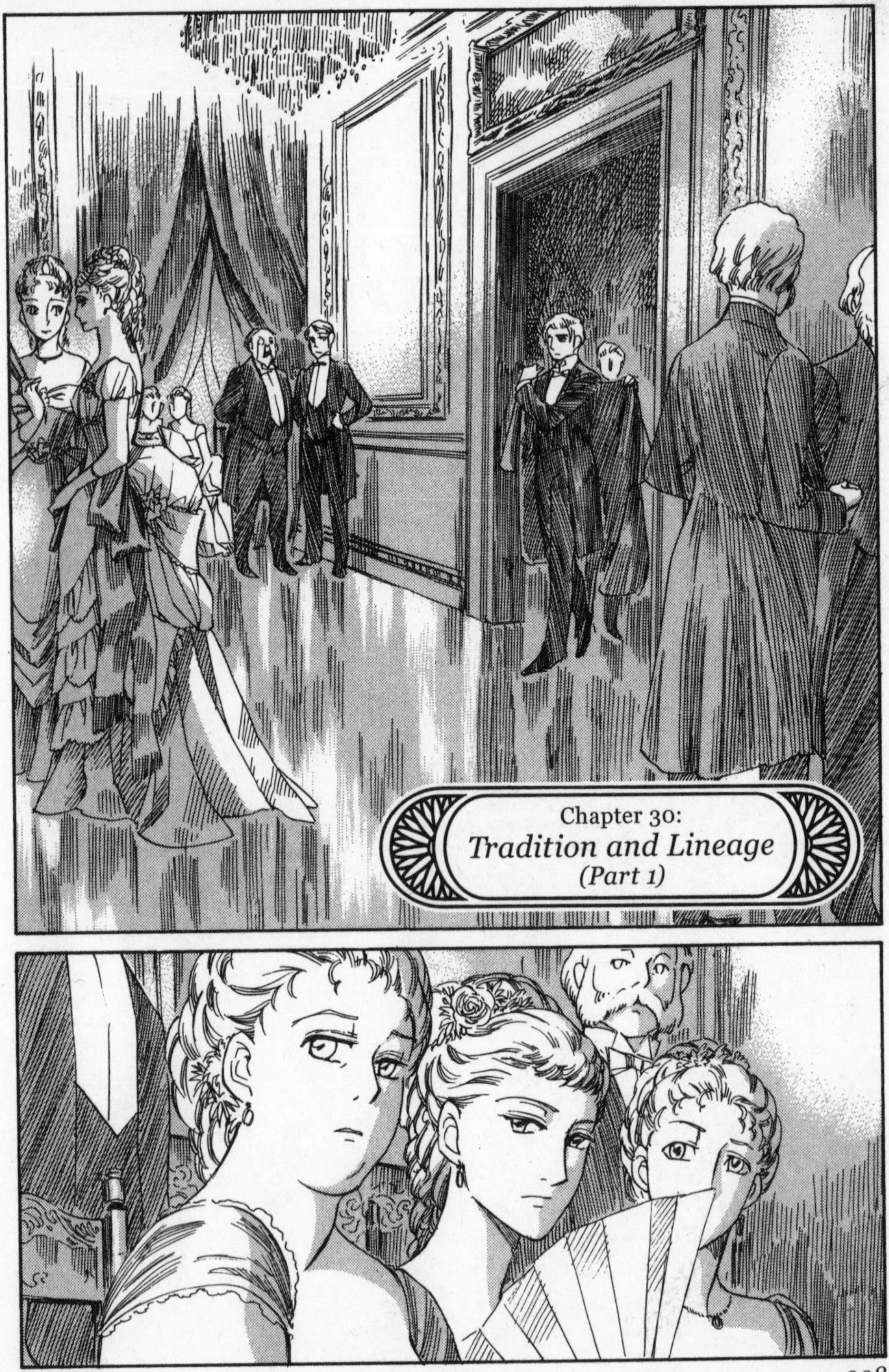
Chapter 30:
Tradition and Lineage
(Part 1)

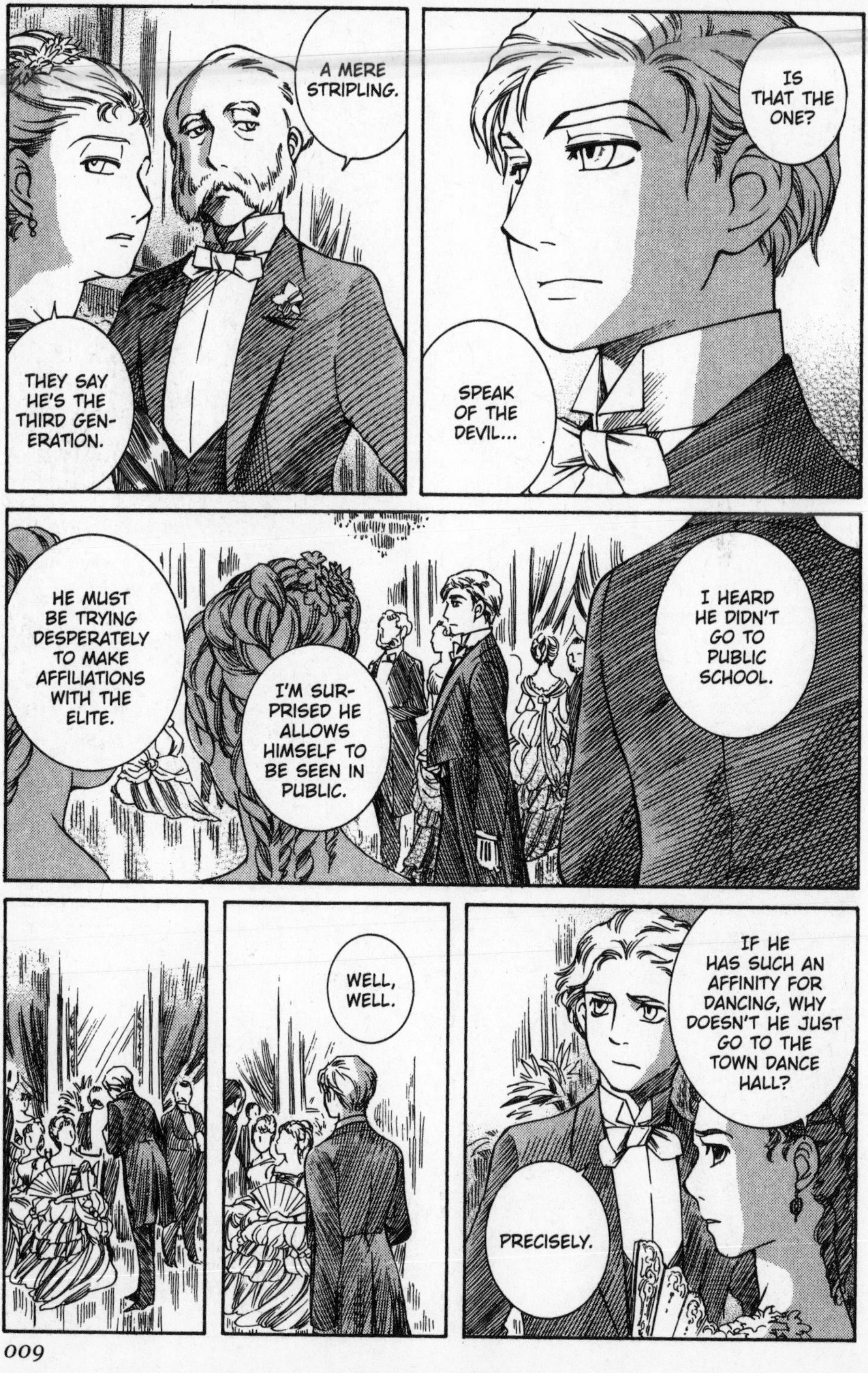
IS THAT THE ONE?
SPEAK OF THE DEVIL...
A MERE STRIPLING.
THEY SAY HE'S THE THIRD GENERATION.
I HEARD HE DIDN'T GO TO PUBLIC SCHOOL.
I'M SURPRISED HE ALLOWS HIMSELF TO BE SEEN IN PUBLIC.
HE MUST BE TRYING DESPERATELY TO MAKE AFFILIATIONS WITH THE ELITE.
IF HE HAS SUCH AN AFFINITY FOR DANCING, WHY DOESN'T HE JUST GO TO THE TOWN DANCE HALL?
PRECISELY.
WELL, WELL.

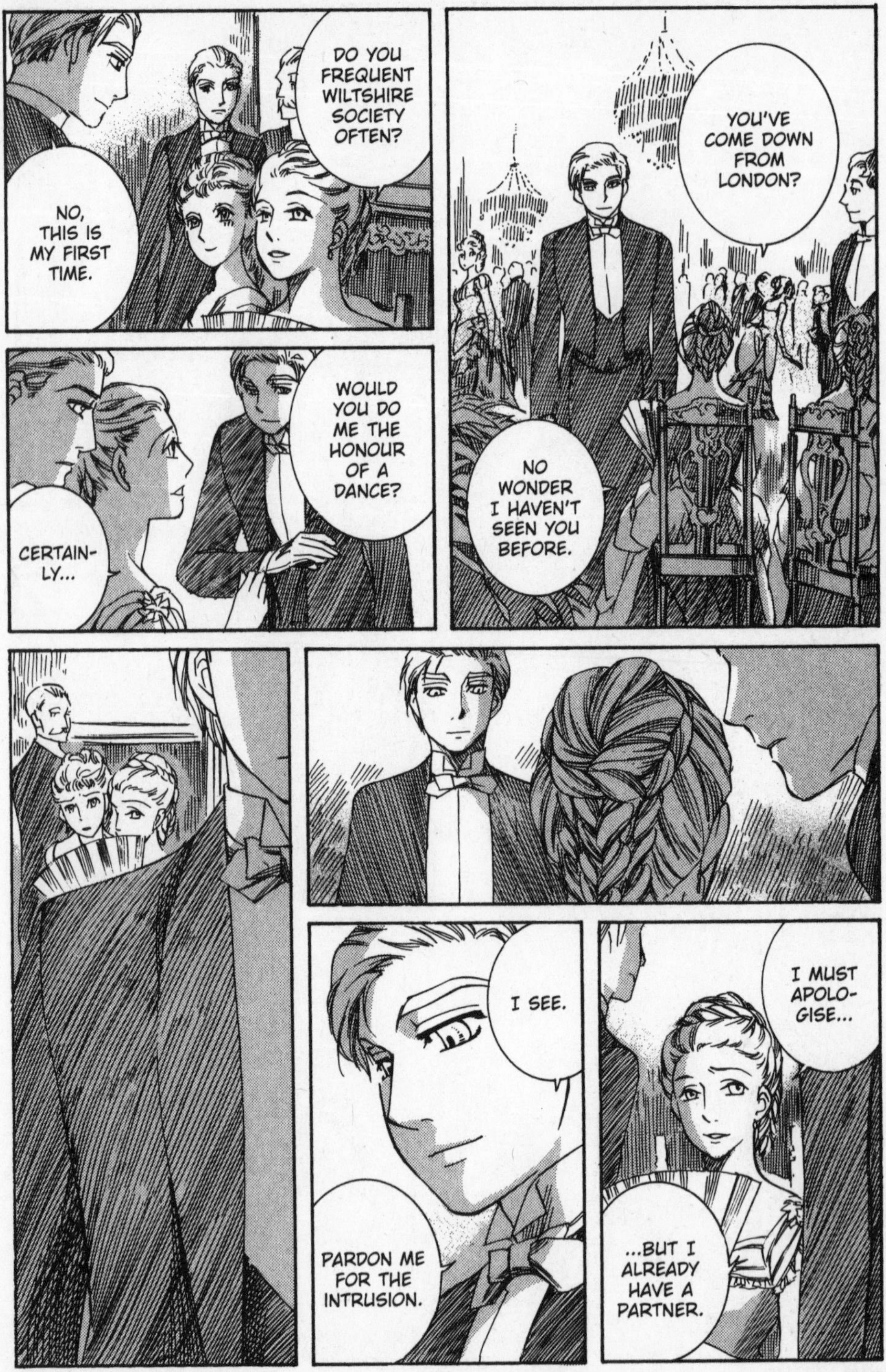
YOU'VE COME DOWN FROM LONDON?
NO WONDER I HAVEN'T SEEN YOU BEFORE.
DO YOU FREQUENT WILTSHIRE SOCIETY OFTEN?
NO, THIS IS MY FIRST TIME.
WOULD YOU DO ME THE HONOUR OF A DANCE?
CERTAIN-LY...
I MUST APOLO-GISE...
...BUT I ALREADY HAVE A PARTNER.
I SEE.
PARDON ME FOR THE INTRUSION.

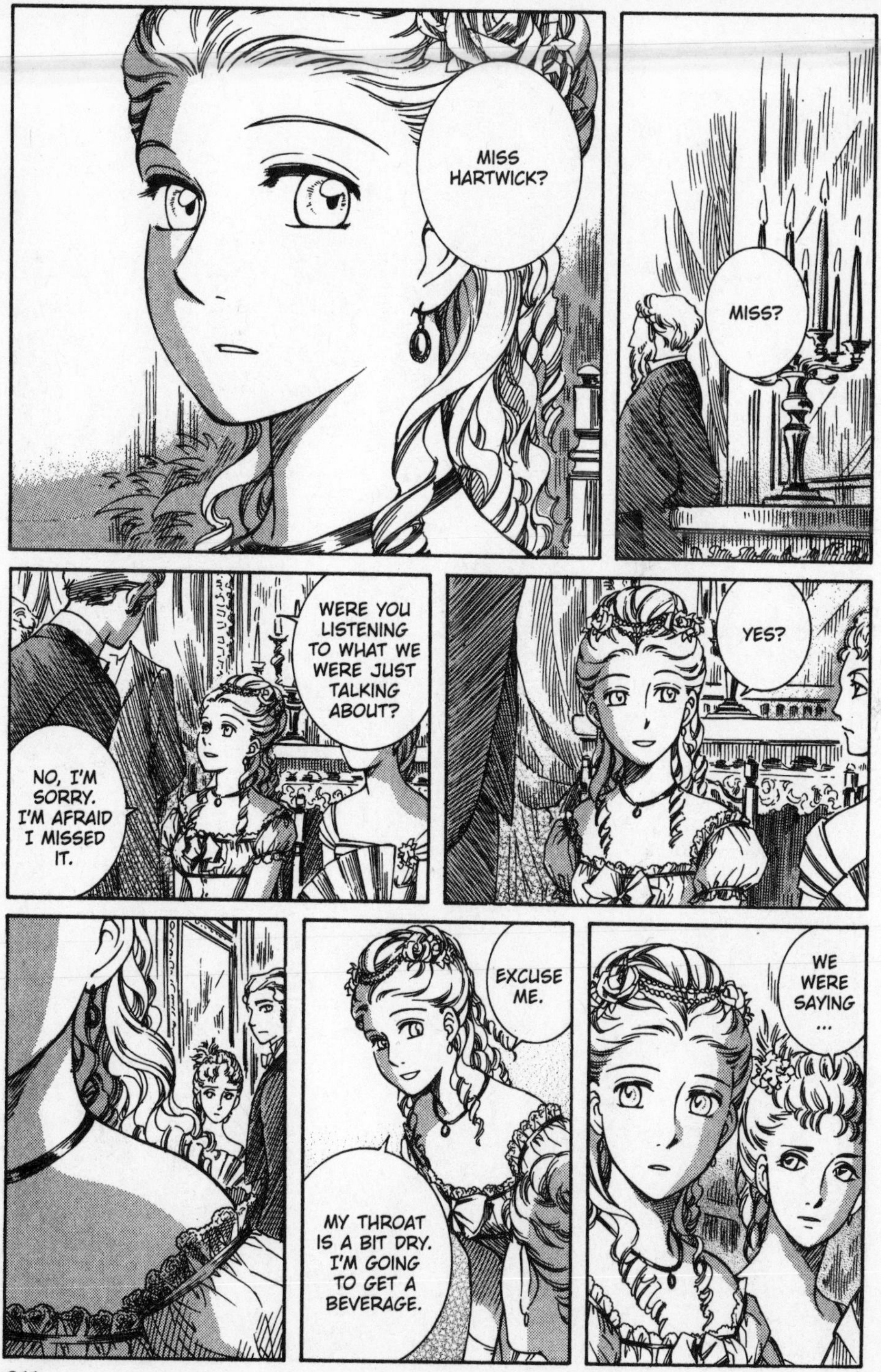
MISS?
MISS HARTWICK?
YES?
WERE YOU LISTENING TO WHAT WE WERE JUST TALKING ABOUT?
NO, I'M SORRY. I'M AFRAID I MISSED IT.
WE WERE SAYING ...
EXCUSE ME.
MY THROAT IS A BIT DRY. I'M GOING TO GET A BEVERAGE.

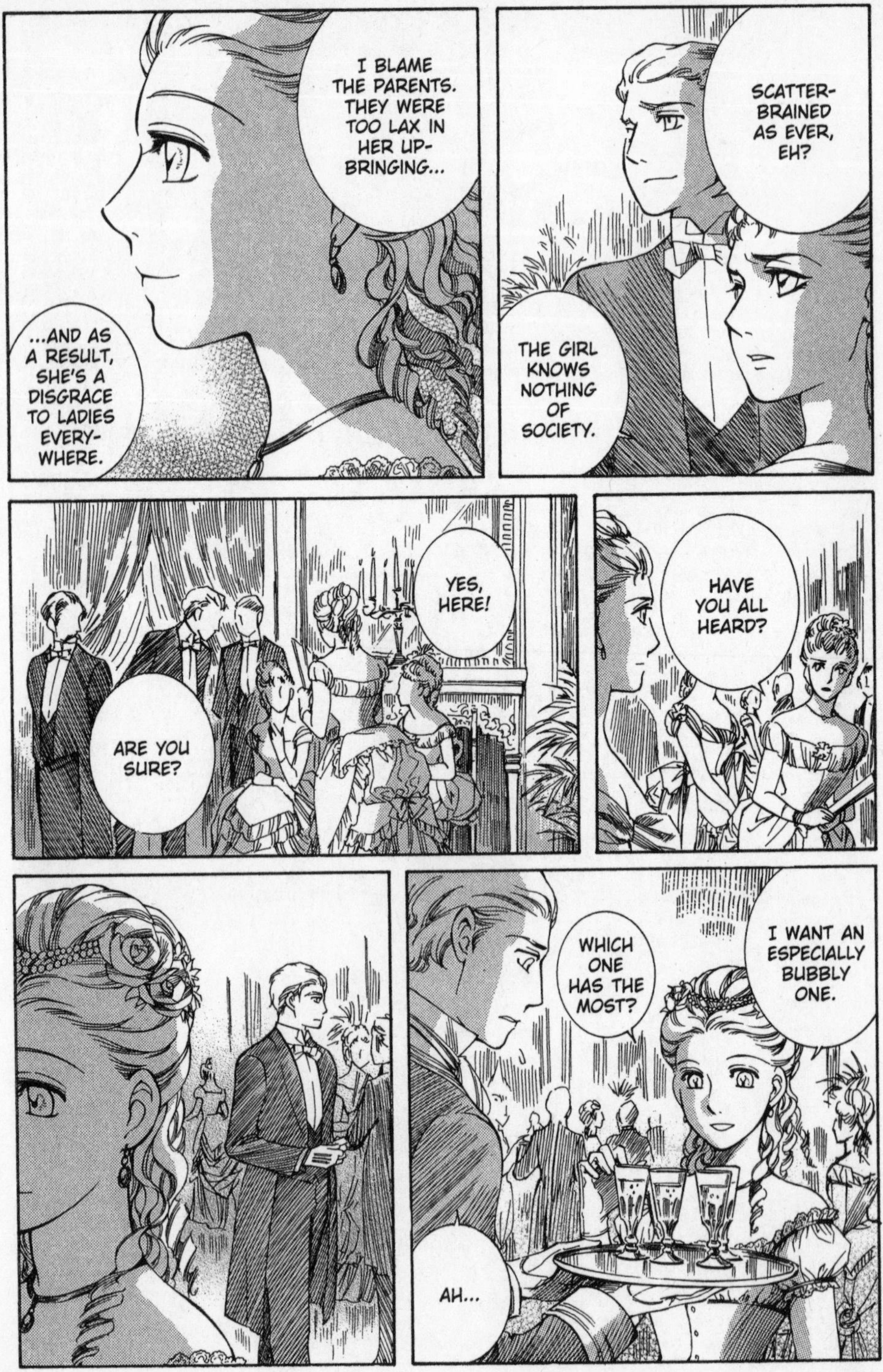
SCATTER-BRAINED AS EVER, EH?
THE GIRL KNOWS NOTHING OF SOCIETY.
I BLAME THE PARENTS. THEY WERE TOO LAX IN HER UP-BRINGING...
...AND AS A RESULT, SHE'S A DISGRACE TO LADIES EVERY-WHERE.
HAVE YOU ALL HEARD?
YES, HERE!
ARE YOU SURE?
I WANT AN ESPECIALLY BUBBLY ONE.
WHICH ONE HAS THE MOST?
AH...

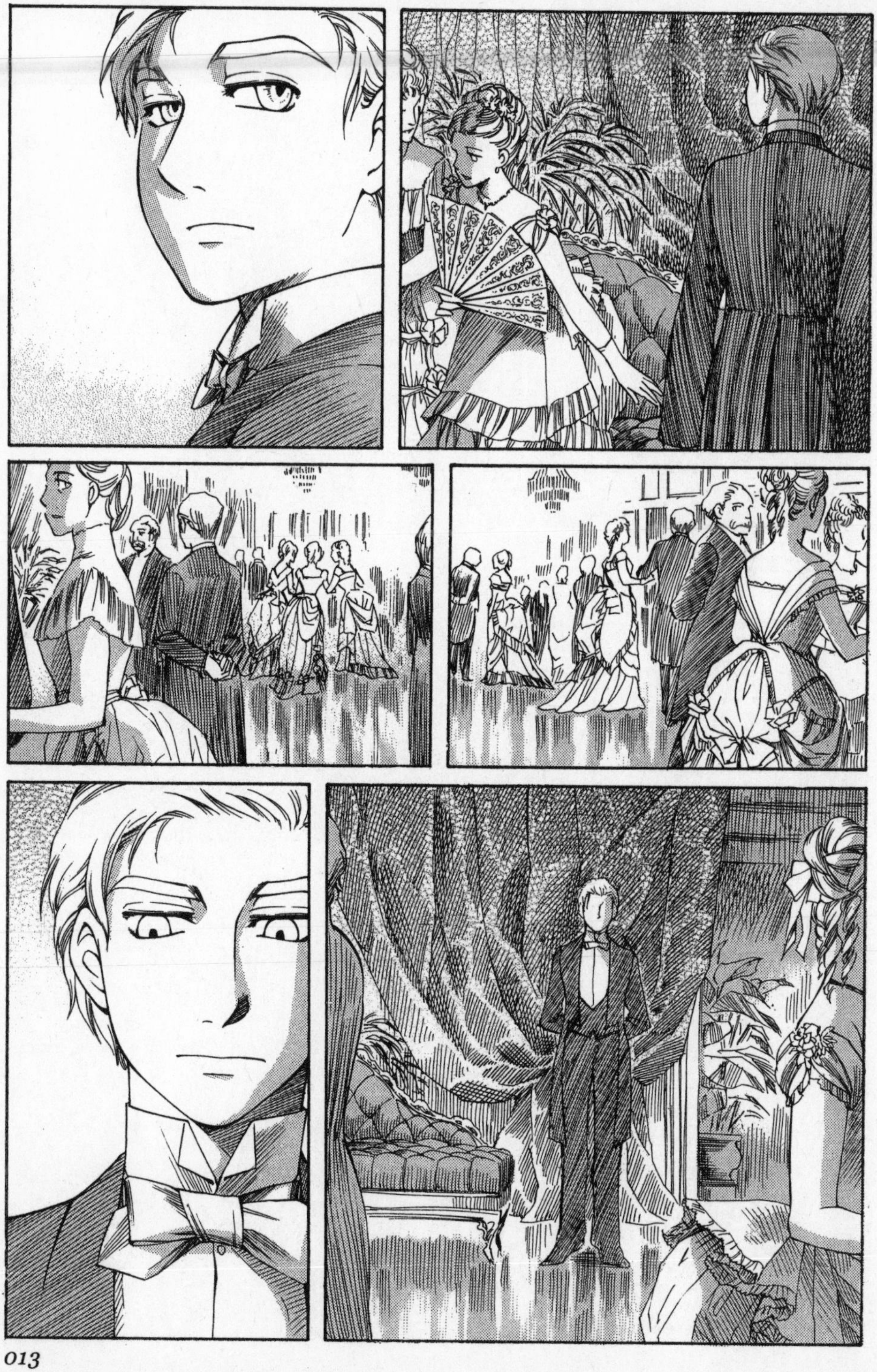

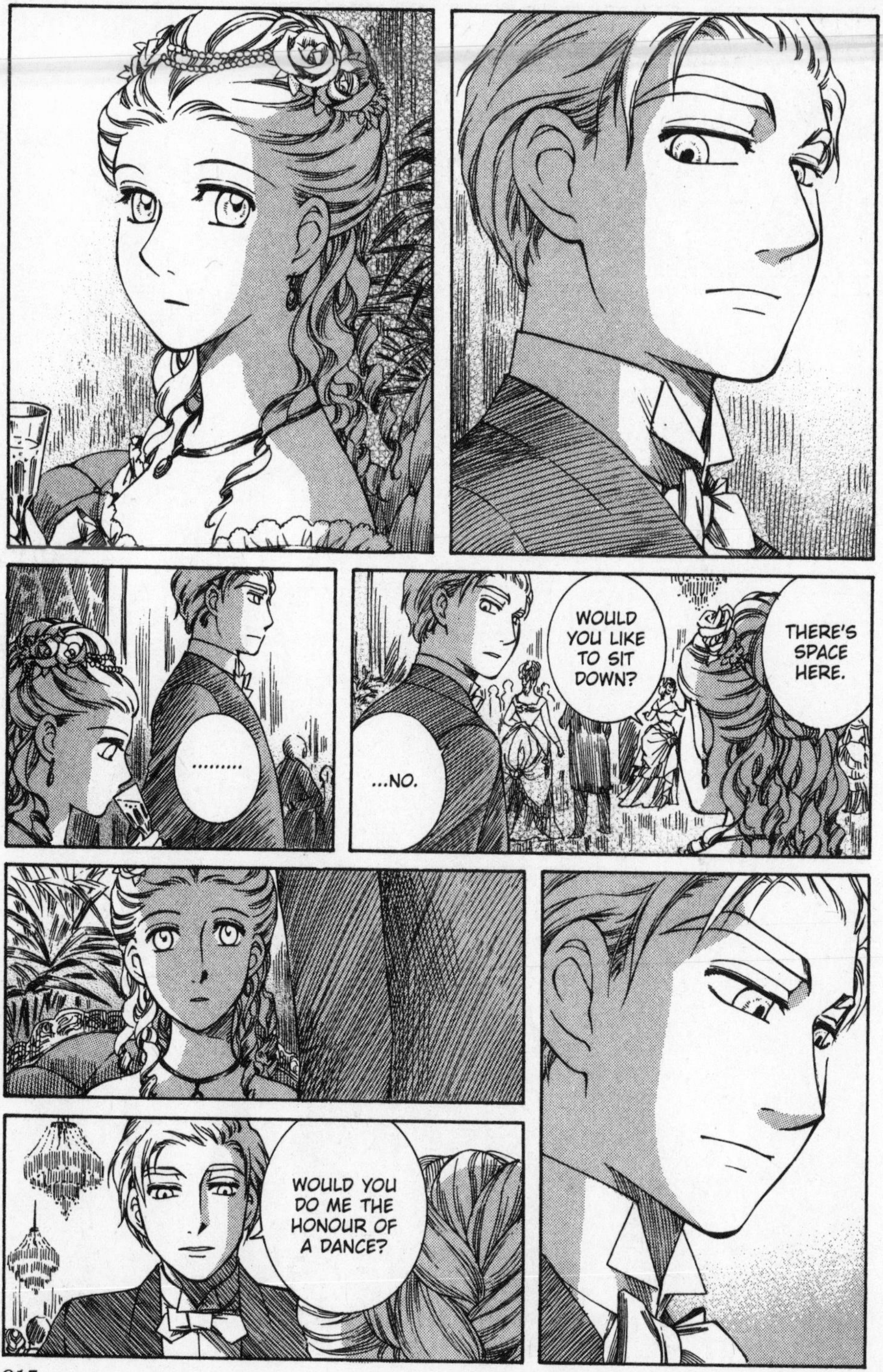
THERE'S SPACE HERE.
WOULD YOU LIKE TO SIT DOWN?
...NO.
....
WOULD YOU DO ME THE HONOUR OF A DANCE?

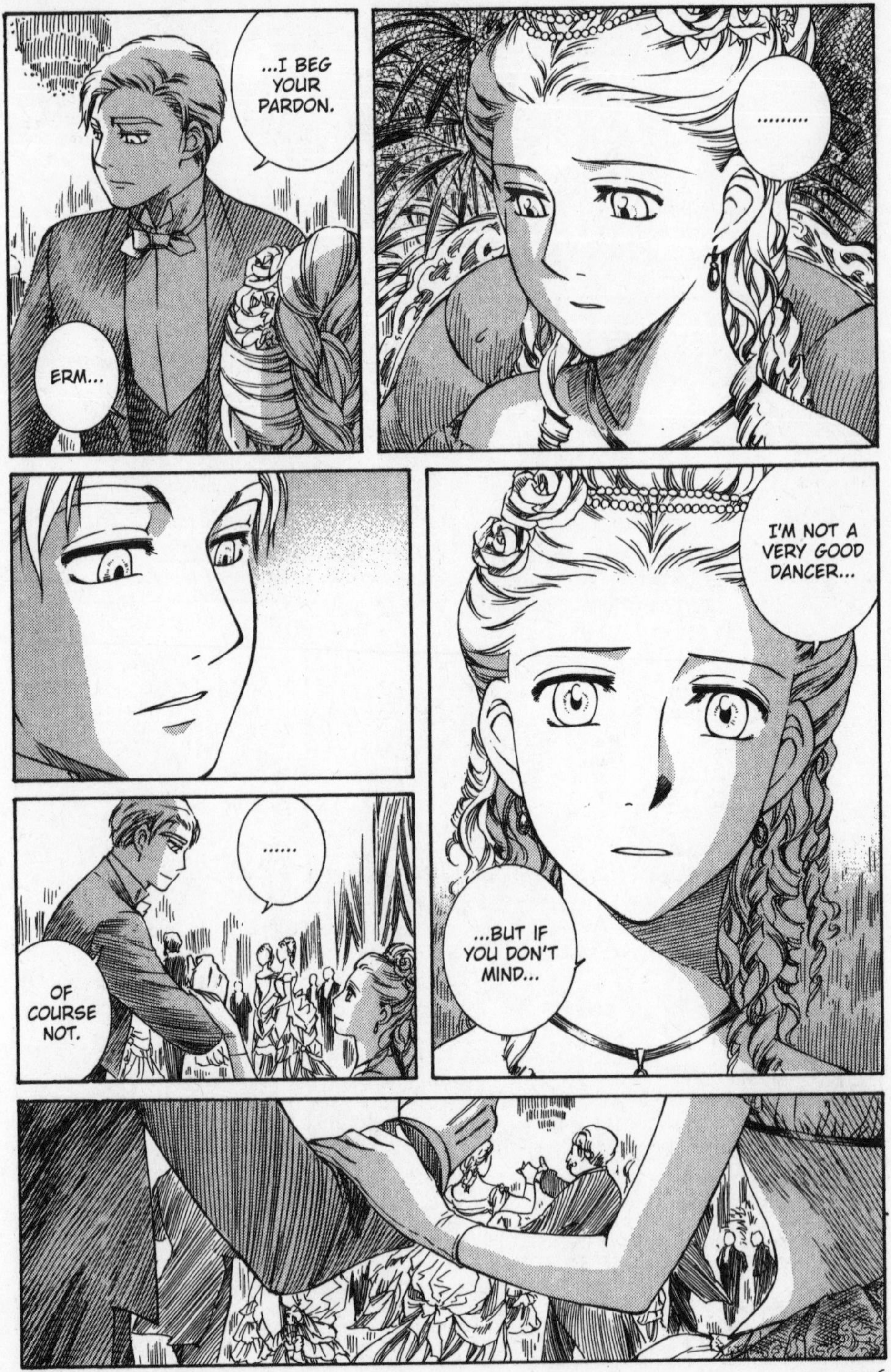
....
...I BEG YOUR PARDON.
ERM...
I'M NOT A VERY GOOD DANCER...
...BUT IF YOU DON'T MIND...
......
OF COURSE NOT.

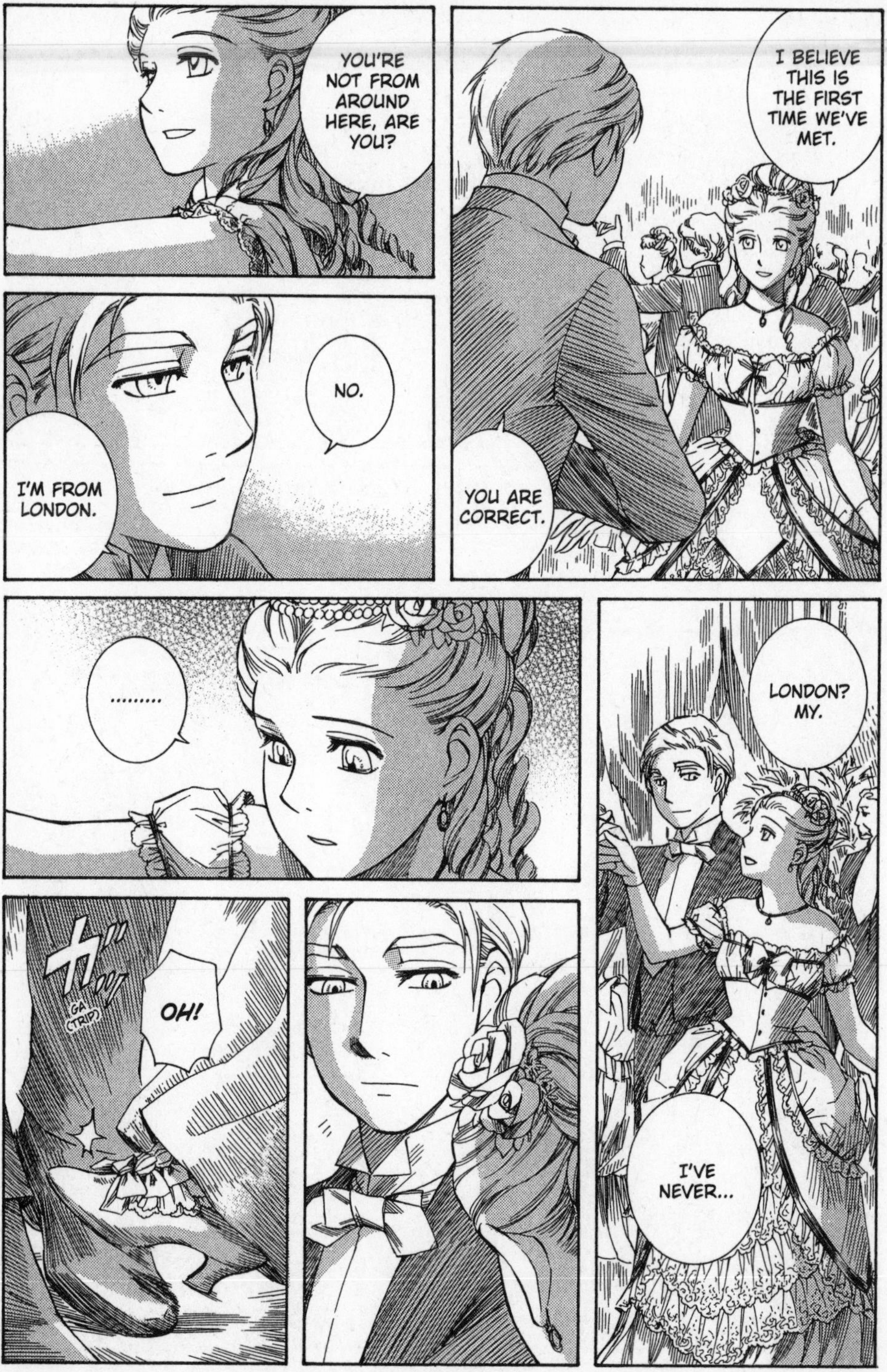
I BELIEVE THIS IS THE FIRST TIME WE'VE MET.
YOU ARE CORRECT.
YOU'RE NOT FROM AROUND HERE, ARE YOU?
NO.
I'M FROM LONDON.
LONDON? MY.
I'VE NEVER...
....
OH!
GA (TRIP)

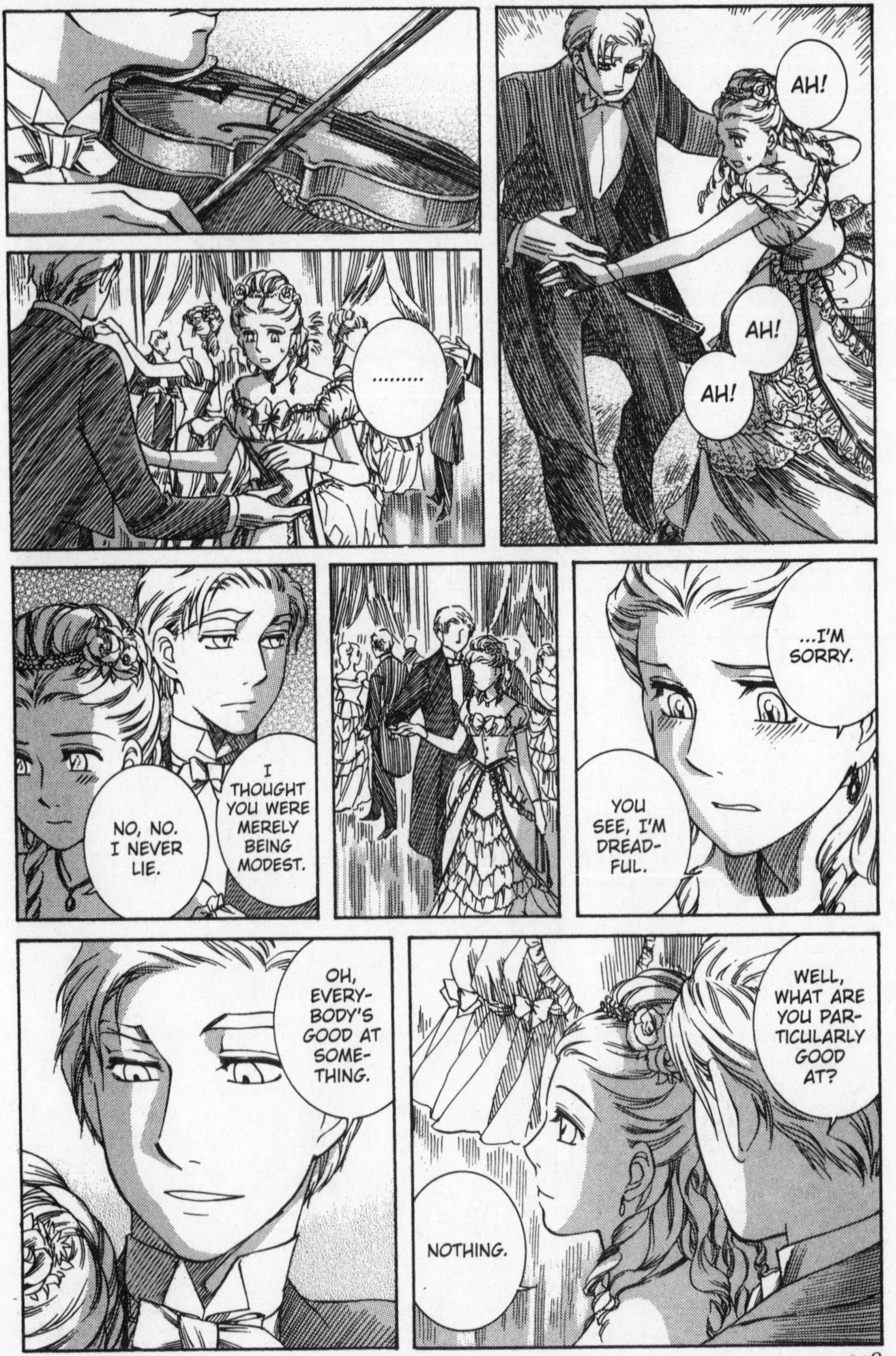
AH!
AH!
AH!
....
...I'M SORRY.
YOU SEE, I'M DREAD-FUL.
I THOUGHT YOU WERE MERELY BEING MODEST.
NO, NO. I NEVER LIE.
WELL, WHAT ARE YOU PAR-TICULARLY GOOD AT?
NOTHING.
OH, EVERY-BODY'S GOOD AT SOME-THING.

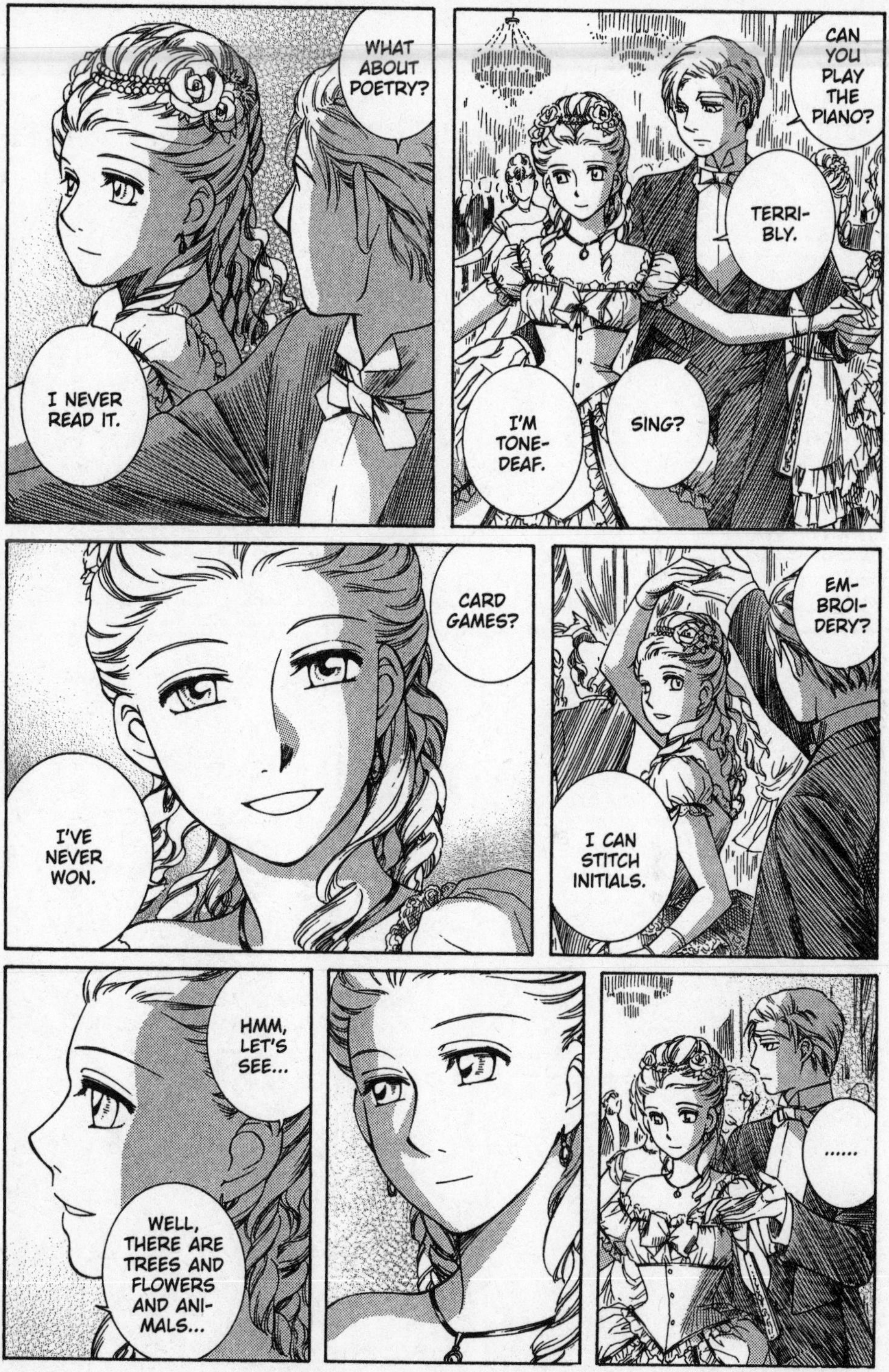
CAN YOU PLAY THE PIANO?
TERRIBLY.
SING?
I'M TONE-DEAF.
WHAT ABOUT POETRY?
I NEVER READ IT.
EMBROIDERY?
I CAN STITCH INITIALS.
CARD GAMES?
I'VE NEVER WON.
......
HMM, LET'S SEE...
WELL, THERE ARE TREES AND FLOWERS AND ANIMALS...

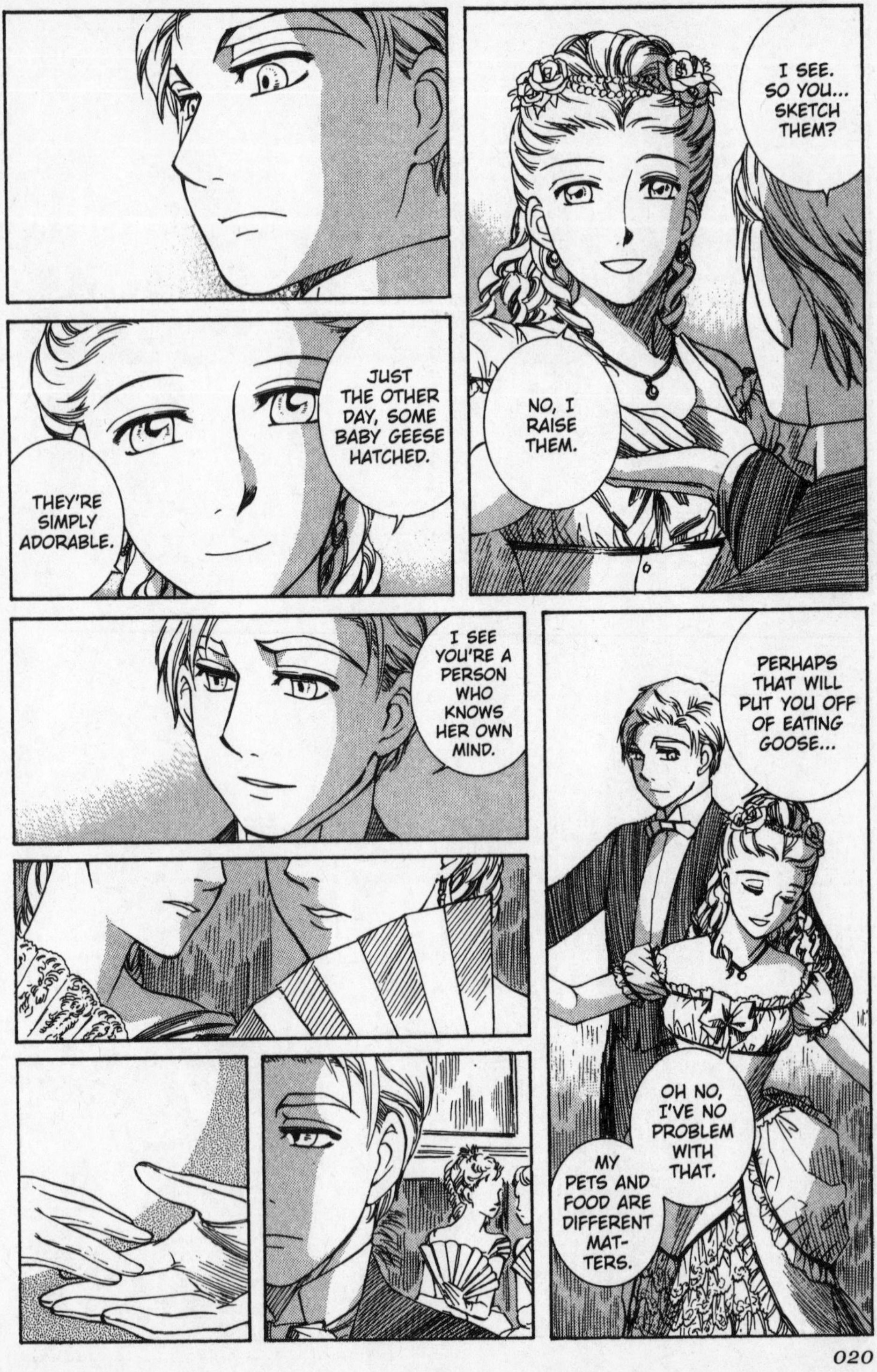
I SEE. SO YOU... SKETCH THEM?
NO, I RAISE THEM.
JUST THE OTHER DAY, SOME BABY GEESE HATCHED.
THEY'RE SIMPLY ADORABLE.
PERHAPS THAT WILL PUT YOU OFF OF EATING GOOSE...
OH NO, I'VE NO PROBLEM WITH THAT.
MY PETS AND FOOD ARE DIFFERENT MAT-TERS.
I SEE YOU'RE A PERSON WHO KNOWS HER OWN MIND.

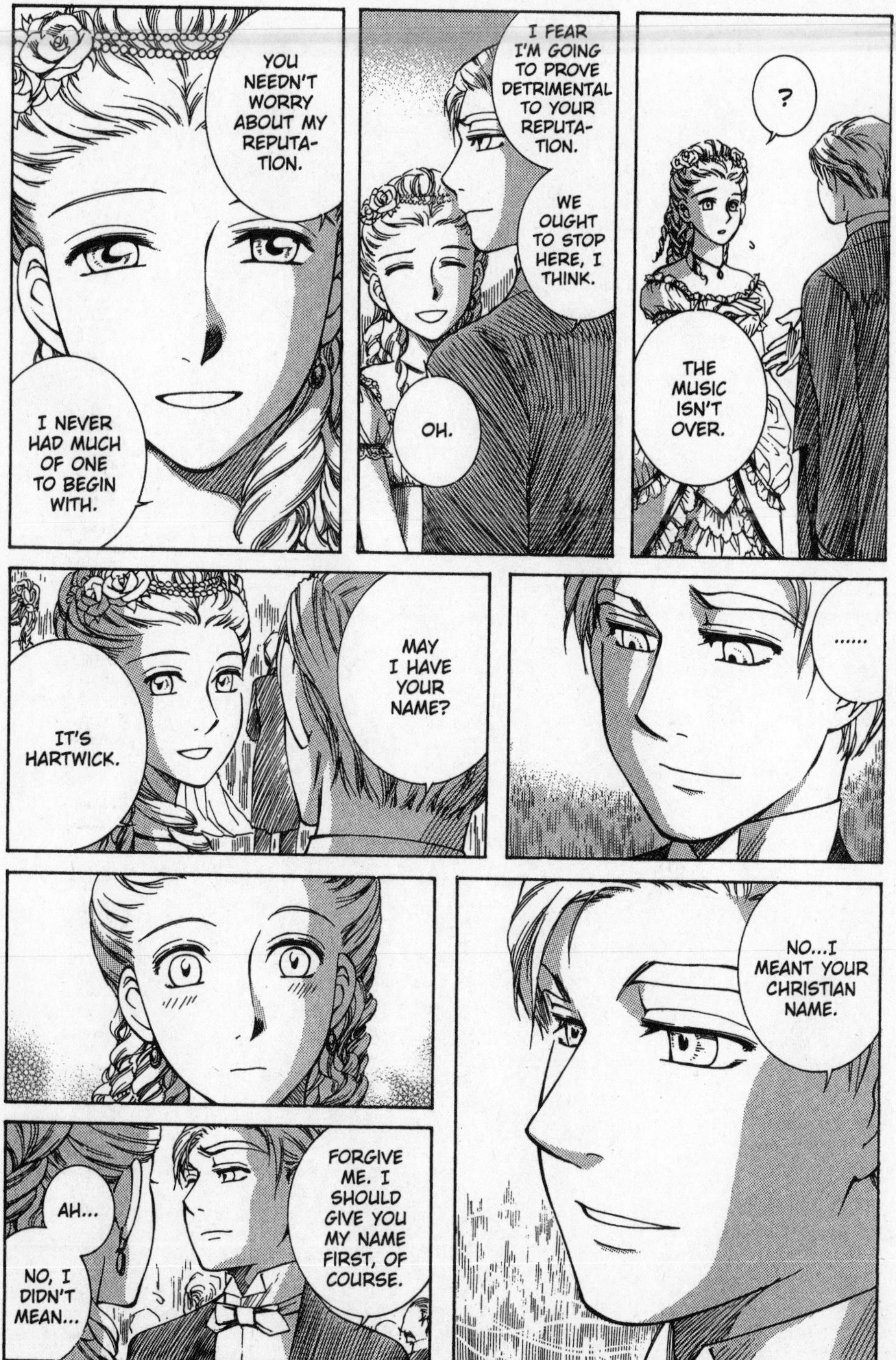
?
THE MUSIC ISN'T OVER.
I FEAR I'M GOING TO PROVE DETRIMENTAL TO YOUR REPUTATION.
WE OUGHT TO STOP HERE, I THINK.
OH.
YOU NEEDN'T WORRY ABOUT MY REPUTATION.
I NEVER HAD MUCH OF ONE TO BEGIN WITH.
......
MAY I HAVE YOUR NAME?
IT'S HARTWICK.
NO...I MEANT YOUR CHRISTIAN NAME.
FORGIVE ME. I SHOULD GIVE YOU MY NAME FIRST, OF COURSE.
AH...
NO, I DIDN'T MEAN...

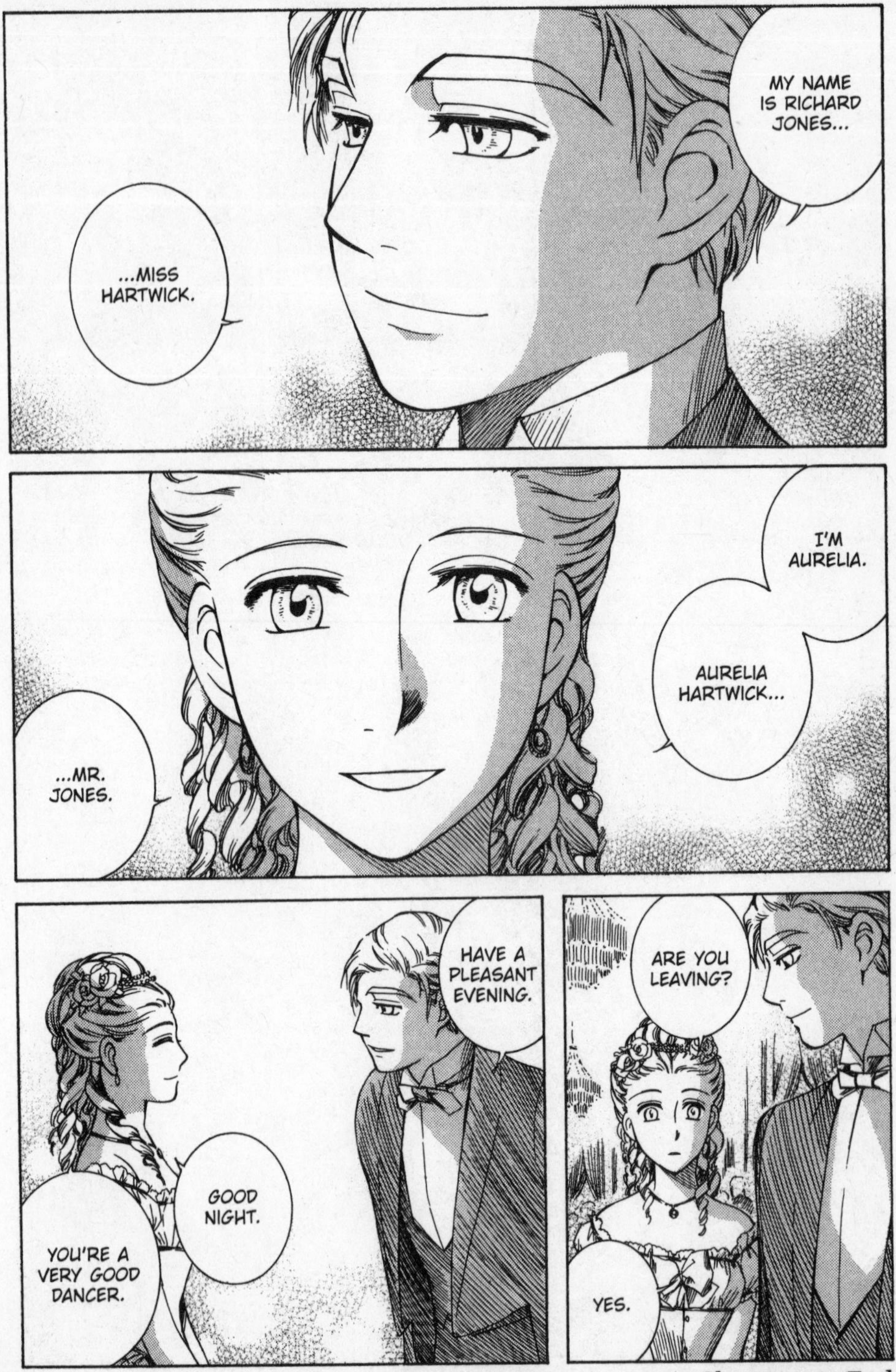
MY NAME IS RICHARD JONES...
...MISS HARTWICK.
I'M AURELIA.
AURELIA HARTWICK...
...MR. JONES.
ARE YOU LEAVING?
YES.
HAVE A PLEASANT EVENING.
GOOD NIGHT.
YOU'RE A VERY GOOD DANCER.

Chapter 30: End

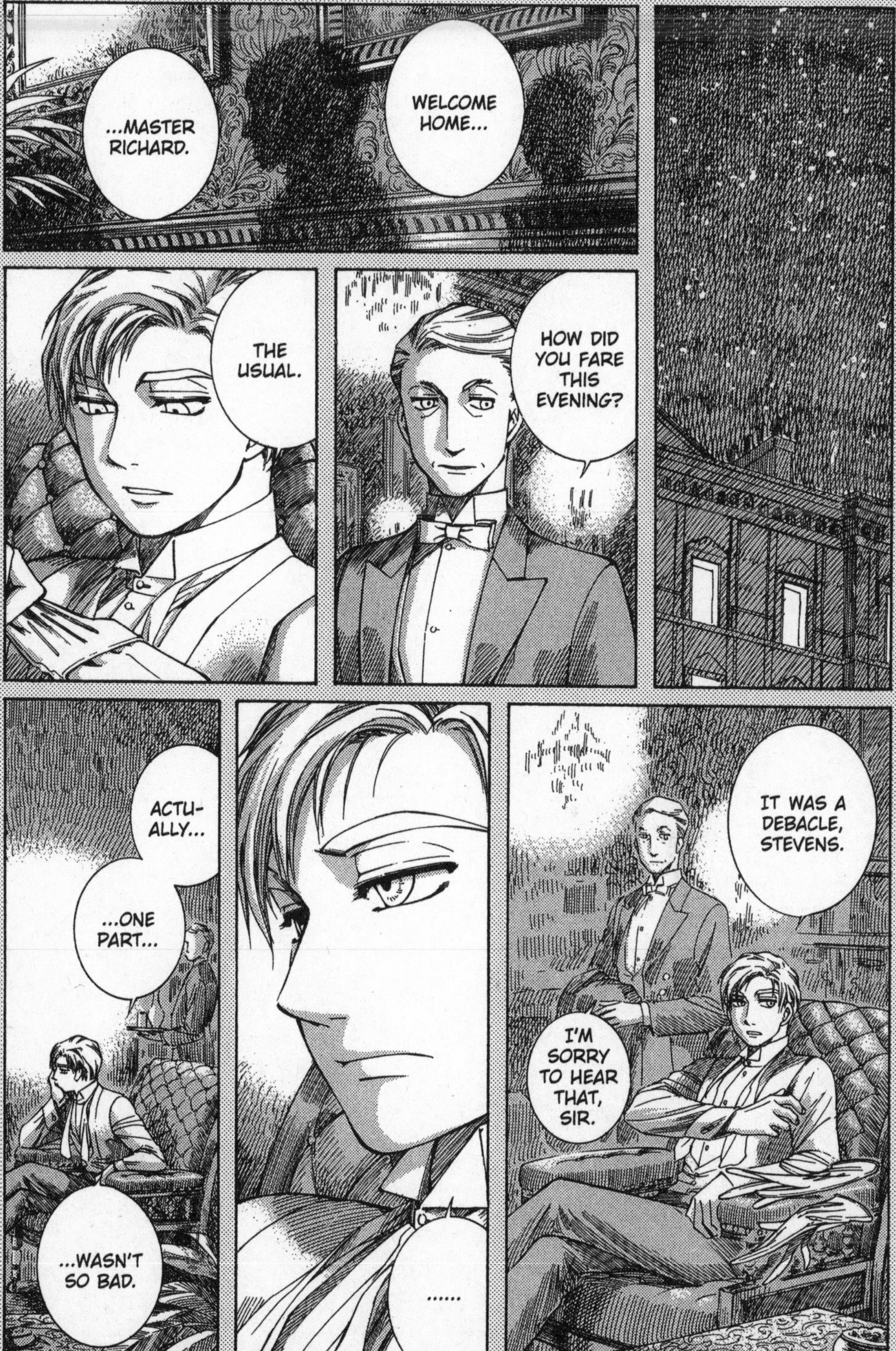
WELCOME HOME...
...MASTER RICHARD.
HOW DID YOU FARE THIS EVENING?
THE USUAL.
IT WAS A DEBACLE, STEVENS.
I'M SORRY TO HEAR THAT, SIR.
......
ACTU-ALLY...
...ONE PART...
...WASN'T SO BAD.

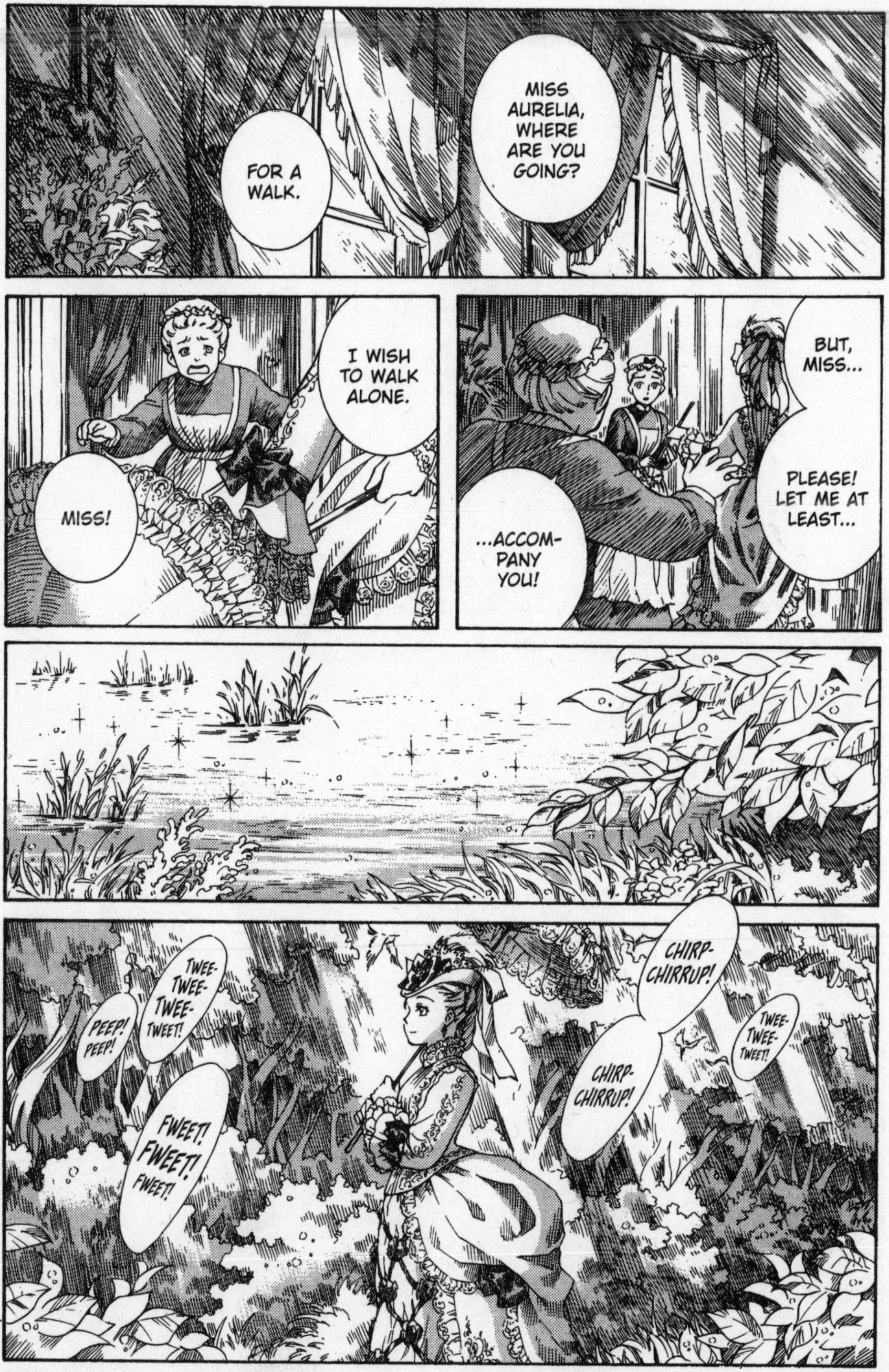
MISS AURELIA, WHERE ARE YOU GOING?
FOR A WALK.
BUT, MISS...
PLEASE! LET ME AT LEAST...
...ACCOMPANY YOU!
I WISH TO WALK ALONE.
MISS!
CHIRP-CHIRRUP!
TWEE-TWEE-TWEET!
CHIRP-CHIRRUP!
TWEE-TWEE-TWEE-TWEET!
PEEP! PEEP!
FWEET! FWEET! FWEET!

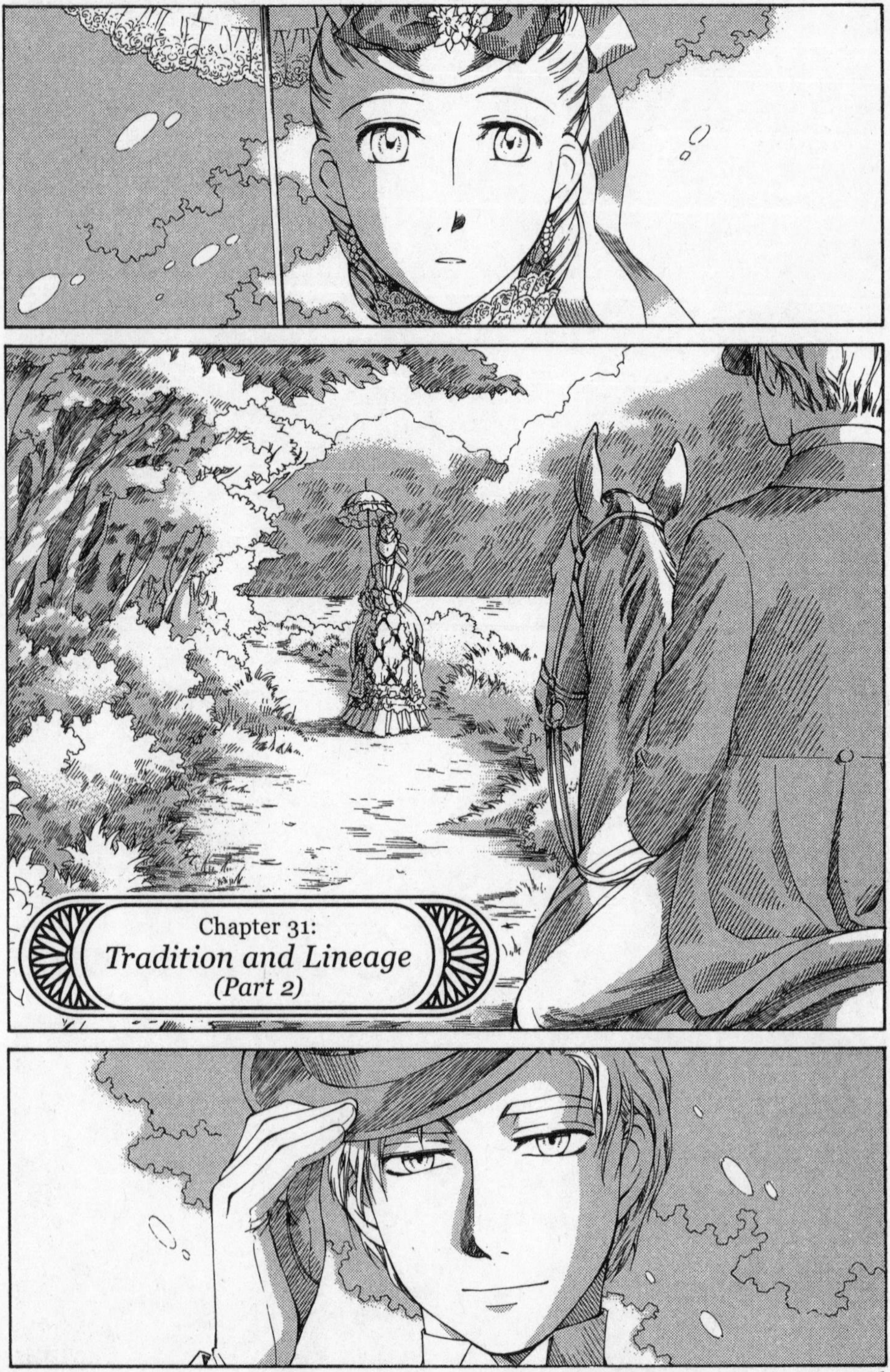
Chapter 31:
Tradition and Lineage
(Part 2)

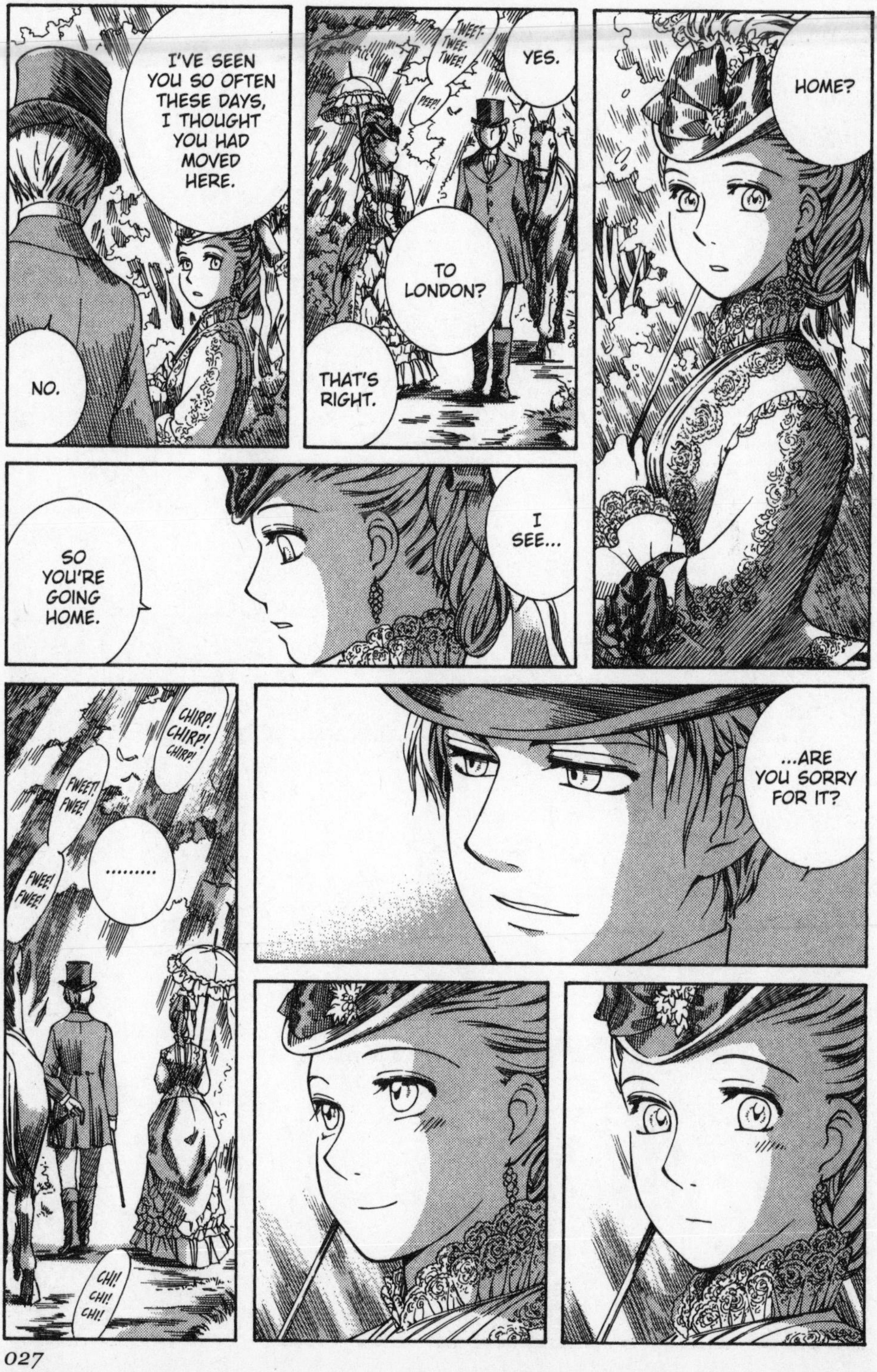
HOME?
YES.
TWEET-TWEE-TWEE!
PEEP!
TO LONDON?
THAT'S RIGHT.
I'VE SEEN YOU SO OFTEN THESE DAYS, I THOUGHT YOU HAD MOVED HERE.
NO.
I SEE...
SO YOU'RE GOING HOME.
...ARE YOU SORRY FOR IT?
CHIRP! CHIRP! CHIRP!
FWEET! FWEE!
....
FWEE! FWEE!
CHI! CHI! CHI!

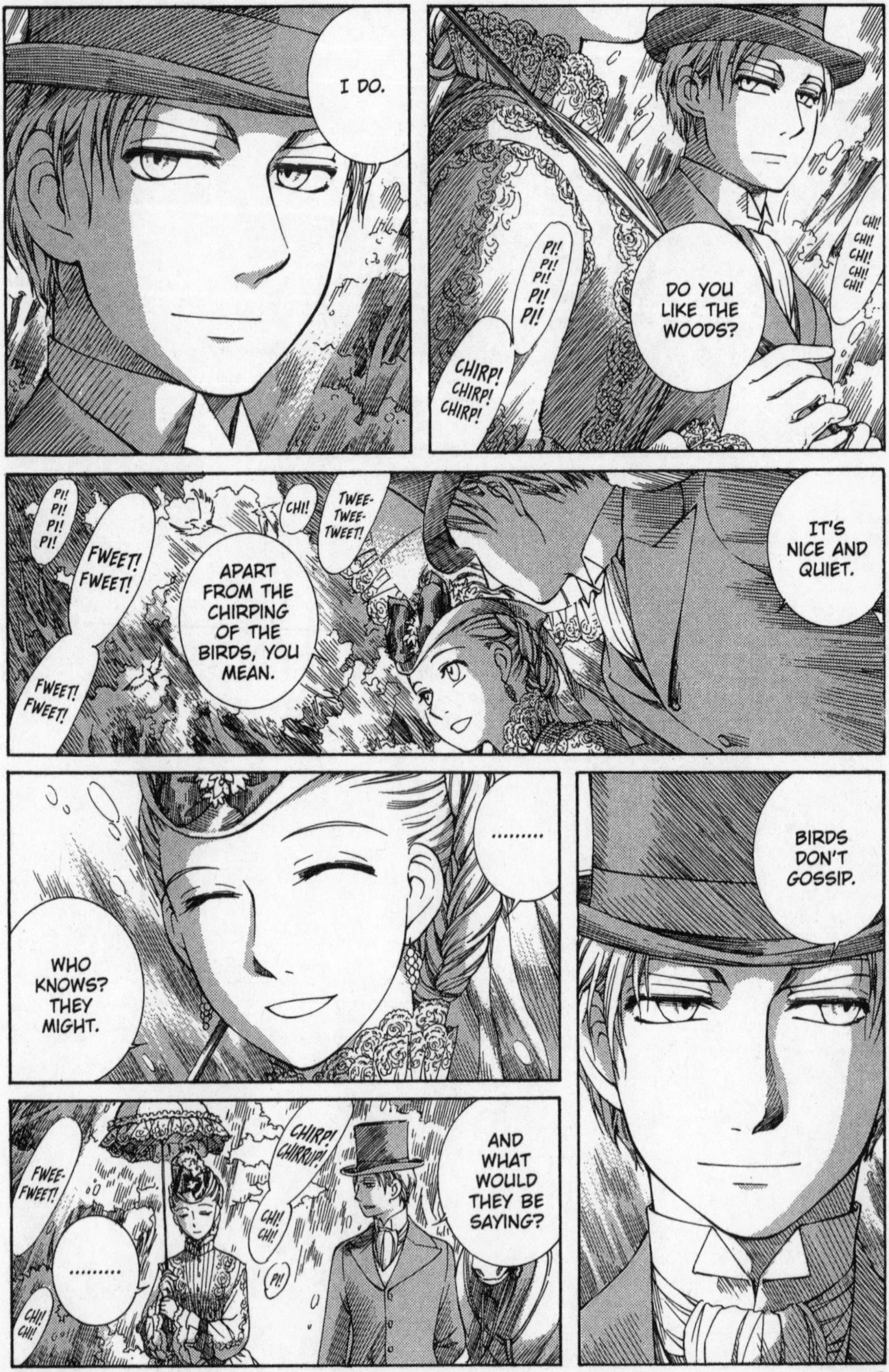
DO YOU LIKE THE WOODS?
CHI! CHI! CHI! CHI! CHI!
PI! PI! PI! PI! PI!
CHIRP! CHIRP! CHIRP!
I DO.
IT'S NICE AND QUIET.
TWEE-TWEE-TWEET!
CHI!
APART FROM THE CHIRPING OF THE BIRDS, YOU MEAN.
PI! PI! PI! PI!
FWEET! FWEET!
FWEET! FWEET!
BIRDS DON'T GOSSIP.
....
WHO KNOWS? THEY MIGHT.
AND WHAT WOULD THEY BE SAYING?
CHIRP! CHIRRUP!
CHI! CHI!
PI!
FWEE-FWEET!
....
CHI! CHI!

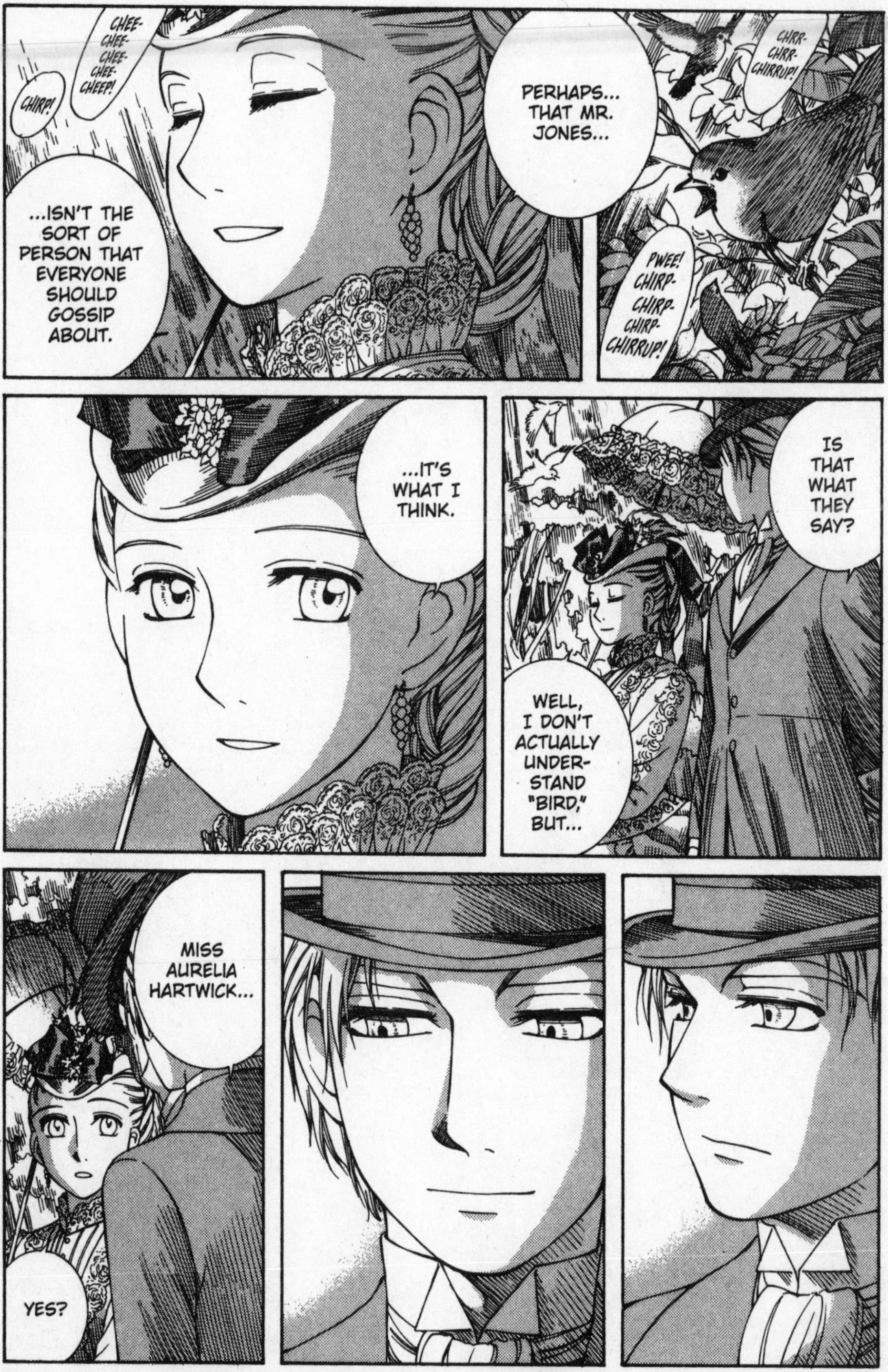
CHRR-CHRR-CHIRRUP!
PWEE! CHIRP-CHIRP-CHIRRUP!
PERHAPS... THAT MR. JONES...
CHEE-CHEE-CHEE-CHEE-CHEEP!
CHIRP!
...ISN'T THE SORT OF PERSON THAT EVERYONE SHOULD GOSSIP ABOUT.
IS THAT WHAT THEY SAY?
WELL, I DON'T ACTUALLY UNDER-STAND "BIRD," BUT...
...IT'S WHAT I THINK.
MISS AURELIA HARTWICK...
YES?

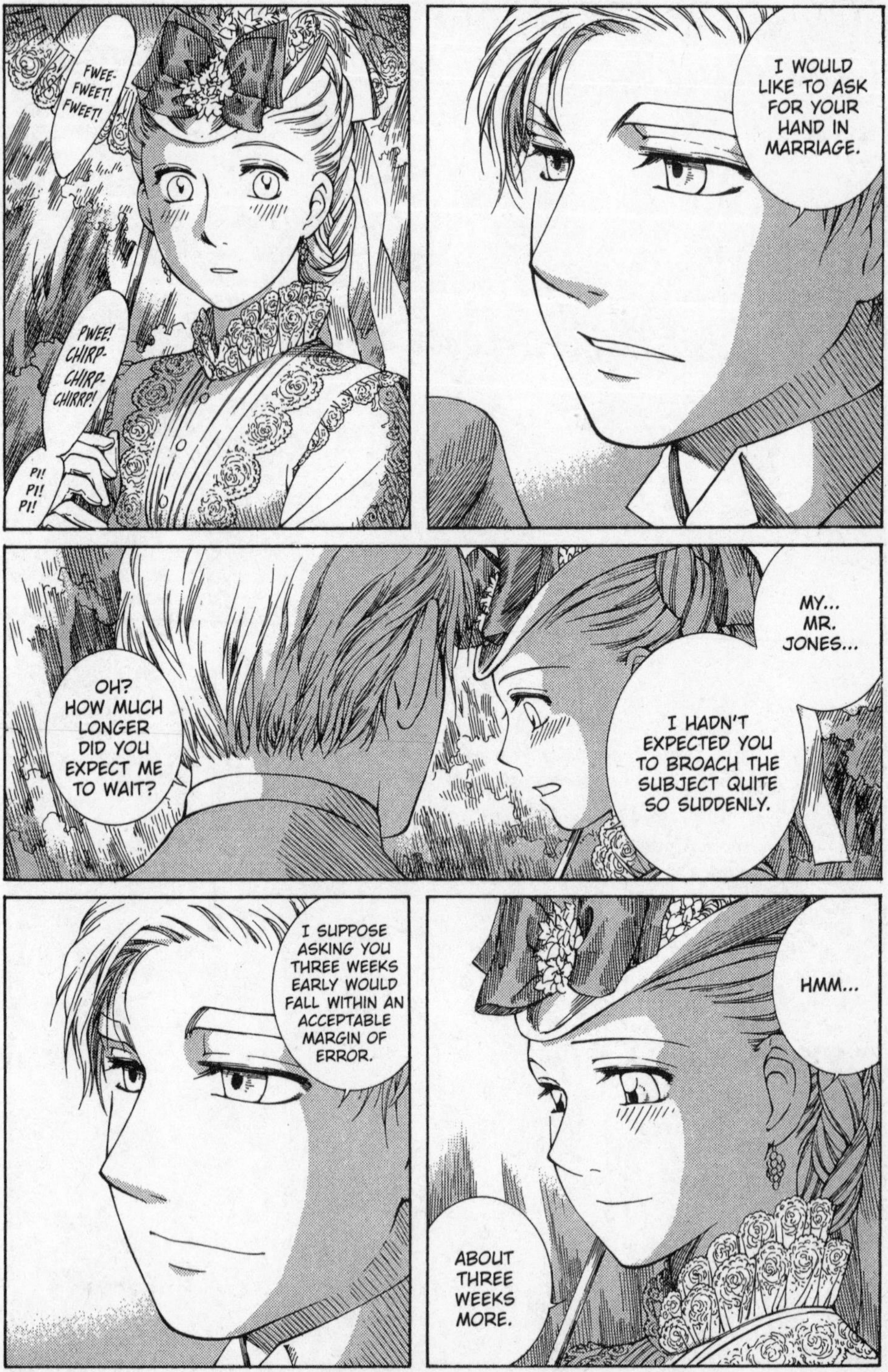
I WOULD LIKE TO ASK FOR YOUR HAND IN MARRIAGE.
FWEE-FWEET! FWEET!
PWEE! CHIRP-CHIRP-CHIRRP!
PI! PI! PI!
MY... MR. JONES...
I HADN'T EXPECTED YOU TO BROACH THE SUBJECT QUITE SO SUDDENLY.
OH? HOW MUCH LONGER DID YOU EXPECT ME TO WAIT?
HMM...
ABOUT THREE WEEKS MORE.
I SUPPOSE ASKING YOU THREE WEEKS EARLY WOULD FALL WITHIN AN ACCEPTABLE MARGIN OF ERROR.

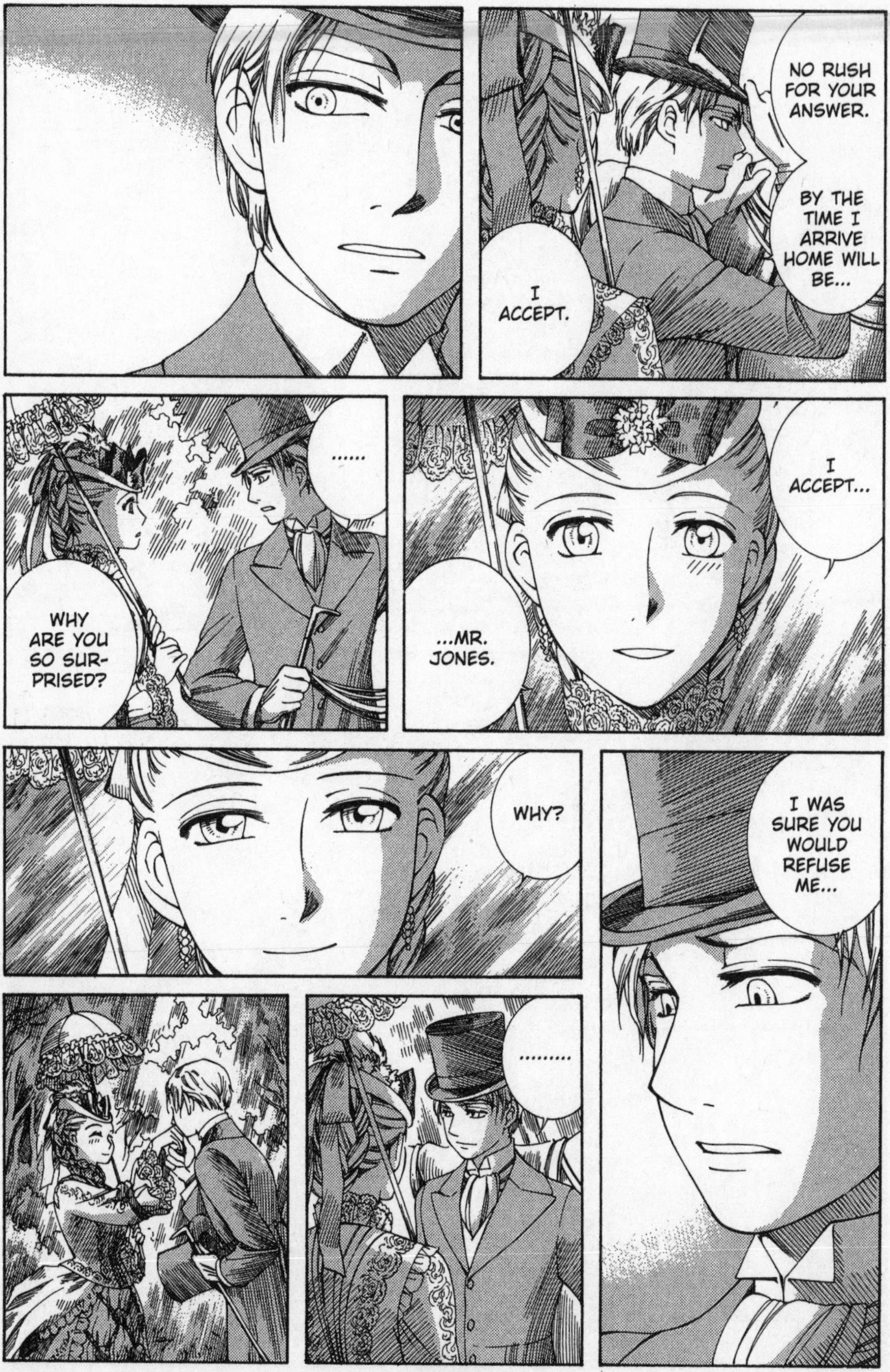
NO RUSH FOR YOUR ANSWER.
BY THE TIME I ARRIVE HOME WILL BE...
I ACCEPT.
I ACCEPT...
...MR. JONES.
......
WHY ARE YOU SO SUR-PRISED?
I WAS SURE YOU WOULD REFUSE ME...
WHY?
....

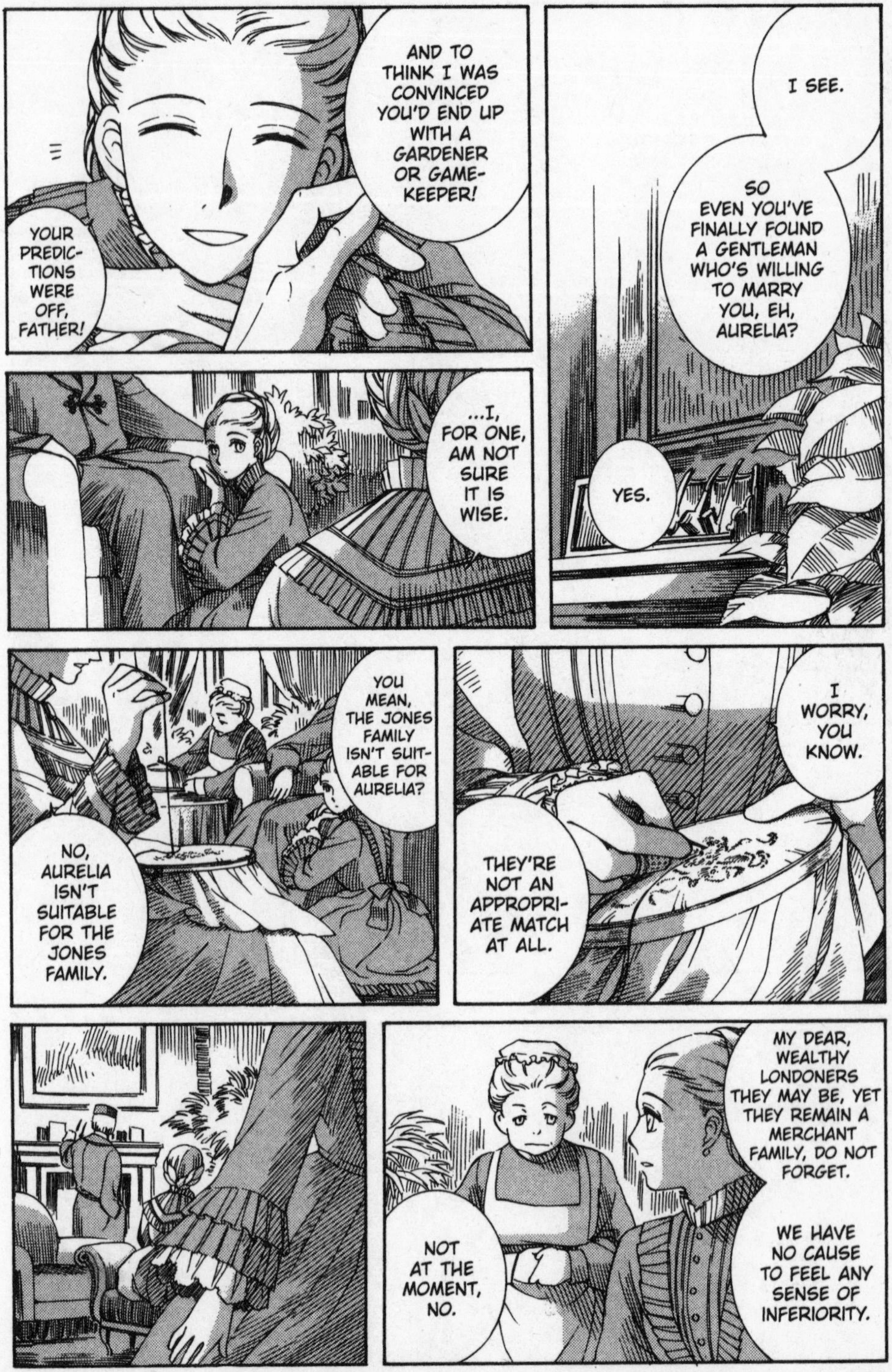
I SEE.
SO EVEN YOU'VE FINALLY FOUND A GENTLEMAN WHO'S WILLING TO MARRY YOU, EH, AURELIA?
YES.
AND TO THINK I WAS CONVINCED YOU'D END UP WITH A GARDENER OR GAME-KEEPER!
YOUR PREDIC-TIONS WERE OFF, FATHER!
...I, FOR ONE, AM NOT SURE IT IS WISE.
I WORRY, YOU KNOW.
THEY'RE NOT AN APPROPRI-ATE MATCH AT ALL.
YOU MEAN, THE JONES FAMILY ISN'T SUIT-ABLE FOR AURELIA?
NO, AURELIA ISN'T SUITABLE FOR THE JONES FAMILY.
MY DEAR, WEALTHY LONDONERS THEY MAY BE, YET THEY REMAIN A MERCHANT FAMILY, DO NOT FORGET.
WE HAVE NO CAUSE TO FEEL ANY SENSE OF INFERIORITY.
NOT AT THE MOMENT, NO.

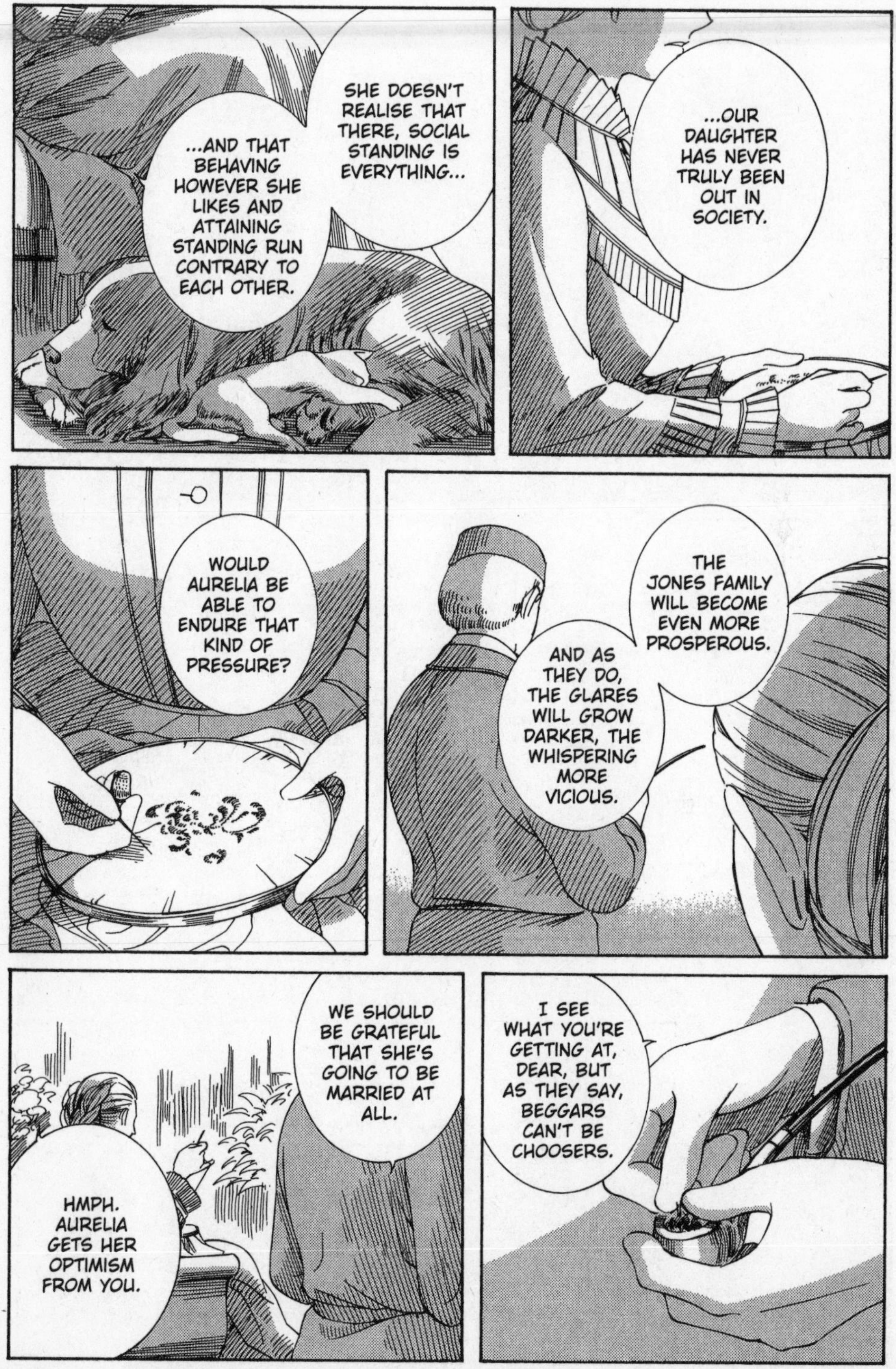
...OUR DAUGHTER HAS NEVER TRULY BEEN OUT IN SOCIETY.
SHE DOESN'T REALISE THAT THERE, SOCIAL STANDING IS EVERYTHING...
...AND THAT BEHAVING HOWEVER SHE LIKES AND ATTAINING STANDING RUN CONTRARY TO EACH OTHER.
THE JONES FAMILY WILL BECOME EVEN MORE PROSPEROUS.
AND AS THEY DO, THE GLARES WILL GROW DARKER, THE WHISPERING MORE VICIOUS.
WOULD AURELIA BE ABLE TO ENDURE THAT KIND OF PRESSURE?
I SEE WHAT YOU'RE GETTING AT, DEAR, BUT AS THEY SAY, BEGGARS CAN'T BE CHOOSERS.
WE SHOULD BE GRATEFUL THAT SHE'S GOING TO BE MARRIED AT ALL.
HMPH. AURELIA GETS HER OPTIMISM FROM YOU.

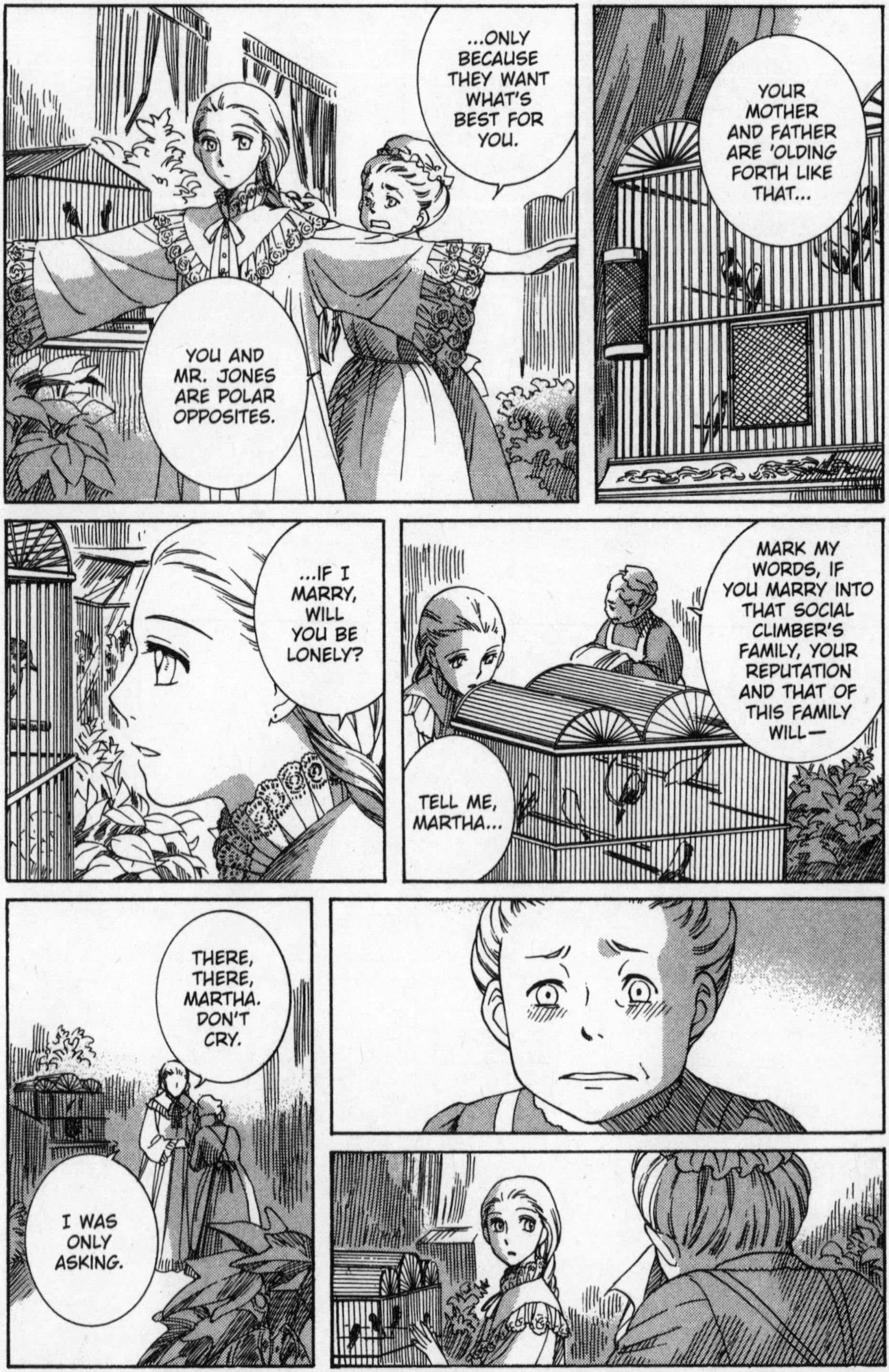
YOUR MOTHER AND FATHER ARE 'OLDING FORTH LIKE THAT...
...ONLY BECAUSE THEY WANT WHAT'S BEST FOR YOU.
YOU AND MR. JONES ARE POLAR OPPOSITES.
MARK MY WORDS, IF YOU MARRY INTO THAT SOCIAL CLIMBER'S FAMILY, YOUR REPUTATION AND THAT OF THIS FAMILY WILL—
TELL ME, MARTHA...
...IF I MARRY, WILL YOU BE LONELY?
THERE, THERE, MARTHA. DON'T CRY.
I WAS ONLY ASKING.

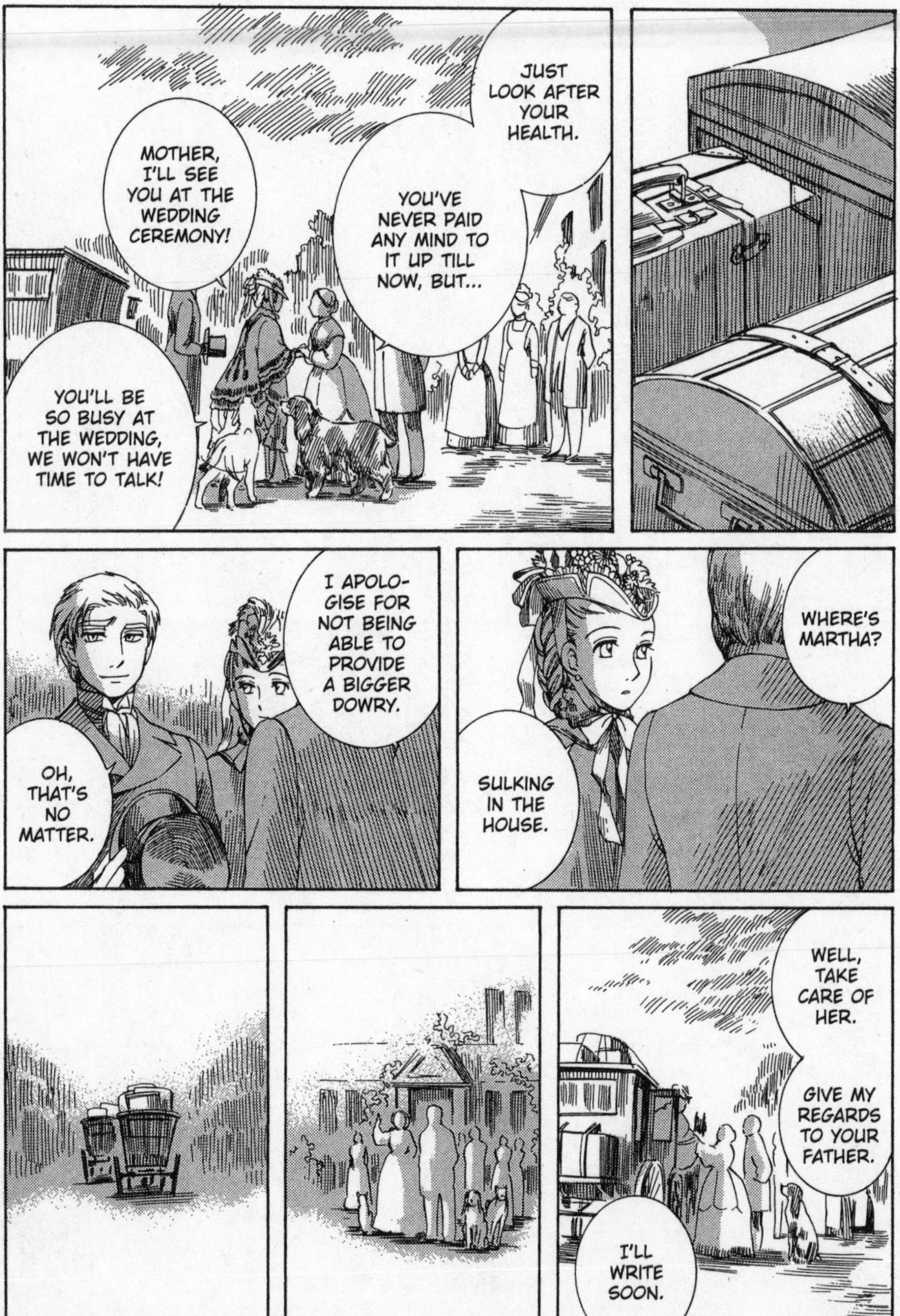

JUST LOOK AFTER YOUR HEALTH.
MOTHER, I'LL SEE YOU AT THE WEDDING CEREMONY!
YOU'VE NEVER PAID ANY MIND TO IT UP TILL NOW, BUT...
YOU'LL BE SO BUSY AT THE WEDDING, WE WON'T HAVE TIME TO TALK!
WHERE'S MARTHA?
SULKING IN THE HOUSE.
I APOLO-GISE FOR NOT BEING ABLE TO PROVIDE A BIGGER DOWRY.
OH, THAT'S NO MATTER.
WELL, TAKE CARE OF HER.
GIVE MY REGARDS TO YOUR FATHER.
I'LL WRITE SOON.

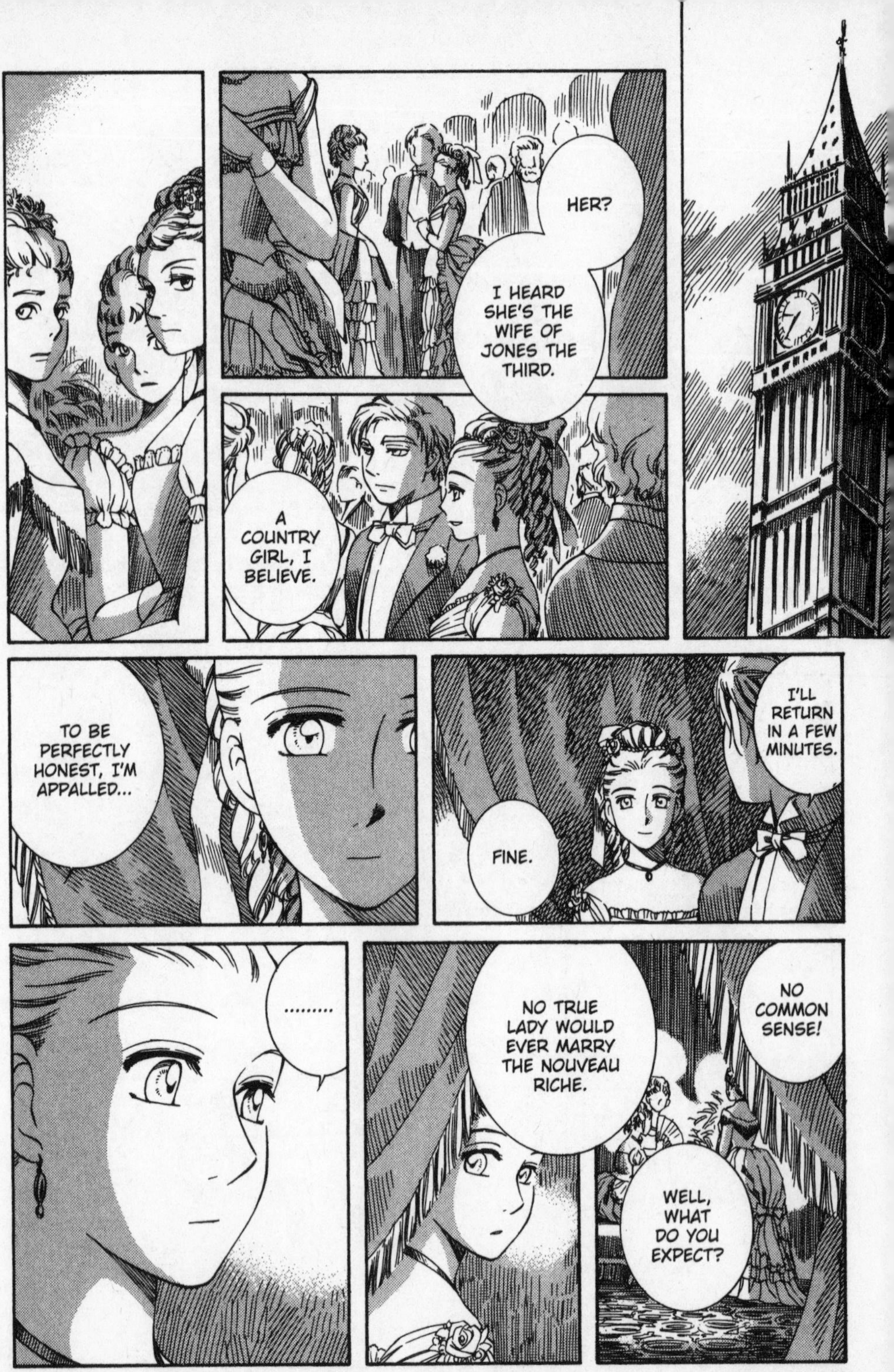
HER?
I HEARD SHE'S THE WIFE OF JONES THE THIRD.
A COUNTRY GIRL, I BELIEVE.
I'LL RETURN IN A FEW MINUTES.
FINE.
TO BE PERFECTLY HONEST, I'M APPALLED...
NO COMMON SENSE!
NO TRUE LADY WOULD EVER MARRY THE NOUVEAU RICHE.
WELL, WHAT DO YOU EXPECT?
....

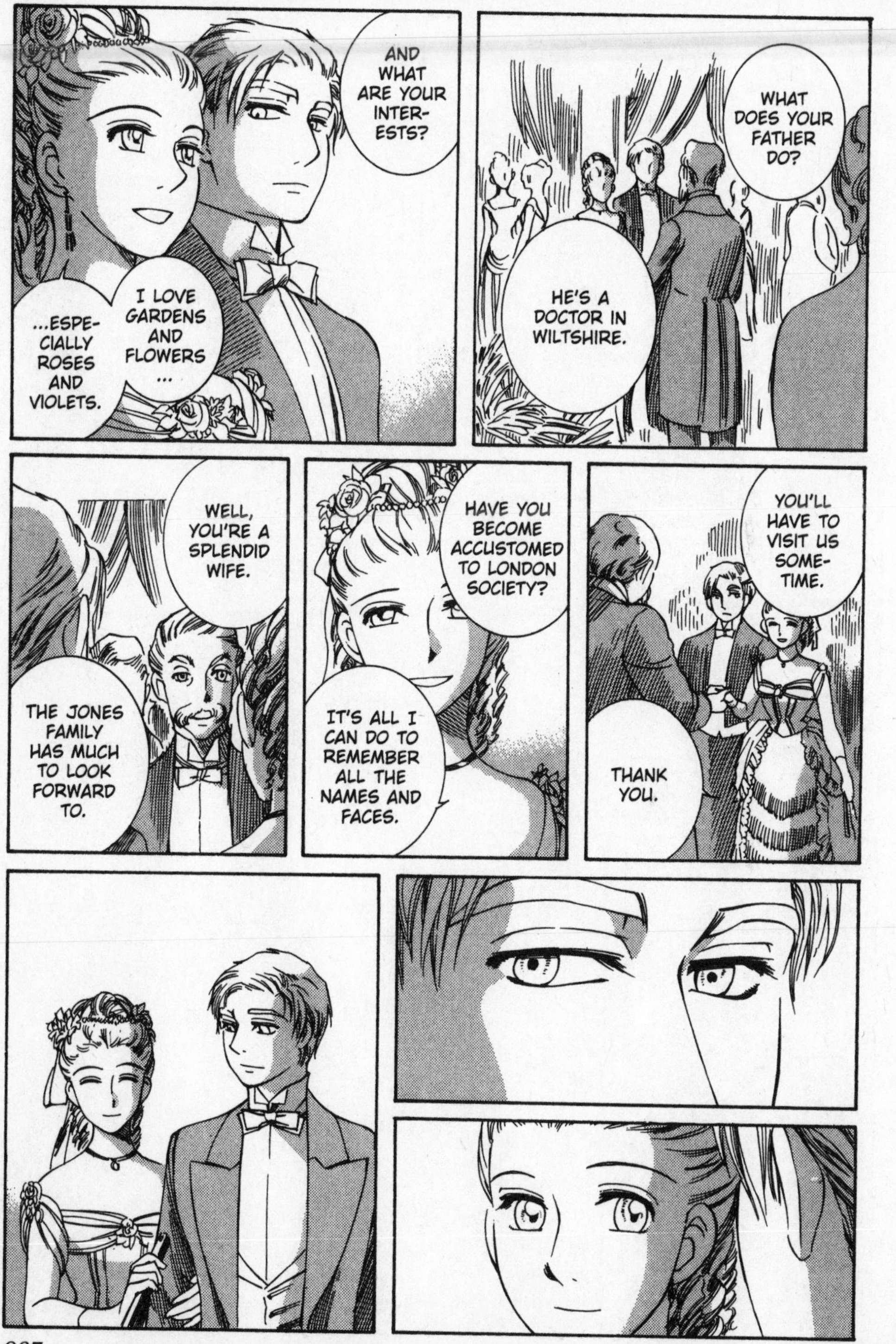
WHAT DOES YOUR FATHER DO?
HE'S A DOCTOR IN WILTSHIRE.
AND WHAT ARE YOUR INTER-ESTS?
I LOVE GARDENS AND FLOWERS ...
...ESPE-CIALLY ROSES AND VIOLETS.
YOU'LL HAVE TO VISIT US SOME-TIME.
THANK YOU.
HAVE YOU BECOME ACCUSTOMED TO LONDON SOCIETY?
IT'S ALL I CAN DO TO REMEMBER ALL THE NAMES AND FACES.
WELL, YOU'RE A SPLENDID WIFE.
THE JONES FAMILY HAS MUCH TO LOOK FORWARD TO.

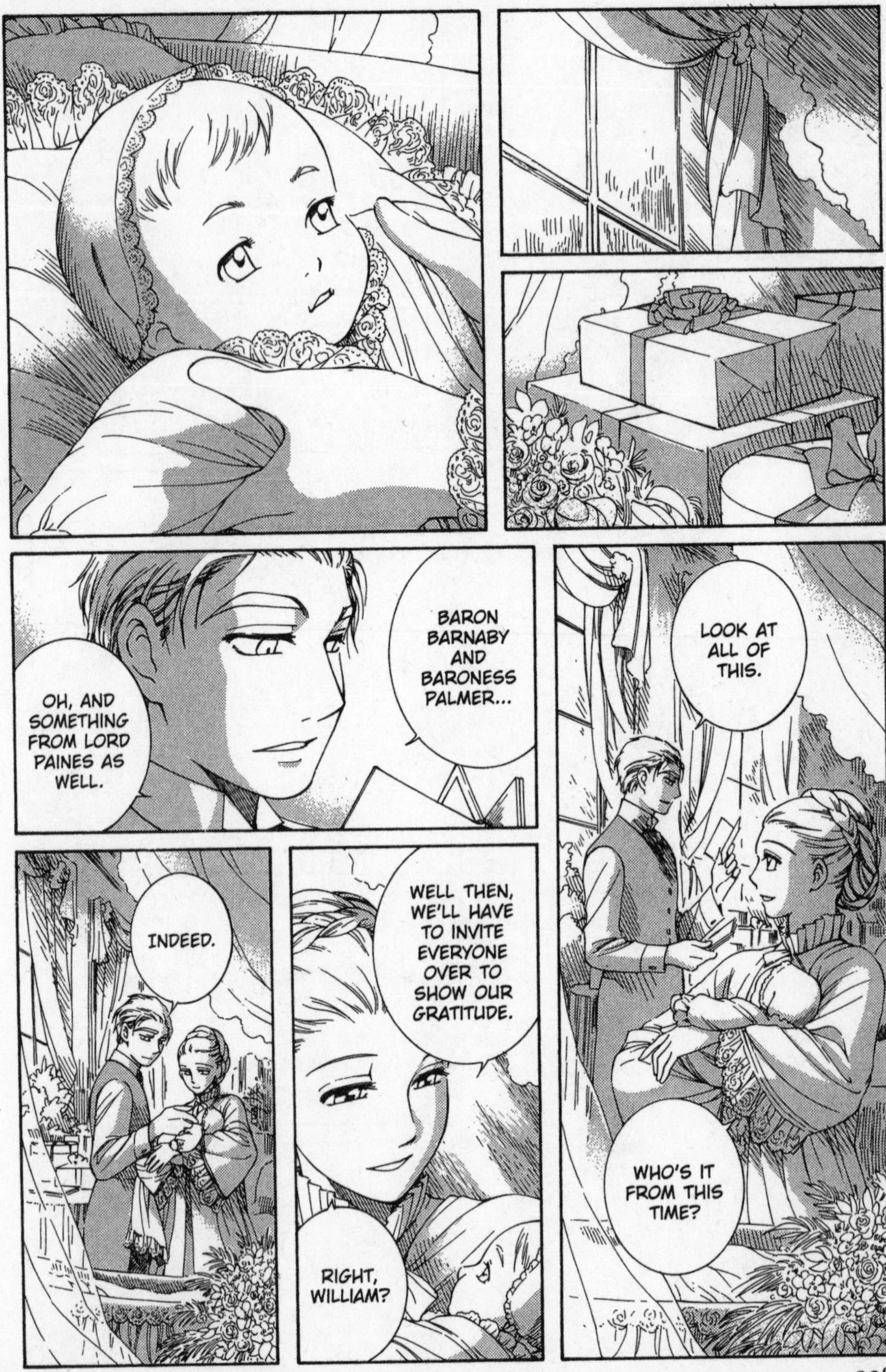
LOOK AT ALL OF THIS.
WHO'S IT FROM THIS TIME?
BARON BARNABY AND BARONESS PALMER...
OH, AND SOMETHING FROM LORD PAINES AS WELL.
WELL THEN, WE'LL HAVE TO INVITE EVERYONE OVER TO SHOW OUR GRATITUDE.
RIGHT, WILLIAM?
INDEED.

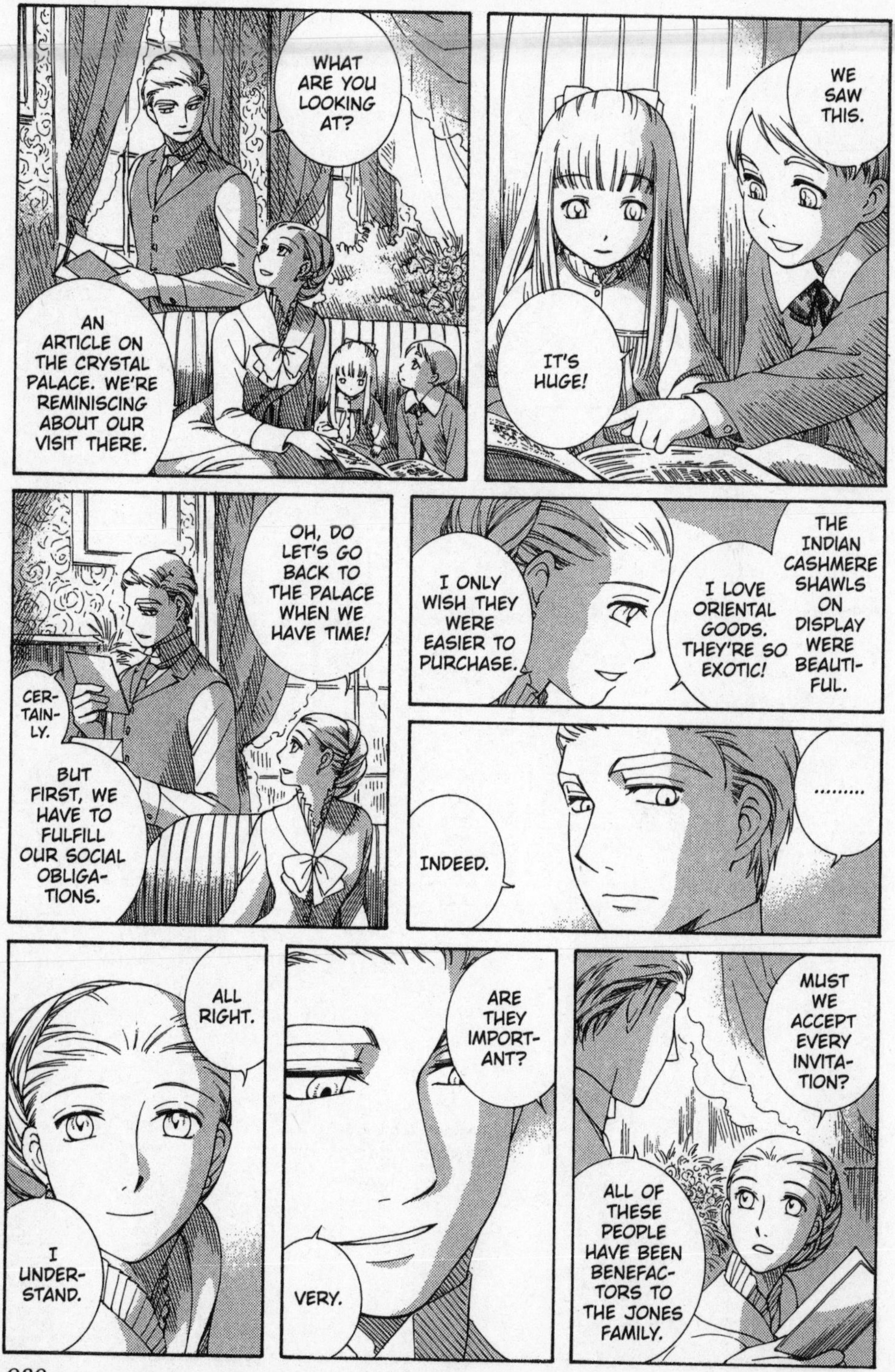
WE SAW THIS.
IT'S HUGE!
WHAT ARE YOU LOOKING AT?
AN ARTICLE ON THE CRYSTAL PALACE. WE'RE REMINISCING ABOUT OUR VISIT THERE.
THE INDIAN CASHMERE SHAWLS ON DISPLAY WERE BEAUTIFUL.
I LOVE ORIENTAL GOODS. THEY'RE SO EXOTIC!
I ONLY WISH THEY WERE EASIER TO PURCHASE.
....
INDEED.
OH, DO LET'S GO BACK TO THE PALACE WHEN WE HAVE TIME!
CERTAINLY.
BUT FIRST, WE HAVE TO FULFILL OUR SOCIAL OBLIGATIONS.
MUST WE ACCEPT EVERY INVITATION?
ALL OF THESE PEOPLE HAVE BEEN BENEFACTORS TO THE JONES FAMILY.
ARE THEY IMPORTANT?
VERY.
ALL RIGHT.
I UNDERSTAND.

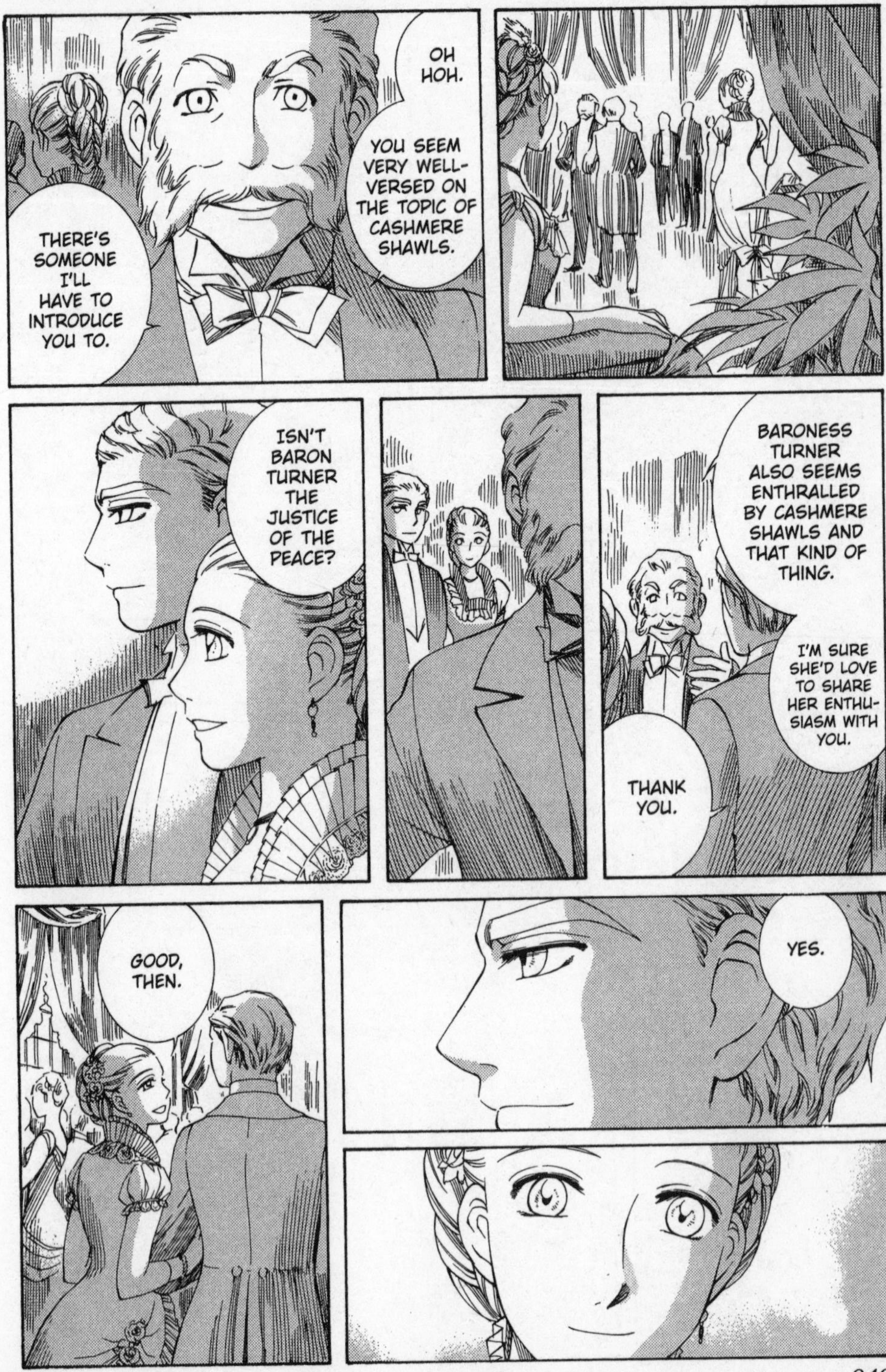
OH HOH.
YOU SEEM VERY WELL-VERSED ON THE TOPIC OF CASHMERE SHAWLS.
THERE'S SOMEONE I'LL HAVE TO INTRODUCE YOU TO.
BARONESS TURNER ALSO SEEMS ENTHRALLED BY CASHMERE SHAWLS AND THAT KIND OF THING.
I'M SURE SHE'D LOVE TO SHARE HER ENTHUSIASM WITH YOU.
THANK YOU.
ISN'T BARON TURNER THE JUSTICE OF THE PEACE?
YES.
GOOD, THEN.

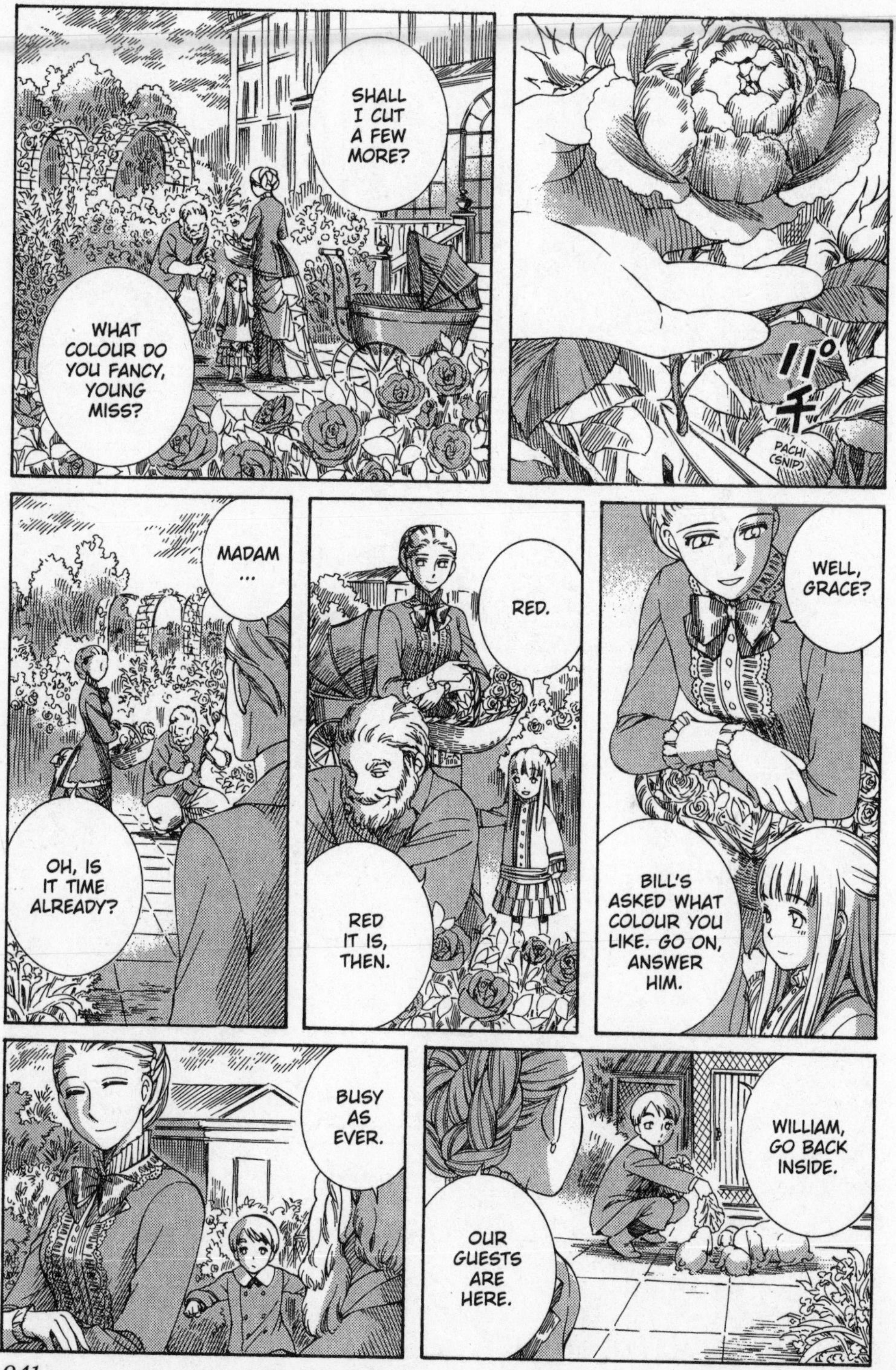
パチ
PACHI (SNIP)
SHALL I CUT A FEW MORE?
WHAT COLOUR DO YOU FANCY, YOUNG MISS?
WELL, GRACE?
BILL'S ASKED WHAT COLOUR YOU LIKE. GO ON, ANSWER HIM.
RED.
RED IT IS, THEN.
MADAM ...
OH, IS IT TIME ALREADY?
WILLIAM, GO BACK INSIDE.
OUR GUESTS ARE HERE.
BUSY AS EVER.

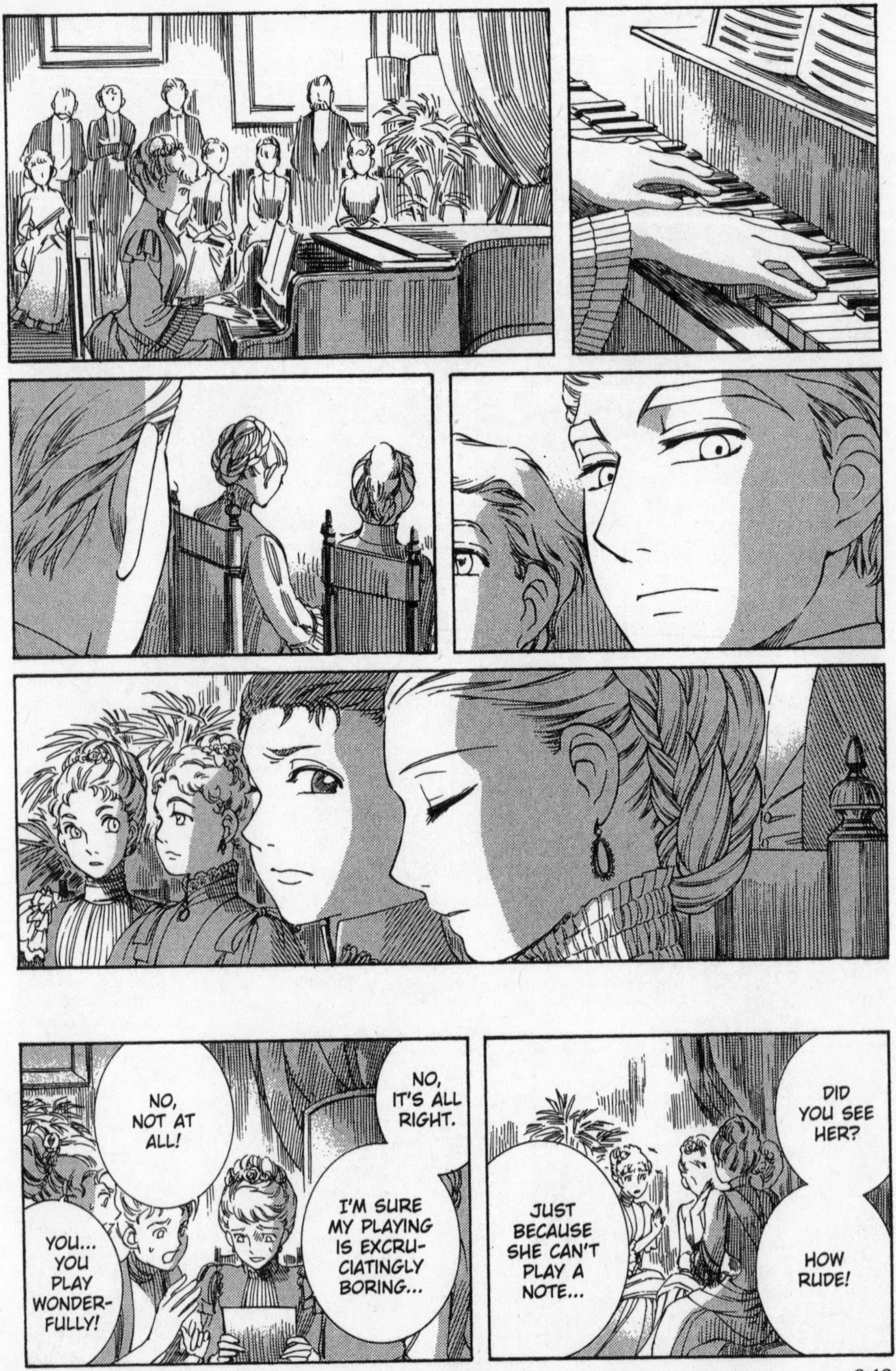
DID YOU SEE HER?
HOW RUDE!
JUST BECAUSE SHE CAN'T PLAY A NOTE...
NO, IT'S ALL RIGHT.
I'M SURE MY PLAYING IS EXCRUCIATINGLY BORING...
NO, NOT AT ALL!
YOU... YOU PLAY WONDERFULLY!

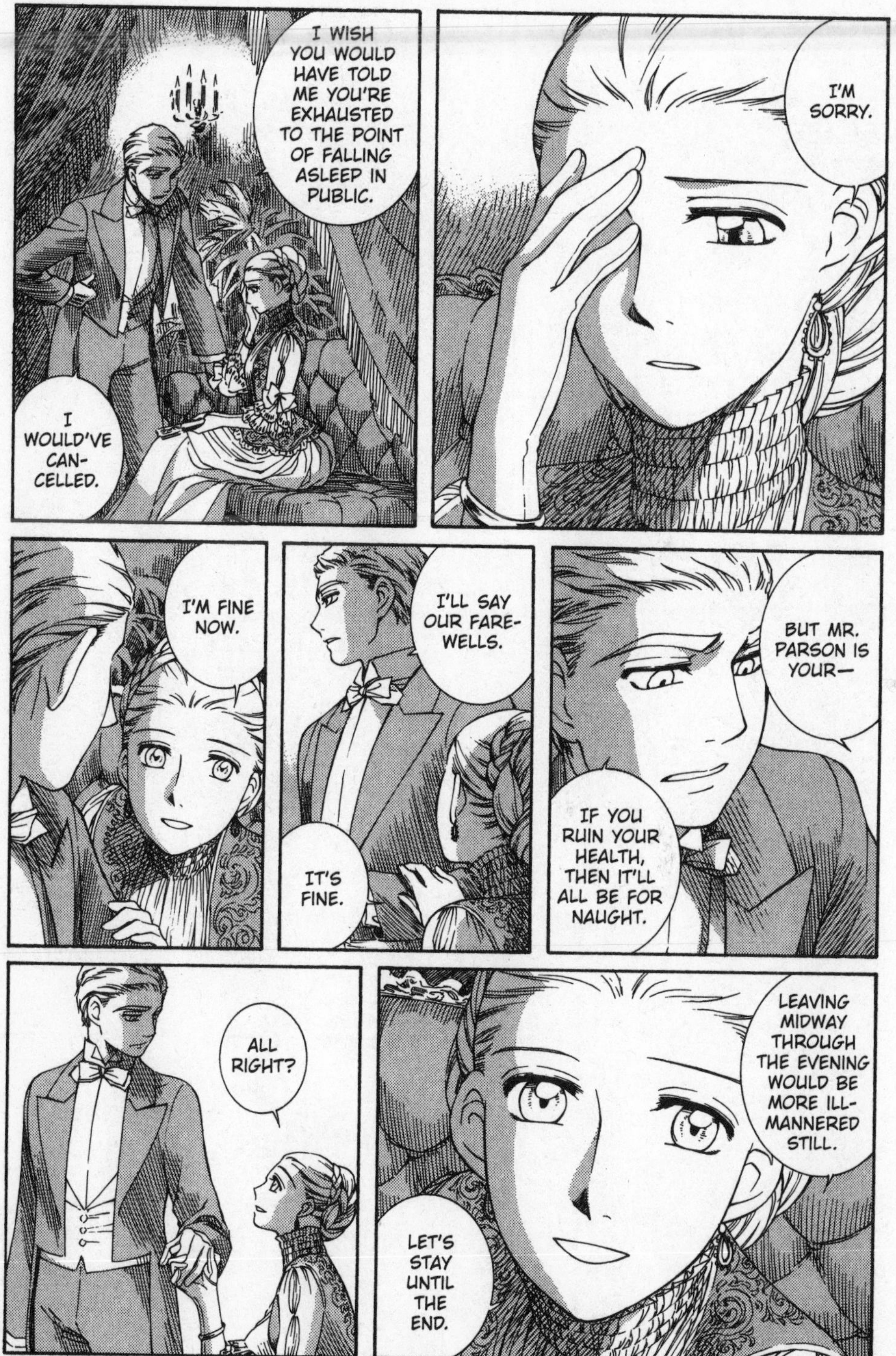
I'M SORRY.
I WISH YOU WOULD HAVE TOLD ME YOU'RE EXHAUSTED TO THE POINT OF FALLING ASLEEP IN PUBLIC.
I WOULD'VE CAN-CELLED.
BUT MR. PARSON IS YOUR—
IF YOU RUIN YOUR HEALTH, THEN IT'LL ALL BE FOR NAUGHT.
I'LL SAY OUR FARE-WELLS.
IT'S FINE.
I'M FINE NOW.
LEAVING MIDWAY THROUGH THE EVENING WOULD BE MORE ILL-MANNERED STILL.
LET'S STAY UNTIL THE END.
ALL RIGHT?

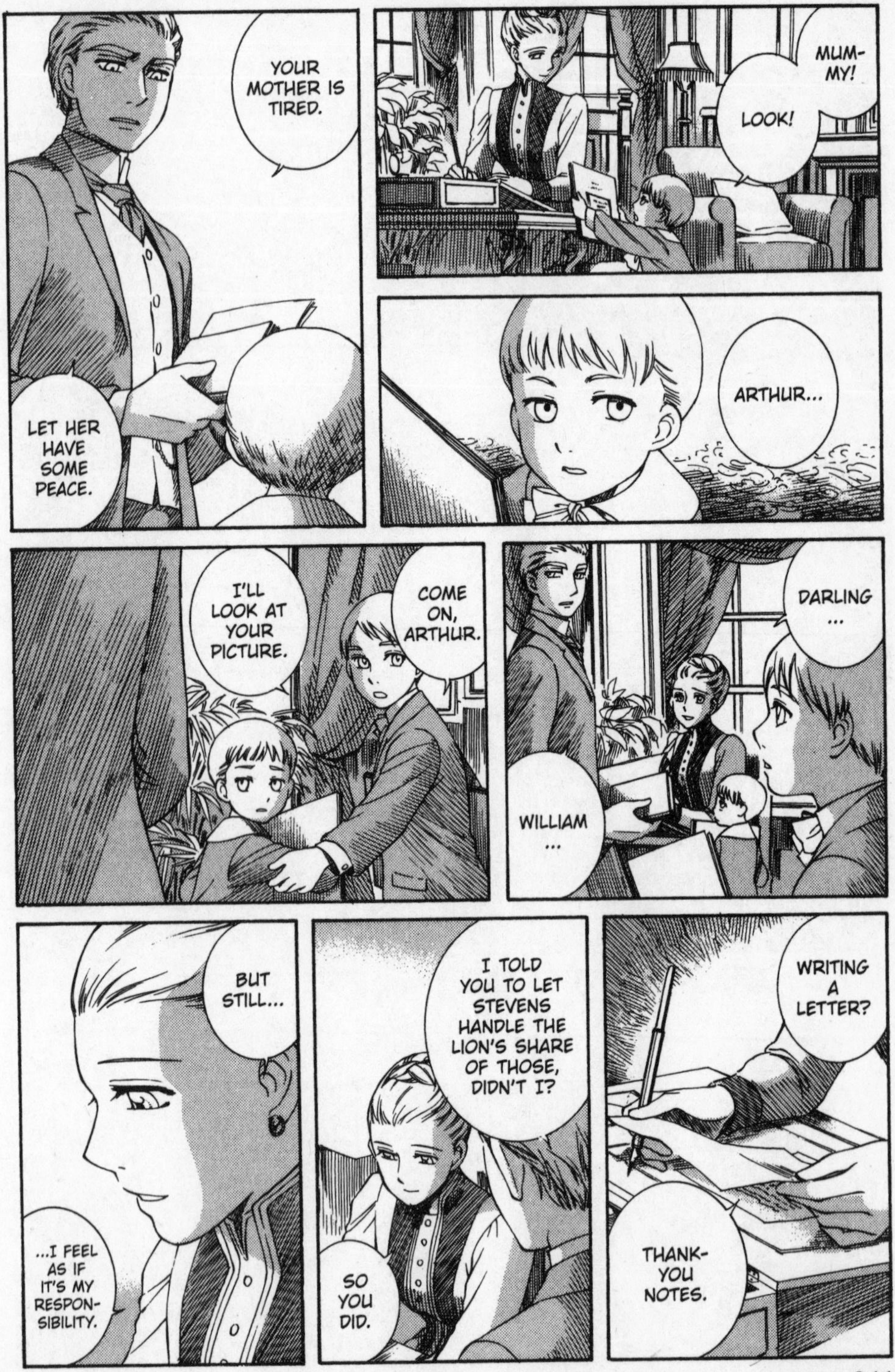
MUMMY!
LOOK!
ARTHUR...
YOUR MOTHER IS TIRED.
LET HER HAVE SOME PEACE.
DARLING...
WILLIAM...
COME ON, ARTHUR.
I'LL LOOK AT YOUR PICTURE.
WRITING A LETTER?
THANK-YOU NOTES.
I TOLD YOU TO LET STEVENS HANDLE THE LION'S SHARE OF THOSE, DIDN'T I?
SO YOU DID.
BUT STILL...
...I FEEL AS IF IT'S MY RESPONSIBILITY.

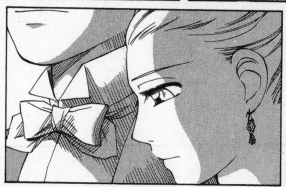

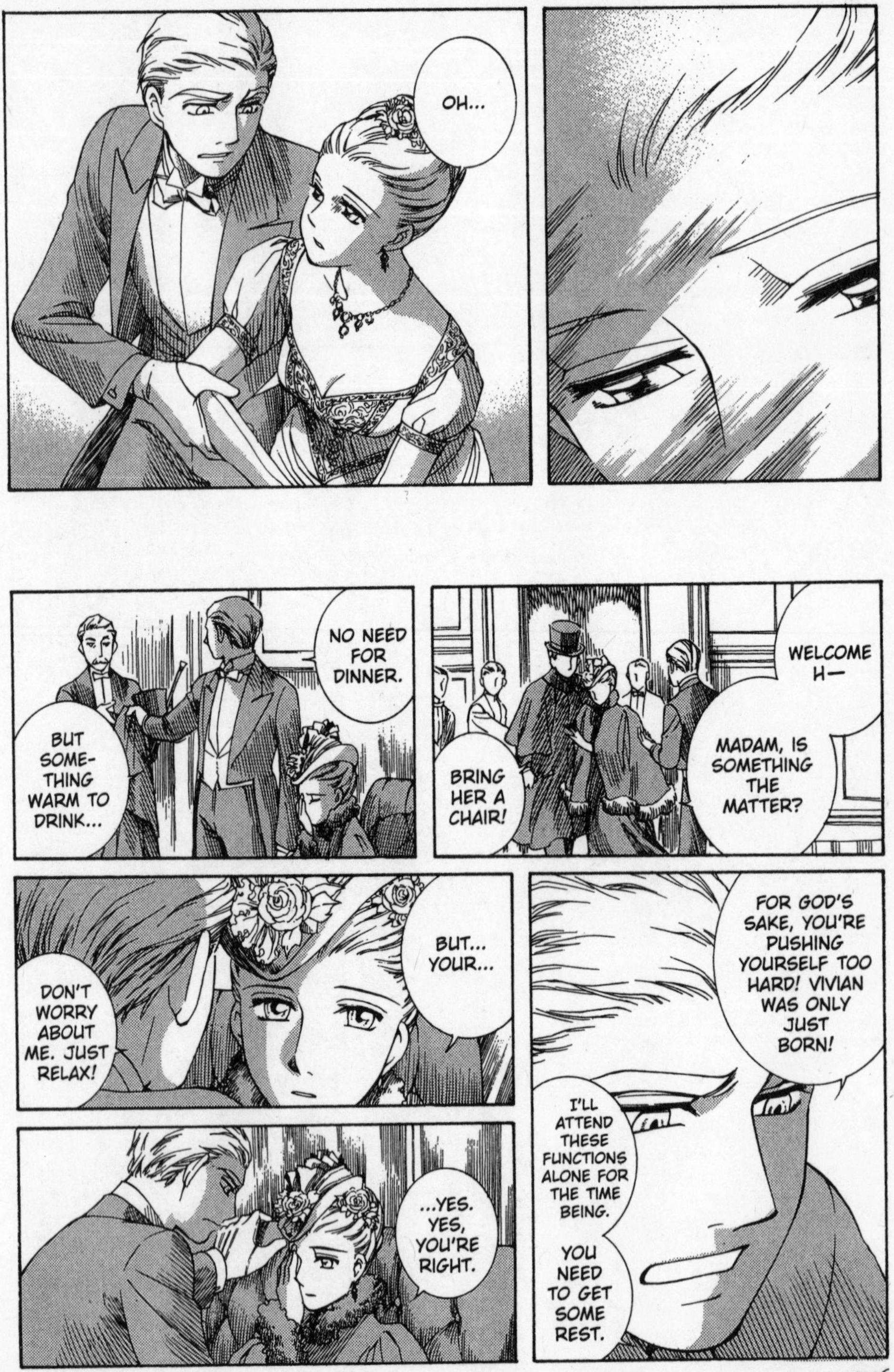
OH...
WELCOME H—
MADAM, IS SOMETHING THE MATTER?
BRING HER A CHAIR!
NO NEED FOR DINNER.
BUT SOMETHING WARM TO DRINK...
FOR GOD'S SAKE, YOU'RE PUSHING YOURSELF TOO HARD! VIVIAN WAS ONLY JUST BORN!
I'LL ATTEND THESE FUNCTIONS ALONE FOR THE TIME BEING.
YOU NEED TO GET SOME REST.
BUT... YOUR...
DON'T WORRY ABOUT ME. JUST RELAX!
...YES. YES, YOU'RE RIGHT.

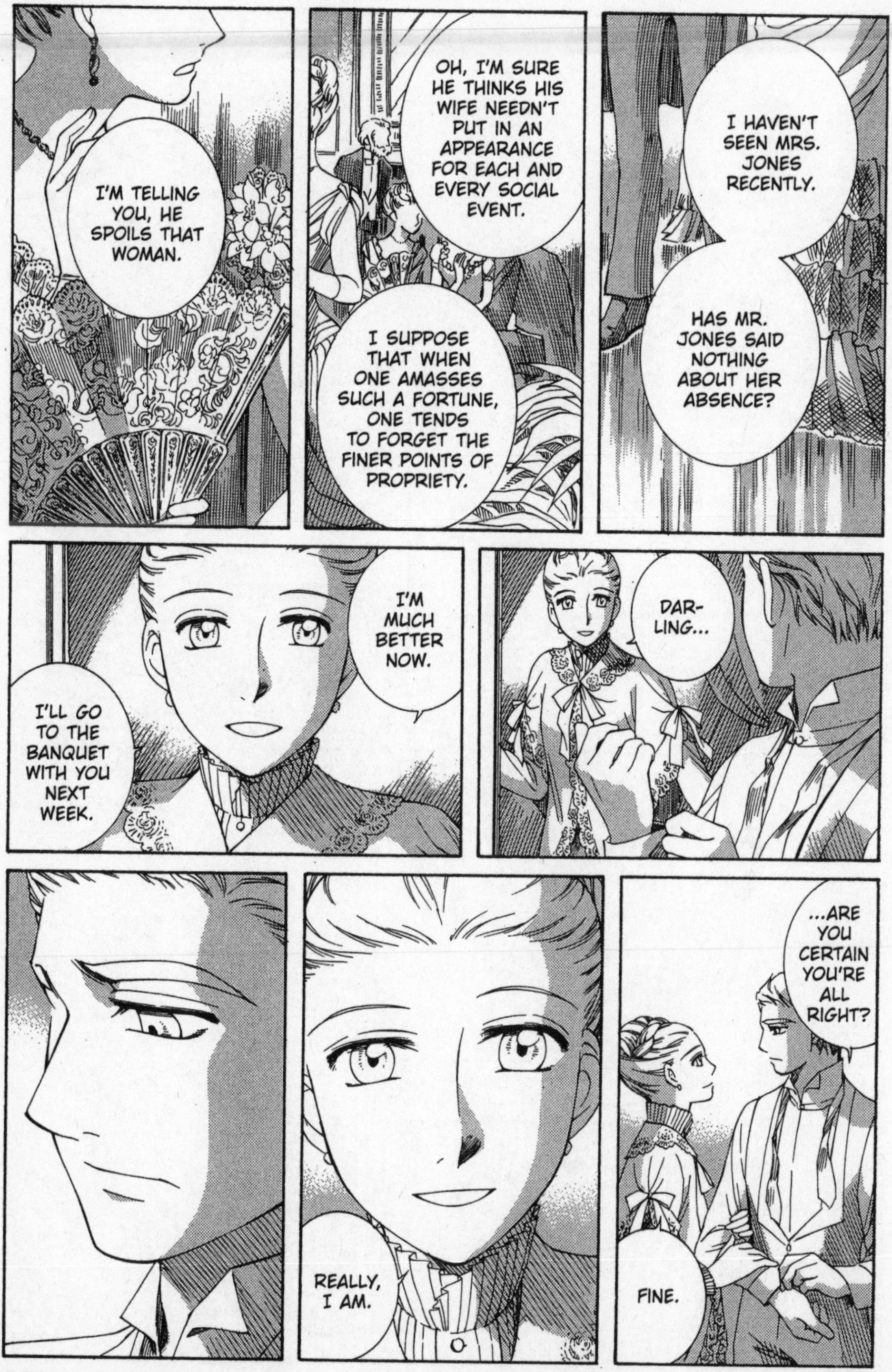
I HAVEN'T SEEN MRS. JONES RECENTLY.
HAS MR. JONES SAID NOTHING ABOUT HER ABSENCE?
OH, I'M SURE HE THINKS HIS WIFE NEEDN'T PUT IN AN APPEARANCE FOR EACH AND EVERY SOCIAL EVENT.
I SUPPOSE THAT WHEN ONE AMASSES SUCH A FORTUNE, ONE TENDS TO FORGET THE FINER POINTS OF PROPRIETY.
I'M TELLING YOU, HE SPOILS THAT WOMAN.
DAR-LING...
I'M MUCH BETTER NOW.
I'LL GO TO THE BANQUET WITH YOU NEXT WEEK.
...ARE YOU CERTAIN YOU'RE ALL RIGHT?
FINE.
REALLY, I AM.

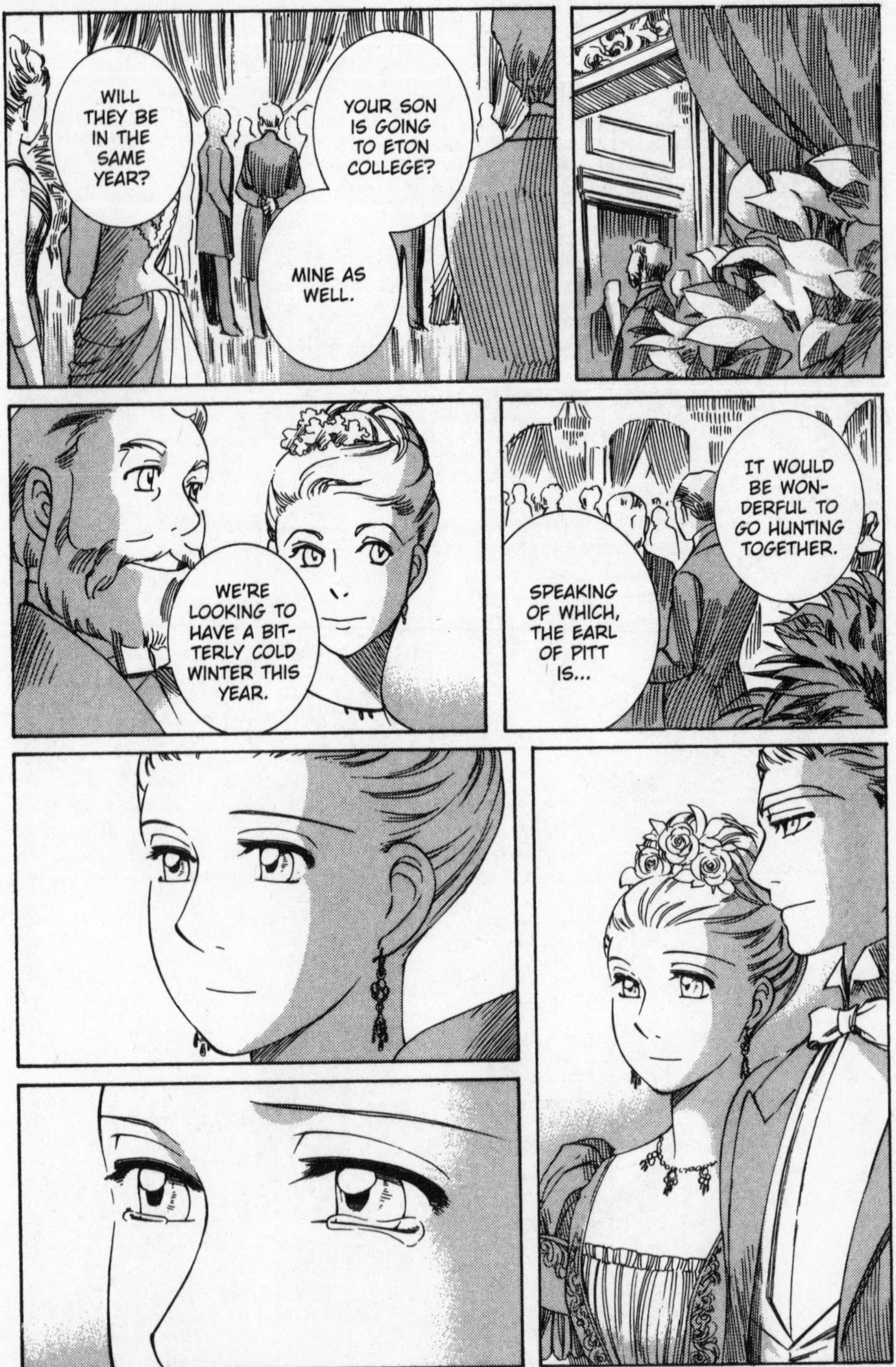
YOUR SON IS GOING TO ETON COLLEGE?
MINE AS WELL.
WILL THEY BE IN THE SAME YEAR?
IT WOULD BE WON-DERFUL TO GO HUNTING TOGETHER.
SPEAKING OF WHICH, THE EARL OF PITT IS...
WE'RE LOOKING TO HAVE A BIT-TERLY COLD WINTER THIS YEAR.

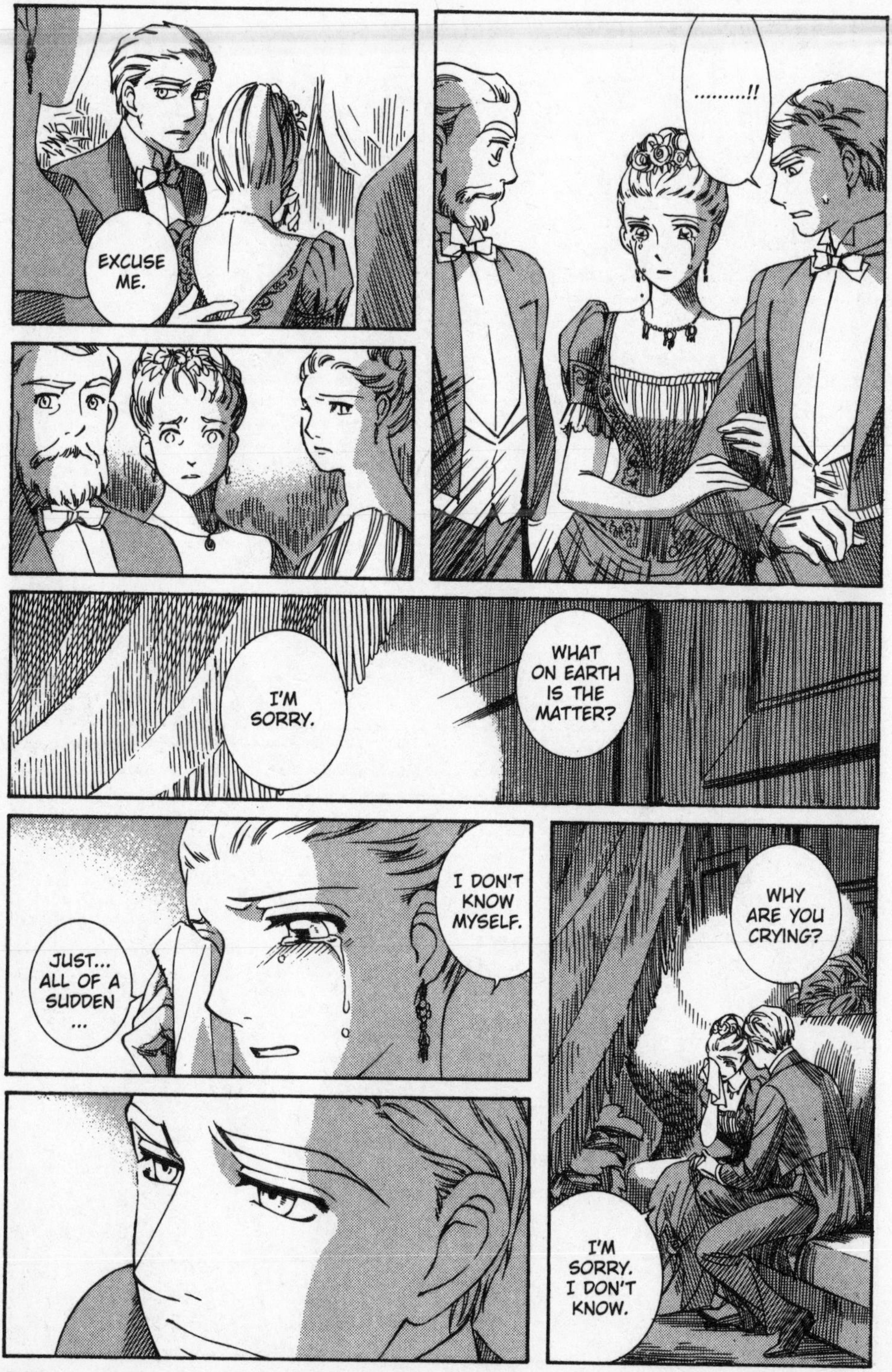
.........!!
EXCUSE ME.
WHAT ON EARTH IS THE MATTER?
I'M SORRY.
WHY ARE YOU CRYING?
I'M SORRY. I DON'T KNOW.
I DON'T KNOW MYSELF.
JUST... ALL OF A SUDDEN ...

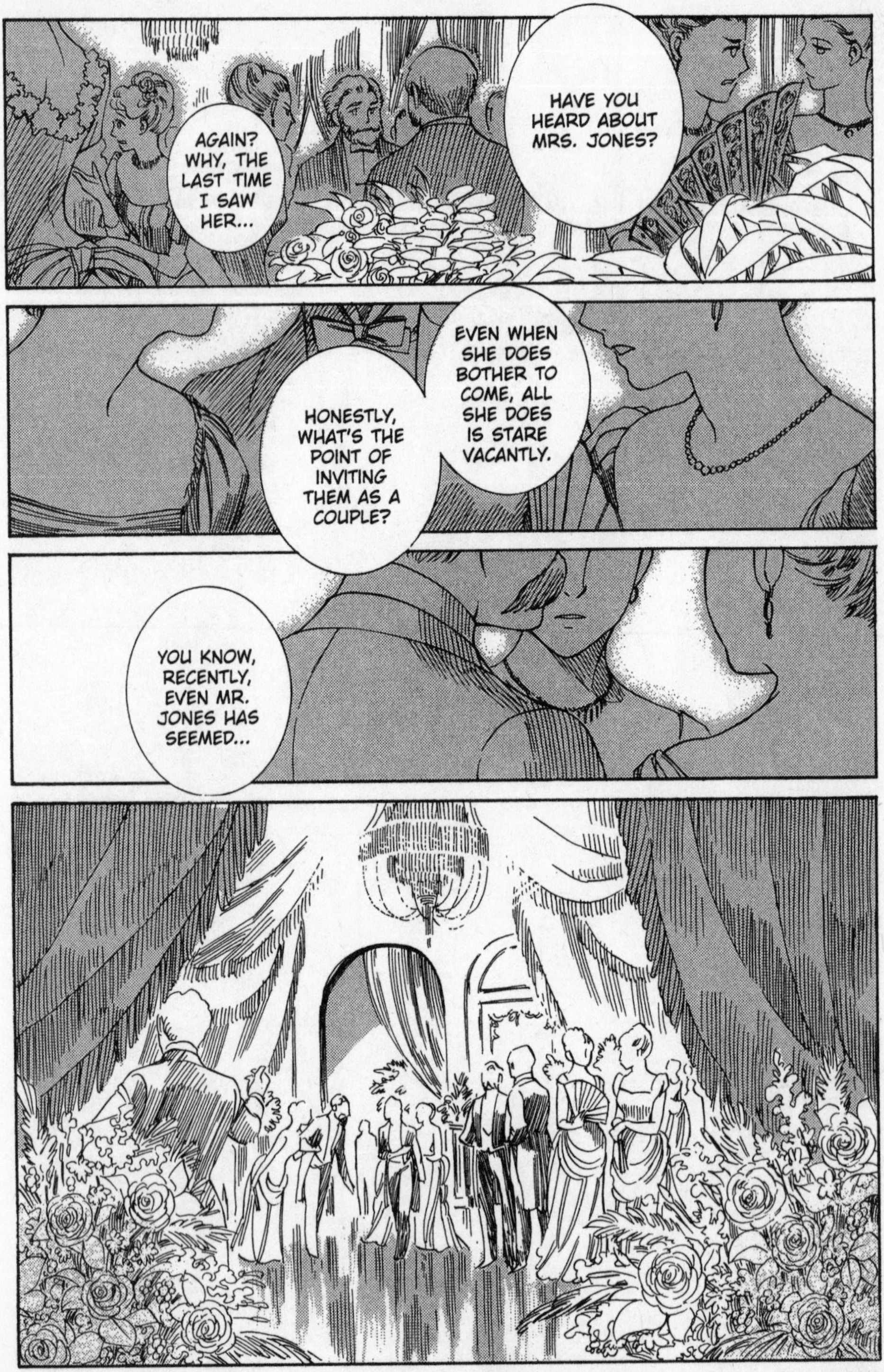
HAVE YOU HEARD ABOUT MRS. JONES?
AGAIN? WHY, THE LAST TIME I SAW HER...
EVEN WHEN SHE DOES BOTHER TO COME, ALL SHE DOES IS STARE VACANTLY.
HONESTLY, WHAT'S THE POINT OF INVITING THEM AS A COUPLE?
YOU KNOW, RECENTLY, EVEN MR. JONES HAS SEEMED...

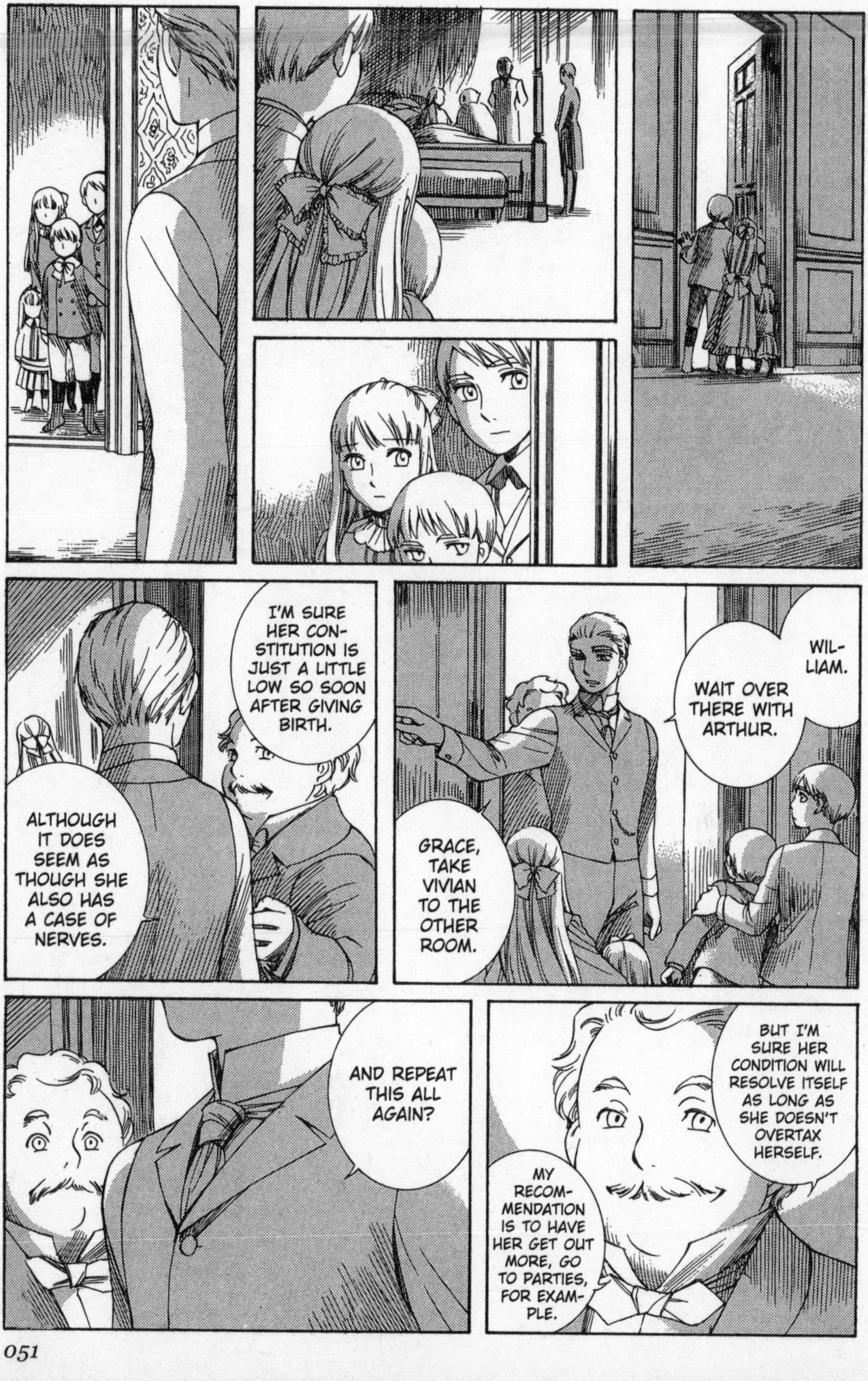
WILLIAM.
WAIT OVER THERE WITH ARTHUR.
GRACE, TAKE VIVIAN TO THE OTHER ROOM.
I'M SURE HER CONSTITUTION IS JUST A LITTLE LOW SO SOON AFTER GIVING BIRTH.
ALTHOUGH IT DOES SEEM AS THOUGH SHE ALSO HAS A CASE OF NERVES.
BUT I'M SURE HER CONDITION WILL RESOLVE ITSELF AS LONG AS SHE DOESN'T OVERTAX HERSELF.
MY RECOMMENDATION IS TO HAVE HER GET OUT MORE, GO TO PARTIES, FOR EXAMPLE.
AND REPEAT THIS ALL AGAIN?

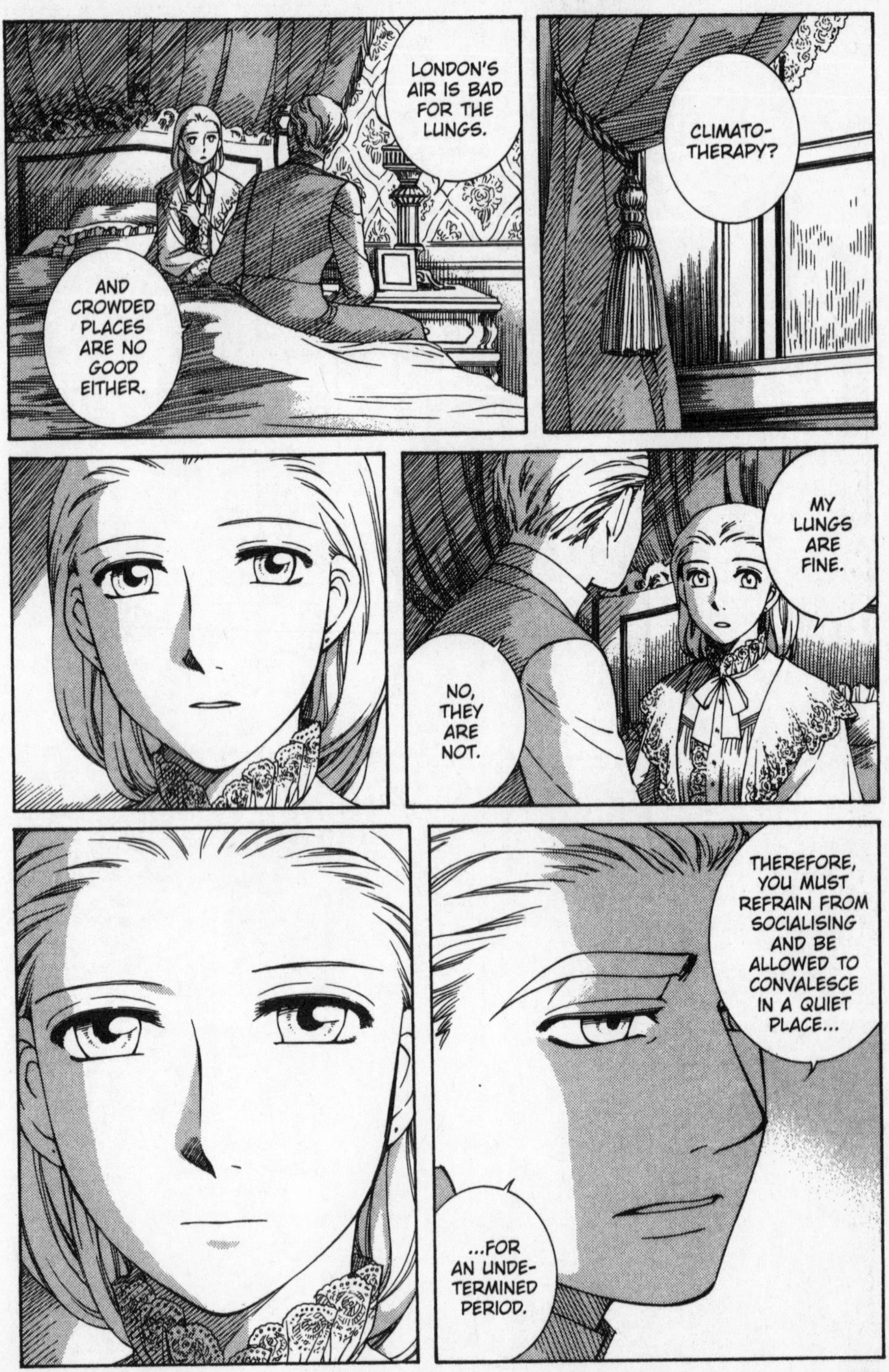
CLIMATO-THERAPY?
LONDON'S AIR IS BAD FOR THE LUNGS.
AND CROWDED PLACES ARE NO GOOD EITHER.
MY LUNGS ARE FINE.
NO, THEY ARE NOT.
THEREFORE, YOU MUST REFRAIN FROM SOCIALISING AND BE ALLOWED TO CONVALESCE IN A QUIET PLACE...
...FOR AN UNDE-TERMINED PERIOD.

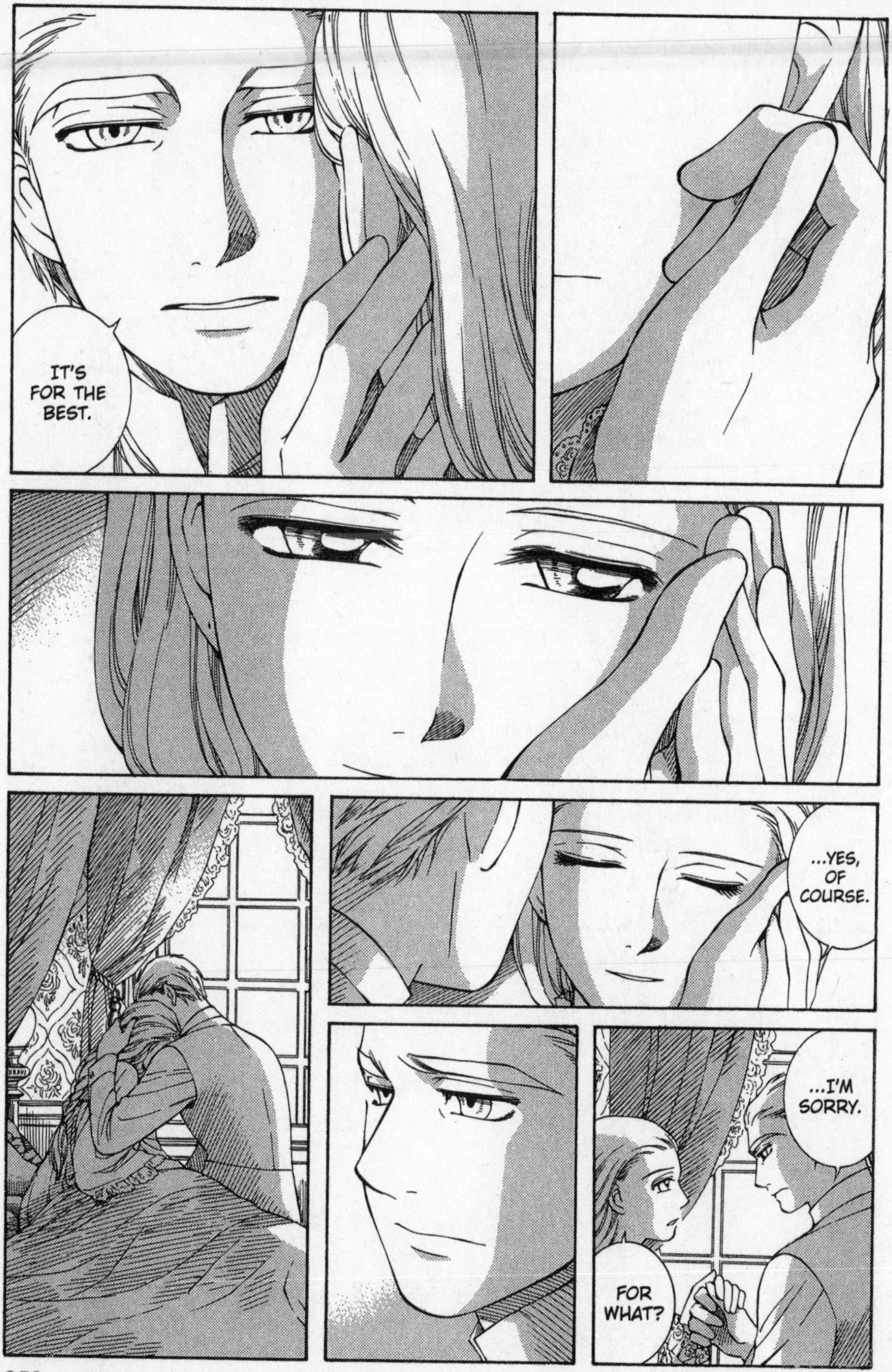
IT'S FOR THE BEST.
...YES, OF COURSE.
...I'M SORRY.
FOR WHAT?

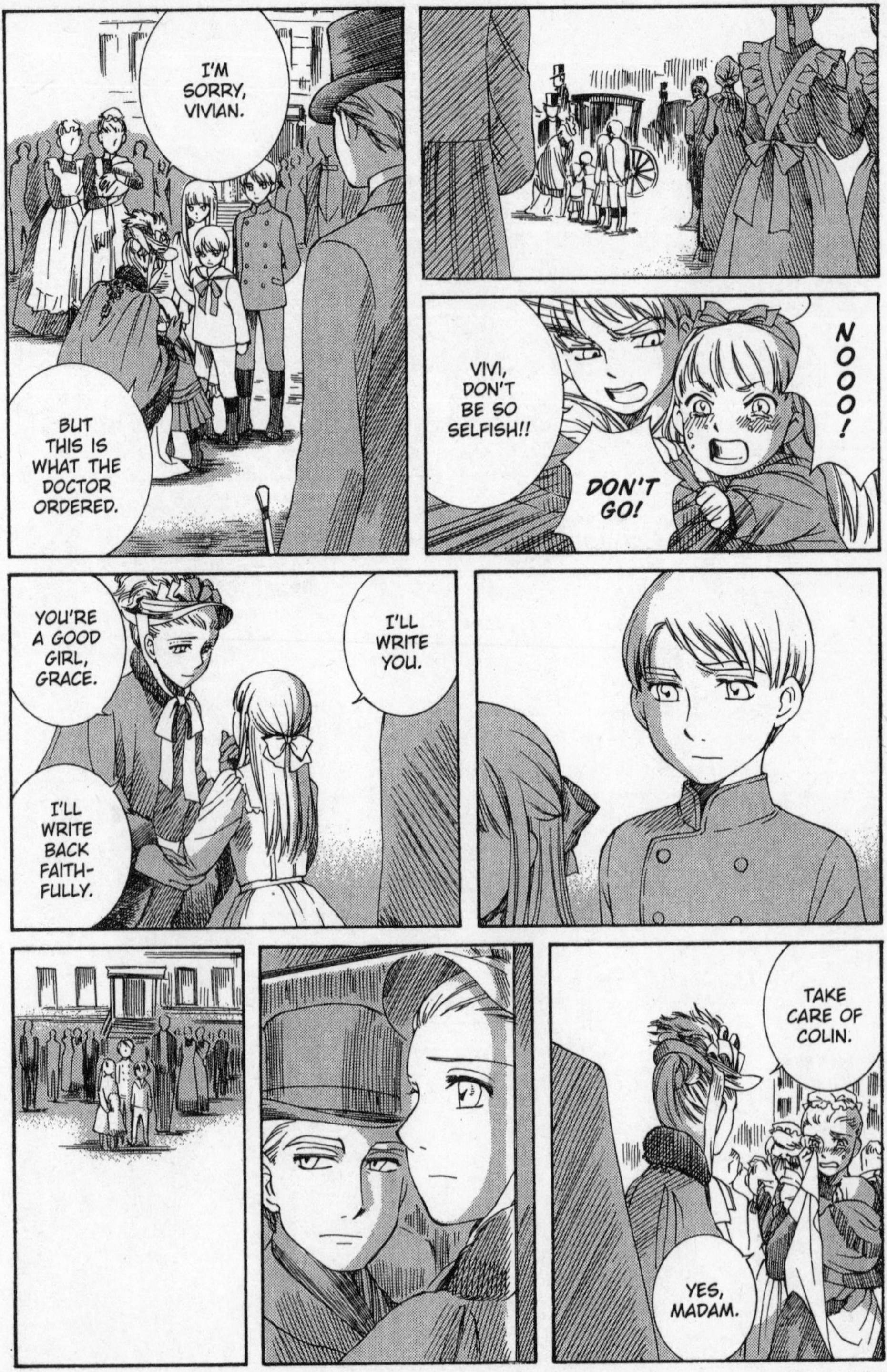
NOOOO!
VIVI, DON'T BE SO SELFISH!!
DON'T GO!
I'M SORRY, VIVIAN.
BUT THIS IS WHAT THE DOCTOR ORDERED.
I'LL WRITE YOU.
YOU'RE A GOOD GIRL, GRACE.
I'LL WRITE BACK FAITH-FULLY.
TAKE CARE OF COLIN.
YES, MADAM.

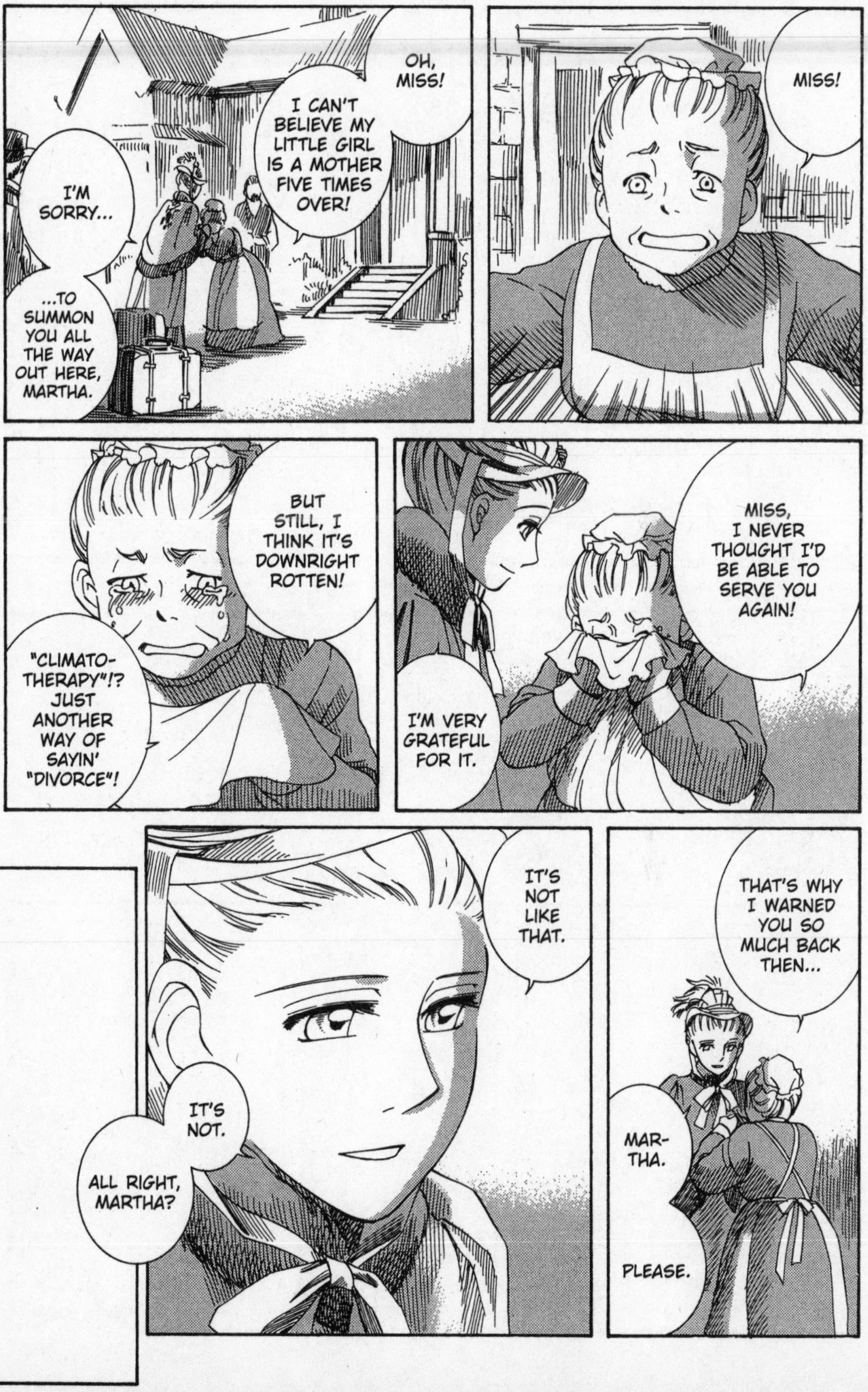
MISS!
OH, MISS!
I CAN'T BELIEVE MY LITTLE GIRL IS A MOTHER FIVE TIMES OVER!
I'M SORRY...
...TO SUMMON YOU ALL THE WAY OUT HERE, MARTHA.
MISS, I NEVER THOUGHT I'D BE ABLE TO SERVE YOU AGAIN!
I'M VERY GRATEFUL FOR IT.
BUT STILL, I THINK IT'S DOWNRIGHT ROTTEN!
"CLIMATO-THERAPY"!? JUST ANOTHER WAY OF SAYIN' "DIVORCE"!
THAT'S WHY I WARNED YOU SO MUCH BACK THEN...
MAR-THA.
PLEASE.
IT'S NOT LIKE THAT.
IT'S NOT.
ALL RIGHT, MARTHA?

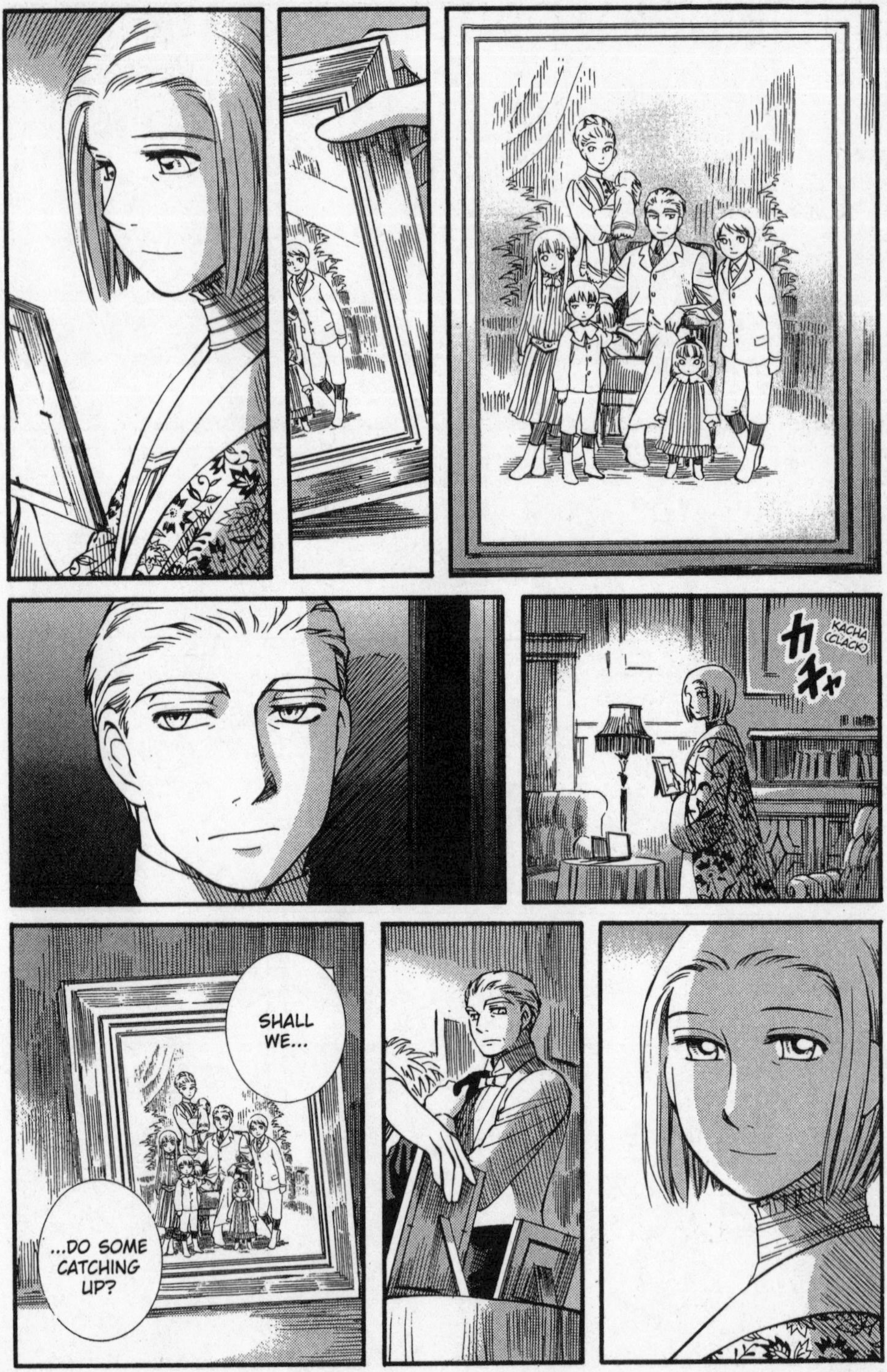
KACHA (CLACK)
カチャ
SHALL WE...
...DO SOME CATCHING UP?

Chapter 31: End

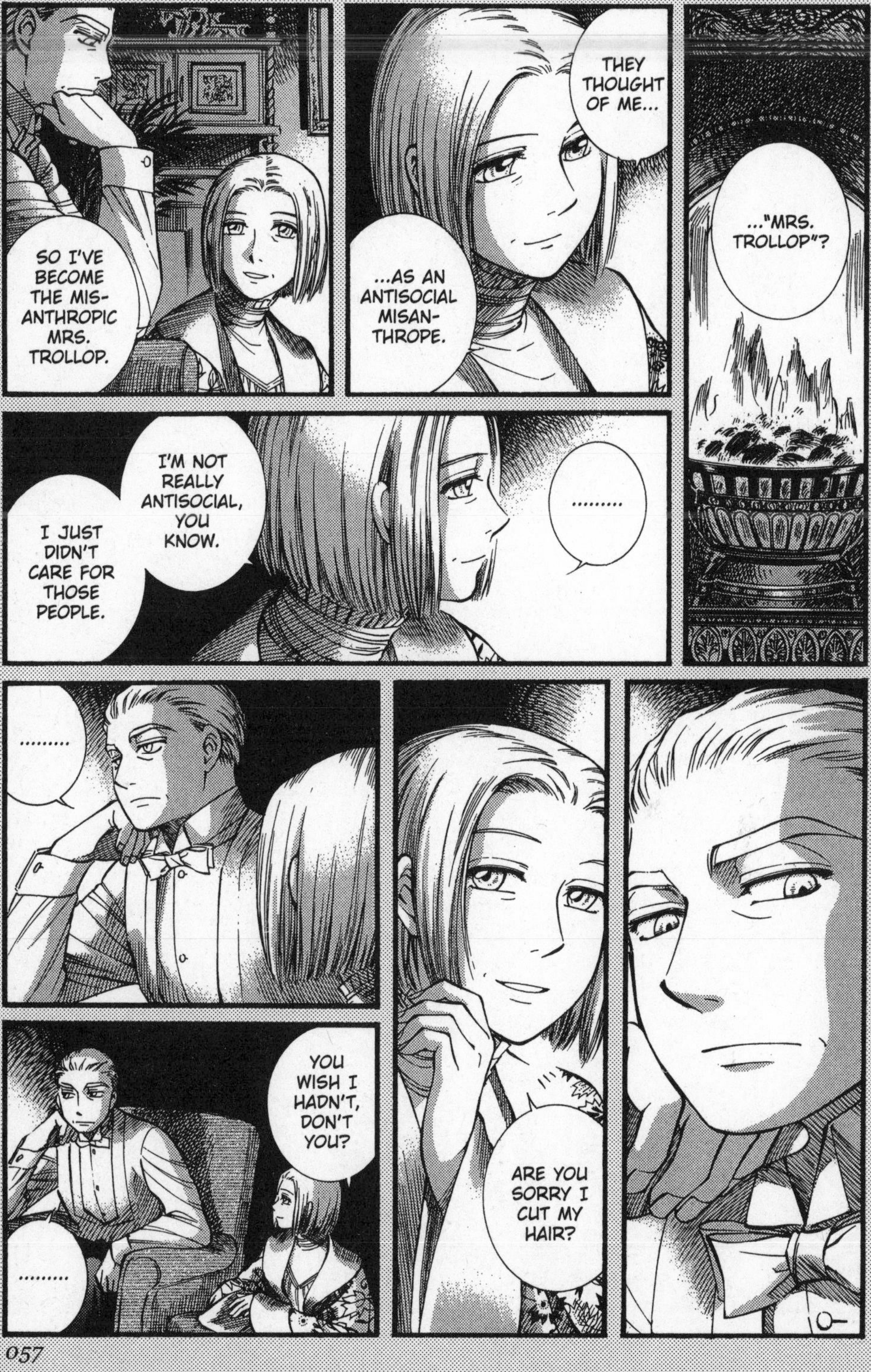
..."MRS. TROLLOP"?
THEY THOUGHT OF ME...
...AS AN ANTISOCIAL MISAN-THROPE.
SO I'VE BECOME THE MIS-ANTHROPIC MRS. TROLLOP.
....
I'M NOT REALLY ANTISOCIAL, YOU KNOW.
I JUST DIDN'T CARE FOR THOSE PEOPLE.
ARE YOU SORRY I CUT MY HAIR?
....
YOU WISH I HADN'T, DON'T YOU?
....

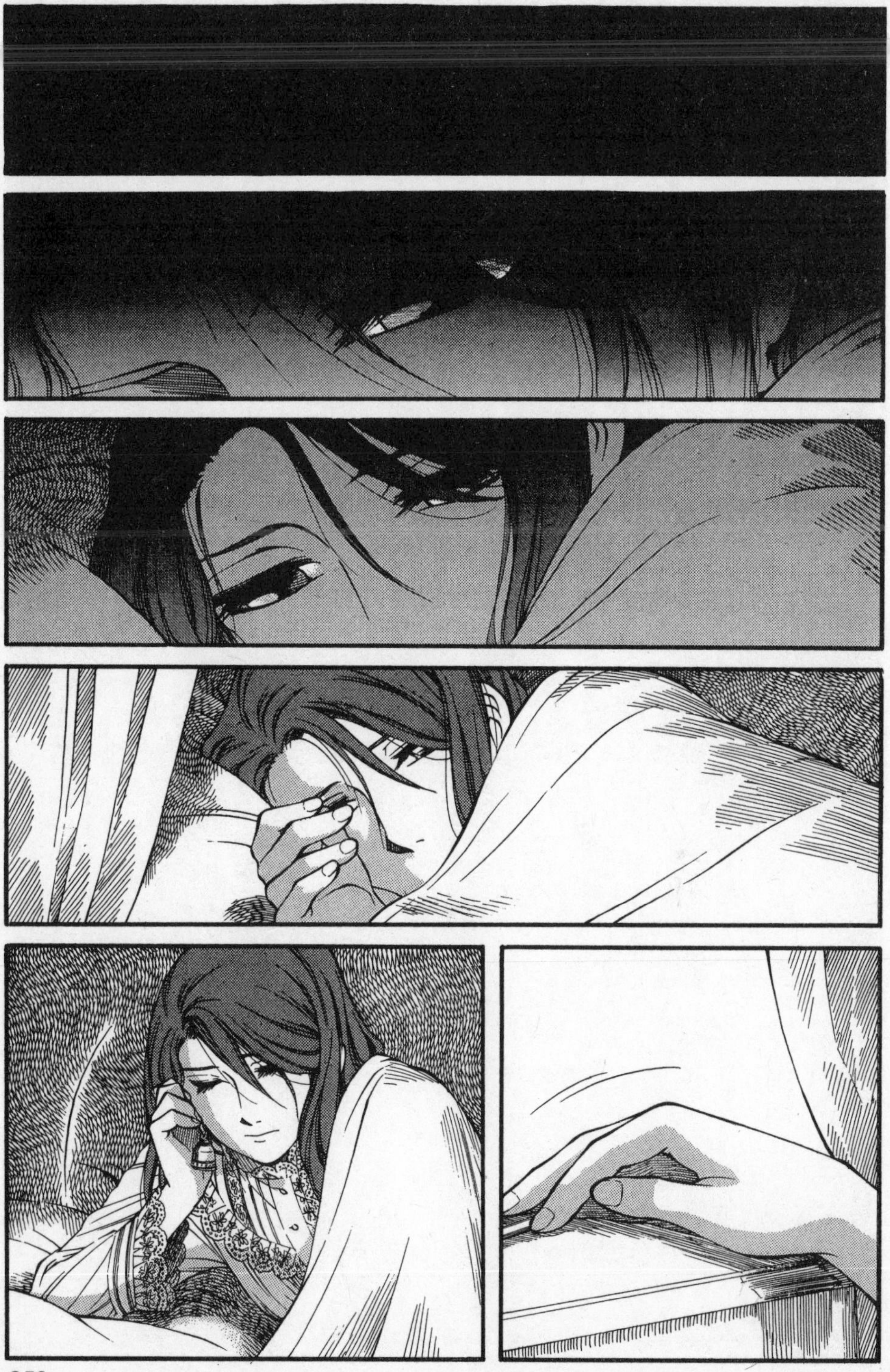

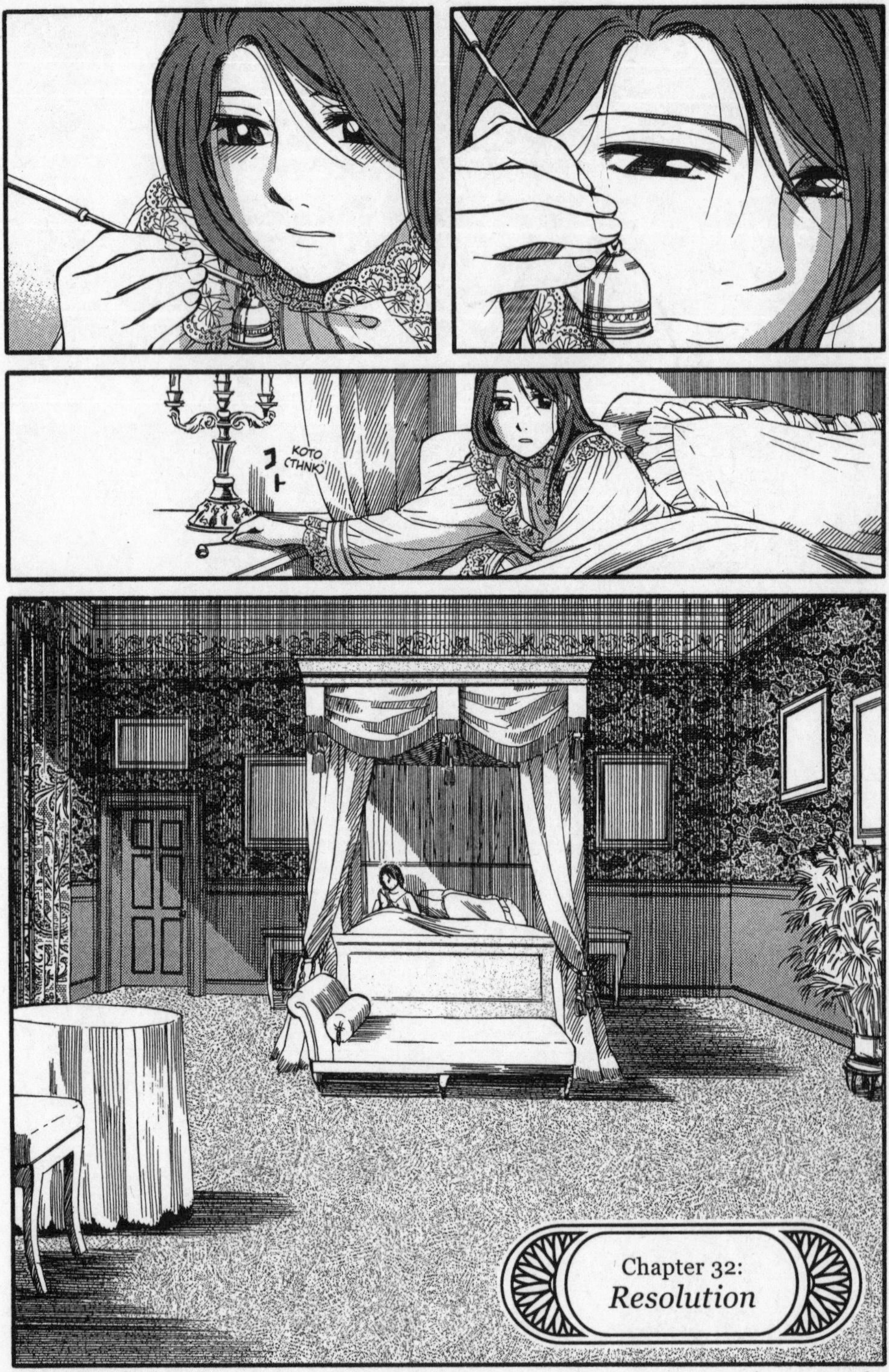
コト
KOTO (THNK)
Chapter 32:
Resolution

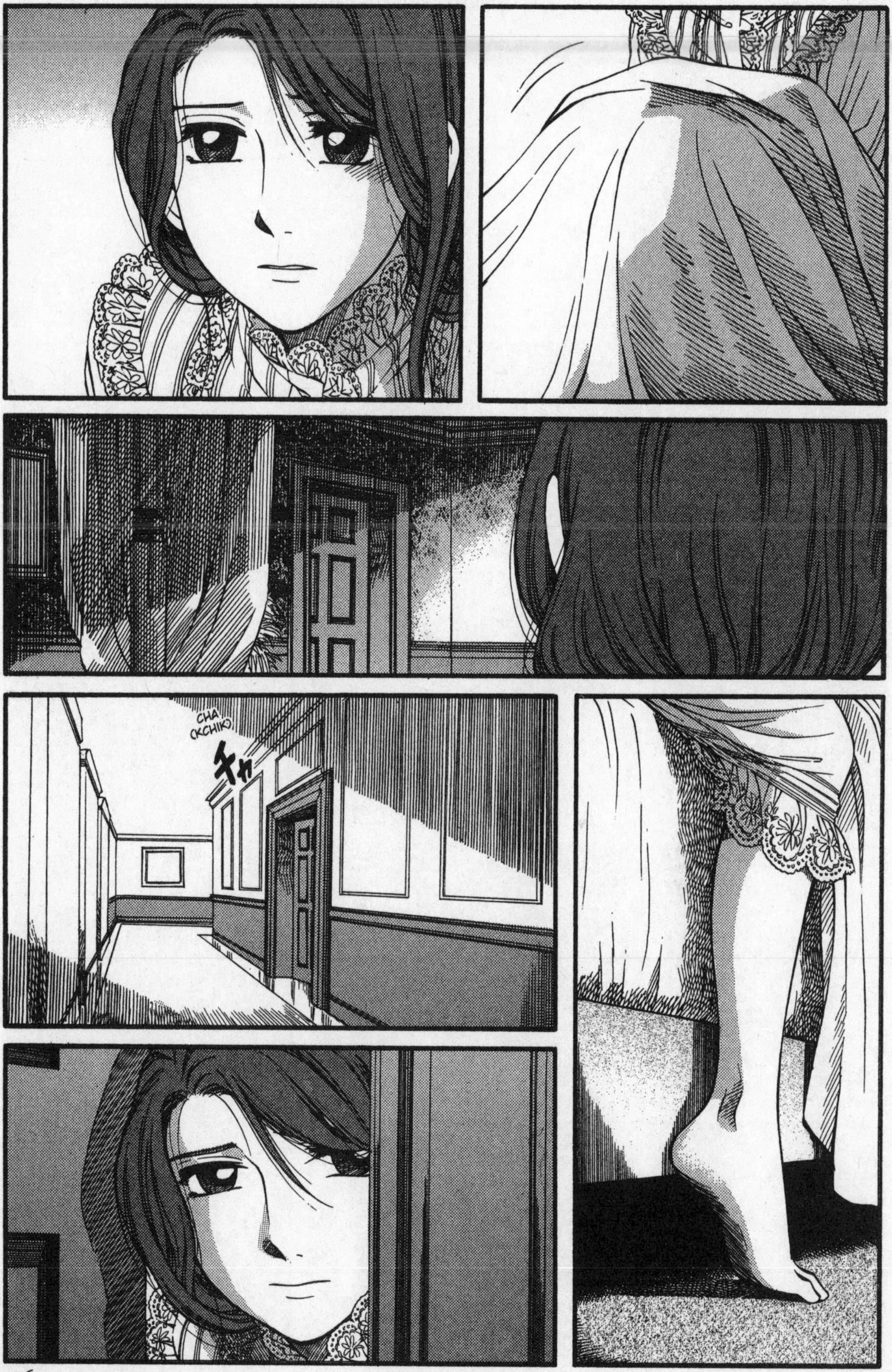
チャ
CHA
(KCHIK)

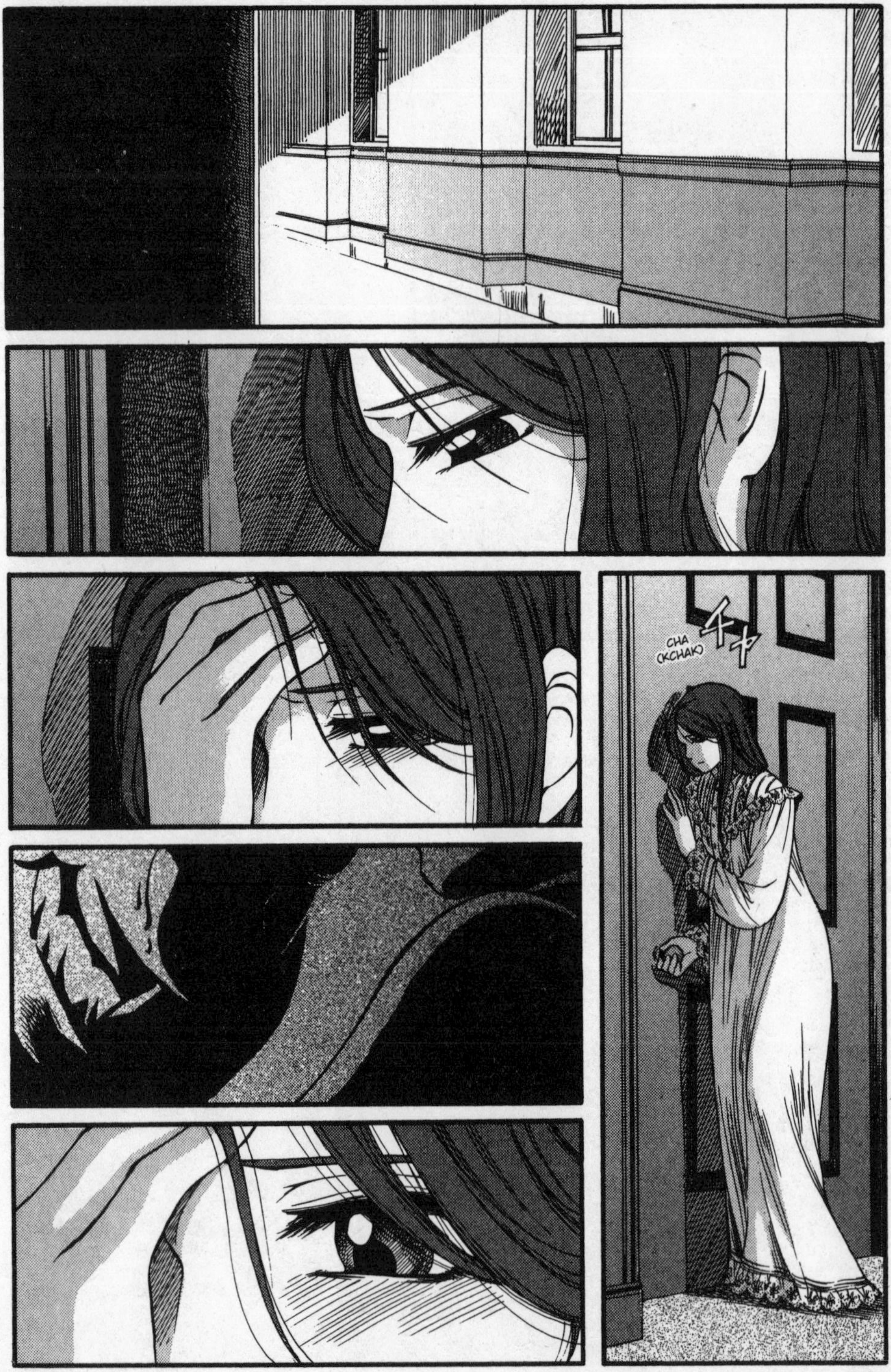
イャ
CHA (KCHAK)

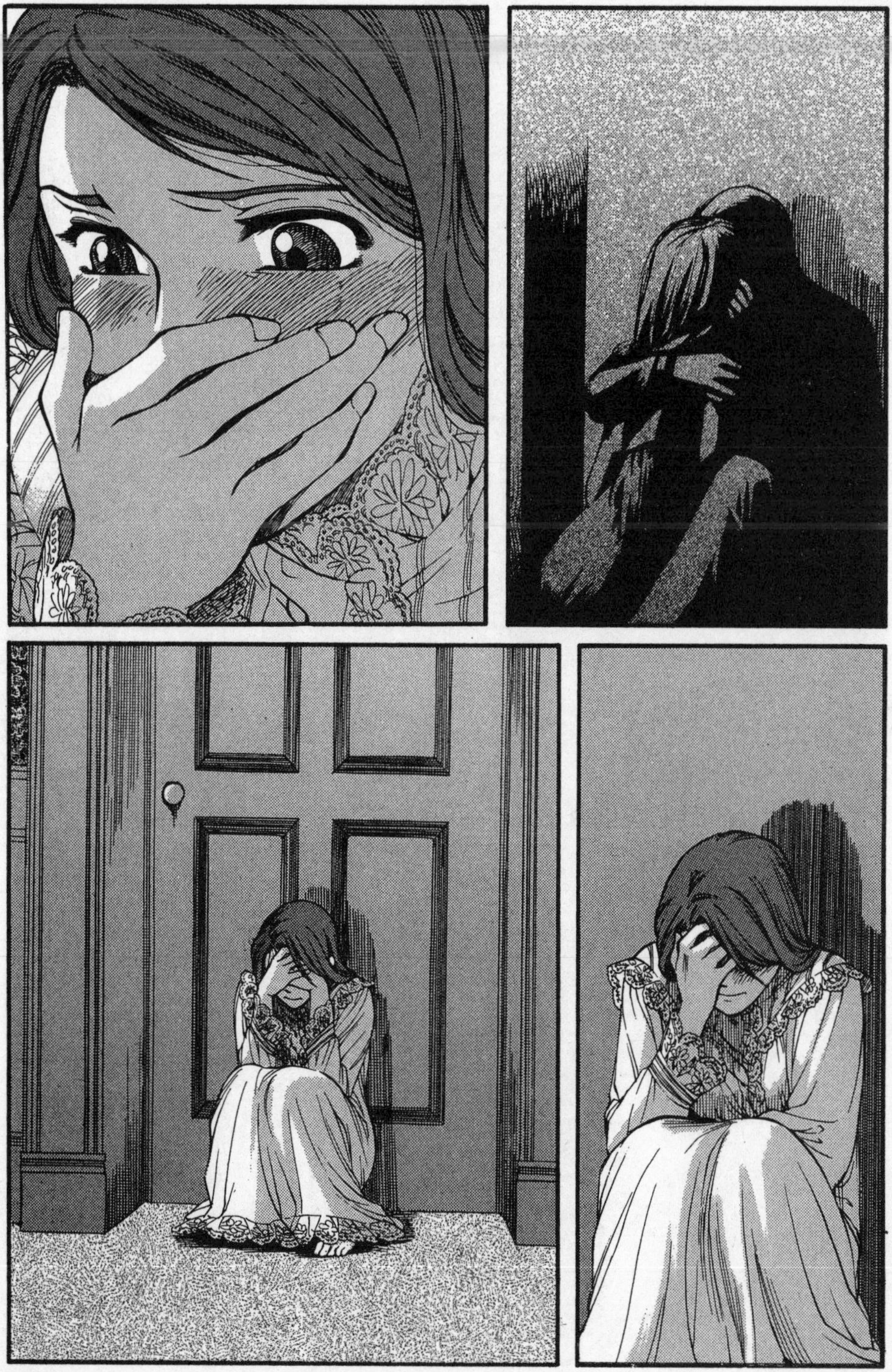

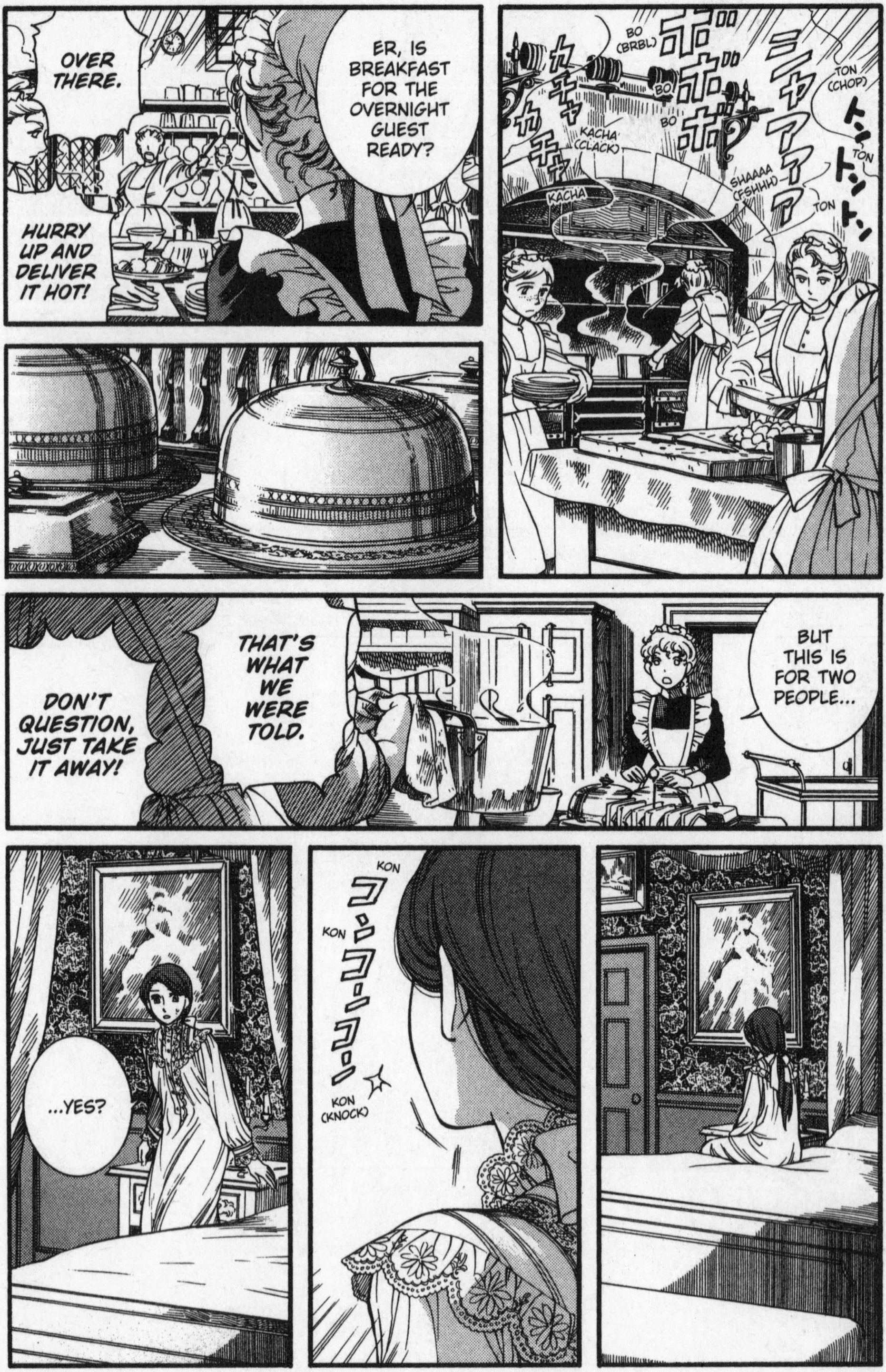
TON (CHOP)
TON
TON
SHAAAA (FSHHH)
BO (BRBL)
BO
BO
KACHA (CLACK)
KACHA
ER, IS BREAKFAST FOR THE OVERNIGHT GUEST READY?
OVER THERE.
HURRY UP AND DELIVER IT HOT!
BUT THIS IS FOR TWO PEOPLE...
THAT'S WHAT WE WERE TOLD.
DON'T QUESTION, JUST TAKE IT AWAY!
KON
KON
KON (KNOCK)
...YES?

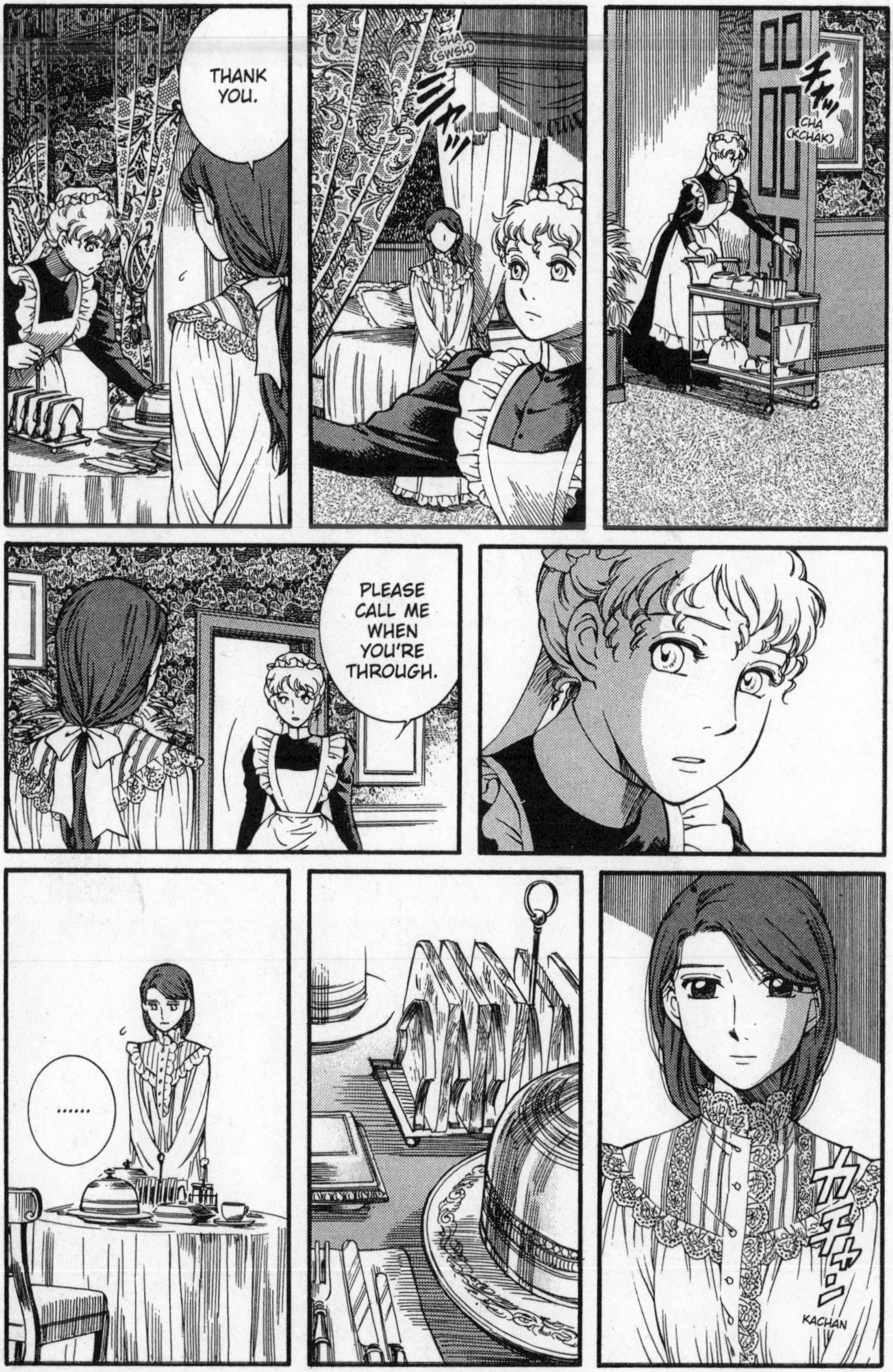

チャッ
CHA (KCHAK)
SHA (SWSH)
シャッ
THANK YOU.
PLEASE CALL ME WHEN YOU'RE THROUGH.
カチャン
KACHAN
......

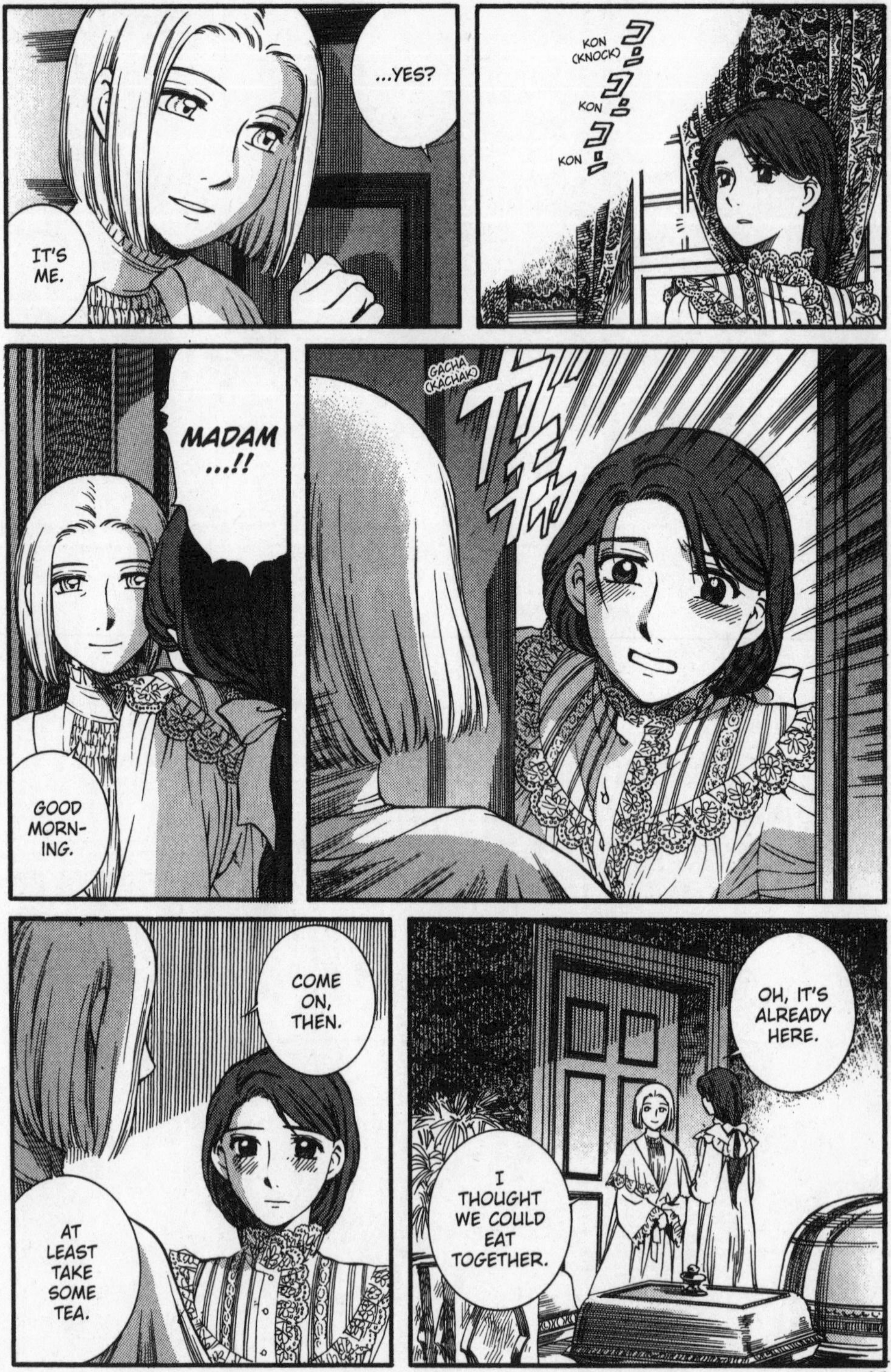
KON (KNOCK)
KON
KON
...YES?
IT'S ME.
GACHA (KACHAK)
MADAM ...!!
GOOD MORNING.
OH, IT'S ALREADY HERE.
I THOUGHT WE COULD EAT TOGETHER.
COME ON, THEN.
AT LEAST TAKE SOME TEA.

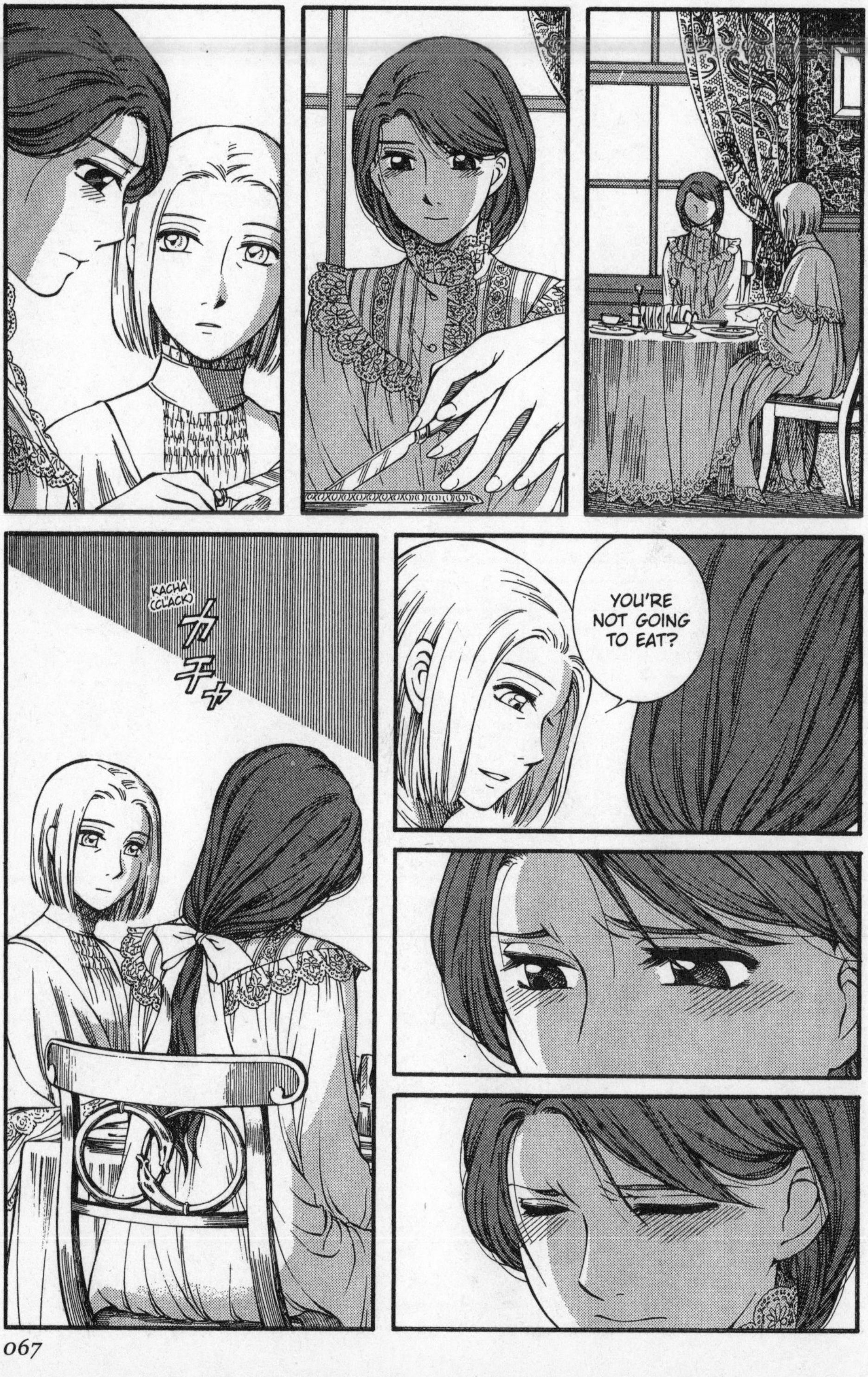
YOU'RE NOT GOING TO EAT?
KACHA (CLACK)
カチャ

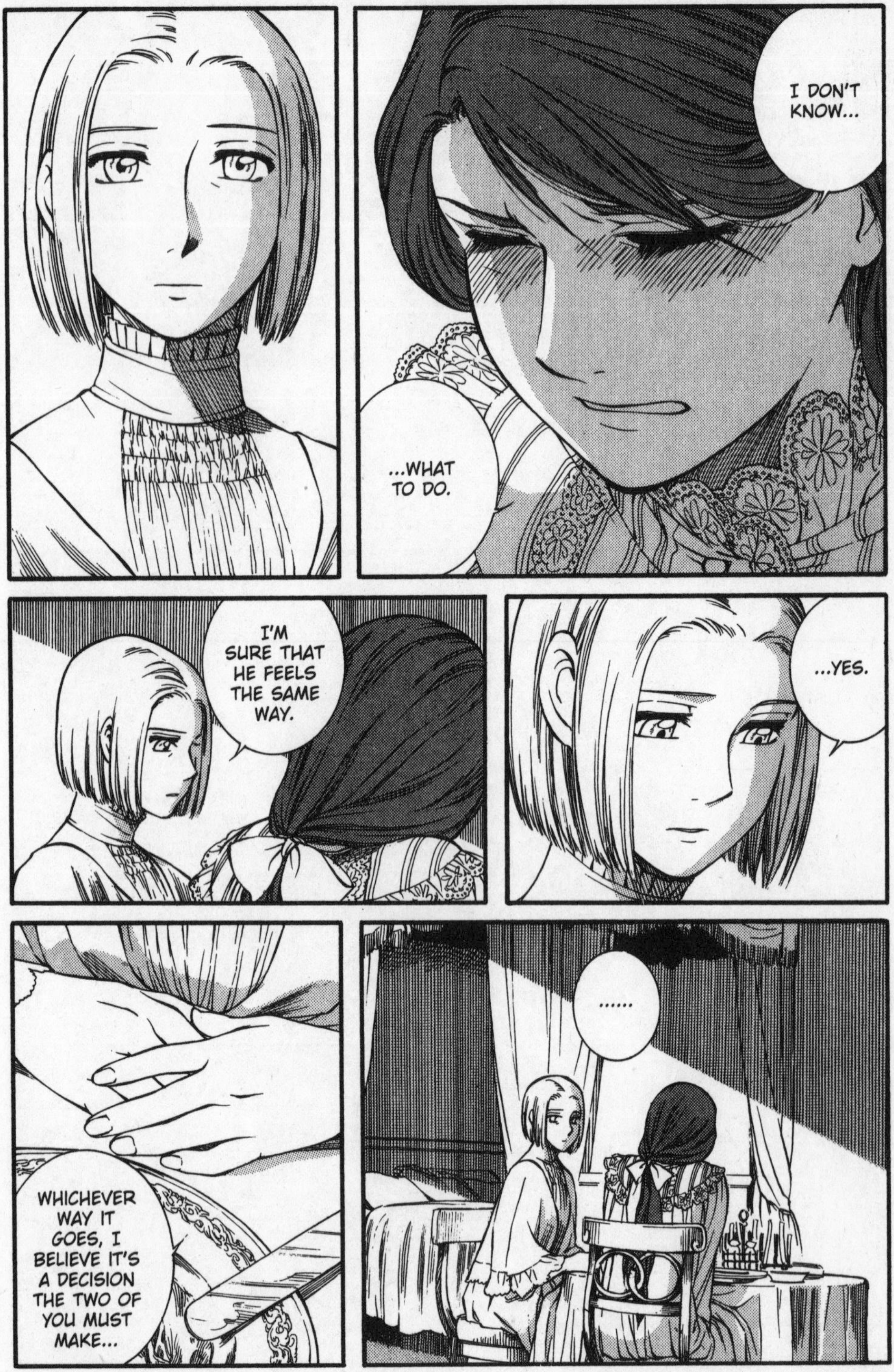
I DON'T KNOW...
...WHAT TO DO.
...YES.
I'M SURE THAT HE FEELS THE SAME WAY.
......
WHICHEVER WAY IT GOES, I BELIEVE IT'S A DECISION THE TWO OF YOU MUST MAKE...

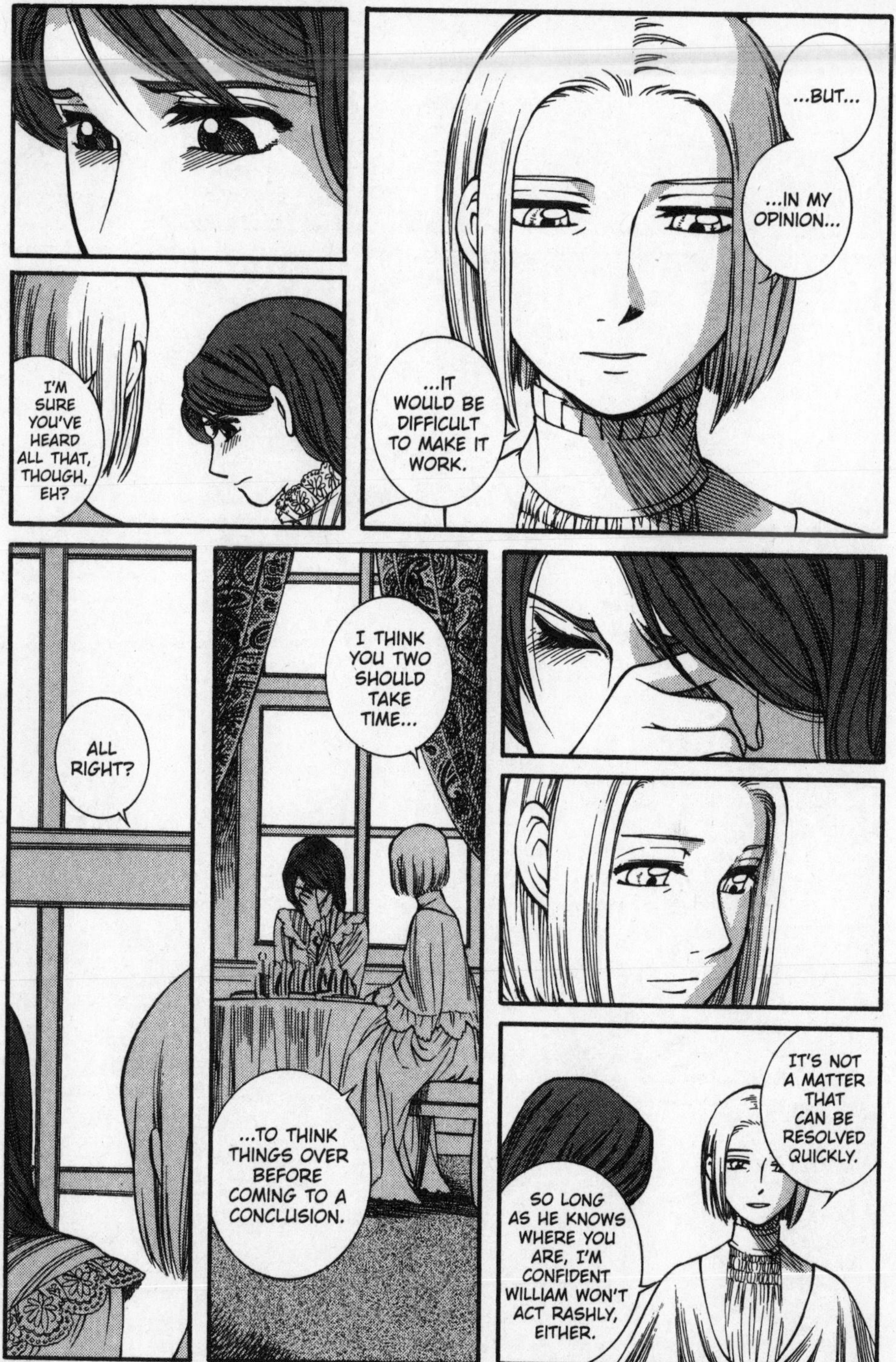
...BUT...
...IN MY OPINION...
...IT WOULD BE DIFFICULT TO MAKE IT WORK.
I'M SURE YOU'VE HEARD ALL THAT, THOUGH, EH?
IT'S NOT A MATTER THAT CAN BE RESOLVED QUICKLY.
SO LONG AS HE KNOWS WHERE YOU ARE, I'M CONFIDENT WILLIAM WON'T ACT RASHLY, EITHER.
I THINK YOU TWO SHOULD TAKE TIME...
...TO THINK THINGS OVER BEFORE COMING TO A CONCLUSION.
ALL RIGHT?

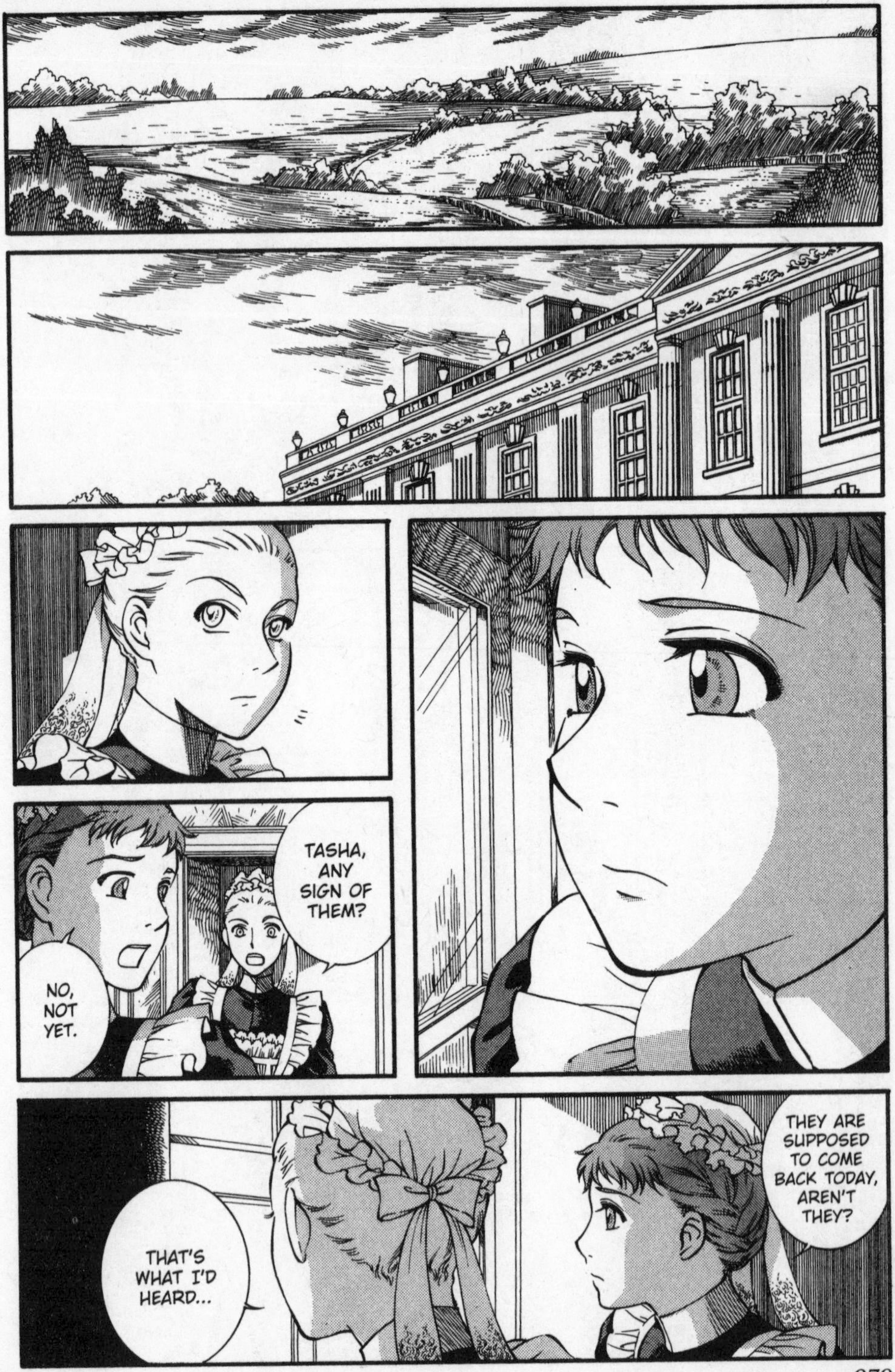
TASHA, ANY SIGN OF THEM?
NO, NOT YET.
THEY ARE SUPPOSED TO COME BACK TODAY, AREN'T THEY?
THAT'S WHAT I'D HEARD...

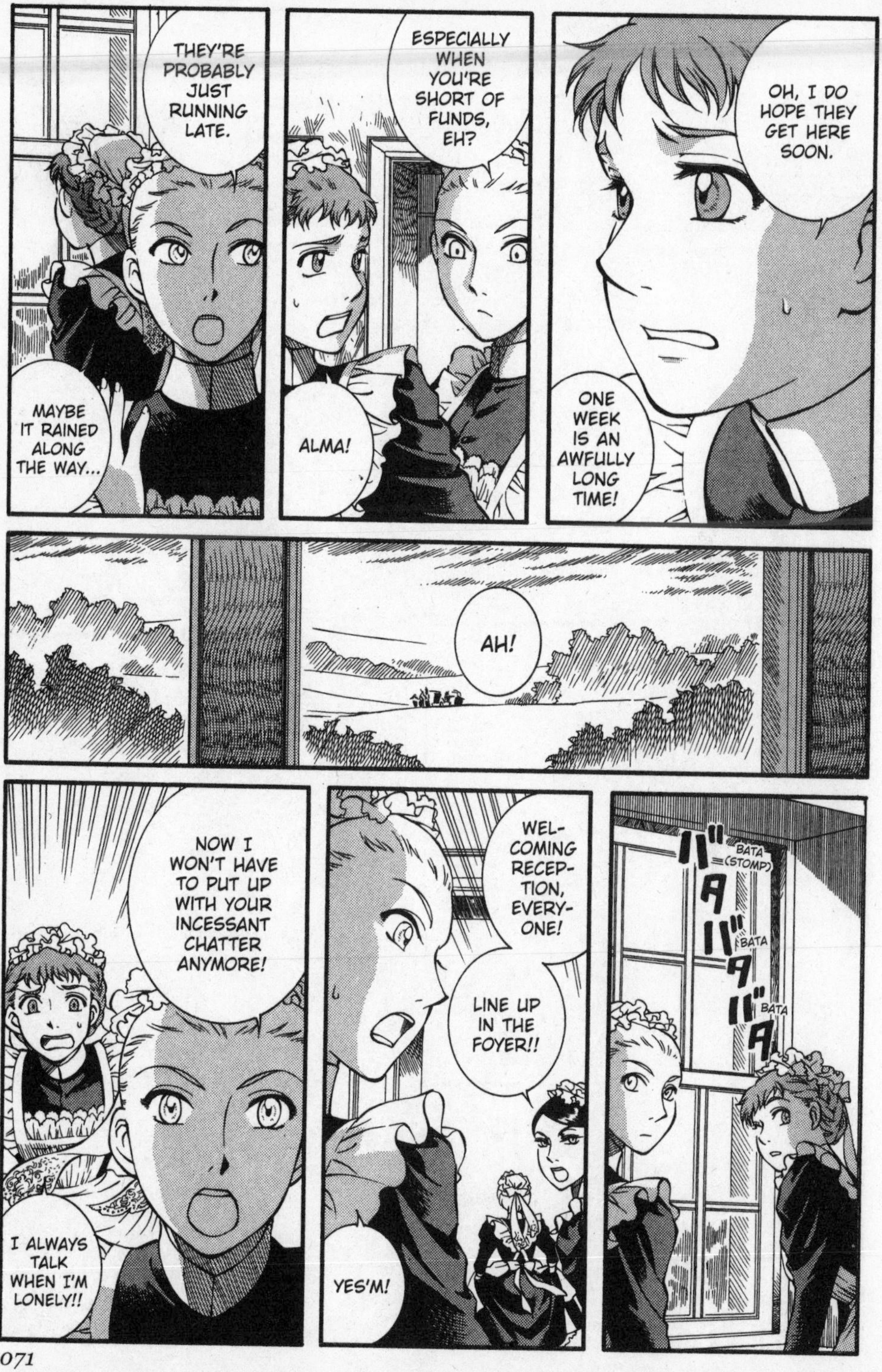
OH, I DO HOPE THEY GET HERE SOON.
ONE WEEK IS AN AWFULLY LONG TIME!
ESPECIALLY WHEN YOU'RE SHORT OF FUNDS, EH?
ALMA!
THEY'RE PROBABLY JUST RUNNING LATE.
MAYBE IT RAINED ALONG THE WAY...
AH!
バタ BATA (STOMP)
バタ BATA
バタ BATA
WEL-COMING RECEP-TION, EVERY-ONE!
LINE UP IN THE FOYER!!
YES'M!
NOW I WON'T HAVE TO PUT UP WITH YOUR INCESSANT CHATTER ANYMORE!
I ALWAYS TALK WHEN I'M LONELY!!

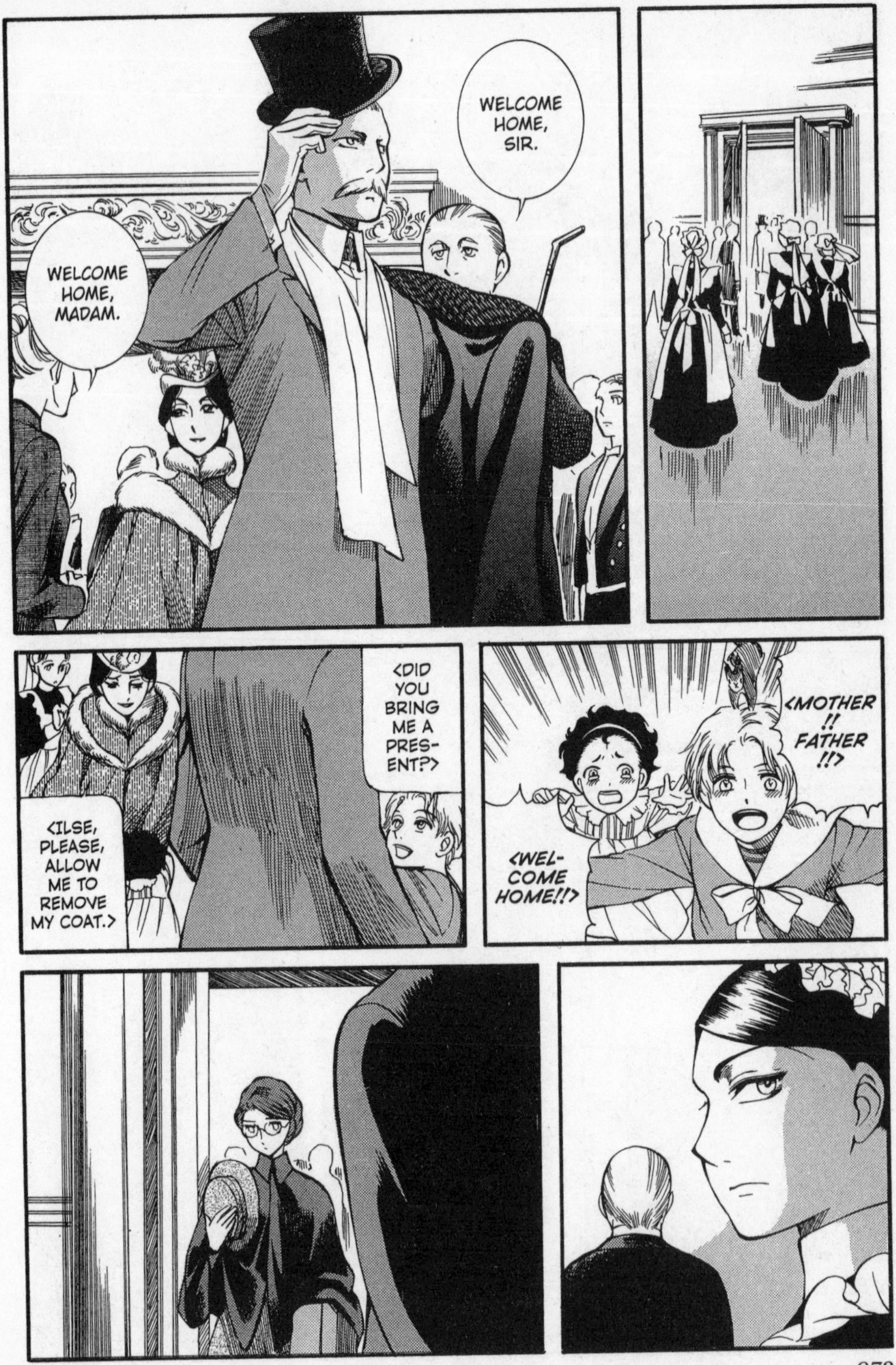
WELCOME HOME, SIR.
WELCOME HOME, MADAM.
<MOTHER!! FATHER!!>
<WEL-COME HOME!!>
<DID YOU BRING ME A PRES-ENT?>
<ILSE, PLEASE, ALLOW ME TO REMOVE MY COAT.>

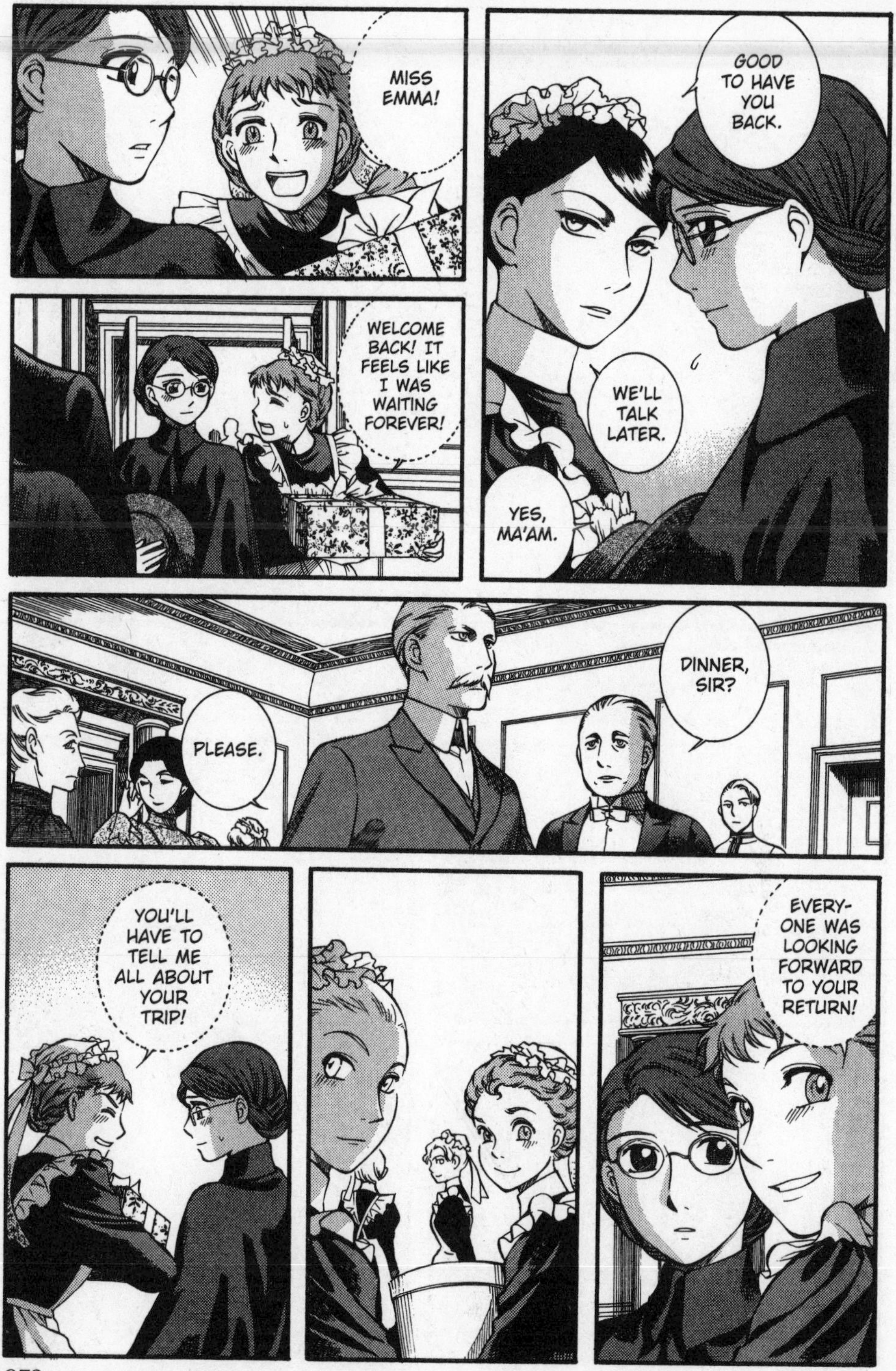

GOOD TO HAVE YOU BACK.
WE'LL TALK LATER.
YES, MA'AM.
MISS EMMA!
WELCOME BACK! IT FEELS LIKE I WAS WAITING FOREVER!
DINNER, SIR?
PLEASE.
EVERY-ONE WAS LOOKING FORWARD TO YOUR RETURN!
YOU'LL HAVE TO TELL ME ALL ABOUT YOUR TRIP!

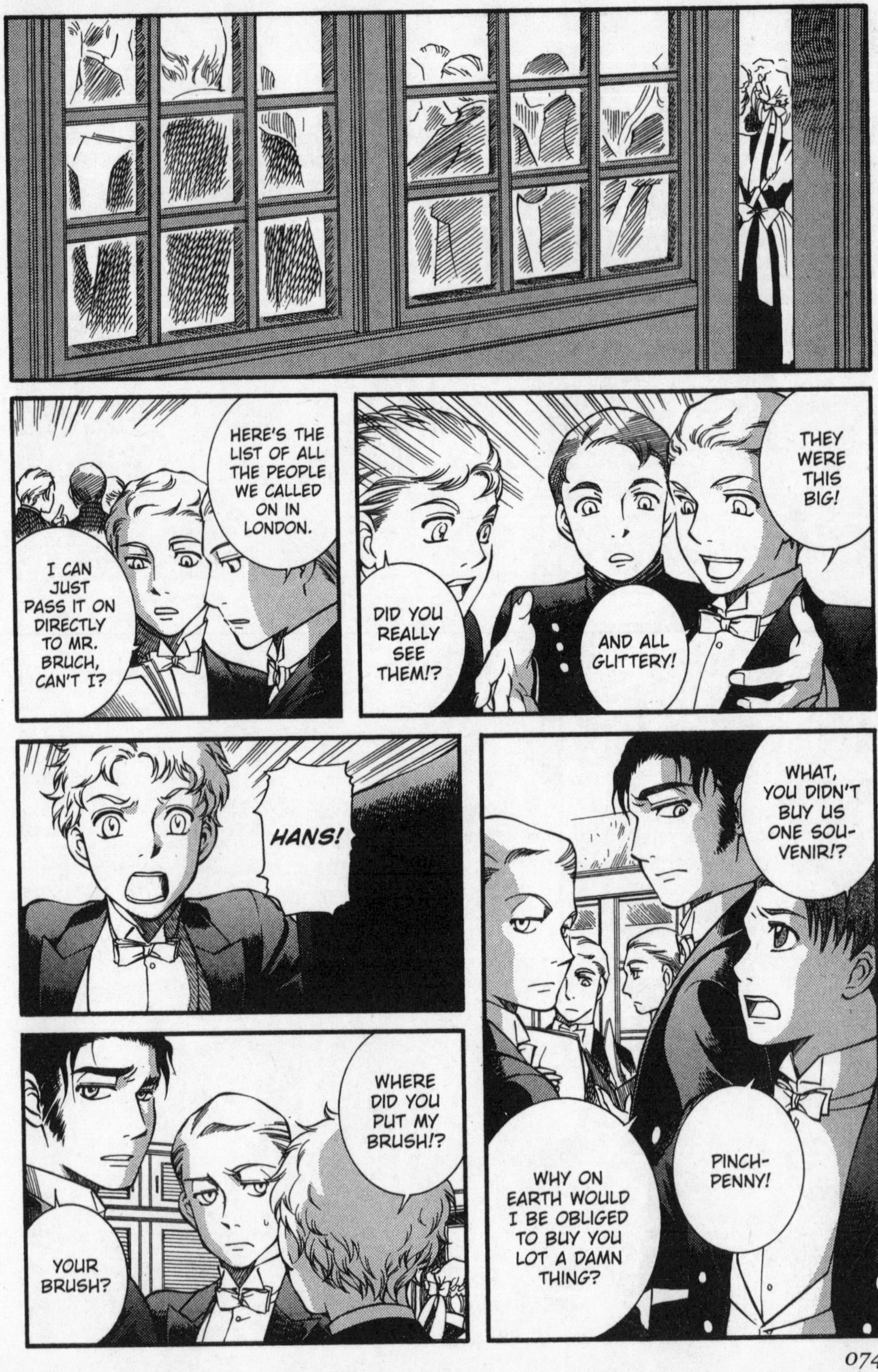
THEY WERE THIS BIG!
AND ALL GLITTERY!
DID YOU REALLY SEE THEM!?
HERE'S THE LIST OF ALL THE PEOPLE WE CALLED ON IN LONDON.
I CAN JUST PASS IT ON DIRECTLY TO MR. BRUCH, CAN'T I?
WHAT, YOU DIDN'T BUY US ONE SOU-VENIR!?
PINCH-PENNY!
WHY ON EARTH WOULD I BE OBLIGED TO BUY YOU LOT A DAMN THING?
HANS!
WHERE DID YOU PUT MY BRUSH!?
YOUR BRUSH?

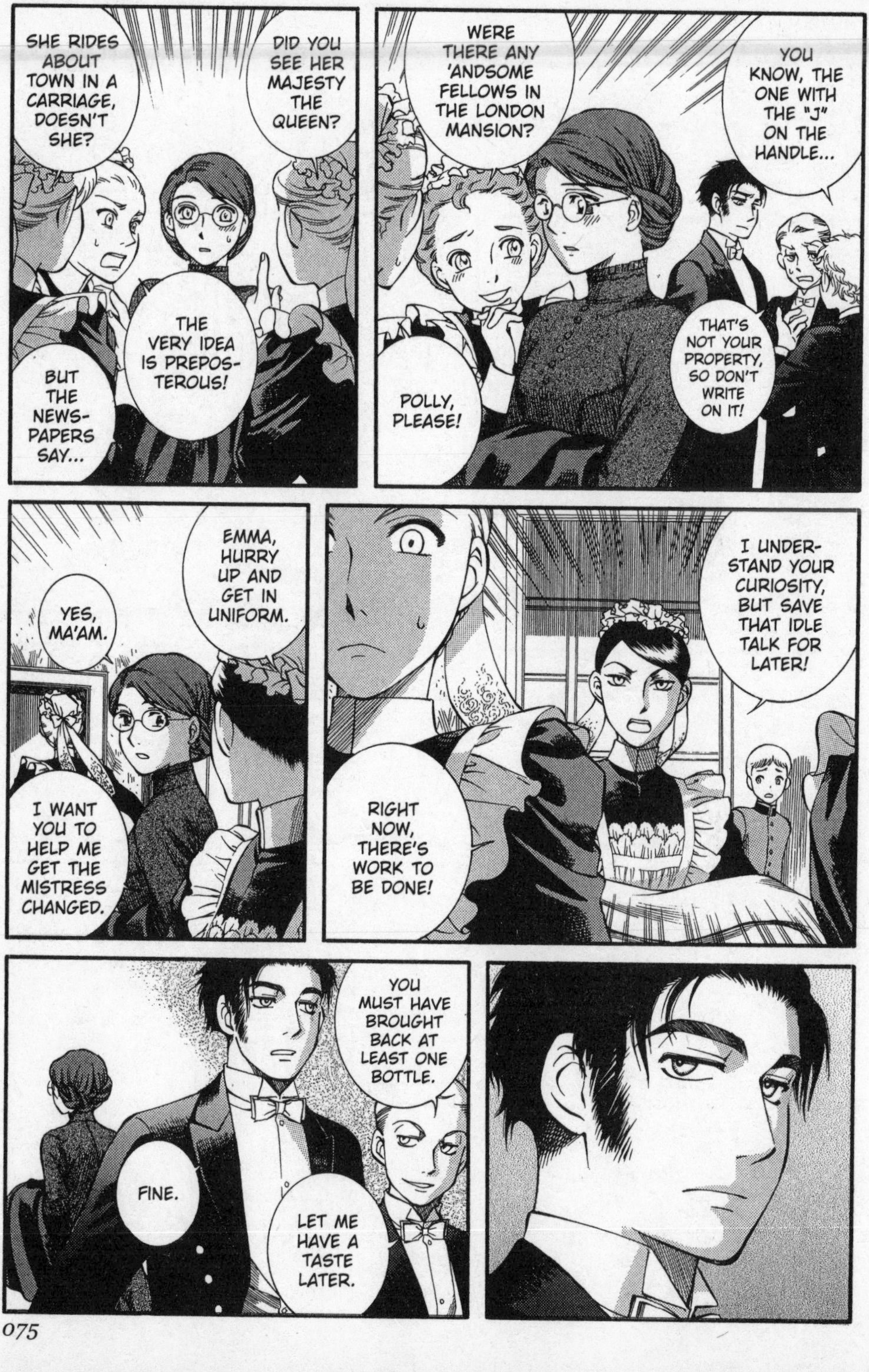
YOU KNOW, THE ONE WITH THE "J" ON THE HANDLE...
WERE THERE ANY 'ANDSOME FELLOWS IN THE LONDON MANSION?
THAT'S NOT YOUR PROPERTY, SO DON'T WRITE ON IT!
POLLY, PLEASE!
DID YOU SEE HER MAJESTY THE QUEEN?
SHE RIDES ABOUT TOWN IN A CARRIAGE, DOESN'T SHE?
THE VERY IDEA IS PREPOSTEROUS!
BUT THE NEWSPAPERS SAY...
I UNDERSTAND YOUR CURIOSITY, BUT SAVE THAT IDLE TALK FOR LATER!
RIGHT NOW, THERE'S WORK TO BE DONE!
EMMA, HURRY UP AND GET IN UNIFORM.
YES, MA'AM.
I WANT YOU TO HELP ME GET THE MISTRESS CHANGED.
YOU MUST HAVE BROUGHT BACK AT LEAST ONE BOTTLE.
FINE.
LET ME HAVE A TASTE LATER.

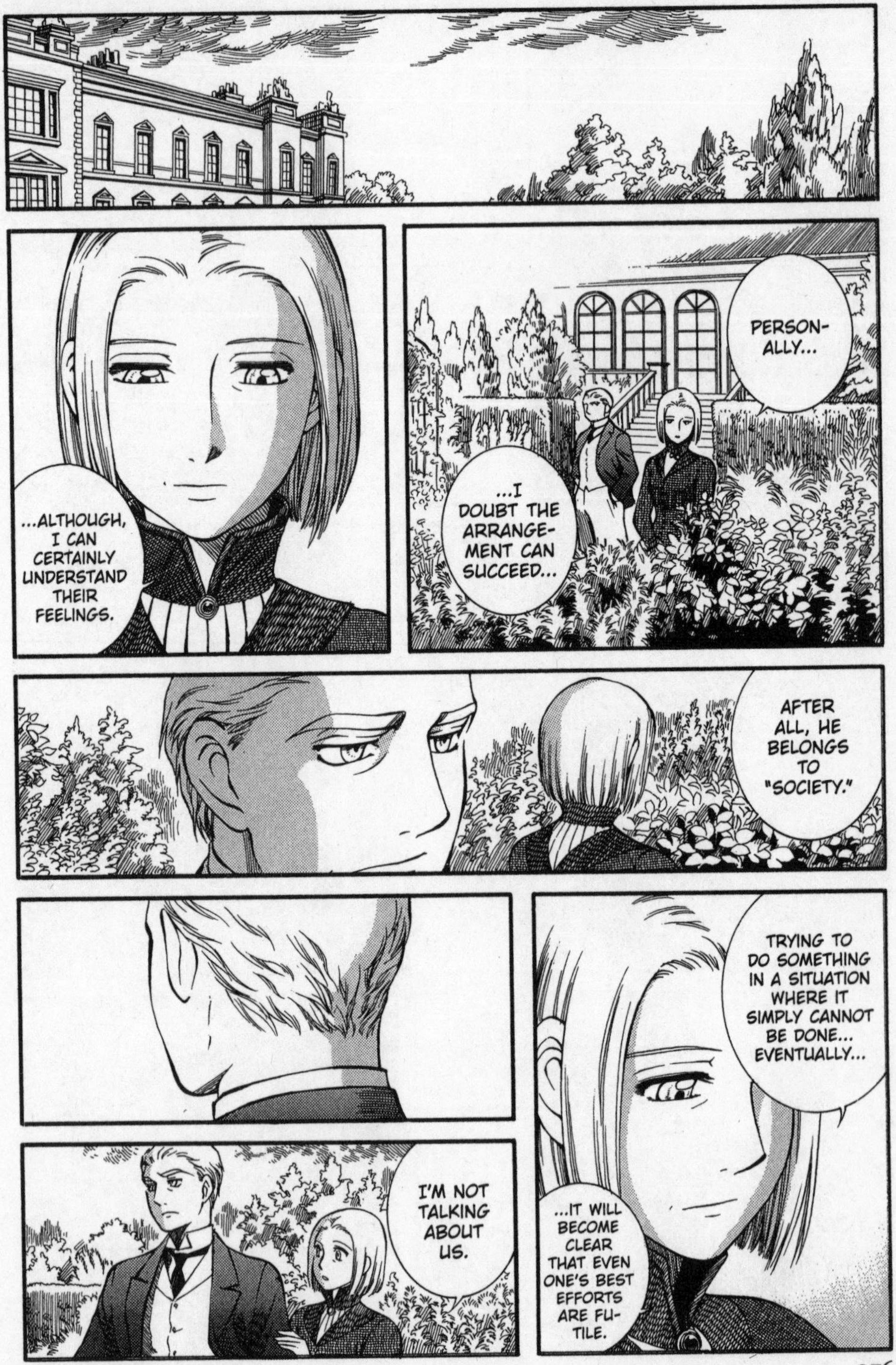
PERSON-ALLY...
...I DOUBT THE ARRANGE-MENT CAN SUCCEED...
...ALTHOUGH, I CAN CERTAINLY UNDERSTAND THEIR FEELINGS.
AFTER ALL, HE BELONGS TO "SOCIETY."
TRYING TO DO SOMETHING IN A SITUATION WHERE IT SIMPLY CANNOT BE DONE... EVENTUALLY...
...IT WILL BECOME CLEAR THAT EVEN ONE'S BEST EFFORTS ARE FU-TILE.
I'M NOT TALKING ABOUT US.

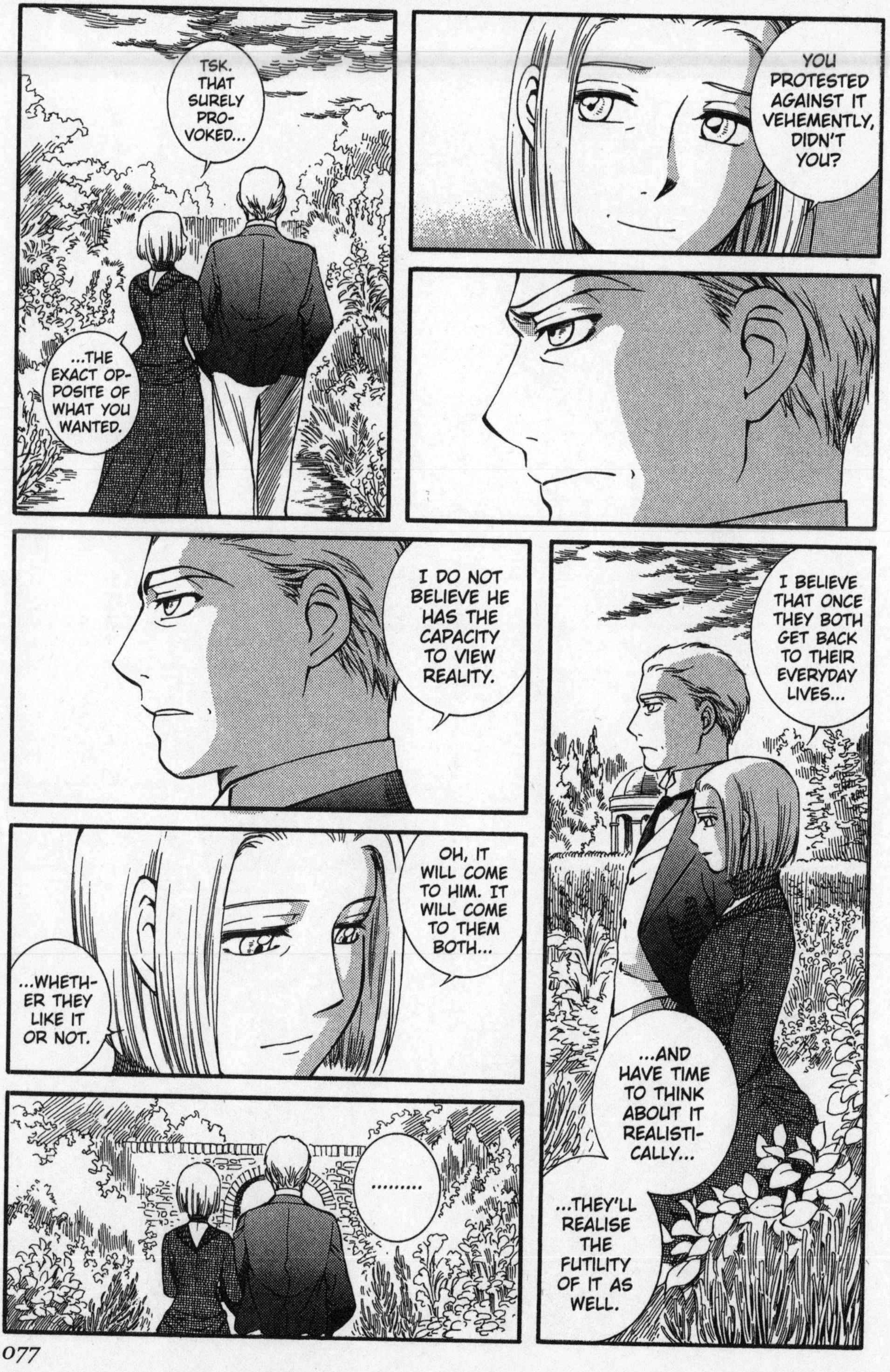
YOU PROTESTED AGAINST IT VEHEMENTLY, DIDN'T YOU?
TSK. THAT SURELY PROVOKED...
...THE EXACT OPPOSITE OF WHAT YOU WANTED.
I BELIEVE THAT ONCE THEY BOTH GET BACK TO THEIR EVERYDAY LIVES...
...AND HAVE TIME TO THINK ABOUT IT REALISTICALLY...
...THEY'LL REALISE THE FUTILITY OF IT AS WELL.
I DO NOT BELIEVE HE HAS THE CAPACITY TO VIEW REALITY.
OH, IT WILL COME TO HIM. IT WILL COME TO THEM BOTH...
...WHETHER THEY LIKE IT OR NOT.
....

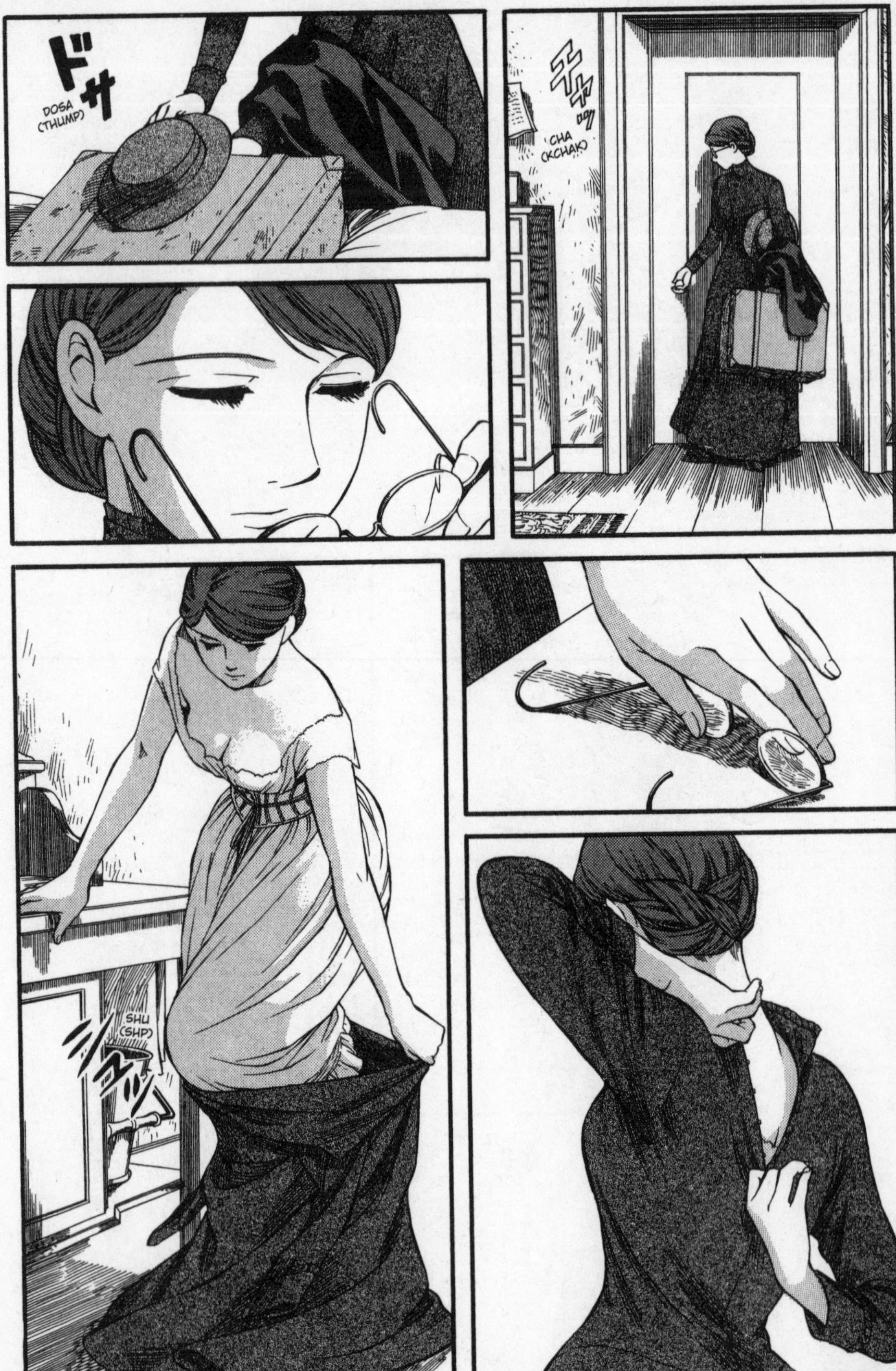
CHA (KCHAK)
ドサ
DOSA (THUMP)
SHU (SHP)

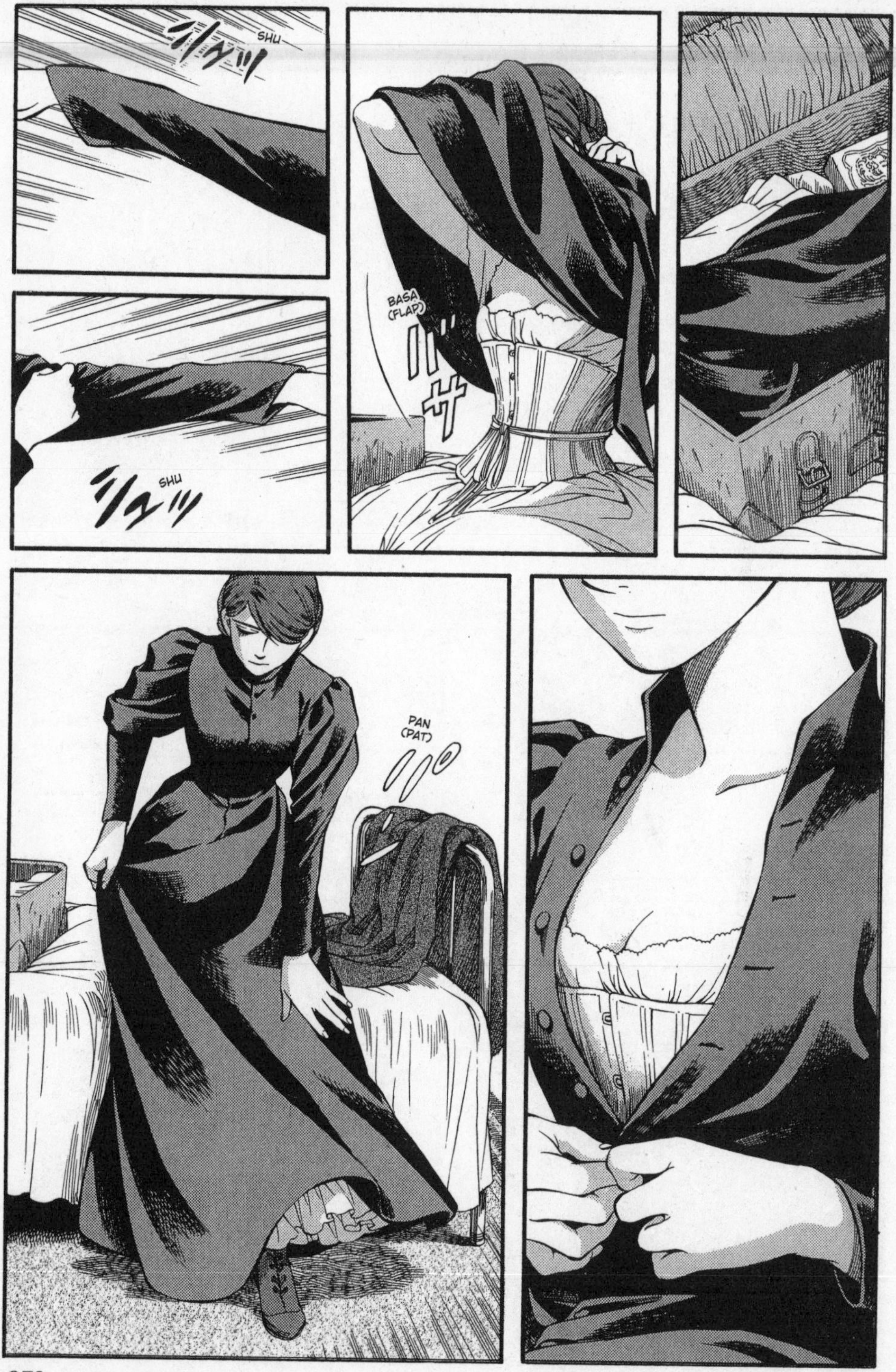
BASA (FLAP)
SHU
SHU
PAN (PAT)

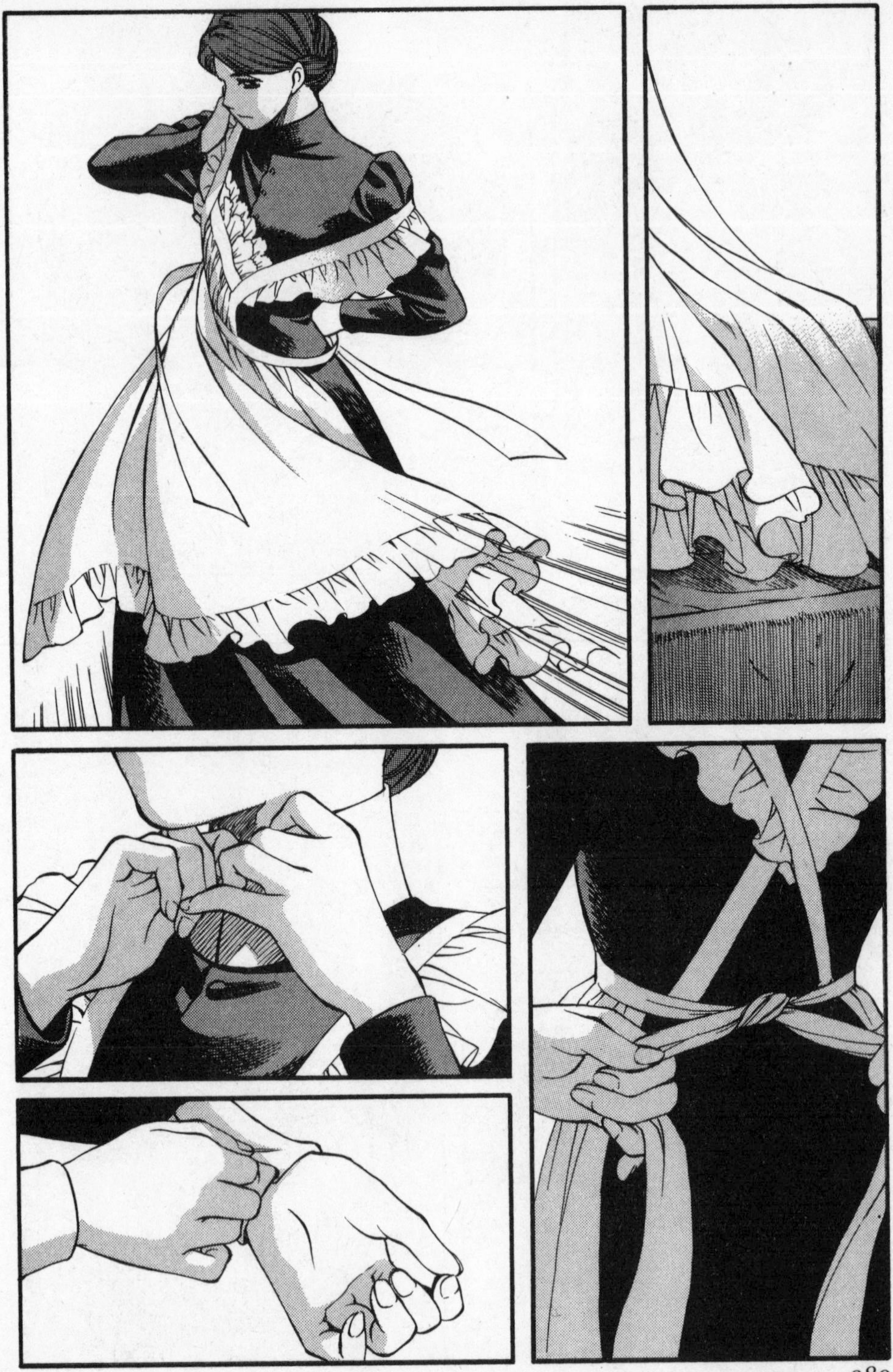

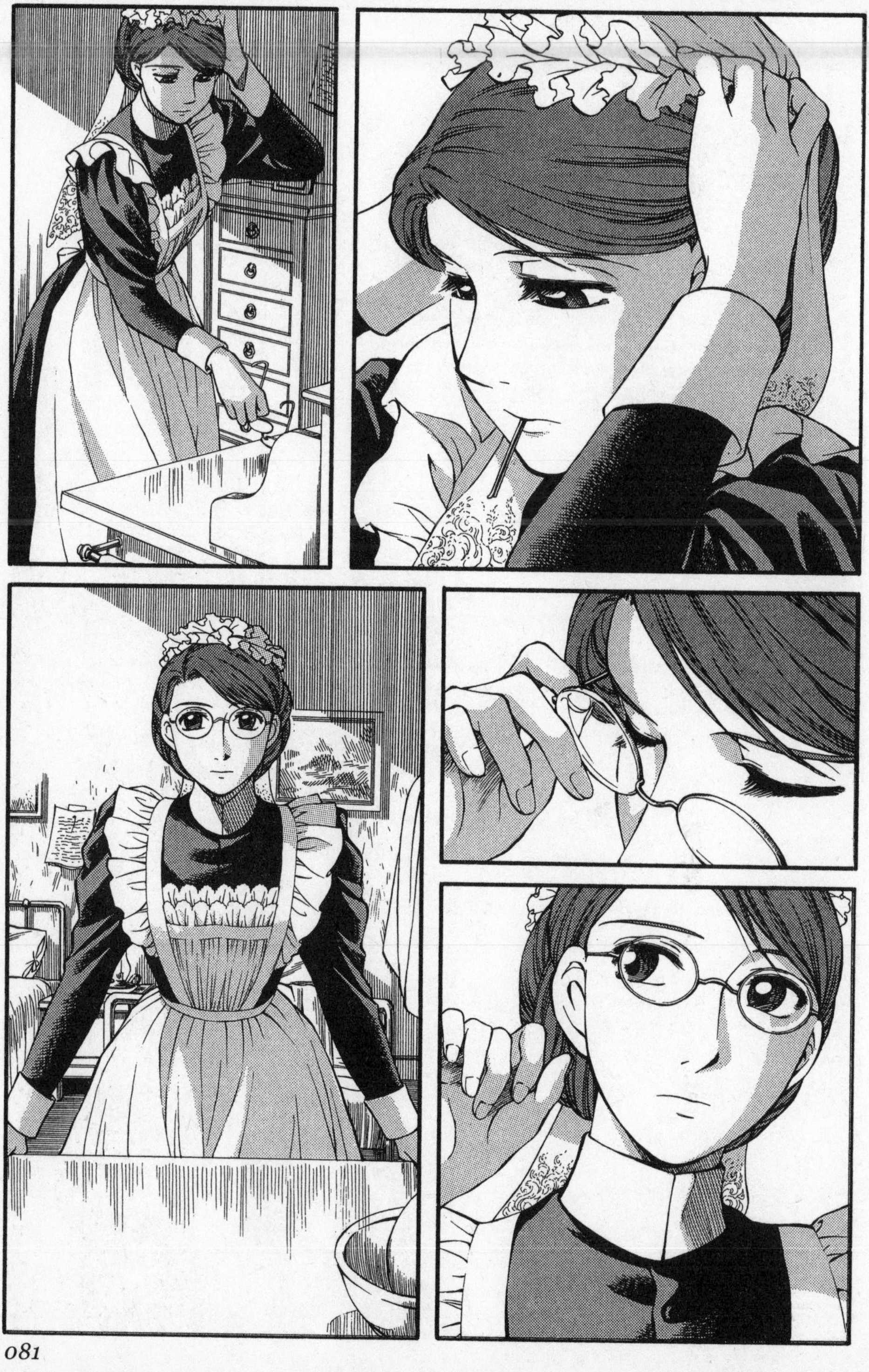

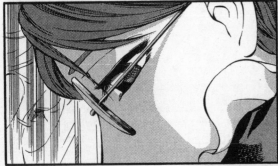

Chapter 32: End

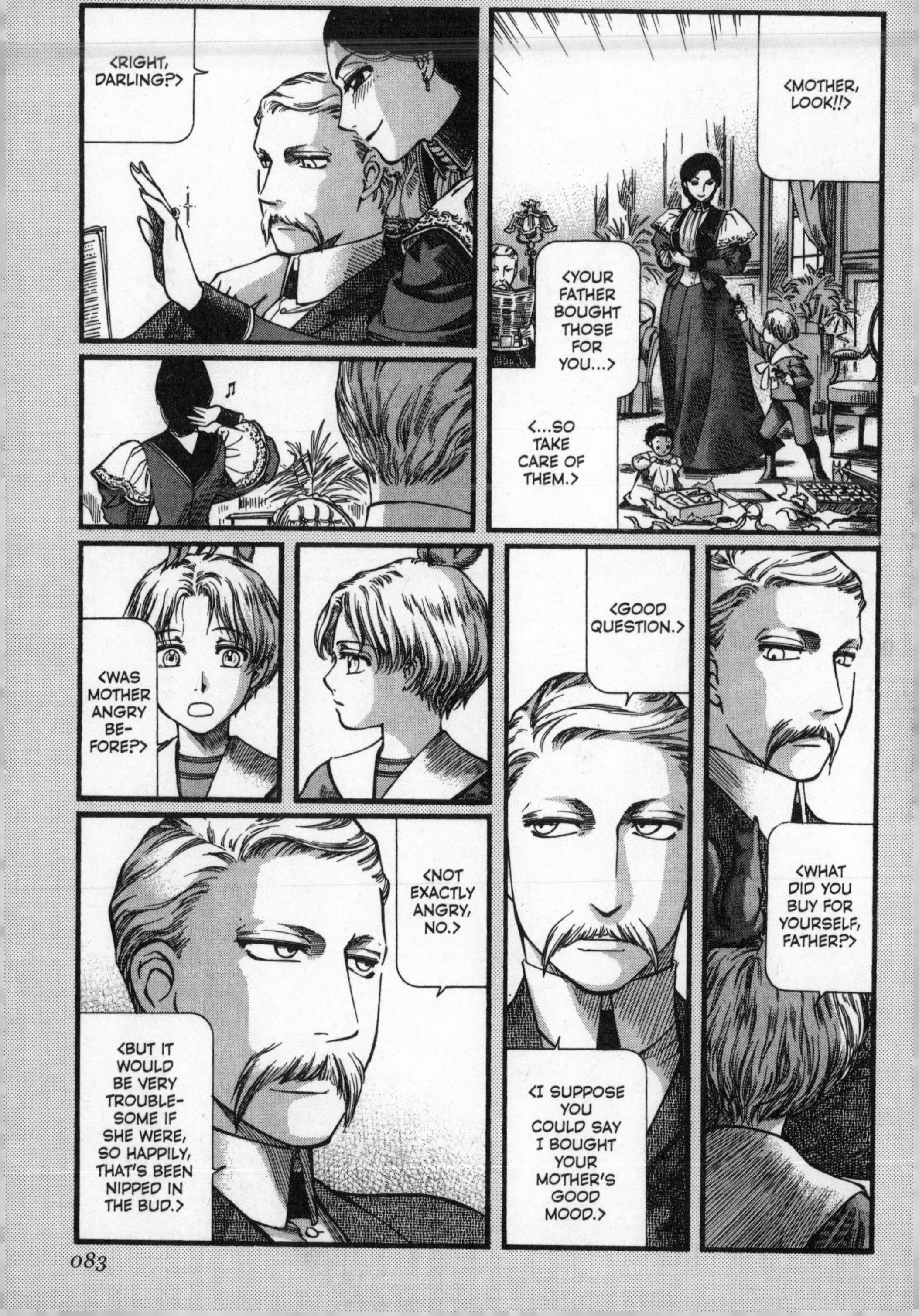
<MOTHER, LOOK!!>
<YOUR FATHER BOUGHT THOSE FOR YOU...>
<...SO TAKE CARE OF THEM.>
<RIGHT, DARLING?>
<WHAT DID YOU BUY FOR YOURSELF, FATHER?>
<GOOD QUESTION.>
<I SUPPOSE YOU COULD SAY I BOUGHT YOUR MOTHER'S GOOD MOOD.>
<WAS MOTHER ANGRY BEFORE?>
<NOT EXACTLY ANGRY, NO.>
<BUT IT WOULD BE VERY TROUBLESOME IF SHE WERE, SO HAPPILY, THAT'S BEEN NIPPED IN THE BUD.>

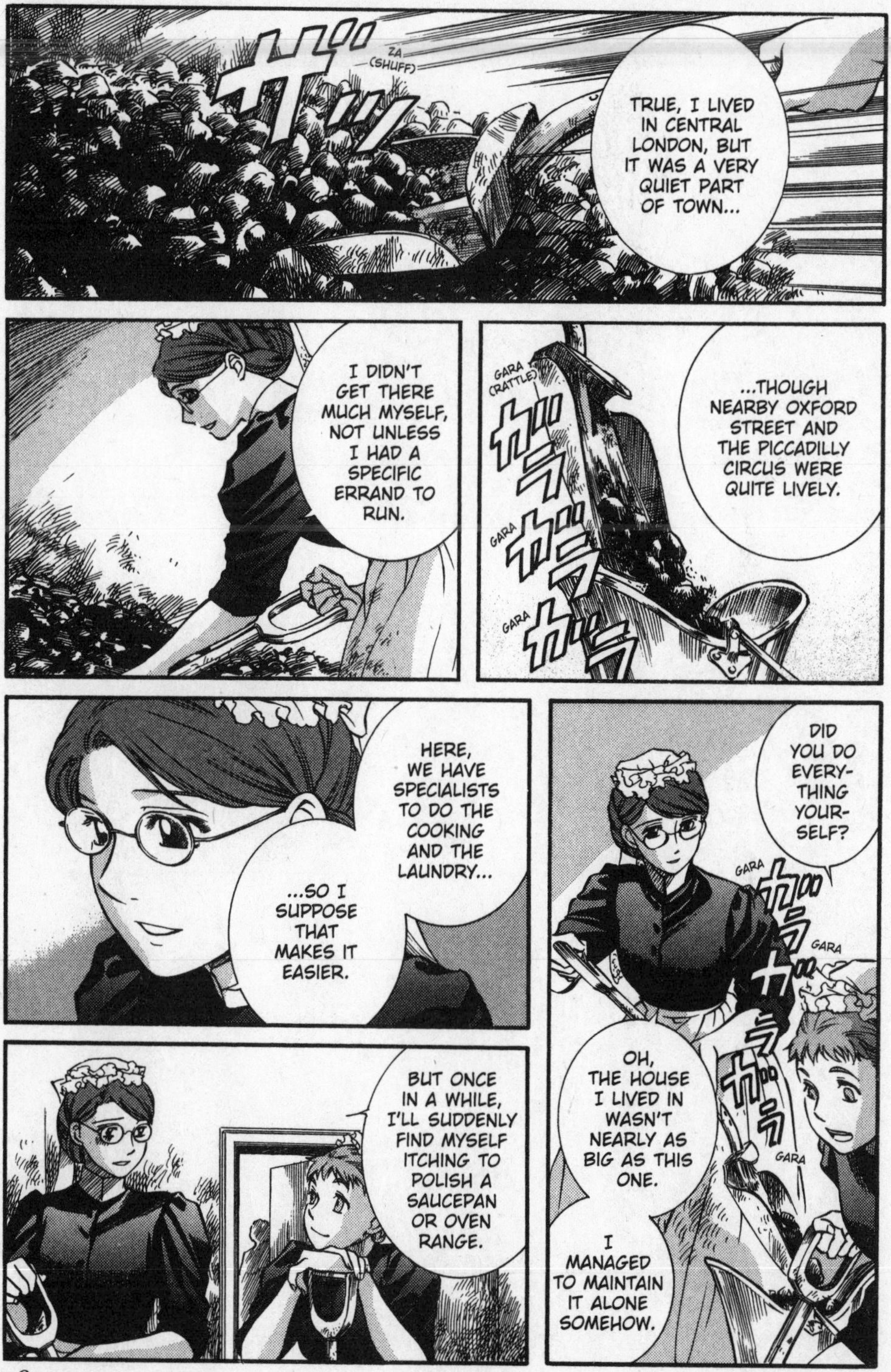
ZA (SHUFF)
TRUE, I LIVED IN CENTRAL LONDON, BUT IT WAS A VERY QUIET PART OF TOWN...
GARA (RATTLE)
GARA
GARA
...THOUGH NEARBY OXFORD STREET AND THE PICCADILLY CIRCUS WERE QUITE LIVELY.
I DIDN'T GET THERE MUCH MYSELF, NOT UNLESS I HAD A SPECIFIC ERRAND TO RUN.
DID YOU DO EVERY-THING YOUR-SELF?
GARA
GARA
GARA
OH, THE HOUSE I LIVED IN WASN'T NEARLY AS BIG AS THIS ONE.
I MANAGED TO MAINTAIN IT ALONE SOMEHOW.
HERE, WE HAVE SPECIALISTS TO DO THE COOKING AND THE LAUNDRY...
...SO I SUPPOSE THAT MAKES IT EASIER.
BUT ONCE IN A WHILE, I'LL SUDDENLY FIND MYSELF ITCHING TO POLISH A SAUCEPAN OR OVEN RANGE.

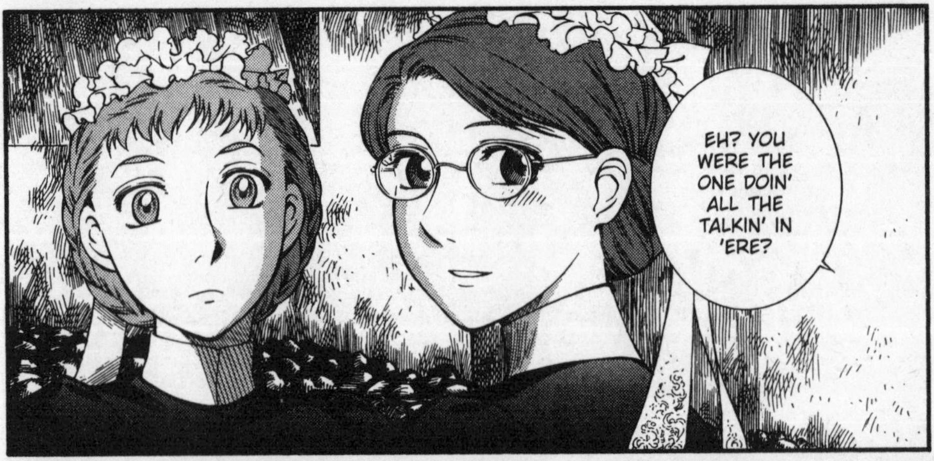
EH? YOU WERE THE ONE DOIN' ALL THE TALKIN' IN 'ERE?

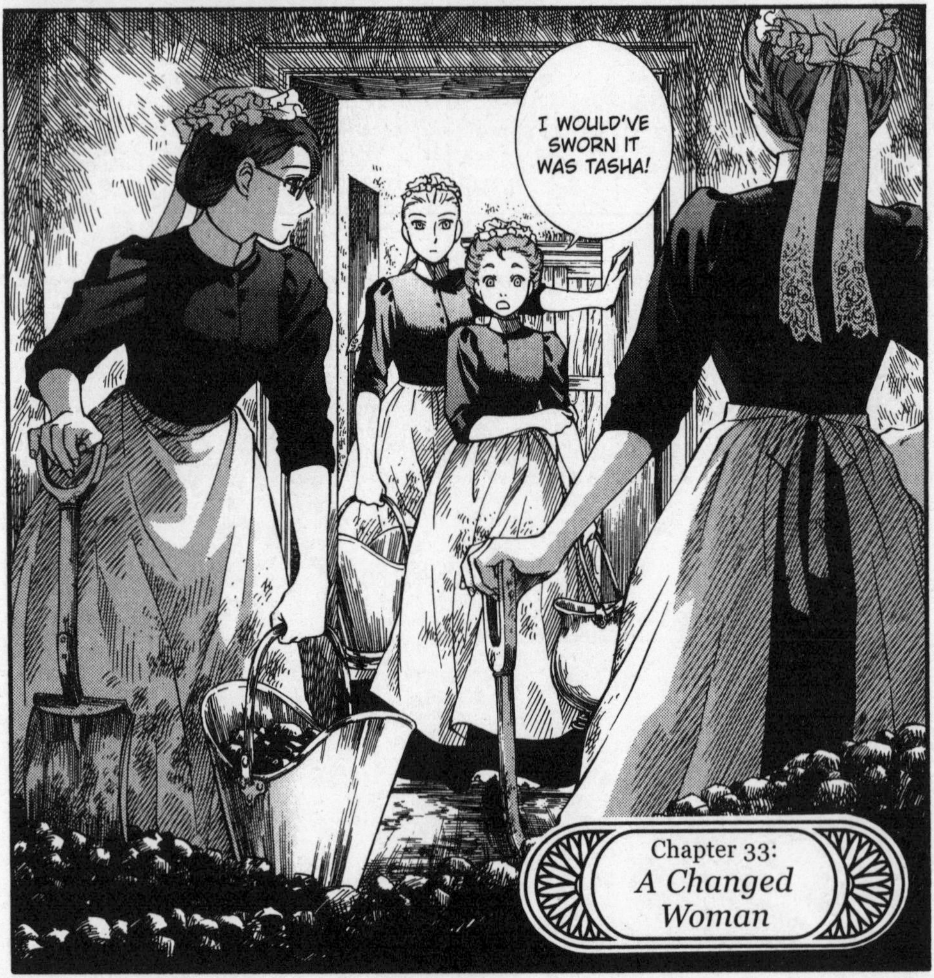
I WOULD'VE SWORN IT WAS TASHA!
Chapter 33: A Changed Woman

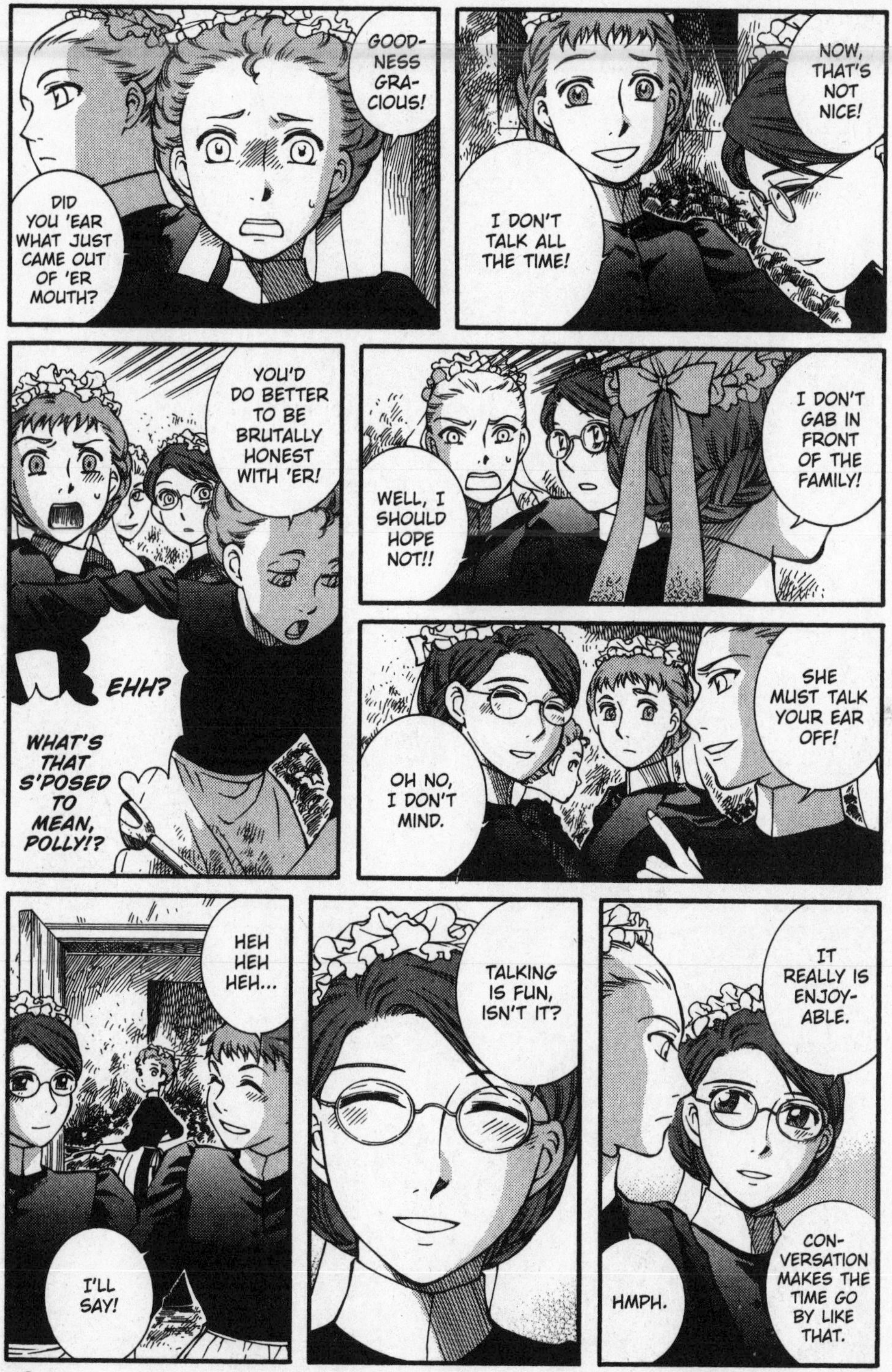
NOW, THAT'S NOT NICE!
I DON'T TALK ALL THE TIME!
GOODNESS GRACIOUS!
DID YOU 'EAR WHAT JUST CAME OUT OF 'ER MOUTH?
I DON'T GAB IN FRONT OF THE FAMILY!
WELL, I SHOULD HOPE NOT!!
SHE MUST TALK YOUR EAR OFF!
OH NO, I DON'T MIND.
YOU'D DO BETTER TO BE BRUTALLY HONEST WITH 'ER!
EHH?
WHAT'S THAT S'POSED TO MEAN, POLLY!?
IT REALLY IS ENJOYABLE.
CONVERSATION MAKES THE TIME GO BY LIKE THAT.
HMPH.
TALKING IS FUN, ISN'T IT?
HEH HEH HEH...
I'LL SAY!

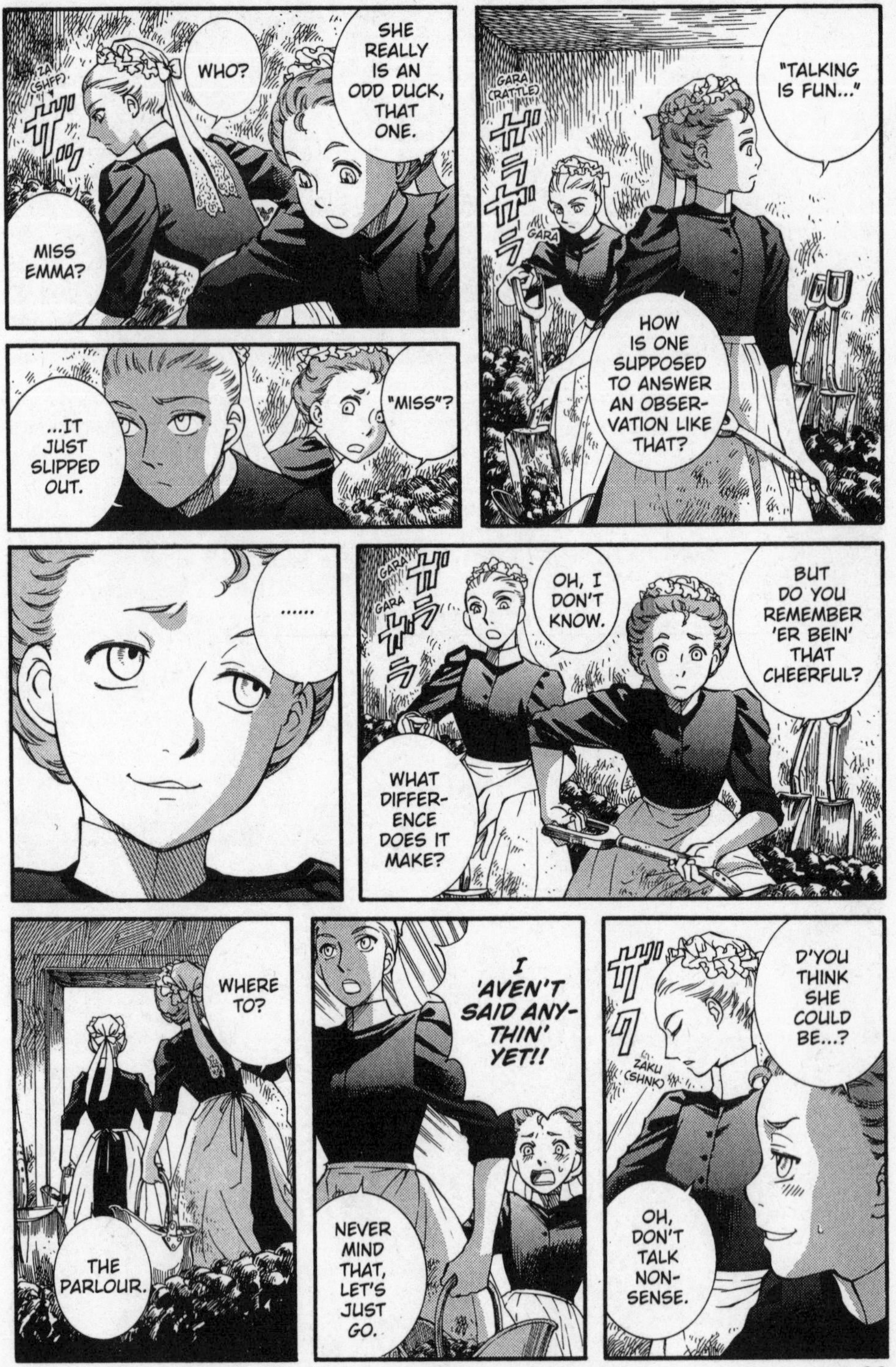

GARA (RATTLE)
GARA
"TALKING IS FUN..."
HOW IS ONE SUPPOSED TO ANSWER AN OBSERVATION LIKE THAT?
SHE REALLY IS AN ODD DUCK, THAT ONE.
WHO?
ZA (SHFF)
MISS EMMA?
"MISS"?
...IT JUST SLIPPED OUT.
BUT DO YOU REMEMBER 'ER BEIN' THAT CHEERFUL?
OH, I DON'T KNOW.
GARA
GARA
WHAT DIFFERENCE DOES IT MAKE?
......
D'YOU THINK SHE COULD BE...?
ZAKU (SHNK)
OH, DON'T TALK NONSENSE.
I 'AVEN'T SAID ANYTHIN' YET!!
NEVER MIND THAT, LET'S JUST GO.
WHERE TO?
THE PARLOUR.

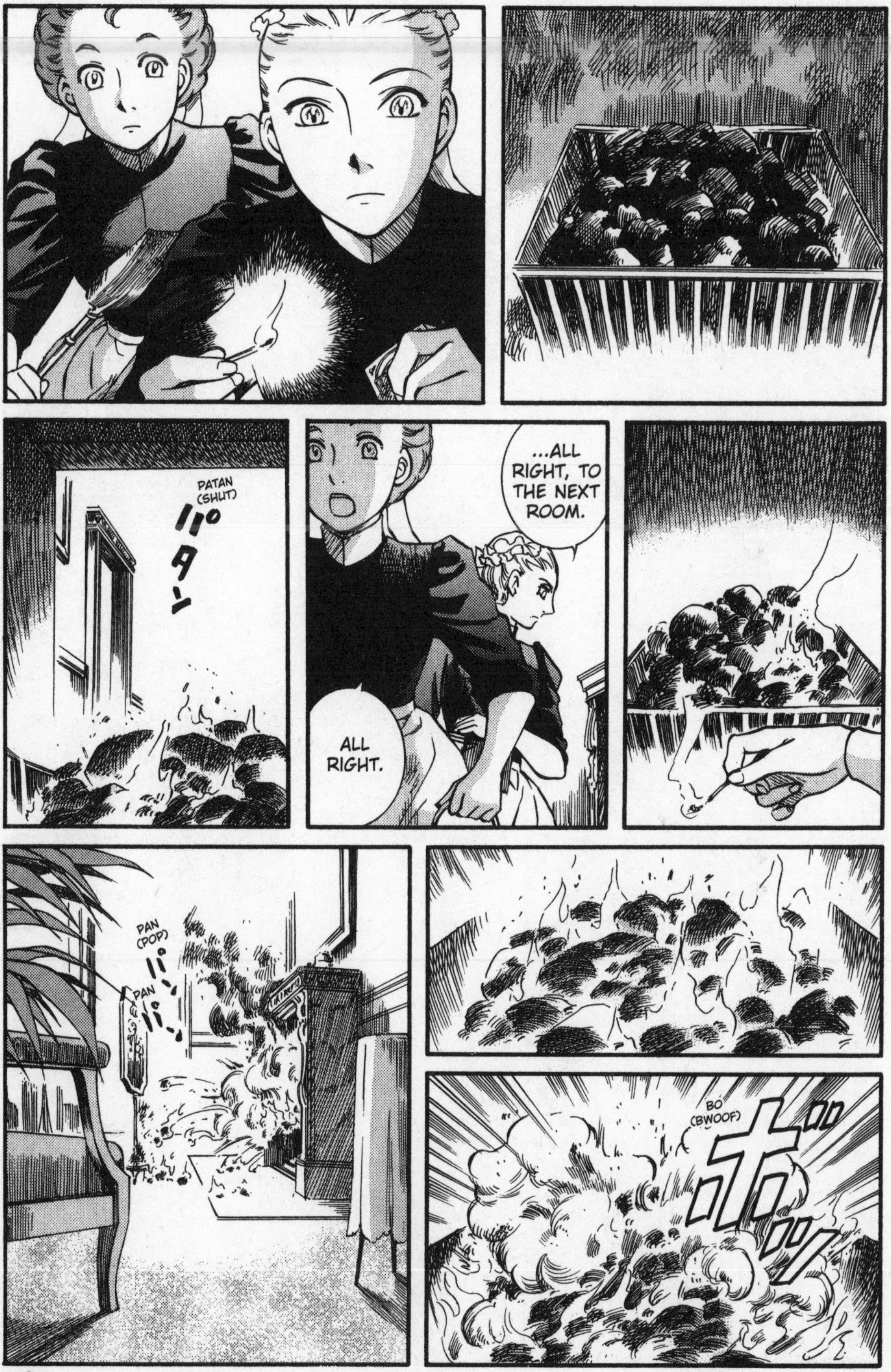
...ALL RIGHT, TO THE NEXT ROOM.
ALL RIGHT.
PATAN (SHUT)
パタン
BO (BWOOF)
ボッ
PAN (POP)
パン
PAN
パン

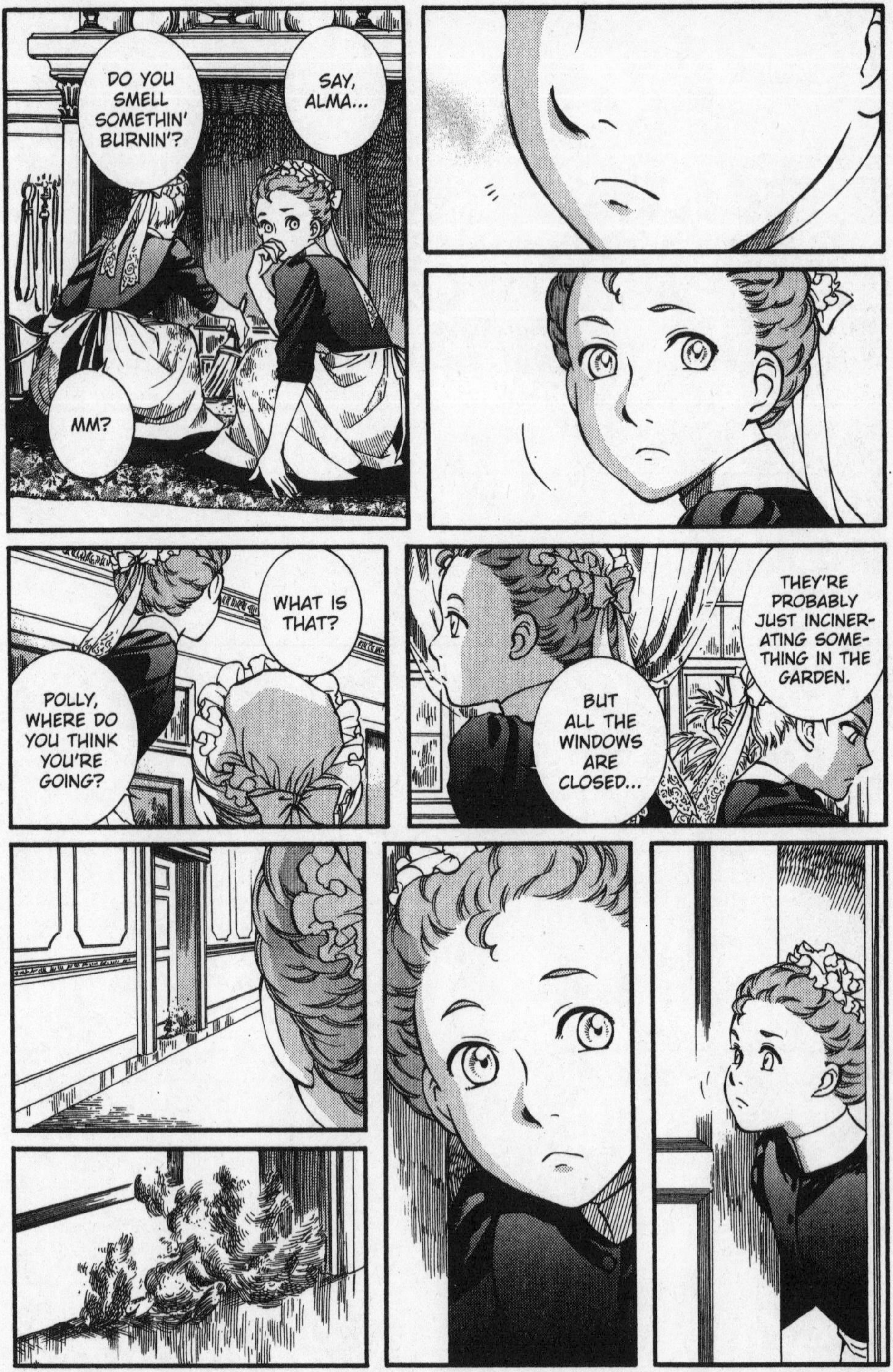
SAY, ALMA...
DO YOU SMELL SOMETHIN' BURNIN'?
MM?
THEY'RE PROBABLY JUST INCINERATING SOMETHING IN THE GARDEN.
BUT ALL THE WINDOWS ARE CLOSED...
WHAT IS THAT?
POLLY, WHERE DO YOU THINK YOU'RE GOING?

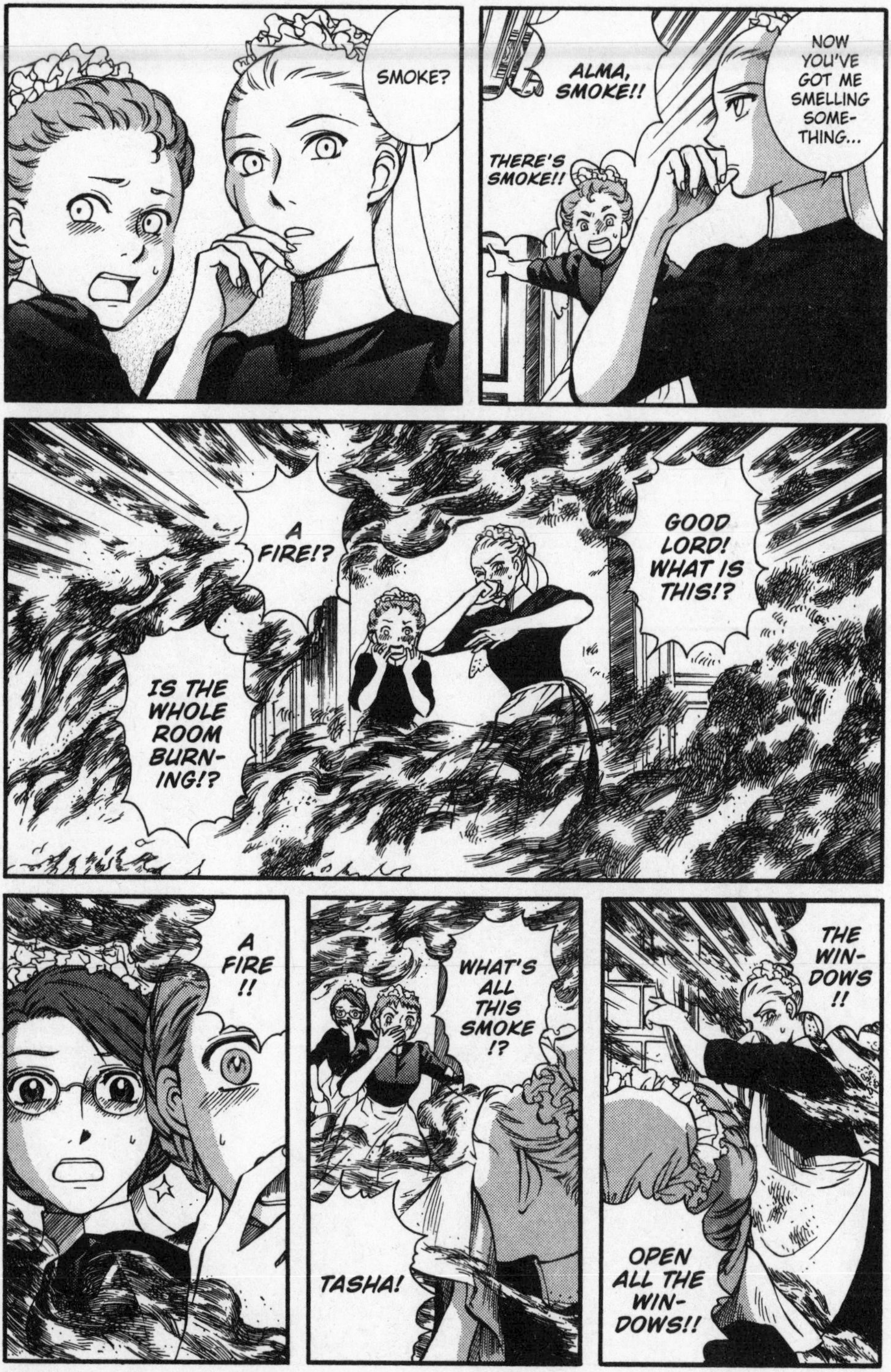
NOW YOU'VE GOT ME SMELLING SOME-THING...
ALMA, SMOKE!!
THERE'S SMOKE!!
SMOKE?
GOOD LORD! WHAT IS THIS!?
A FIRE!?
IS THE WHOLE ROOM BURN-ING!?
THE WIN-DOWS!!
OPEN ALL THE WIN-DOWS!!
WHAT'S ALL THIS SMOKE!?
TASHA!
A FIRE!!

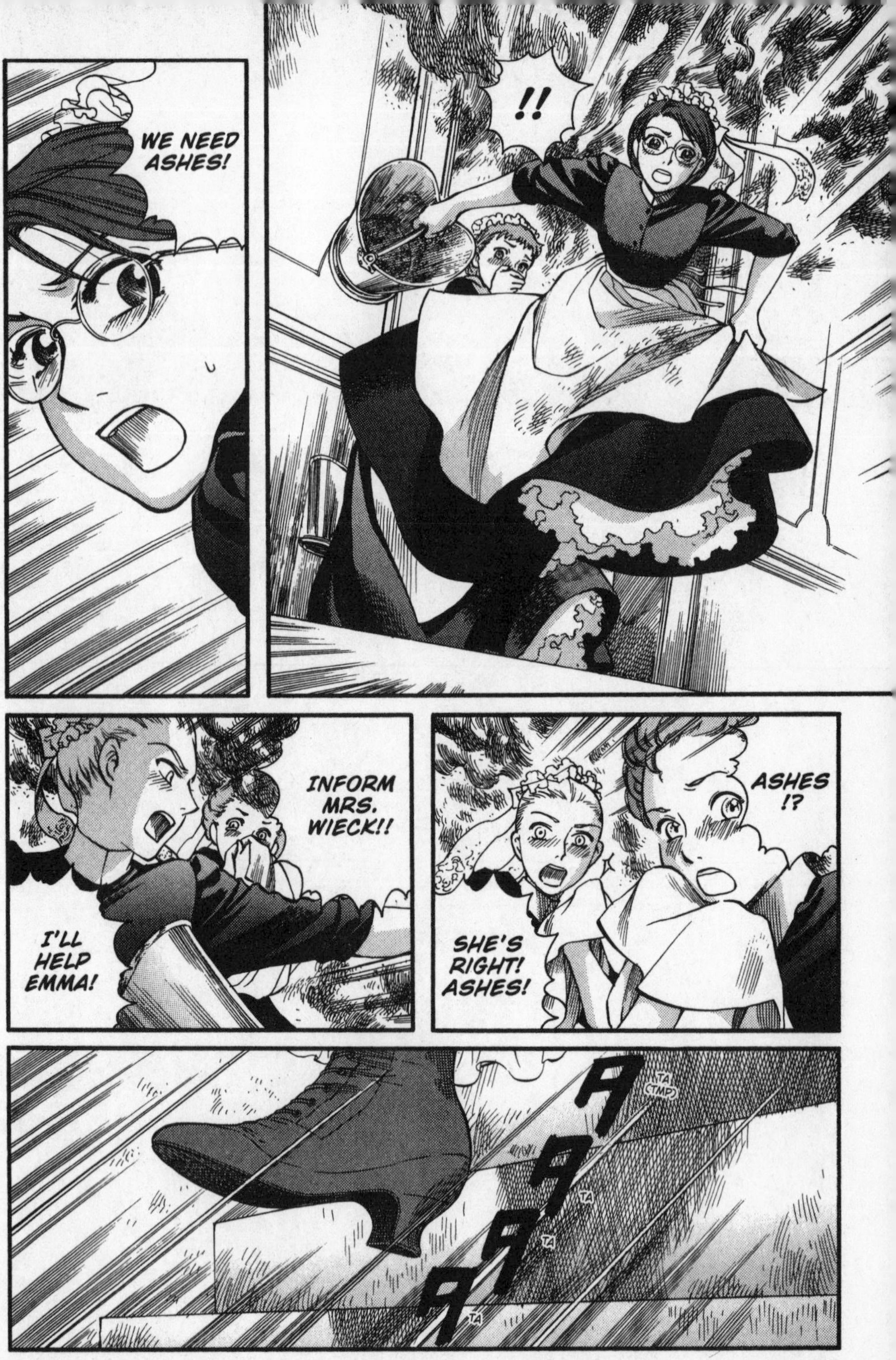

!!
WE NEED ASHES!
ASHES!?
SHE'S RIGHT! ASHES!
INFORM MRS. WIECK!!
I'LL HELP EMMA!
TA (TMP)
TA
TA
TA

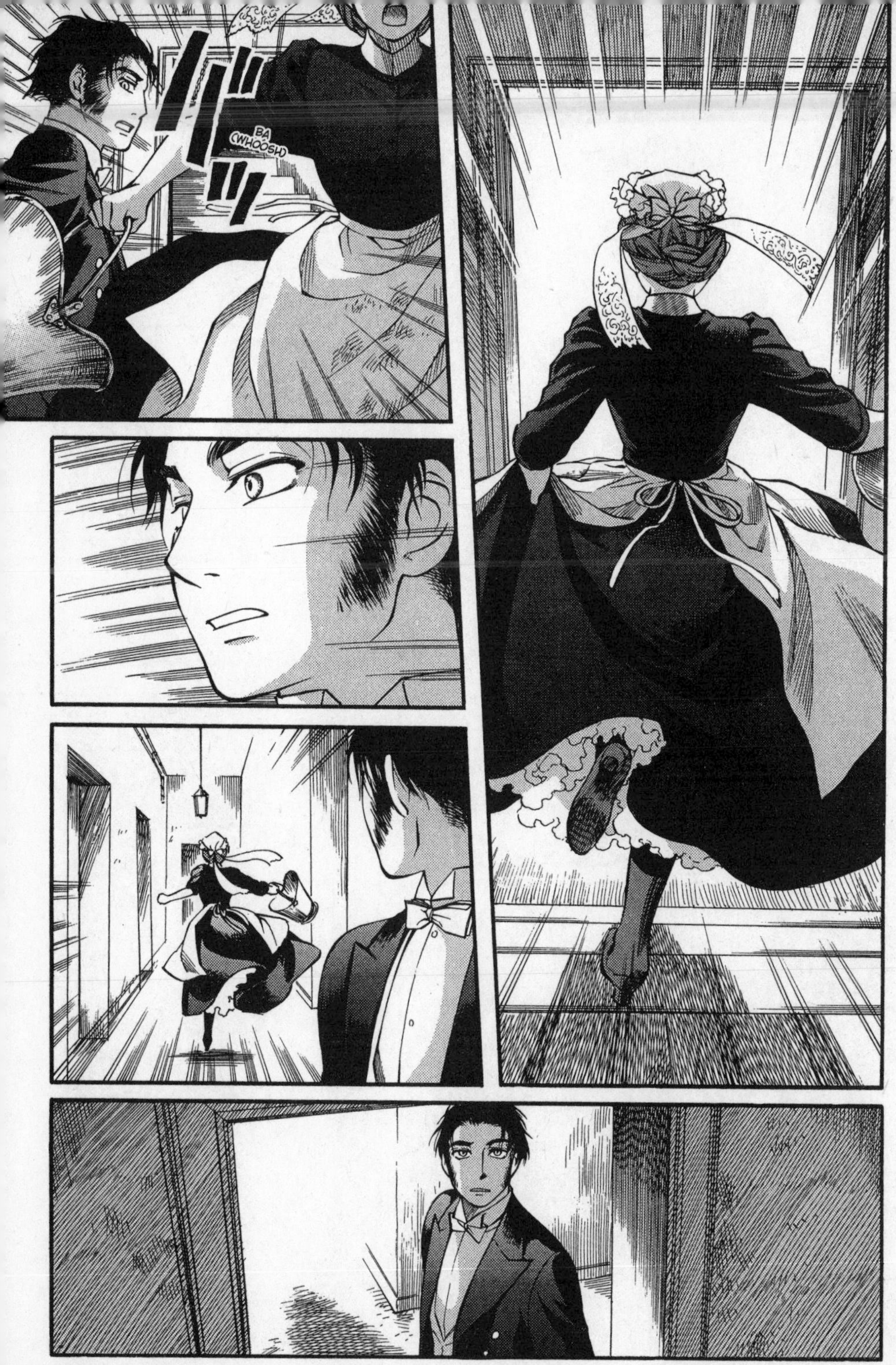
BA (WHOOSH)

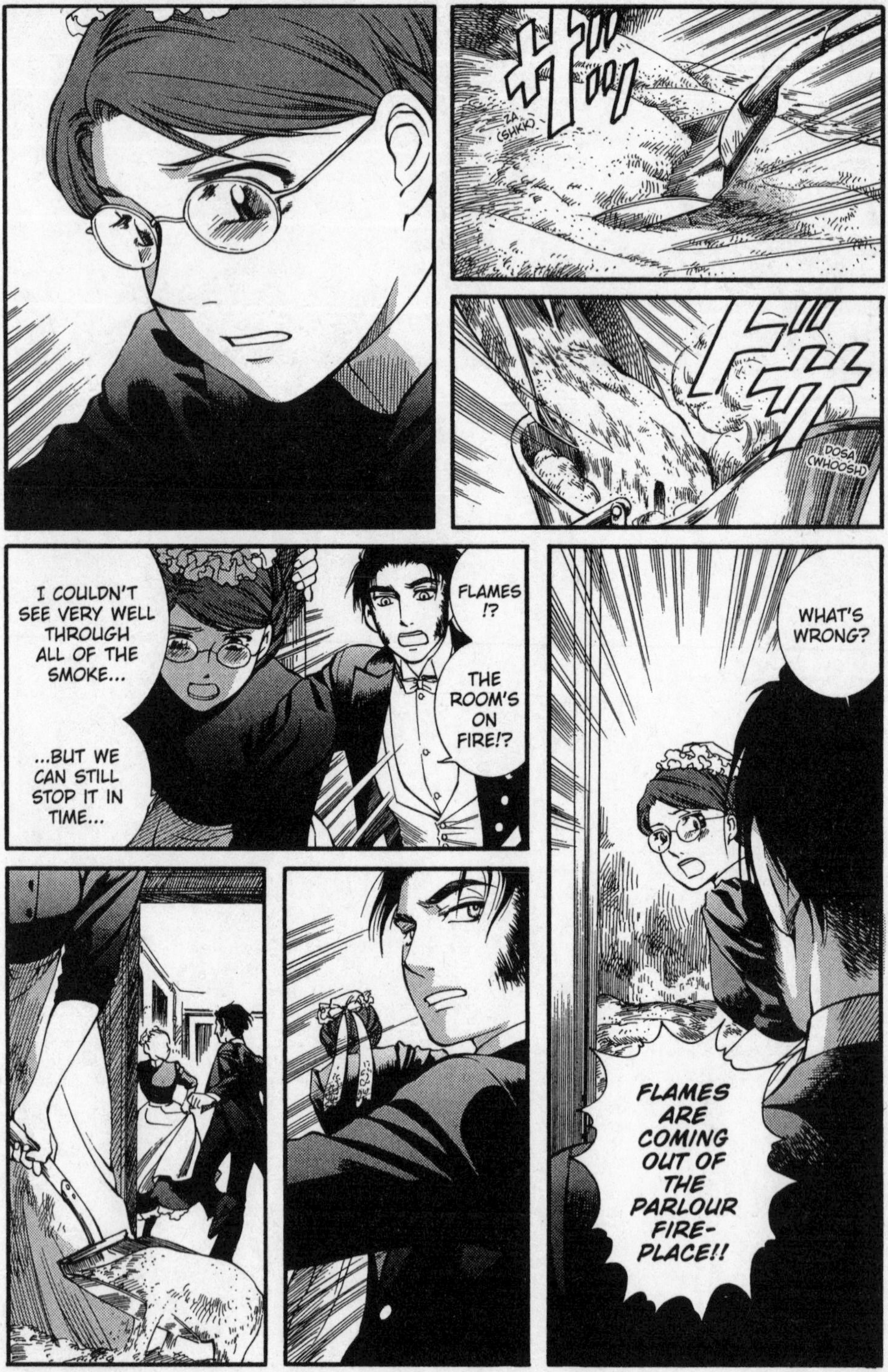
ZA (SHKK)
DOSA (WHOOSH)
WHAT'S WRONG?
FLAMES ARE COMING OUT OF THE PARLOUR FIRE-PLACE!!
FLAMES !?
THE ROOM'S ON FIRE!?
I COULDN'T SEE VERY WELL THROUGH ALL OF THE SMOKE...
...BUT WE CAN STILL STOP IT IN TIME...

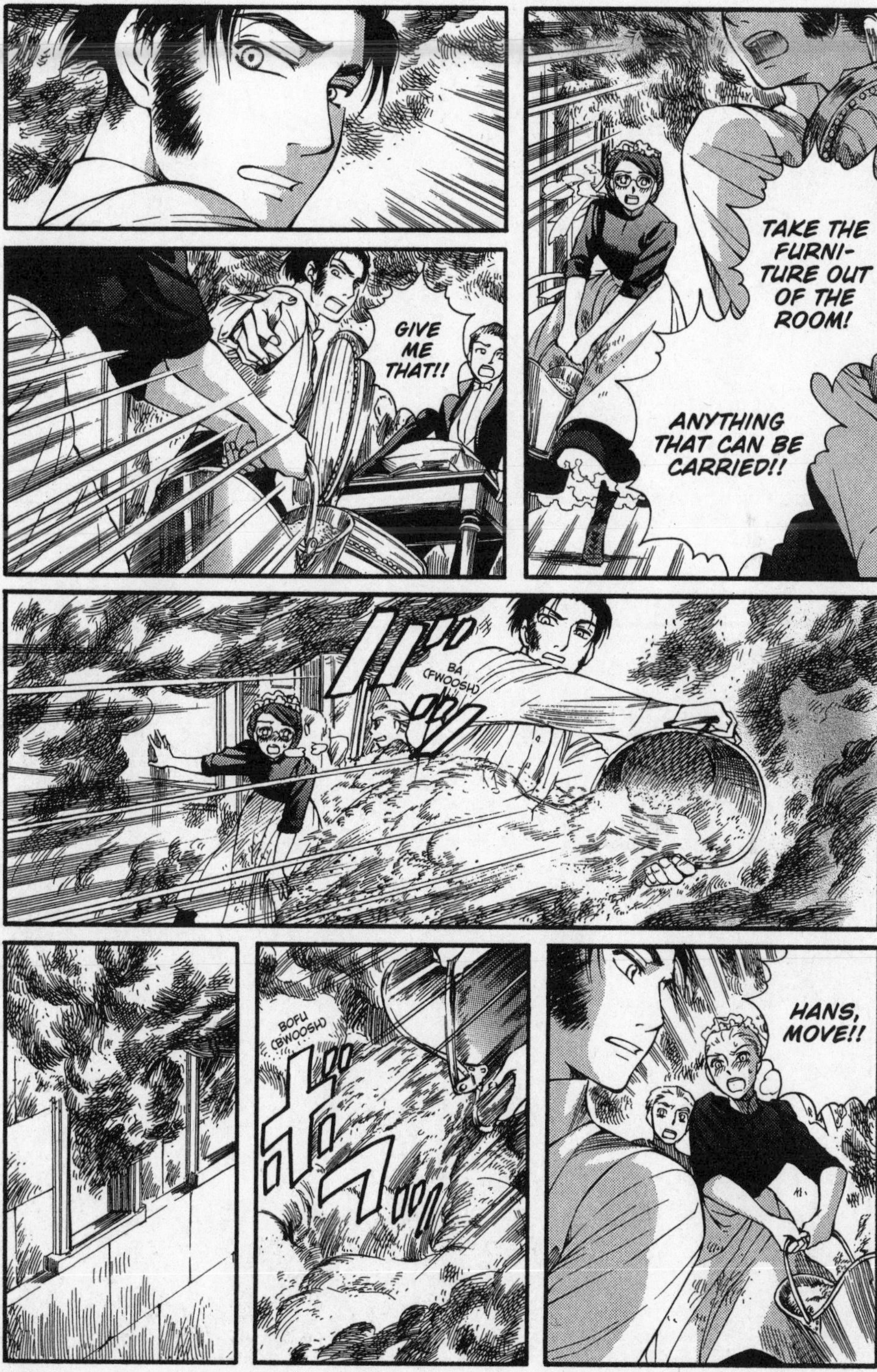
TAKE THE FURNITURE OUT OF THE ROOM!
ANYTHING THAT CAN BE CARRIED!!
GIVE ME THAT!!
BA (FWOOSH)
HANS, MOVE!!
BOFU (BWOOSH)

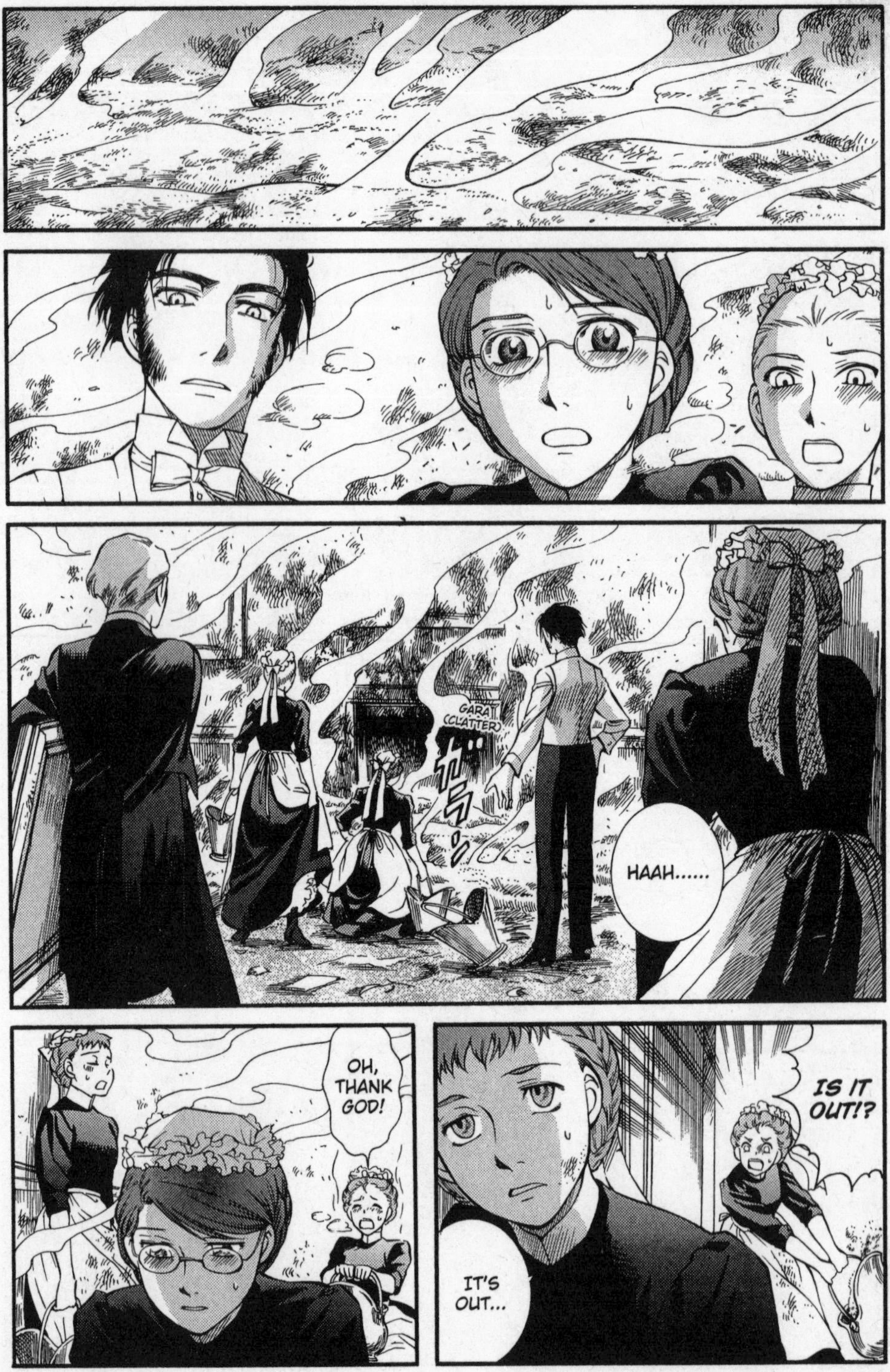
GARA (CLATTER)
ガラ
HAAH......
IS IT OUT!?
IT'S OUT...
OH, THANK GOD!

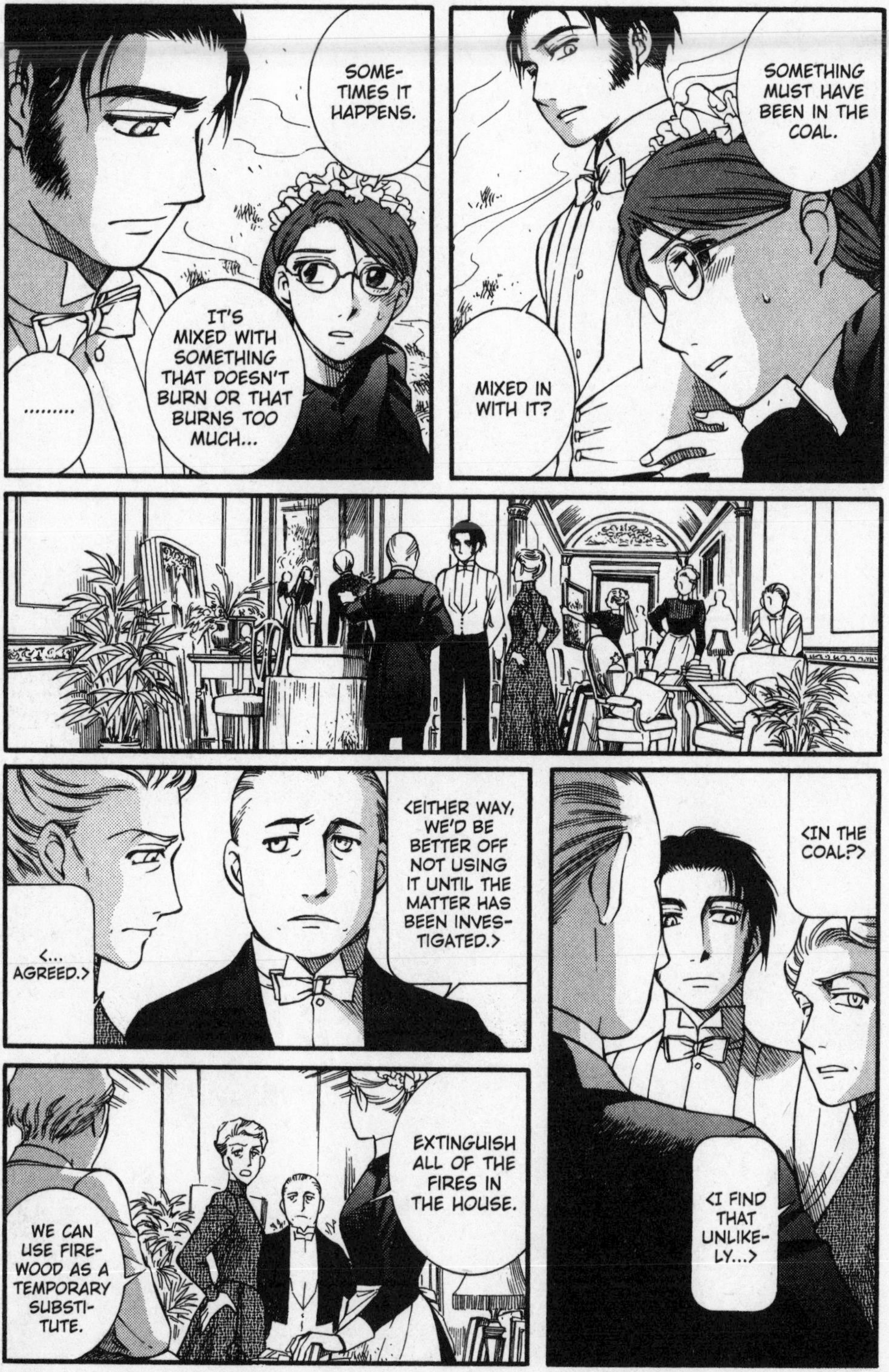
SOMETHING MUST HAVE BEEN IN THE COAL.
MIXED IN WITH IT?
SOME-TIMES IT HAPPENS.
IT'S MIXED WITH SOMETHING THAT DOESN'T BURN OR THAT BURNS TOO MUCH...
....
<IN THE COAL?>
<I FIND THAT UNLIKE-LY...>
<EITHER WAY, WE'D BE BETTER OFF NOT USING IT UNTIL THE MATTER HAS BEEN INVES-TIGATED.>
<... AGREED.>
EXTINGUISH ALL OF THE FIRES IN THE HOUSE.
WE CAN USE FIRE-WOOD AS A TEMPORARY SUBSTI-TUTE.

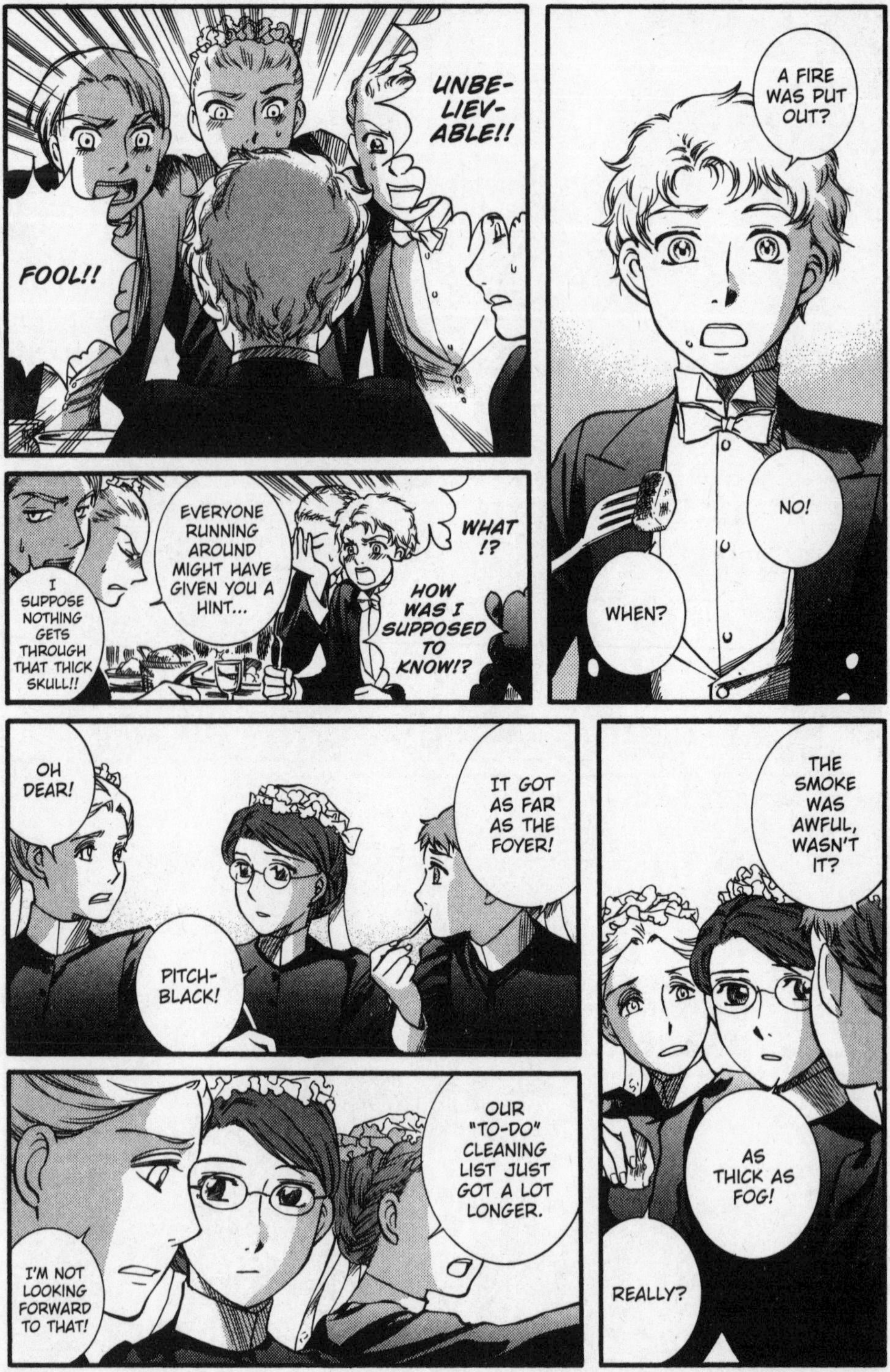
A FIRE WAS PUT OUT?
NO!
WHEN?
UNBELIEVABLE!!
FOOL!!
WHAT!?
HOW WAS I SUPPOSED TO KNOW!?
EVERYONE RUNNING AROUND MIGHT HAVE GIVEN YOU A HINT...
I SUPPOSE NOTHING GETS THROUGH THAT THICK SKULL!!
THE SMOKE WAS AWFUL, WASN'T IT?
AS THICK AS FOG!
REALLY?
IT GOT AS FAR AS THE FOYER!
OH DEAR!
PITCH-BLACK!
OUR "TO-DO" CLEANING LIST JUST GOT A LOT LONGER.
I'M NOT LOOKING FORWARD TO THAT!

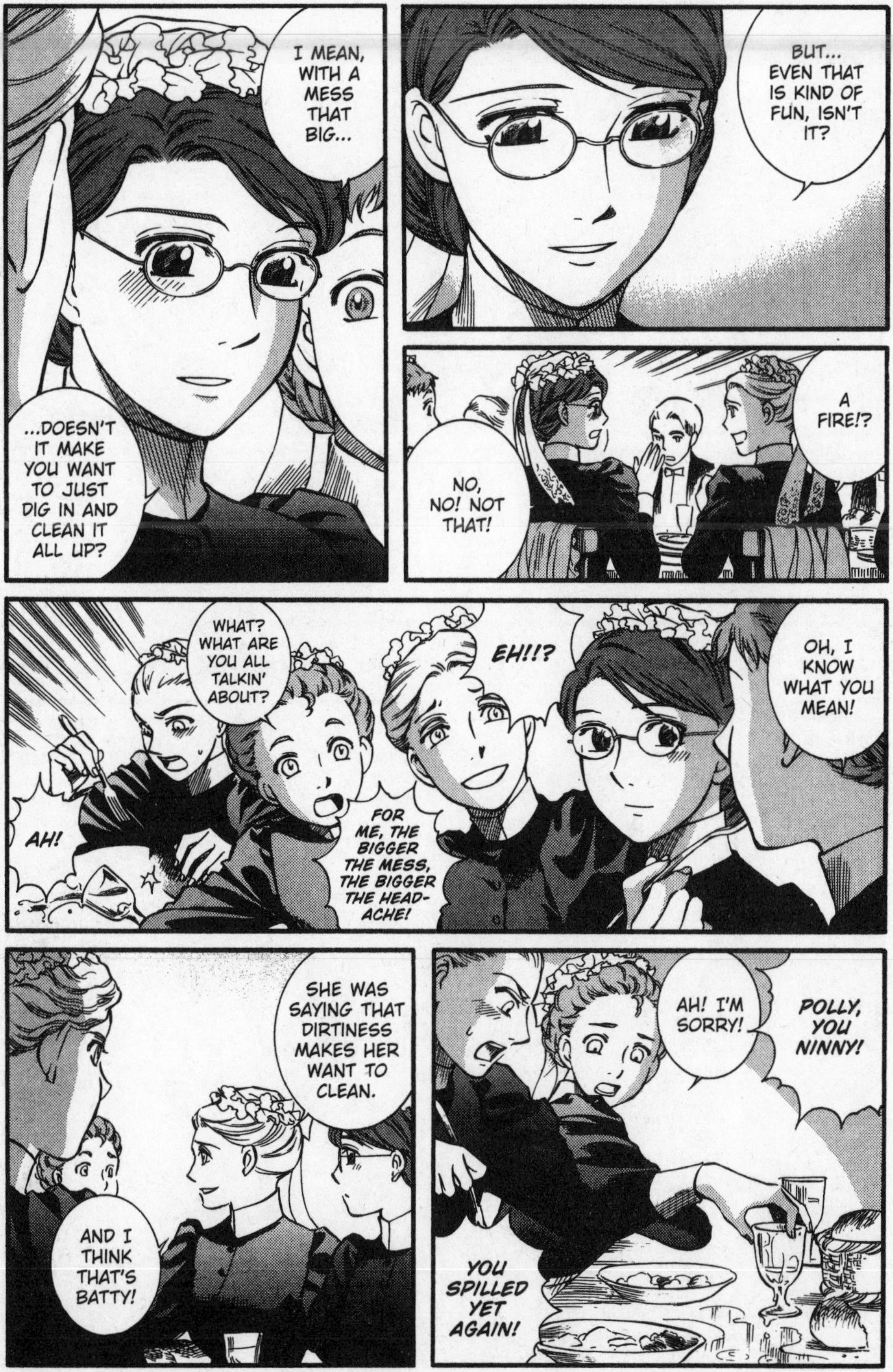
BUT... EVEN THAT IS KIND OF FUN, ISN'T IT?
A FIRE!?
NO, NO! NOT THAT!
I MEAN, WITH A MESS THAT BIG...
...DOESN'T IT MAKE YOU WANT TO JUST DIG IN AND CLEAN IT ALL UP?
OH, I KNOW WHAT YOU MEAN!
EH!!?
FOR ME, THE BIGGER THE MESS, THE BIGGER THE HEAD-ACHE!
WHAT? WHAT ARE YOU ALL TALKIN' ABOUT?
AH!
POLLY, YOU NINNY!
AH! I'M SORRY!
YOU SPILLED YET AGAIN!
SHE WAS SAYING THAT DIRTINESS MAKES HER WANT TO CLEAN.
AND I THINK THAT'S BATTY!

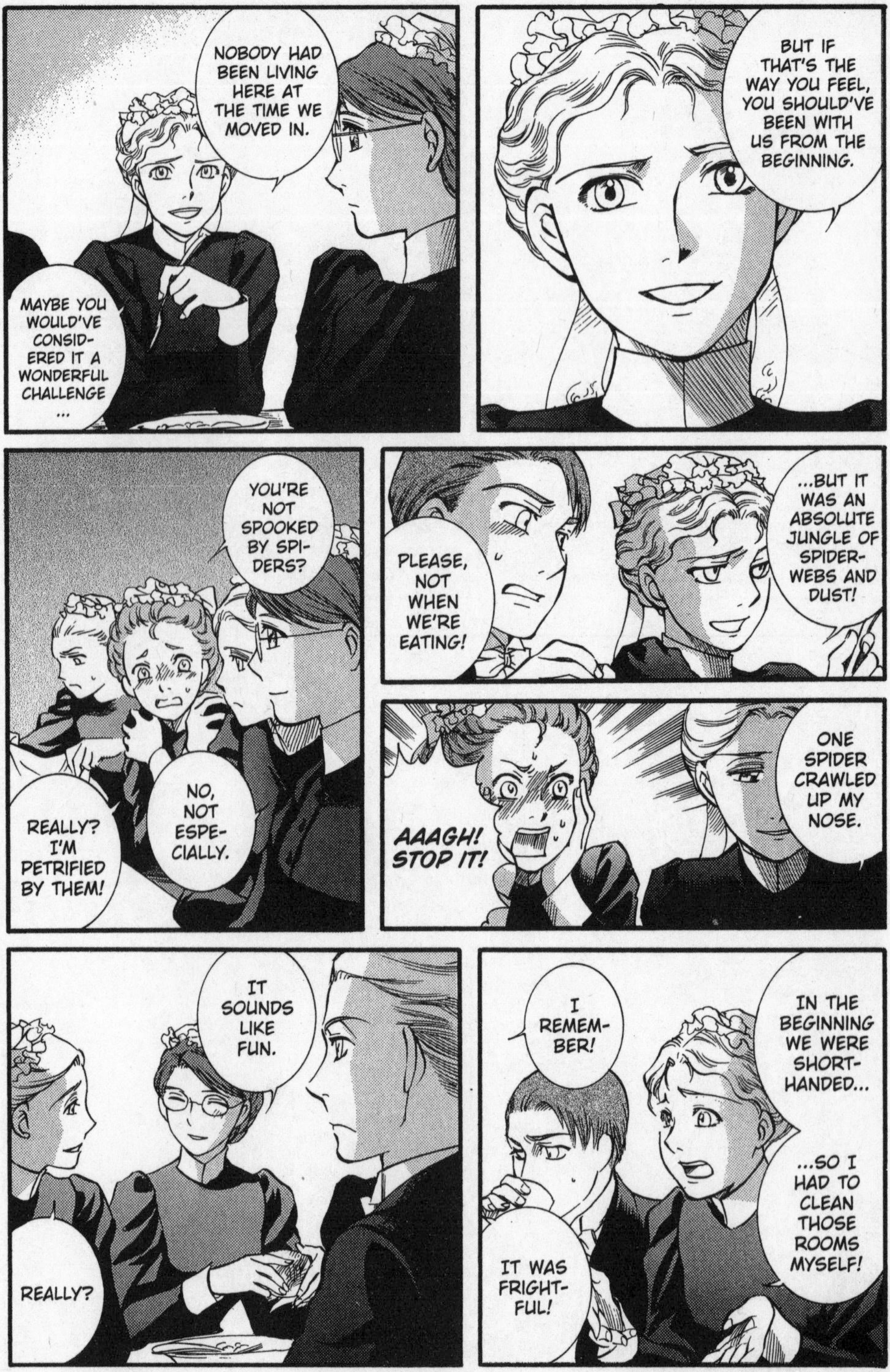
BUT IF THAT'S THE WAY YOU FEEL, YOU SHOULD'VE BEEN WITH US FROM THE BEGINNING.
NOBODY HAD BEEN LIVING HERE AT THE TIME WE MOVED IN.
MAYBE YOU WOULD'VE CONSID-ERED IT A WONDERFUL CHALLENGE ...
...BUT IT WAS AN ABSOLUTE JUNGLE OF SPIDER-WEBS AND DUST!
PLEASE, NOT WHEN WE'RE EATING!
ONE SPIDER CRAWLED UP MY NOSE.
AAAGH! STOP IT!
YOU'RE NOT SPOOKED BY SPI-DERS?
NO, NOT ESPE-CIALLY.
REALLY? I'M PETRIFIED BY THEM!
IN THE BEGINNING WE WERE SHORT-HANDED...
I REMEMBER!
...SO I HAD TO CLEAN THOSE ROOMS MYSELF!
IT WAS FRIGHT-FUL!
IT SOUNDS LIKE FUN.
REALLY?

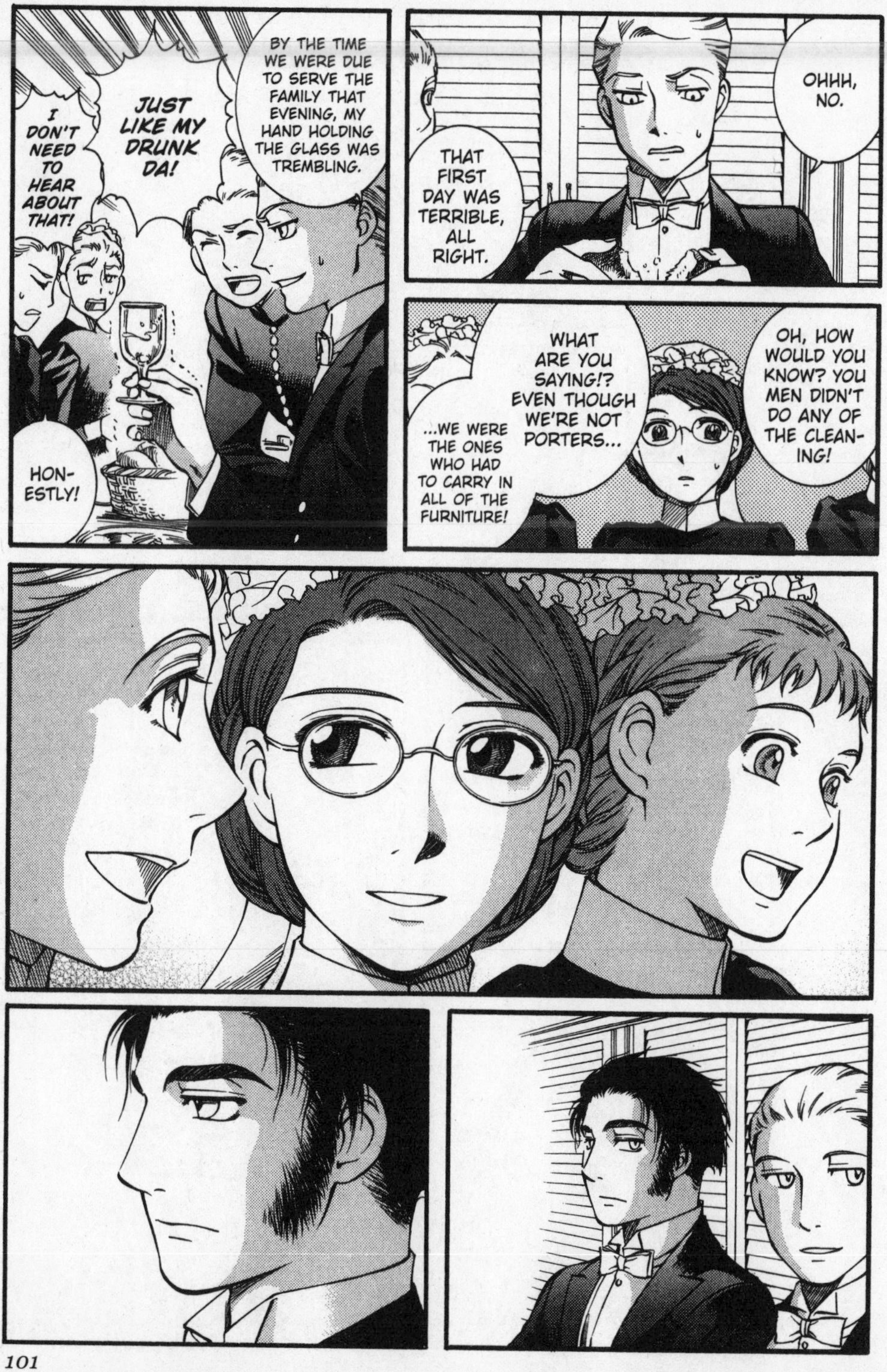
OHHH, NO.
THAT FIRST DAY WAS TERRIBLE, ALL RIGHT.
OH, HOW WOULD YOU KNOW? YOU MEN DIDN'T DO ANY OF THE CLEANING!
WHAT ARE YOU SAYING!? EVEN THOUGH WE'RE NOT PORTERS...
...WE WERE THE ONES WHO HAD TO CARRY IN ALL OF THE FURNITURE!
BY THE TIME WE WERE DUE TO SERVE THE FAMILY THAT EVENING, MY HAND HOLDING THE GLASS WAS TREMBLING.
JUST LIKE MY DRUNK DA!
I DON'T NEED TO HEAR ABOUT THAT!
HON-ESTLY!

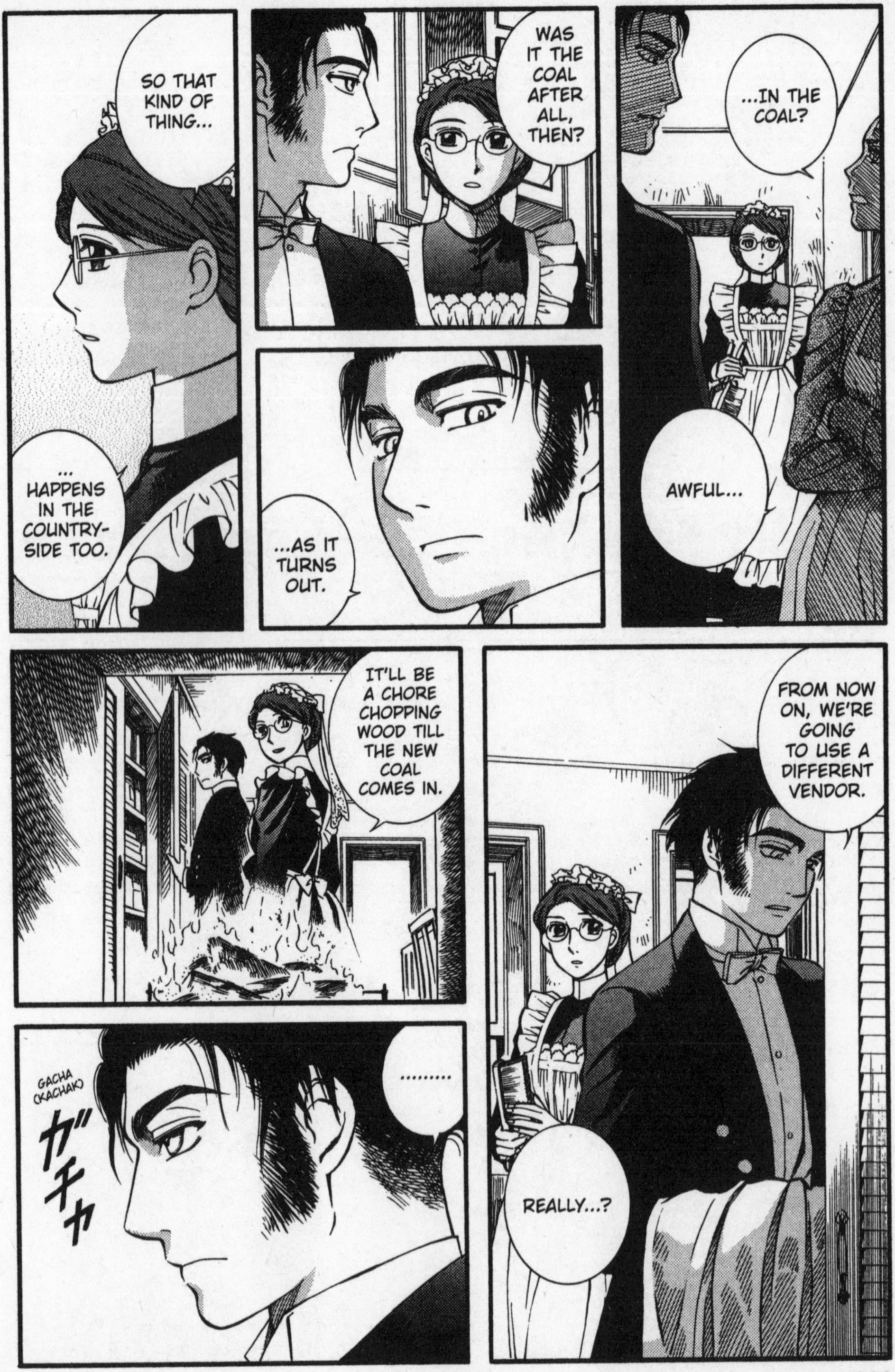
...IN THE COAL?
AWFUL...
WAS IT THE COAL AFTER ALL, THEN?
...AS IT TURNS OUT.
SO THAT KIND OF THING...
... HAPPENS IN THE COUNTRY-SIDE TOO.
FROM NOW ON, WE'RE GOING TO USE A DIFFERENT VENDOR.
REALLY...?
IT'LL BE A CHORE CHOPPING WOOD TILL THE NEW COAL COMES IN.
....
GACHA (KACHAK)
ガチャ

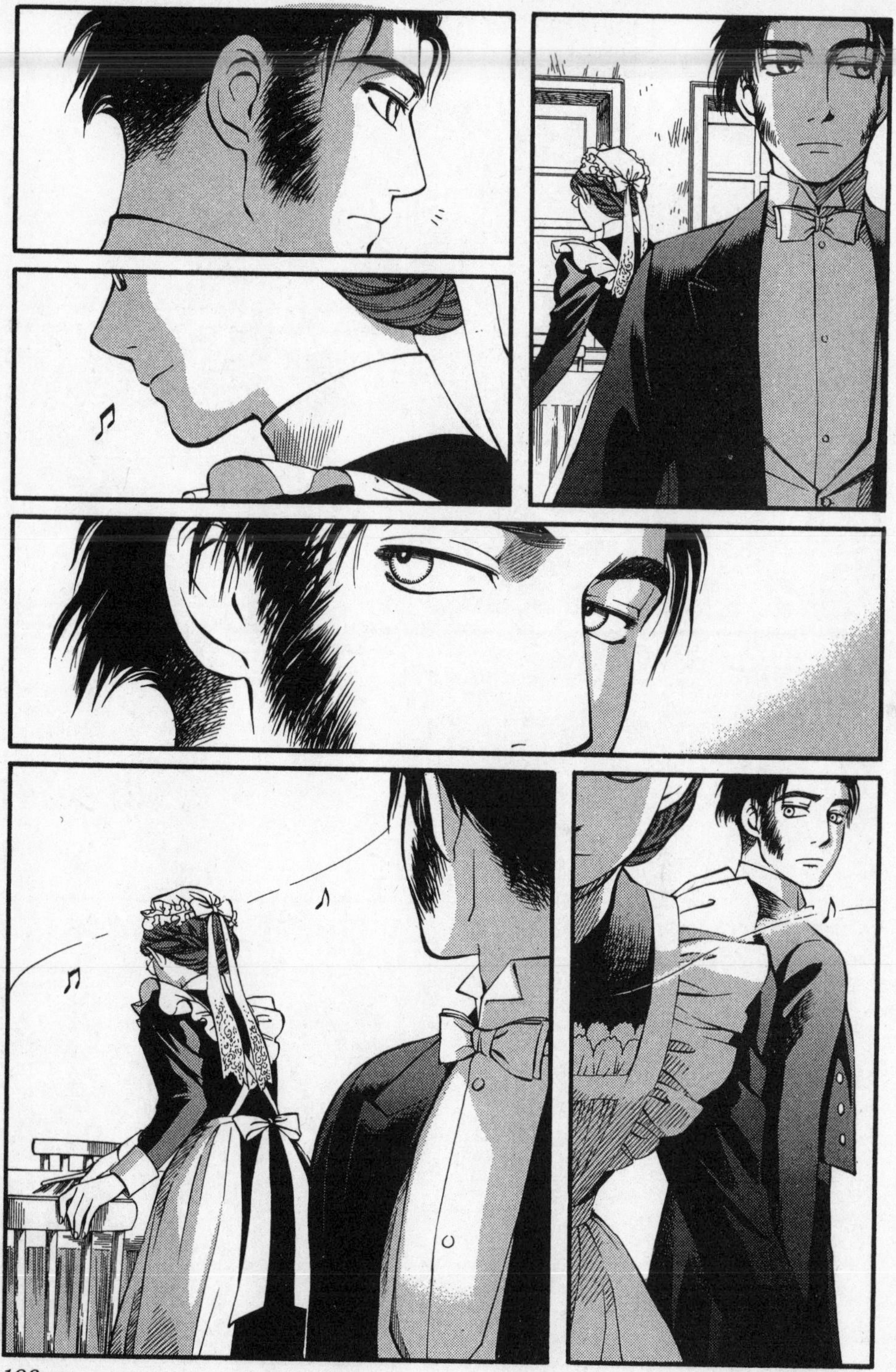

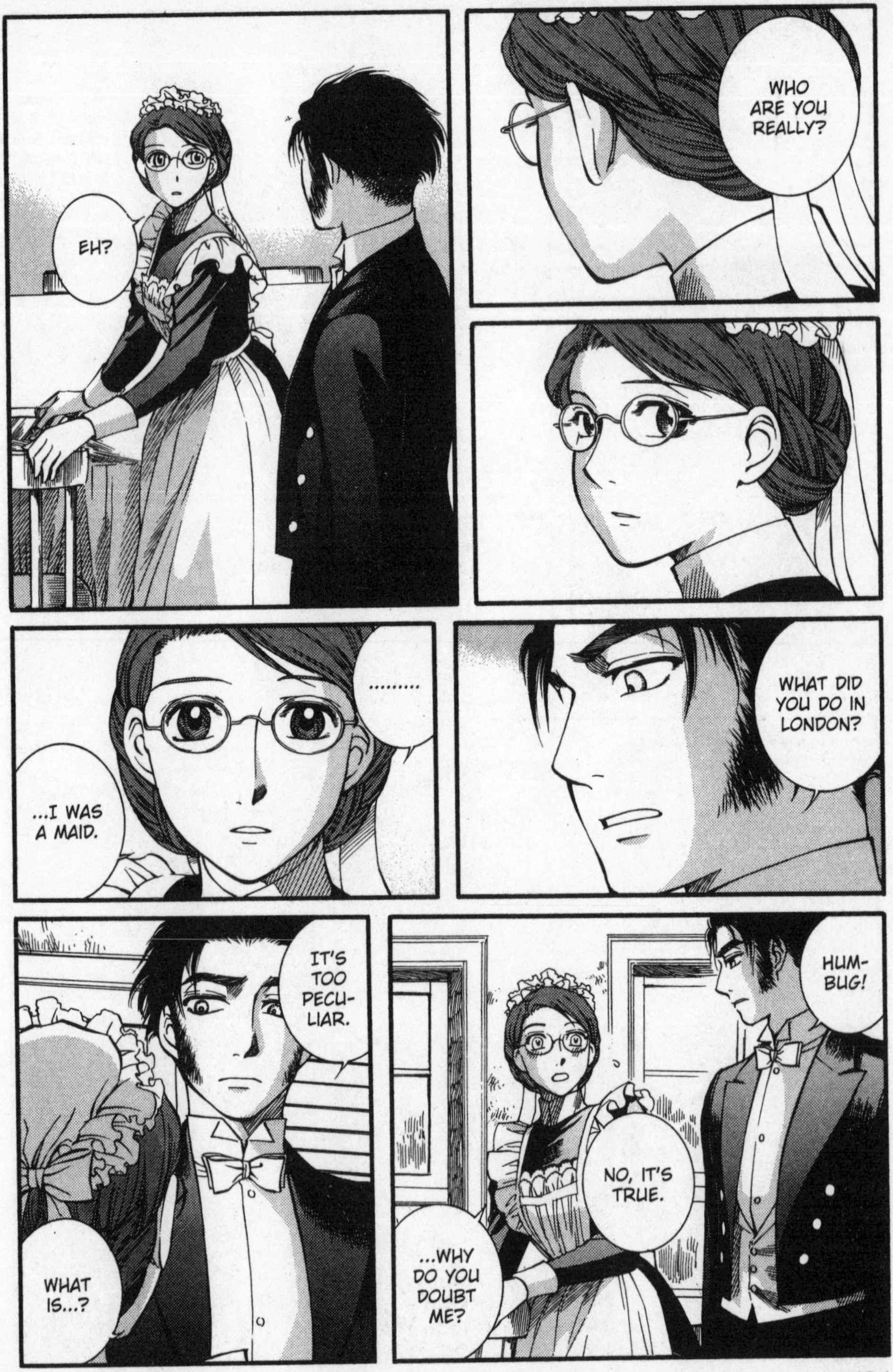
WHO ARE YOU REALLY?
EH?
WHAT DID YOU DO IN LONDON?
....
...I WAS A MAID.
HUM-BUG!
NO, IT'S TRUE.
...WHY DO YOU DOUBT ME?
IT'S TOO PECULIAR.
WHAT IS...?

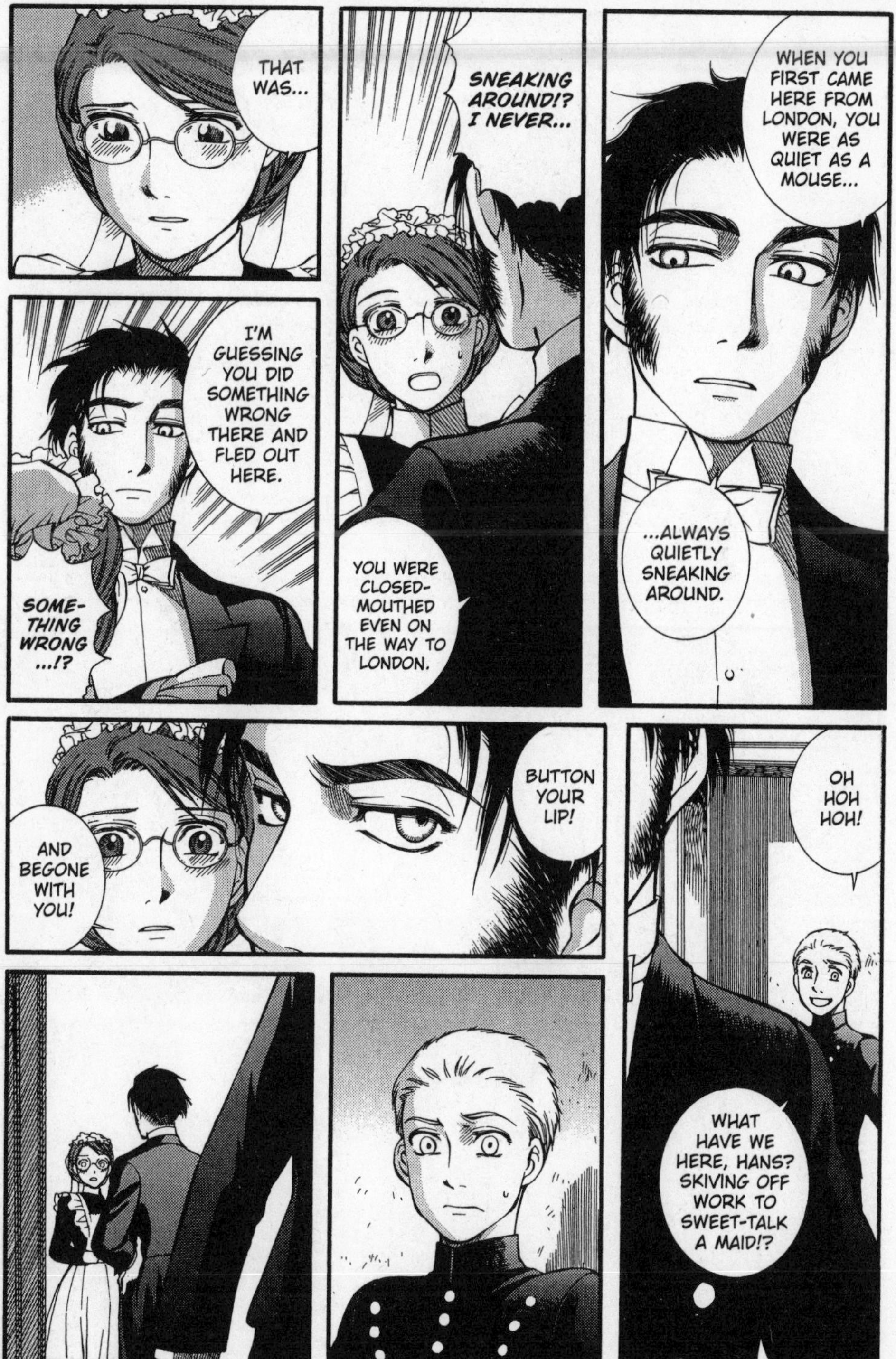
WHEN YOU FIRST CAME HERE FROM LONDON, YOU WERE AS QUIET AS A MOUSE...
...ALWAYS QUIETLY SNEAKING AROUND.
SNEAKING AROUND!? I NEVER...
YOU WERE CLOSED-MOUTHED EVEN ON THE WAY TO LONDON.
THAT WAS...
I'M GUESSING YOU DID SOMETHING WRONG THERE AND FLED OUT HERE.
SOME-THING WRONG ...!?
OH HOH HOH!
WHAT HAVE WE HERE, HANS? SKIVING OFF WORK TO SWEET-TALK A MAID!?
BUTTON YOUR LIP!
AND BEGONE WITH YOU!

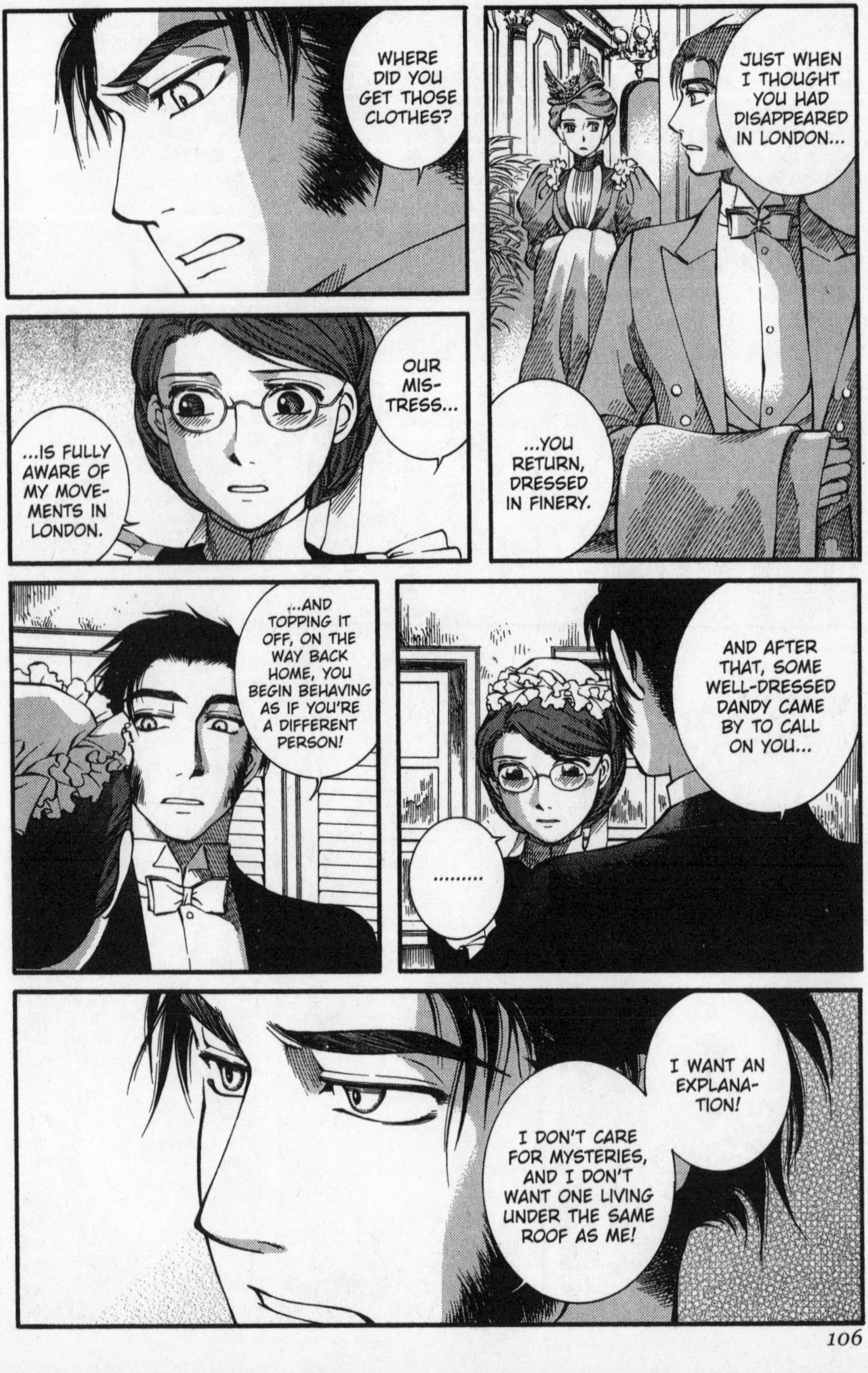
JUST WHEN I THOUGHT YOU HAD DISAPPEARED IN LONDON...
...YOU RETURN, DRESSED IN FINERY.
WHERE DID YOU GET THOSE CLOTHES?
OUR MIS-TRESS...
...IS FULLY AWARE OF MY MOVE-MENTS IN LONDON.
AND AFTER THAT, SOME WELL-DRESSED DANDY CAME BY TO CALL ON YOU...
....
...AND TOPPING IT OFF, ON THE WAY BACK HOME, YOU BEGIN BEHAVING AS IF YOU'RE A DIFFERENT PERSON!
I WANT AN EXPLANA-TION!
I DON'T CARE FOR MYSTERIES, AND I DON'T WANT ONE LIVING UNDER THE SAME ROOF AS ME!

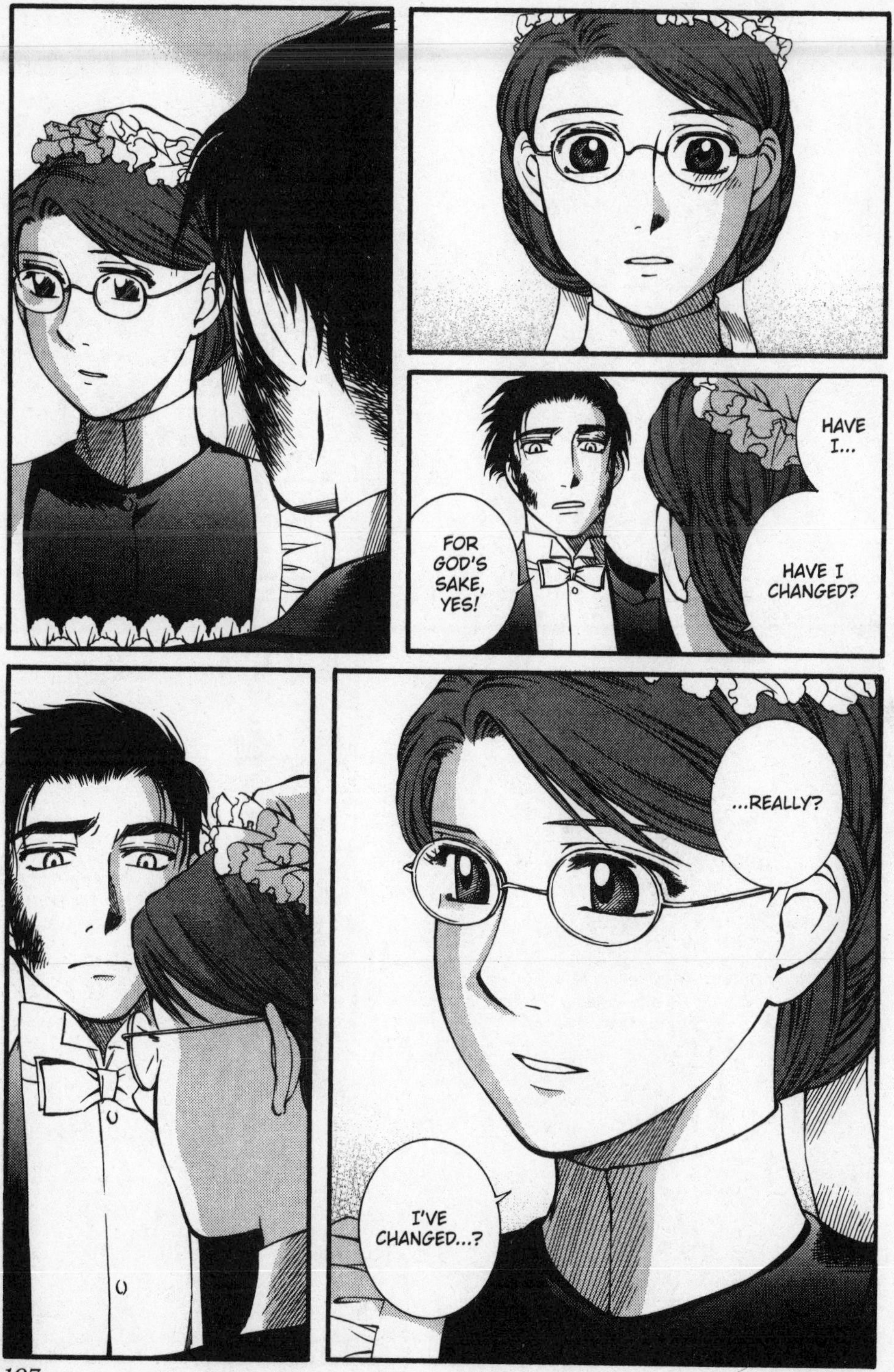
HAVE I...
HAVE I CHANGED?
FOR GOD'S SAKE, YES!
...REALLY?
I'VE CHANGED...?

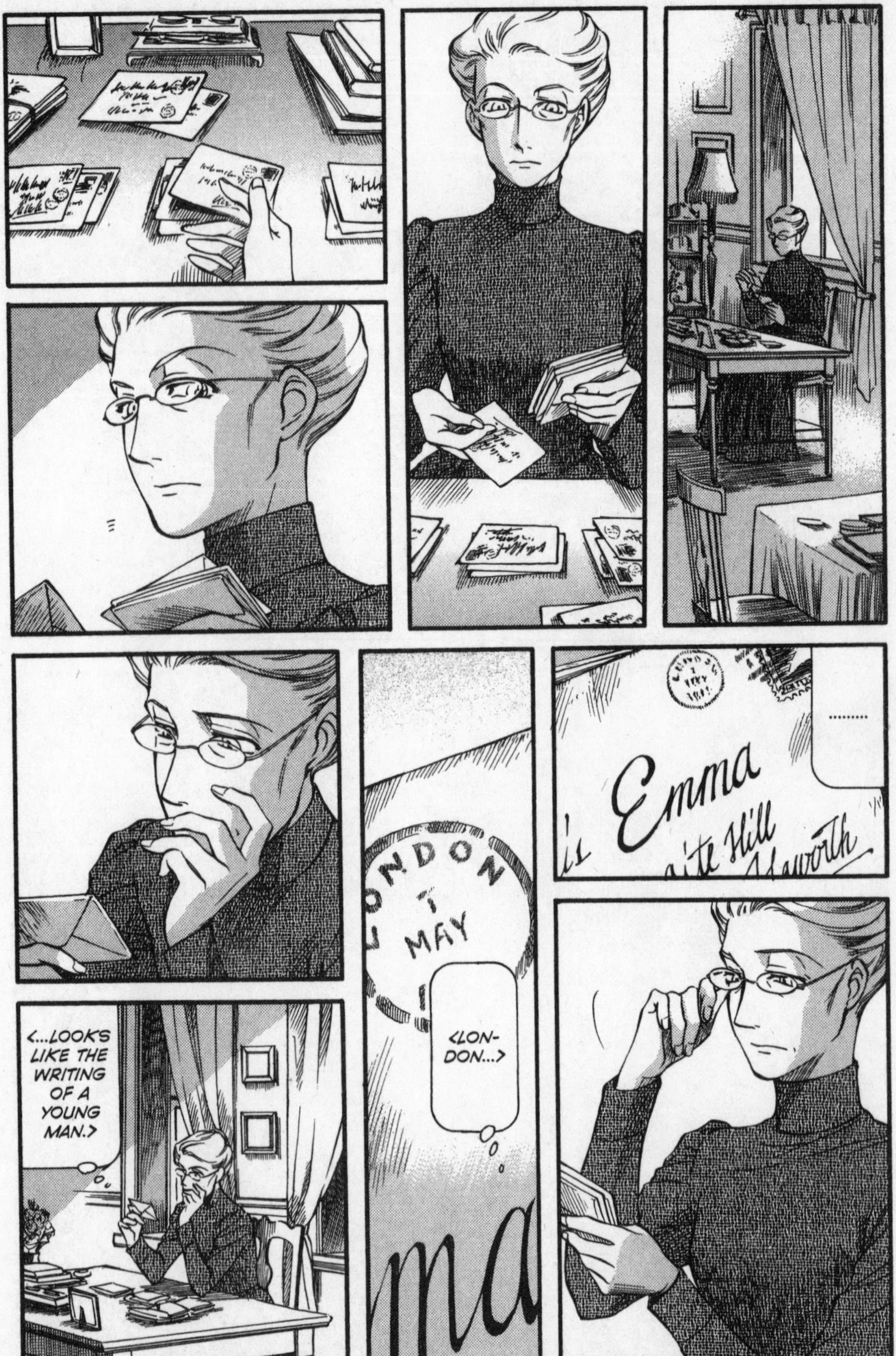
Emma
....
LONDON
1
MAY
<LON-
DON...>
<...LOOKS
LIKE THE
WRITING
OF A
YOUNG
MAN.>

Chapter 33: End

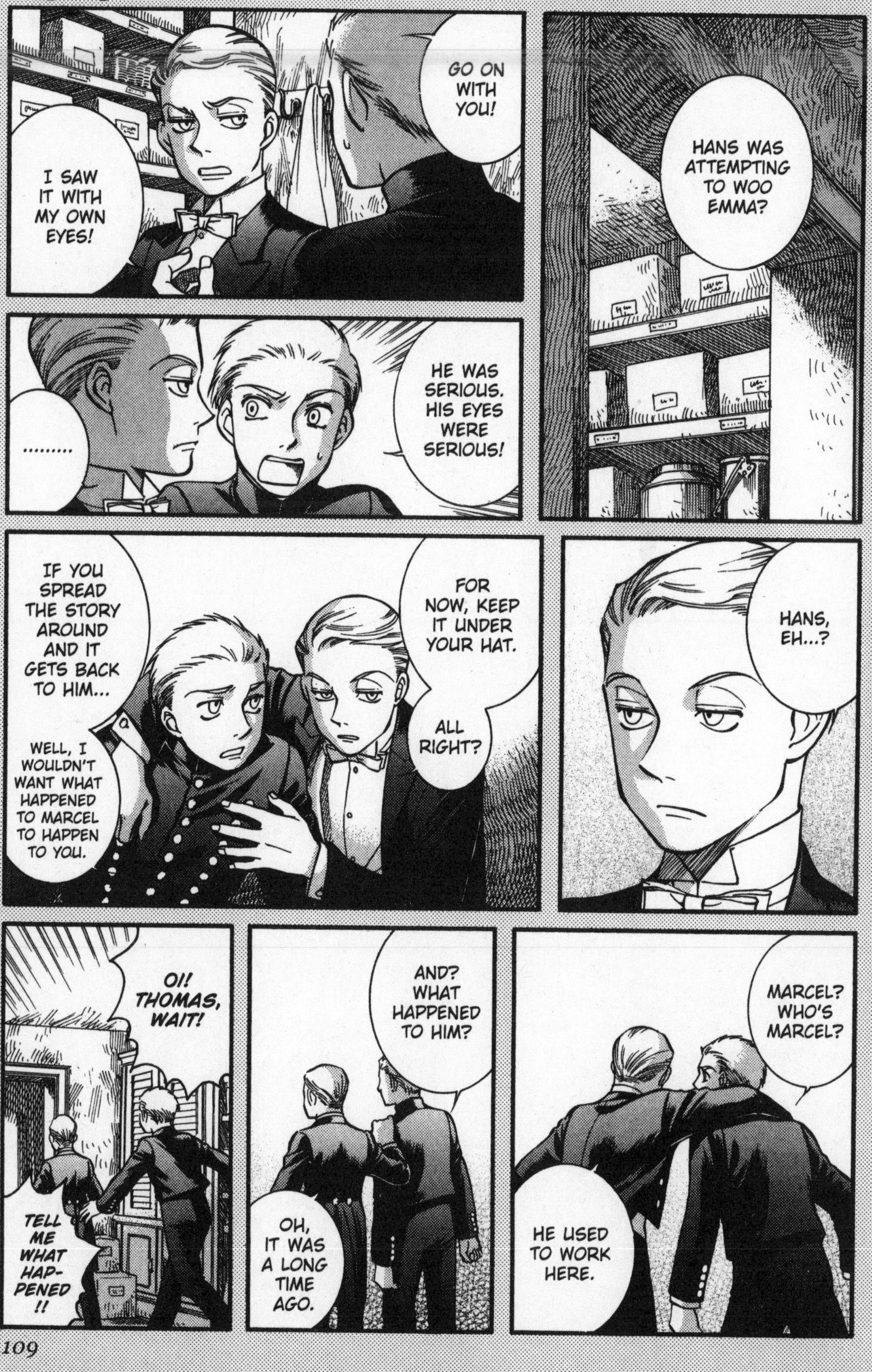
HANS WAS ATTEMPTING TO WOO EMMA?
GO ON WITH YOU!
I SAW IT WITH MY OWN EYES!
HE WAS SERIOUS. HIS EYES WERE SERIOUS!
....
HANS, EH...?
FOR NOW, KEEP IT UNDER YOUR HAT.
ALL RIGHT?
IF YOU SPREAD THE STORY AROUND AND IT GETS BACK TO HIM...
WELL, I WOULDN'T WANT WHAT HAPPENED TO MARCEL TO HAPPEN TO YOU.
MARCEL? WHO'S MARCEL?
HE USED TO WORK HERE.
AND? WHAT HAPPENED TO HIM?
OH, IT WAS A LONG TIME AGO.
OI! THOMAS, WAIT!
TELL ME WHAT HAP-PENED!!

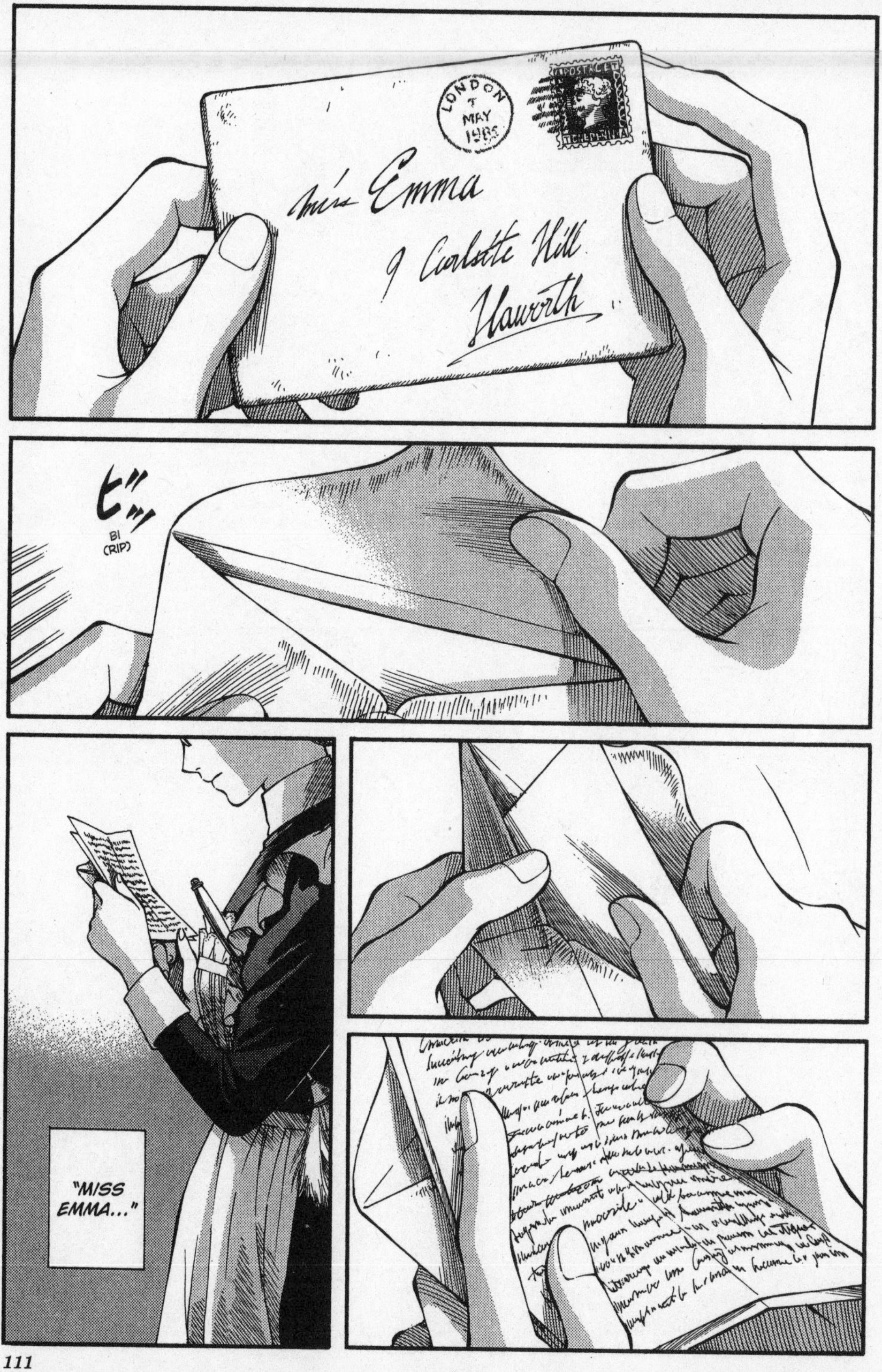
ビッ
BI
(RIP)
"MISS
EMMA..."

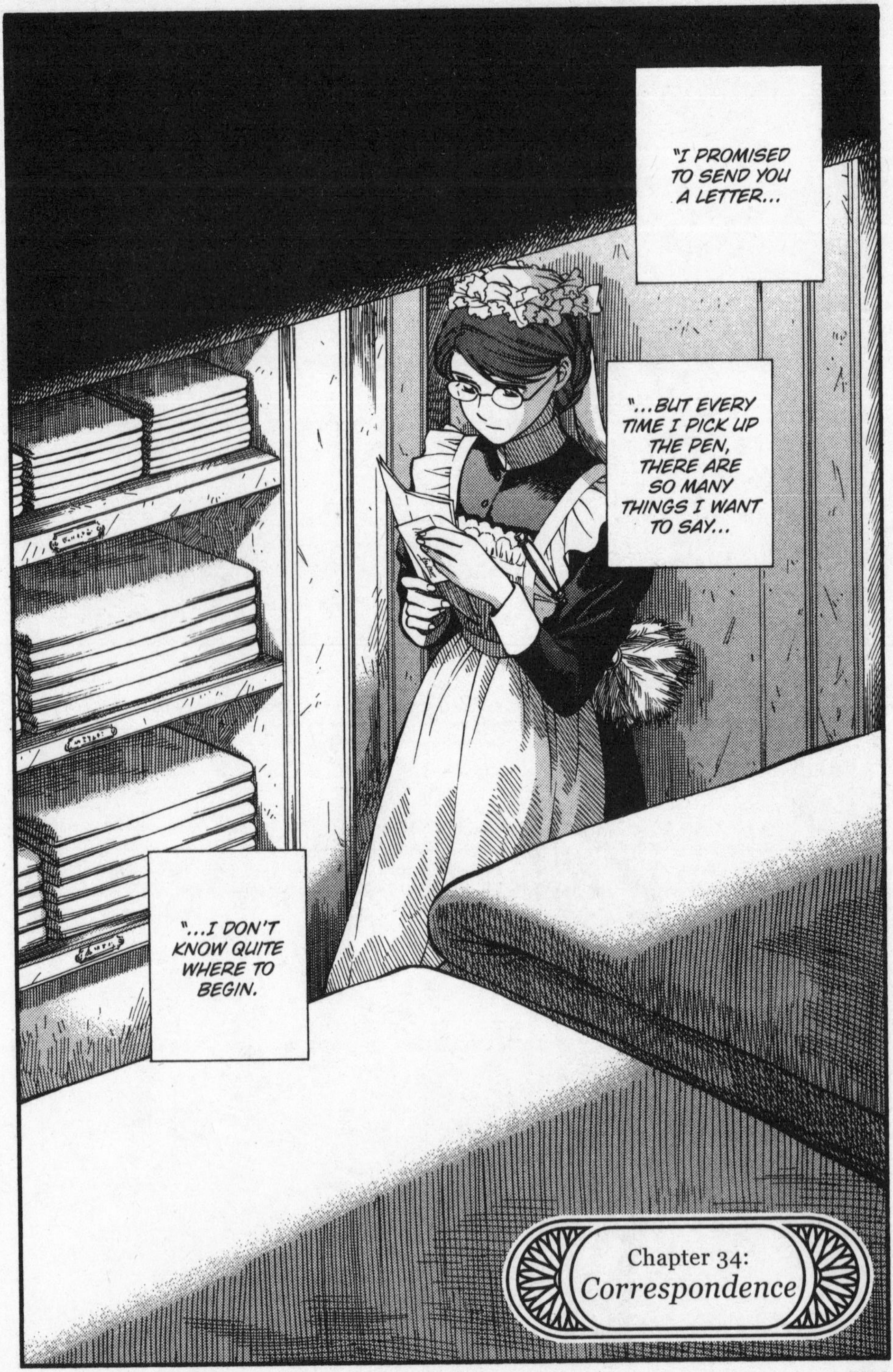
"I PROMISED TO SEND YOU A LETTER...
"...BUT EVERY TIME I PICK UP THE PEN, THERE ARE SO MANY THINGS I WANT TO SAY...
"...I DON'T KNOW QUITE WHERE TO BEGIN.
Chapter 34: Correspondence

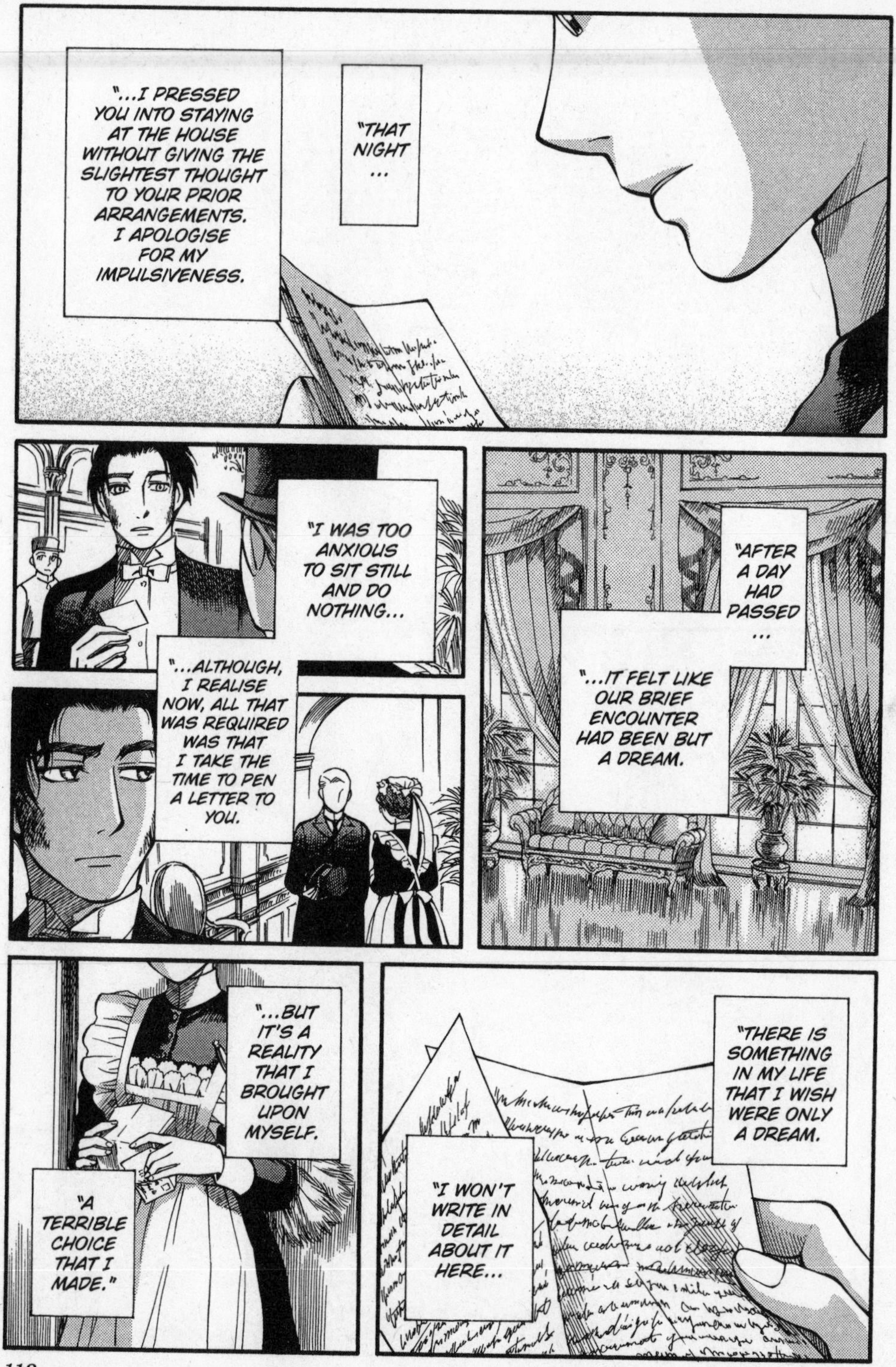
"THAT NIGHT ...
"...I PRESSED YOU INTO STAYING AT THE HOUSE WITHOUT GIVING THE SLIGHTEST THOUGHT TO YOUR PRIOR ARRANGEMENTS. I APOLOGISE FOR MY IMPULSIVENESS.
"AFTER A DAY HAD PASSED ...
"...IT FELT LIKE OUR BRIEF ENCOUNTER HAD BEEN BUT A DREAM.
"I WAS TOO ANXIOUS TO SIT STILL AND DO NOTHING...
"...ALTHOUGH, I REALISE NOW, ALL THAT WAS REQUIRED WAS THAT I TAKE THE TIME TO PEN A LETTER TO YOU.
"THERE IS SOMETHING IN MY LIFE THAT I WISH WERE ONLY A DREAM.
"I WON'T WRITE IN DETAIL ABOUT IT HERE...
"...BUT IT'S A REALITY THAT I BROUGHT UPON MYSELF.
"A TERRIBLE CHOICE THAT I MADE."

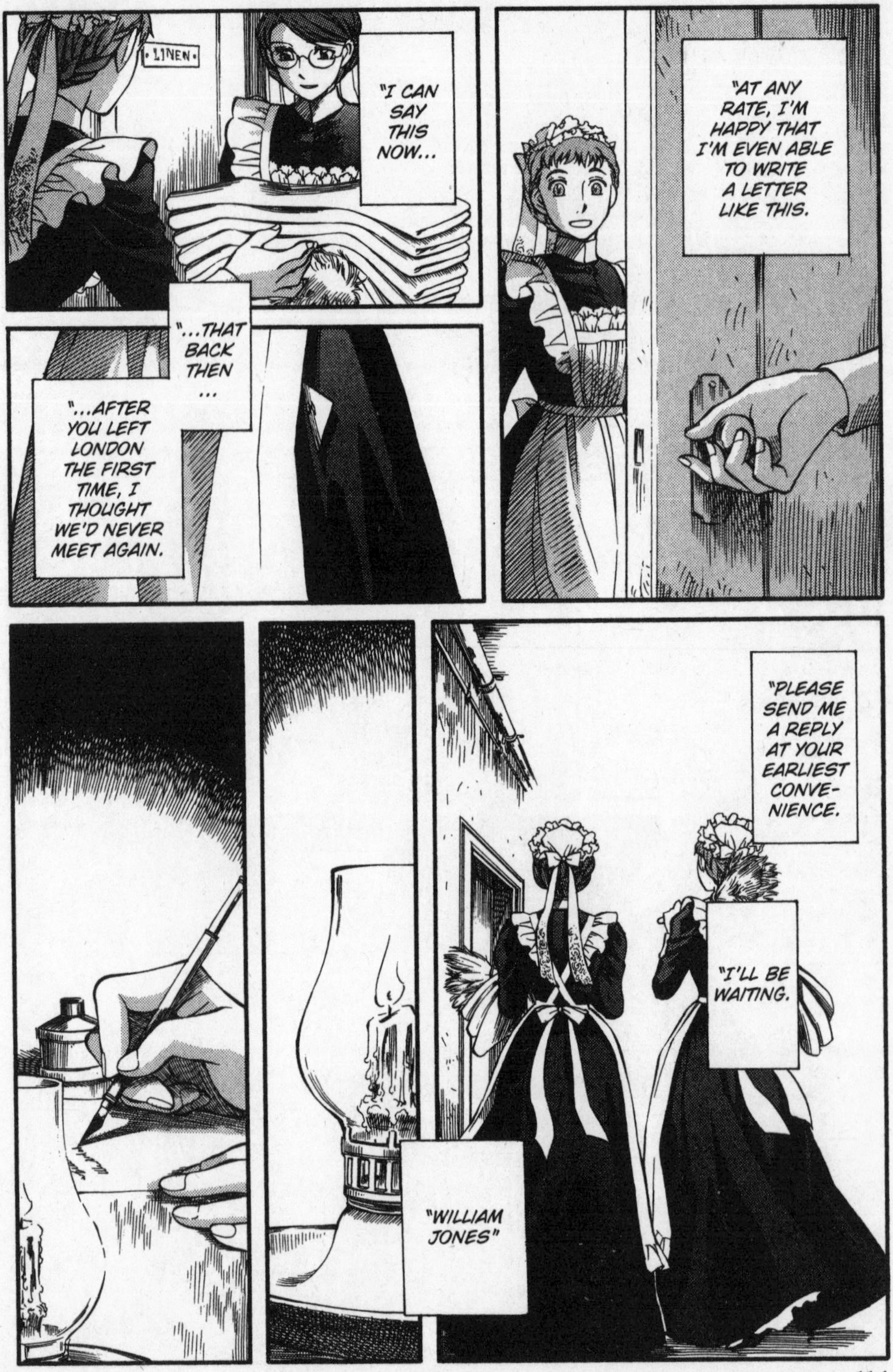
"AT ANY RATE, I'M HAPPY THAT I'M EVEN ABLE TO WRITE A LETTER LIKE THIS.
LINEN
"I CAN SAY THIS NOW...
"...THAT BACK THEN...
"...AFTER YOU LEFT LONDON THE FIRST TIME, I THOUGHT WE'D NEVER MEET AGAIN.
"PLEASE SEND ME A REPLY AT YOUR EARLIEST CONVE-NIENCE.
"I'LL BE WAITING.
"WILLIAM JONES"

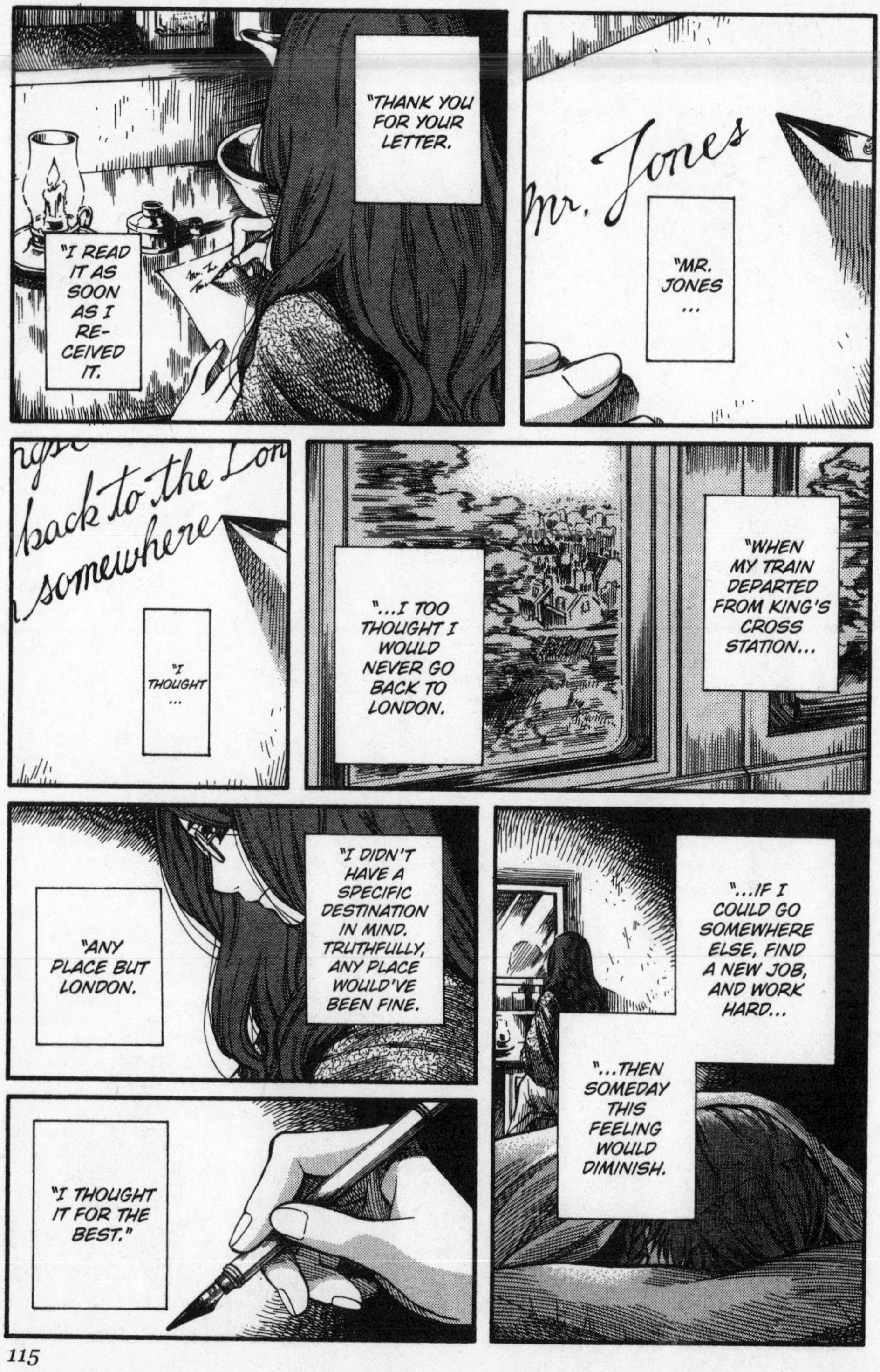
Mr. Jones
"MR. JONES ...
"THANK YOU FOR YOUR LETTER.
"I READ IT AS SOON AS I RE-CEIVED IT.
"WHEN MY TRAIN DEPARTED FROM KING'S CROSS STATION...
"...I TOO THOUGHT I WOULD NEVER GO BACK TO LONDON.
back to the Lon
somewhere
"I THOUGHT ...
"...IF I COULD GO SOMEWHERE ELSE, FIND A NEW JOB, AND WORK HARD...
"...THEN SOMEDAY THIS FEELING WOULD DIMINISH.
"I DIDN'T HAVE A SPECIFIC DESTINATION IN MIND. TRUTHFULLY, ANY PLACE WOULD'VE BEEN FINE.
"ANY PLACE BUT LONDON.
"I THOUGHT IT FOR THE BEST."

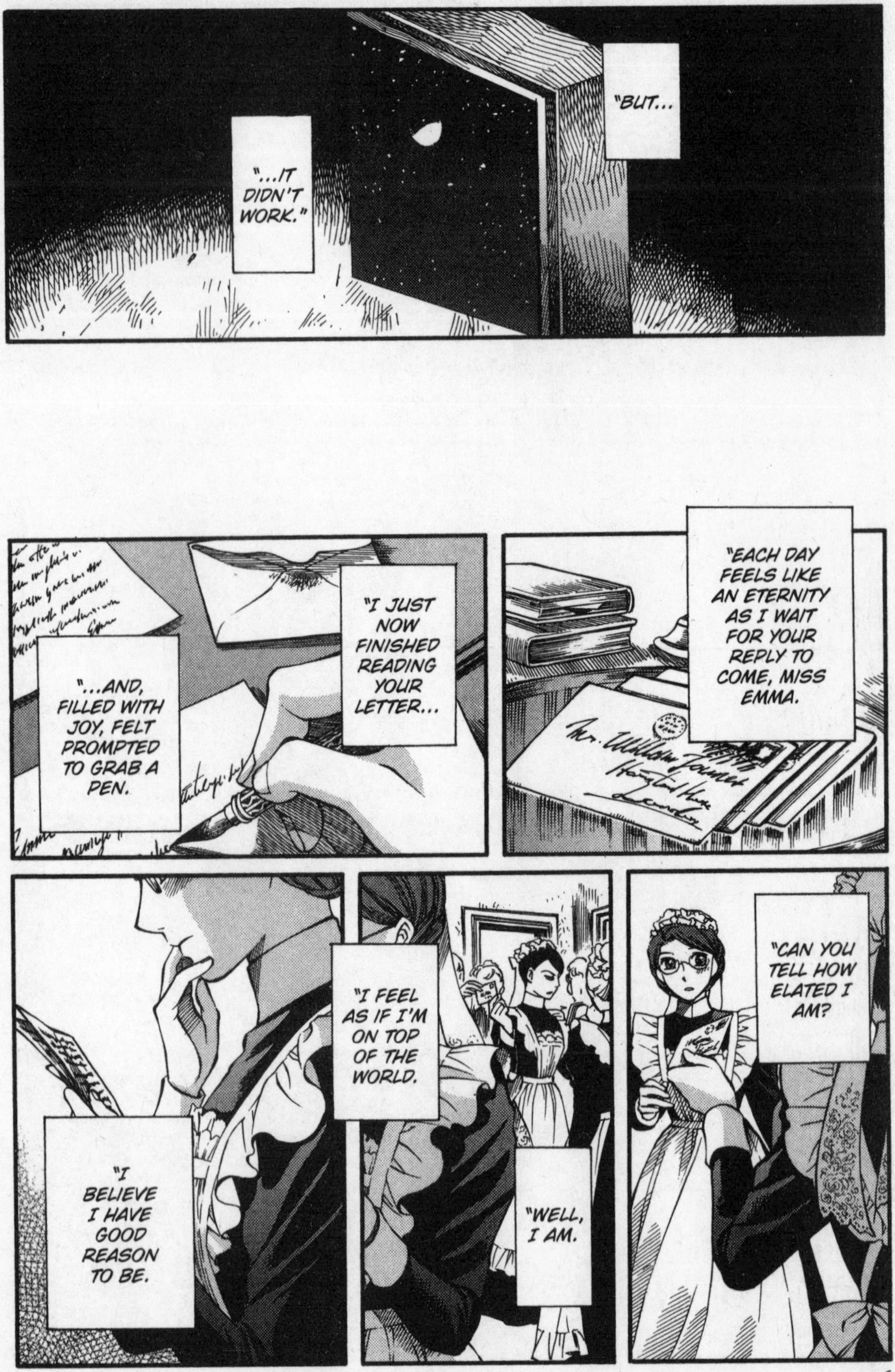
"BUT...
"...IT DIDN'T WORK."
"EACH DAY FEELS LIKE AN ETERNITY AS I WAIT FOR YOUR REPLY TO COME, MISS EMMA.
"I JUST NOW FINISHED READING YOUR LETTER...
"...AND, FILLED WITH JOY, FELT PROMPTED TO GRAB A PEN.
"CAN YOU TELL HOW ELATED I AM?
"WELL, I AM.
"I FEEL AS IF I'M ON TOP OF THE WORLD.
"I BELIEVE I HAVE GOOD REASON TO BE.

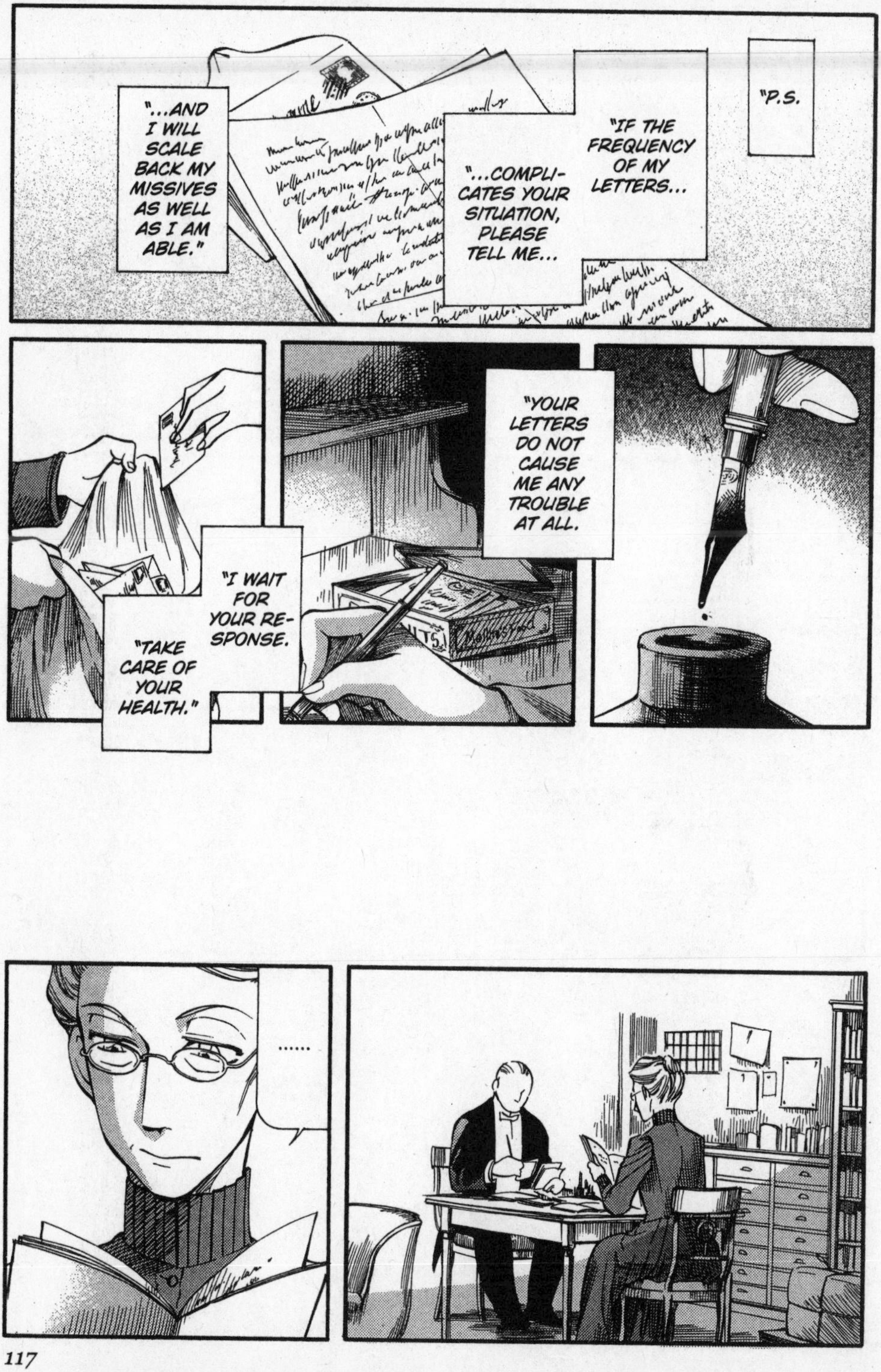
"P.S.
"IF THE FREQUENCY OF MY LETTERS...
"...COMPLICATES YOUR SITUATION, PLEASE TELL ME...
"...AND I WILL SCALE BACK MY MISSIVES AS WELL AS I AM ABLE."
"YOUR LETTERS DO NOT CAUSE ME ANY TROUBLE AT ALL.
"I WAIT FOR YOUR RESPONSE.
"TAKE CARE OF YOUR HEALTH."
......

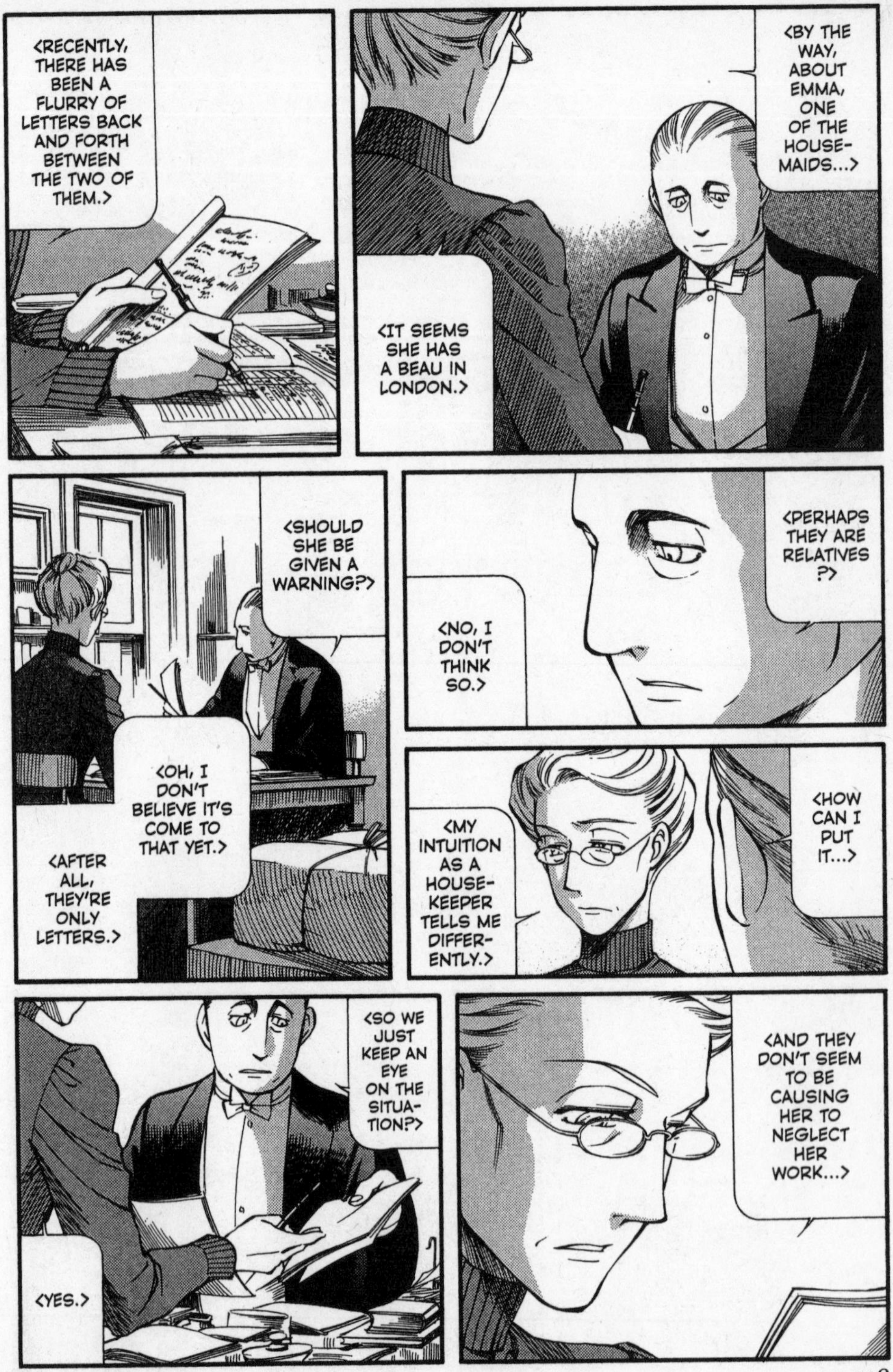
<BY THE WAY, ABOUT EMMA, ONE OF THE HOUSE-MAIDS...>
<IT SEEMS SHE HAS A BEAU IN LONDON.>
<RECENTLY, THERE HAS BEEN A FLURRY OF LETTERS BACK AND FORTH BETWEEN THE TWO OF THEM.>
<PERHAPS THEY ARE RELATIVES?>
<NO, I DON'T THINK SO.>
<HOW CAN I PUT IT...>
<MY INTUITION AS A HOUSE-KEEPER TELLS ME DIFFER-ENTLY.>
<SHOULD SHE BE GIVEN A WARNING?>
<OH, I DON'T BELIEVE IT'S COME TO THAT YET.>
<AFTER ALL, THEY'RE ONLY LETTERS.>
<AND THEY DON'T SEEM TO BE CAUSING HER TO NEGLECT HER WORK...>
<SO WE JUST KEEP AN EYE ON THE SITUA-TION?>
<YES.>

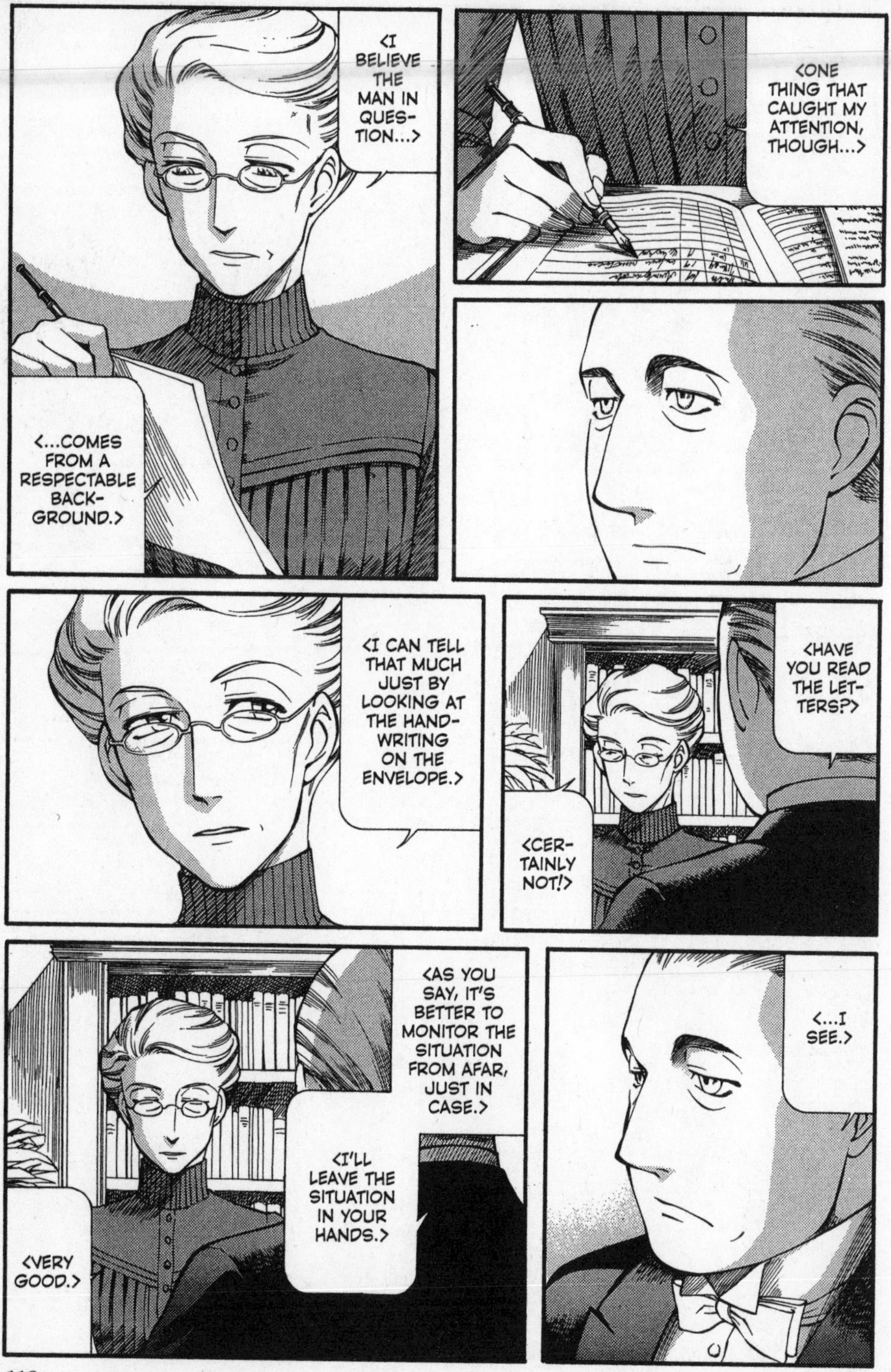
<ONE THING THAT CAUGHT MY ATTENTION, THOUGH...>
<I BELIEVE THE MAN IN QUESTION...>
<...COMES FROM A RESPECTABLE BACKGROUND.>
<HAVE YOU READ THE LETTERS?>
<CERTAINLY NOT!>
<I CAN TELL THAT MUCH JUST BY LOOKING AT THE HANDWRITING ON THE ENVELOPE.>
<...I SEE.>
<AS YOU SAY, IT'S BETTER TO MONITOR THE SITUATION FROM AFAR, JUST IN CASE.>
<I'LL LEAVE THE SITUATION IN YOUR HANDS.>
<VERY GOOD.>

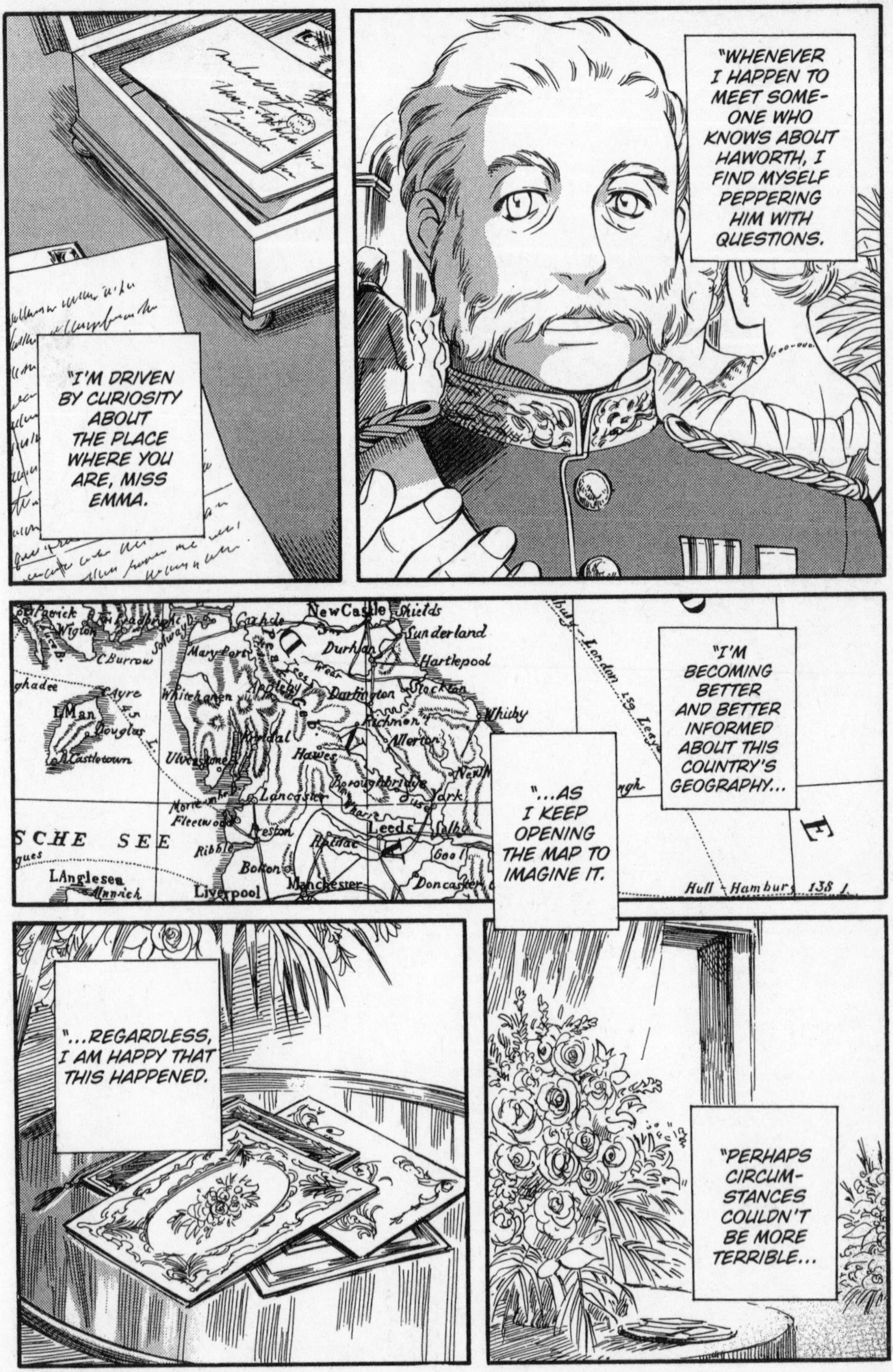
"WHENEVER I HAPPEN TO MEET SOME-ONE WHO KNOWS ABOUT HAWORTH, I FIND MYSELF PEPPERING HIM WITH QUESTIONS.
"I'M DRIVEN BY CURIOSITY ABOUT THE PLACE WHERE YOU ARE, MISS EMMA.
"I'M BECOMING BETTER AND BETTER INFORMED ABOUT THIS COUNTRY'S GEOGRAPHY...
"...AS I KEEP OPENING THE MAP TO IMAGINE IT.
NewCastle
Shields
Sunderland
Durham
Hartlepool
Mary Port
Whitehaven
Appleby
Darlington
Stockton
Whitby
Douglas
Castletown
Kendal
Hawes
Boroughbridge
York
Lancaster
Fleetwood
Preston
Leeds
SCHE SEE
Ribble
Bolton
Manchester
Liverpool
Hull - Hamburg 138
"PERHAPS CIRCUM-STANCES COULDN'T BE MORE TERRIBLE...
"...REGARDLESS, I AM HAPPY THAT THIS HAPPENED.

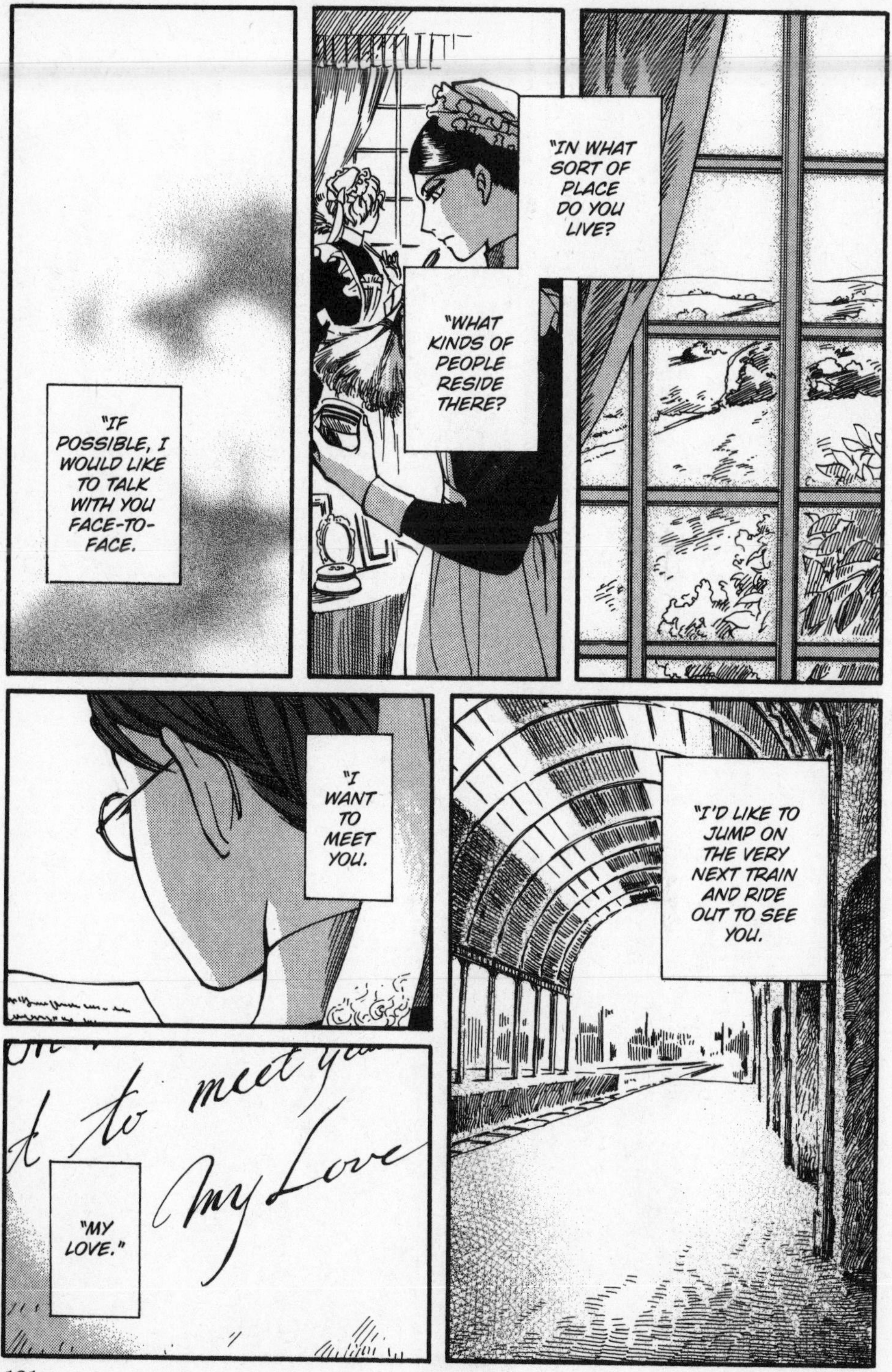
"IN WHAT SORT OF PLACE DO YOU LIVE?
"WHAT KINDS OF PEOPLE RESIDE THERE?
"IF POSSIBLE, I WOULD LIKE TO TALK WITH YOU FACE-TO-FACE.
"I'D LIKE TO JUMP ON THE VERY NEXT TRAIN AND RIDE OUT TO SEE YOU.
"I WANT TO MEET YOU.
t to meet
My Love
"MY LOVE."

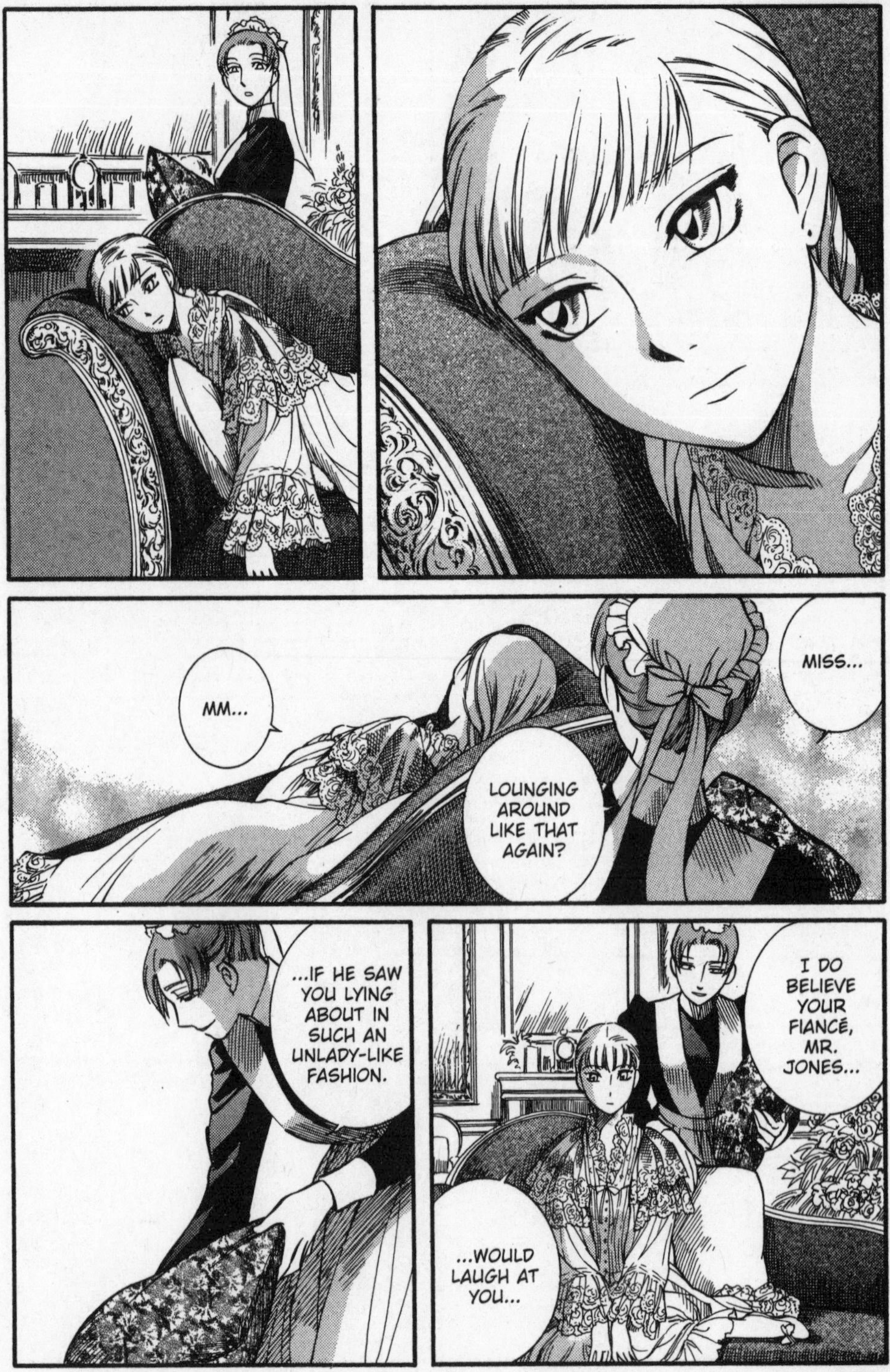
MISS...
LOUNGING AROUND LIKE THAT AGAIN?
MM...
I DO BELIEVE YOUR FIANCÉ, MR. JONES...
...WOULD LAUGH AT YOU...
...IF HE SAW YOU LYING ABOUT IN SUCH AN UNLADY-LIKE FASHION.

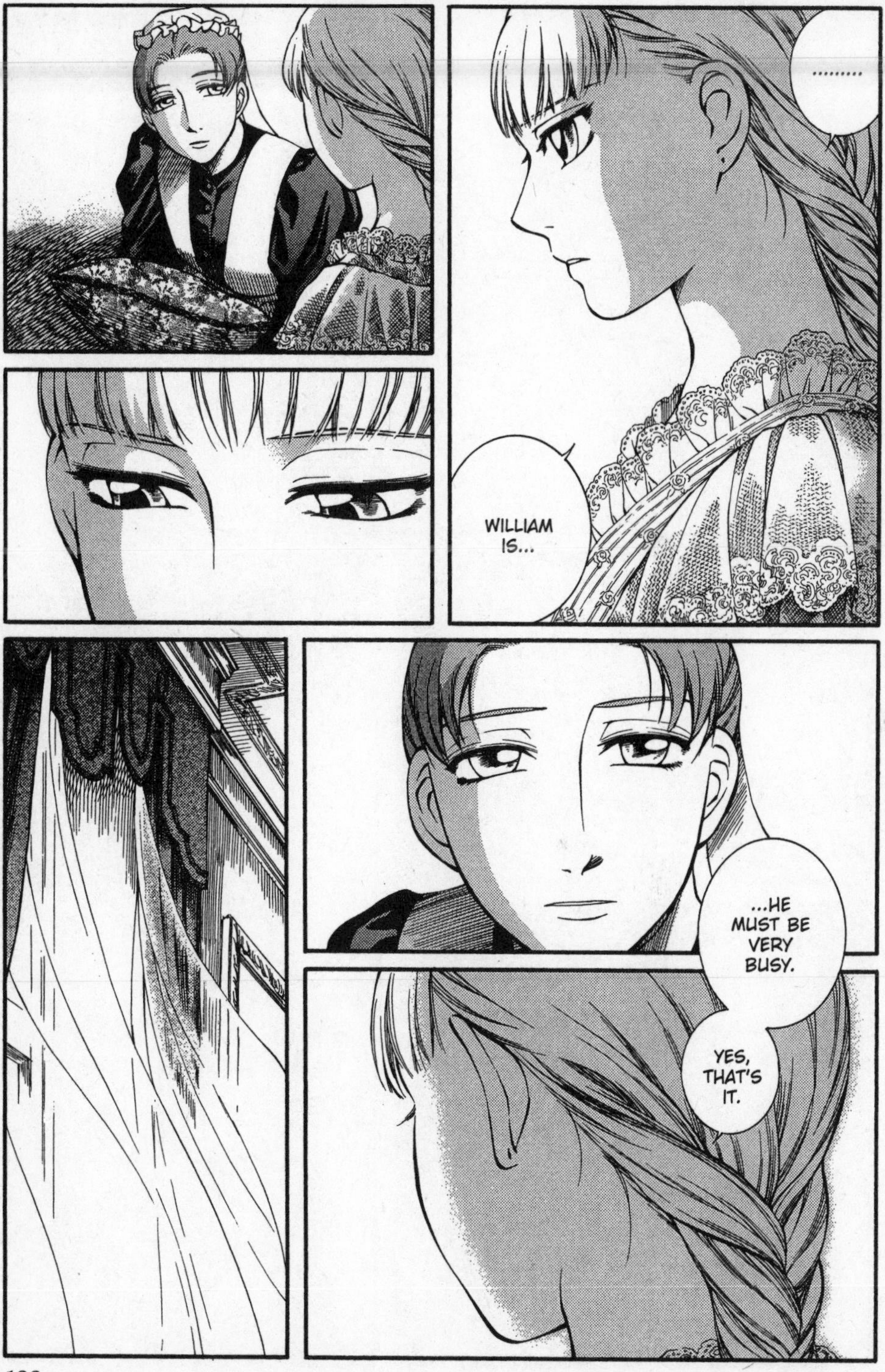

....
WILLIAM IS...
...HE MUST BE VERY BUSY.
YES, THAT'S IT.

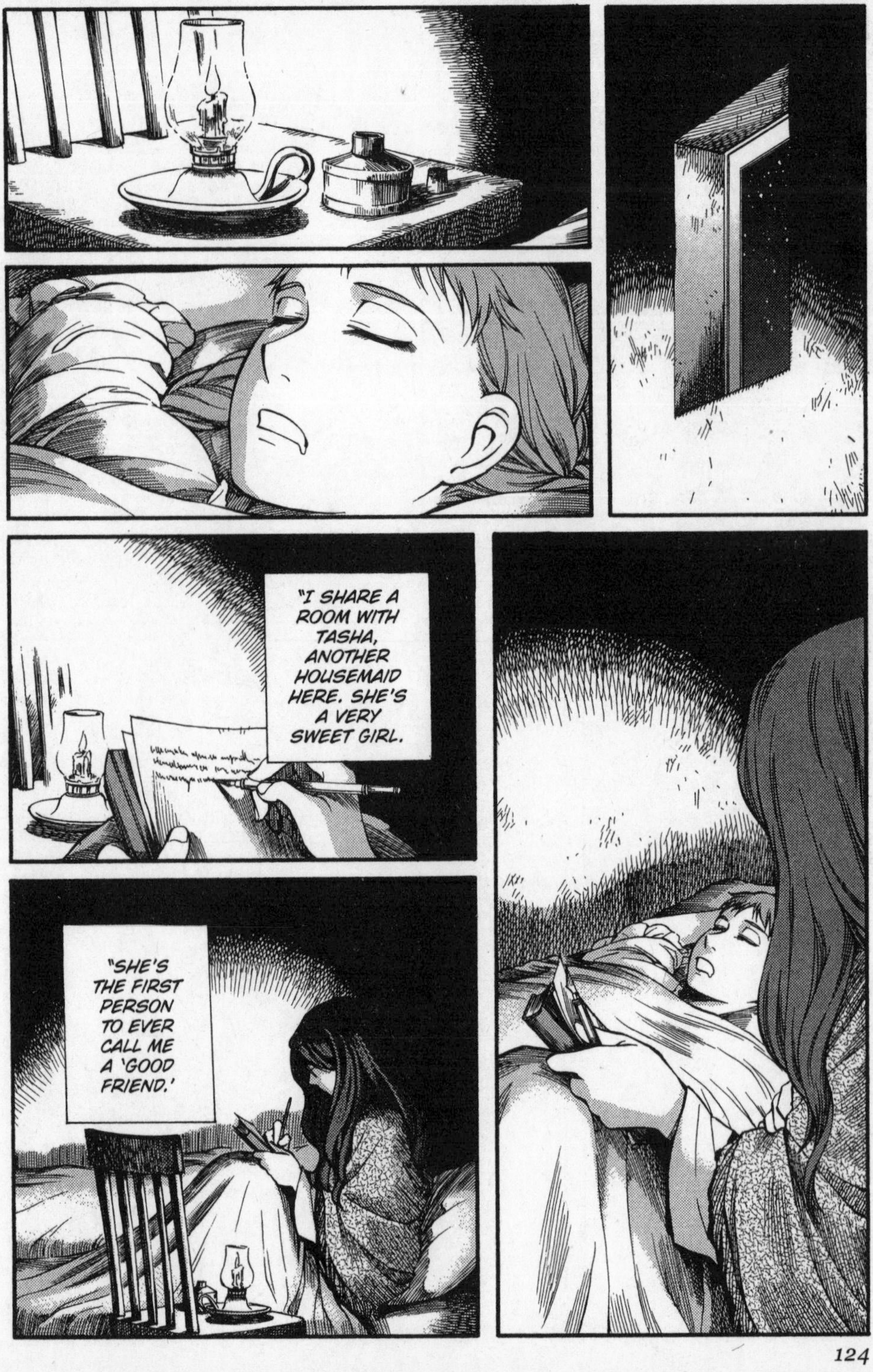
"I SHARE A ROOM WITH TASHA, ANOTHER HOUSEMAID HERE. SHE'S A VERY SWEET GIRL.
"SHE'S THE FIRST PERSON TO EVER CALL ME A 'GOOD FRIEND.'

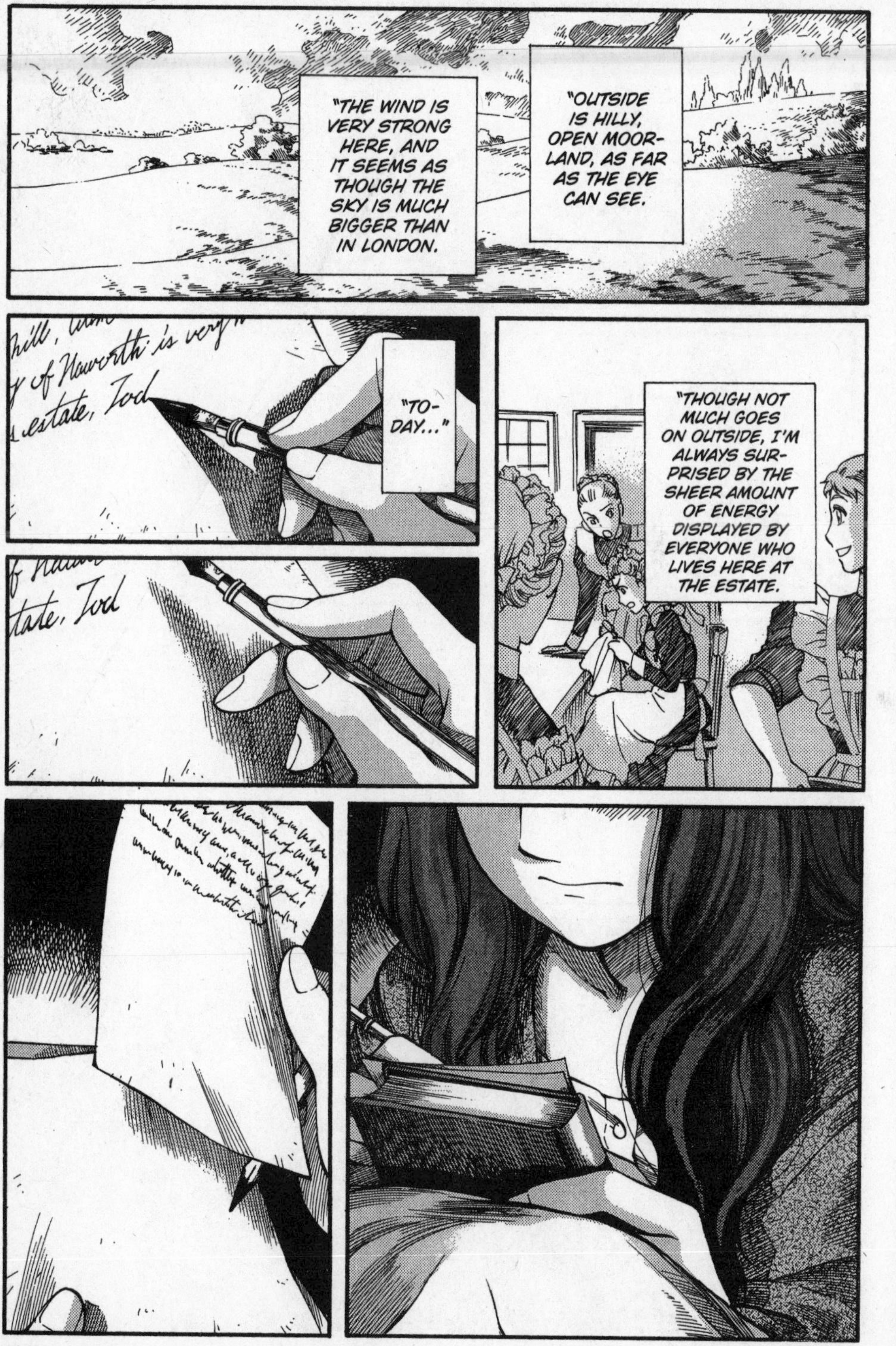

"OUTSIDE IS HILLY, OPEN MOORLAND, AS FAR AS THE EYE CAN SEE.
"THE WIND IS VERY STRONG HERE, AND IT SEEMS AS THOUGH THE SKY IS MUCH BIGGER THAN IN LONDON.
"THOUGH NOT MUCH GOES ON OUTSIDE, I'M ALWAYS SURPRISED BY THE SHEER AMOUNT OF ENERGY DISPLAYED BY EVERYONE WHO LIVES HERE AT THE ESTATE.
"TODAY..."

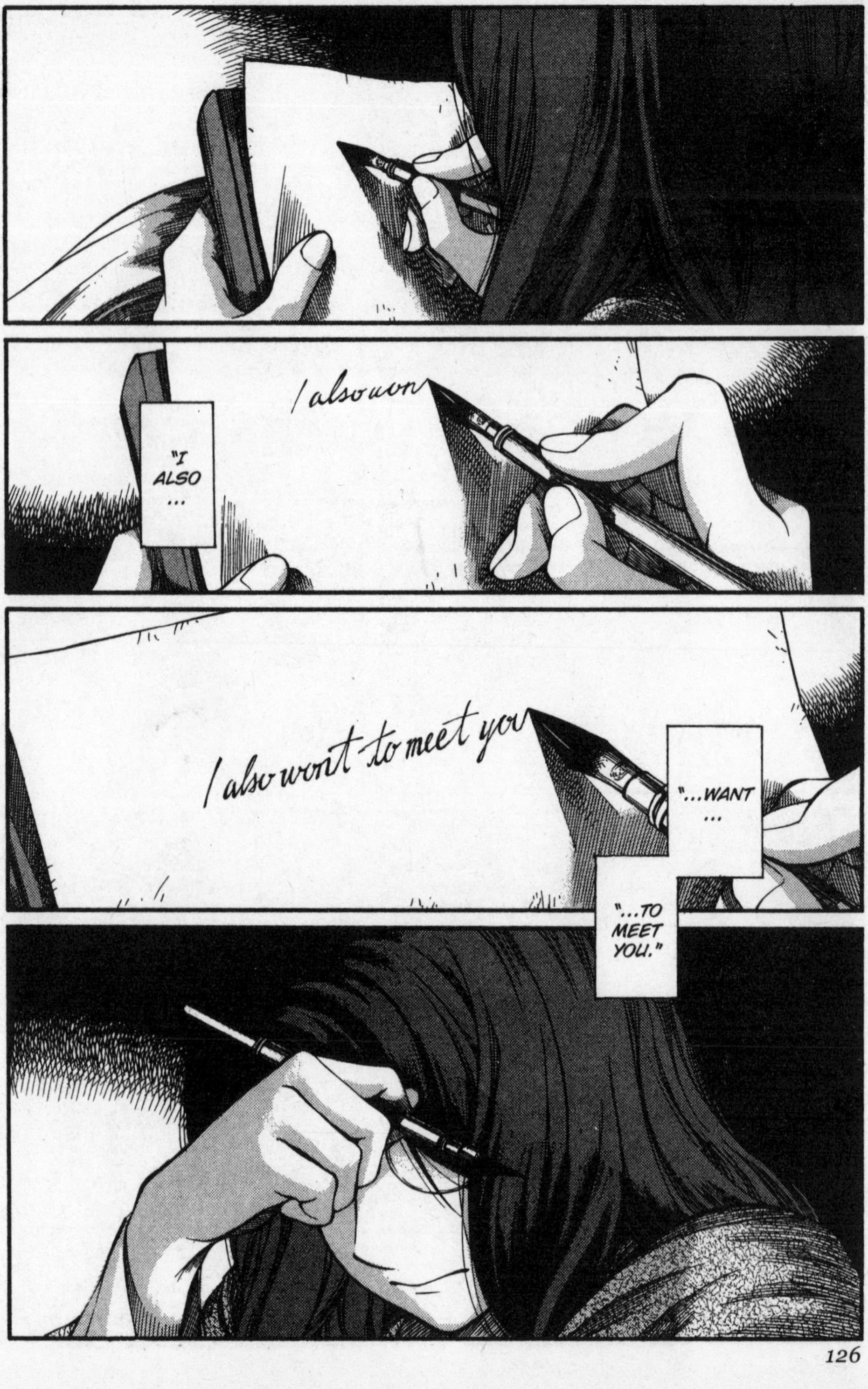
I also won
"I ALSO ...
I also wont to meet you
"...WANT ...
"...TO MEET YOU."

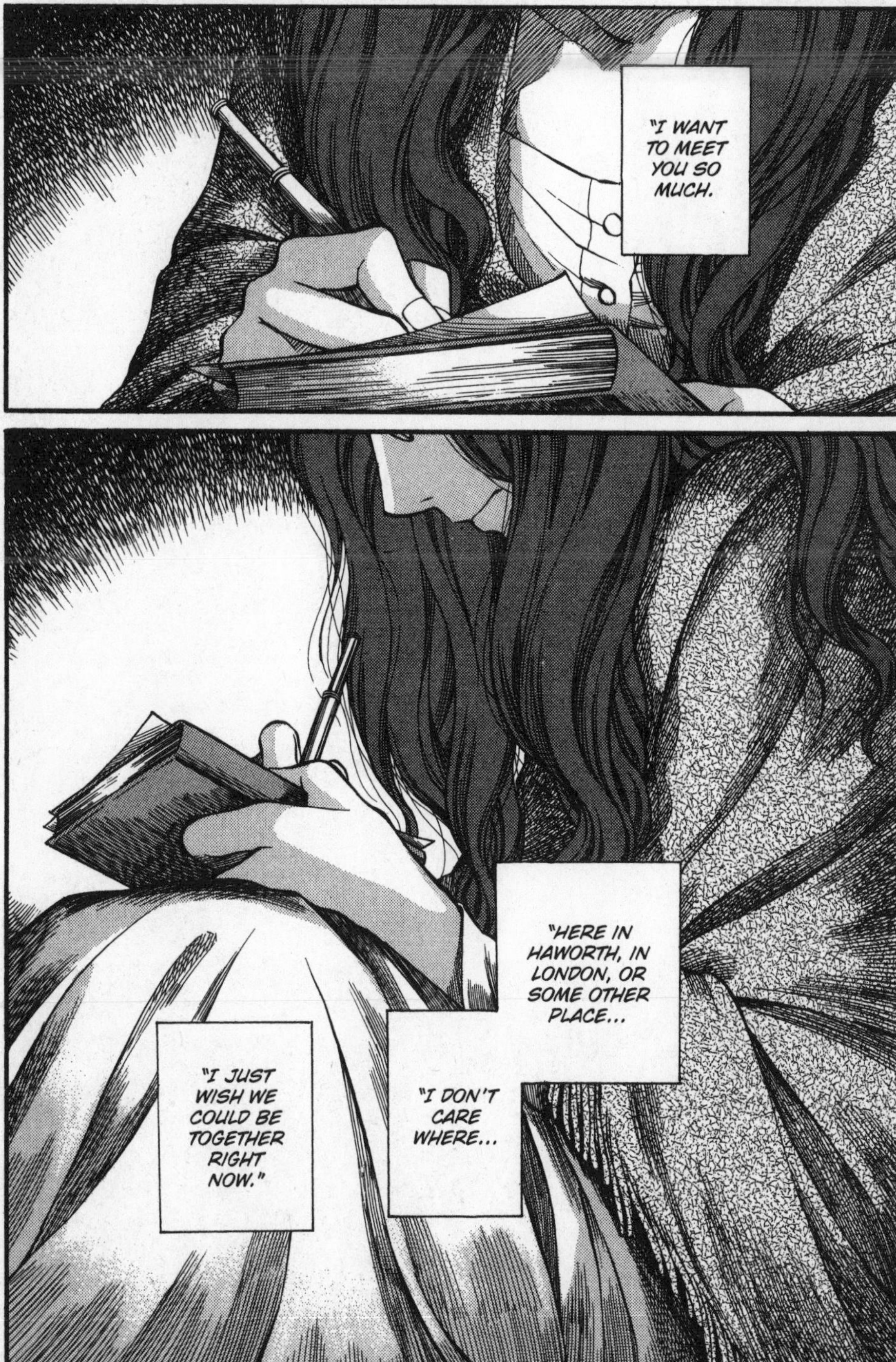
"I WANT TO MEET YOU SO MUCH.
"HERE IN HAWORTH, IN LONDON, OR SOME OTHER PLACE...
"I DON'T CARE WHERE...
"I JUST WISH WE COULD BE TOGETHER RIGHT NOW."

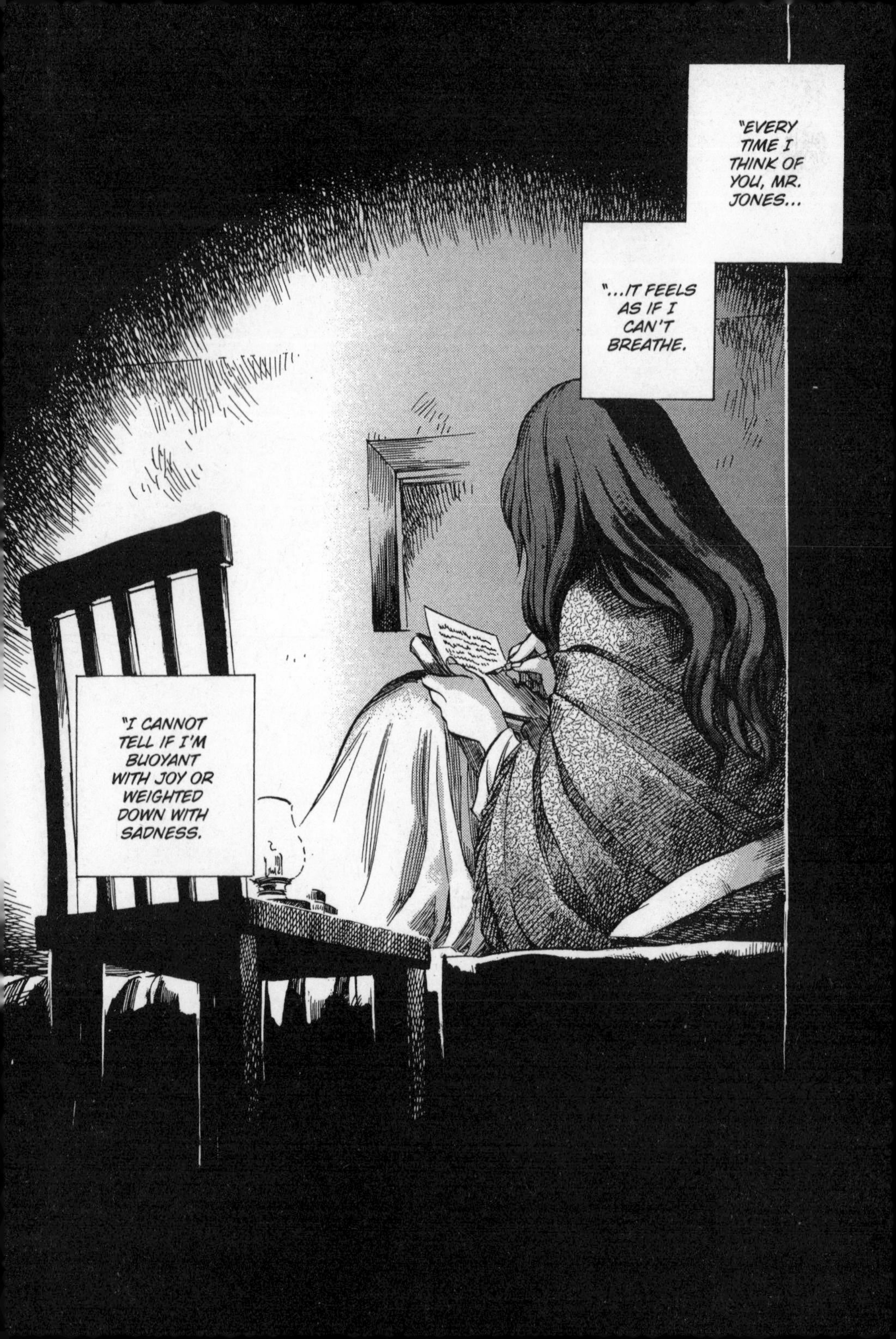
"EVERY TIME I THINK OF YOU, MR. JONES...
"...IT FEELS AS IF I CAN'T BREATHE.
"I CANNOT TELL IF I'M BUOYANT WITH JOY OR WEIGHTED DOWN WITH SADNESS.

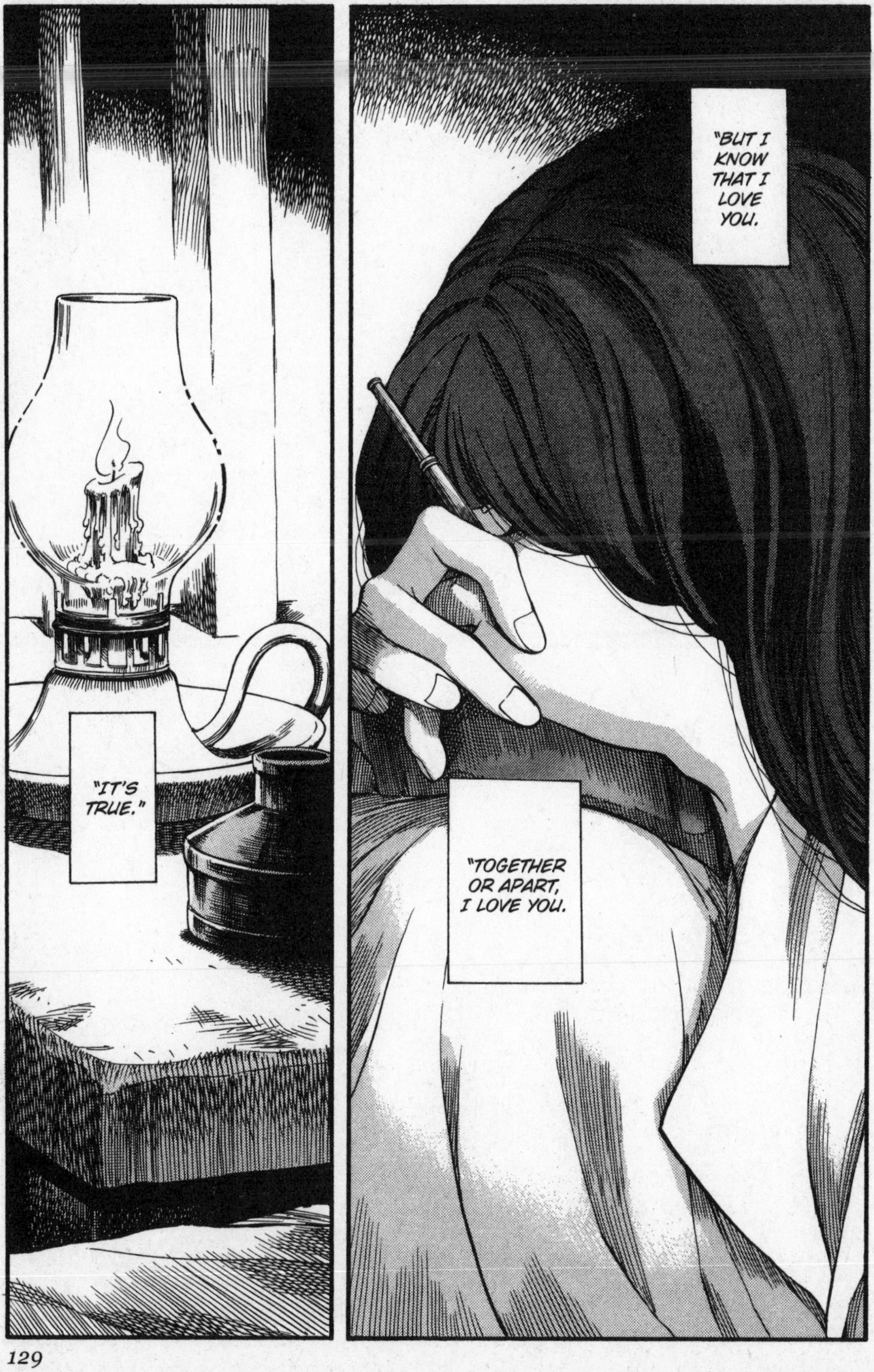
"BUT I KNOW THAT I LOVE YOU.
"TOGETHER OR APART, I LOVE YOU.
"IT'S TRUE."

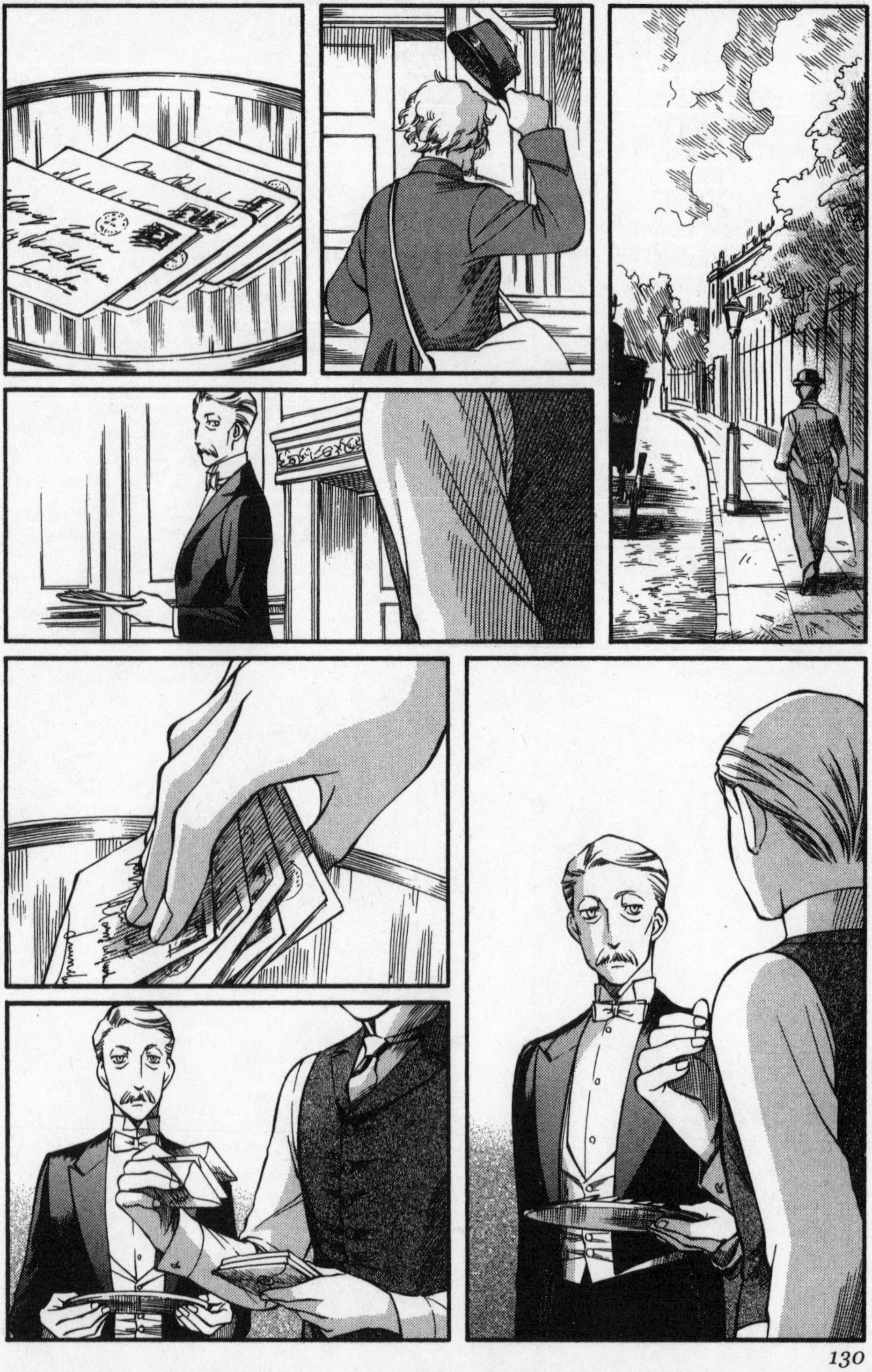

Mr. William Jones
19 Hamstedshere
London

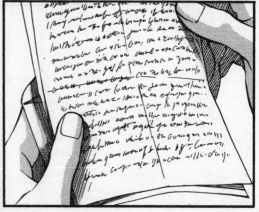

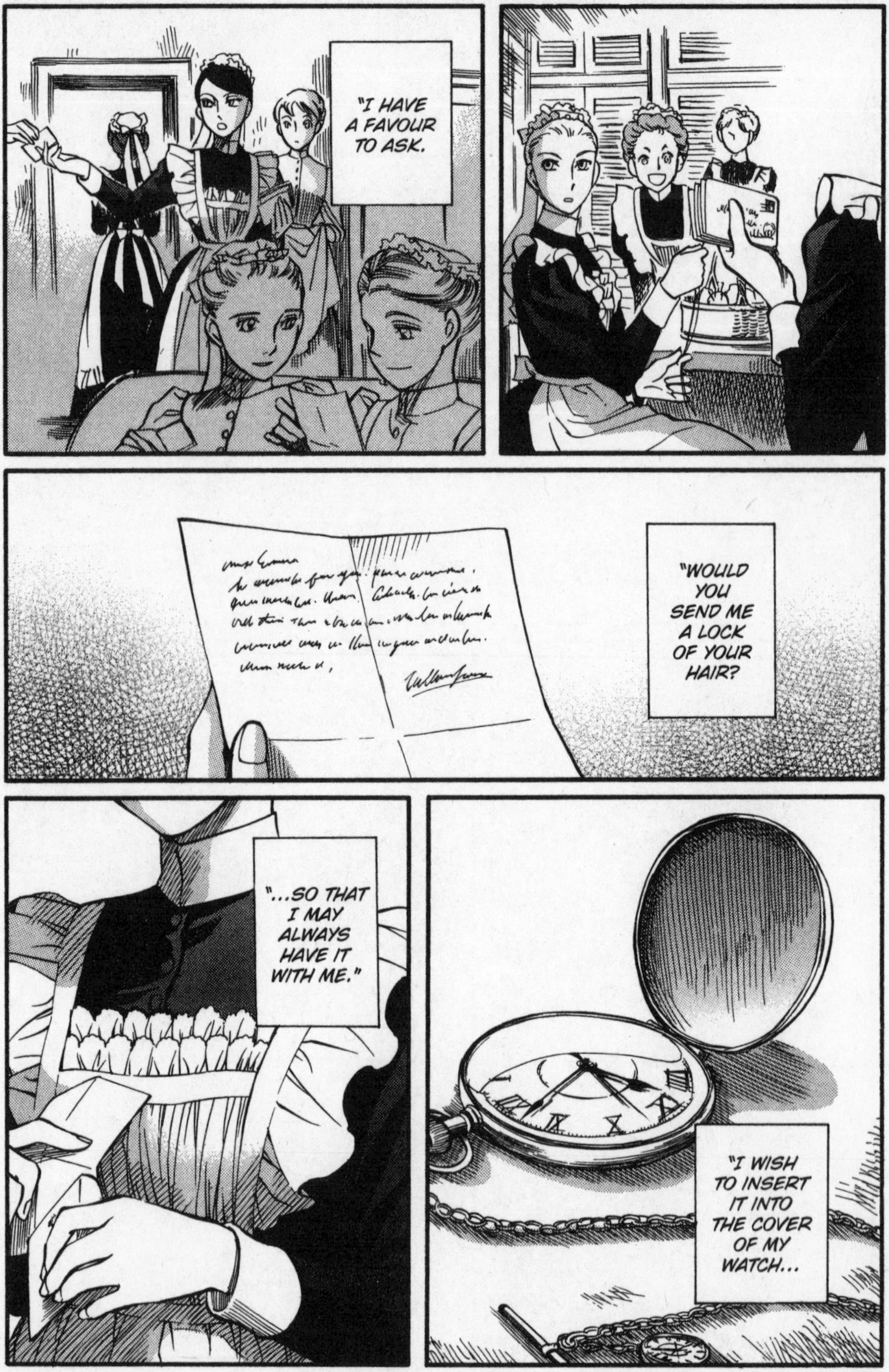
"I HAVE A FAVOUR TO ASK.
"WOULD YOU SEND ME A LOCK OF YOUR HAIR?
"I WISH TO INSERT IT INTO THE COVER OF MY WATCH...
"...SO THAT I MAY ALWAYS HAVE IT WITH ME."

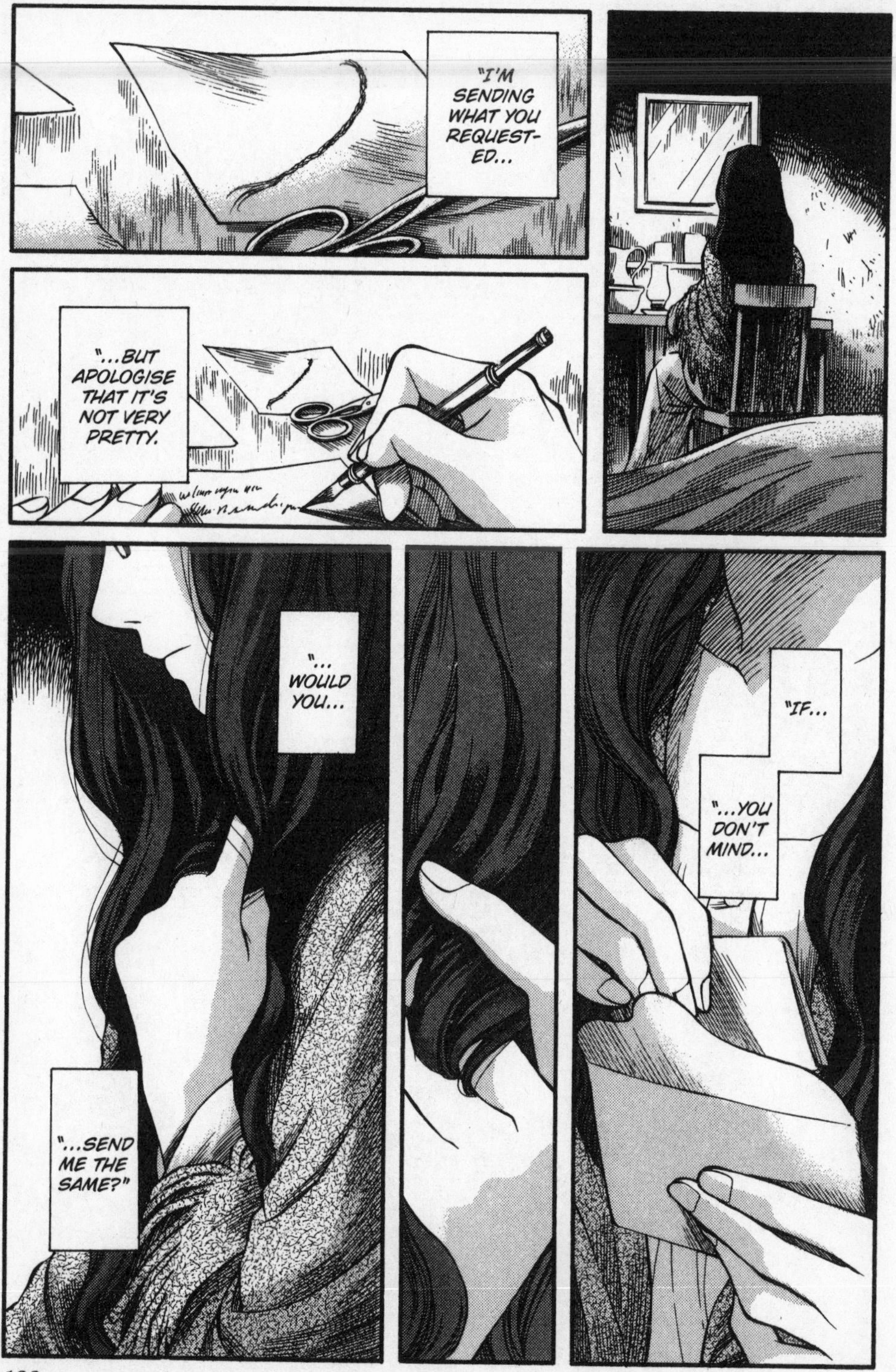
"I'M SENDING WHAT YOU REQUEST-ED...
"...BUT APOLOGISE THAT IT'S NOT VERY PRETTY.
"IF...
"...YOU DON'T MIND...
"...WOULD YOU...
"...SEND ME THE SAME?"

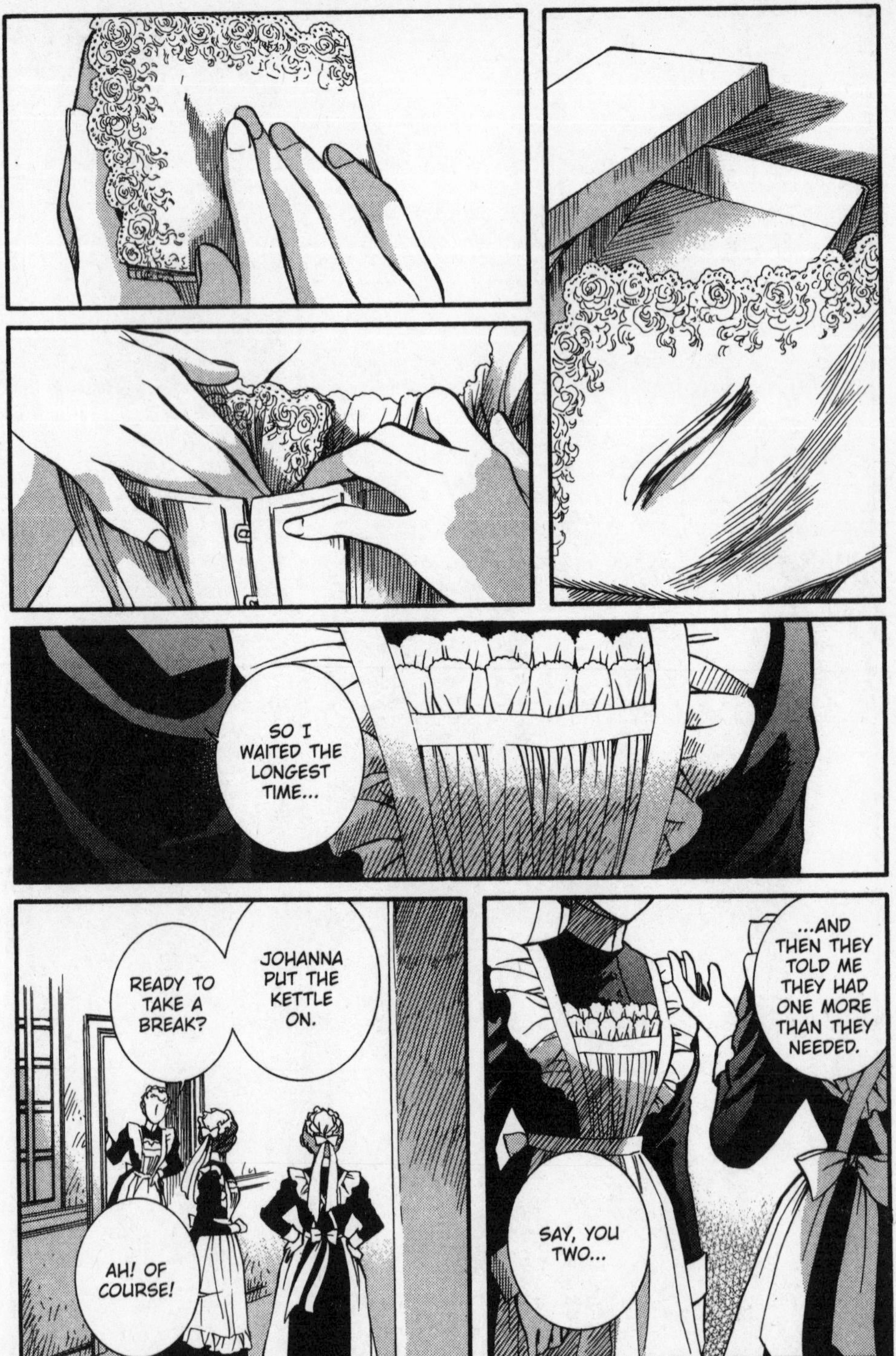
SO I WAITED THE LONGEST TIME...
...AND THEN THEY TOLD ME THEY HAD ONE MORE THAN THEY NEEDED.
SAY, YOU TWO...
JOHANNA PUT THE KETTLE ON.
READY TO TAKE A BREAK?
AH! OF COURSE!

Chapter 34: End

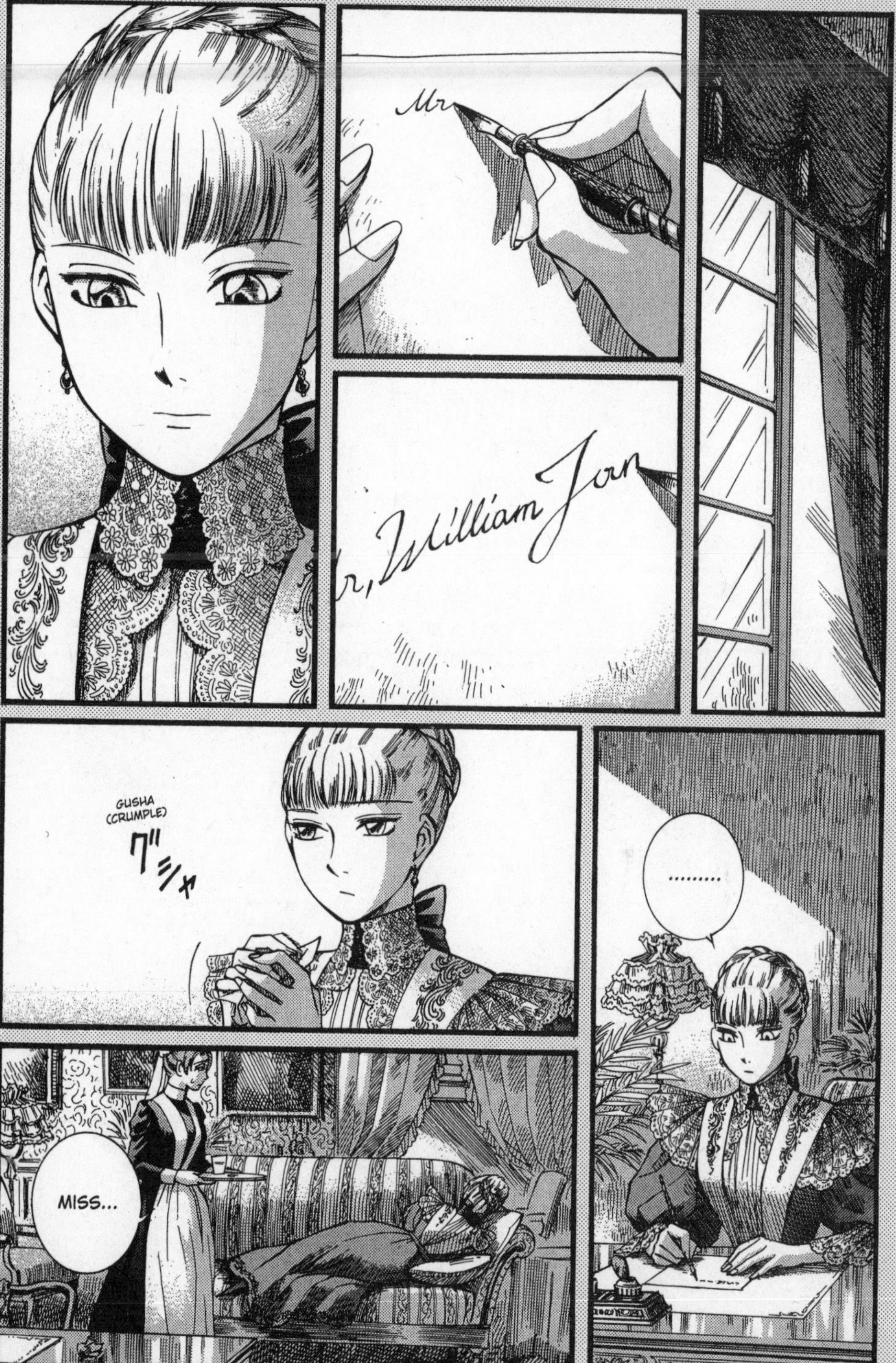
Mr
r, William Jon
....
GUSHA (CRUMPLE)
グシャ
MISS...

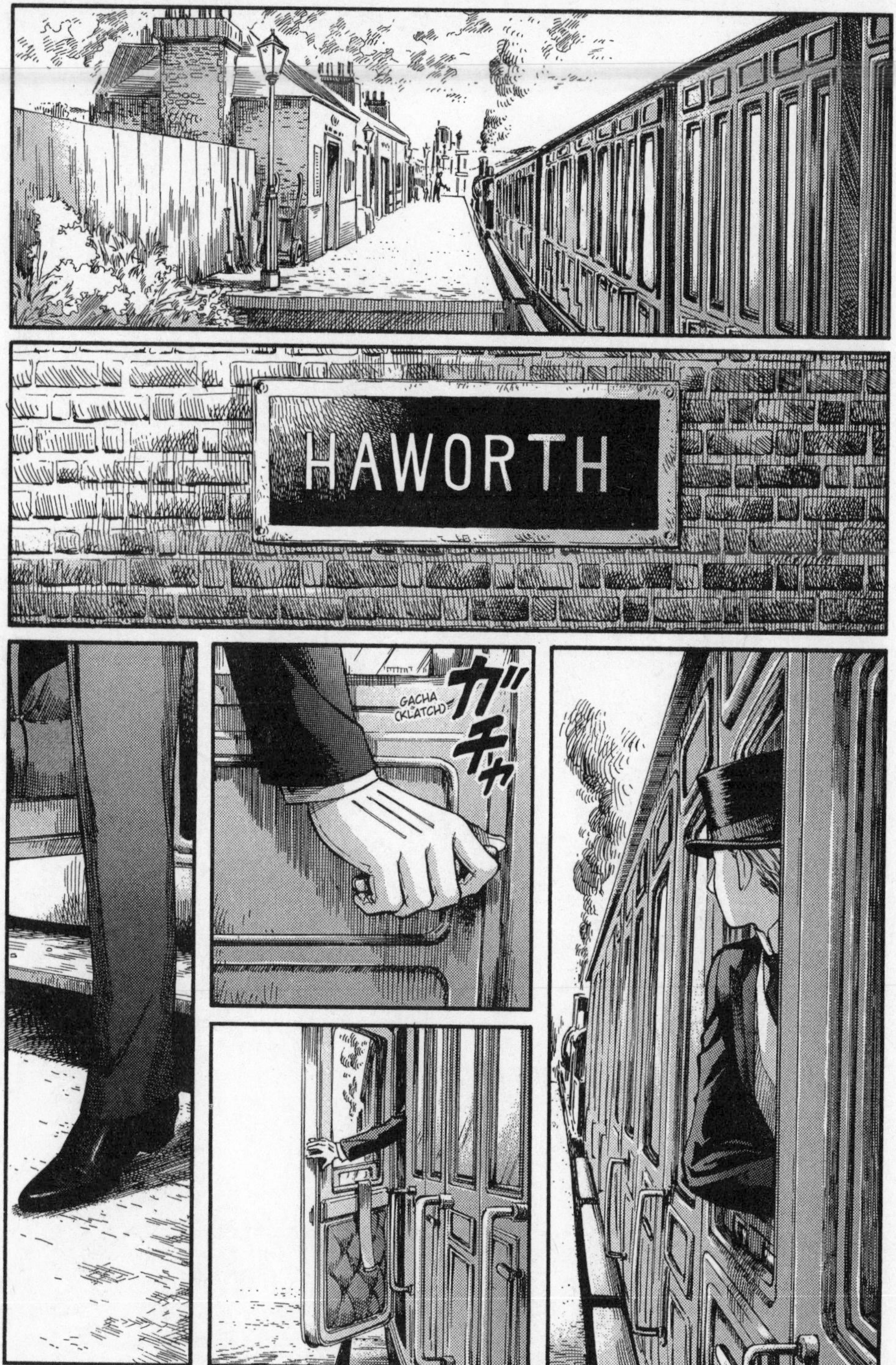
HAWORTH
ガチャ
GACHA (KLATCH)

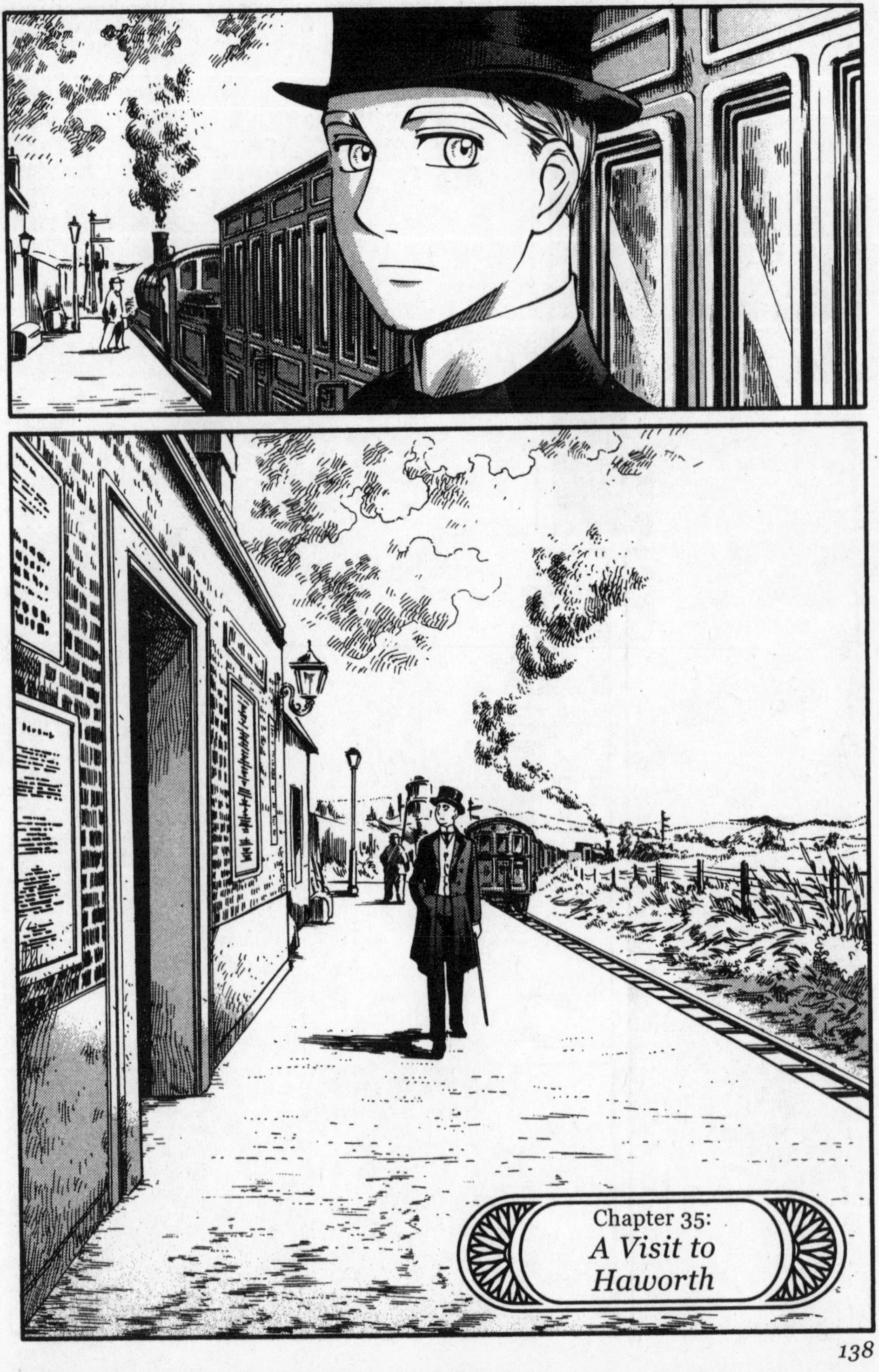
Chapter 35:
A Visit to
Haworth

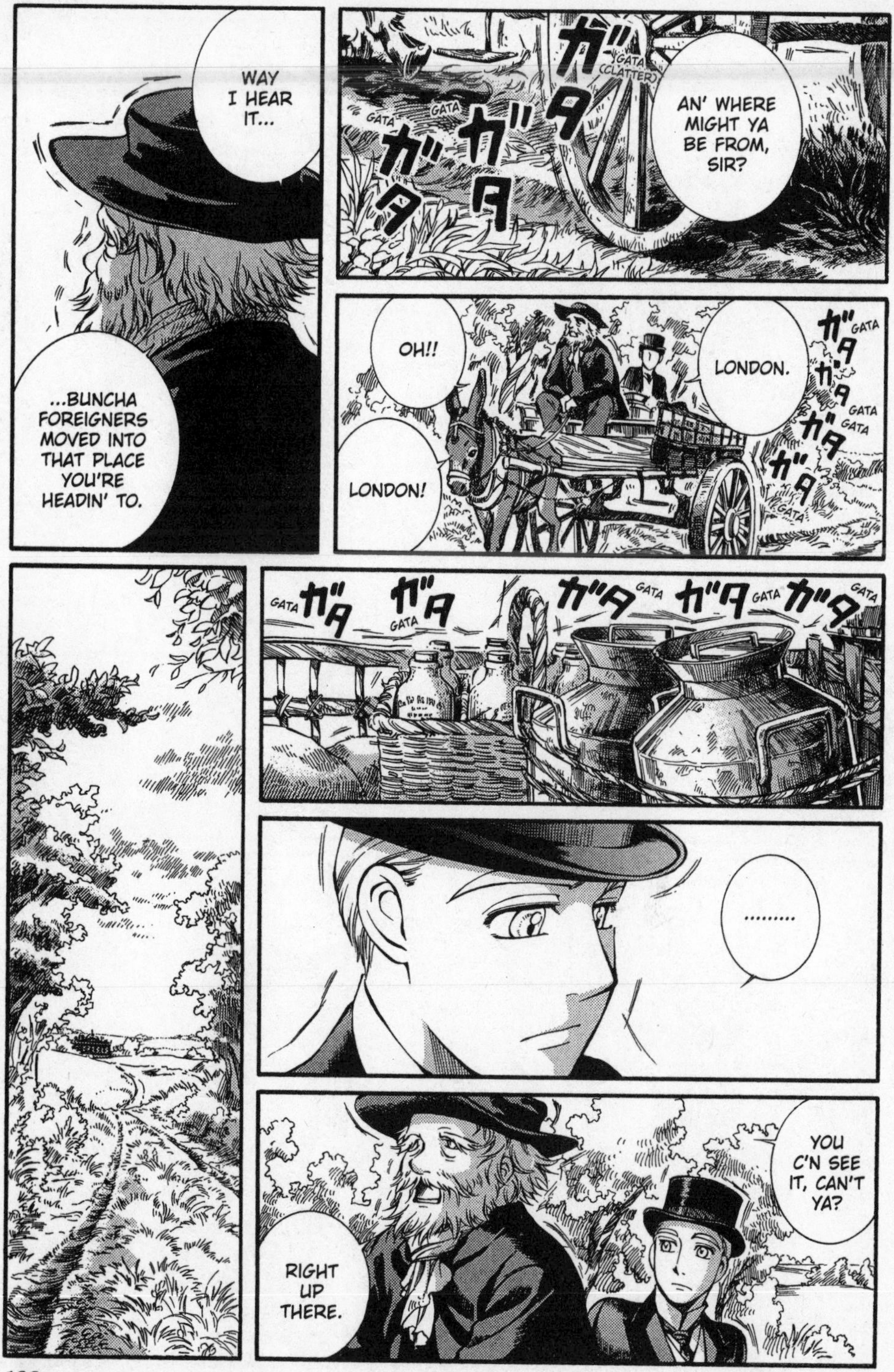
ガタ
GATA (CLATTER)
AN' WHERE MIGHT YA BE FROM, SIR?
ガタ GATA
ガタ GATA
ガタ GATA
ガタ GATA
ガタ GATA
ガタ GATA
LONDON.
OH!!
LONDON!
WAY I HEAR IT...
...BUNCHA FOREIGNERS MOVED INTO THAT PLACE YOU'RE HEADIN' TO.
ガタ GATA
ガタ GATA
ガタ GATA
ガタ GATA
ガタ GATA
....
YOU C'N SEE IT, CAN'T YA?
RIGHT UP THERE.

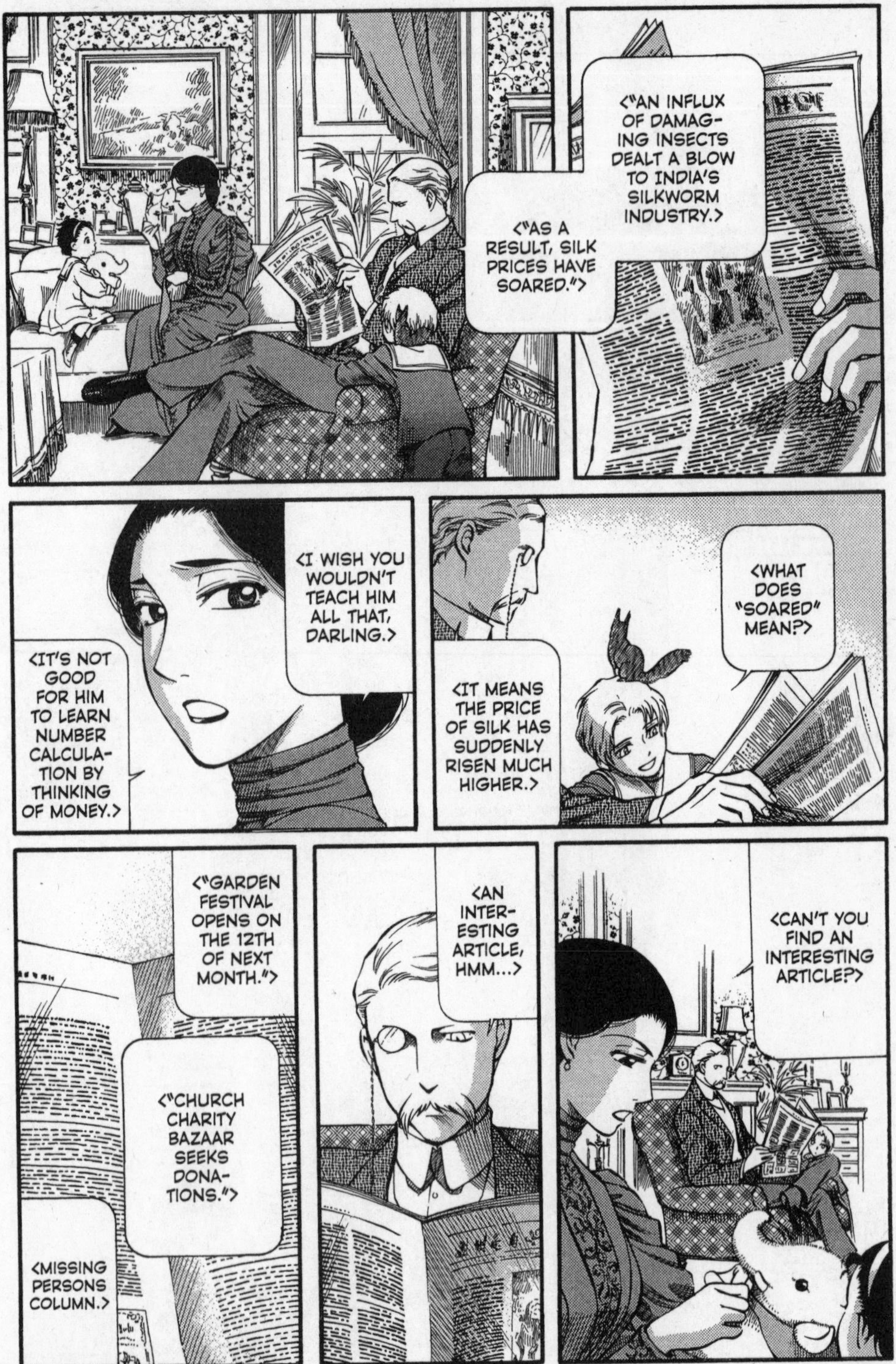
<"AN INFLUX OF DAMAGING INSECTS DEALT A BLOW TO INDIA'S SILKWORM INDUSTRY.>
<"AS A RESULT, SILK PRICES HAVE SOARED.">
<WHAT DOES "SOARED" MEAN?>
<IT MEANS THE PRICE OF SILK HAS SUDDENLY RISEN MUCH HIGHER.>
<I WISH YOU WOULDN'T TEACH HIM ALL THAT, DARLING.>
<IT'S NOT GOOD FOR HIM TO LEARN NUMBER CALCULATION BY THINKING OF MONEY.>
<CAN'T YOU FIND AN INTERESTING ARTICLE?>
<AN INTERESTING ARTICLE, HMM...>
<"GARDEN FESTIVAL OPENS ON THE 12TH OF NEXT MONTH.">
<"CHURCH CHARITY BAZAAR SEEKS DONATIONS.">
<MISSING PERSONS COLUMN.>

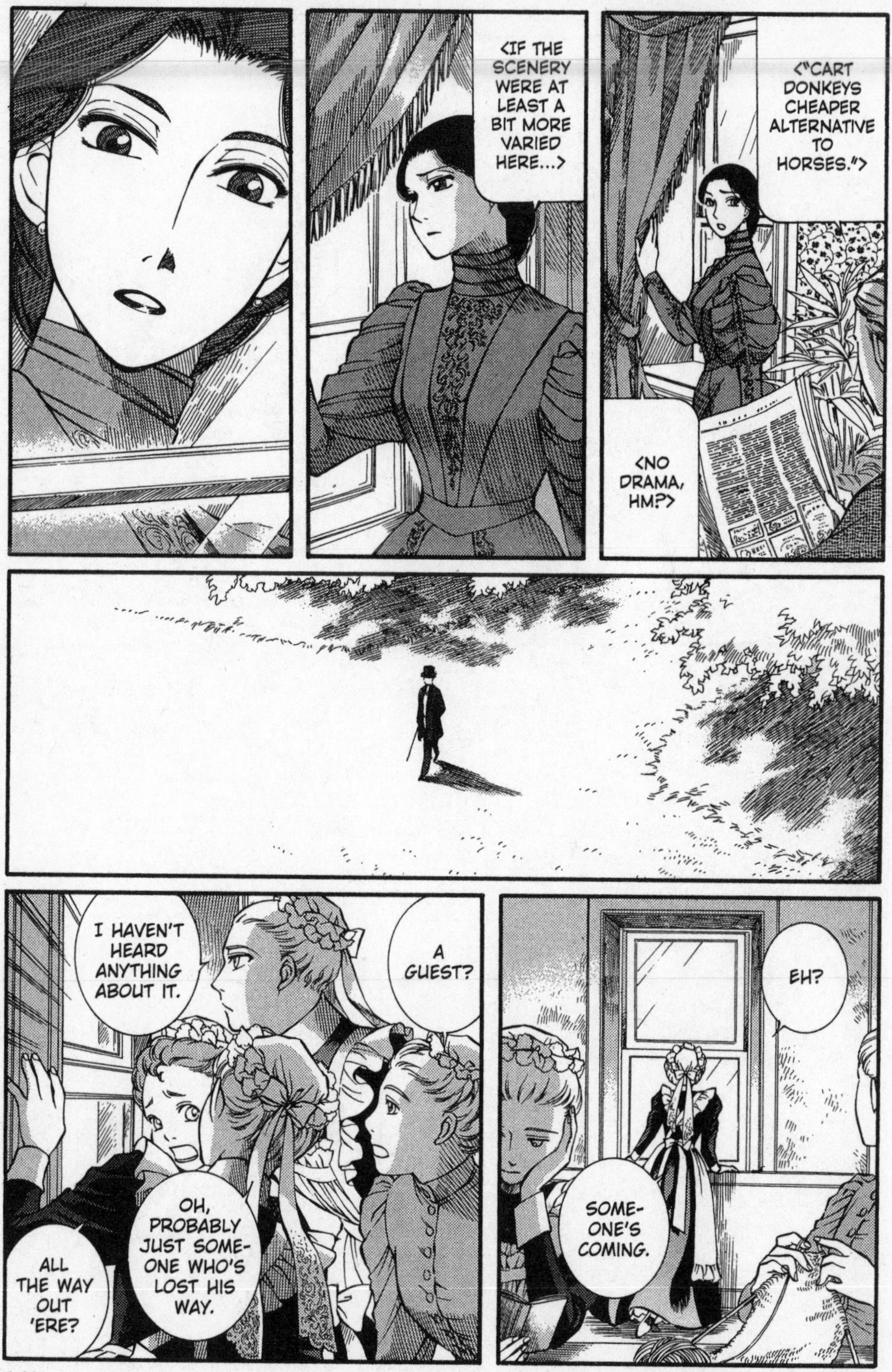

<"CART DONKEYS CHEAPER ALTERNATIVE TO HORSES.">
<NO DRAMA, HM?>
<IF THE SCENERY WERE AT LEAST A BIT MORE VARIED HERE...>
EH?
SOME-ONE'S COMING.
A GUEST?
I HAVEN'T HEARD ANYTHING ABOUT IT.
OH, PROBABLY JUST SOME-ONE WHO'S LOST HIS WAY.
ALL THE WAY OUT 'ERE?

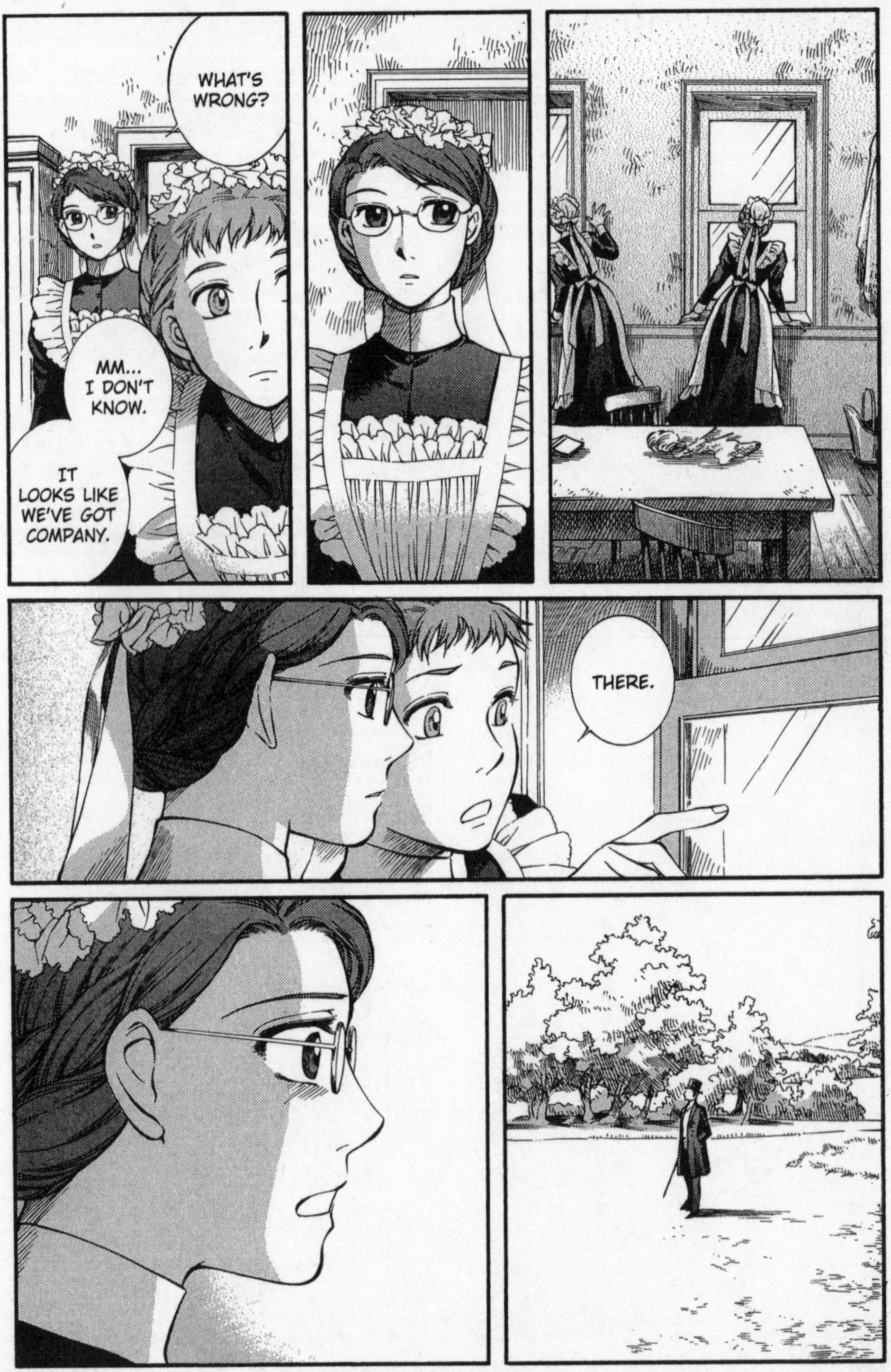
WHAT'S WRONG?
MM... I DON'T KNOW.
IT LOOKS LIKE WE'VE GOT COMPANY.
THERE.

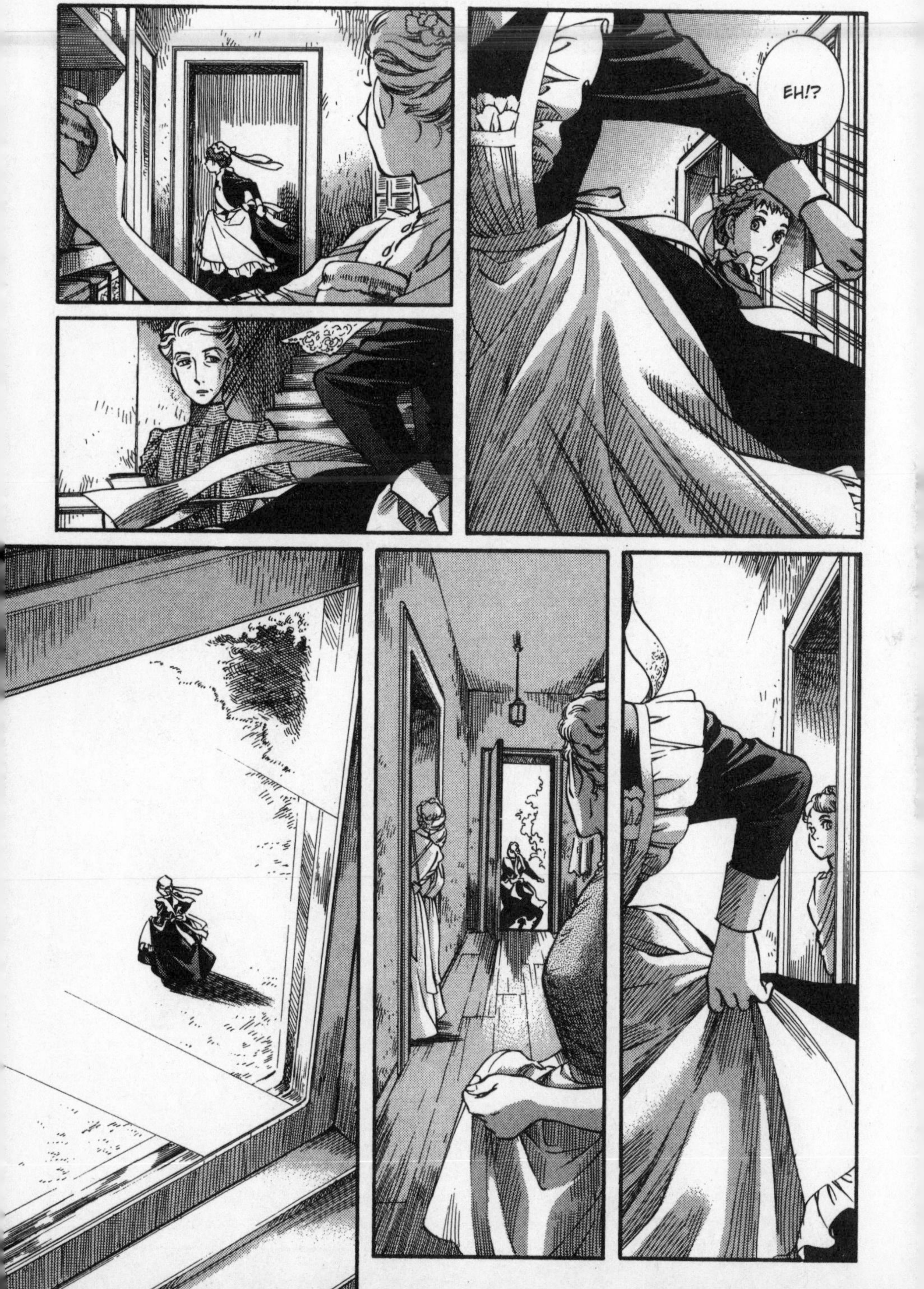
EH!?

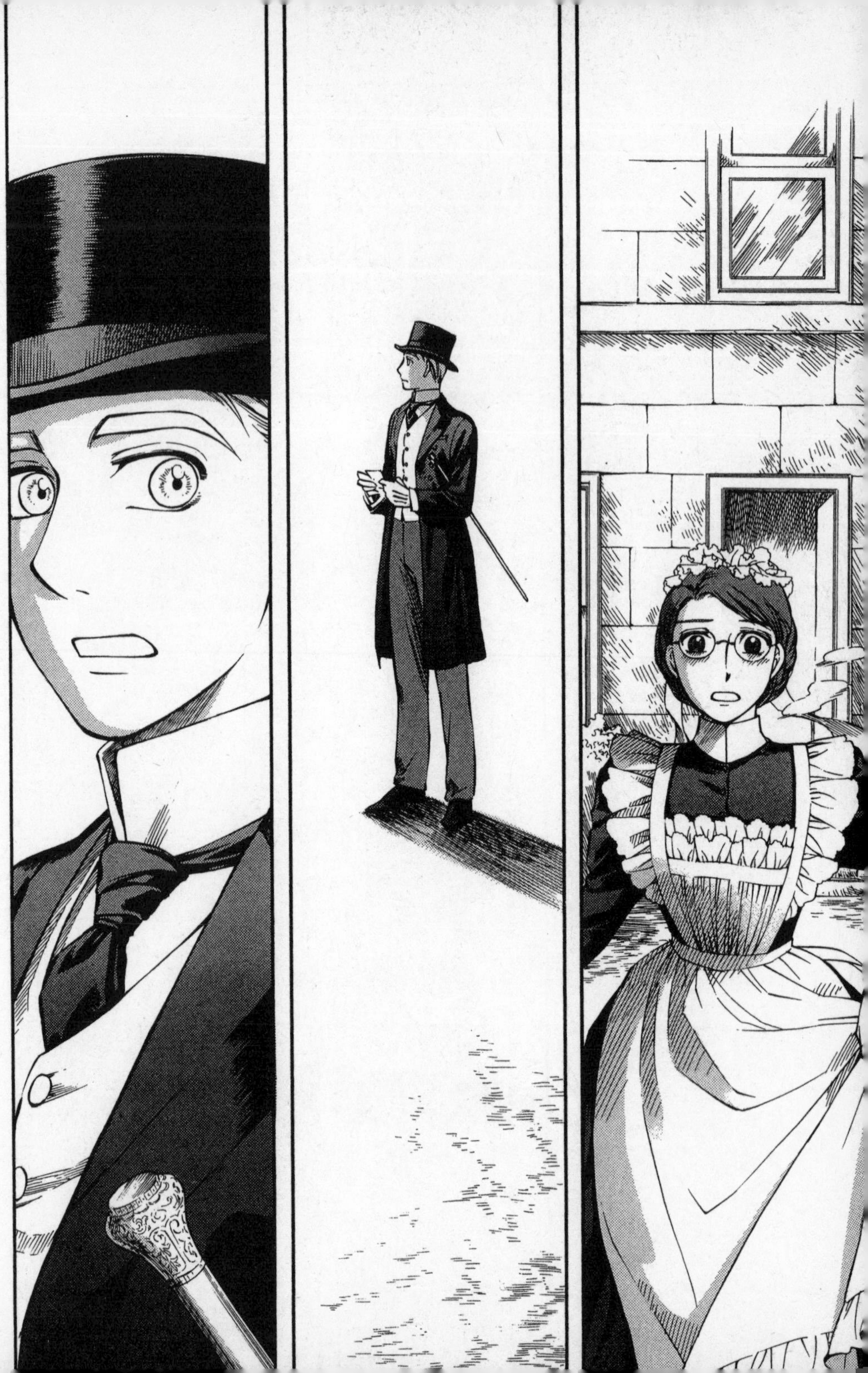

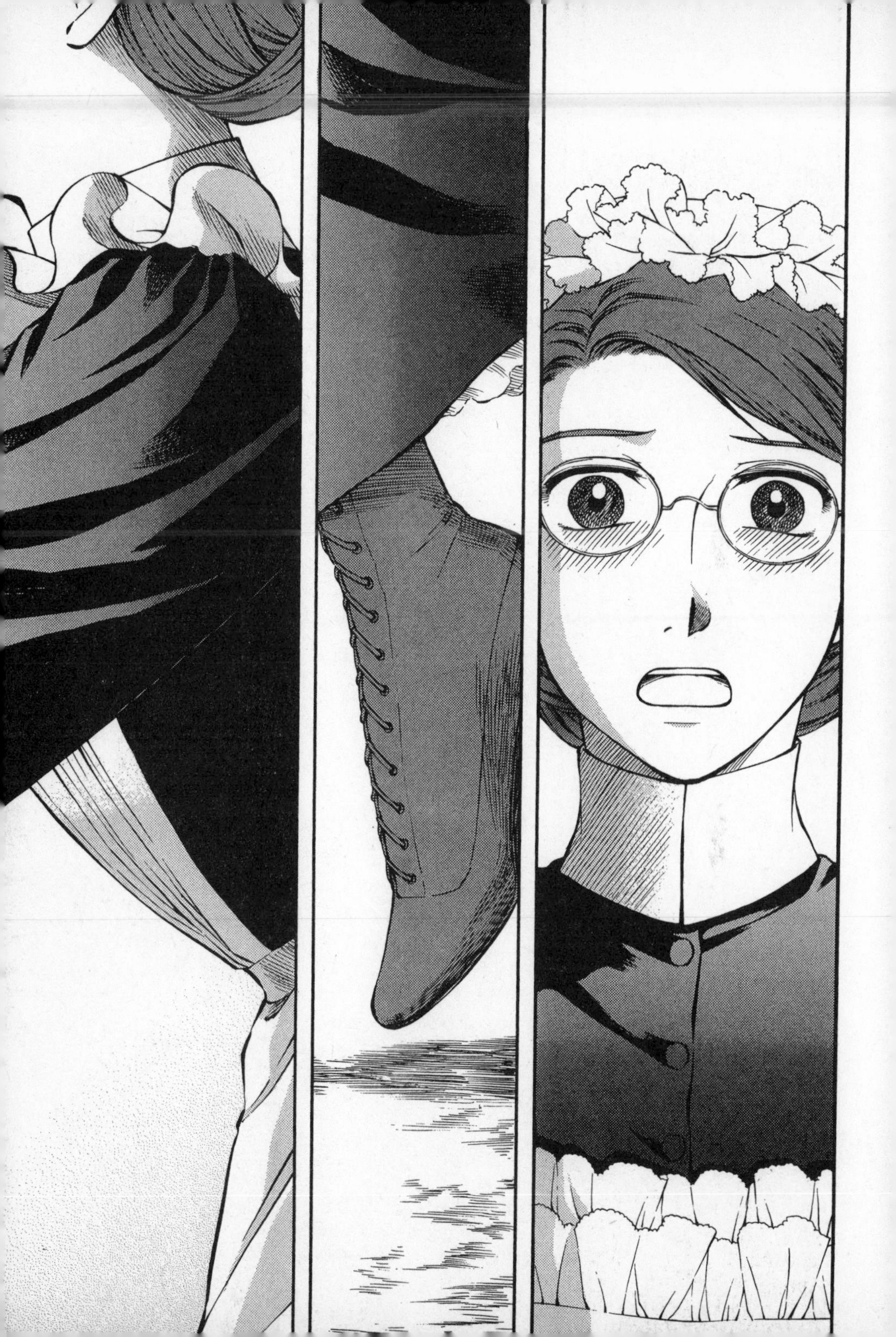

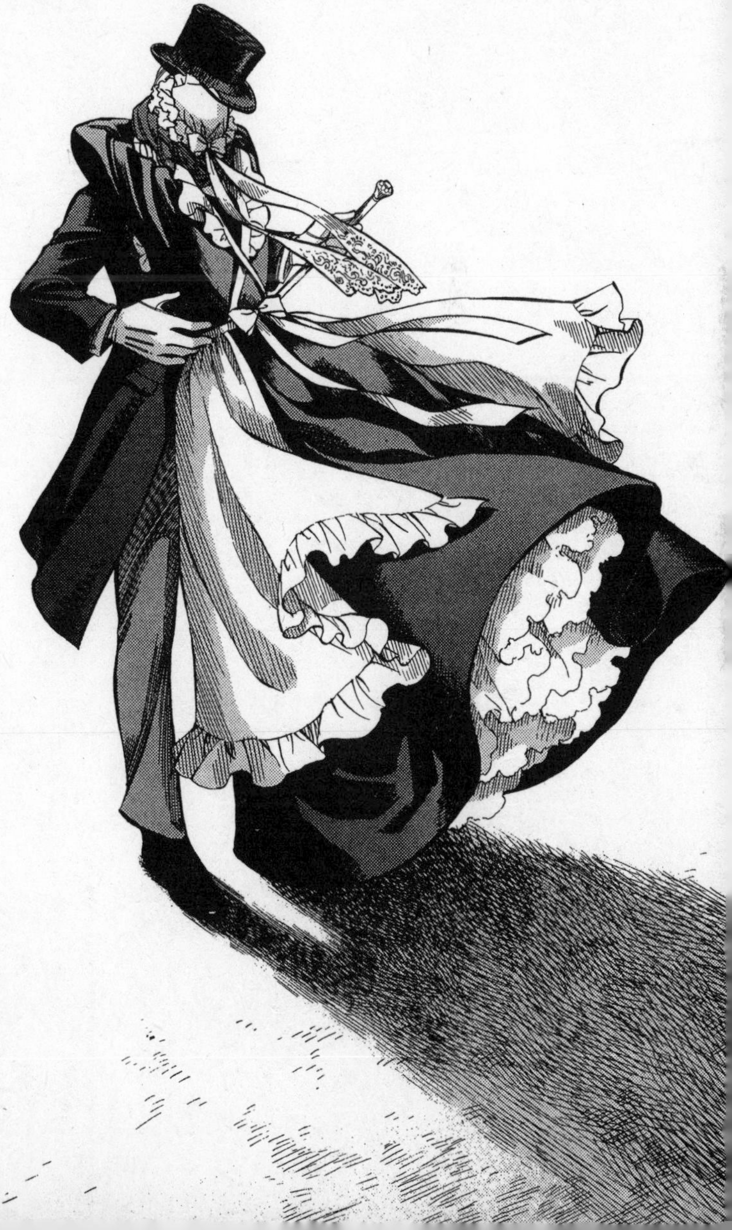

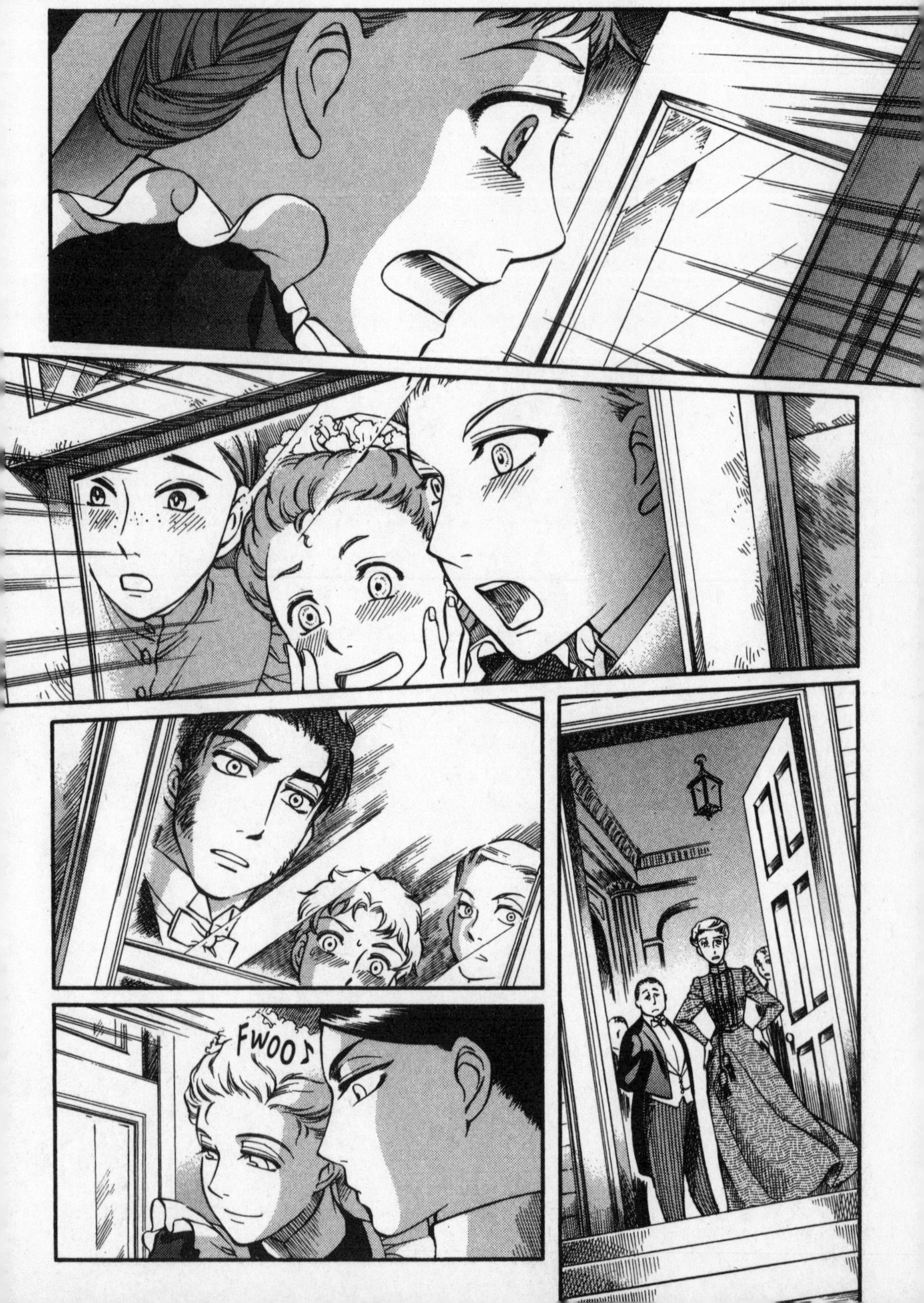
FWOO

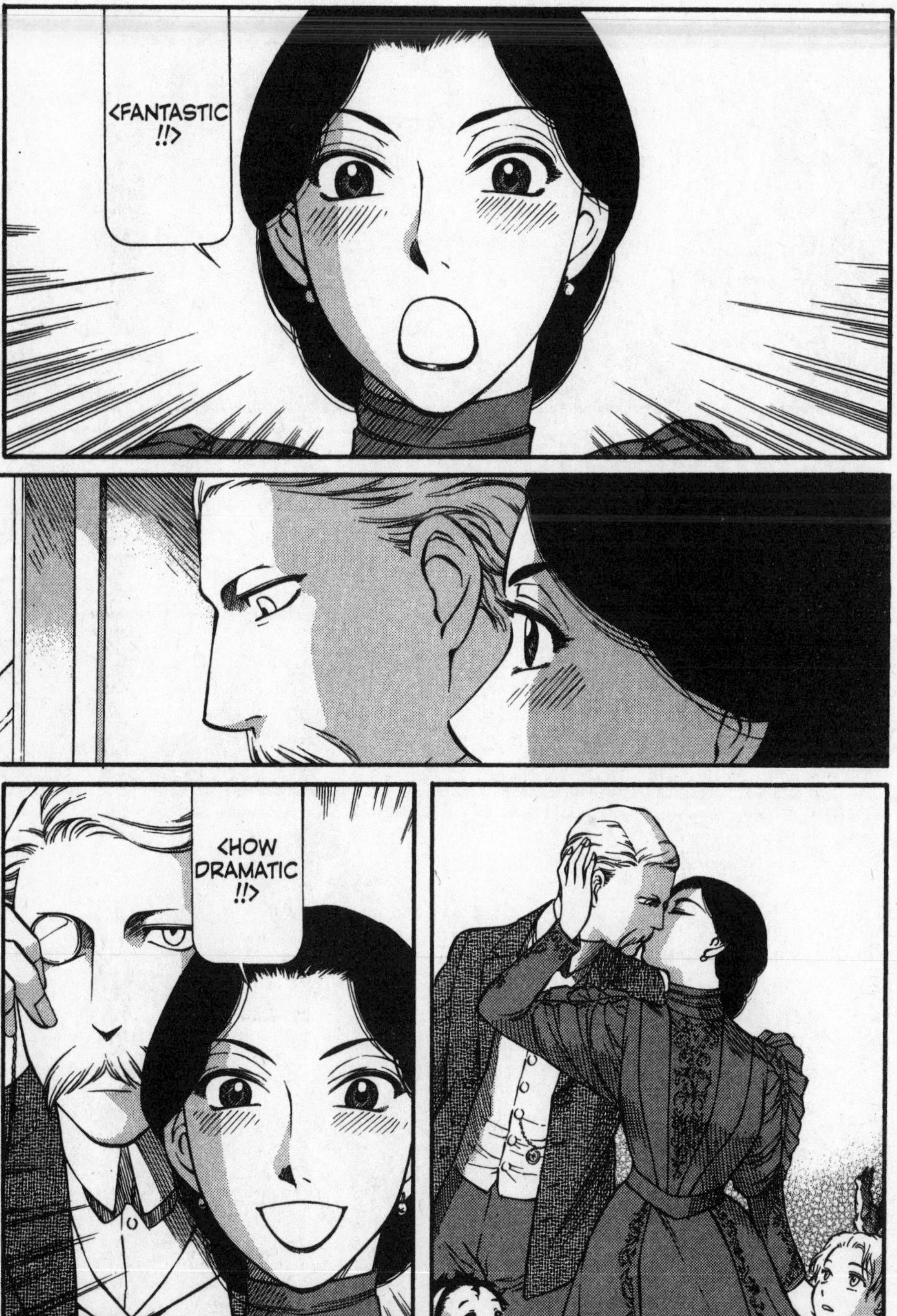
<FANTASTIC !!>
<HOW DRAMATIC !!>

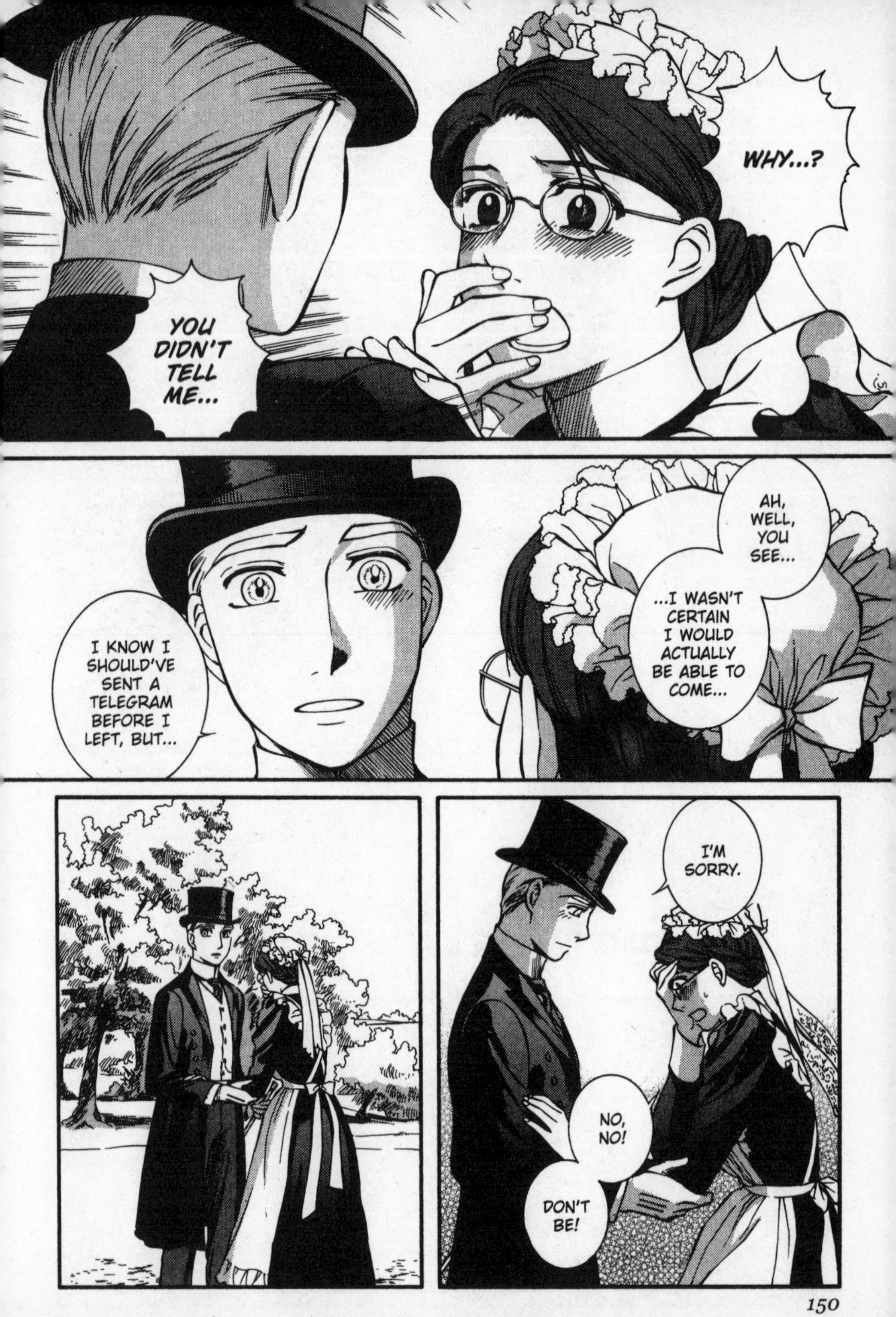
WHY...?
YOU DIDN'T TELL ME...
AH, WELL, YOU SEE...
...I WASN'T CERTAIN I WOULD ACTUALLY BE ABLE TO COME...
I KNOW I SHOULD'VE SENT A TELEGRAM BEFORE I LEFT, BUT...
I'M SORRY.
NO, NO!
DON'T BE!

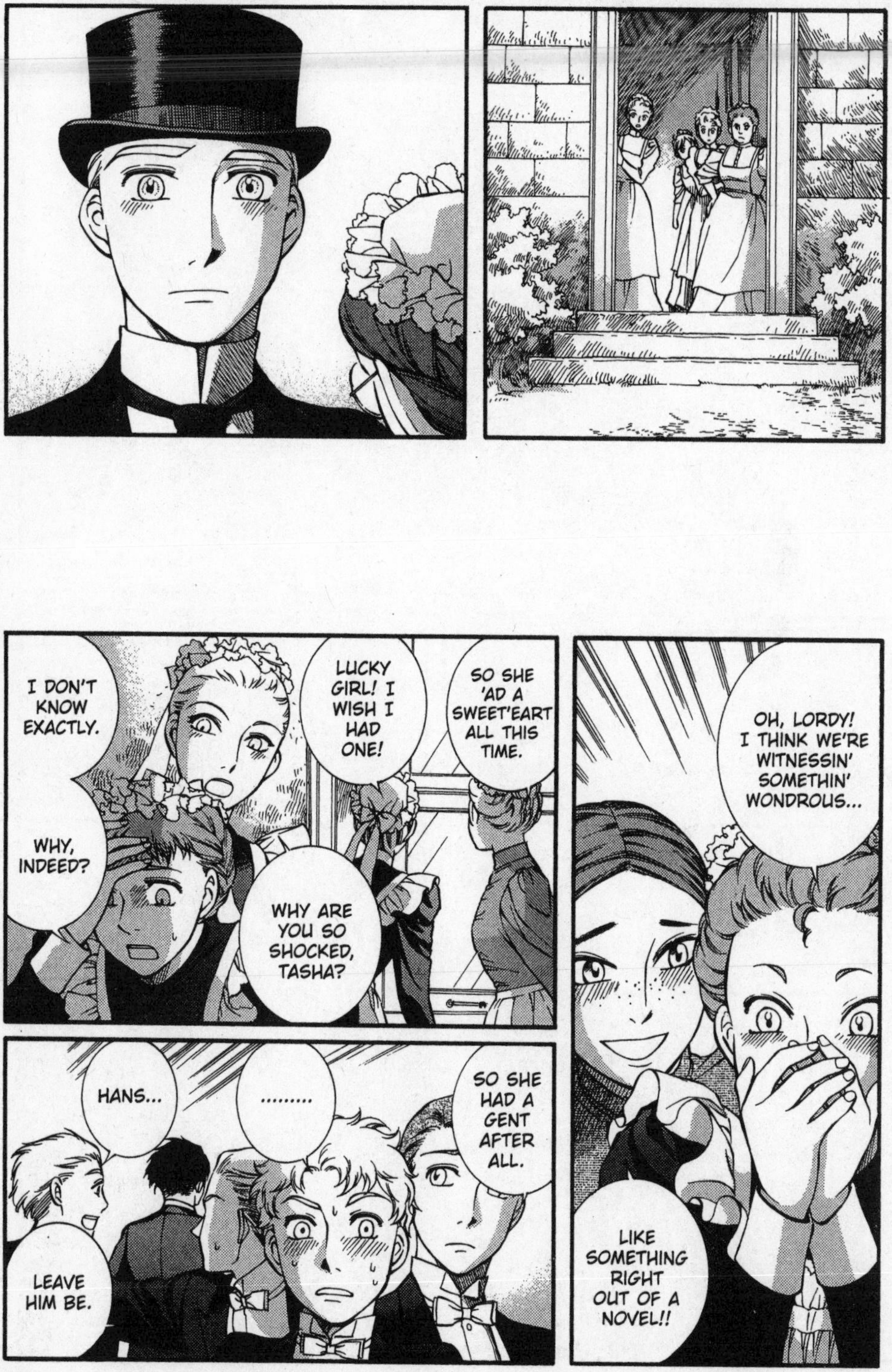
OH, LORDY! I THINK WE'RE WITNESSIN' SOMETHIN' WONDROUS...
LIKE SOMETHING RIGHT OUT OF A NOVEL!!
SO SHE 'AD A SWEET'EART ALL THIS TIME.
LUCKY GIRL! I WISH I HAD ONE!
WHY ARE YOU SO SHOCKED, TASHA?
WHY, INDEED?
I DON'T KNOW EXACTLY.
SO SHE HAD A GENT AFTER ALL.
....
HANS...
LEAVE HIM BE.

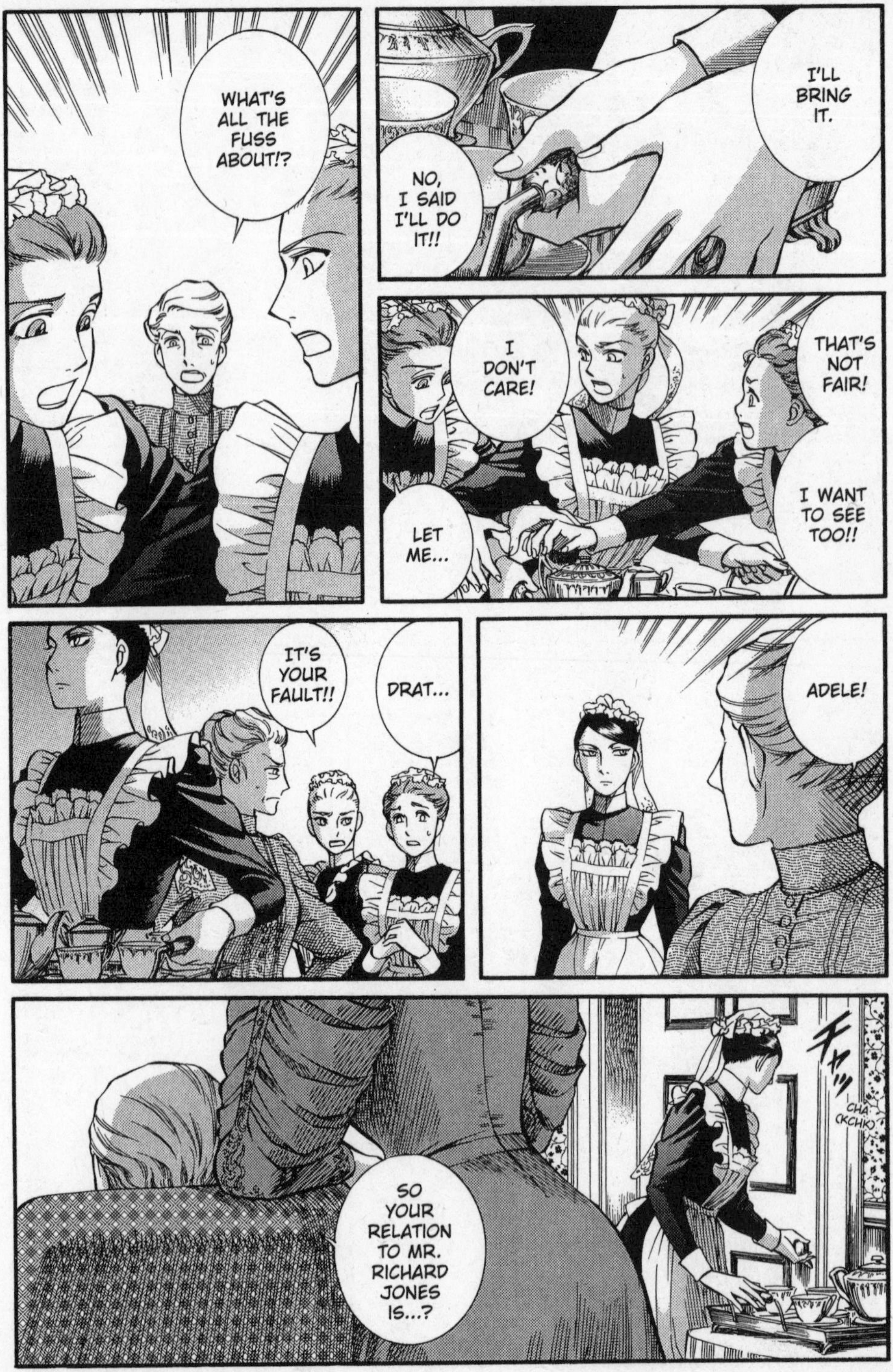
I'LL BRING IT.
NO, I SAID I'LL DO IT!!
THAT'S NOT FAIR!
I DON'T CARE!
I WANT TO SEE TOO!!
LET ME...
WHAT'S ALL THE FUSS ABOUT!?
ADELE!
DRAT...
IT'S YOUR FAULT!!
チャッ
CHA (KCHK)
SO YOUR RELATION TO MR. RICHARD JONES IS...?

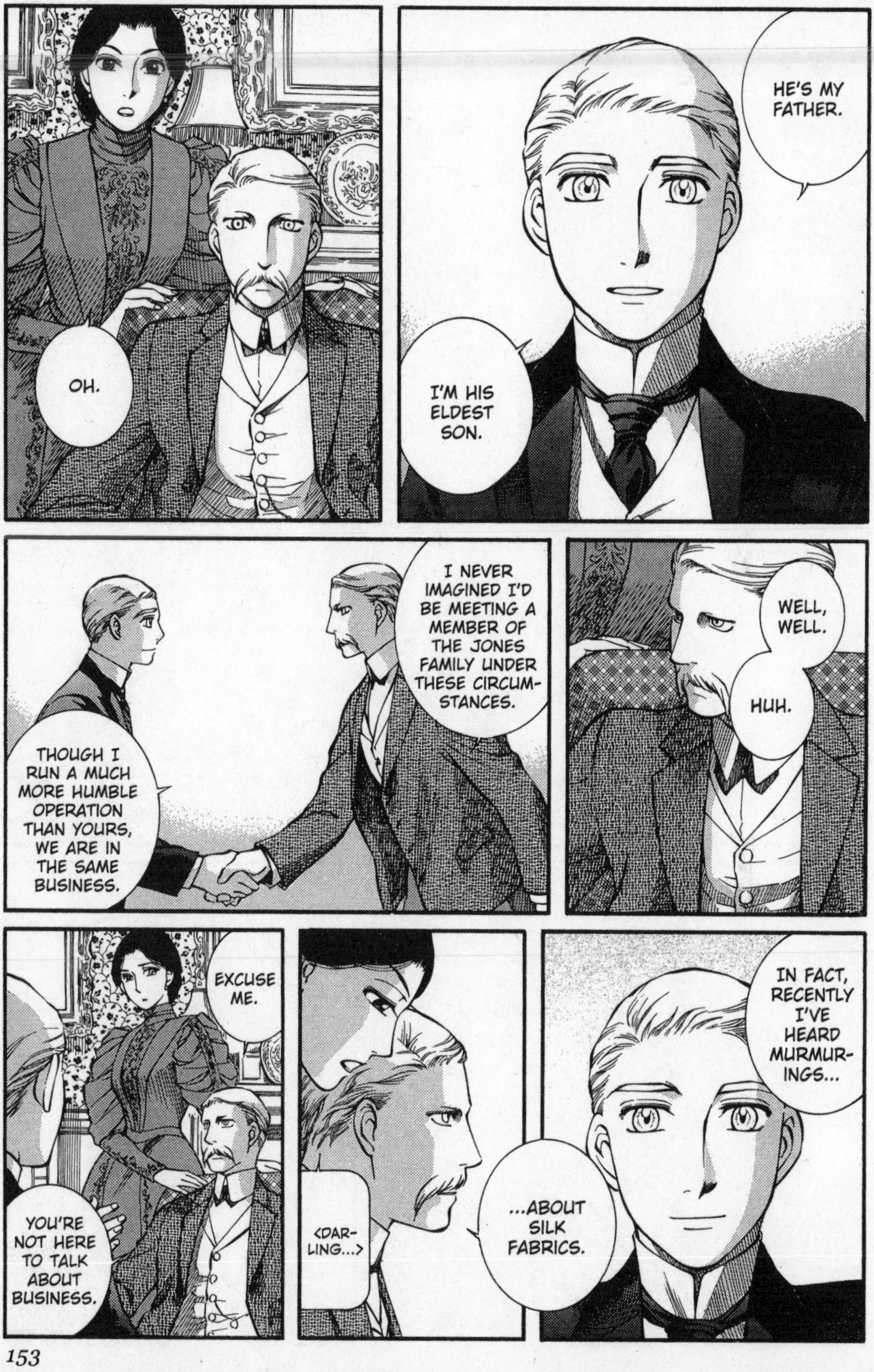

HE'S MY FATHER.
I'M HIS ELDEST SON.
OH.
WELL, WELL.
HUH.
I NEVER IMAGINED I'D BE MEETING A MEMBER OF THE JONES FAMILY UNDER THESE CIRCUMSTANCES.
THOUGH I RUN A MUCH MORE HUMBLE OPERATION THAN YOURS, WE ARE IN THE SAME BUSINESS.
IN FACT, RECENTLY I'VE HEARD MURMURINGS...
...ABOUT SILK FABRICS.
<DARLING...>
EXCUSE ME.
YOU'RE NOT HERE TO TALK ABOUT BUSINESS.

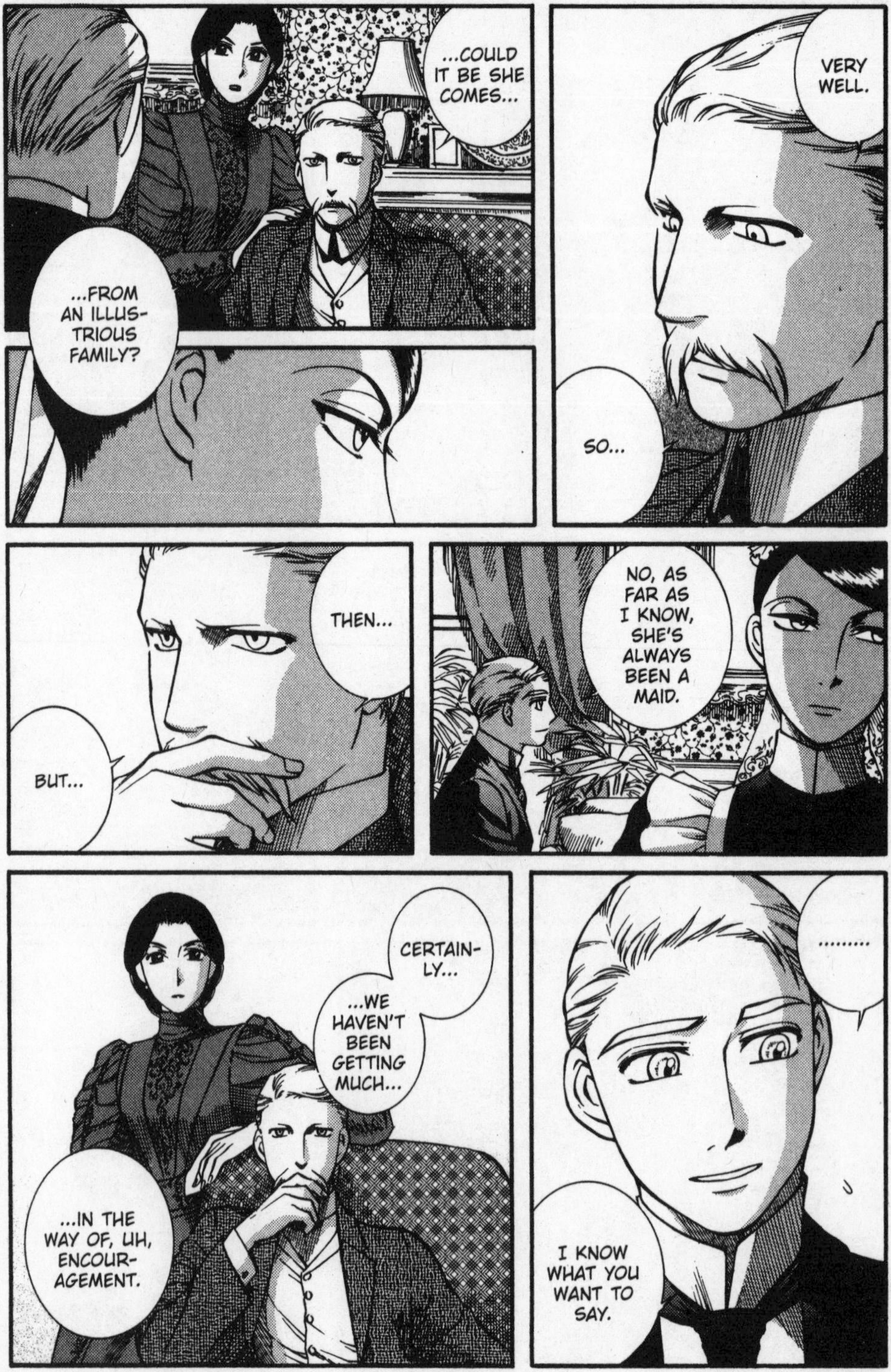
VERY WELL.
SO...
...COULD IT BE SHE COMES...
...FROM AN ILLUS-TRIOUS FAMILY?
NO, AS FAR AS I KNOW, SHE'S ALWAYS BEEN A MAID.
THEN...
BUT...
....
I KNOW WHAT YOU WANT TO SAY.
CERTAIN-LY...
...WE HAVEN'T BEEN GETTING MUCH...
...IN THE WAY OF, UH, ENCOUR-AGEMENT.

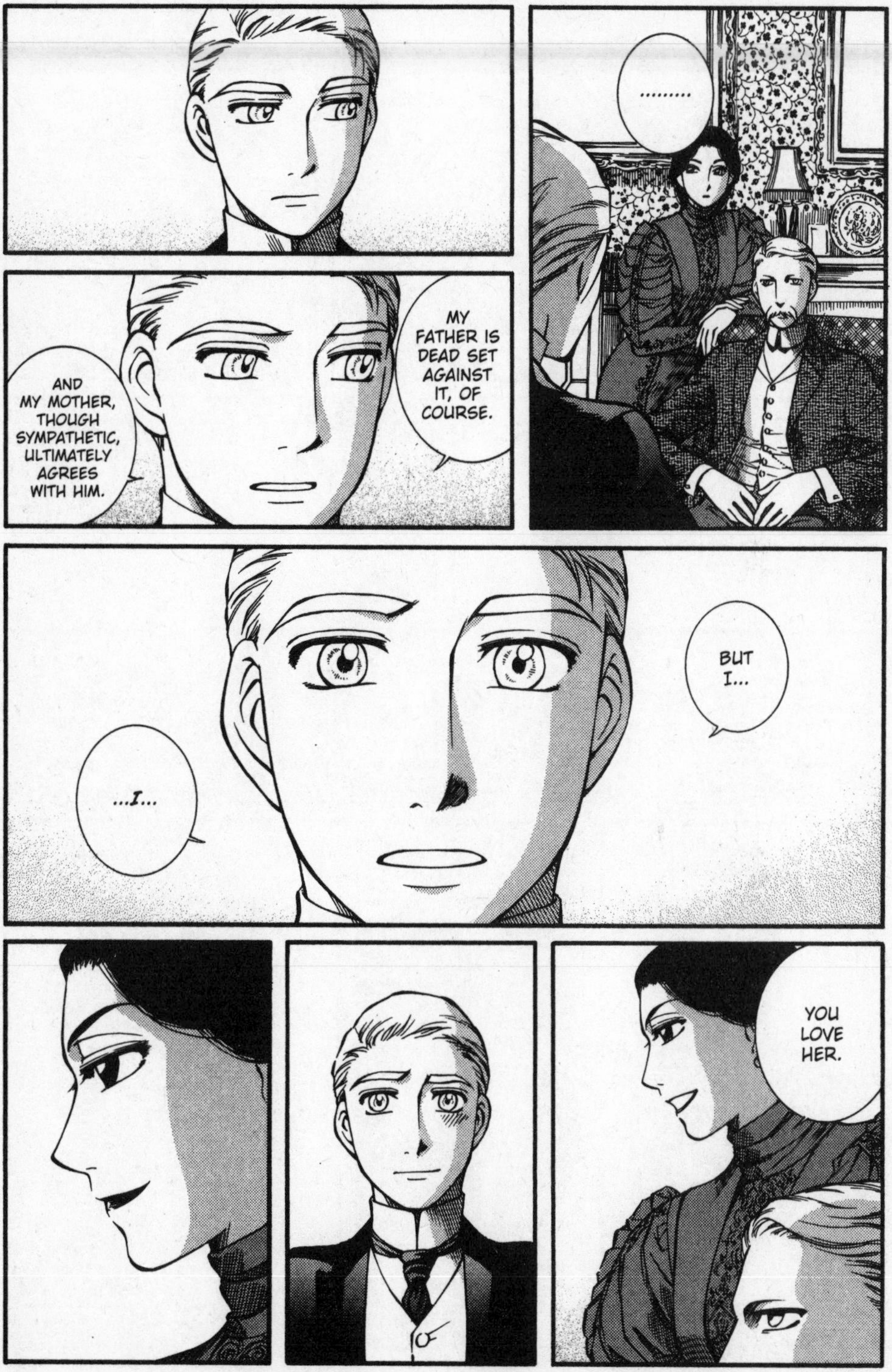
....
MY FATHER IS DEAD SET AGAINST IT, OF COURSE.
AND MY MOTHER, THOUGH SYMPATHETIC, ULTIMATELY AGREES WITH HIM.
BUT I...
...I...
YOU LOVE HER.

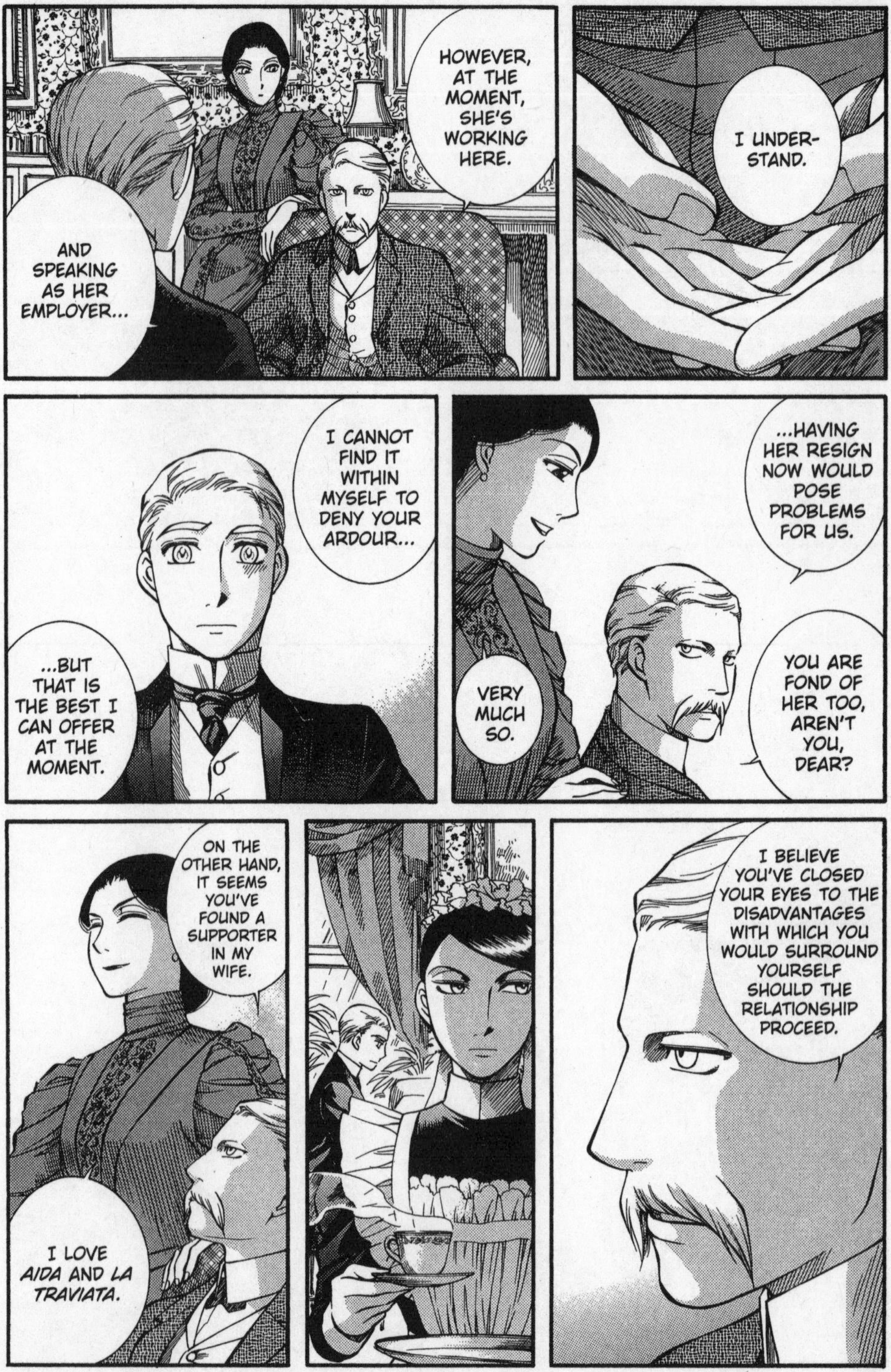
I UNDER-STAND.
HOWEVER, AT THE MOMENT, SHE'S WORKING HERE.
AND SPEAKING AS HER EMPLOYER...
...HAVING HER RESIGN NOW WOULD POSE PROBLEMS FOR US.
YOU ARE FOND OF HER TOO, AREN'T YOU, DEAR?
VERY MUCH SO.
I CANNOT FIND IT WITHIN MYSELF TO DENY YOUR ARDOUR...
...BUT THAT IS THE BEST I CAN OFFER AT THE MOMENT.
I BELIEVE YOU'VE CLOSED YOUR EYES TO THE DISADVANTAGES WITH WHICH YOU WOULD SURROUND YOURSELF SHOULD THE RELATIONSHIP PROCEED.
ON THE OTHER HAND, IT SEEMS YOU'VE FOUND A SUPPORTER IN MY WIFE.
I LOVE *AIDA* AND *LA TRAVIATA*.

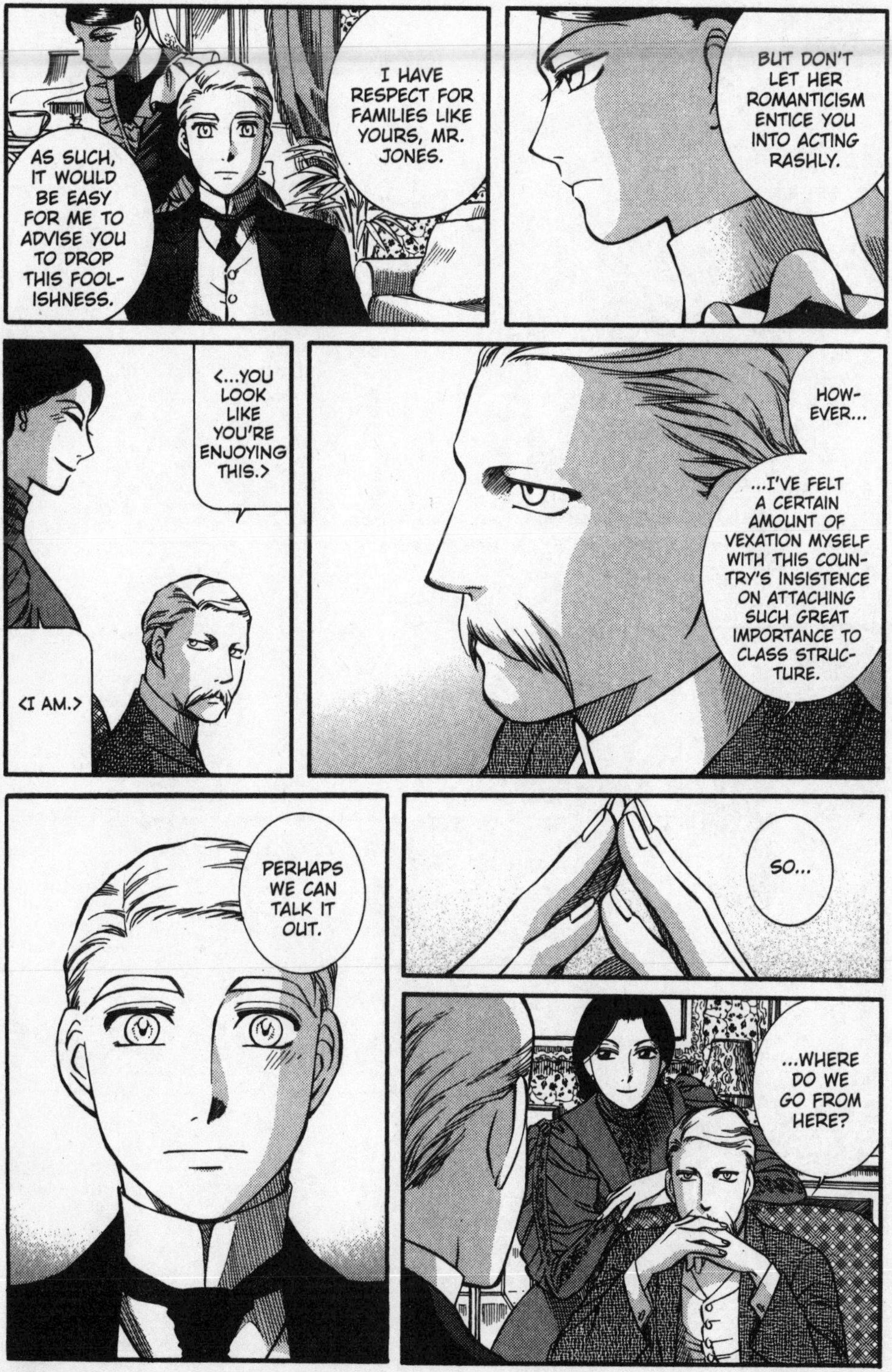
BUT DON'T LET HER ROMANTICISM ENTICE YOU INTO ACTING RASHLY.
I HAVE RESPECT FOR FAMILIES LIKE YOURS, MR. JONES.
AS SUCH, IT WOULD BE EASY FOR ME TO ADVISE YOU TO DROP THIS FOOL-ISHNESS.
HOW-EVER...
...I'VE FELT A CERTAIN AMOUNT OF VEXATION MYSELF WITH THIS COUN-TRY'S INSISTENCE ON ATTACHING SUCH GREAT IMPORTANCE TO CLASS STRUC-TURE.
<...YOU LOOK LIKE YOU'RE ENJOYING THIS.>
<I AM.>
SO...
...WHERE DO WE GO FROM HERE?
PERHAPS WE CAN TALK IT OUT.

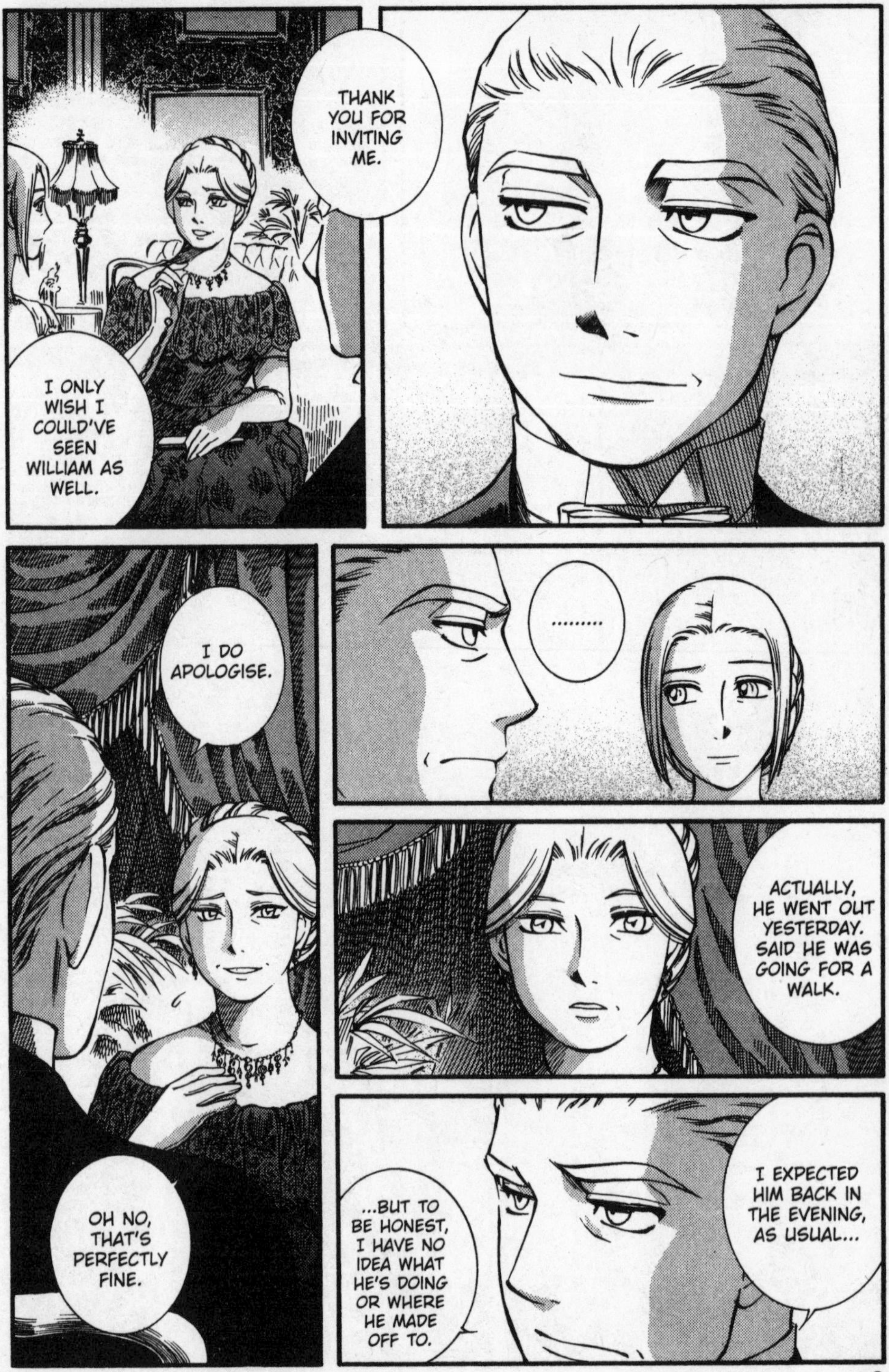
THANK YOU FOR INVITING ME.
I ONLY WISH I COULD'VE SEEN WILLIAM AS WELL.
....
ACTUALLY, HE WENT OUT YESTERDAY. SAID HE WAS GOING FOR A WALK.
I EXPECTED HIM BACK IN THE EVENING, AS USUAL...
...BUT TO BE HONEST, I HAVE NO IDEA WHAT HE'S DOING OR WHERE HE MADE OFF TO.
I DO APOLOGISE.
OH NO, THAT'S PERFECTLY FINE.

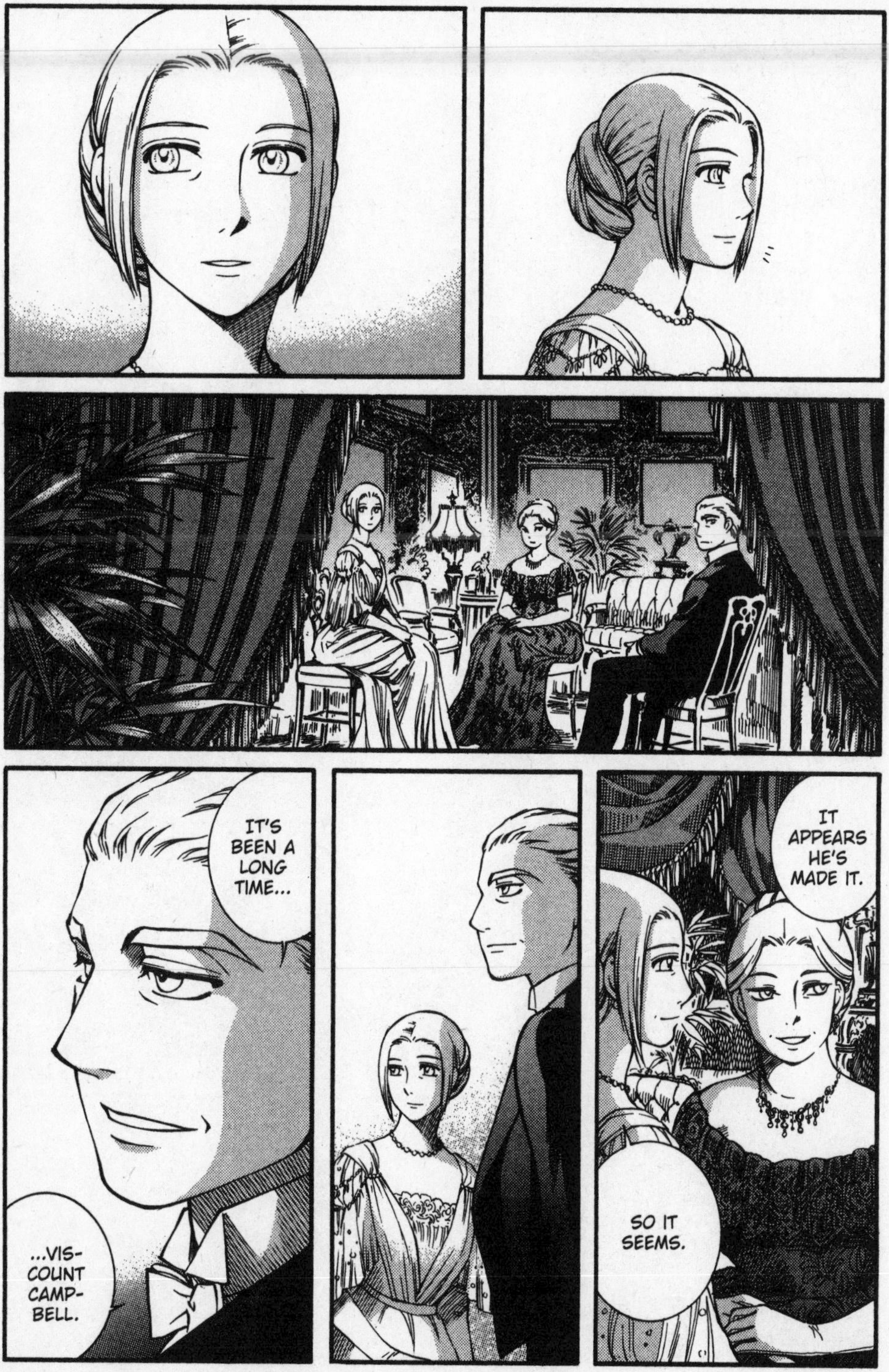
IT APPEARS HE'S MADE IT.
SO IT SEEMS.
IT'S BEEN A LONG TIME...
...VIS-COUNT CAMP-BELL.

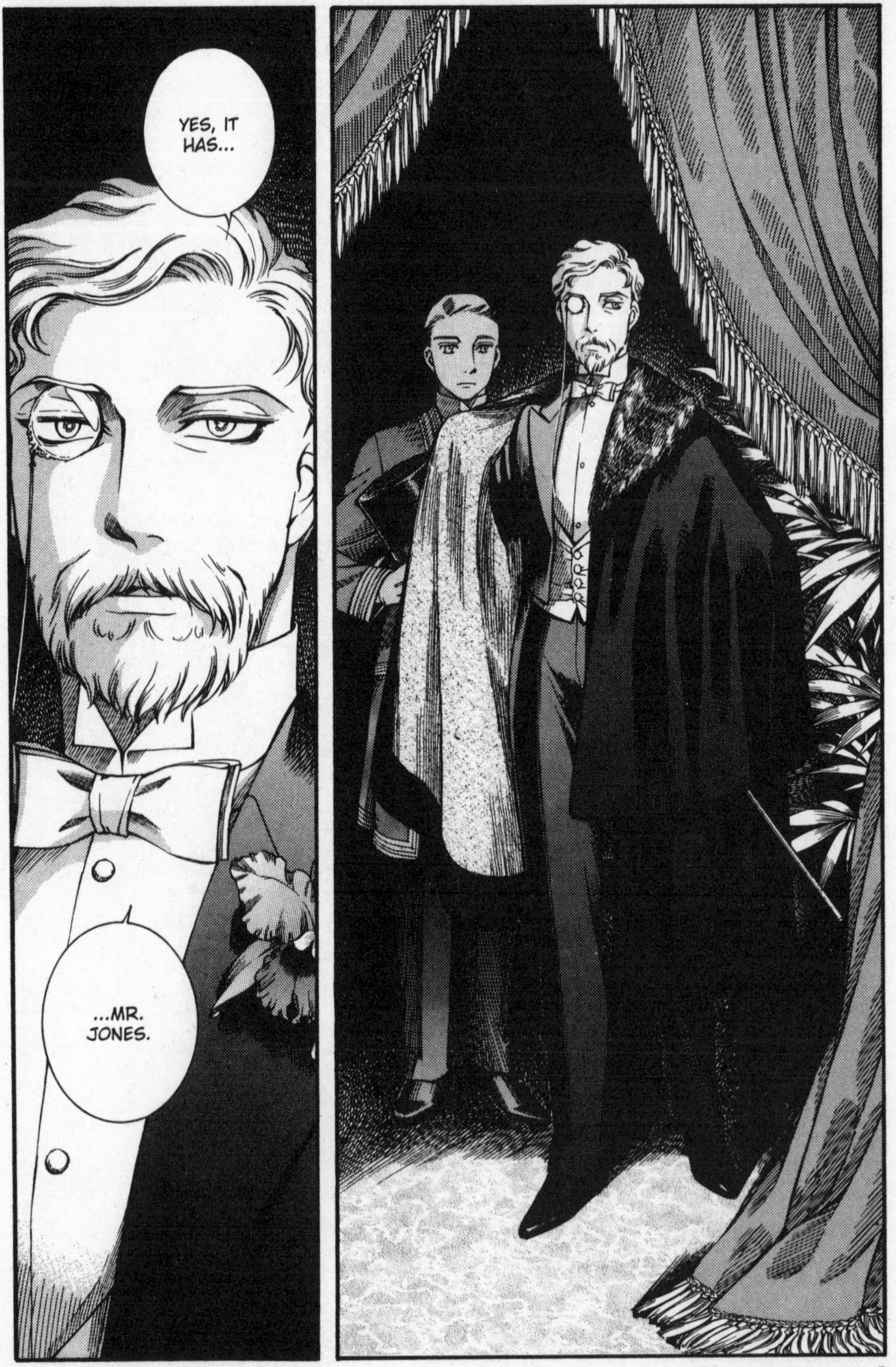
YES, IT HAS...
...MR. JONES.

Chapter 35: End

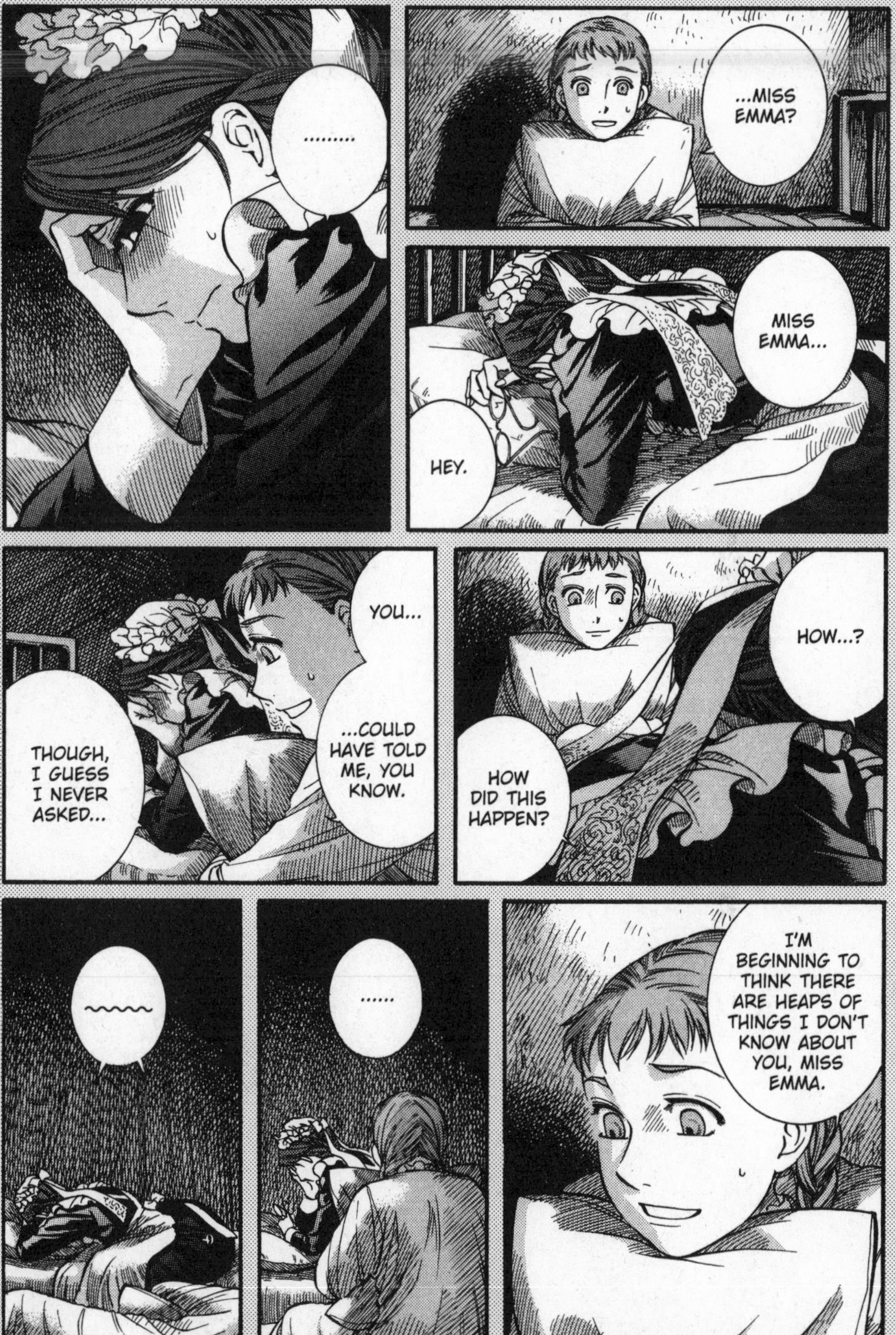
...MISS EMMA?
MISS EMMA...
HEY.
....
HOW...?
HOW DID THIS HAPPEN?
YOU...
...COULD HAVE TOLD ME, YOU KNOW.
THOUGH, I GUESS I NEVER ASKED...
I'M BEGINNING TO THINK THERE ARE HEAPS OF THINGS I DON'T KNOW ABOUT YOU, MISS EMMA.
......
~~~~
~~~~

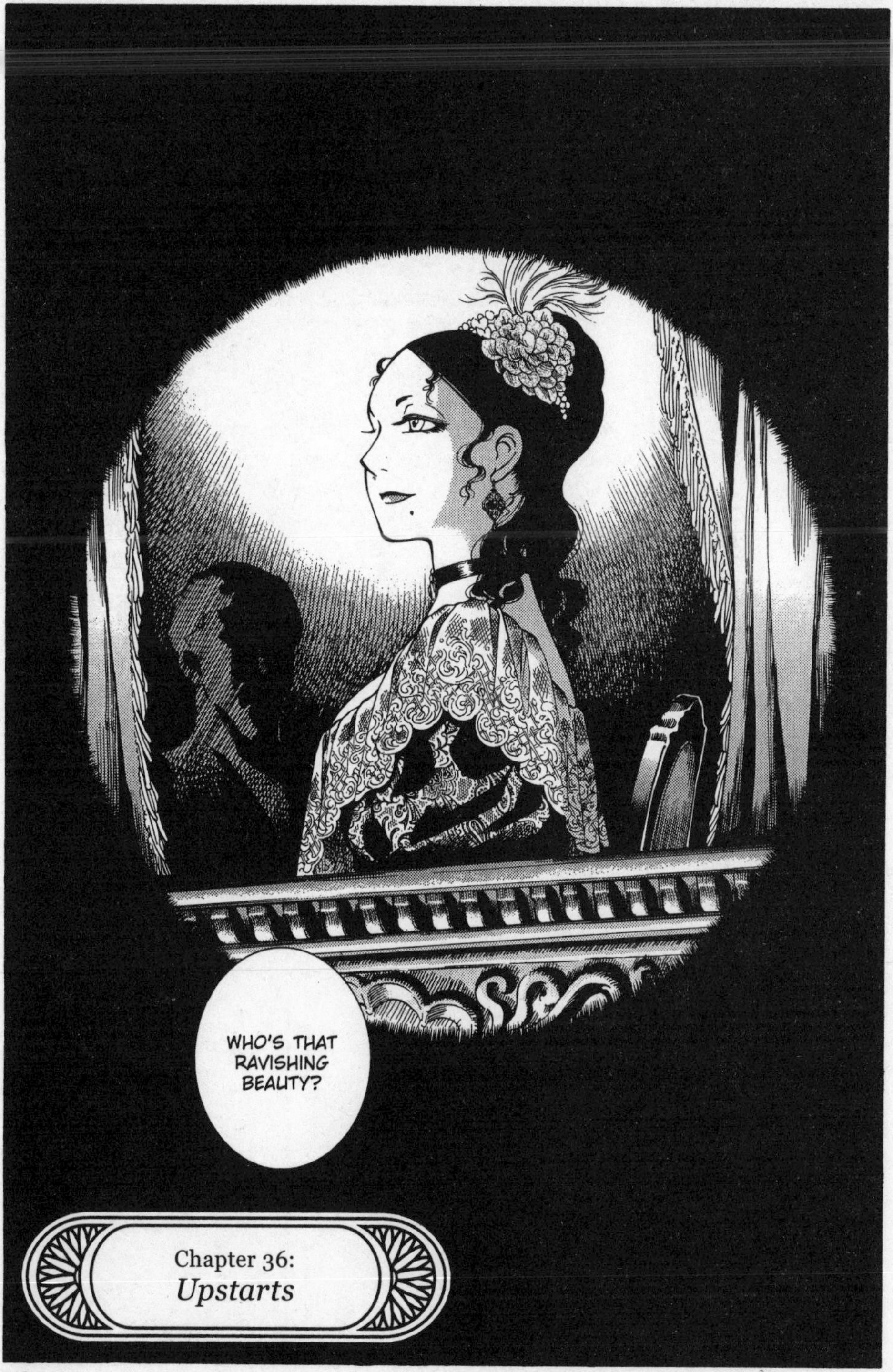
WHO'S THAT RAVISHING BEAUTY?

Chapter 36: *Upstarts*

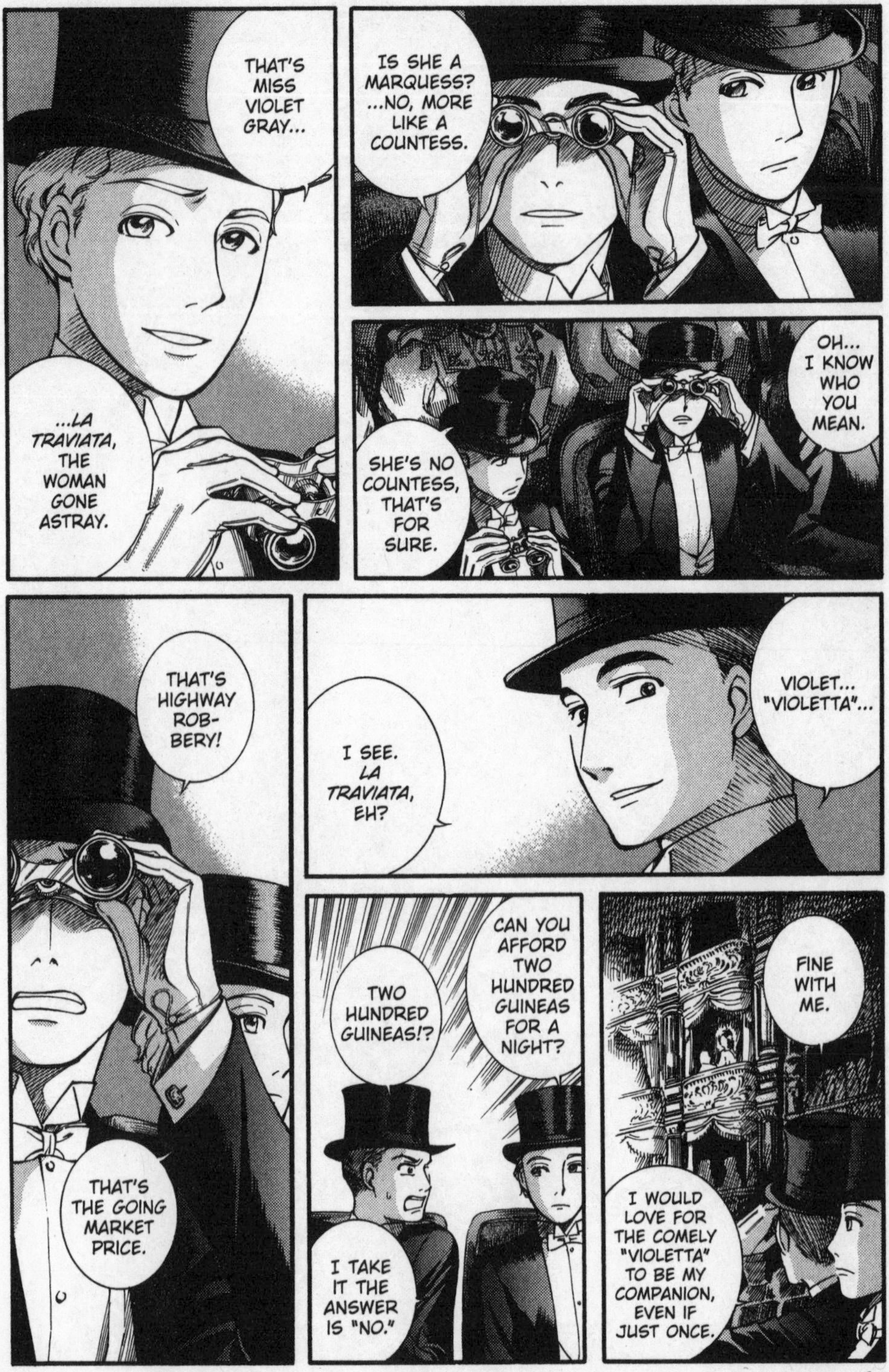
IS SHE A MARQUESS? ...NO, MORE LIKE A COUNTESS.
OH... I KNOW WHO YOU MEAN.
SHE'S NO COUNTESS, THAT'S FOR SURE.
THAT'S MISS VIOLET GRAY...
...*LA TRAVIATA*, THE WOMAN GONE ASTRAY.
VIOLET... "VIOLETTA"...
I SEE. *LA TRAVIATA*, EH?
FINE WITH ME.
I WOULD LOVE FOR THE COMELY "VIOLETTA" TO BE MY COMPANION, EVEN IF JUST ONCE.
CAN YOU AFFORD TWO HUNDRED GUINEAS FOR A NIGHT?
TWO HUNDRED GUINEAS!?
I TAKE IT THE ANSWER IS "NO."
THAT'S HIGHWAY ROB-BERY!
THAT'S THE GOING MARKET PRICE.

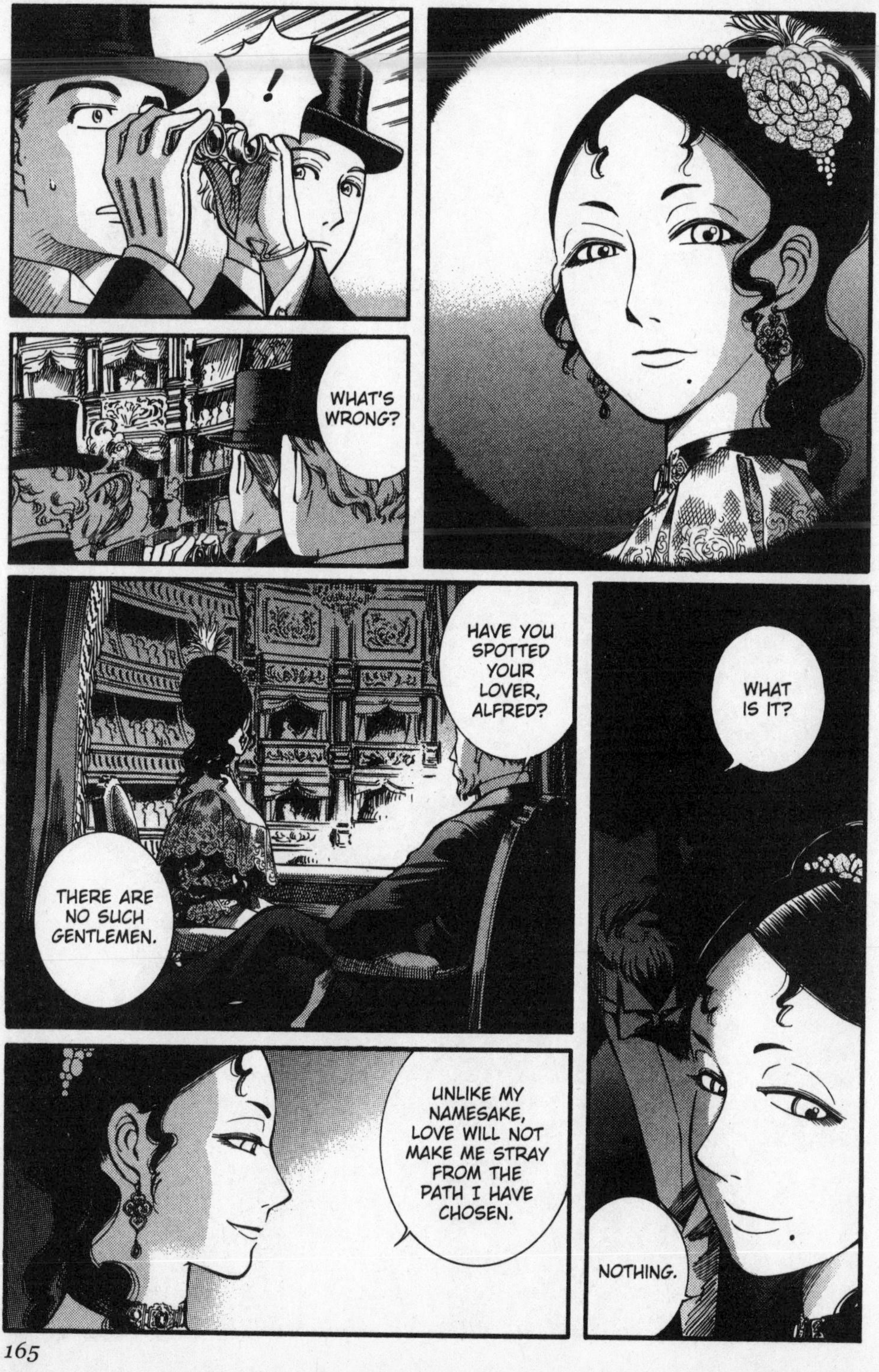
!
WHAT'S WRONG?
WHAT IS IT?
NOTHING.
HAVE YOU SPOTTED YOUR LOVER, ALFRED?
THERE ARE NO SUCH GENTLEMEN.
UNLIKE MY NAMESAKE, LOVE WILL NOT MAKE ME STRAY FROM THE PATH I HAVE CHOSEN.

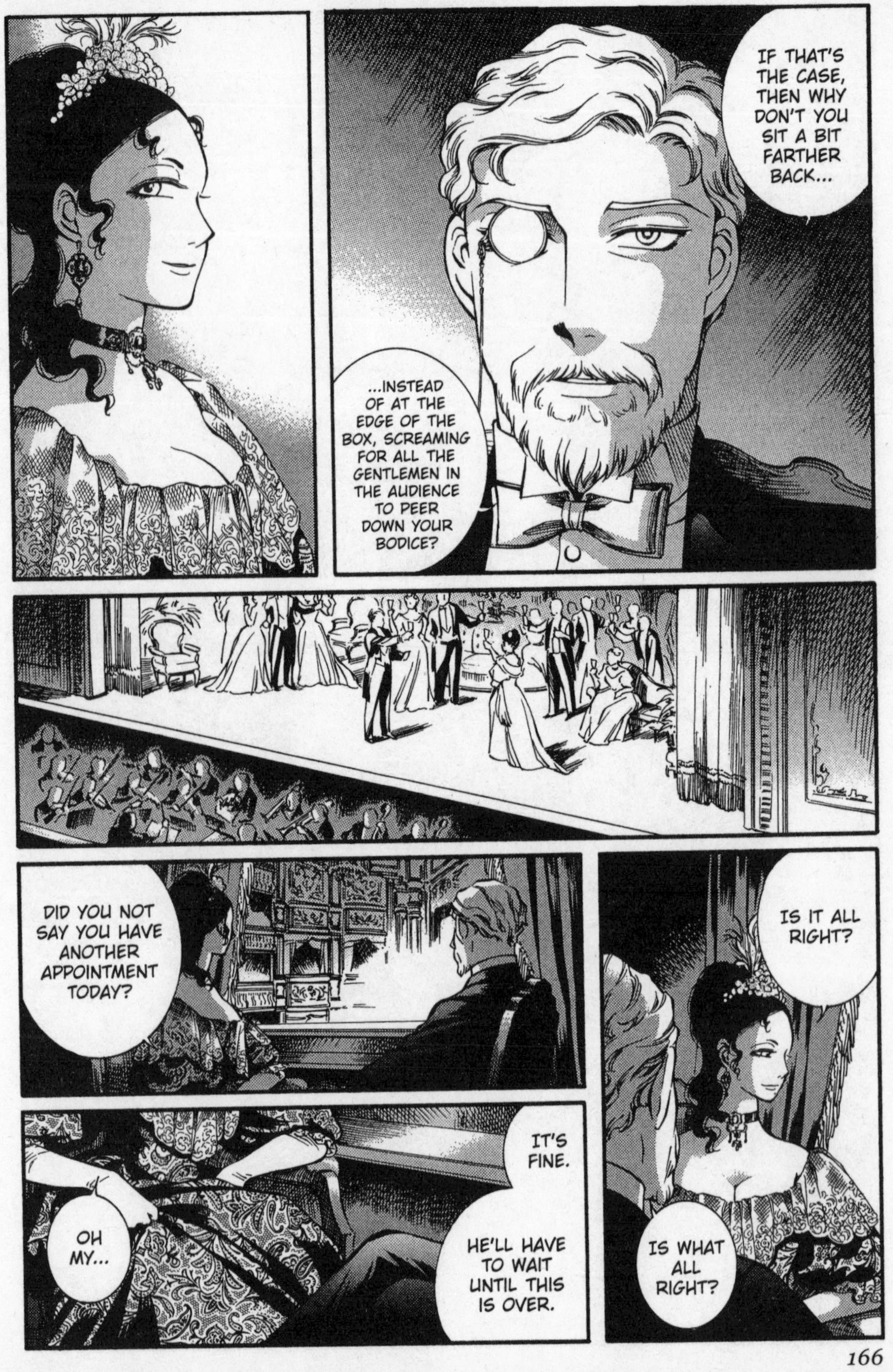
IF THAT'S THE CASE, THEN WHY DON'T YOU SIT A BIT FARTHER BACK...
...INSTEAD OF AT THE EDGE OF THE BOX, SCREAMING FOR ALL THE GENTLEMEN IN THE AUDIENCE TO PEER DOWN YOUR BODICE?
IS IT ALL RIGHT?
IS WHAT ALL RIGHT?
DID YOU NOT SAY YOU HAVE ANOTHER APPOINTMENT TODAY?
IT'S FINE.
HE'LL HAVE TO WAIT UNTIL THIS IS OVER.
OH MY...

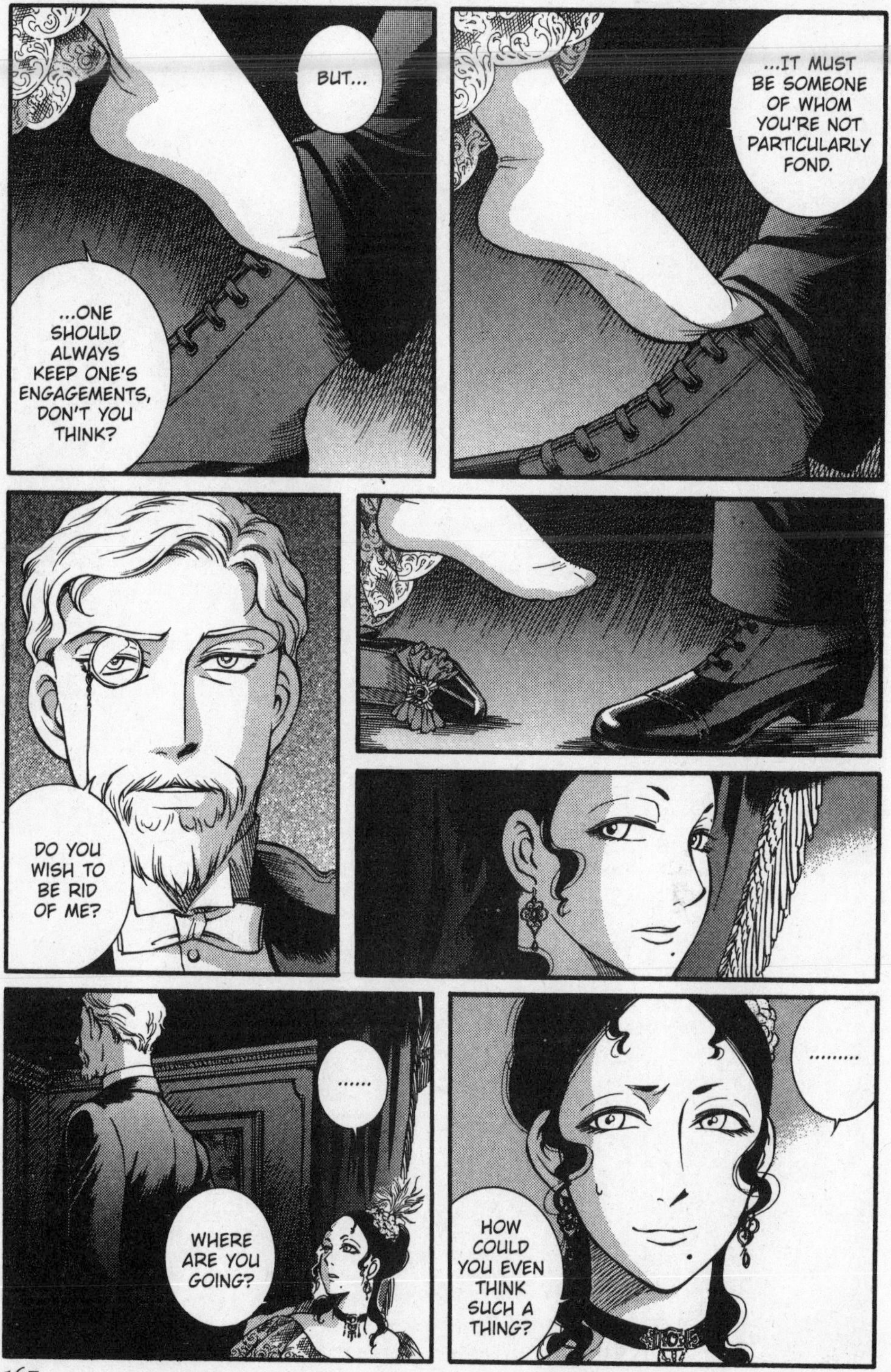
...IT MUST BE SOMEONE OF WHOM YOU'RE NOT PARTICULARLY FOND.
BUT...
...ONE SHOULD ALWAYS KEEP ONE'S ENGAGEMENTS, DON'T YOU THINK?
DO YOU WISH TO BE RID OF ME?
....
HOW COULD YOU EVEN THINK SUCH A THING?
......
WHERE ARE YOU GOING?

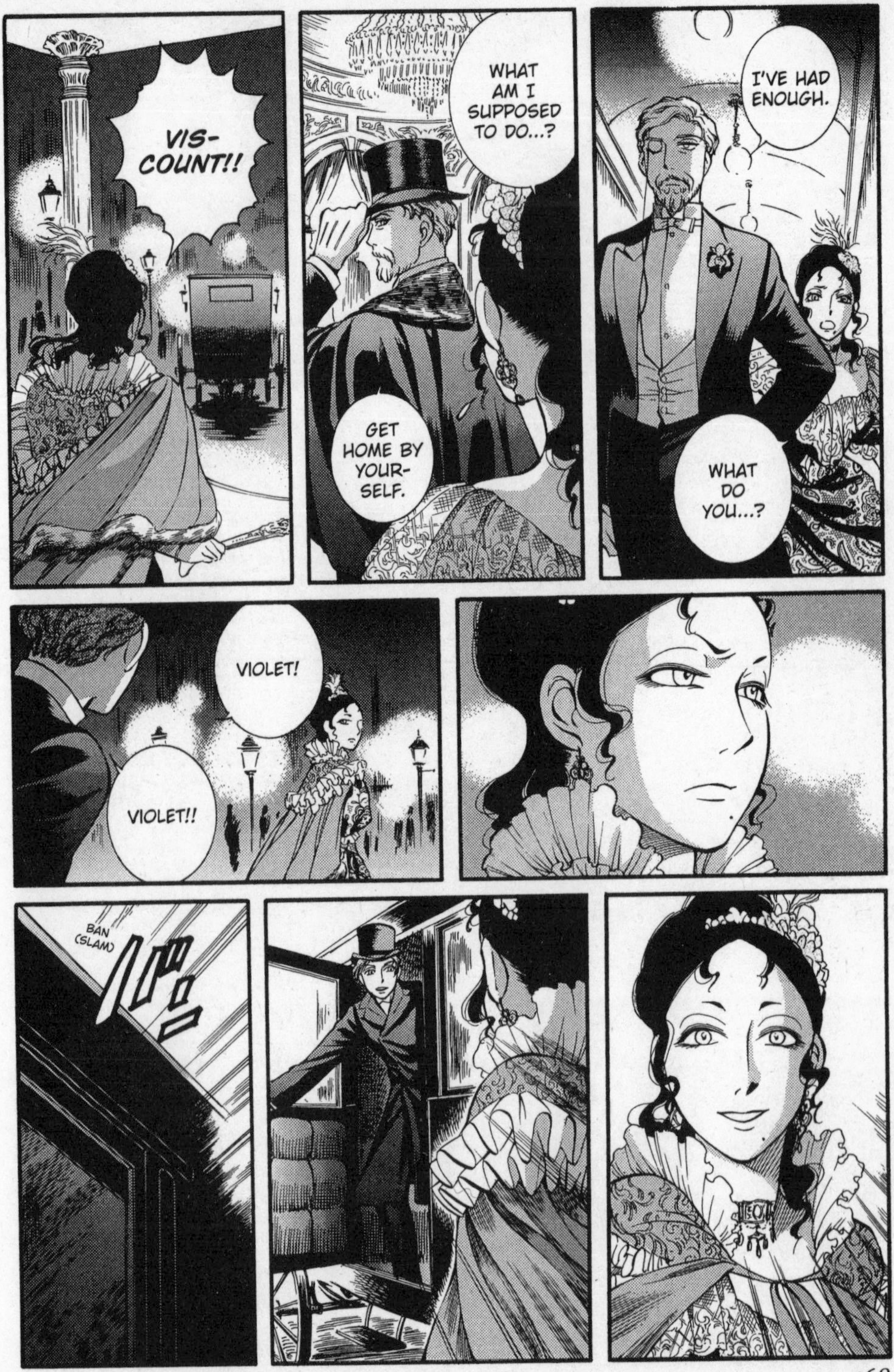
I'VE HAD ENOUGH.
WHAT DO YOU...?
WHAT AM I SUPPOSED TO DO...?
GET HOME BY YOURSELF.
VIS-COUNT!!
VIOLET!
VIOLET!!
BAN (SLAM)

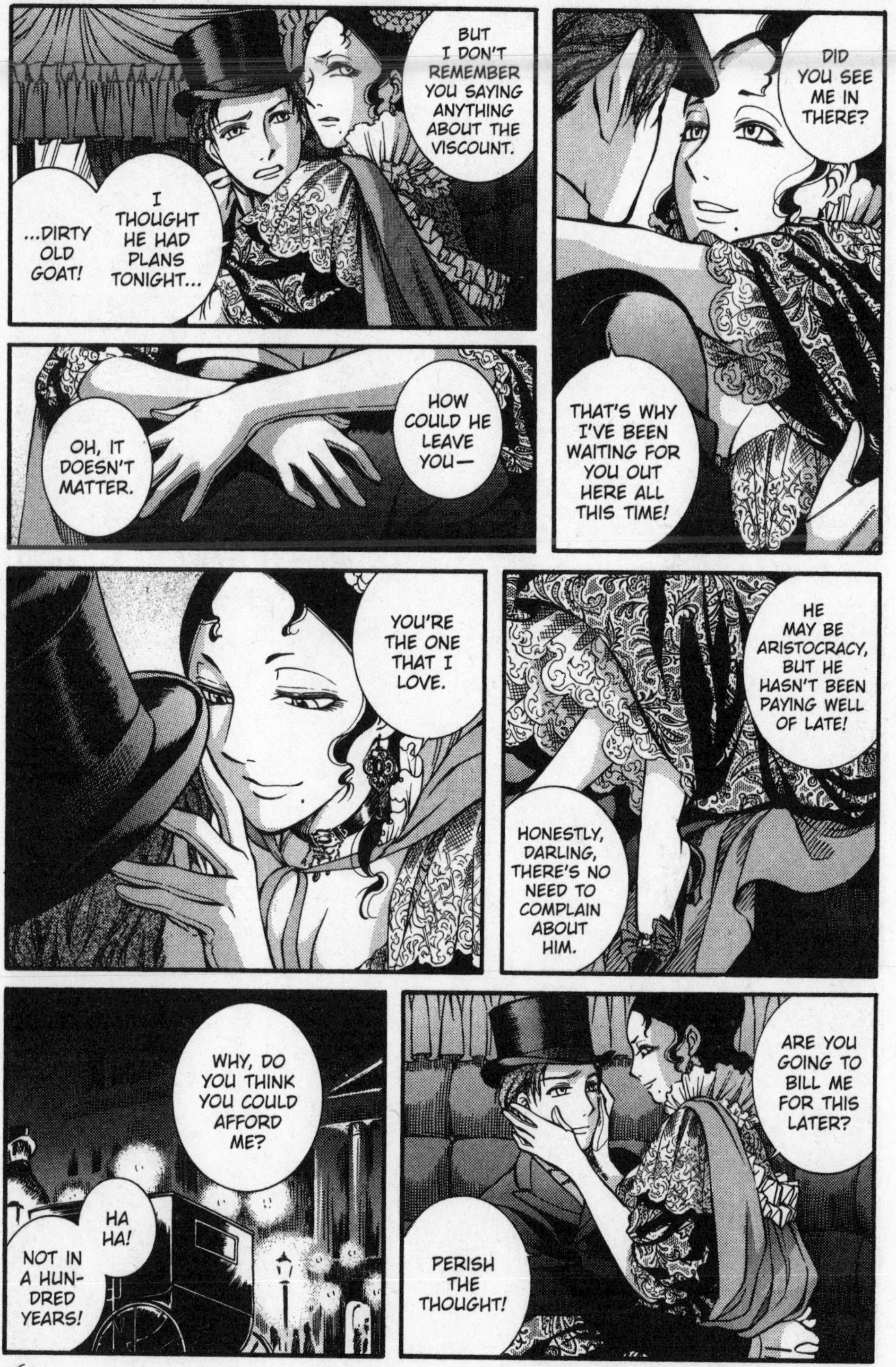
DID YOU SEE ME IN THERE?
THAT'S WHY I'VE BEEN WAITING FOR YOU OUT HERE ALL THIS TIME!
BUT I DON'T REMEMBER YOU SAYING ANYTHING ABOUT THE VISCOUNT.
I THOUGHT HE HAD PLANS TONIGHT...
...DIRTY OLD GOAT!
HOW COULD HE LEAVE YOU—
OH, IT DOESN'T MATTER.
HE MAY BE ARISTOCRACY, BUT HE HASN'T BEEN PAYING WELL OF LATE!
HONESTLY, DARLING, THERE'S NO NEED TO COMPLAIN ABOUT HIM.
YOU'RE THE ONE THAT I LOVE.
ARE YOU GOING TO BILL ME FOR THIS LATER?
PERISH THE THOUGHT!
WHY, DO YOU THINK YOU COULD AFFORD ME?
HA HA!
NOT IN A HUN-DRED YEARS!

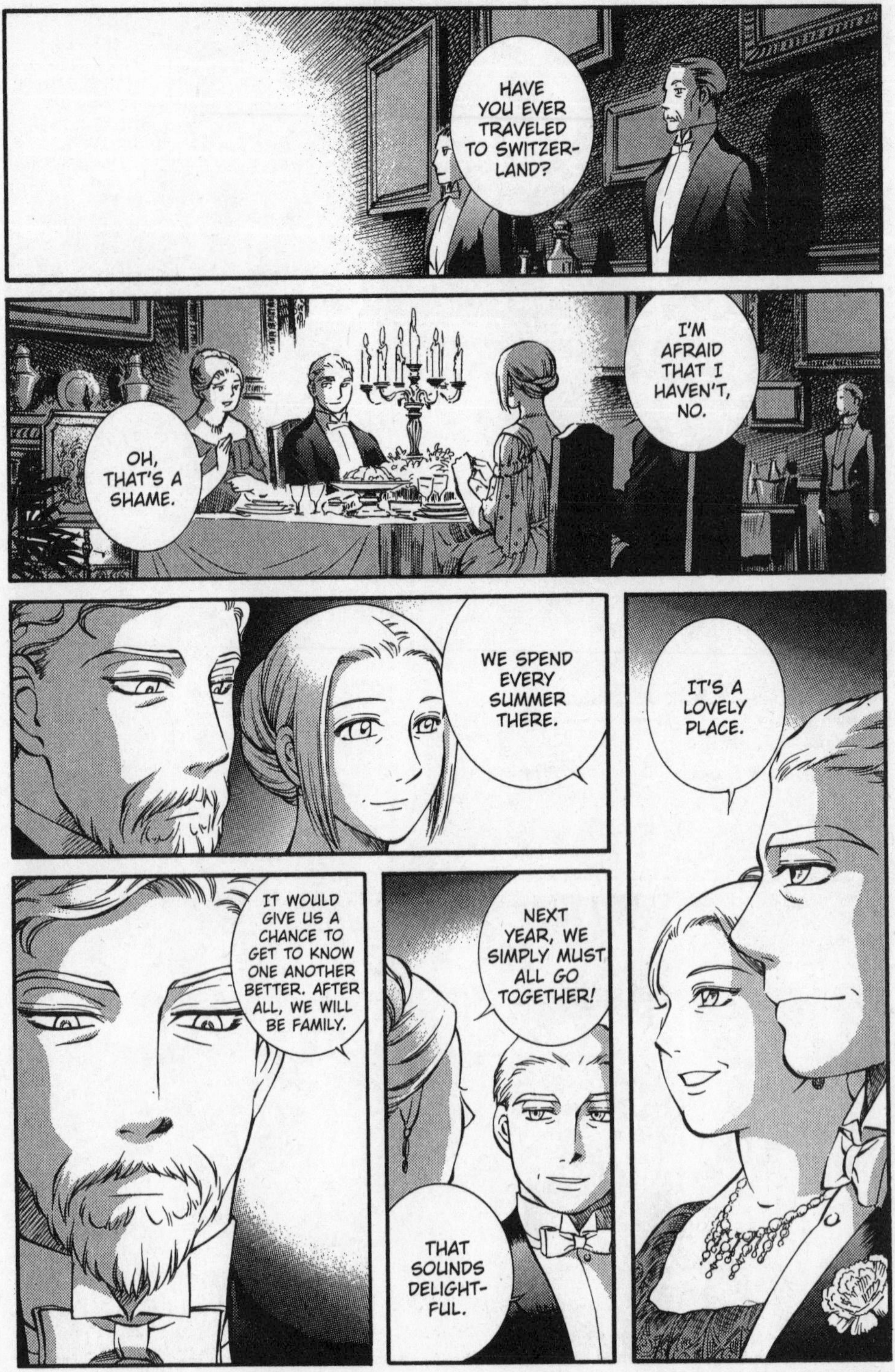
HAVE YOU EVER TRAVELED TO SWITZER-LAND?
I'M AFRAID THAT I HAVEN'T, NO.
OH, THAT'S A SHAME.
IT'S A LOVELY PLACE.
WE SPEND EVERY SUMMER THERE.
NEXT YEAR, WE SIMPLY MUST ALL GO TOGETHER!
THAT SOUNDS DELIGHT-FUL.
IT WOULD GIVE US A CHANCE TO GET TO KNOW ONE ANOTHER BETTER. AFTER ALL, WE WILL BE FAMILY.

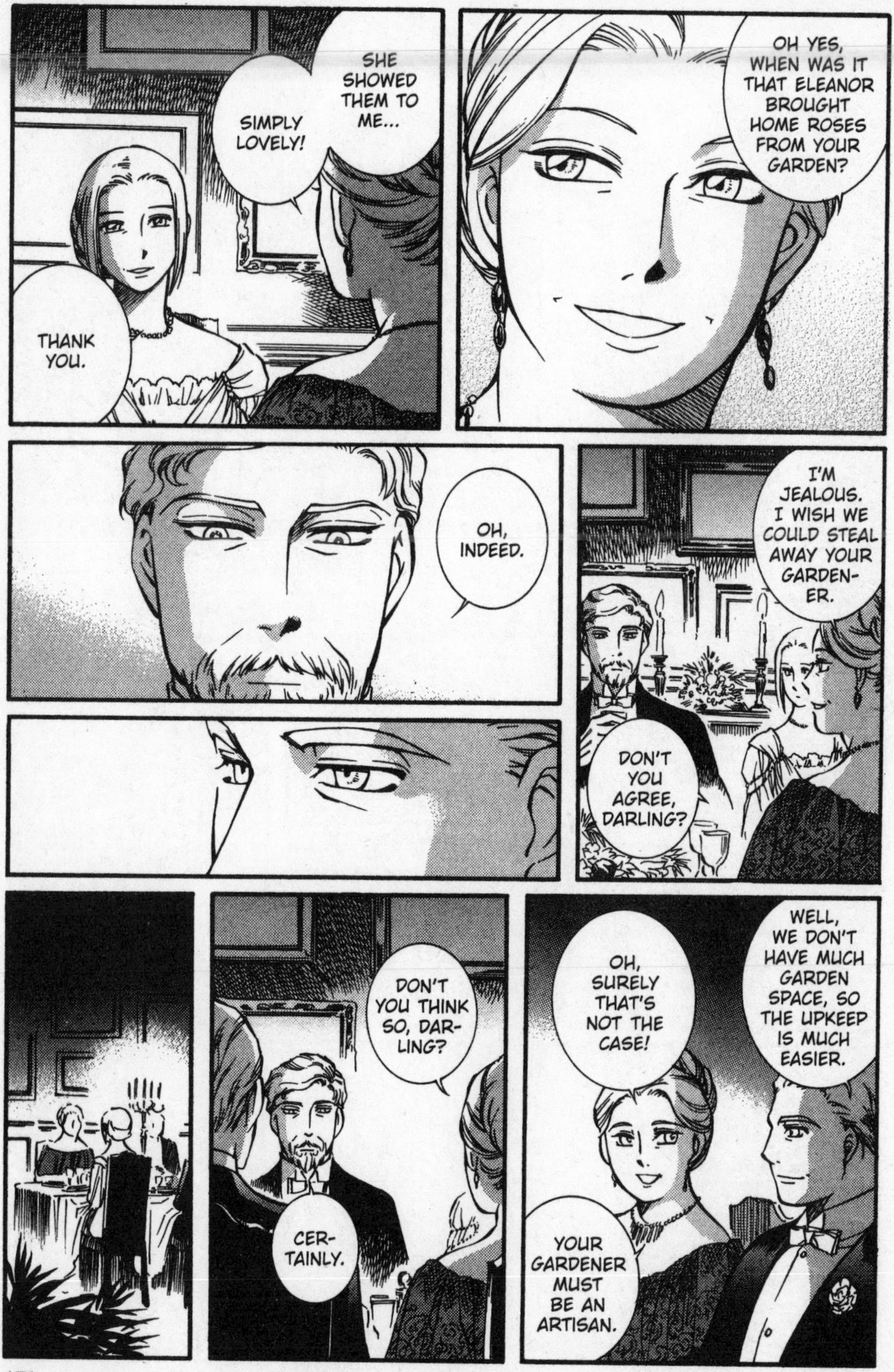
OH YES, WHEN WAS IT THAT ELEANOR BROUGHT HOME ROSES FROM YOUR GARDEN?
SHE SHOWED THEM TO ME...
SIMPLY LOVELY!
THANK YOU.
I'M JEALOUS. I WISH WE COULD STEAL AWAY YOUR GARDEN-ER.
DON'T YOU AGREE, DARLING?
OH, INDEED.
WELL, WE DON'T HAVE MUCH GARDEN SPACE, SO THE UPKEEP IS MUCH EASIER.
OH, SURELY THAT'S NOT THE CASE!
YOUR GARDENER MUST BE AN ARTISAN.
DON'T YOU THINK SO, DAR-LING?
CER-TAINLY.

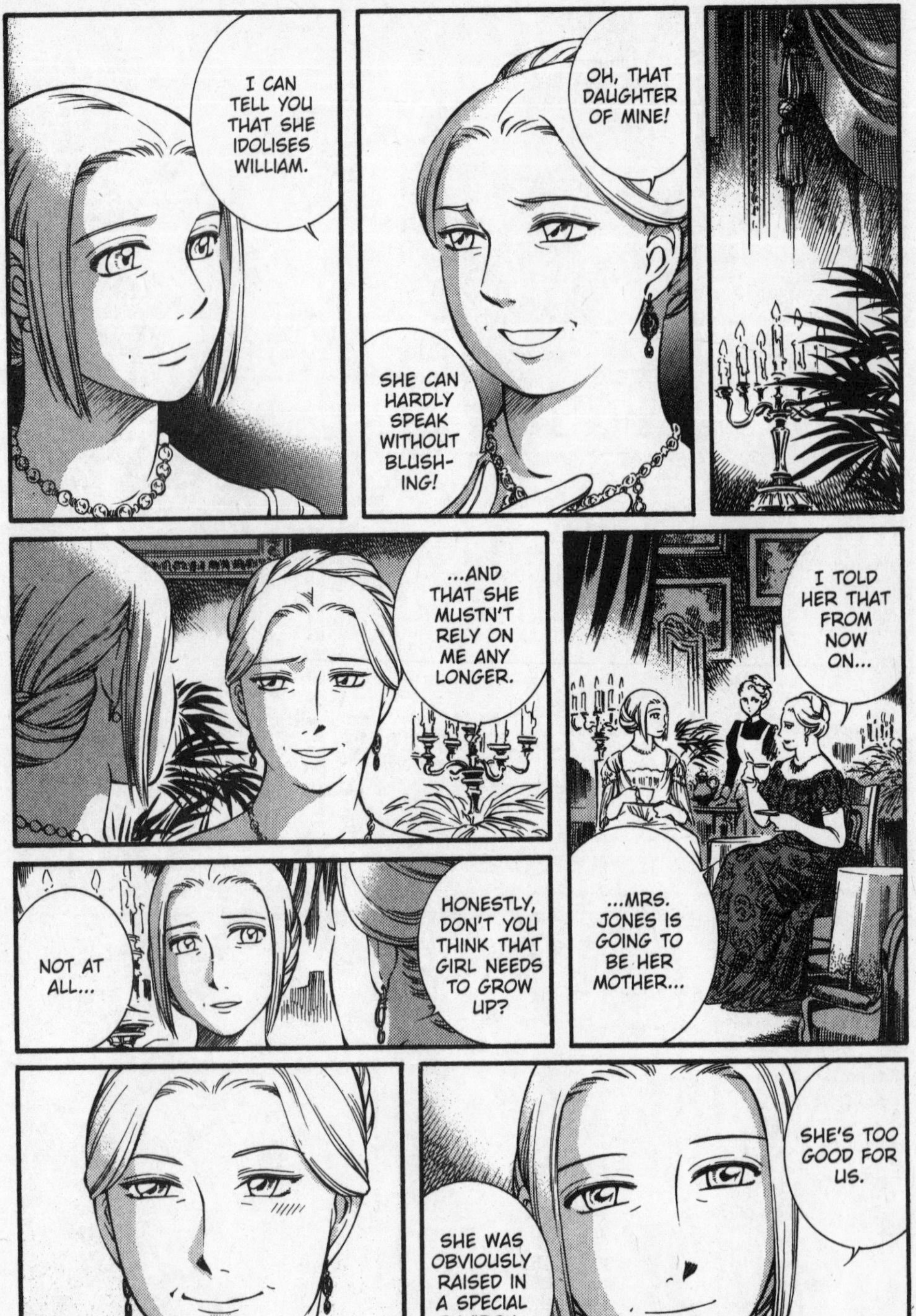
OH, THAT DAUGHTER OF MINE!
SHE CAN HARDLY SPEAK WITHOUT BLUSHING!
I CAN TELL YOU THAT SHE IDOLISES WILLIAM.
I TOLD HER THAT FROM NOW ON...
...MRS. JONES IS GOING TO BE HER MOTHER...
...AND THAT SHE MUSTN'T RELY ON ME ANY LONGER.
HONESTLY, DON'T YOU THINK THAT GIRL NEEDS TO GROW UP?
NOT AT ALL...
SHE'S TOO GOOD FOR US.
SHE WAS OBVIOUSLY RAISED IN A SPECIAL ENVIRON-MENT.

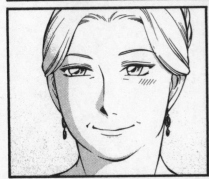

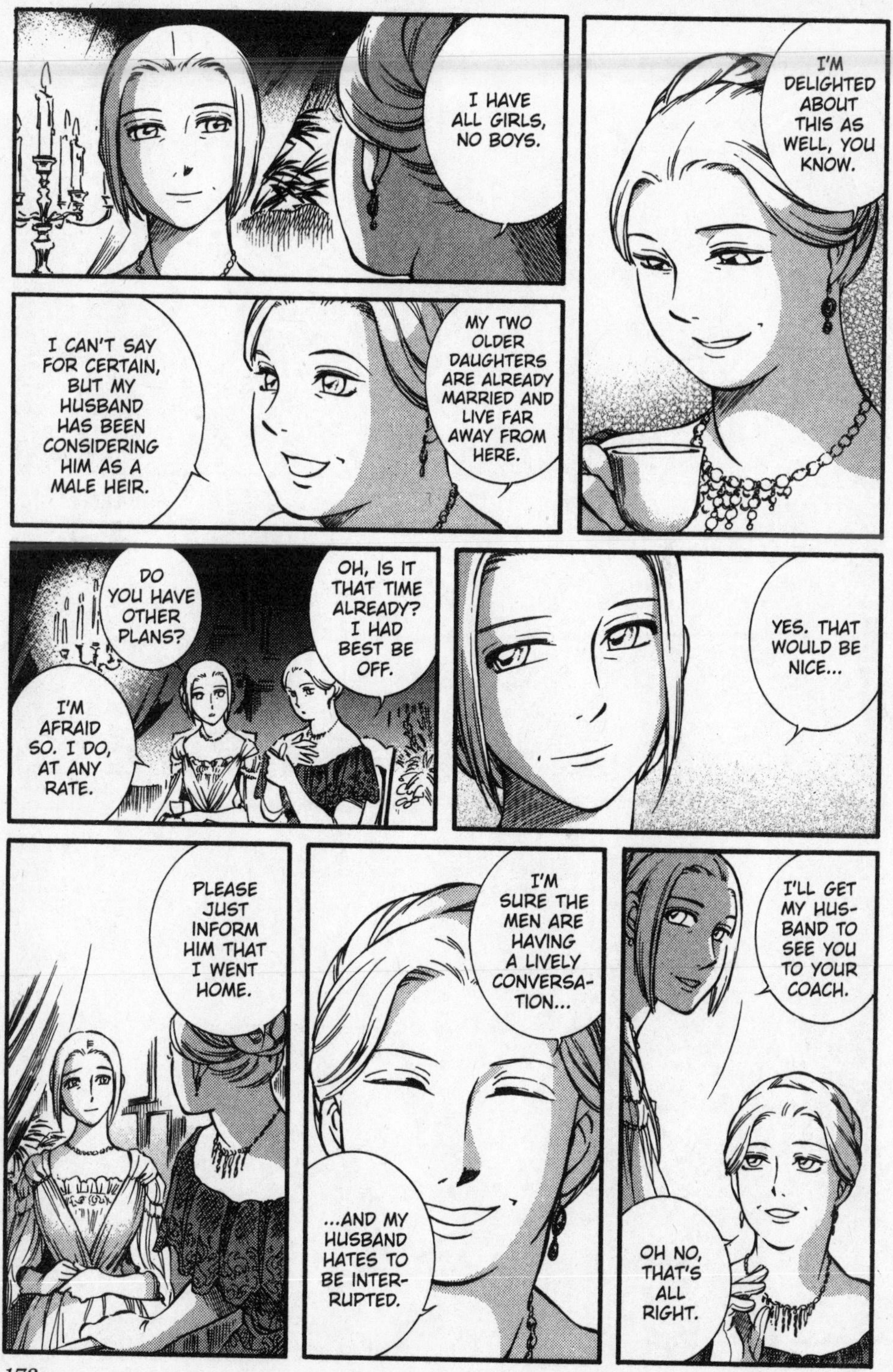
I'M DELIGHTED ABOUT THIS AS WELL, YOU KNOW.
I HAVE ALL GIRLS, NO BOYS.
MY TWO OLDER DAUGHTERS ARE ALREADY MARRIED AND LIVE FAR AWAY FROM HERE.
I CAN'T SAY FOR CERTAIN, BUT MY HUSBAND HAS BEEN CONSIDERING HIM AS A MALE HEIR.
YES. THAT WOULD BE NICE...
OH, IS IT THAT TIME ALREADY? I HAD BEST BE OFF.
DO YOU HAVE OTHER PLANS?
I'M AFRAID SO. I DO, AT ANY RATE.
I'LL GET MY HUS-BAND TO SEE YOU TO YOUR COACH.
OH NO, THAT'S ALL RIGHT.
I'M SURE THE MEN ARE HAVING A LIVELY CONVERSA-TION...
...AND MY HUSBAND HATES TO BE INTER-RUPTED.
PLEASE JUST INFORM HIM THAT I WENT HOME.

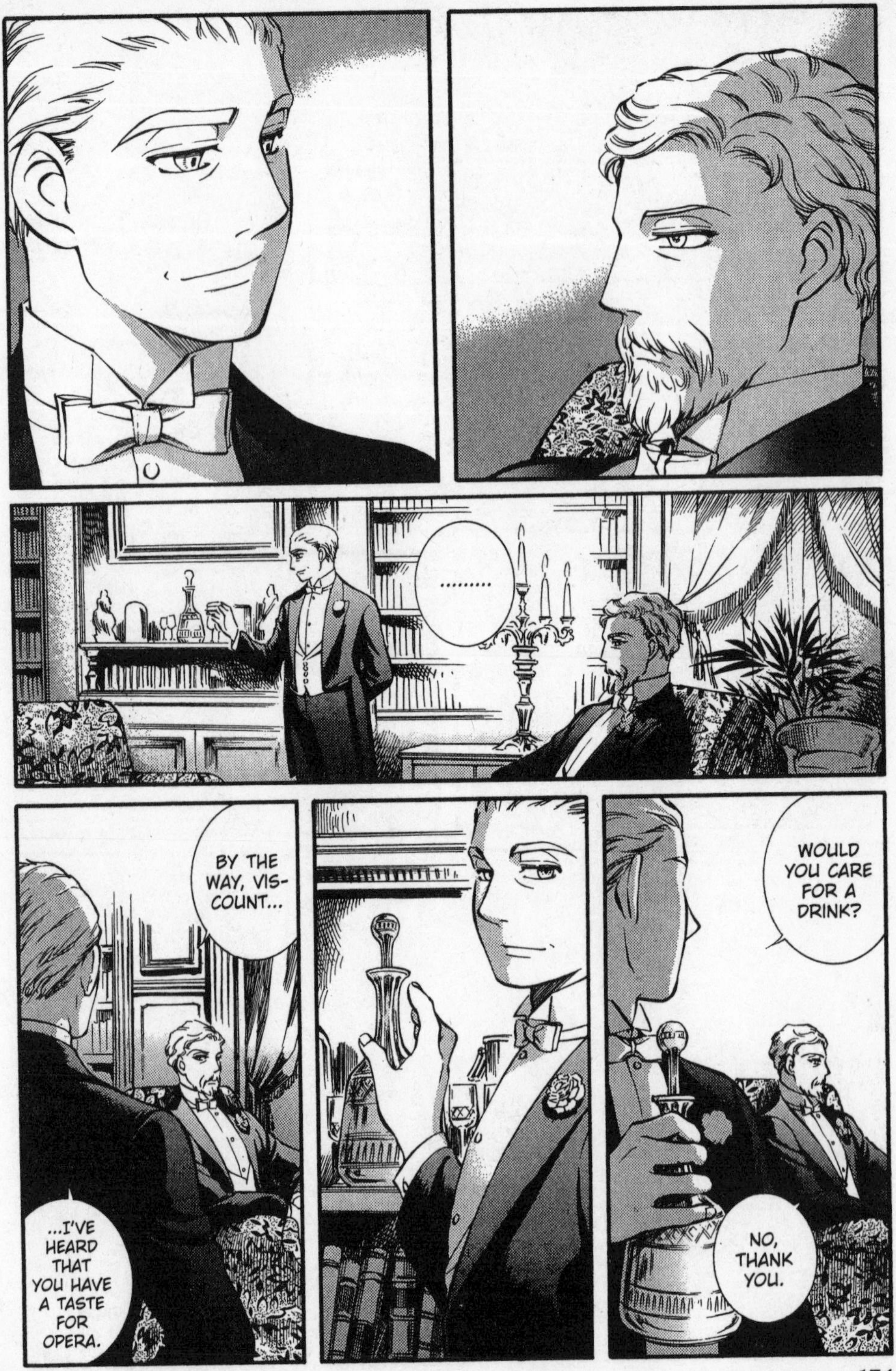
....
WOULD YOU CARE FOR A DRINK?
NO, THANK YOU.
BY THE WAY, VIS-COUNT...
...I'VE HEARD THAT YOU HAVE A TASTE FOR OPERA.

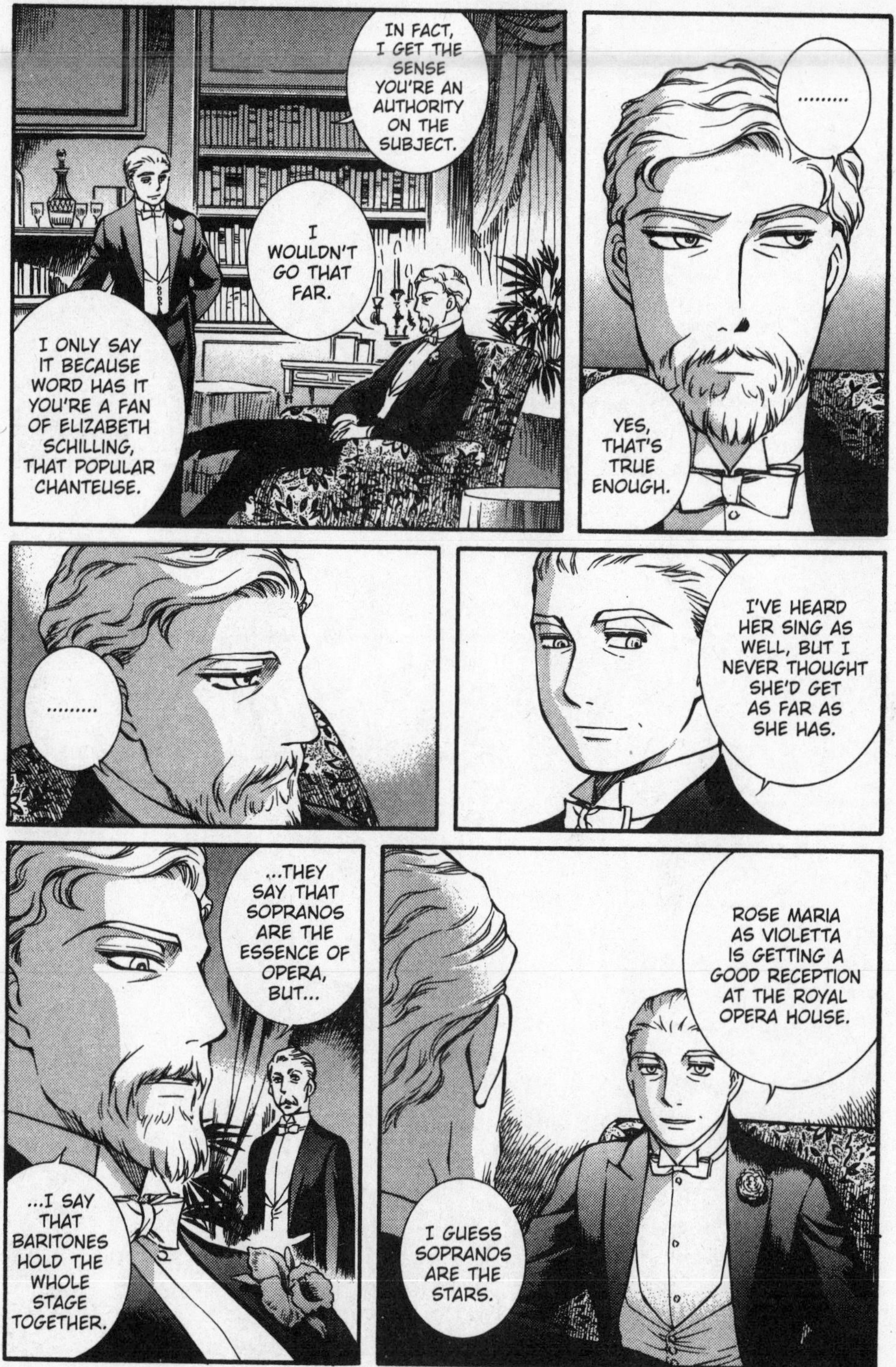
....
YES, THAT'S TRUE ENOUGH.
IN FACT, I GET THE SENSE YOU'RE AN AUTHORITY ON THE SUBJECT.
I WOULDN'T GO THAT FAR.
I ONLY SAY IT BECAUSE WORD HAS IT YOU'RE A FAN OF ELIZABETH SCHILLING, THAT POPULAR CHANTEUSE.
I'VE HEARD HER SING AS WELL, BUT I NEVER THOUGHT SHE'D GET AS FAR AS SHE HAS.
....
ROSE MARIA AS VIOLETTA IS GETTING A GOOD RECEPTION AT THE ROYAL OPERA HOUSE.
I GUESS SOPRANOS ARE THE STARS.
...THEY SAY THAT SOPRANOS ARE THE ESSENCE OF OPERA, BUT...
...I SAY THAT BARITONES HOLD THE WHOLE STAGE TOGETHER.

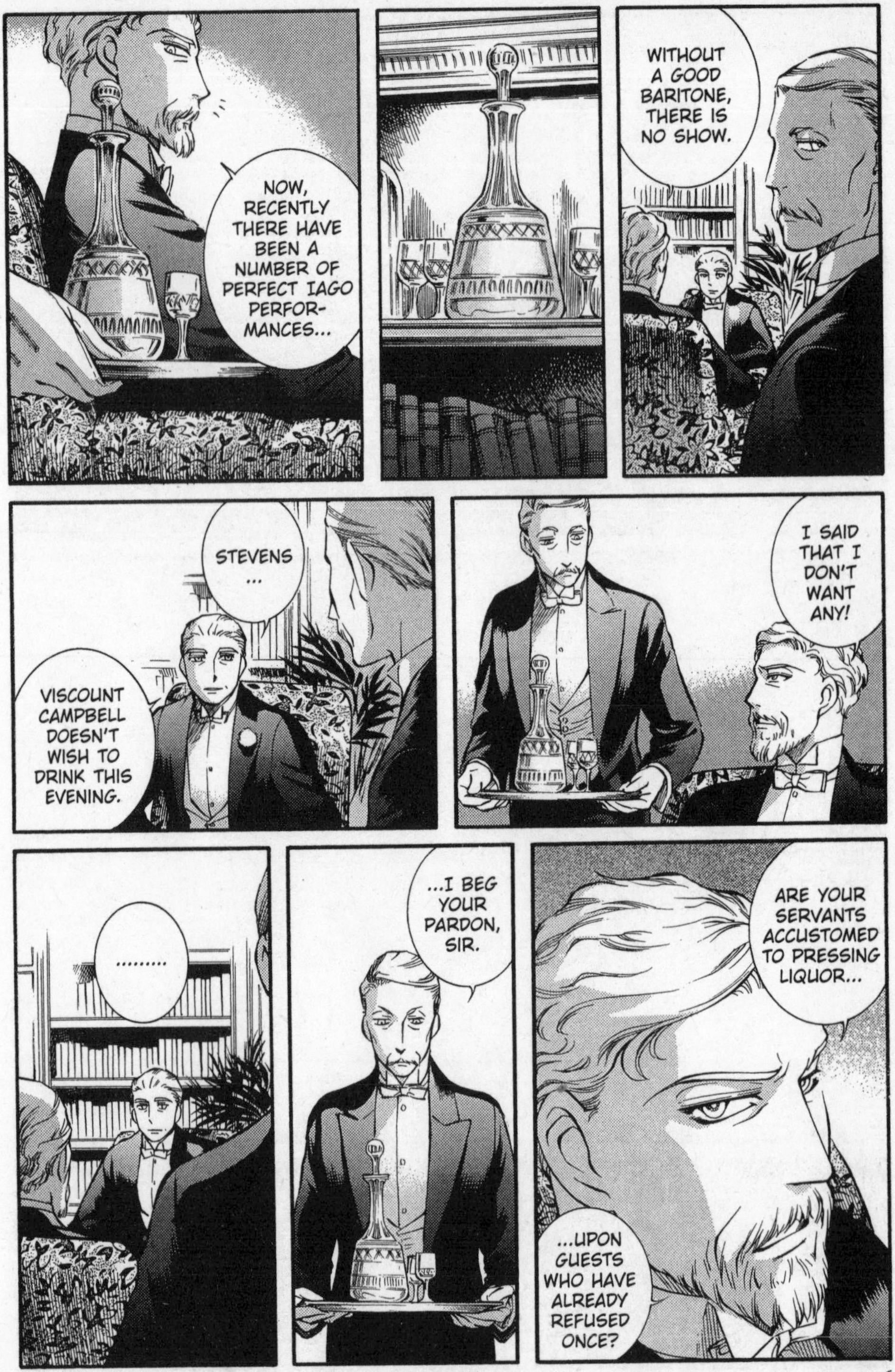
WITHOUT A GOOD BARITONE, THERE IS NO SHOW.
NOW, RECENTLY THERE HAVE BEEN A NUMBER OF PERFECT IAGO PERFORMANCES...
I SAID THAT I DON'T WANT ANY!
STEVENS ...
VISCOUNT CAMPBELL DOESN'T WISH TO DRINK THIS EVENING.
ARE YOUR SERVANTS ACCUSTOMED TO PRESSING LIQUOR...
...UPON GUESTS WHO HAVE ALREADY REFUSED ONCE?
...I BEG YOUR PARDON, SIR.
....

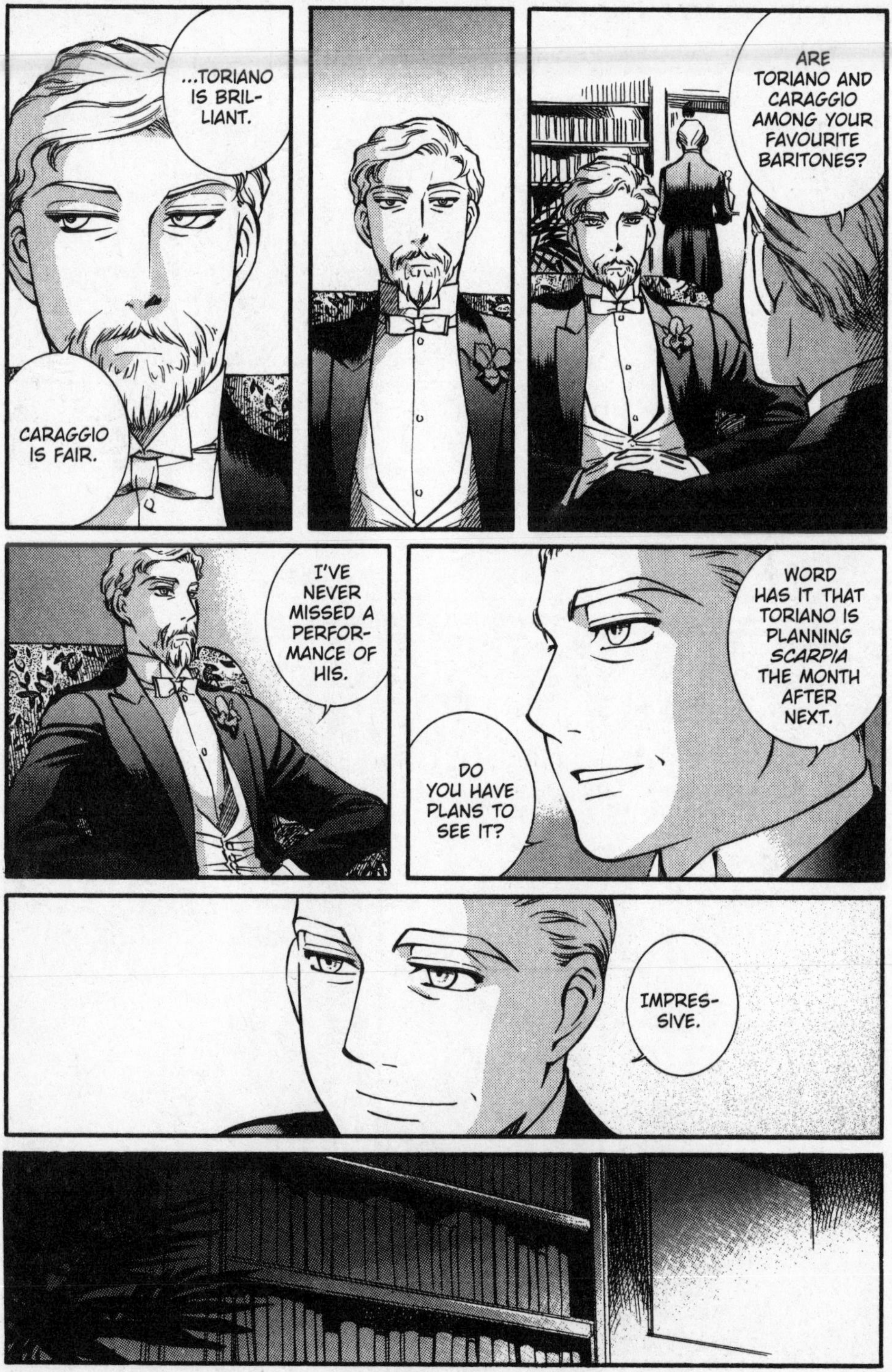
ARE TORIANO AND CARAGGIO AMONG YOUR FAVOURITE BARITONES?
...TORIANO IS BRILLIANT.
CARAGGIO IS FAIR.
WORD HAS IT THAT TORIANO IS PLANNING *SCARPIA* THE MONTH AFTER NEXT.
DO YOU HAVE PLANS TO SEE IT?
I'VE NEVER MISSED A PERFORMANCE OF HIS.
IMPRESSIVE.

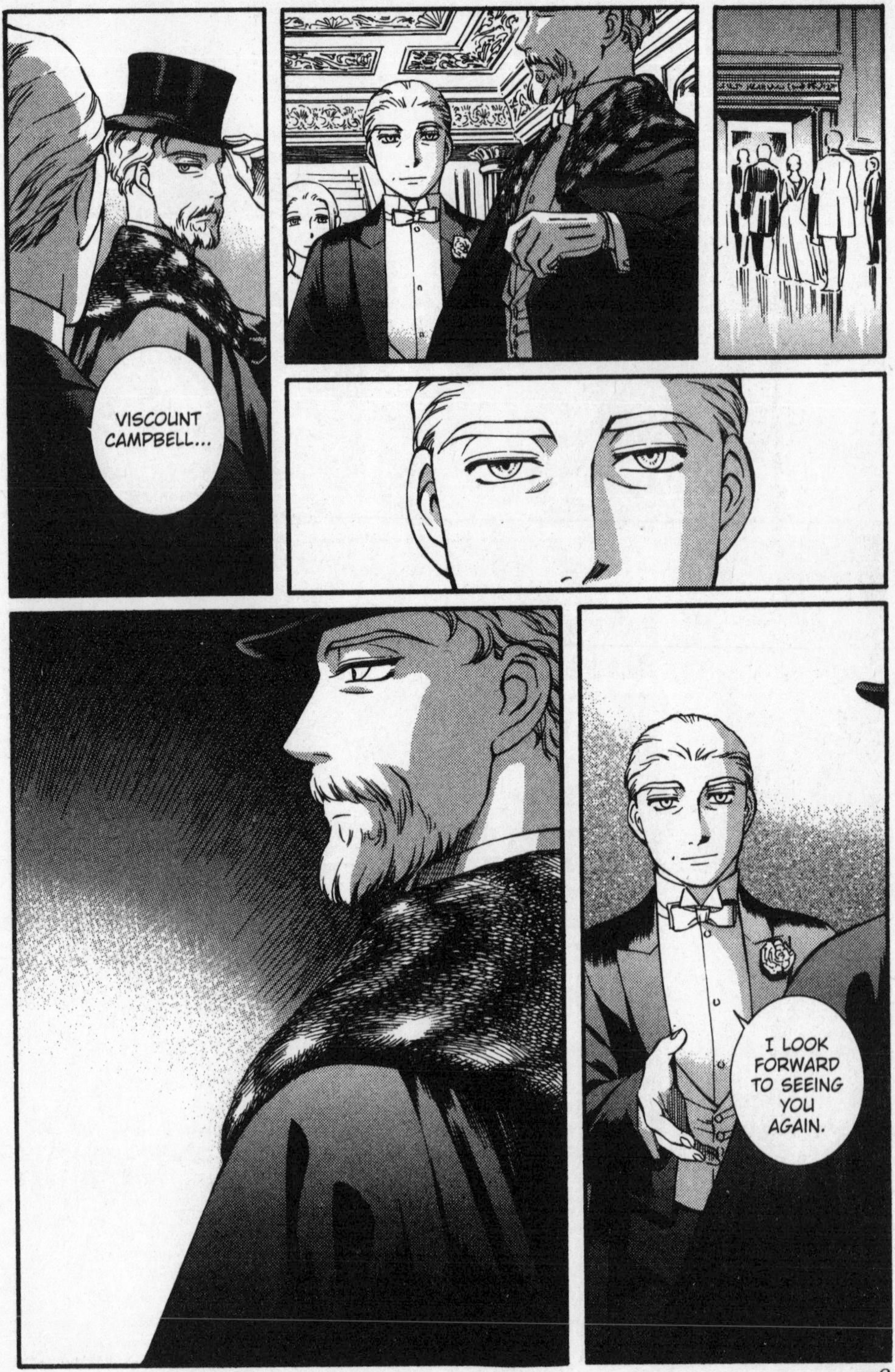
VISCOUNT CAMPBELL...
I LOOK FORWARD TO SEEING YOU AGAIN.

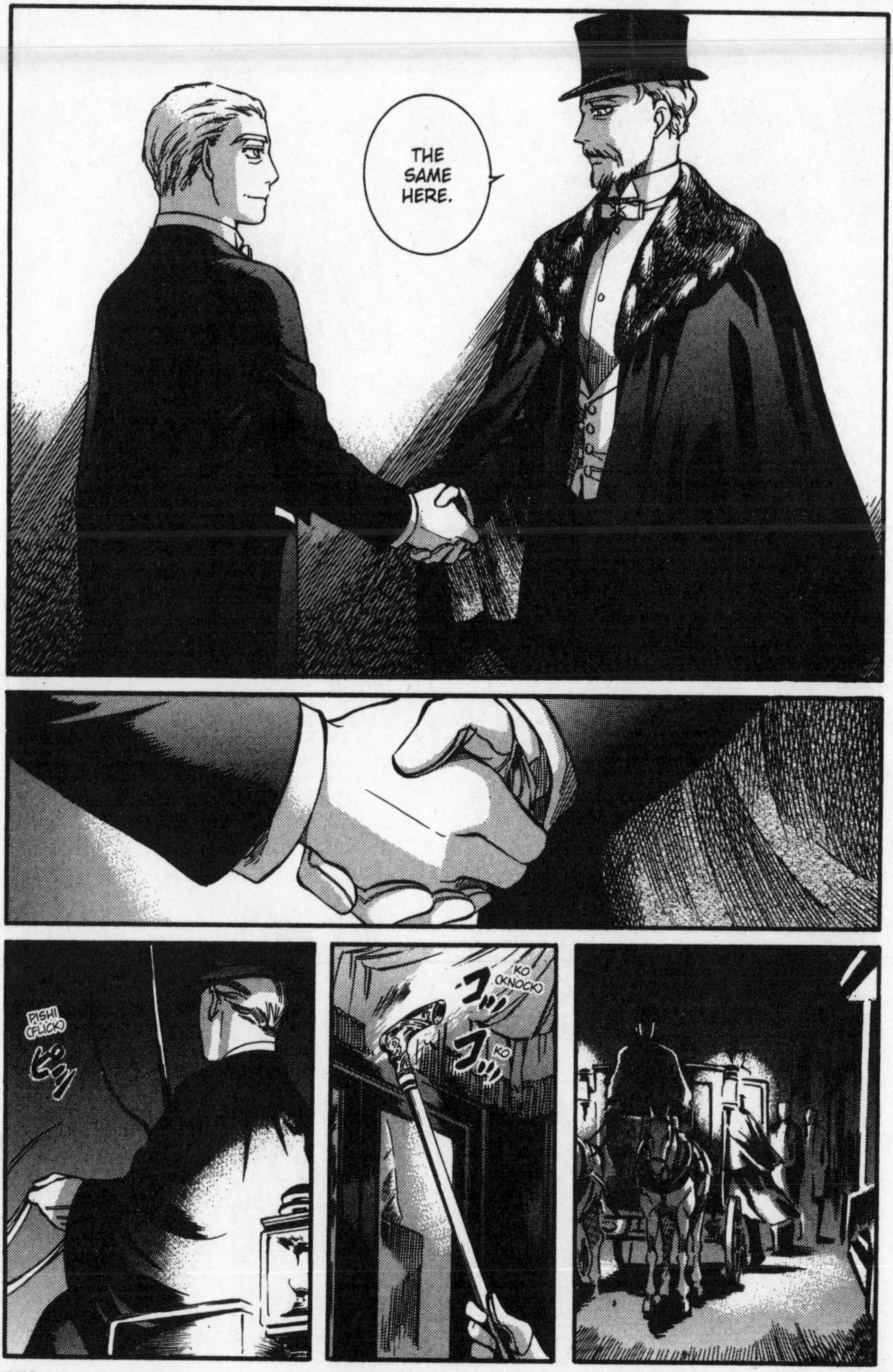
THE SAME HERE.
KO (KNOCK)
KO
PISHI (FLICK)

ガラ
ガラ
ガラ GARA (RATTLE)
ガラ GARA
ガラ GARA

....

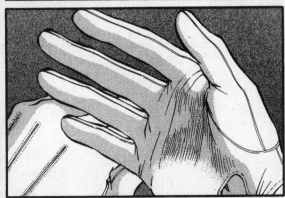

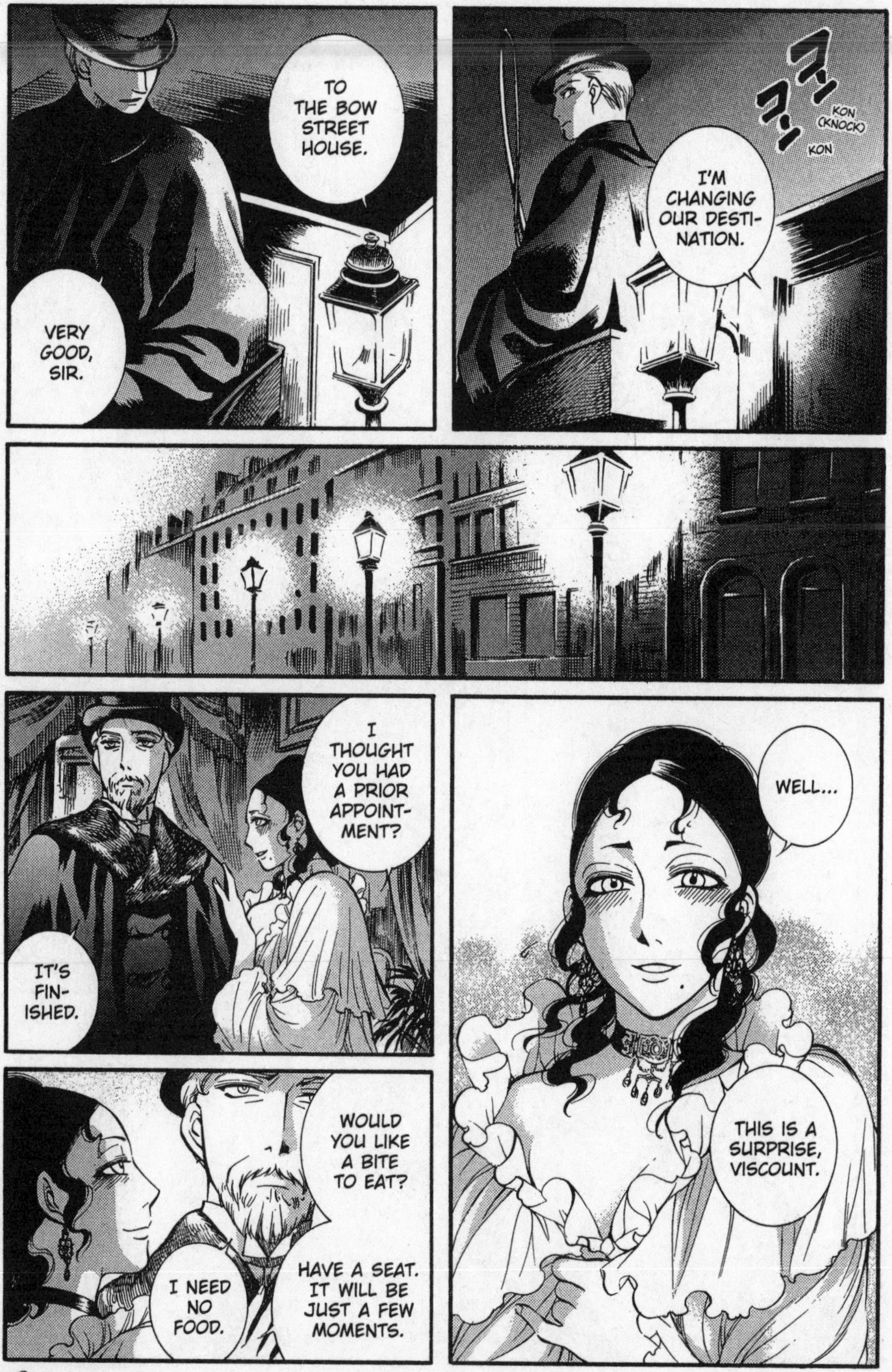
KON (KNOCK)
KON
I'M CHANGING OUR DESTI-NATION.
TO THE BOW STREET HOUSE.
VERY GOOD, SIR.
WELL...
THIS IS A SURPRISE, VISCOUNT.
I THOUGHT YOU HAD A PRIOR APPOINT-MENT?
IT'S FIN-ISHED.
WOULD YOU LIKE A BITE TO EAT?
HAVE A SEAT. IT WILL BE JUST A FEW MOMENTS.
I NEED NO FOOD.

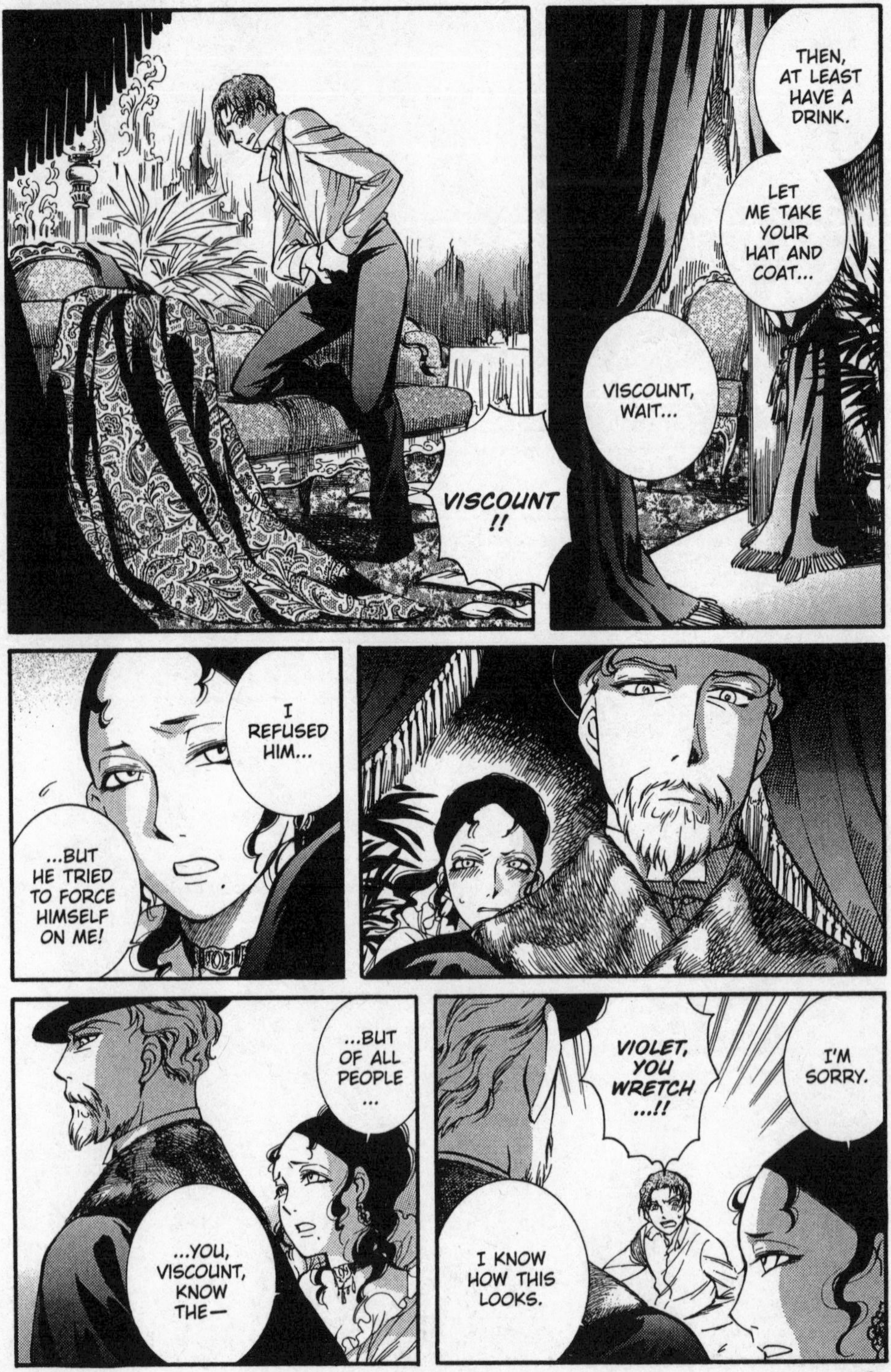
THEN, AT LEAST HAVE A DRINK.
LET ME TAKE YOUR HAT AND COAT...
VISCOUNT, WAIT...
VISCOUNT!!
I REFUSED HIM...
...BUT HE TRIED TO FORCE HIMSELF ON ME!
I'M SORRY.
VIOLET, YOU WRETCH...!!
I KNOW HOW THIS LOOKS.
...BUT OF ALL PEOPLE...
...YOU, VISCOUNT, KNOW THE—

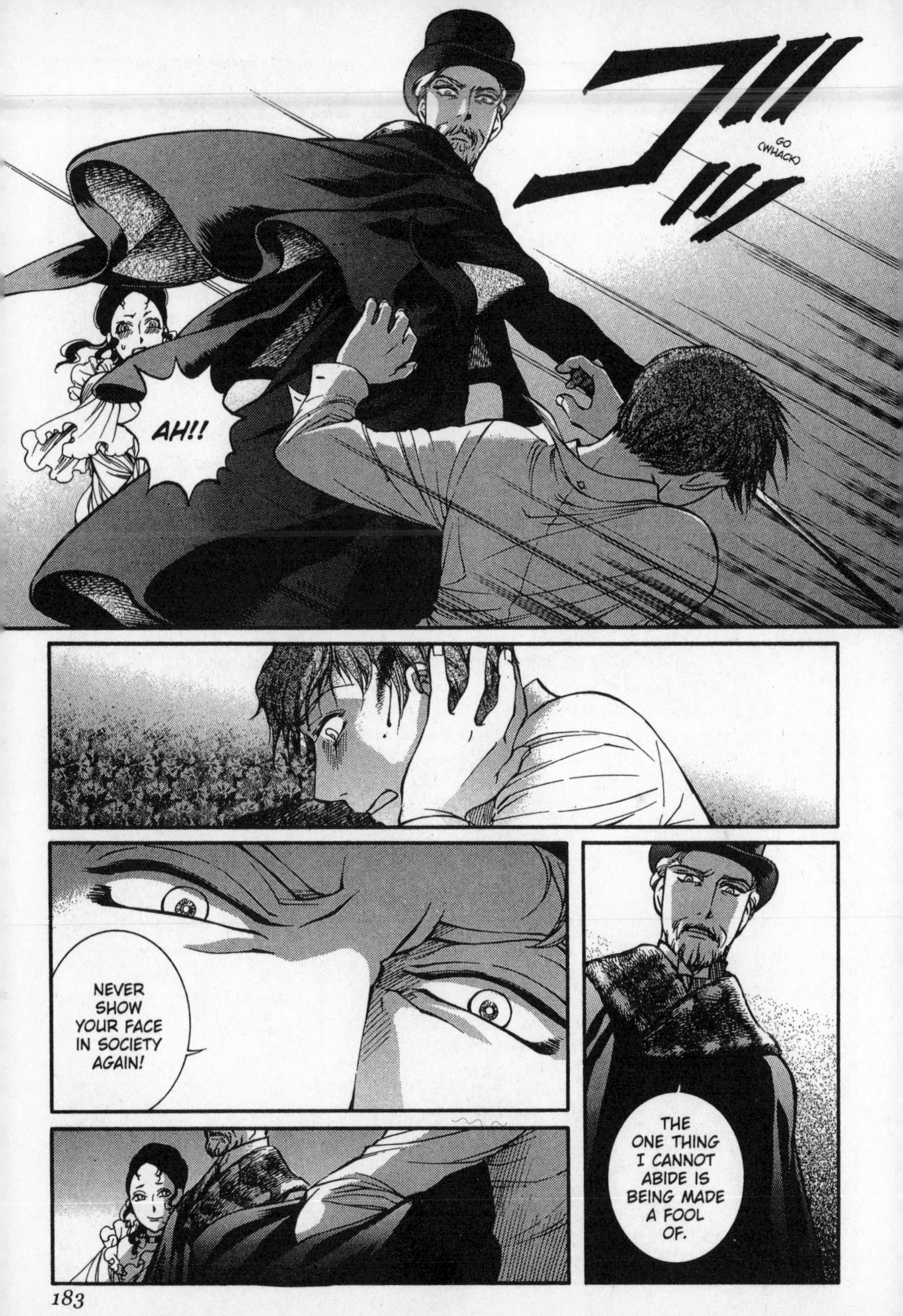
GO (WHACK)
AH!!
THE ONE THING I CANNOT ABIDE IS BEING MADE A FOOL OF.
NEVER SHOW YOUR FACE IN SOCIETY AGAIN!

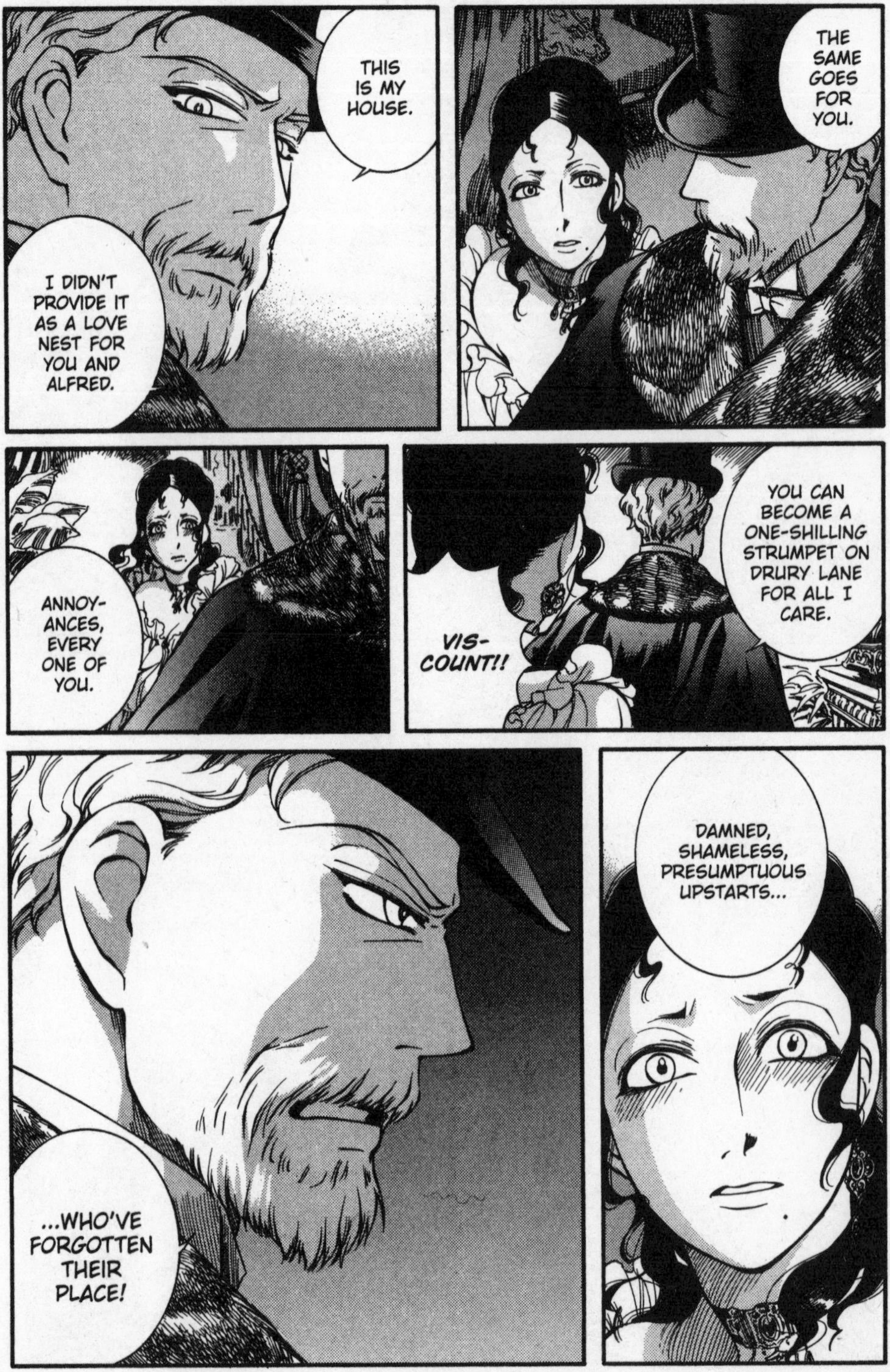
THE SAME GOES FOR YOU.
THIS IS MY HOUSE.
I DIDN'T PROVIDE IT AS A LOVE NEST FOR YOU AND ALFRED.
YOU CAN BECOME A ONE-SHILLING STRUMPET ON DRURY LANE FOR ALL I CARE.
VIS-COUNT!!
ANNOY-ANCES, EVERY ONE OF YOU.
DAMNED, SHAMELESS, PRESUMPTUOUS UPSTARTS...
...WHO'VE FORGOTTEN THEIR PLACE!

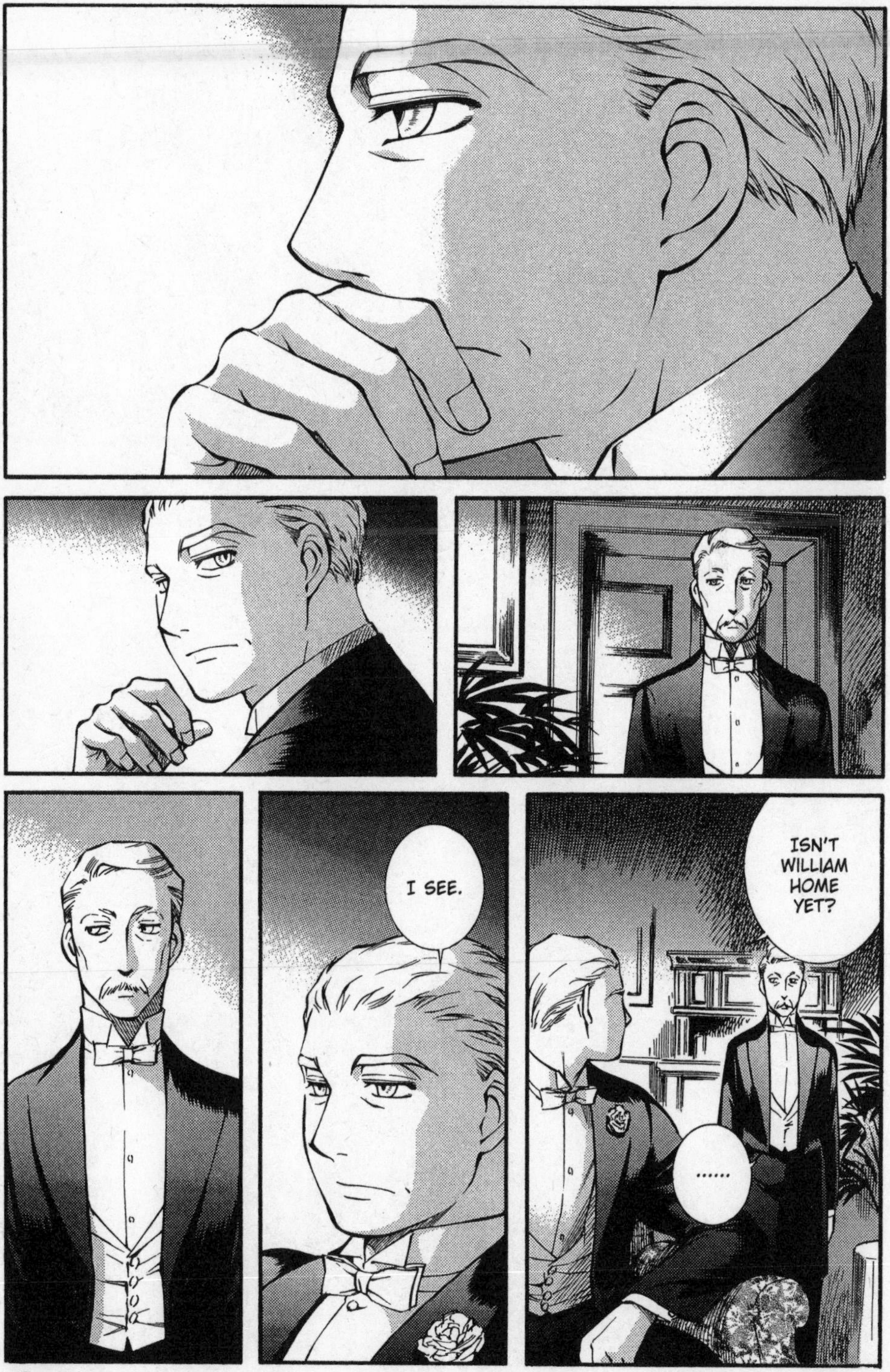
ISN'T WILLIAM HOME YET?
......
I SEE.

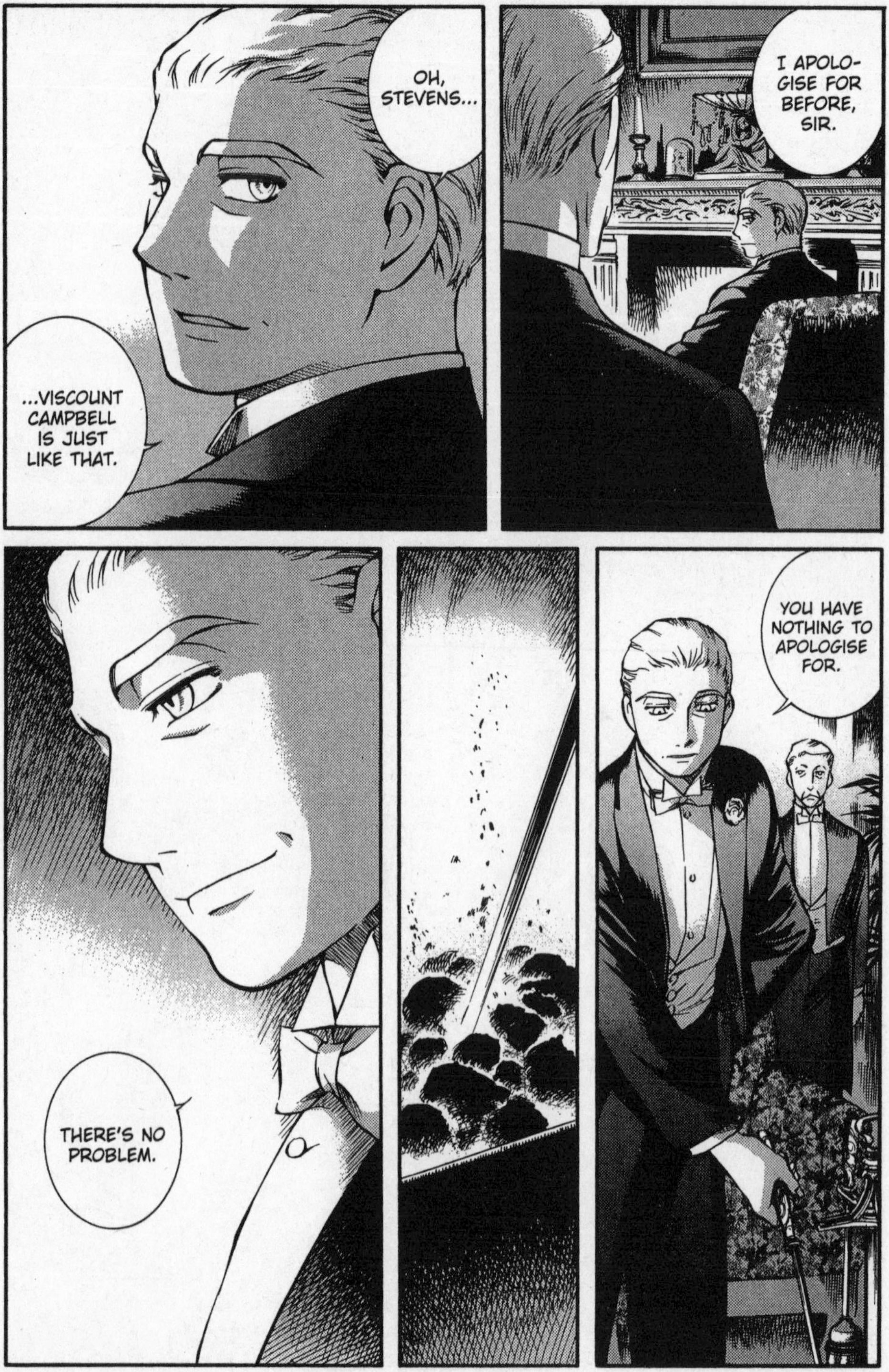
I APOLOGISE FOR BEFORE, SIR.
OH, STEVENS...
...VISCOUNT CAMPBELL IS JUST LIKE THAT.
YOU HAVE NOTHING TO APOLOGISE FOR.
THERE'S NO PROBLEM.

Chapter 36: End

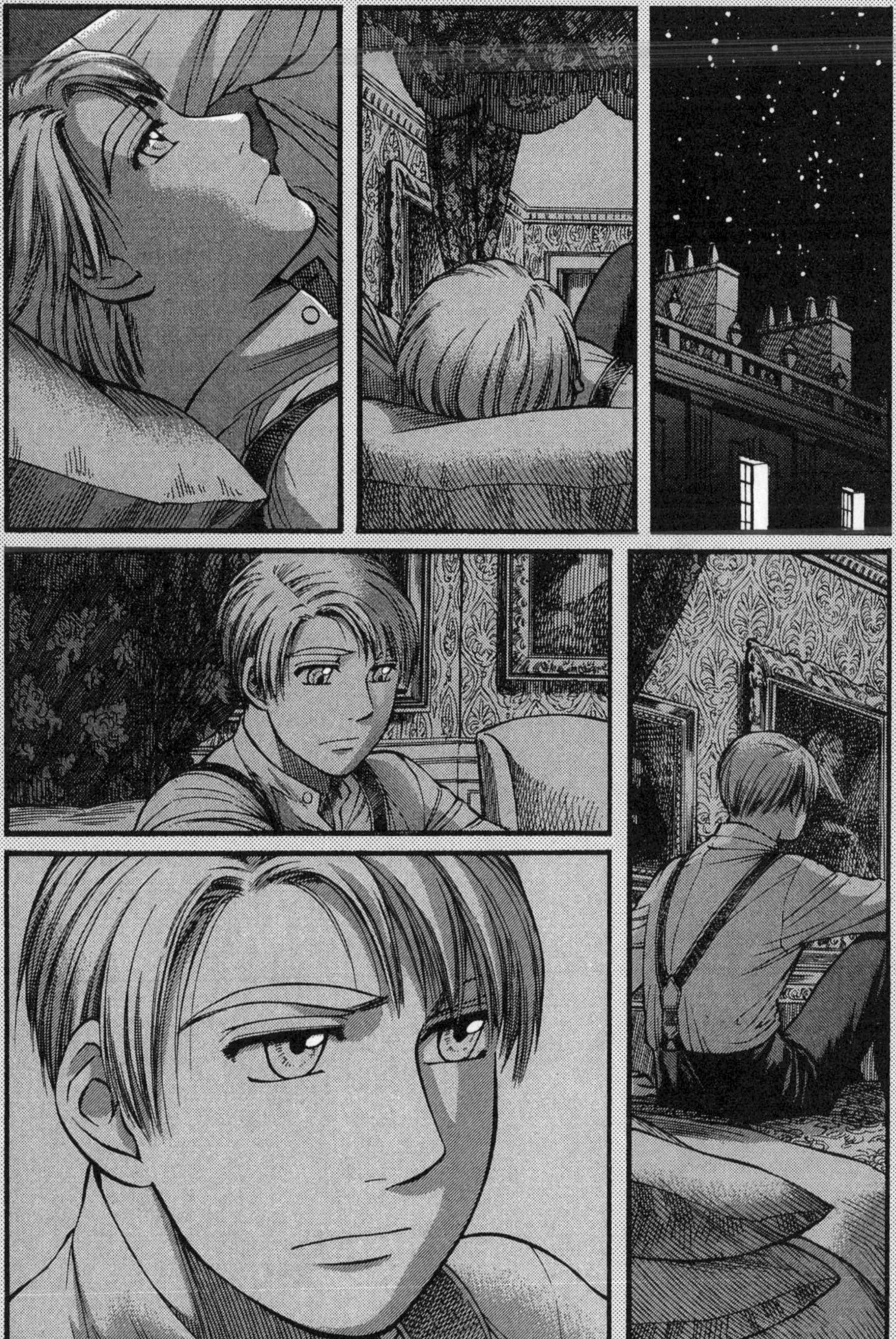

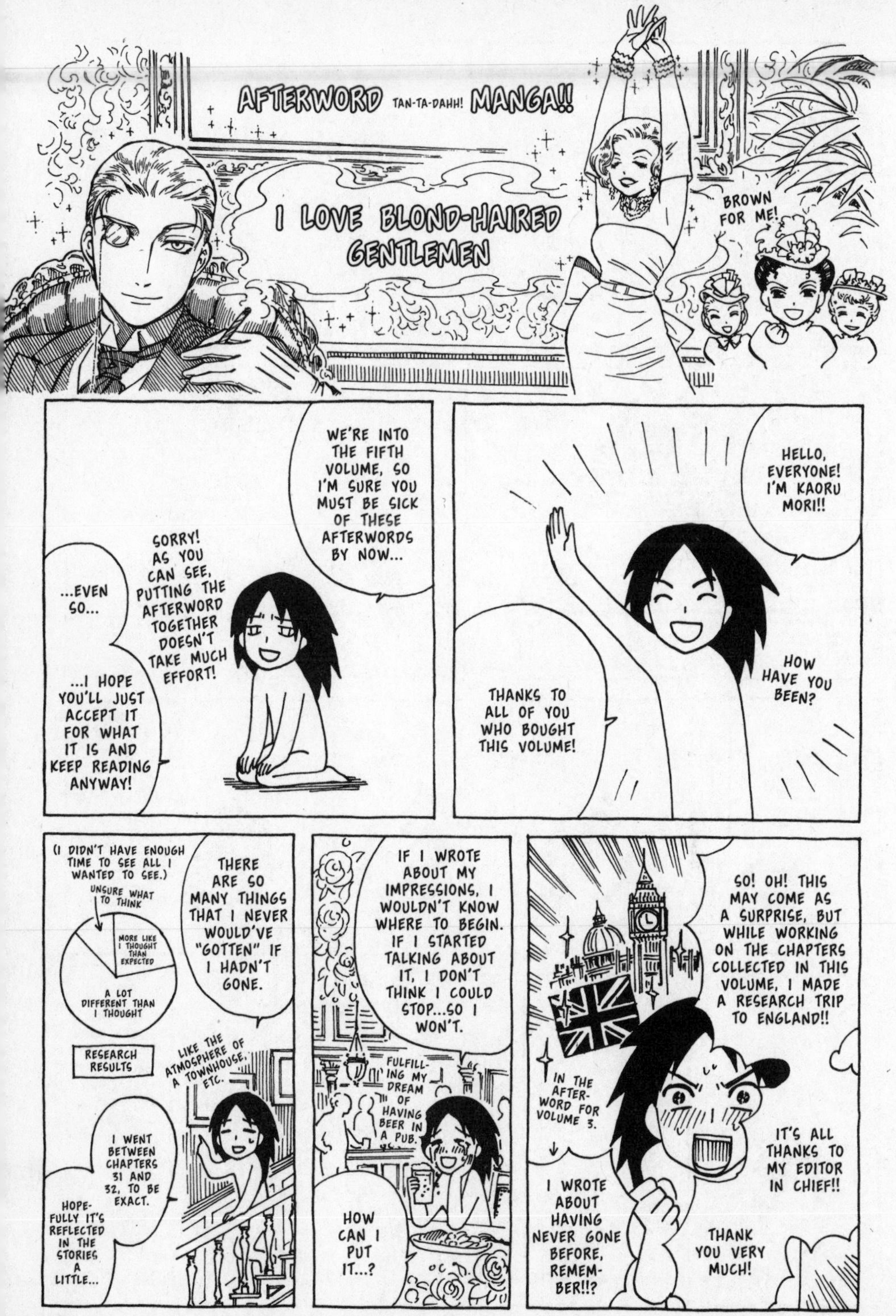
AFTERWORD TAN-TA-DAHH! MANGA!!
I LOVE BLOND-HAIRED GENTLEMEN
BROWN FOR ME!
HELLO, EVERYONE! I'M KAORU MORI!!
HOW HAVE YOU BEEN?
THANKS TO ALL OF YOU WHO BOUGHT THIS VOLUME!
WE'RE INTO THE FIFTH VOLUME, SO I'M SURE YOU MUST BE SICK OF THESE AFTERWORDS BY NOW...
SORRY! AS YOU CAN SEE, PUTTING THE AFTERWORD TOGETHER DOESN'T TAKE MUCH EFFORT!
...EVEN SO...
...I HOPE YOU'LL JUST ACCEPT IT FOR WHAT IT IS AND KEEP READING ANYWAY!
SO! OH! THIS MAY COME AS A SURPRISE, BUT WHILE WORKING ON THE CHAPTERS COLLECTED IN THIS VOLUME, I MADE A RESEARCH TRIP TO ENGLAND!!
IN THE AFTERWORD FOR VOLUME 3.
IT'S ALL THANKS TO MY EDITOR IN CHIEF!!
I WROTE ABOUT HAVING NEVER GONE BEFORE, REMEMBER!!?
THANK YOU VERY MUCH!
IF I WROTE ABOUT MY IMPRESSIONS, I WOULDN'T KNOW WHERE TO BEGIN. IF I STARTED TALKING ABOUT IT, I DON'T THINK I COULD STOP...SO I WON'T.
FULFILLING MY DREAM OF HAVING BEER IN A PUB.
HOW CAN I PUT IT...?
THERE ARE SO MANY THINGS THAT I NEVER WOULD'VE "GOTTEN" IF I HADN'T GONE.
(I DIDN'T HAVE ENOUGH TIME TO SEE ALL I WANTED TO SEE.)
UNSURE WHAT TO THINK
MORE LIKE I THOUGHT THAN EXPECTED
A LOT DIFFERENT THAN I THOUGHT
RESEARCH RESULTS
LIKE THE ATMOSPHERE OF A TOWNHOUSE, ETC.
I WENT BETWEEN CHAPTERS 31 AND 32, TO BE EXACT.
HOPEFULLY IT'S REFLECTED IN THE STORIES A LITTLE...

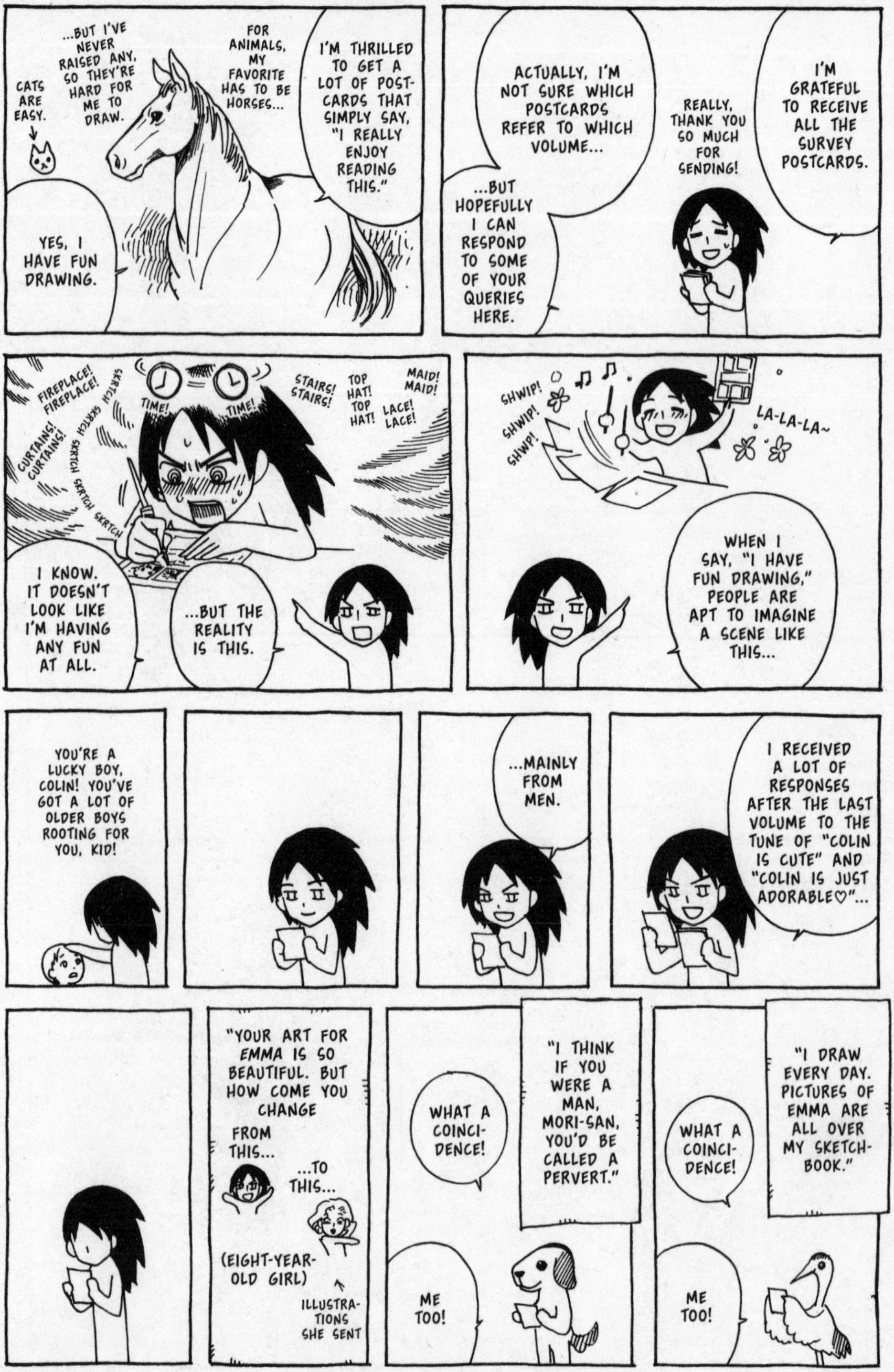
I'M GRATEFUL TO RECEIVE ALL THE SURVEY POSTCARDS.
REALLY, THANK YOU SO MUCH FOR SENDING!
ACTUALLY, I'M NOT SURE WHICH POSTCARDS REFER TO WHICH VOLUME...
...BUT HOPEFULLY I CAN RESPOND TO SOME OF YOUR QUERIES HERE.
I'M THRILLED TO GET A LOT OF POST-CARDS THAT SIMPLY SAY, "I REALLY ENJOY READING THIS."
FOR ANIMALS, MY FAVORITE HAS TO BE HORSES...
...BUT I'VE NEVER RAISED ANY, SO THEY'RE HARD FOR ME TO DRAW.
CATS ARE EASY.
YES, I HAVE FUN DRAWING.
WHEN I SAY, "I HAVE FUN DRAWING," PEOPLE ARE APT TO IMAGINE A SCENE LIKE THIS...
LA-LA-LA~
SHWIP! SHWIP! SHWP!
...BUT THE REALITY IS THIS.
I KNOW. IT DOESN'T LOOK LIKE I'M HAVING ANY FUN AT ALL.
MAID! MAID!
LACE! LACE!
TOP HAT! TOP HAT!
STAIRS! STAIRS!
TIME! TIME!
FIREPLACE! FIREPLACE!
CURTAINS! CURTAINS!
SKRTCH SKRTCH SKRTCH SKRTCH SKRTCH
I RECEIVED A LOT OF RESPONSES AFTER THE LAST VOLUME TO THE TUNE OF "COLIN IS CUTE" AND "COLIN IS JUST ADORABLE♡"...
...MAINLY FROM MEN.
YOU'RE A LUCKY BOY, COLIN! YOU'VE GOT A LOT OF OLDER BOYS ROOTING FOR YOU, KID!
"I DRAW EVERY DAY. PICTURES OF EMMA ARE ALL OVER MY SKETCH-BOOK."
WHAT A COINCI-DENCE!
ME TOO!
"I THINK IF YOU WERE A MAN, MORI-SAN, YOU'D BE CALLED A PERVERT."
WHAT A COINCI-DENCE!
ME TOO!
"YOUR ART FOR EMMA IS SO BEAUTIFUL. BUT HOW COME YOU CHANGE
FROM THIS...
...TO THIS...
(EIGHT-YEAR-OLD GIRL)
ILLUSTRA-TIONS SHE SENT

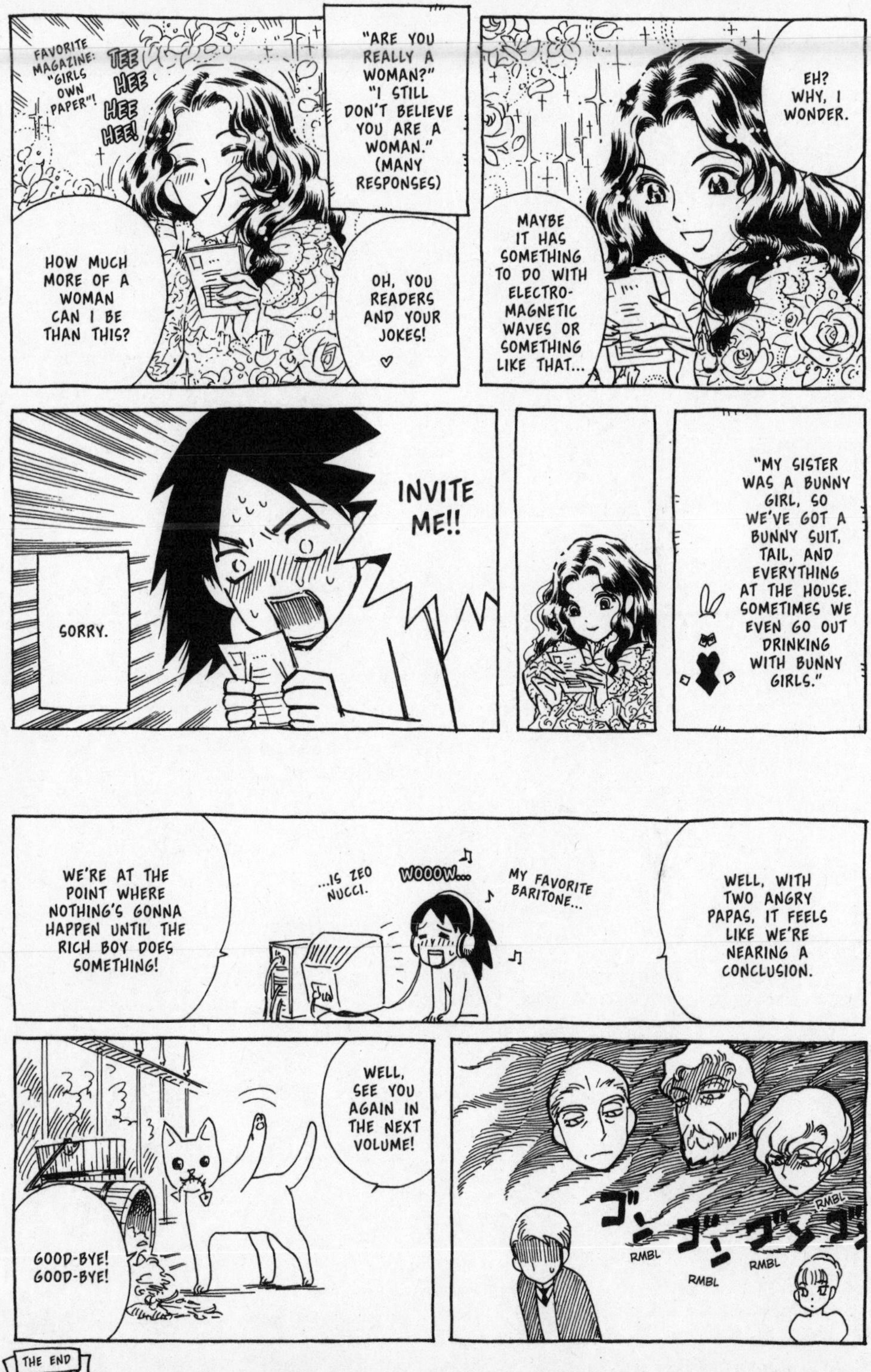
EH? WHY, I WONDER.
MAYBE IT HAS SOMETHING TO DO WITH ELECTRO-MAGNETIC WAVES OR SOMETHING LIKE THAT...
"ARE YOU REALLY A WOMAN?" "I STILL DON'T BELIEVE YOU ARE A WOMAN." (MANY RESPONSES)
OH, YOU READERS AND YOUR JOKES! ♡
TEE HEE HEE HEE!
FAVORITE MAGAZINE: "GIRLS OWN PAPER"!
HOW MUCH MORE OF A WOMAN CAN I BE THAN THIS?
"MY SISTER WAS A BUNNY GIRL, SO WE'VE GOT A BUNNY SUIT, TAIL, AND EVERYTHING AT THE HOUSE. SOMETIMES WE EVEN GO OUT DRINKING WITH BUNNY GIRLS."
INVITE ME!!
SORRY.
WELL, WITH TWO ANGRY PAPAS, IT FEELS LIKE WE'RE NEARING A CONCLUSION.
MY FAVORITE BARITONE...
WOOOW...
...IS ZEO NUCCI.
WE'RE AT THE POINT WHERE NOTHING'S GONNA HAPPEN UNTIL THE RICH BOY DOES SOMETHING!
RMBL
RMBL
RMBL
RMBL
WELL, SEE YOU AGAIN IN THE NEXT VOLUME!
GOOD-BYE! GOOD-BYE!
THE END

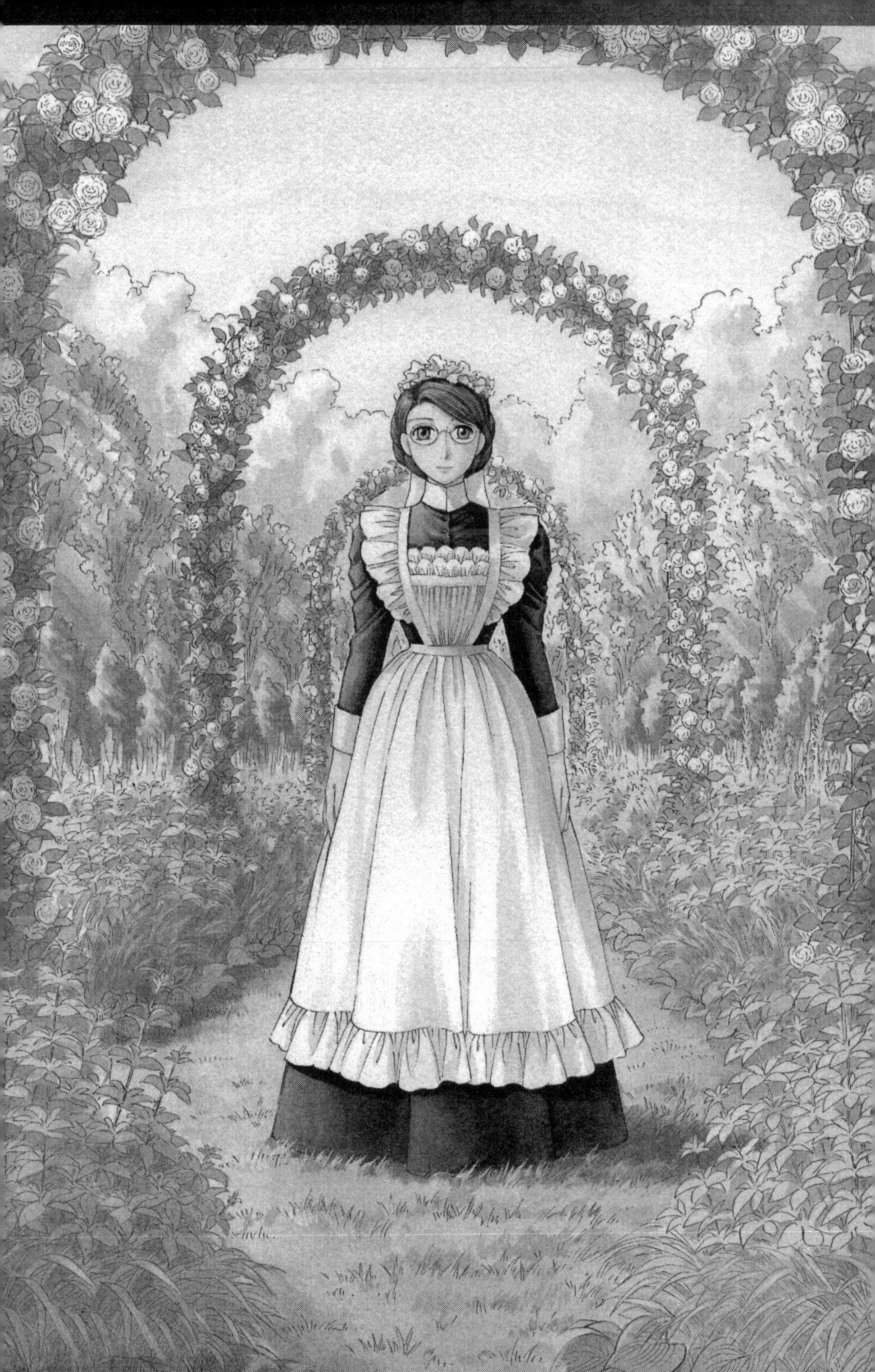

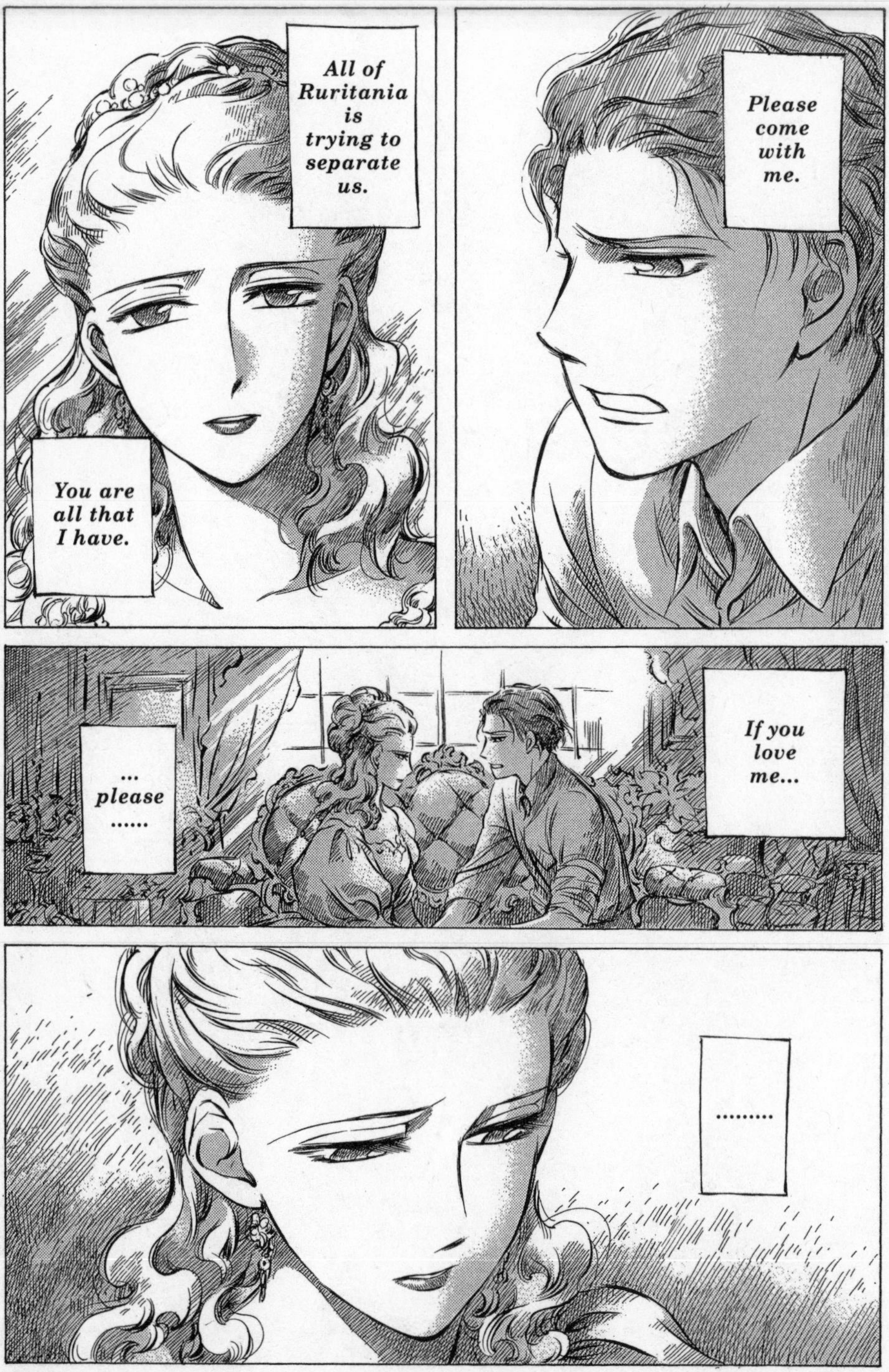
Please come with me.
All of Ruritania is trying to separate us.
You are all that I have.
If you love me...
... please ......
....

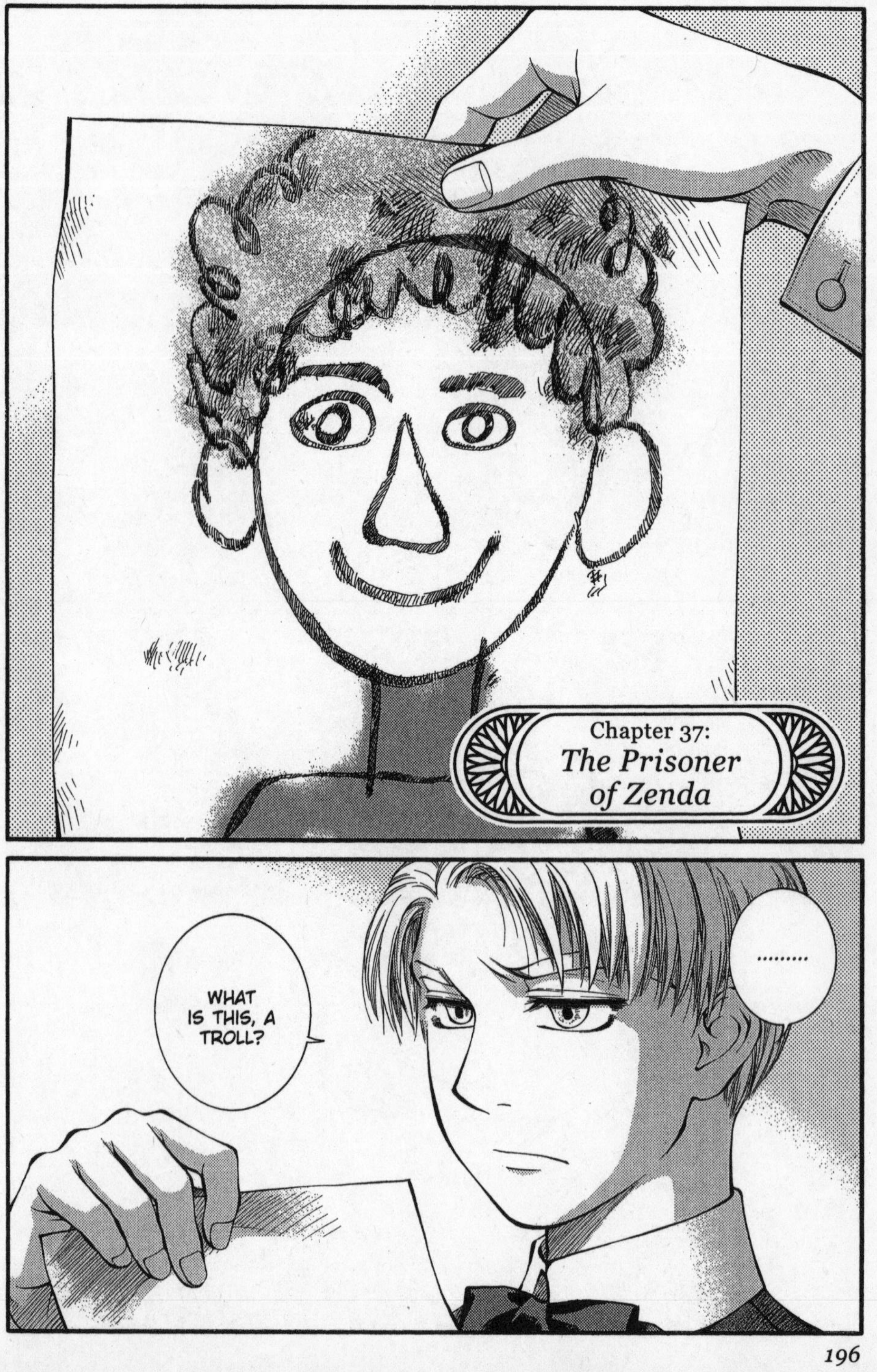
Chapter 37:
The Prisoner of Zenda
....
WHAT IS THIS, A TROLL?

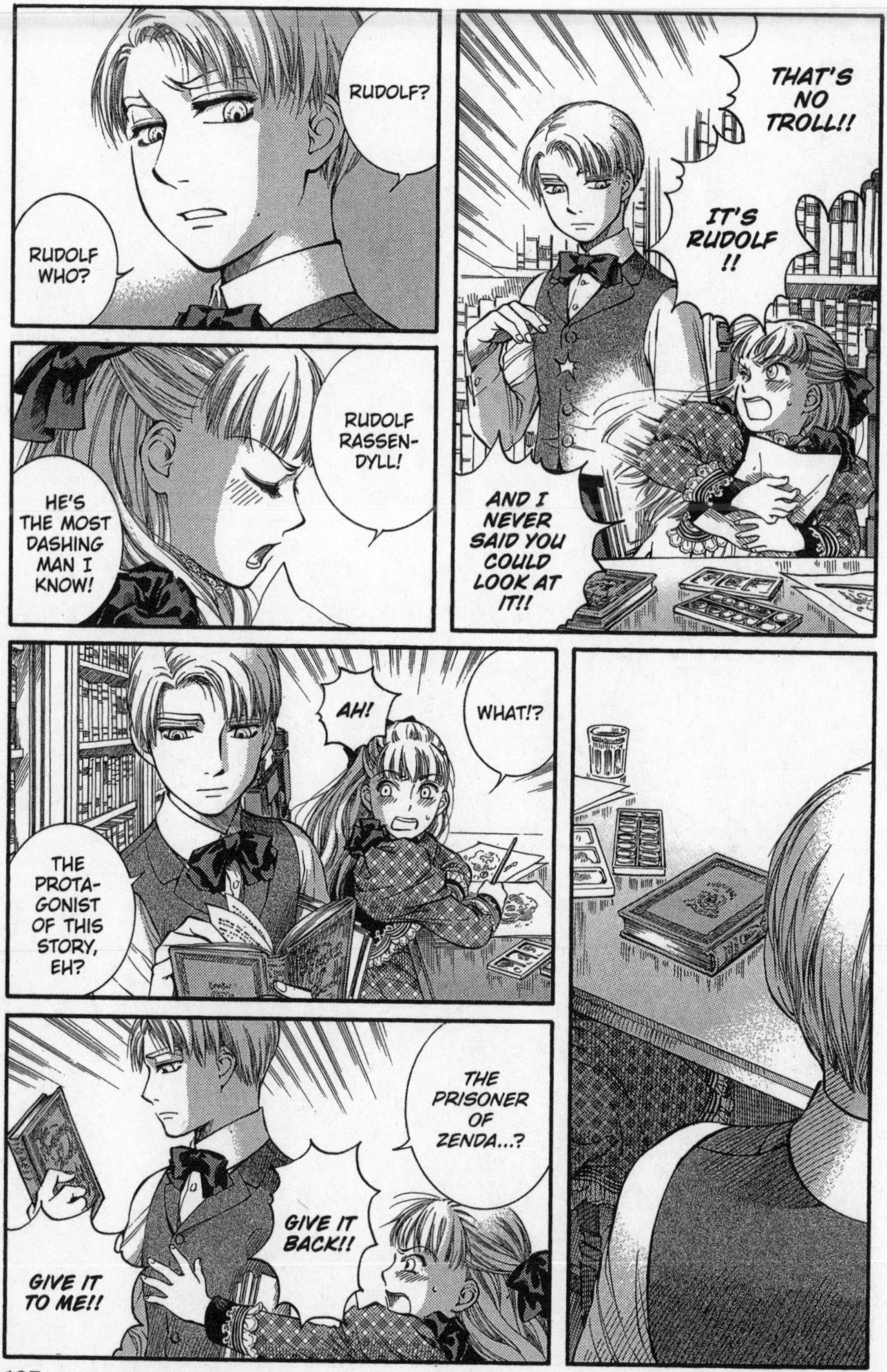
THAT'S NO TROLL!!
IT'S RUDOLF !!
AND I NEVER SAID YOU COULD LOOK AT IT!!
RUDOLF?
RUDOLF WHO?
RUDOLF RASSEN-DYLL!
HE'S THE MOST DASHING MAN I KNOW!
WHAT!?
AH!
THE PROTA-GONIST OF THIS STORY, EH?
THE PRISONER OF ZENDA...?
GIVE IT BACK!!
GIVE IT TO ME!!

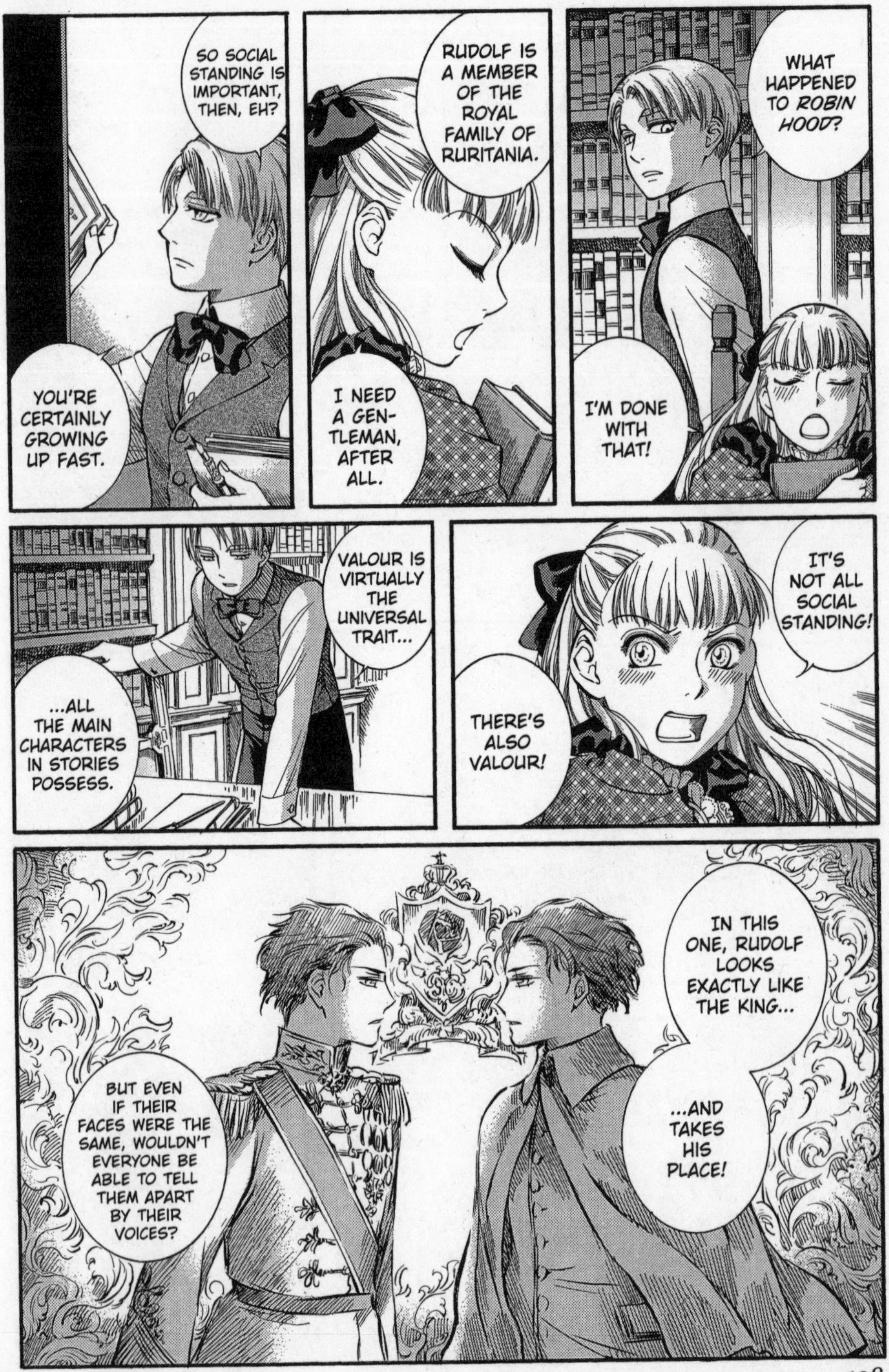
WHAT HAPPENED TO *ROBIN HOOD*?
I'M DONE WITH THAT!
RUDOLF IS A MEMBER OF THE ROYAL FAMILY OF RURITANIA.
I NEED A GENTLEMAN, AFTER ALL.
SO SOCIAL STANDING IS IMPORTANT, THEN, EH?
YOU'RE CERTAINLY GROWING UP FAST.
IT'S NOT ALL SOCIAL STANDING!
THERE'S ALSO VALOUR!
VALOUR IS VIRTUALLY THE UNIVERSAL TRAIT...
...ALL THE MAIN CHARACTERS IN STORIES POSSESS.
IN THIS ONE, RUDOLF LOOKS EXACTLY LIKE THE KING...
...AND TAKES HIS PLACE!
BUT EVEN IF THEIR FACES WERE THE SAME, WOULDN'T EVERYONE BE ABLE TO TELL THEM APART BY THEIR VOICES?

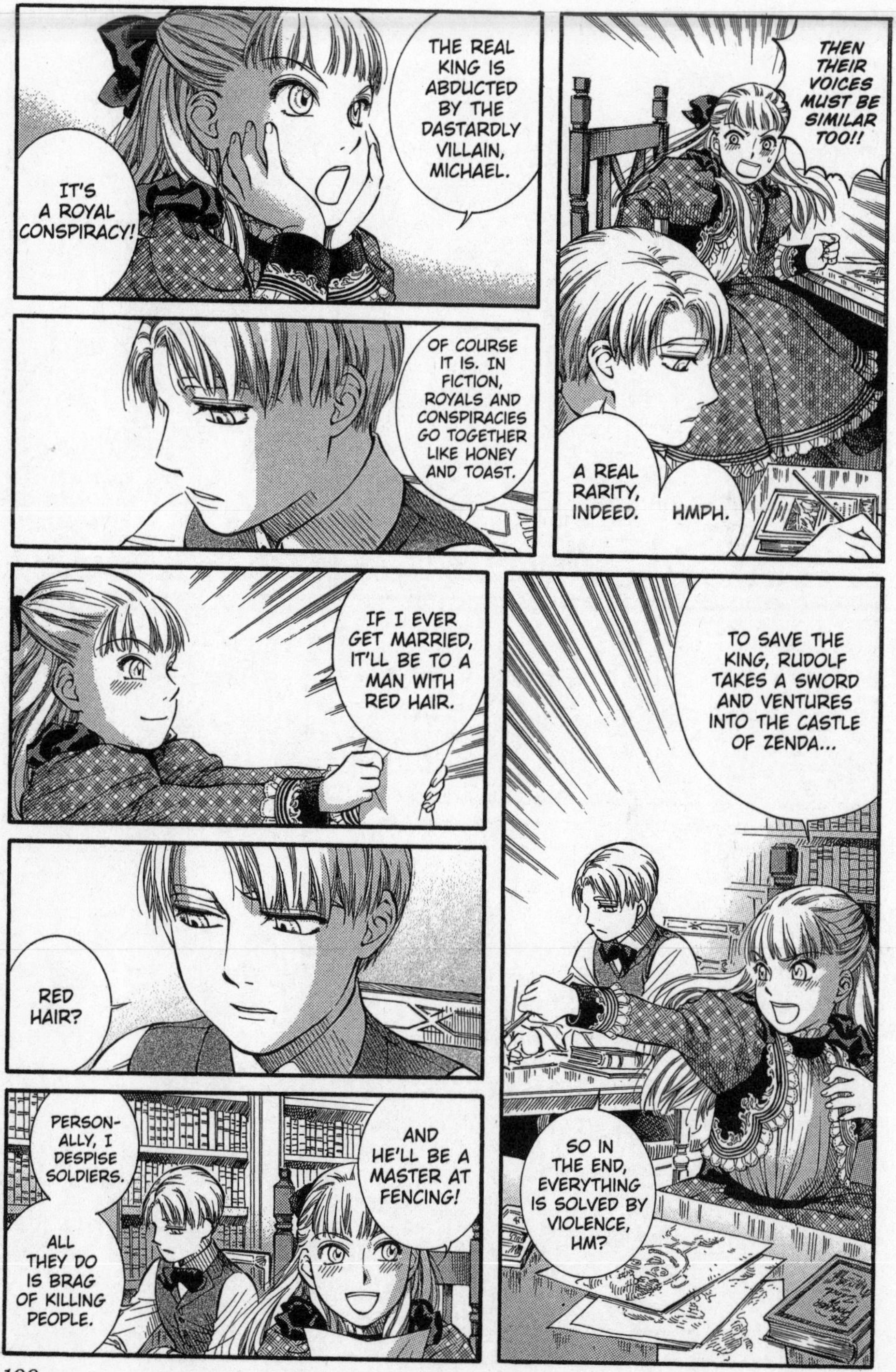
THEN THEIR VOICES MUST BE SIMILAR TOO!!
HMPH.
A REAL RARITY, INDEED.
THE REAL KING IS ABDUCTED BY THE DASTARDLY VILLAIN, MICHAEL.
IT'S A ROYAL CONSPIRACY!
OF COURSE IT IS. IN FICTION, ROYALS AND CONSPIRACIES GO TOGETHER LIKE HONEY AND TOAST.
TO SAVE THE KING, RUDOLF TAKES A SWORD AND VENTURES INTO THE CASTLE OF ZENDA...
SO IN THE END, EVERYTHING IS SOLVED BY VIOLENCE, HM?
IF I EVER GET MARRIED, IT'LL BE TO A MAN WITH RED HAIR.
RED HAIR?
AND HE'LL BE A MASTER AT FENCING!
PERSON-ALLY, I DESPISE SOLDIERS.
ALL THEY DO IS BRAG OF KILLING PEOPLE.

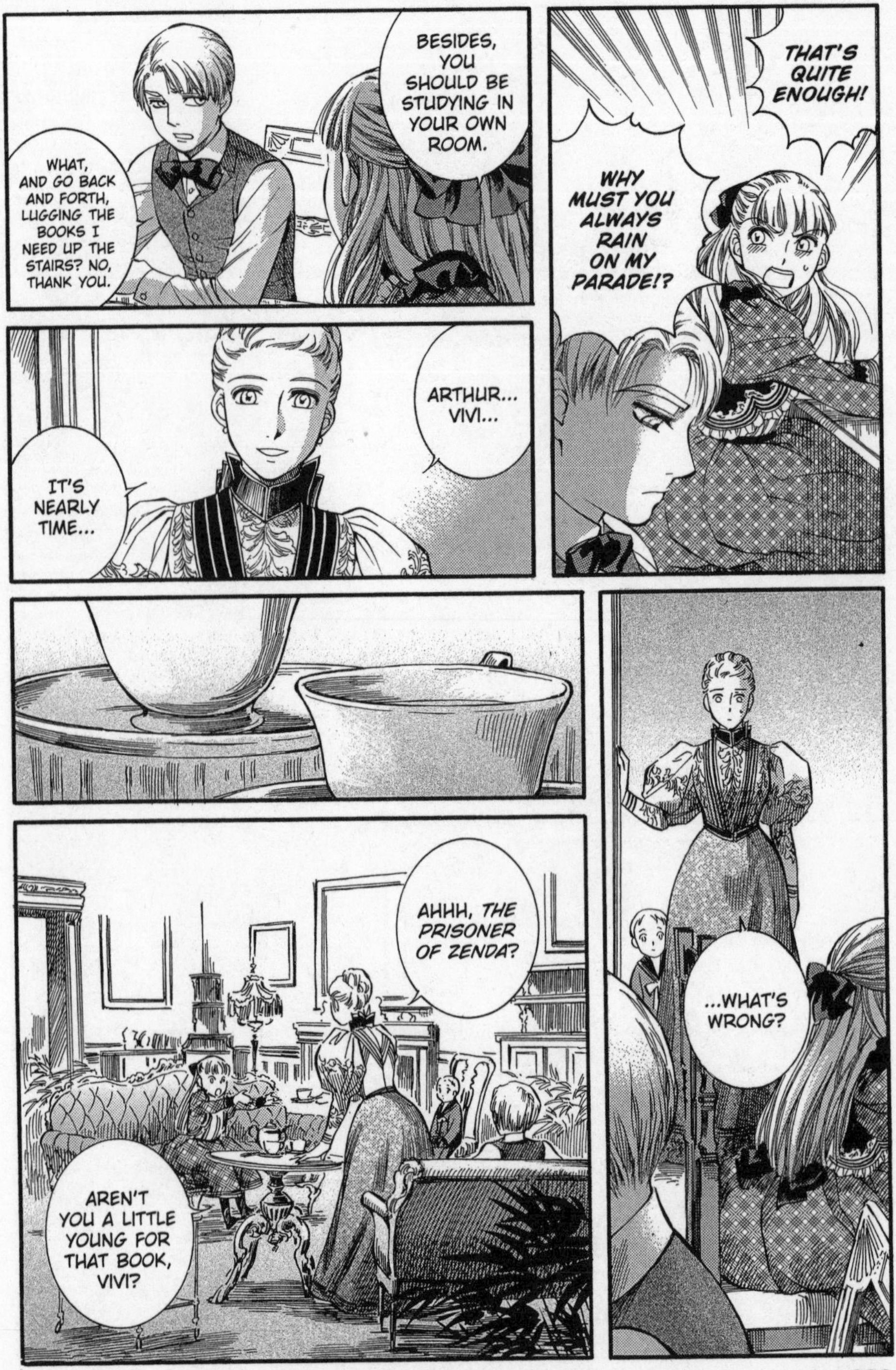
THAT'S QUITE ENOUGH!
WHY MUST YOU ALWAYS RAIN ON MY PARADE!?
BESIDES, YOU SHOULD BE STUDYING IN YOUR OWN ROOM.
WHAT, AND GO BACK AND FORTH, LUGGING THE BOOKS I NEED UP THE STAIRS? NO, THANK YOU.
ARTHUR... VIVI...
IT'S NEARLY TIME...
...WHAT'S WRONG?
AHHH, *THE PRISONER OF ZENDA?*
AREN'T YOU A LITTLE YOUNG FOR THAT BOOK, VIVI?

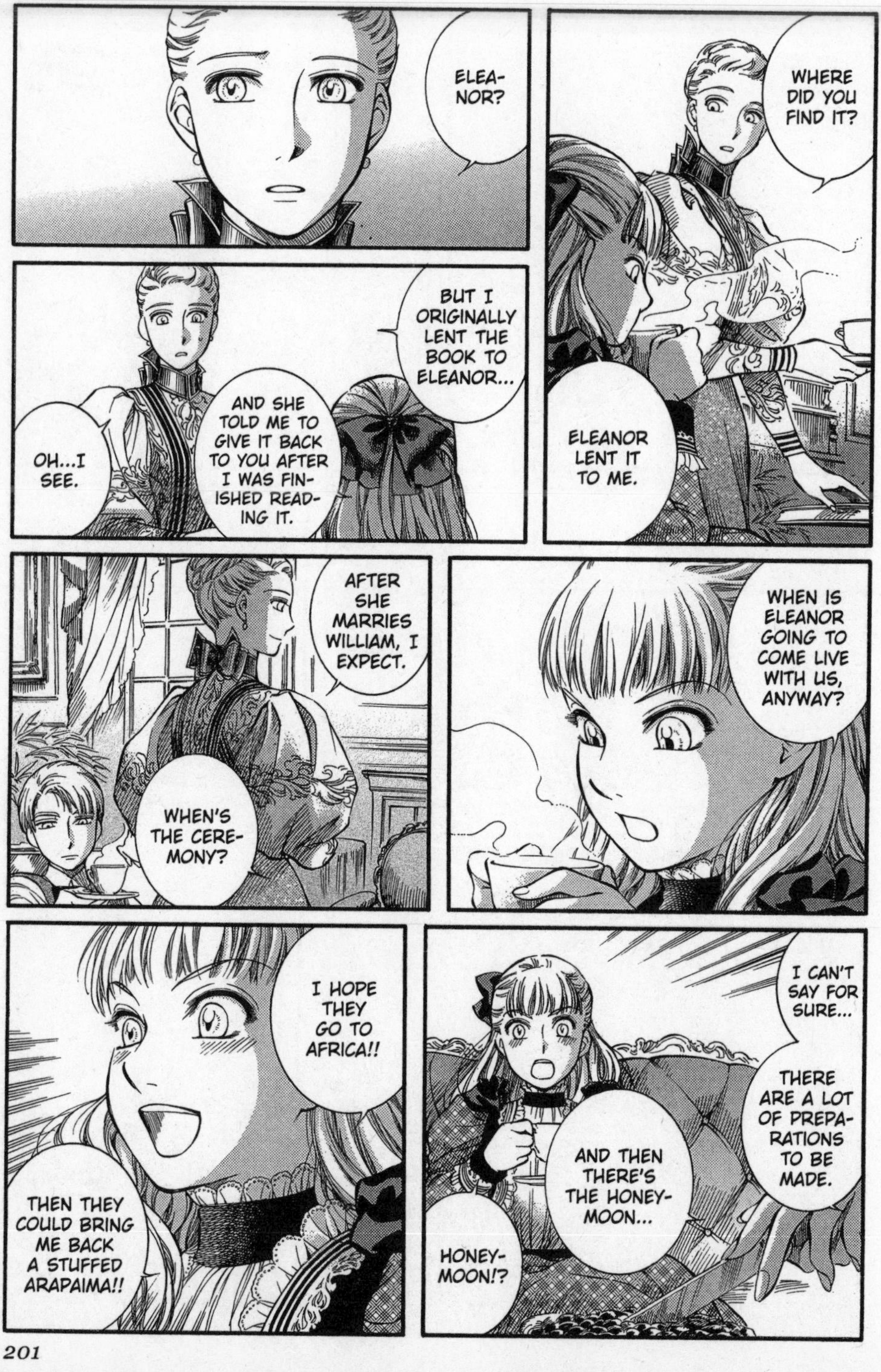
WHERE DID YOU FIND IT?
ELEANOR LENT IT TO ME.
ELEA-NOR?
BUT I ORIGINALLY LENT THE BOOK TO ELEANOR...
AND SHE TOLD ME TO GIVE IT BACK TO YOU AFTER I WAS FIN-ISHED READ-ING IT.
OH...I SEE.
WHEN IS ELEANOR GOING TO COME LIVE WITH US, ANYWAY?
AFTER SHE MARRIES WILLIAM, I EXPECT.
WHEN'S THE CERE-MONY?
I CAN'T SAY FOR SURE...
THERE ARE A LOT OF PREPA-RATIONS TO BE MADE.
AND THEN THERE'S THE HONEY-MOON...
HONEY-MOON!?
I HOPE THEY GO TO AFRICA!!
THEN THEY COULD BRING ME BACK A STUFFED ARAPAIMA!!

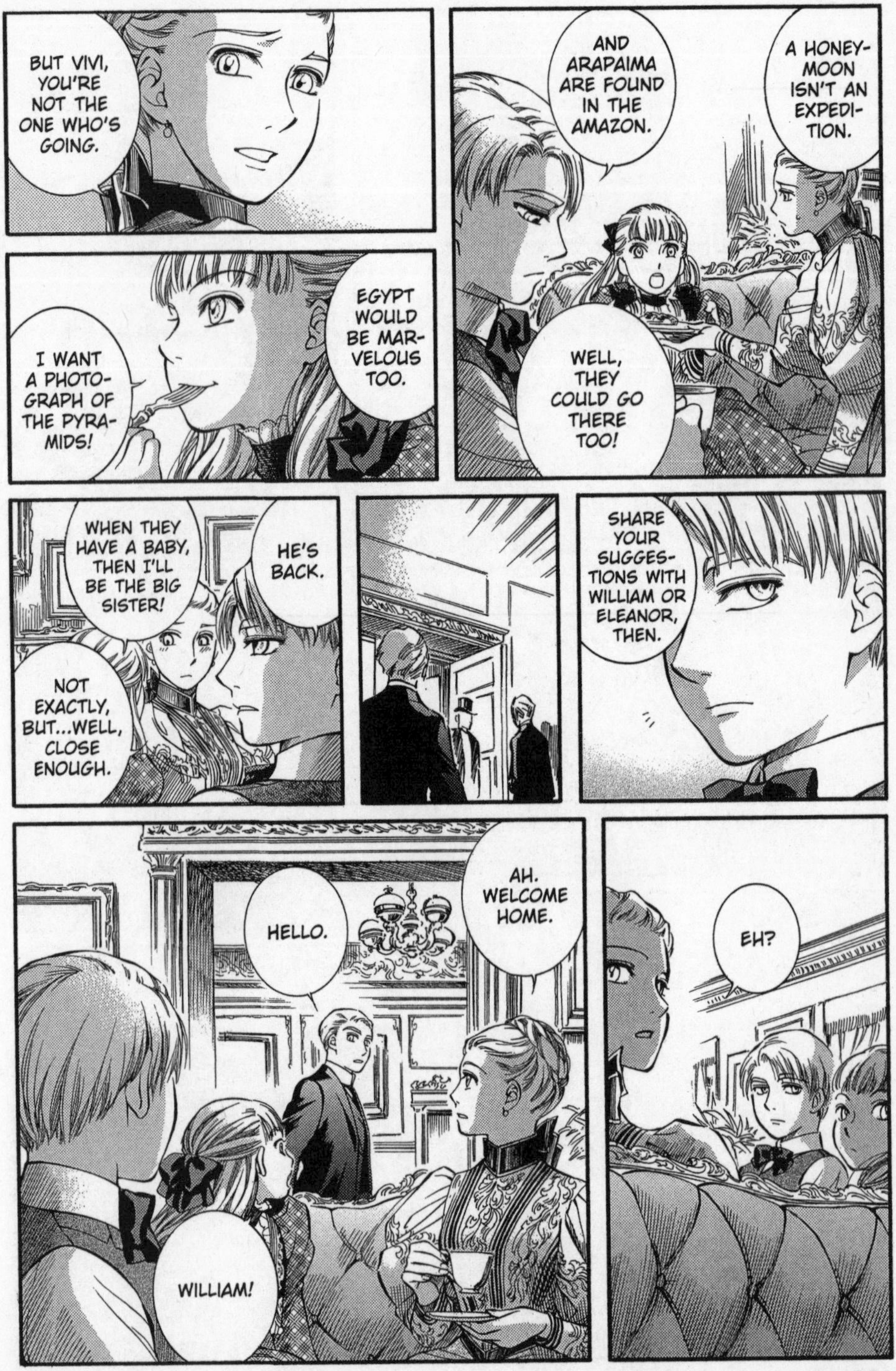
A HONEY-MOON ISN'T AN EXPEDI-TION.
AND ARAPAIMA ARE FOUND IN THE AMAZON.
WELL, THEY COULD GO THERE TOO!
BUT VIVI, YOU'RE NOT THE ONE WHO'S GOING.
EGYPT WOULD BE MAR-VELOUS TOO.
I WANT A PHOTO-GRAPH OF THE PYRA-MIDS!
SHARE YOUR SUGGES-TIONS WITH WILLIAM OR ELEANOR, THEN.
HE'S BACK.
WHEN THEY HAVE A BABY, THEN I'LL BE THE BIG SISTER!
NOT EXACTLY, BUT...WELL, CLOSE ENOUGH.
EH?
AH. WELCOME HOME.
HELLO.
WILLIAM!

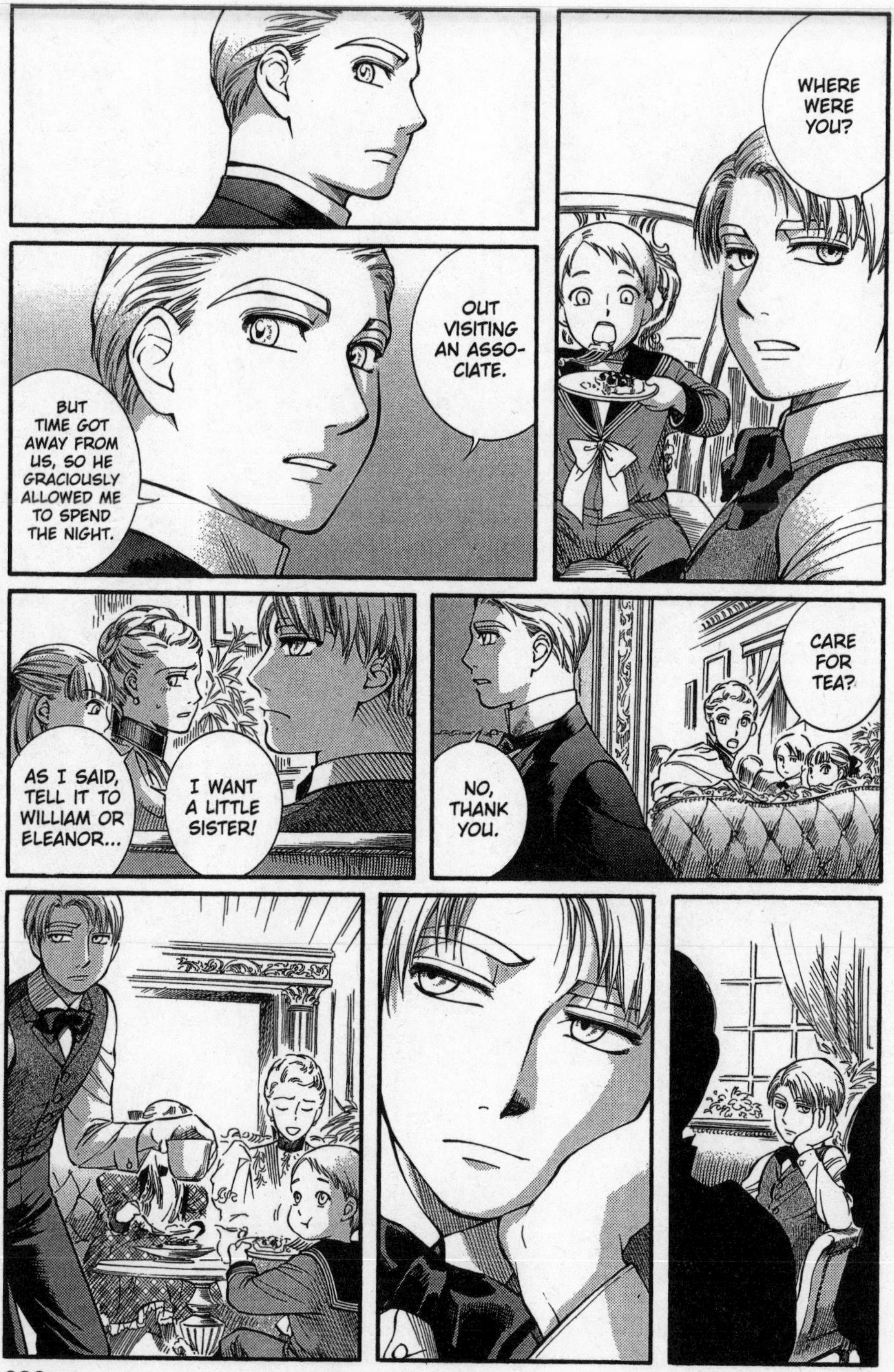
WHERE WERE YOU?
OUT VISITING AN ASSO-CIATE.
BUT TIME GOT AWAY FROM US, SO HE GRACIOUSLY ALLOWED ME TO SPEND THE NIGHT.
CARE FOR TEA?
NO, THANK YOU.
I WANT A LITTLE SISTER!
AS I SAID, TELL IT TO WILLIAM OR ELEANOR...

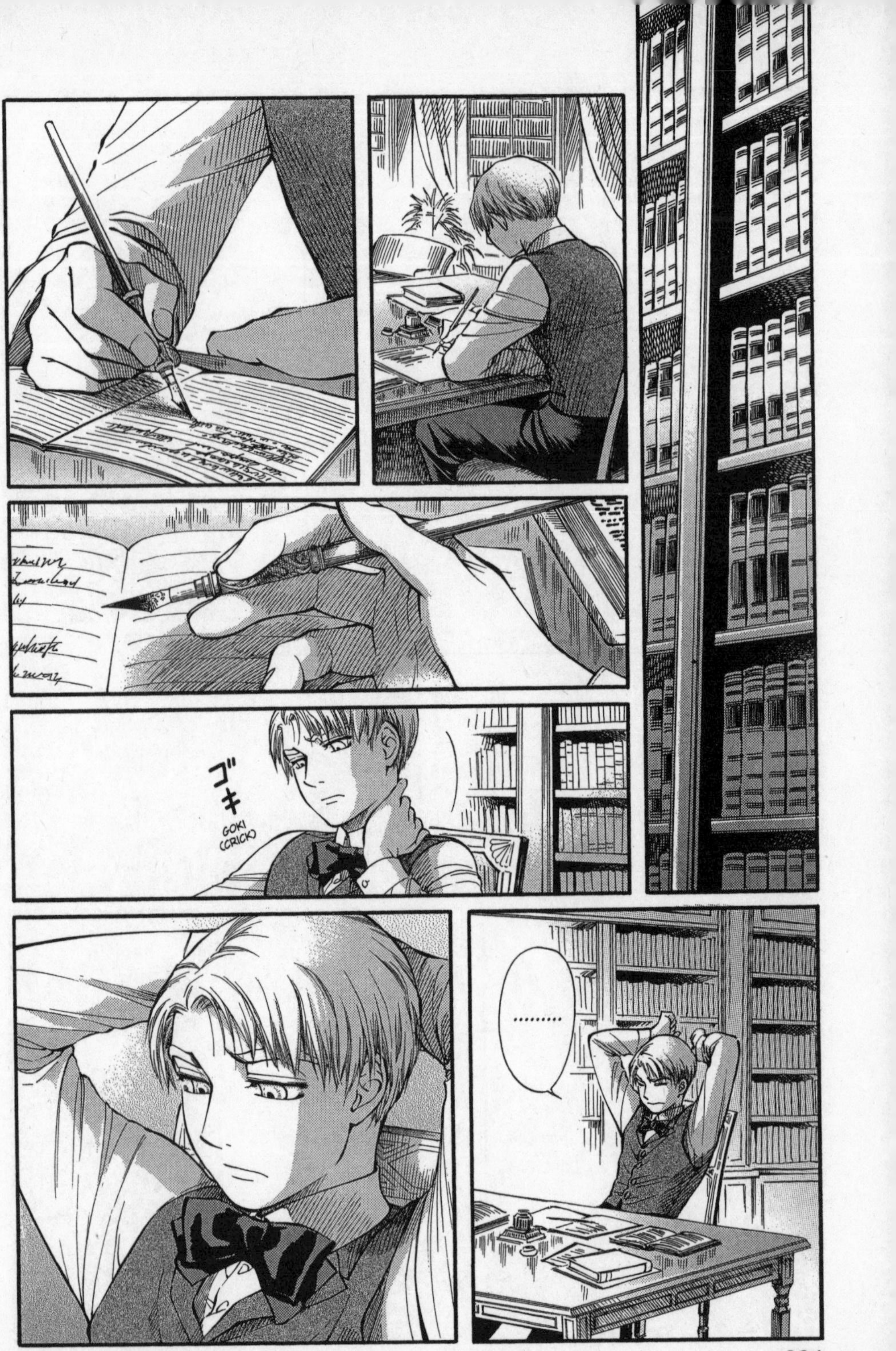

ゴキ
GOKI (CRICK)
....

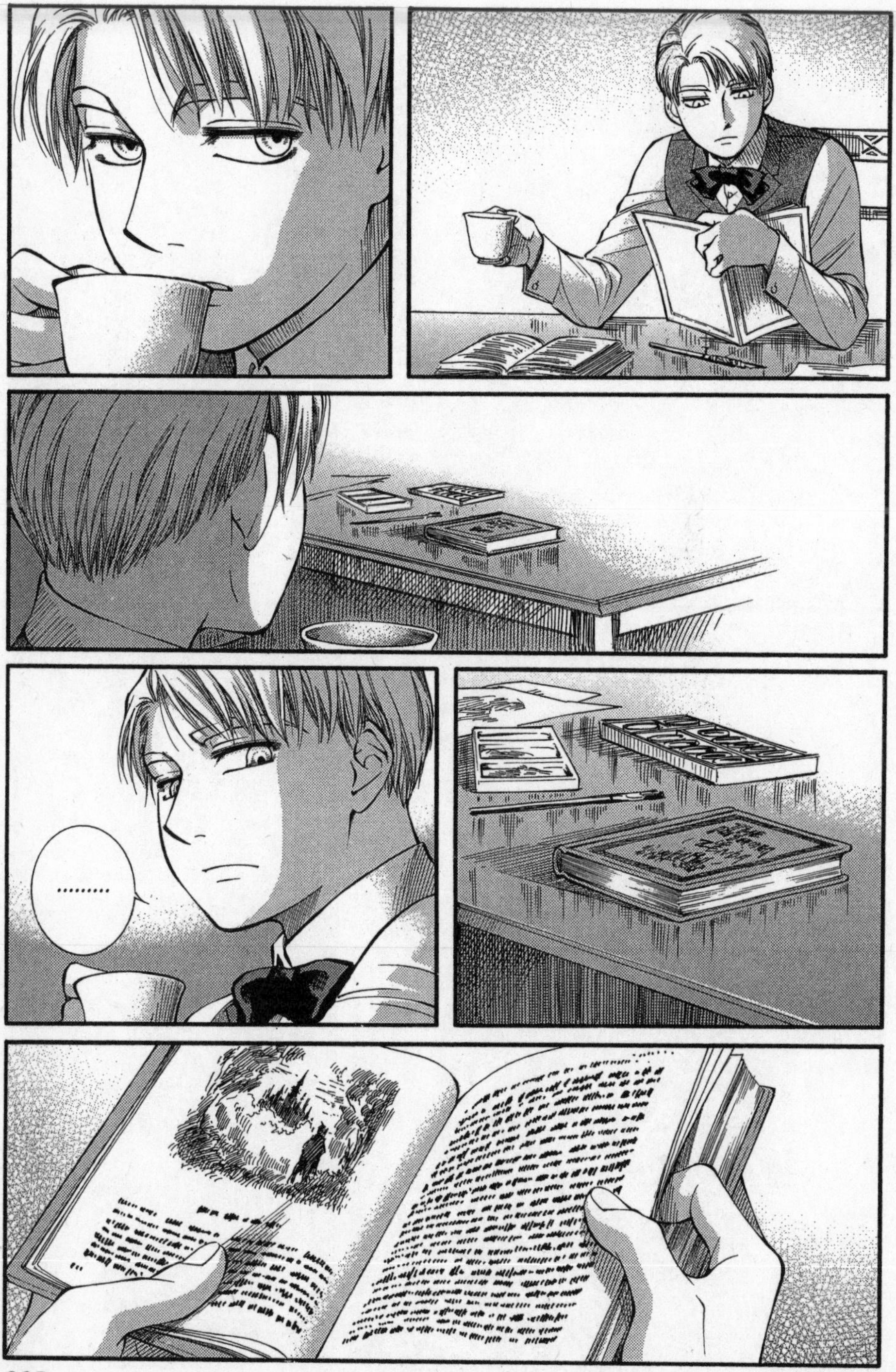
....

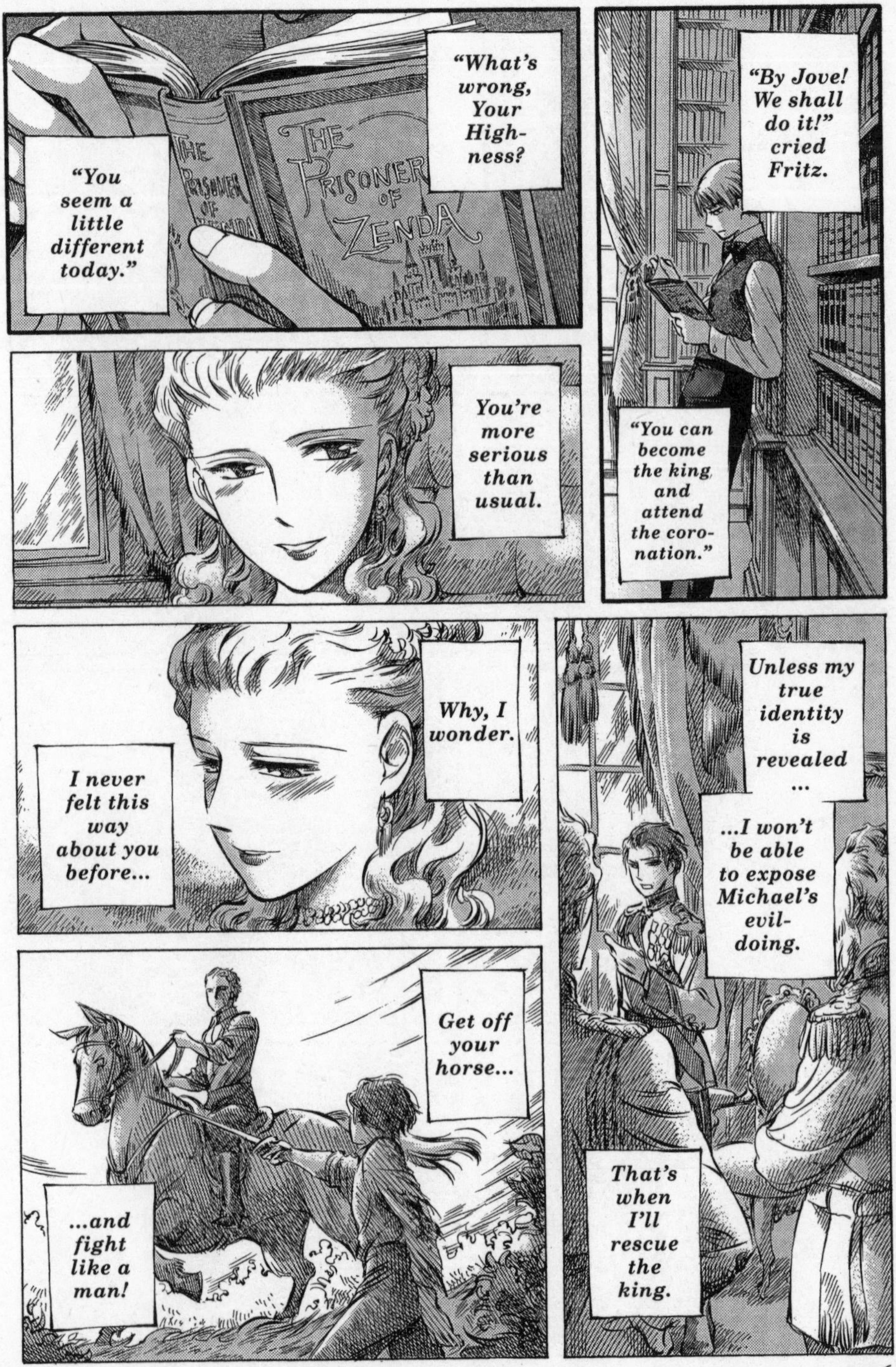
"By Jove! We shall do it!" cried Fritz.
"You can become the king and attend the coro-nation."
"What's wrong, Your High-ness?
THE PRISONER OF ZENDA
"You seem a little different today."
You're more serious than usual.
Unless my true identity is revealed ...
...I won't be able to expose Michael's evil-doing.
That's when I'll rescue the king.
Why, I wonder.
I never felt this way about you before...
Get off your horse...
...and fight like a man!

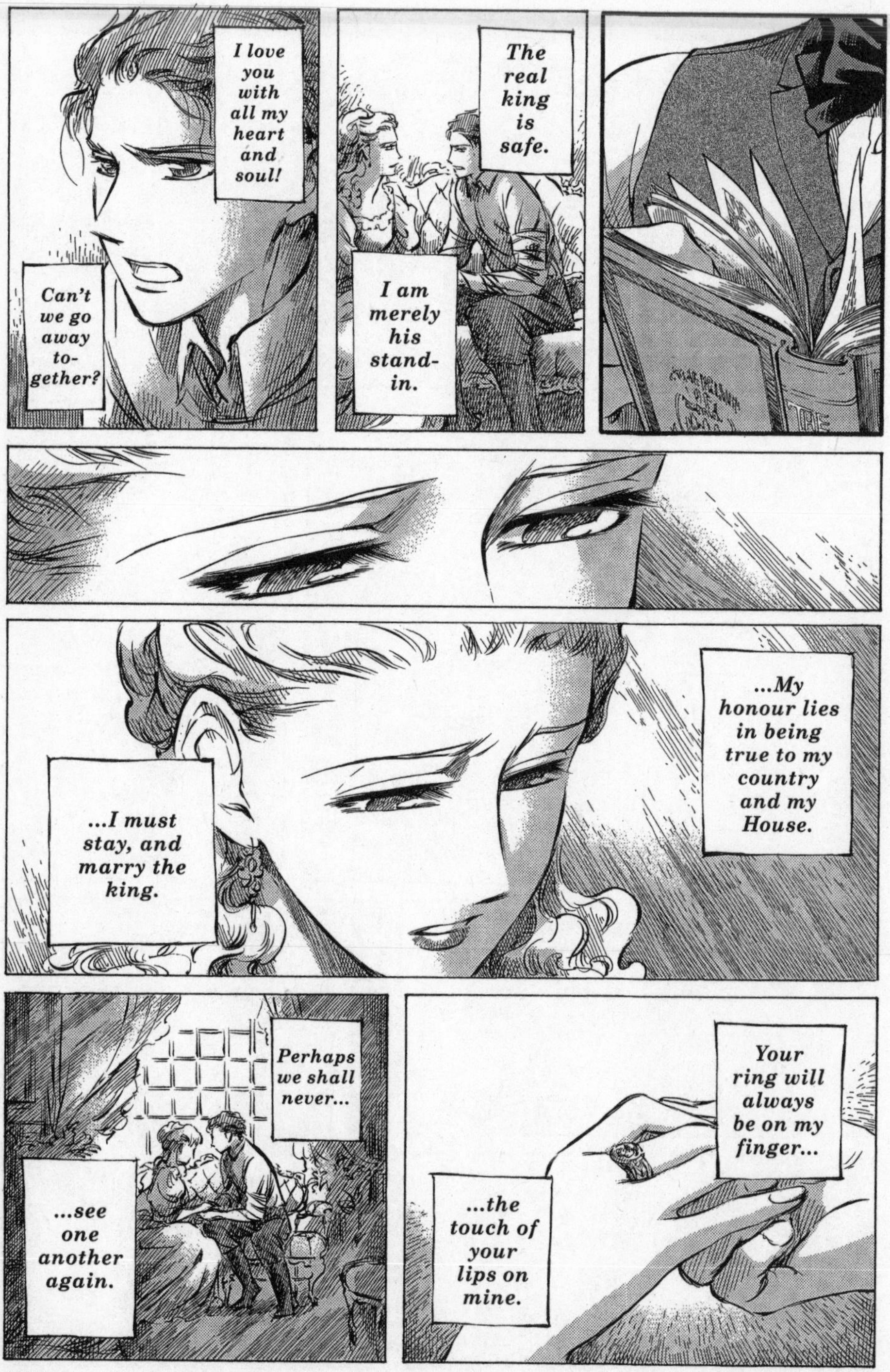
The real king is safe.
I am merely his stand-in.
I love you with all my heart and soul!
Can't we go away together?
...My honour lies in being true to my country and my House.
...I must stay, and marry the king.
Your ring will always be on my finger...
...the touch of your lips on mine.
Perhaps we shall never...
...see one another again.

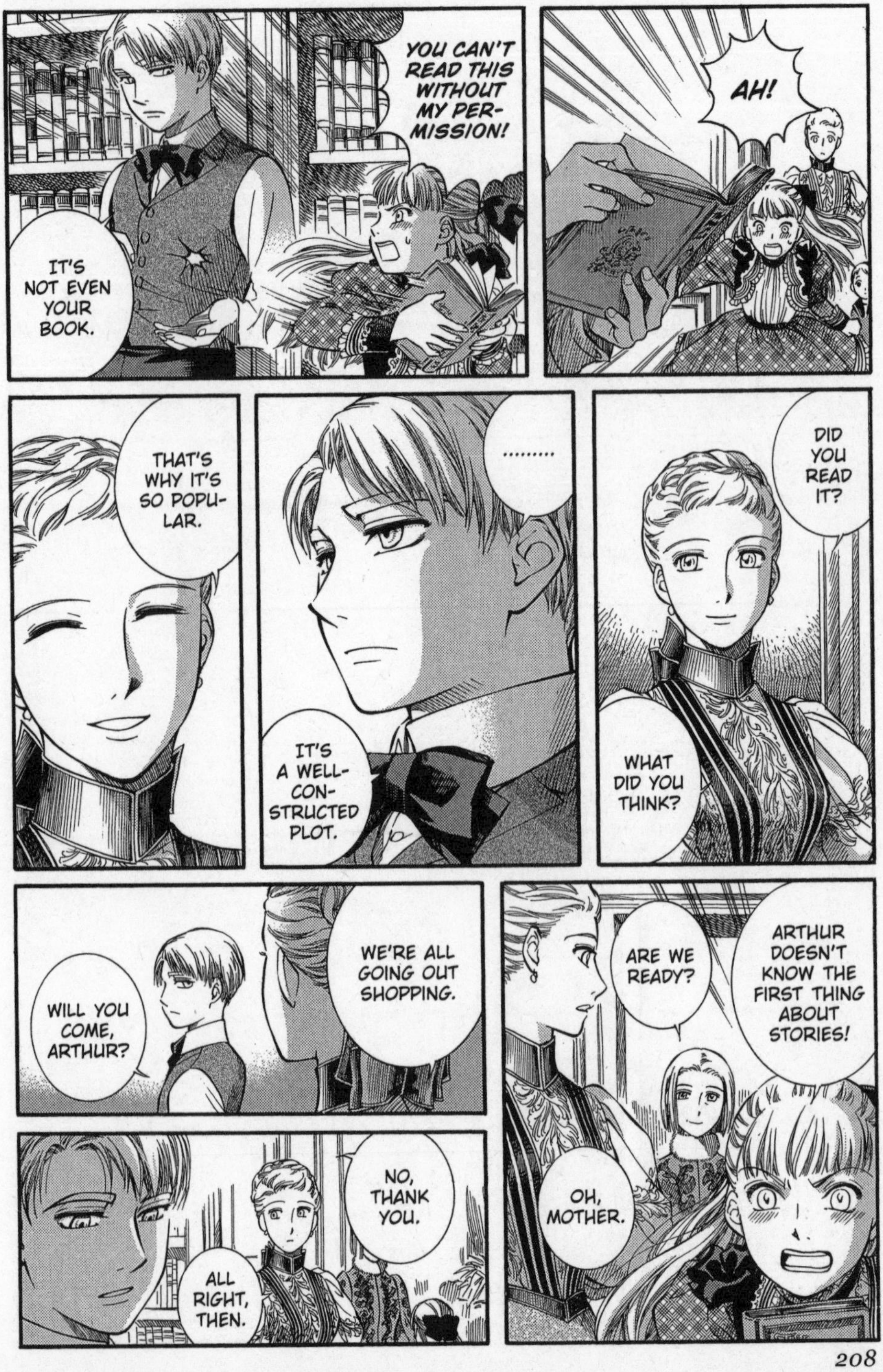
AH!
YOU CAN'T READ THIS WITHOUT MY PER-MISSION!
IT'S NOT EVEN YOUR BOOK.
DID YOU READ IT?
WHAT DID YOU THINK?
....
IT'S A WELL-CONSTRUCTED PLOT.
THAT'S WHY IT'S SO POPU-LAR.
ARTHUR DOESN'T KNOW THE FIRST THING ABOUT STORIES!
ARE WE READY?
OH, MOTHER.
WE'RE ALL GOING OUT SHOPPING.
WILL YOU COME, ARTHUR?
NO, THANK YOU.
ALL RIGHT, THEN.

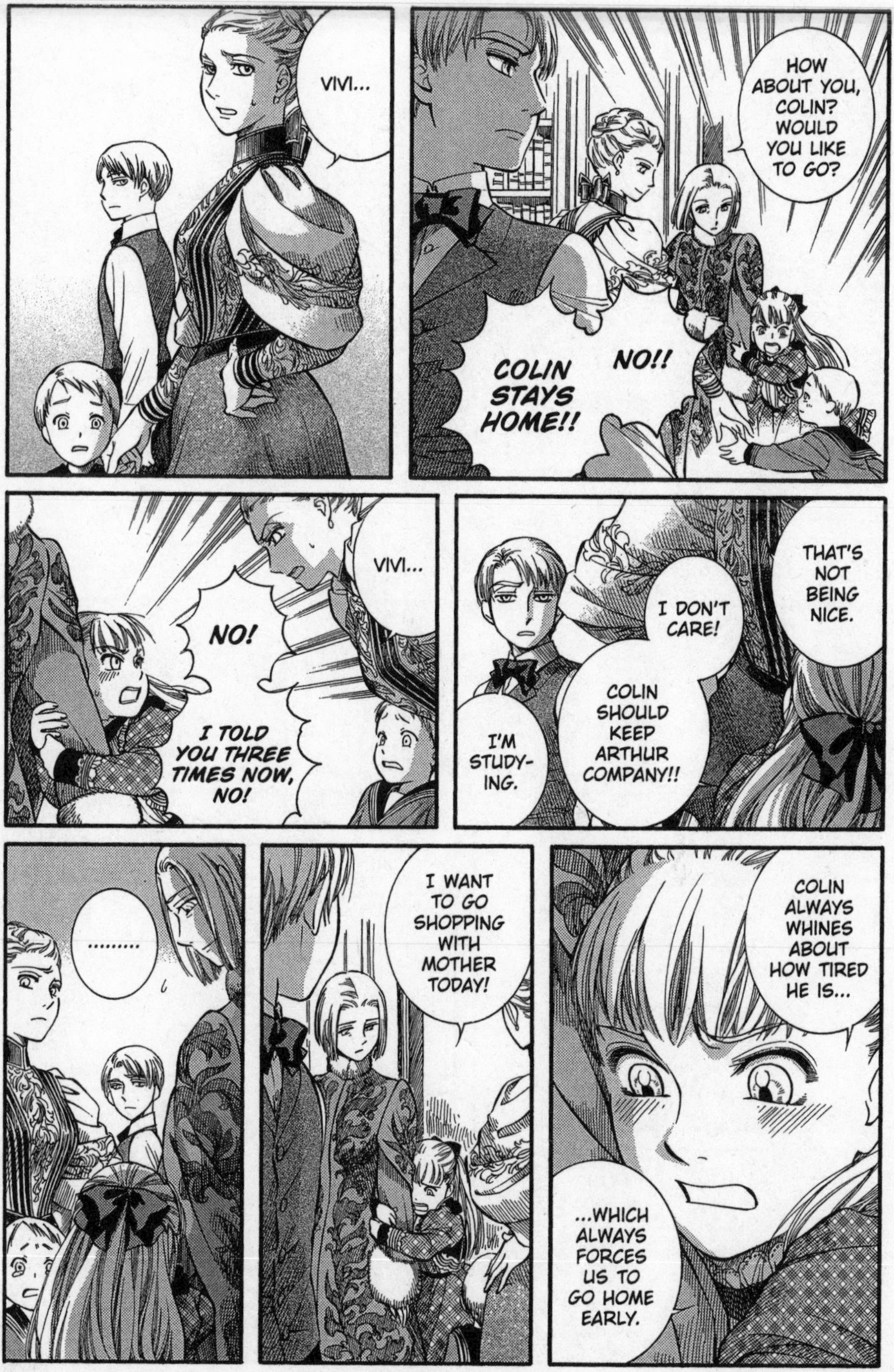
HOW ABOUT YOU, COLIN? WOULD YOU LIKE TO GO?
NO!!
COLIN STAYS HOME!!
VIVI...
THAT'S NOT BEING NICE.
I DON'T CARE!
COLIN SHOULD KEEP ARTHUR COMPANY!!
I'M STUDY-ING.
VIVI...
NO!
I TOLD YOU THREE TIMES NOW, NO!
COLIN ALWAYS WHINES ABOUT HOW TIRED HE IS...
...WHICH ALWAYS FORCES US TO GO HOME EARLY.
I WANT TO GO SHOPPING WITH MOTHER TODAY!
....

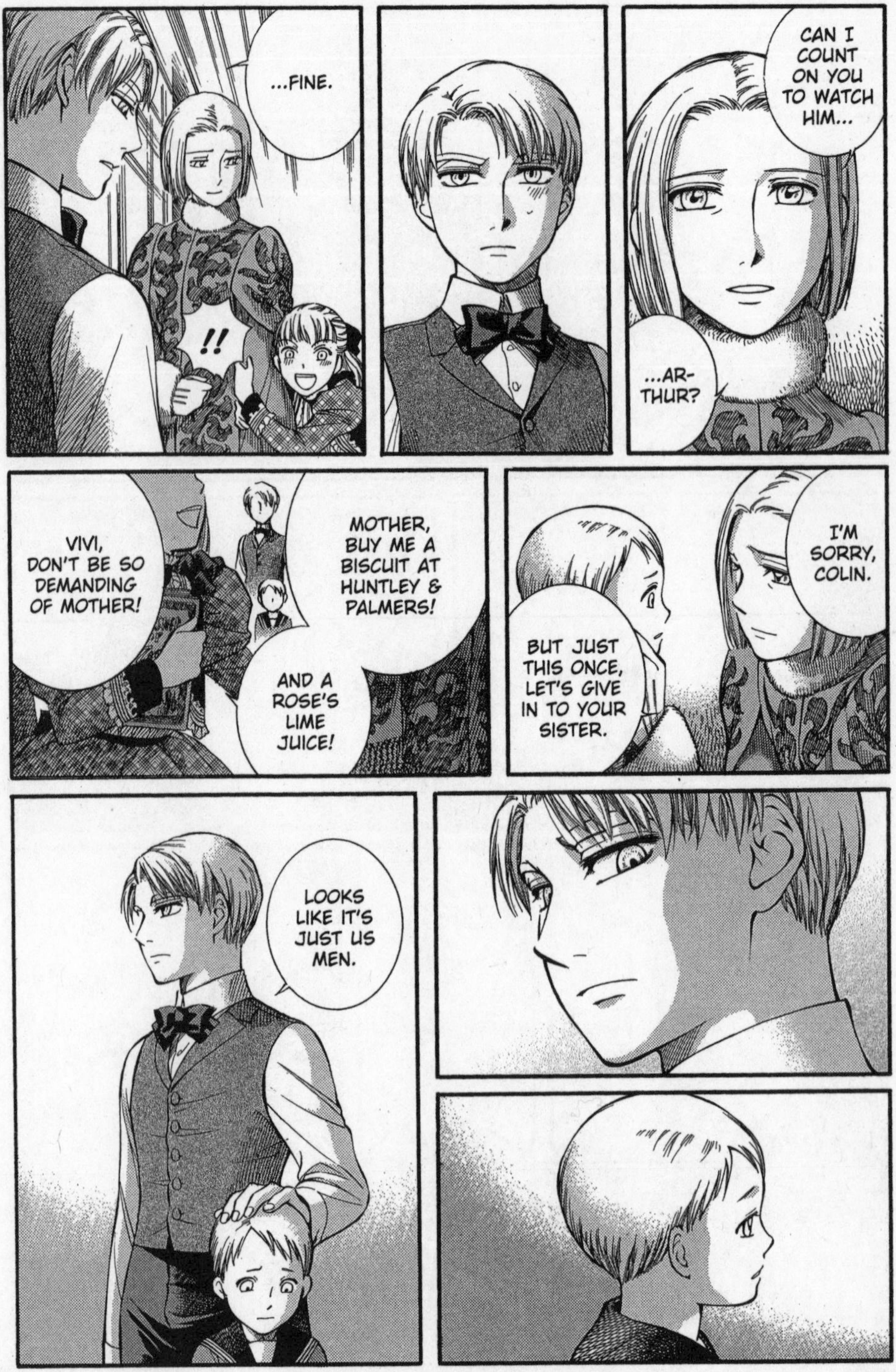
CAN I COUNT ON YOU TO WATCH HIM...
...AR-THUR?
...FINE.
!!
I'M SORRY, COLIN.
BUT JUST THIS ONCE, LET'S GIVE IN TO YOUR SISTER.
MOTHER, BUY ME A BISCUIT AT HUNTLEY & PALMERS!
AND A ROSE'S LIME JUICE!
VIVI, DON'T BE SO DEMANDING OF MOTHER!
LOOKS LIKE IT'S JUST US MEN.

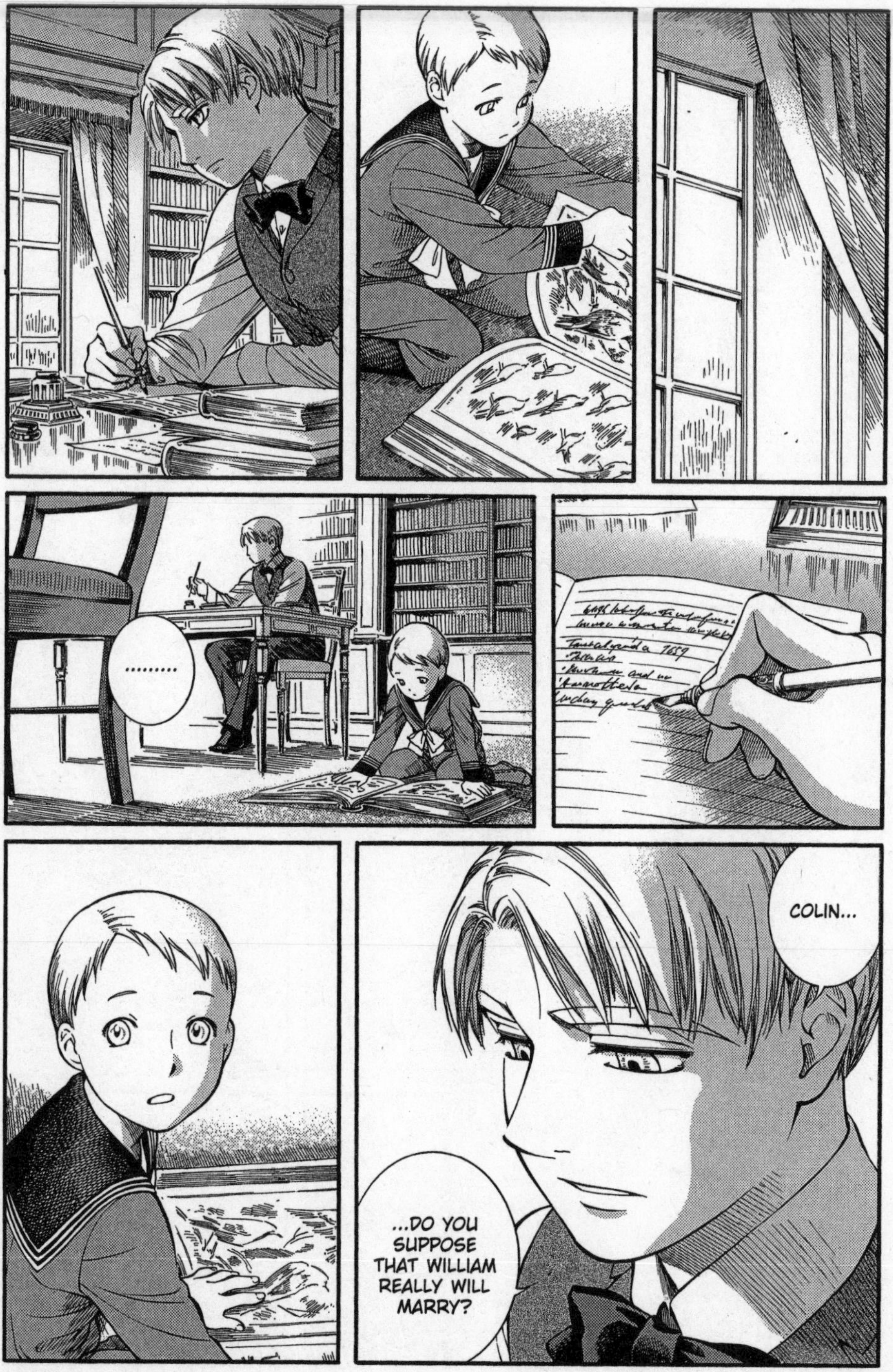
....
COLIN...
...DO YOU SUPPOSE THAT WILLIAM REALLY WILL MARRY?

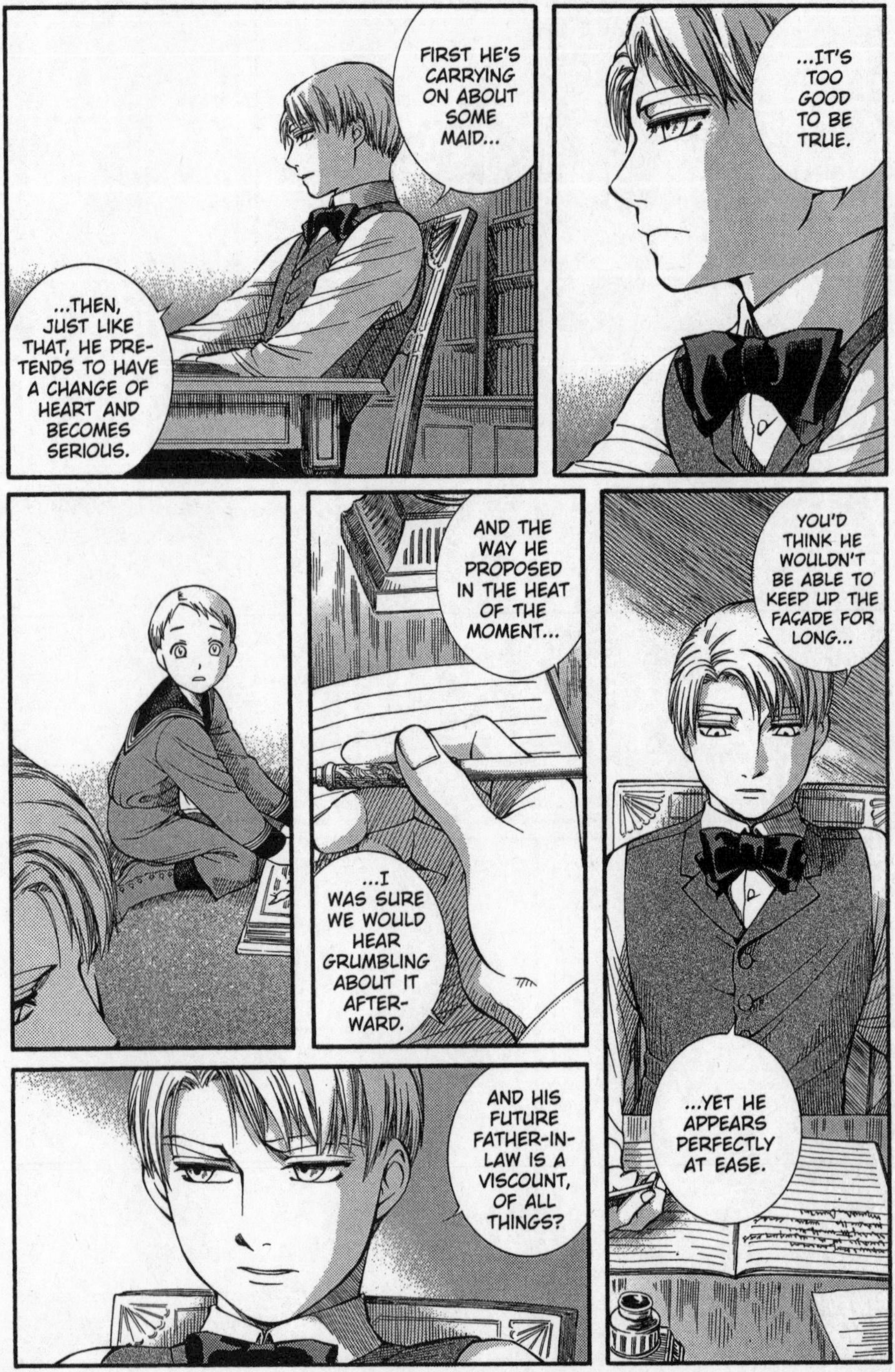
...IT'S TOO GOOD TO BE TRUE.
FIRST HE'S CARRYING ON ABOUT SOME MAID...
...THEN, JUST LIKE THAT, HE PRETENDS TO HAVE A CHANGE OF HEART AND BECOMES SERIOUS.
YOU'D THINK HE WOULDN'T BE ABLE TO KEEP UP THE FAÇADE FOR LONG...
...YET HE APPEARS PERFECTLY AT EASE.
AND THE WAY HE PROPOSED IN THE HEAT OF THE MOMENT...
...I WAS SURE WE WOULD HEAR GRUMBLING ABOUT IT AFTERWARD.
AND HIS FUTURE FATHER-IN-LAW IS A VISCOUNT, OF ALL THINGS?

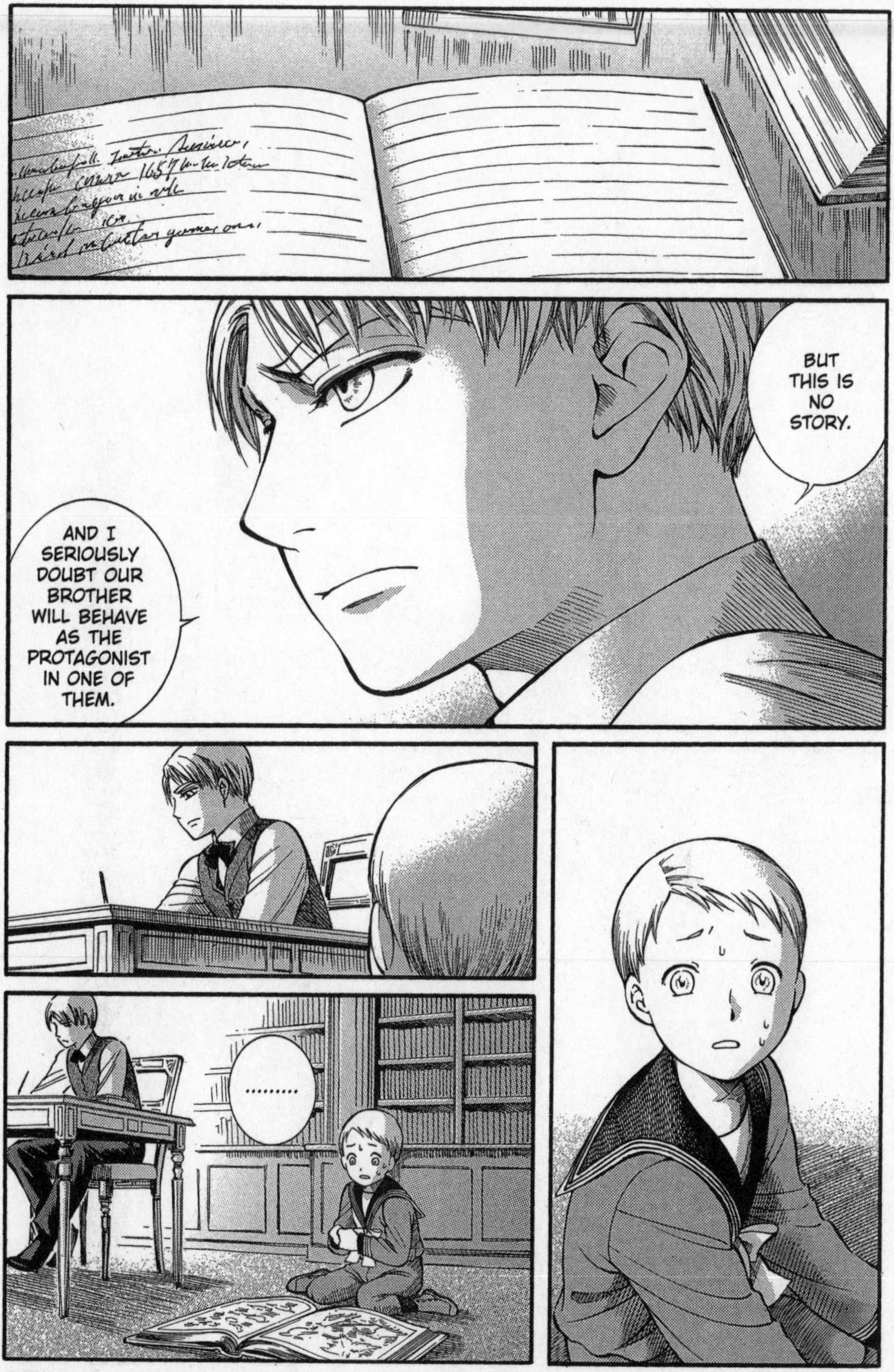
BUT THIS IS NO STORY.
AND I SERIOUSLY DOUBT OUR BROTHER WILL BEHAVE AS THE PROTAGONIST IN ONE OF THEM.
....

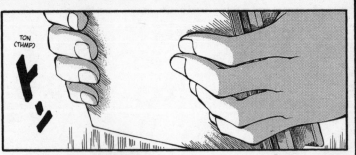

TON
(THMP)
トン

GYU
(TIGHT)
ギュッ

CHA
(CKCHAK)
チャッ

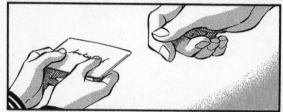

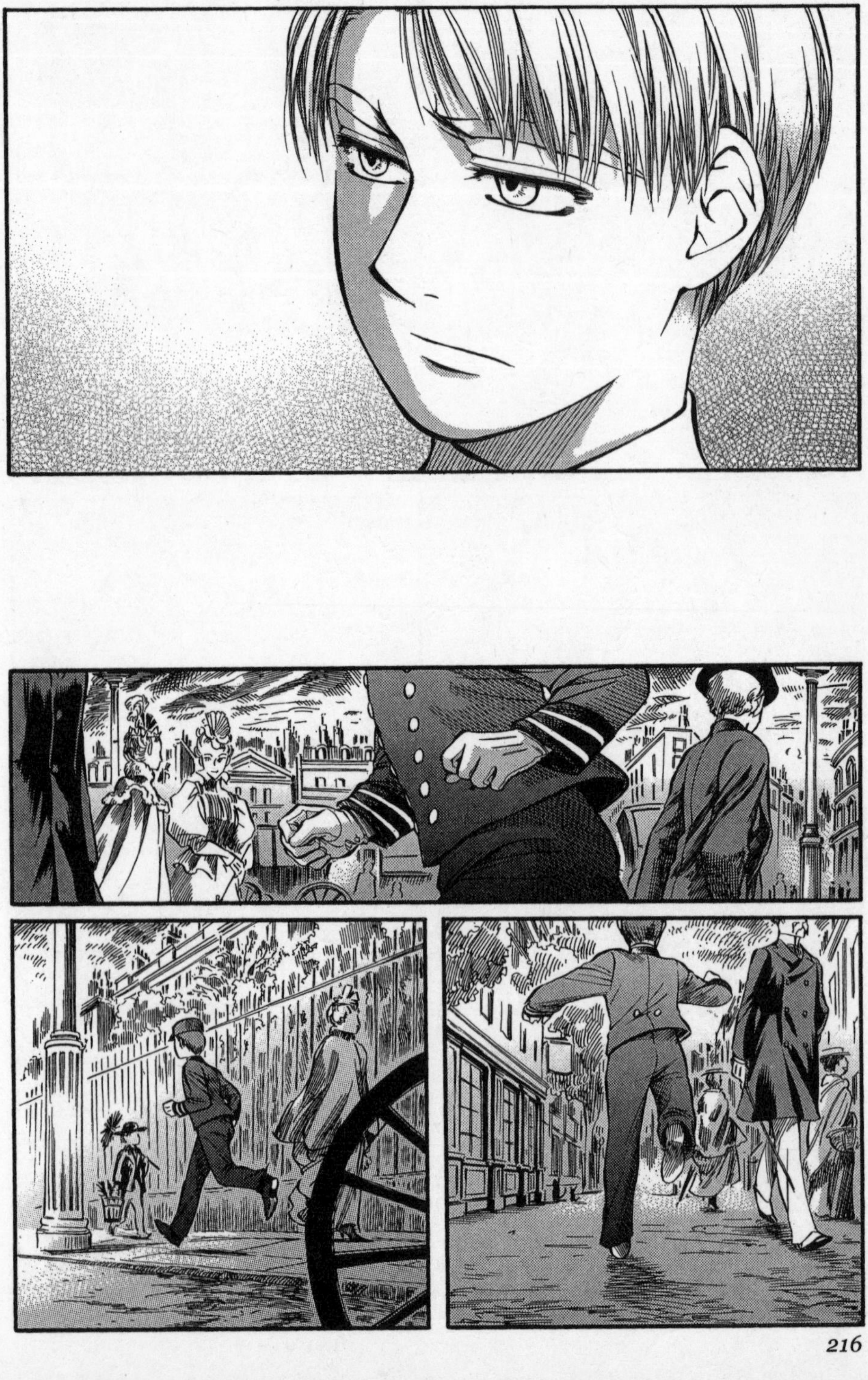

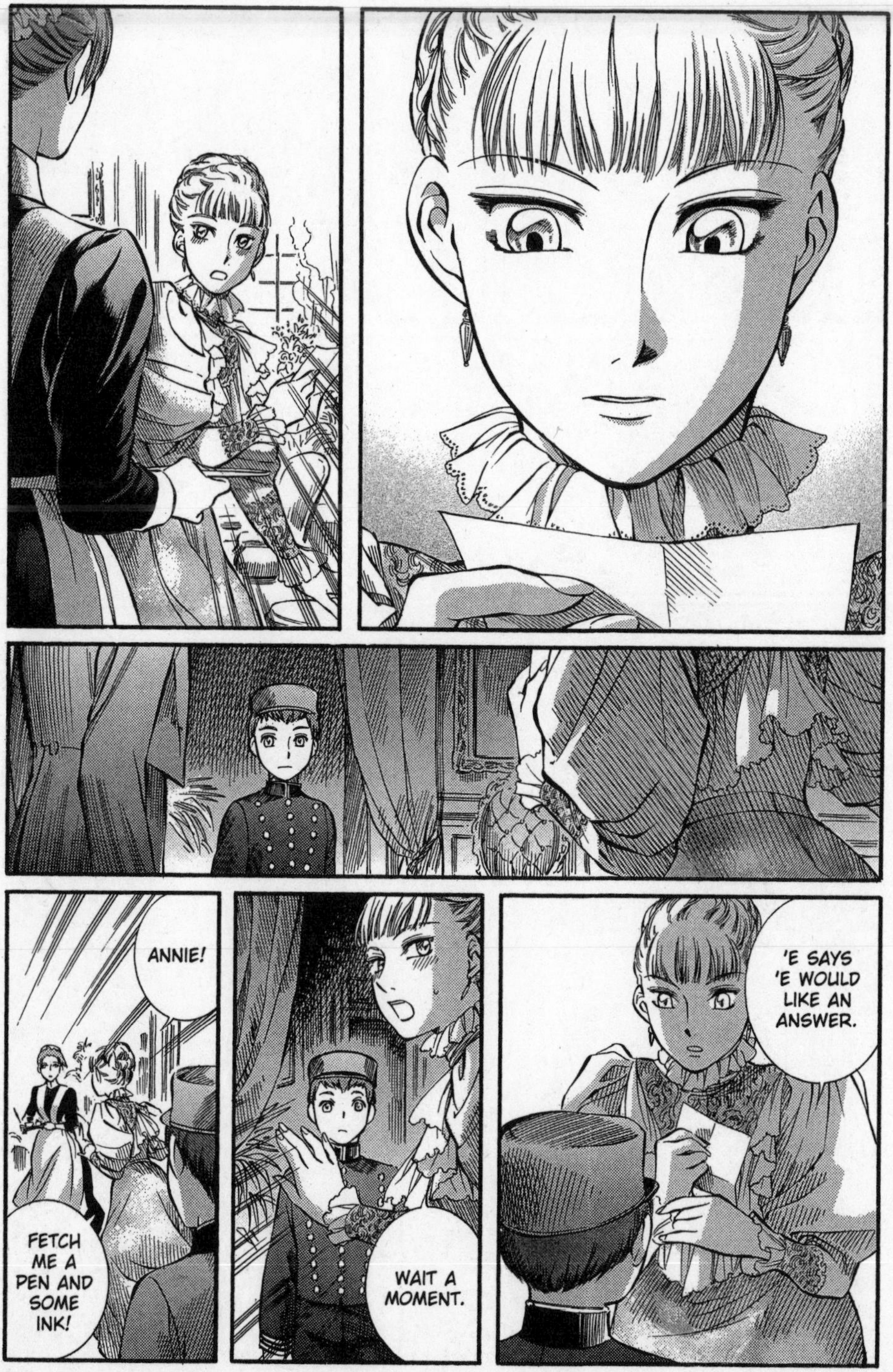
'E SAYS 'E WOULD LIKE AN ANSWER.
WAIT A MOMENT.
ANNIE!
FETCH ME A PEN AND SOME INK!

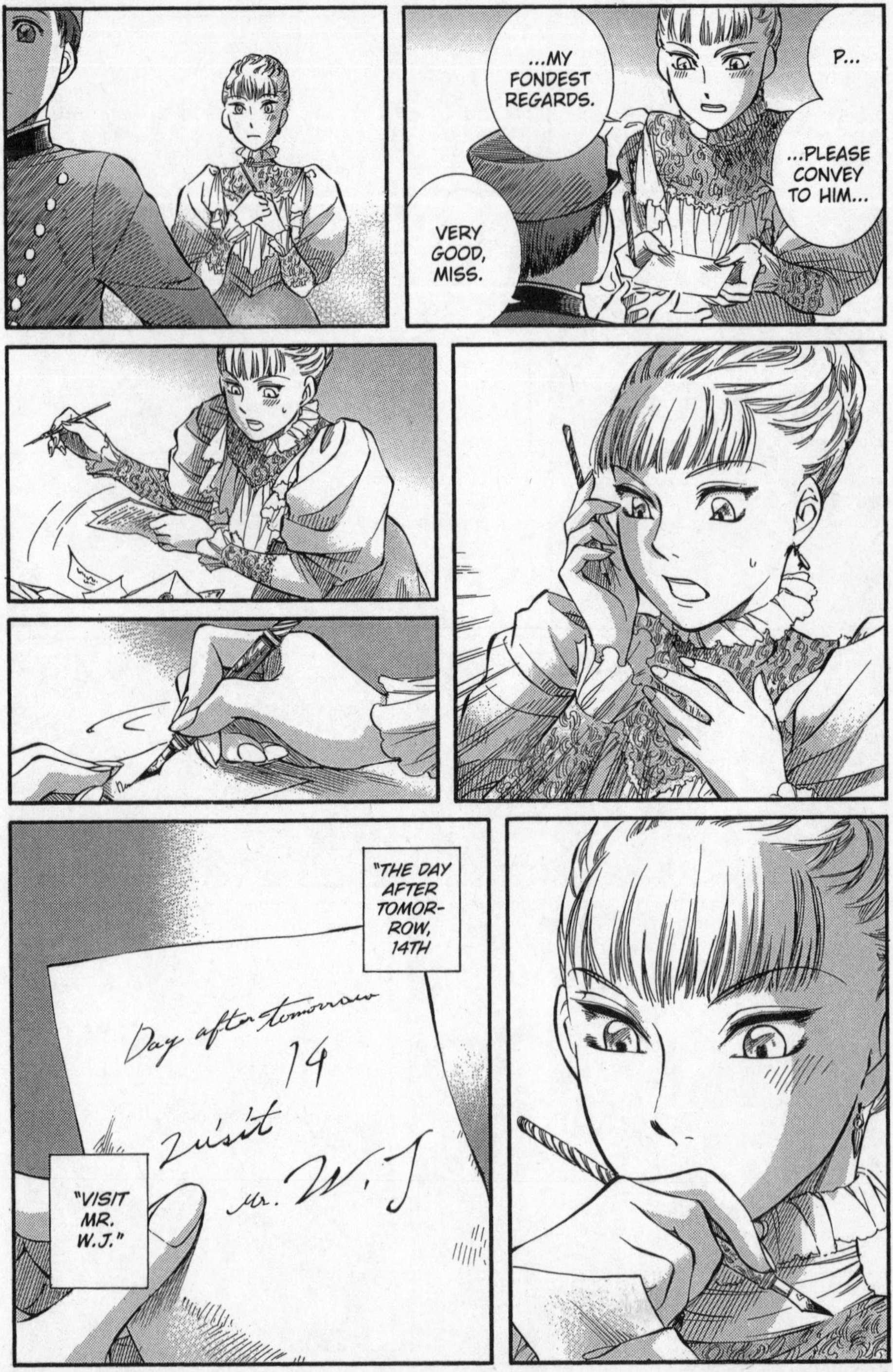
P...
...PLEASE CONVEY TO HIM...
...MY FONDEST REGARDS.
VERY GOOD, MISS.
"THE DAY AFTER TOMOR-ROW, 14TH
Day after tomorrow
14
visit
Mr. W. J
"VISIT MR. W.J."

Chapter 37: End

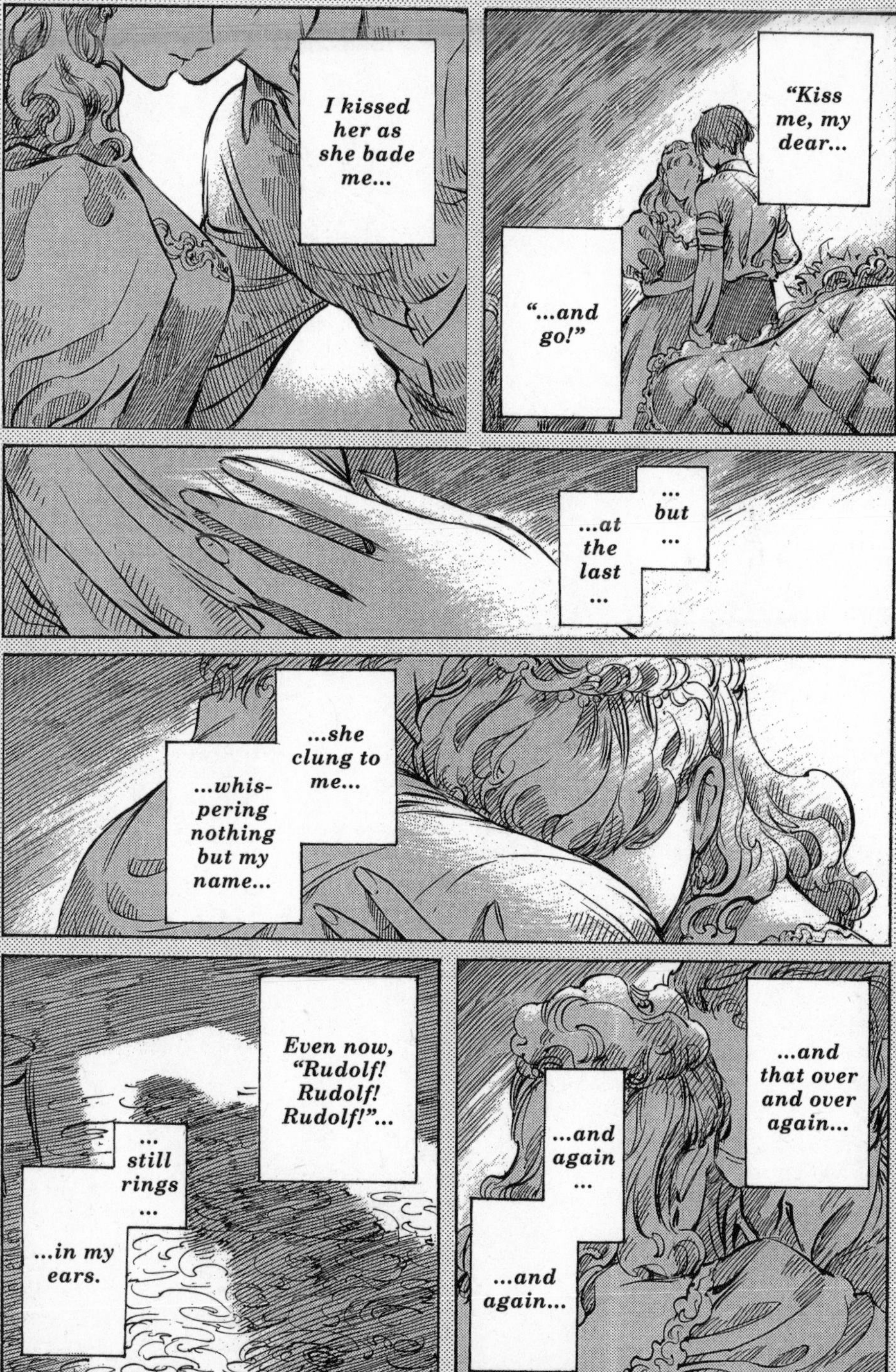
"Kiss me, my dear...
"...and go!"
I kissed her as she bade me...
... but ...
...at the last ...
...she clung to me...
...whispering nothing but my name...
...and that over and over again...
...and again ...
...and again...
Even now, "Rudolf! Rudolf! Rudolf!"...
... still rings ...
...in my ears.

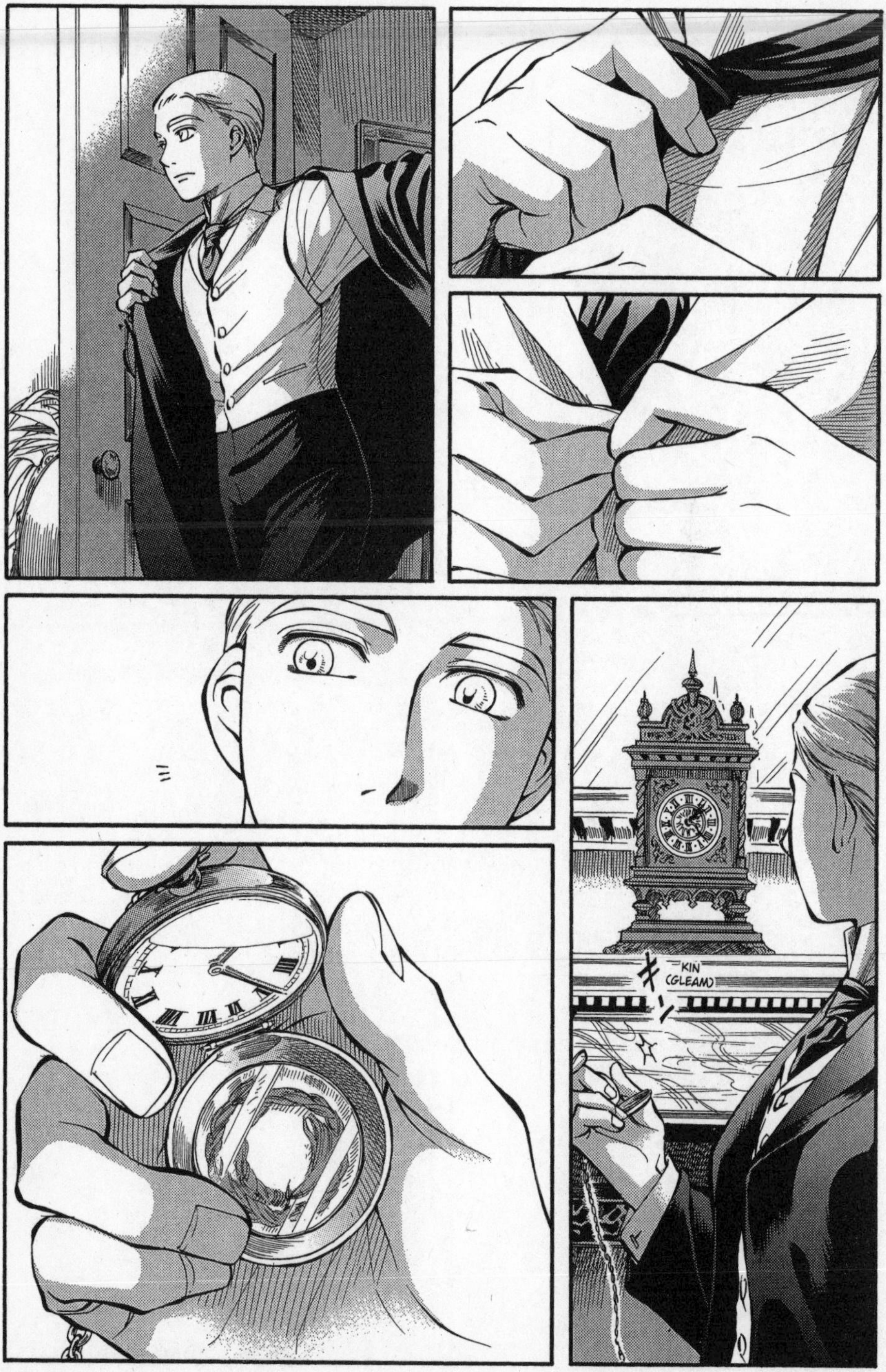
KIN
(GLEAM)

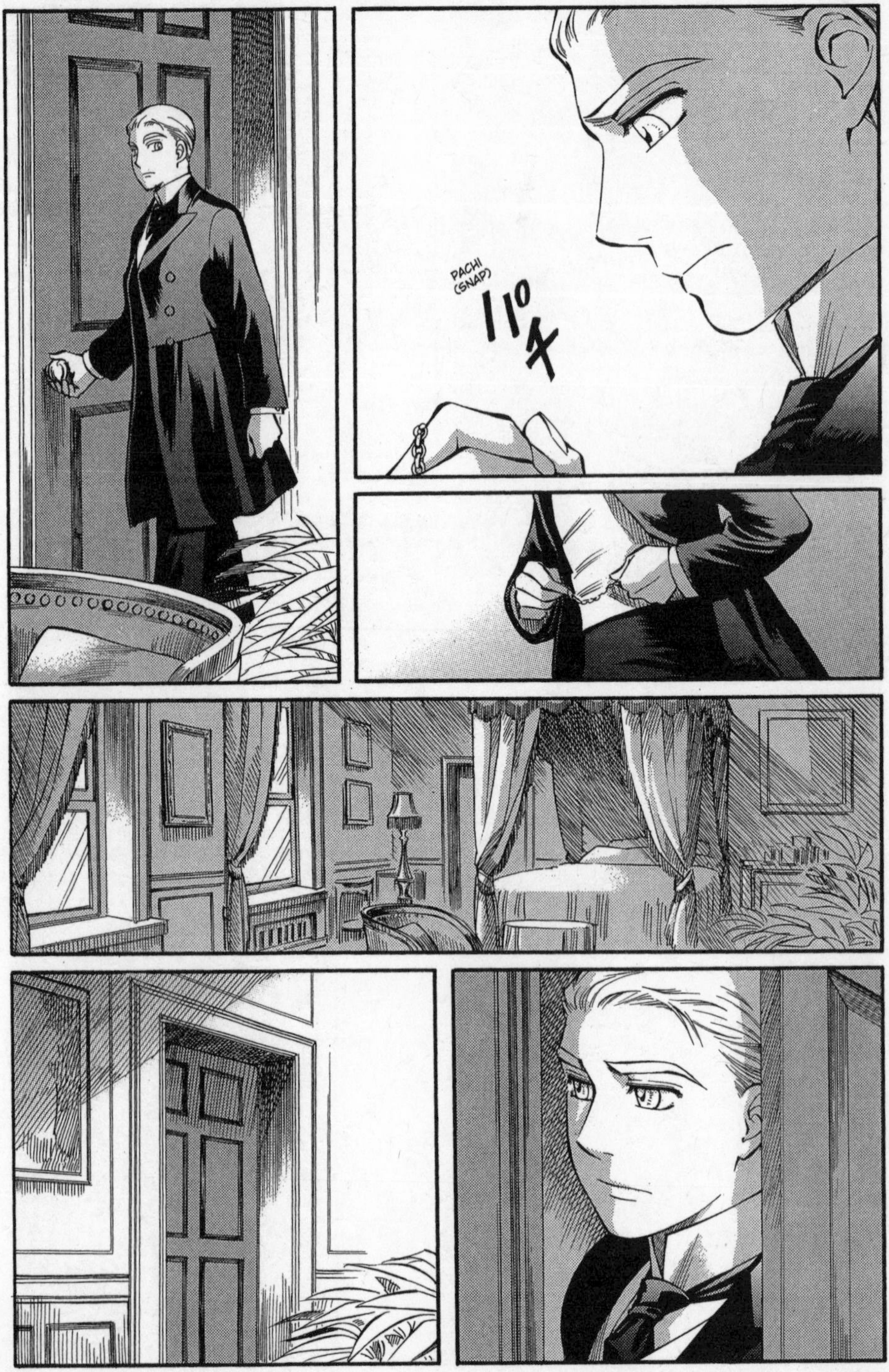
PACHI (SNAP)
パチ

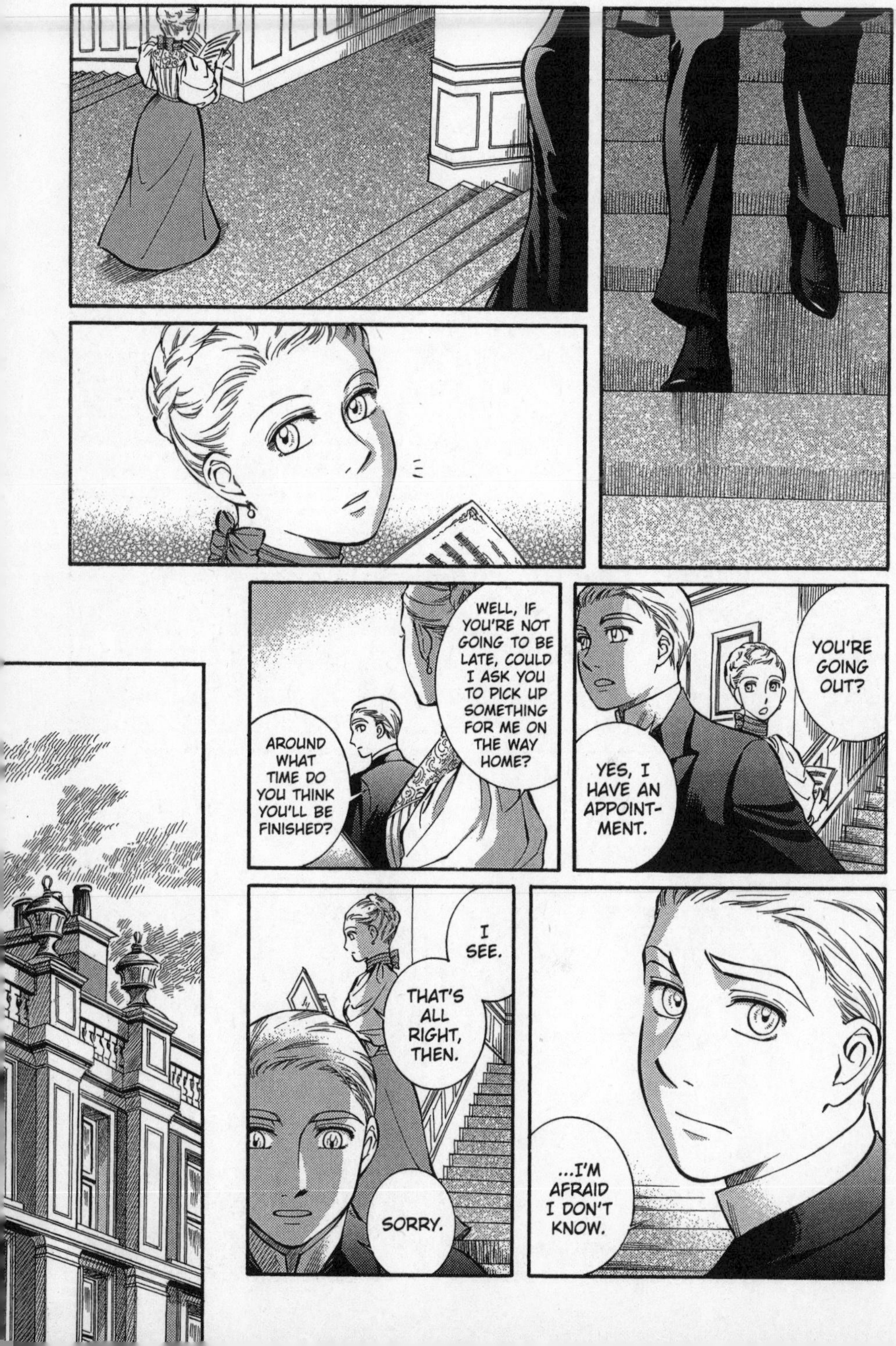
YOU'RE GOING OUT?
YES, I HAVE AN APPOINTMENT.
WELL, IF YOU'RE NOT GOING TO BE LATE, COULD I ASK YOU TO PICK UP SOMETHING FOR ME ON THE WAY HOME?
AROUND WHAT TIME DO YOU THINK YOU'LL BE FINISHED?
...I'M AFRAID I DON'T KNOW.
I SEE.
THAT'S ALL RIGHT, THEN.
SORRY.

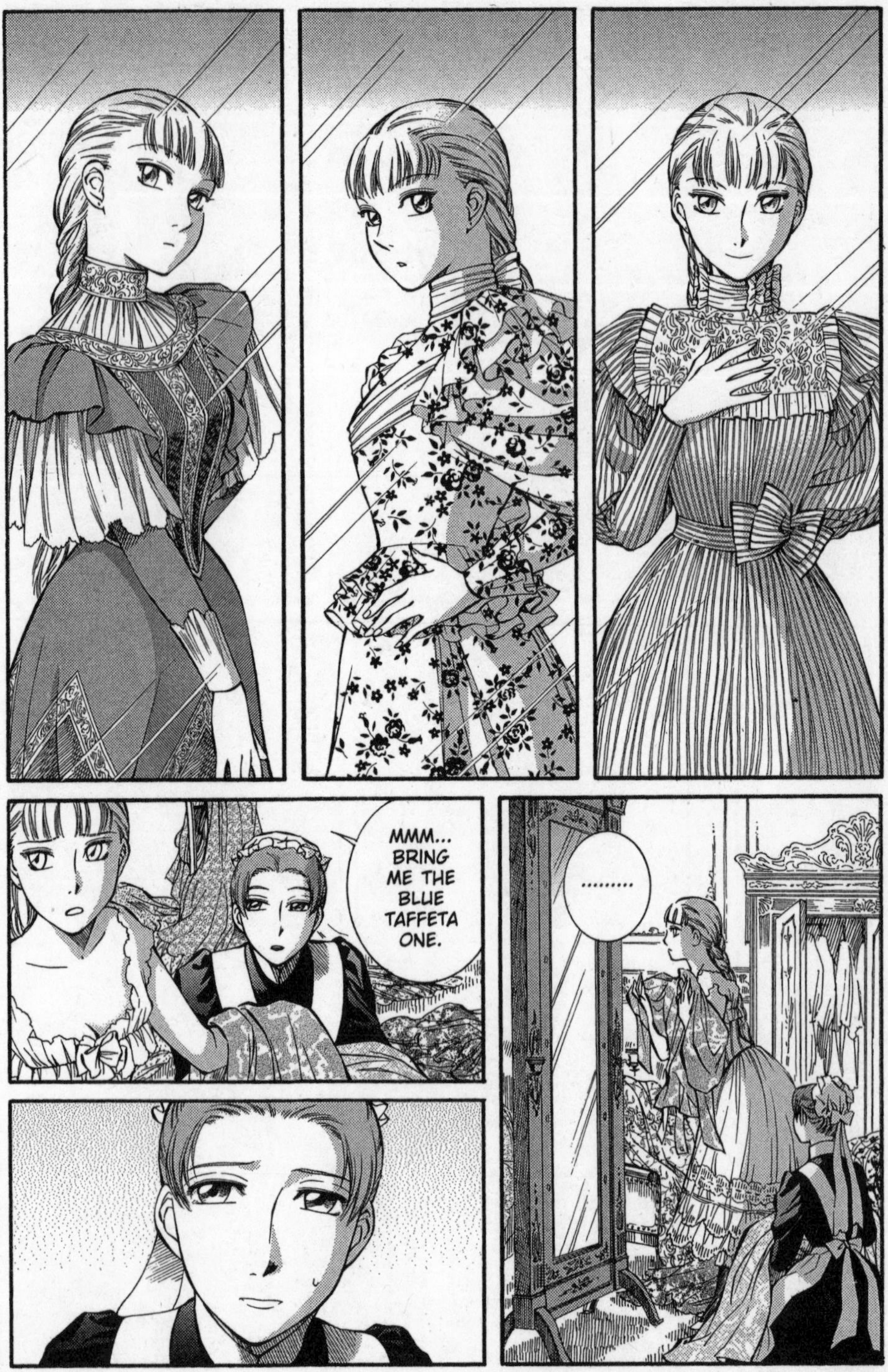
....
MMM... BRING ME THE BLUE TAFFETA ONE.

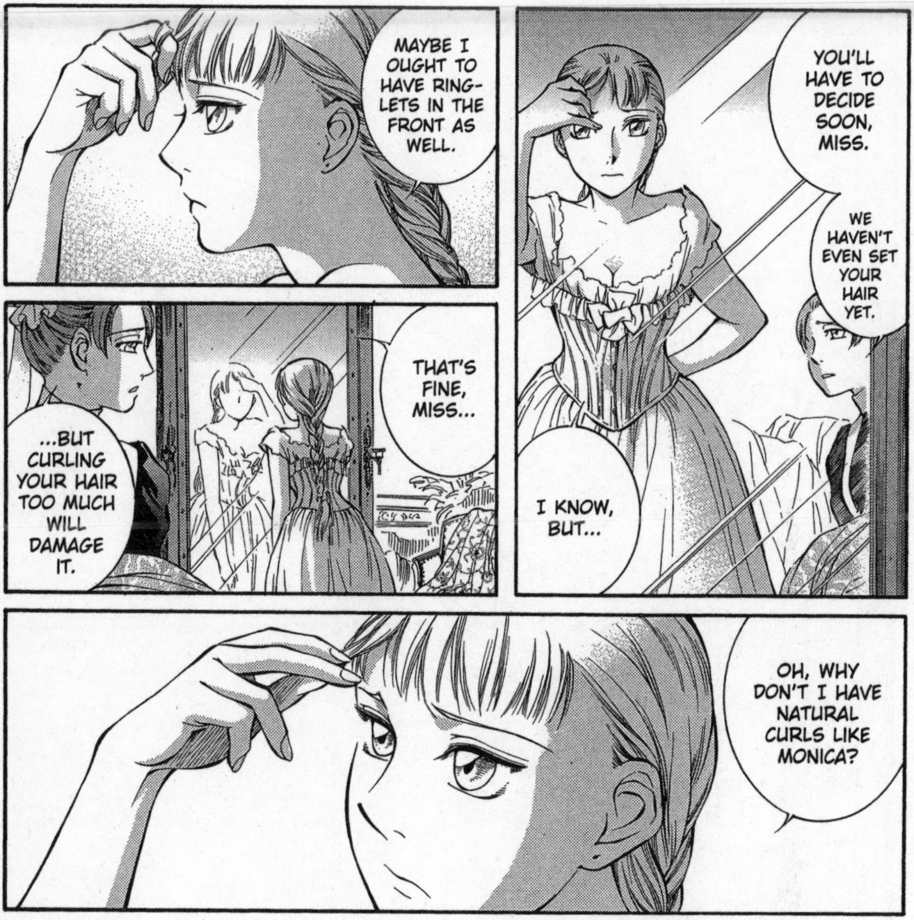
YOU'LL HAVE TO DECIDE SOON, MISS.
WE HAVEN'T EVEN SET YOUR HAIR YET.
I KNOW, BUT...
MAYBE I OUGHT TO HAVE RING-LETS IN THE FRONT AS WELL.
THAT'S FINE, MISS...
...BUT CURLING YOUR HAIR TOO MUCH WILL DAMAGE IT.
OH, WHY DON'T I HAVE NATURAL CURLS LIKE MONICA?

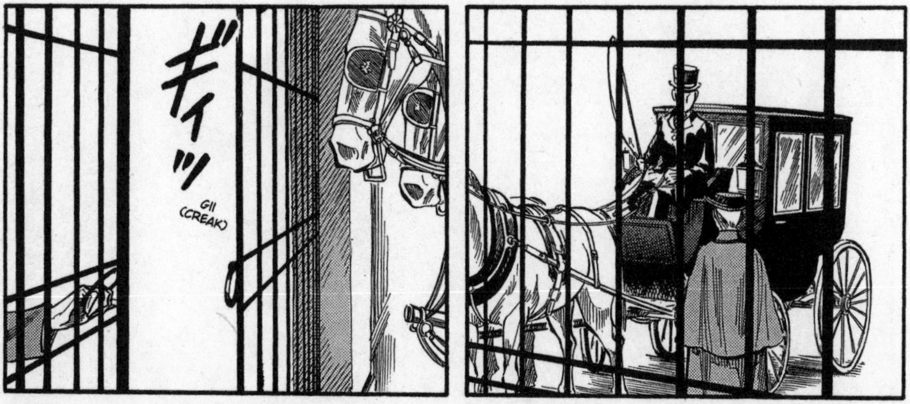
ギィッ
GII (CREAK)

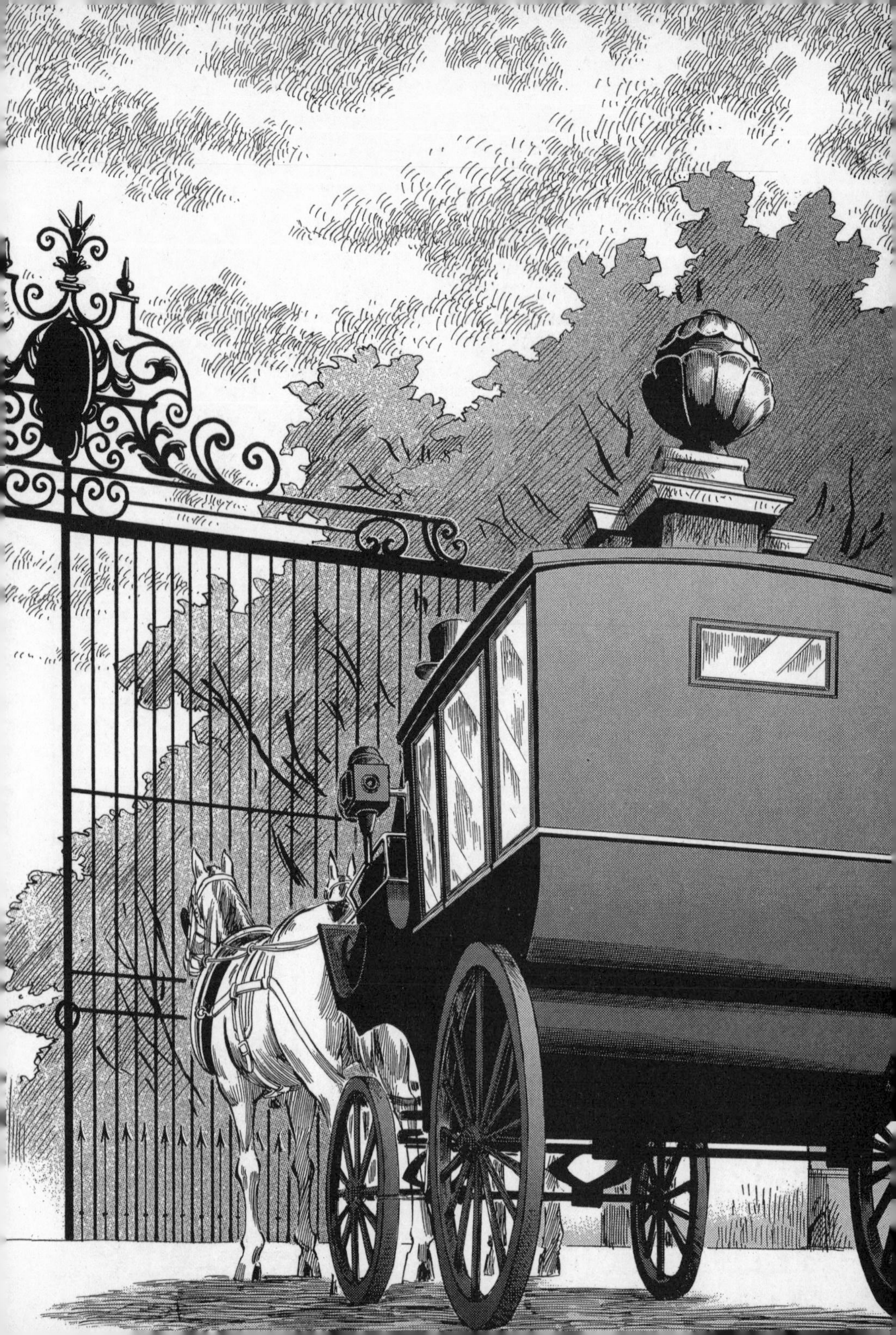

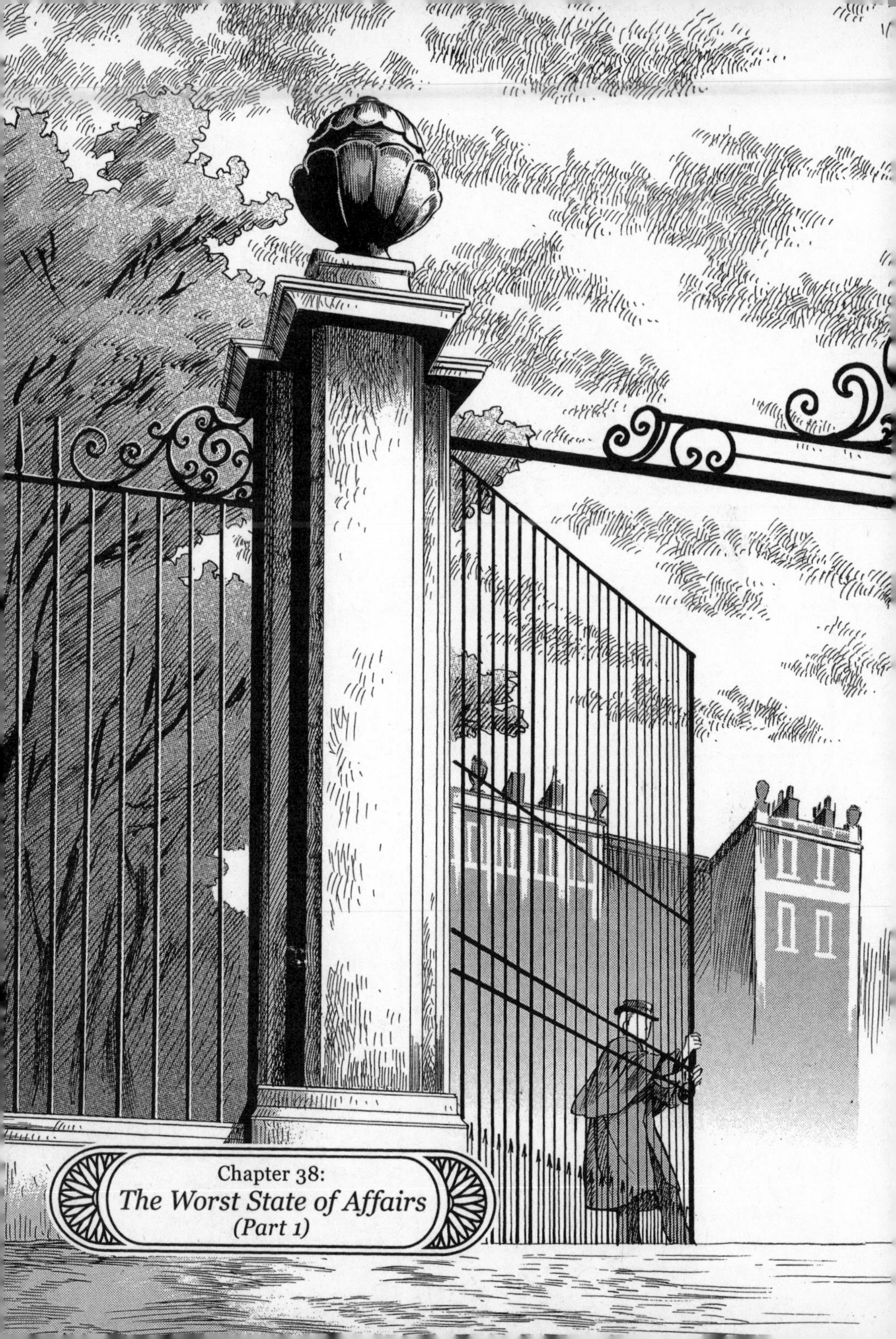
Chapter 38:
The Worst State of Affairs
(Part 1)

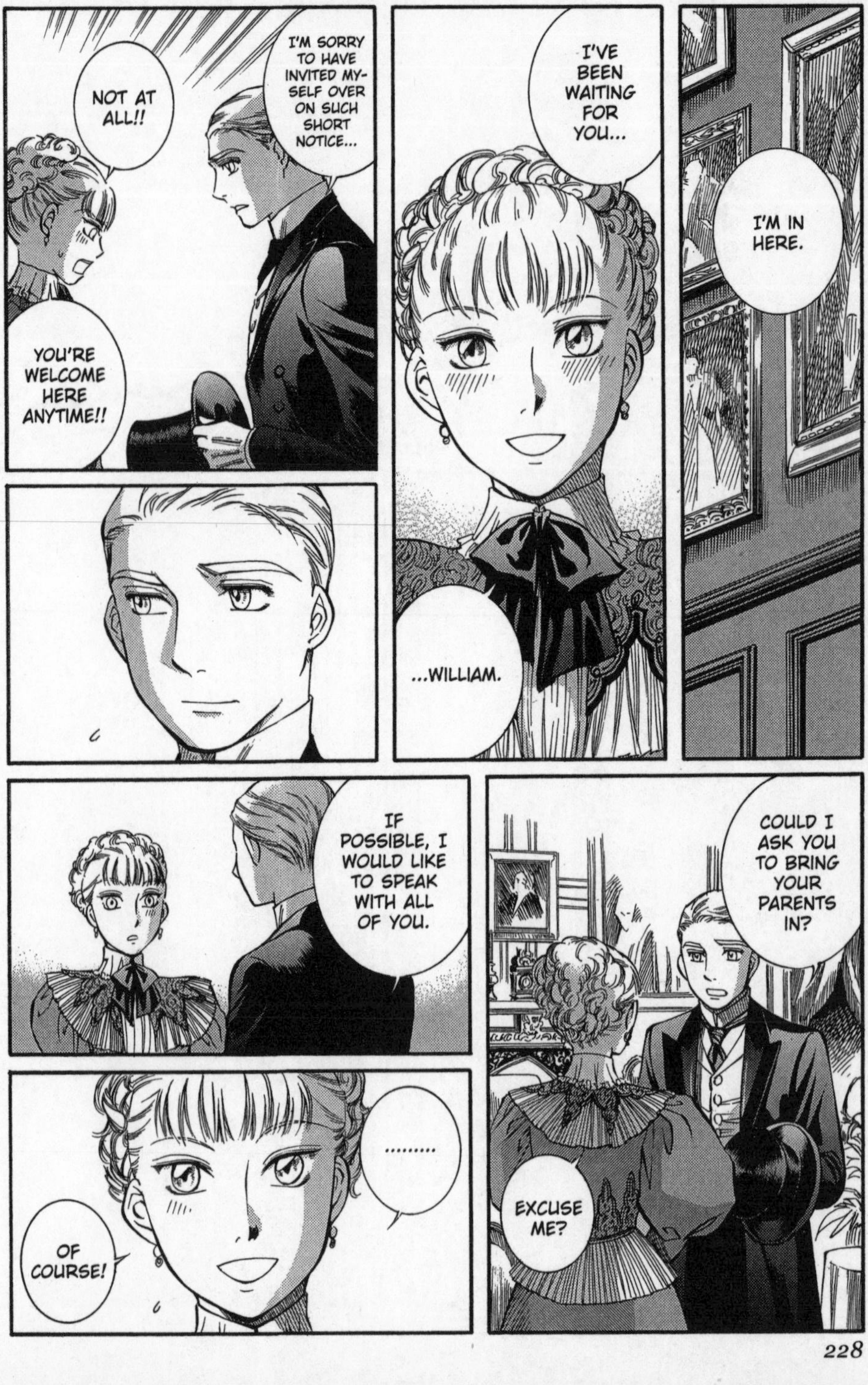
I'M IN HERE.
I'VE BEEN WAITING FOR YOU...
...WILLIAM.
I'M SORRY TO HAVE INVITED MY-SELF OVER ON SUCH SHORT NOTICE...
NOT AT ALL!!
YOU'RE WELCOME HERE ANYTIME!!
COULD I ASK YOU TO BRING YOUR PARENTS IN?
EXCUSE ME?
IF POSSIBLE, I WOULD LIKE TO SPEAK WITH ALL OF YOU.
....
OF COURSE!

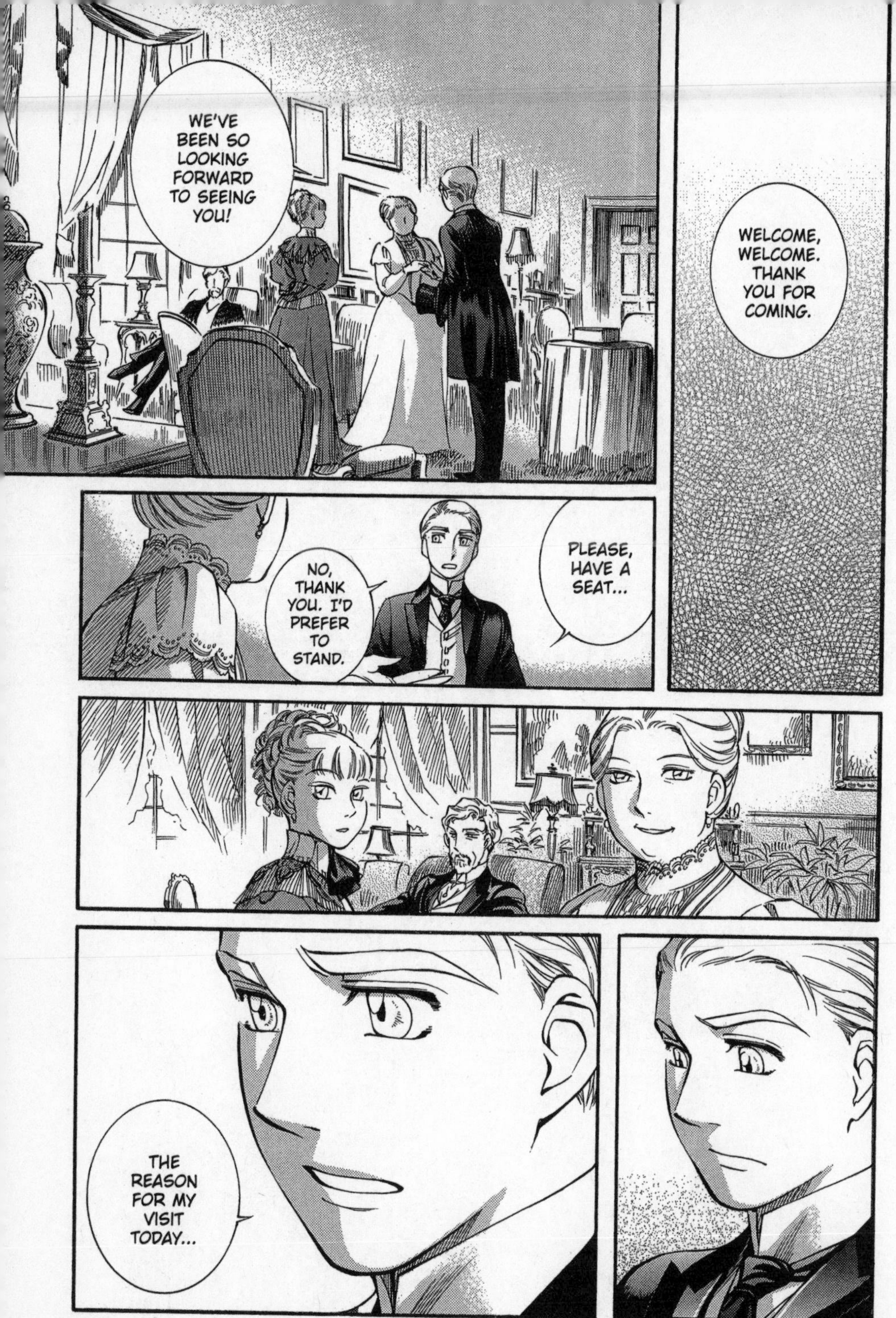
WELCOME, WELCOME. THANK YOU FOR COMING.
WE'VE BEEN SO LOOKING FORWARD TO SEEING YOU!
PLEASE, HAVE A SEAT...
NO, THANK YOU. I'D PREFER TO STAND.
THE REASON FOR MY VISIT TODAY...

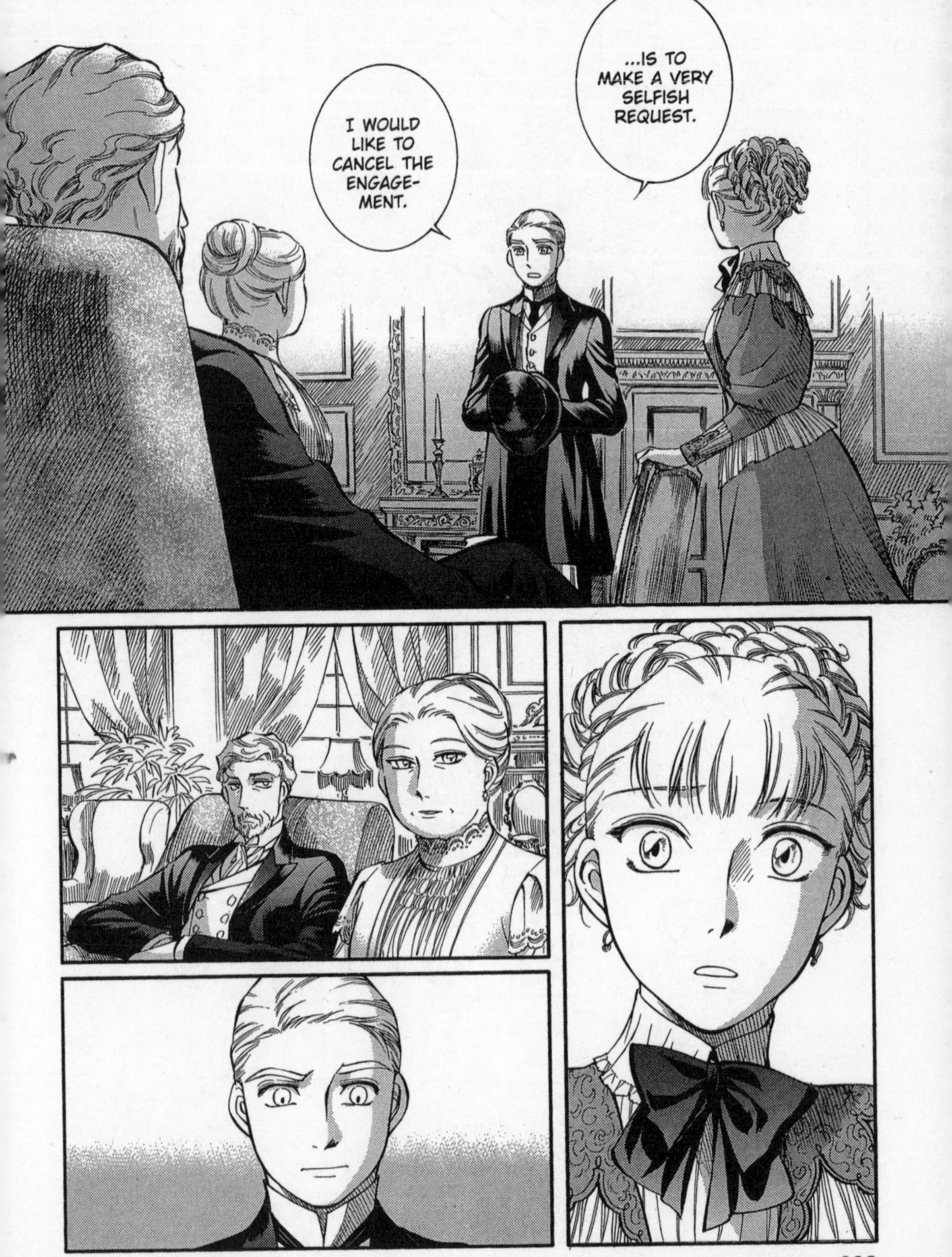
...IS TO MAKE A VERY SELFISH REQUEST.
I WOULD LIKE TO CANCEL THE ENGAGE-MENT.

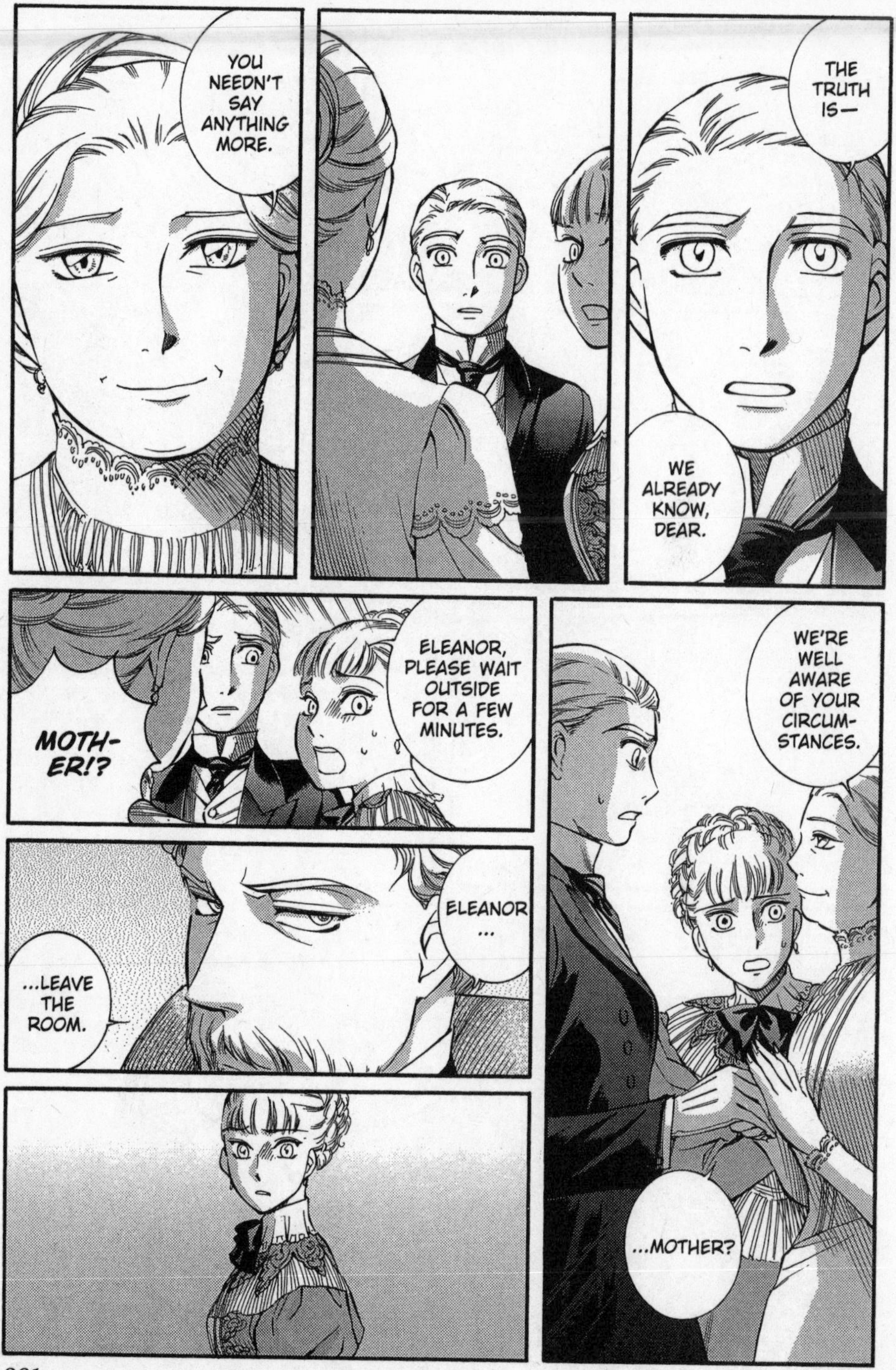
THE TRUTH IS—
WE ALREADY KNOW, DEAR.
YOU NEEDN'T SAY ANYTHING MORE.
WE'RE WELL AWARE OF YOUR CIRCUM-STANCES.
...MOTHER?
ELEANOR, PLEASE WAIT OUTSIDE FOR A FEW MINUTES.
MOTH-ER!?
ELEANOR ...
...LEAVE THE ROOM.

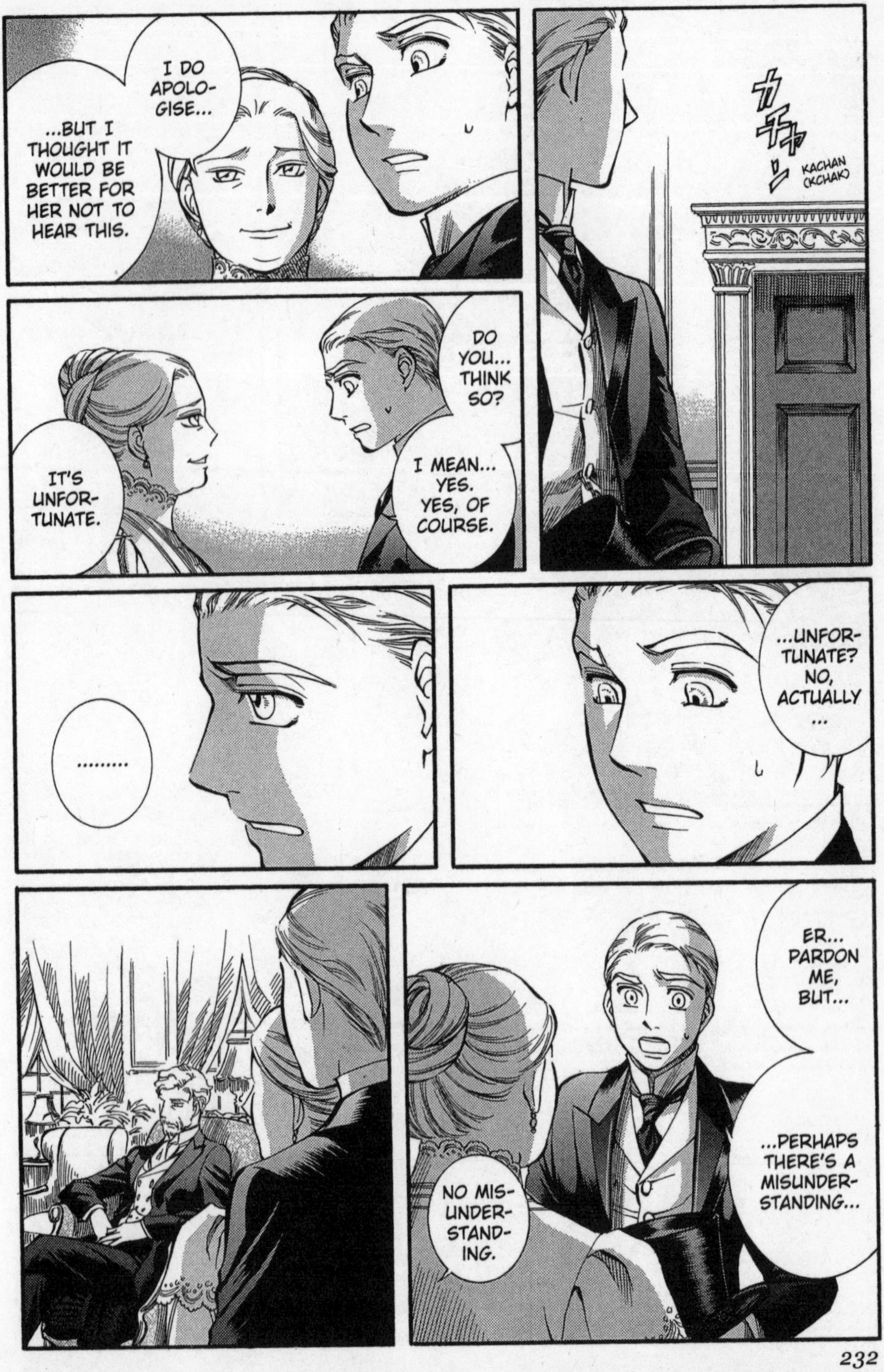
カチャッ
KACHAN (KCHAK)
I DO APOLOGISE...
...BUT I THOUGHT IT WOULD BE BETTER FOR HER NOT TO HEAR THIS.
DO YOU... THINK SO?
I MEAN... YES. YES, OF COURSE.
IT'S UNFORTUNATE.
...UNFORTUNATE? NO, ACTUALLY ...
....
ER... PARDON ME, BUT...
...PERHAPS THERE'S A MISUNDERSTANDING...
NO MISUNDERSTANDING.

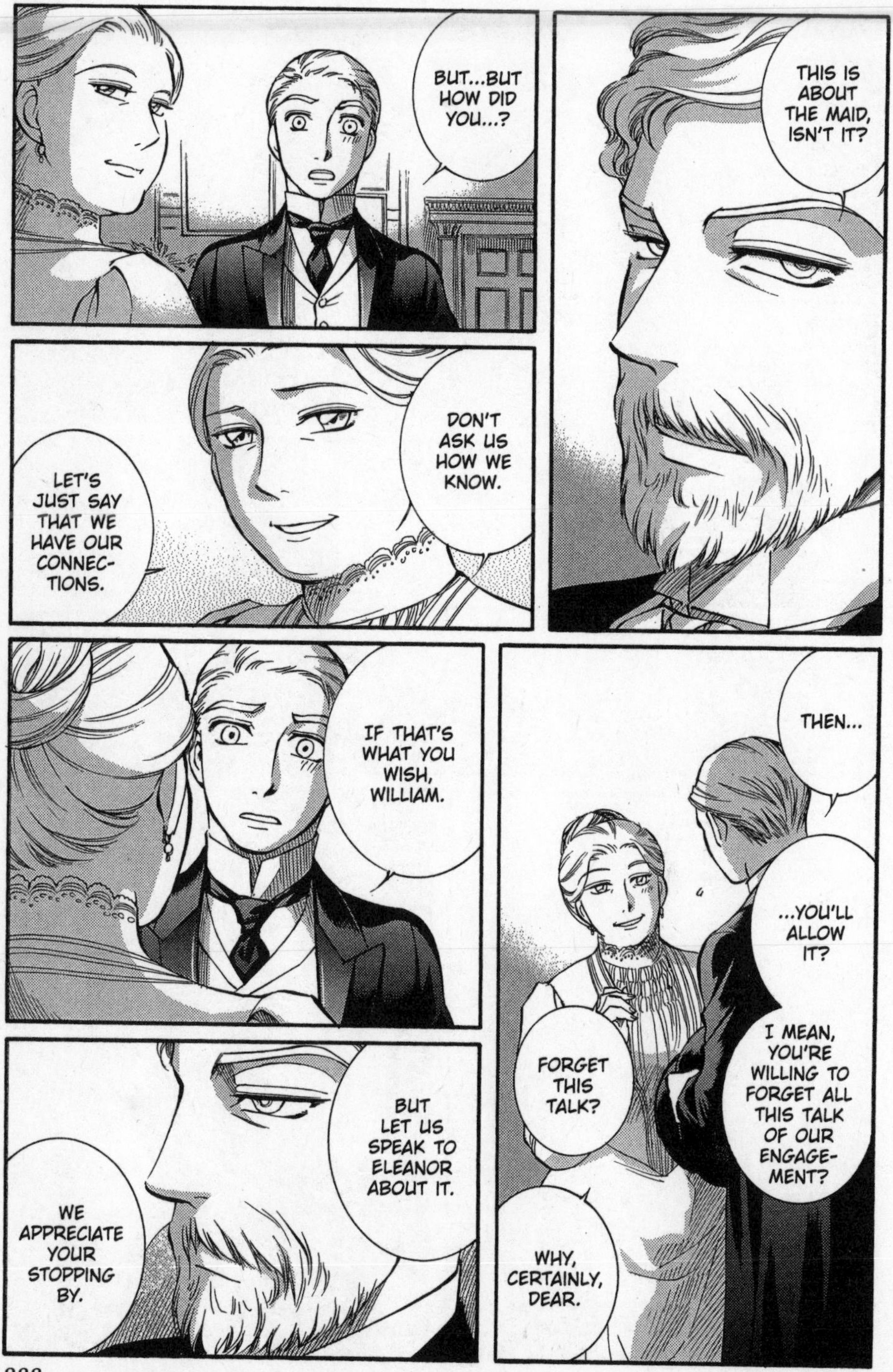
THIS IS ABOUT THE MAID, ISN'T IT?
BUT...BUT HOW DID YOU...?
DON'T ASK US HOW WE KNOW.
LET'S JUST SAY THAT WE HAVE OUR CONNEC-TIONS.
THEN...
...YOU'LL ALLOW IT?
I MEAN, YOU'RE WILLING TO FORGET ALL THIS TALK OF OUR ENGAGE-MENT?
FORGET THIS TALK?
WHY, CERTAINLY, DEAR.
IF THAT'S WHAT YOU WISH, WILLIAM.
BUT LET US SPEAK TO ELEANOR ABOUT IT.
WE APPRECIATE YOUR STOPPING BY.

THAT...

...WENT WELL...I THINK?

....

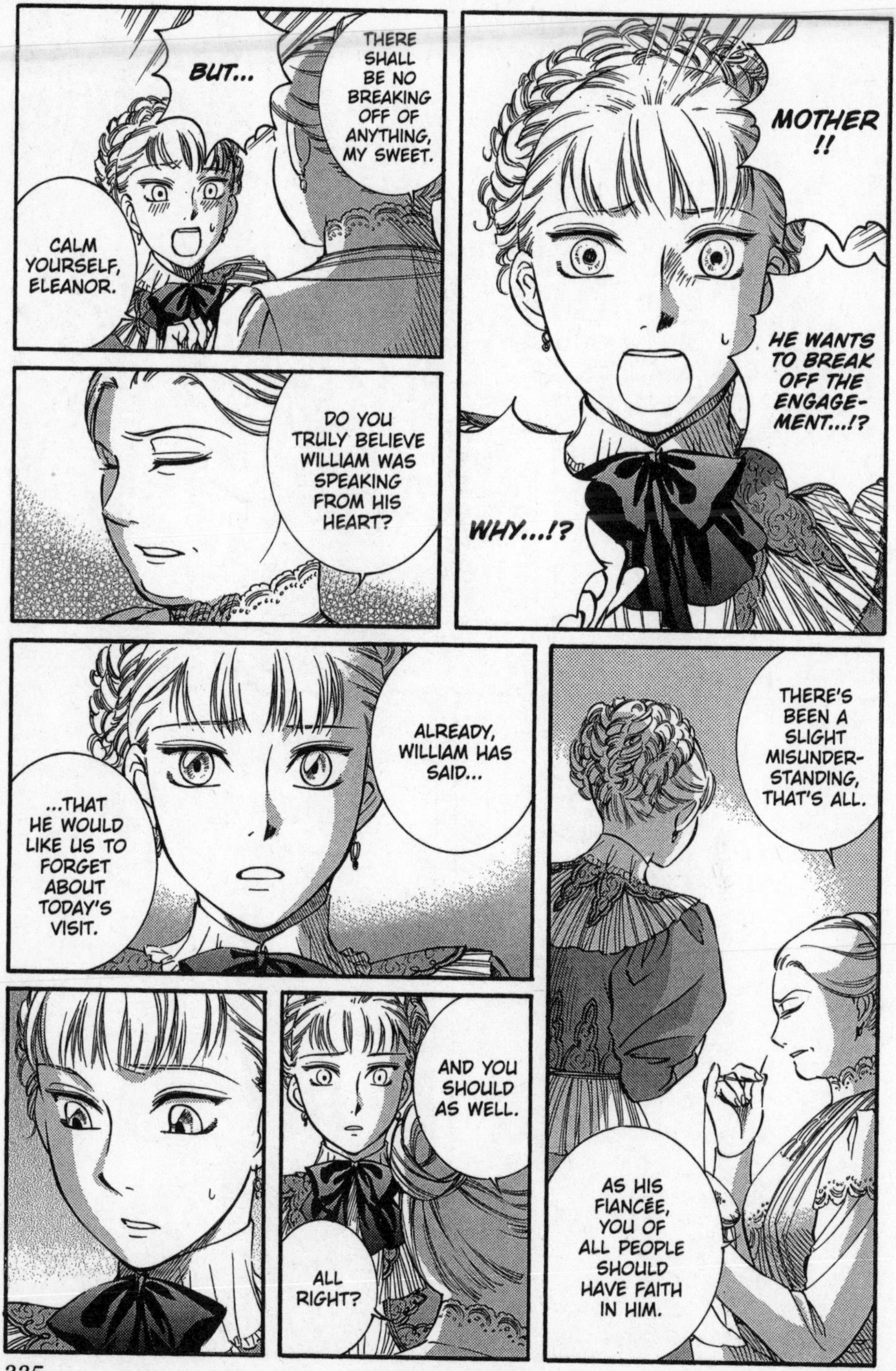
MOTHER!!
HE WANTS TO BREAK OFF THE ENGAGEMENT...!?
WHY...!?
THERE SHALL BE NO BREAKING OFF OF ANYTHING, MY SWEET.
BUT...
CALM YOURSELF, ELEANOR.
DO YOU TRULY BELIEVE WILLIAM WAS SPEAKING FROM HIS HEART?
THERE'S BEEN A SLIGHT MISUNDERSTANDING, THAT'S ALL.
AS HIS FIANCÉE, YOU OF ALL PEOPLE SHOULD HAVE FAITH IN HIM.
ALREADY, WILLIAM HAS SAID...
...THAT HE WOULD LIKE US TO FORGET ABOUT TODAY'S VISIT.
AND YOU SHOULD AS WELL.
ALL RIGHT?

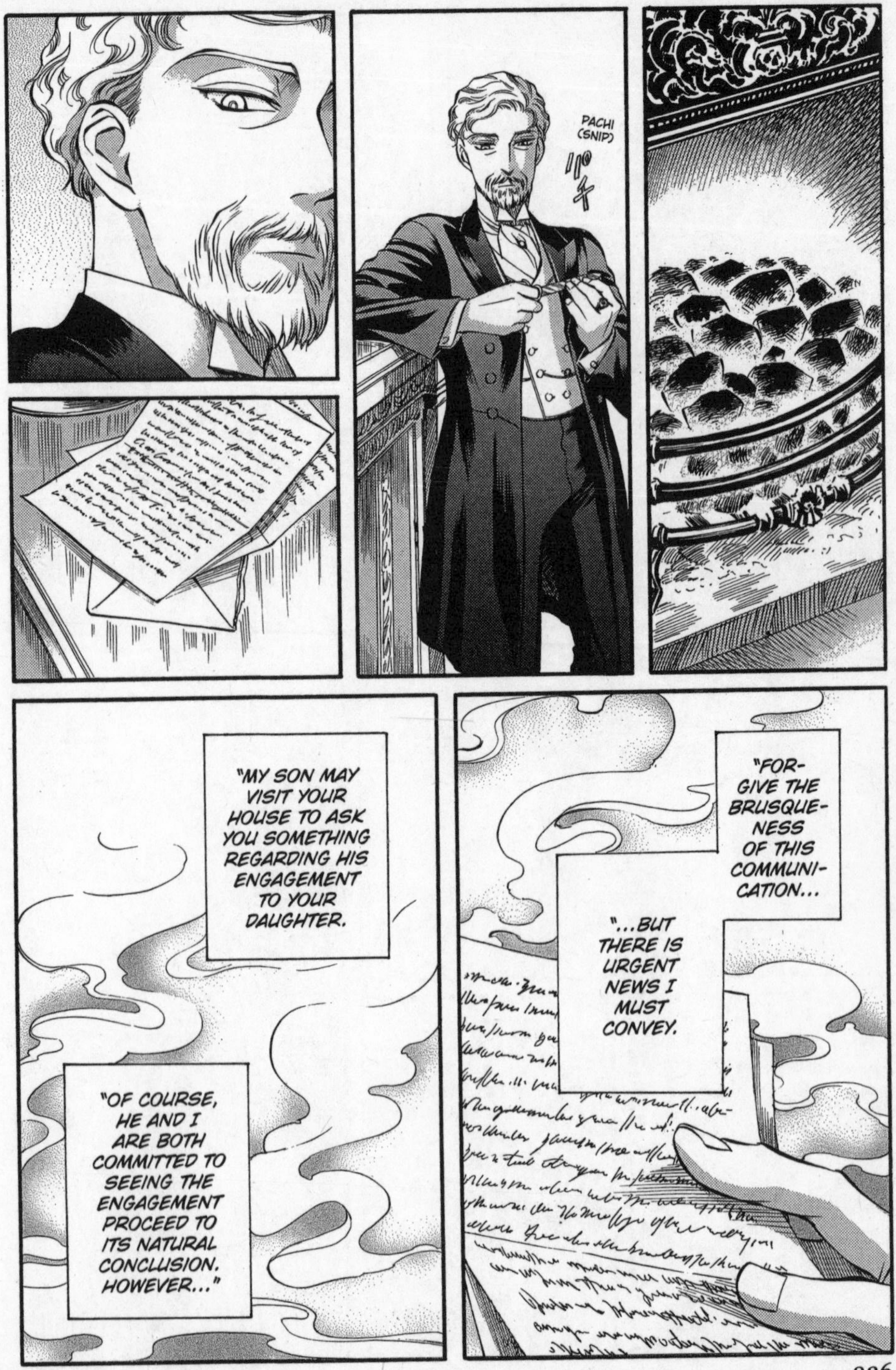
PACHI (SNIP)
"FOR-GIVE THE BRUSQUE-NESS OF THIS COMMUNI-CATION...
"...BUT THERE IS URGENT NEWS I MUST CONVEY.
"MY SON MAY VISIT YOUR HOUSE TO ASK YOU SOMETHING REGARDING HIS ENGAGEMENT TO YOUR DAUGHTER.
"OF COURSE, HE AND I ARE BOTH COMMITTED TO SEEING THE ENGAGEMENT PROCEED TO ITS NATURAL CONCLUSION. HOWEVER..."

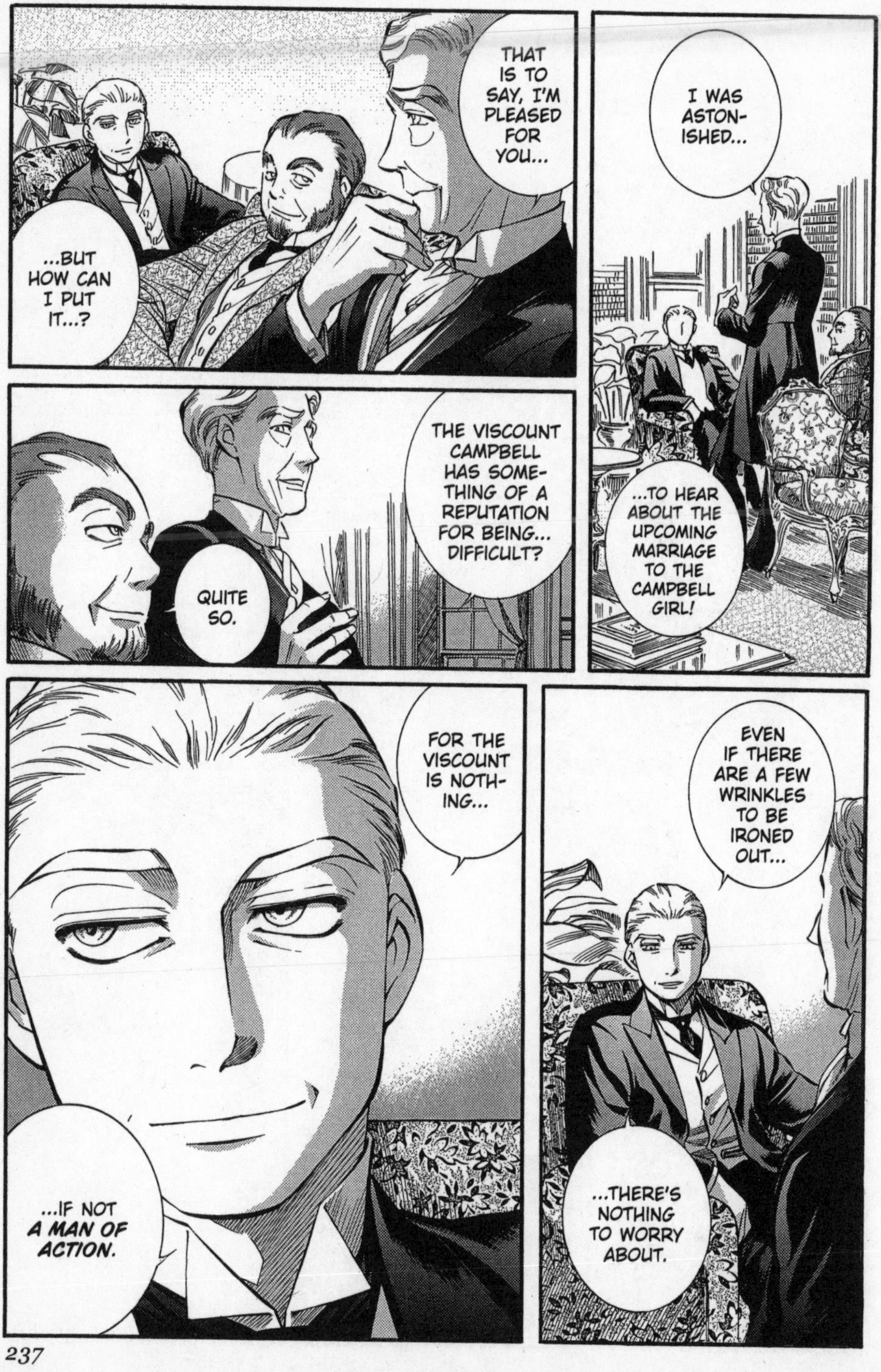
I WAS ASTONISHED...
...TO HEAR ABOUT THE UPCOMING MARRIAGE TO THE CAMPBELL GIRL!
THAT IS TO SAY, I'M PLEASED FOR YOU...
...BUT HOW CAN I PUT IT...?
THE VISCOUNT CAMPBELL HAS SOMETHING OF A REPUTATION FOR BEING... DIFFICULT?
QUITE SO.
EVEN IF THERE ARE A FEW WRINKLES TO BE IRONED OUT...
...THERE'S NOTHING TO WORRY ABOUT.
FOR THE VISCOUNT IS NOTHING...
...IF NOT *A MAN OF ACTION*.

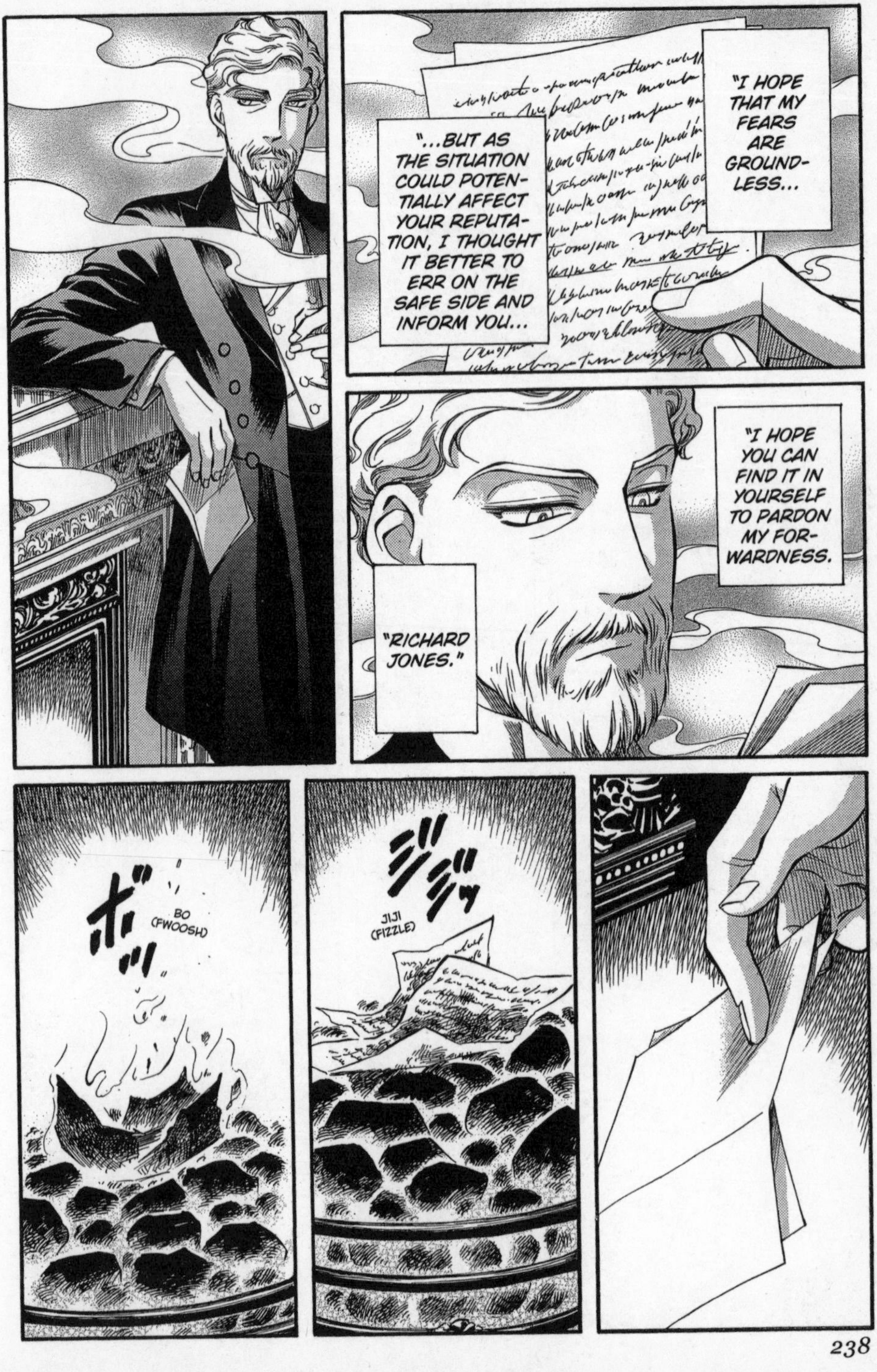
"I HOPE THAT MY FEARS ARE GROUNDLESS...
"...BUT AS THE SITUATION COULD POTENTIALLY AFFECT YOUR REPUTATION, I THOUGHT IT BETTER TO ERR ON THE SAFE SIDE AND INFORM YOU...
"I HOPE YOU CAN FIND IT IN YOURSELF TO PARDON MY FORWARDNESS.
"RICHARD JONES."
JIJI (FIZZLE)
BO (FWOOSH)

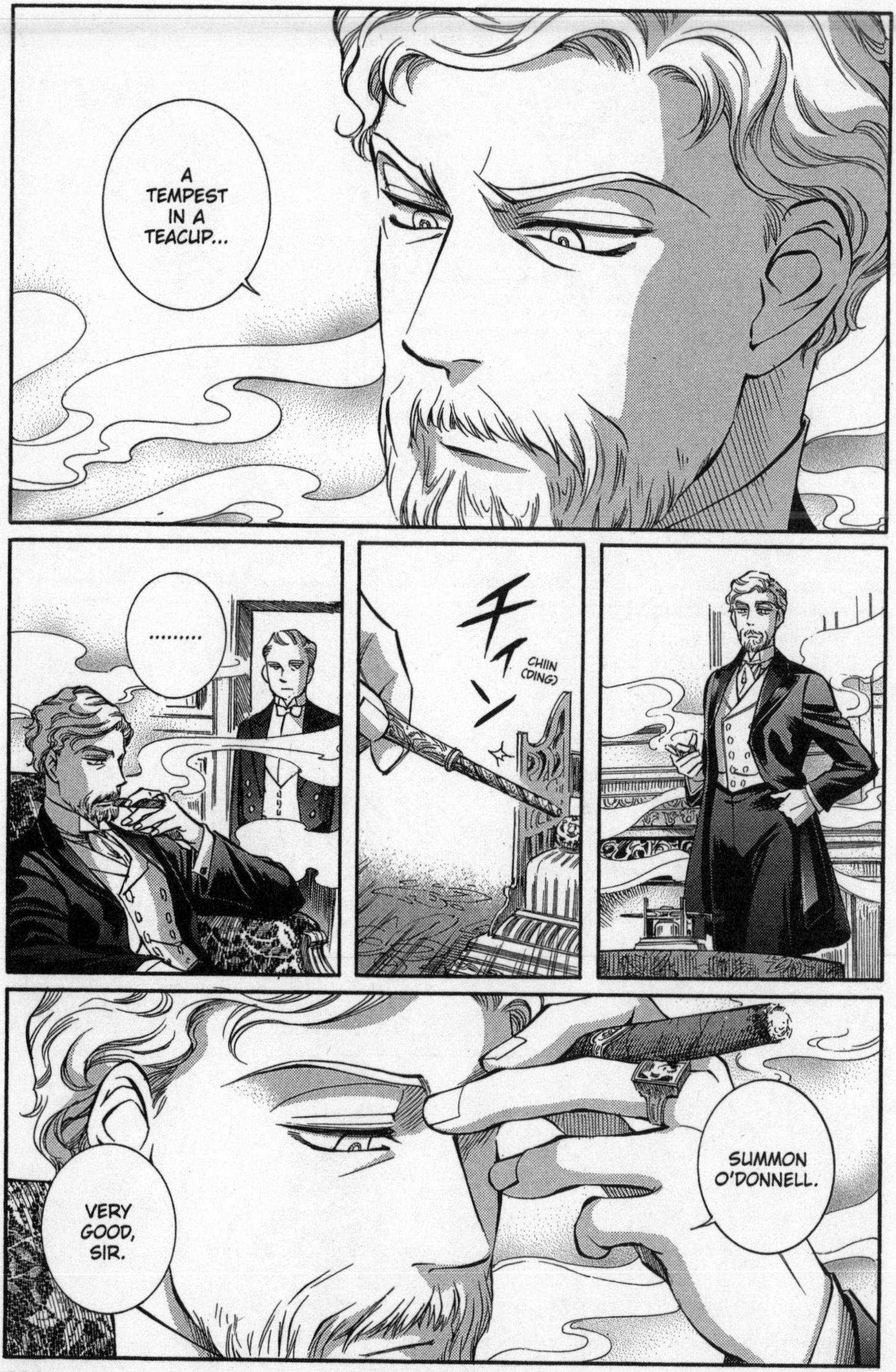
A TEMPEST IN A TEACUP...
チィン
CHIIN (DING)
....
SUMMON O'DONNELL.
VERY GOOD, SIR.

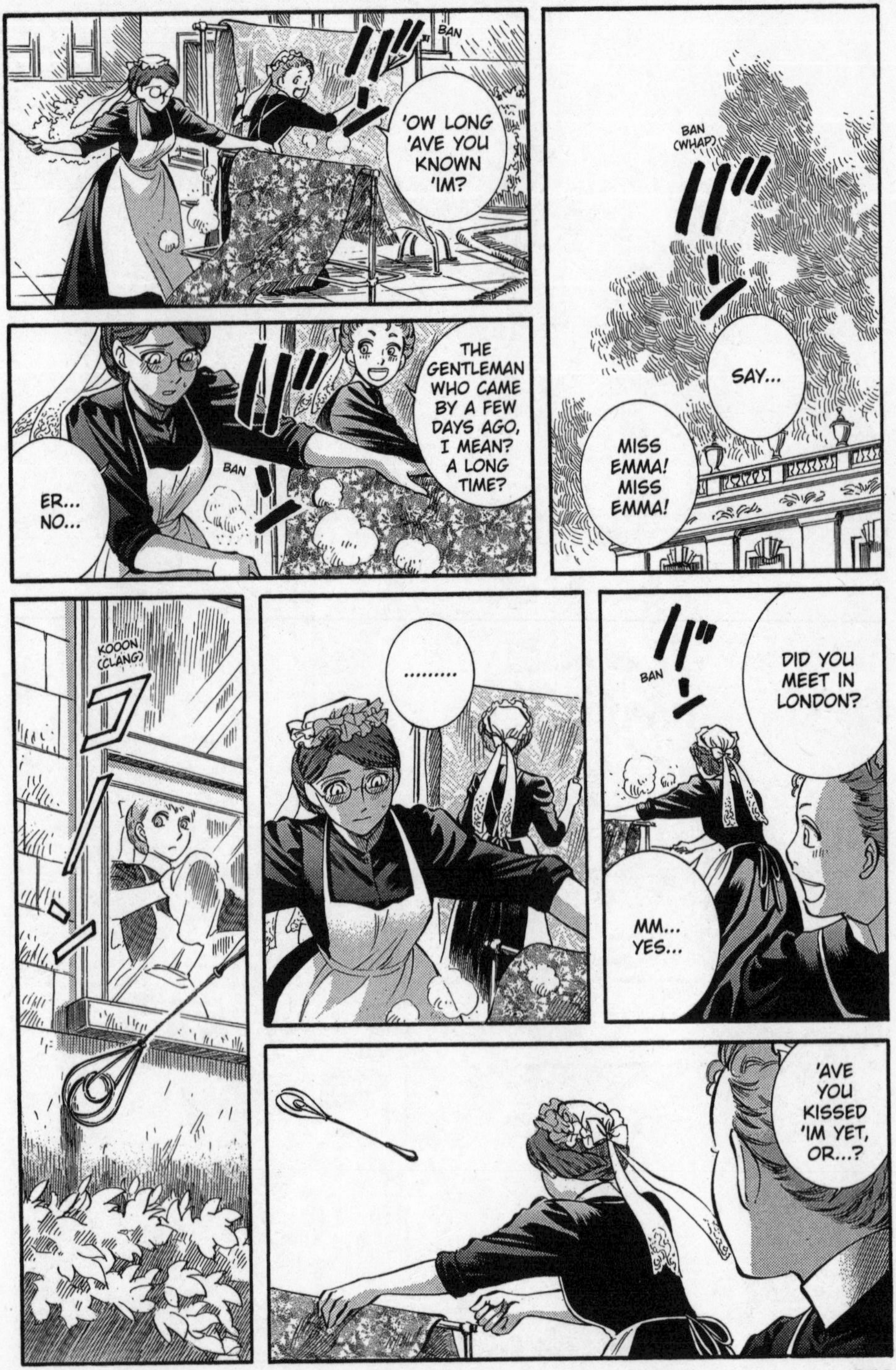

BAN (WHAP)
SAY...
MISS EMMA! MISS EMMA!
BAN
'OW LONG 'AVE YOU KNOWN 'IM?
THE GENTLEMAN WHO CAME BY A FEW DAYS AGO, I MEAN? A LONG TIME?
BAN
ER... NO...
BAN
DID YOU MEET IN LONDON?
MM... YES...
....
'AVE YOU KISSED 'IM YET, OR...?
KOOON (CLANG)

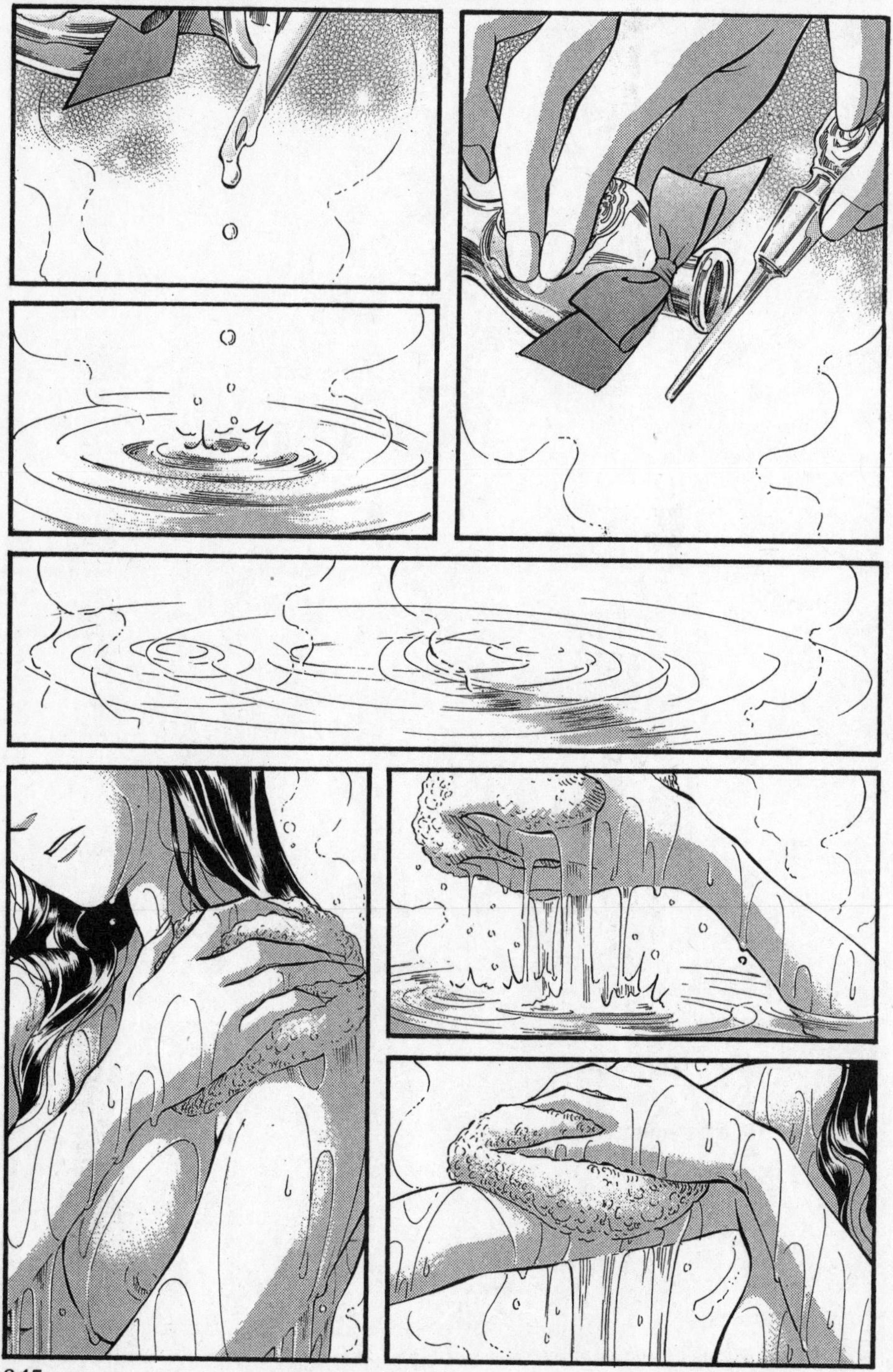

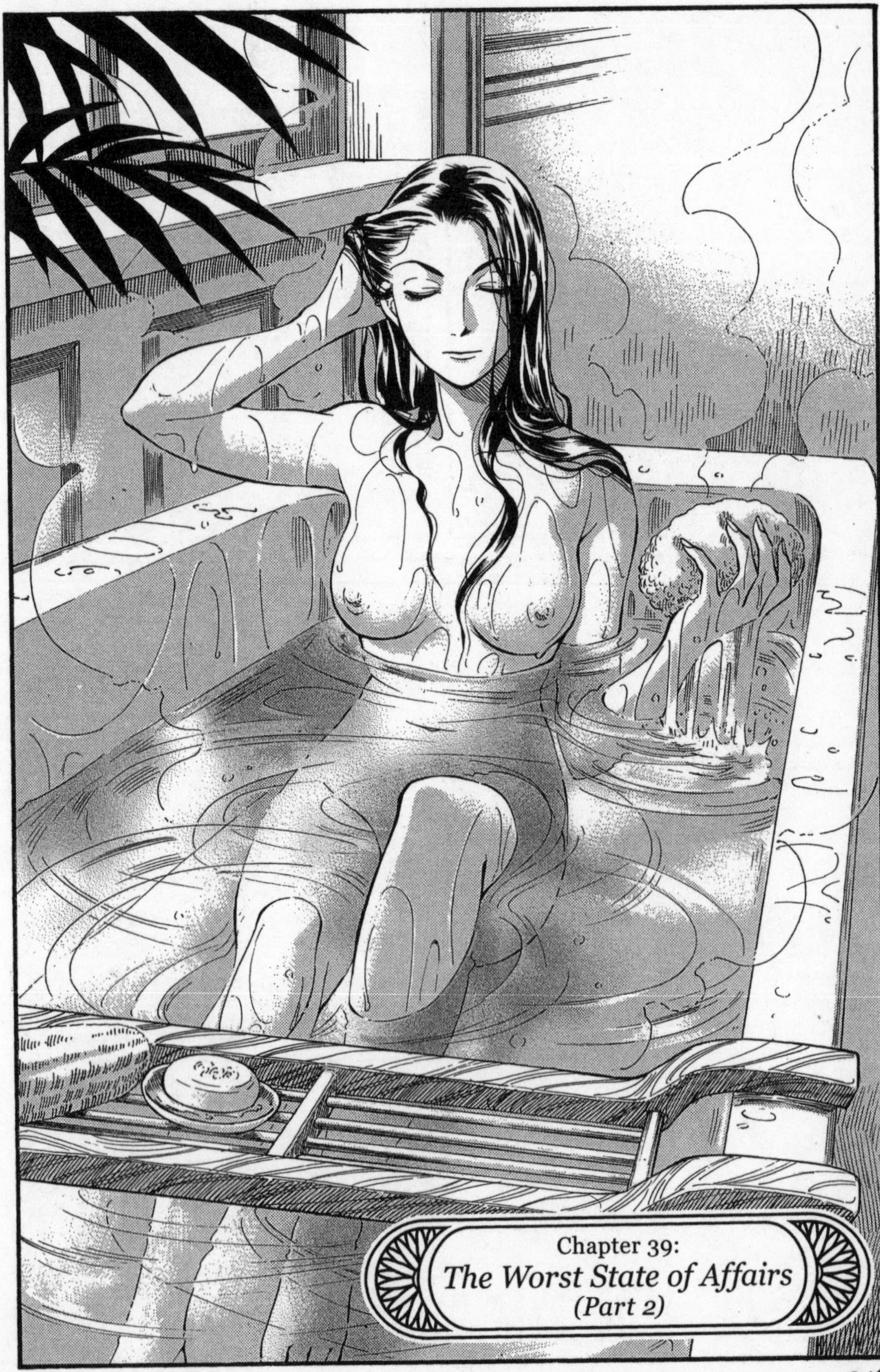
Chapter 39:
The Worst State of Affairs
(Part 2)

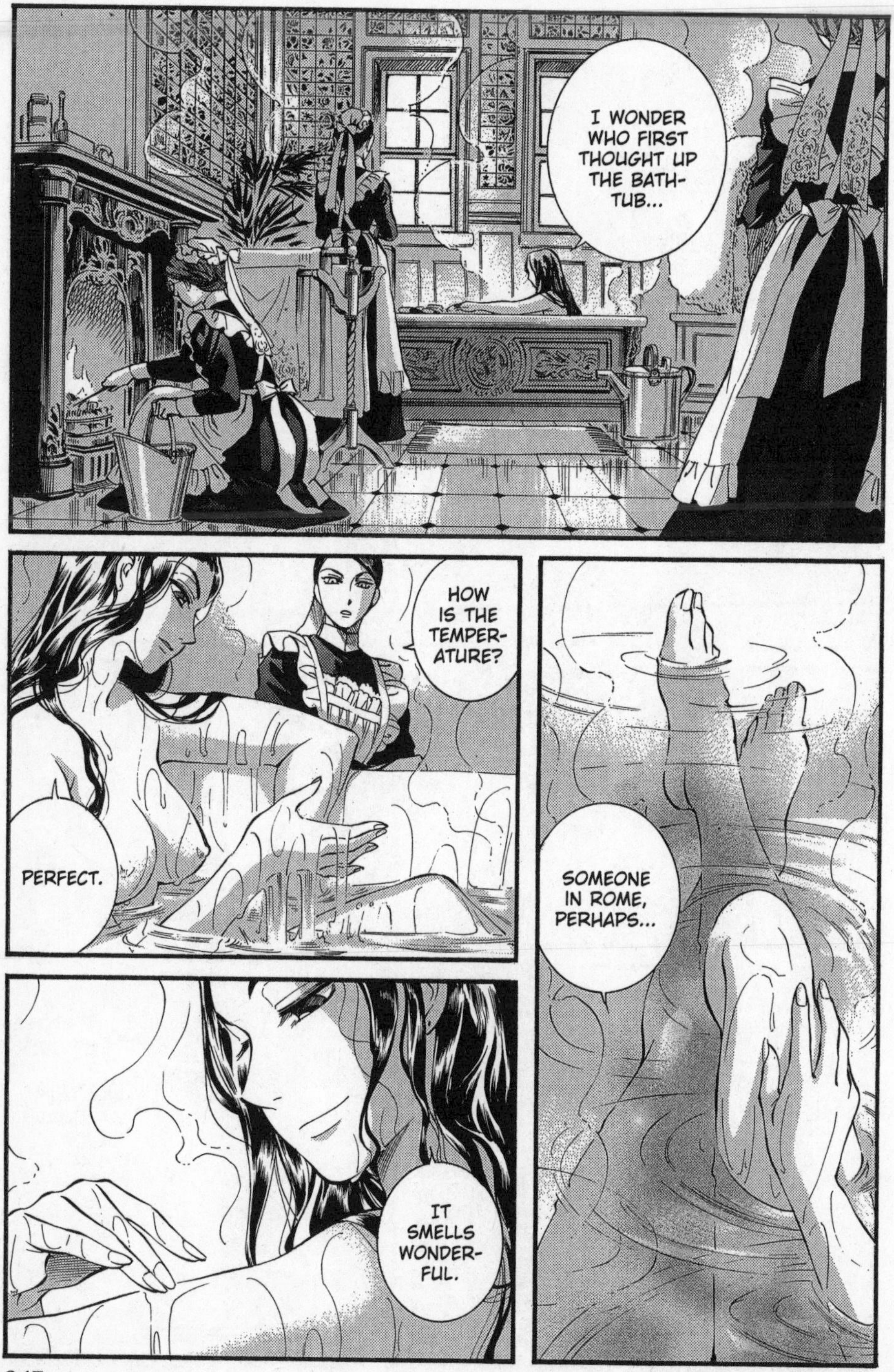
I WONDER WHO FIRST THOUGHT UP THE BATH-TUB...
SOMEONE IN ROME, PERHAPS...
HOW IS THE TEMPER-ATURE?
PERFECT.
IT SMELLS WONDER-FUL.

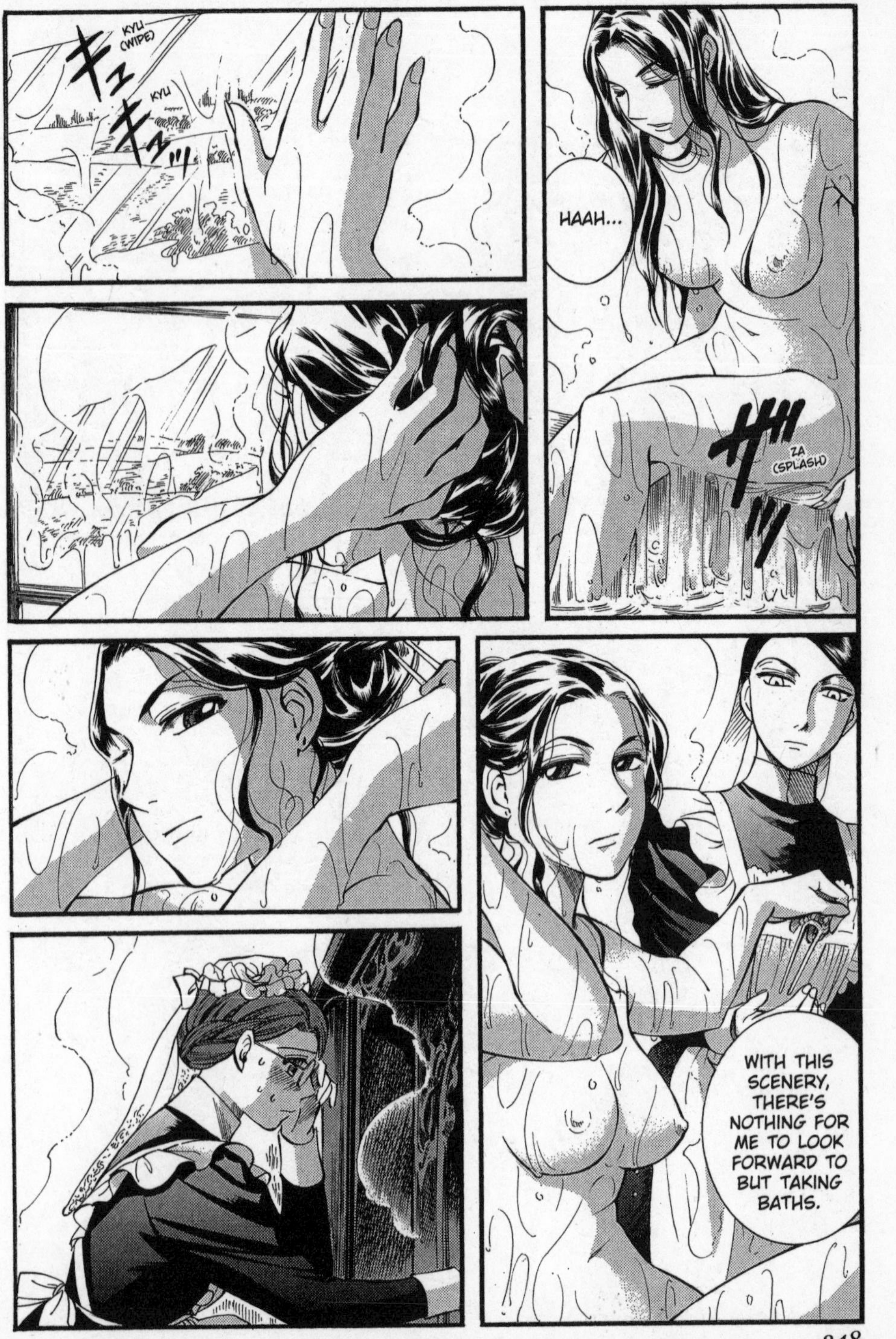
HAAH...
ZA (SPLASH)
KYU (WIPE)
KYU
WITH THIS SCENERY, THERE'S NOTHING FOR ME TO LOOK FORWARD TO BUT TAKING BATHS.

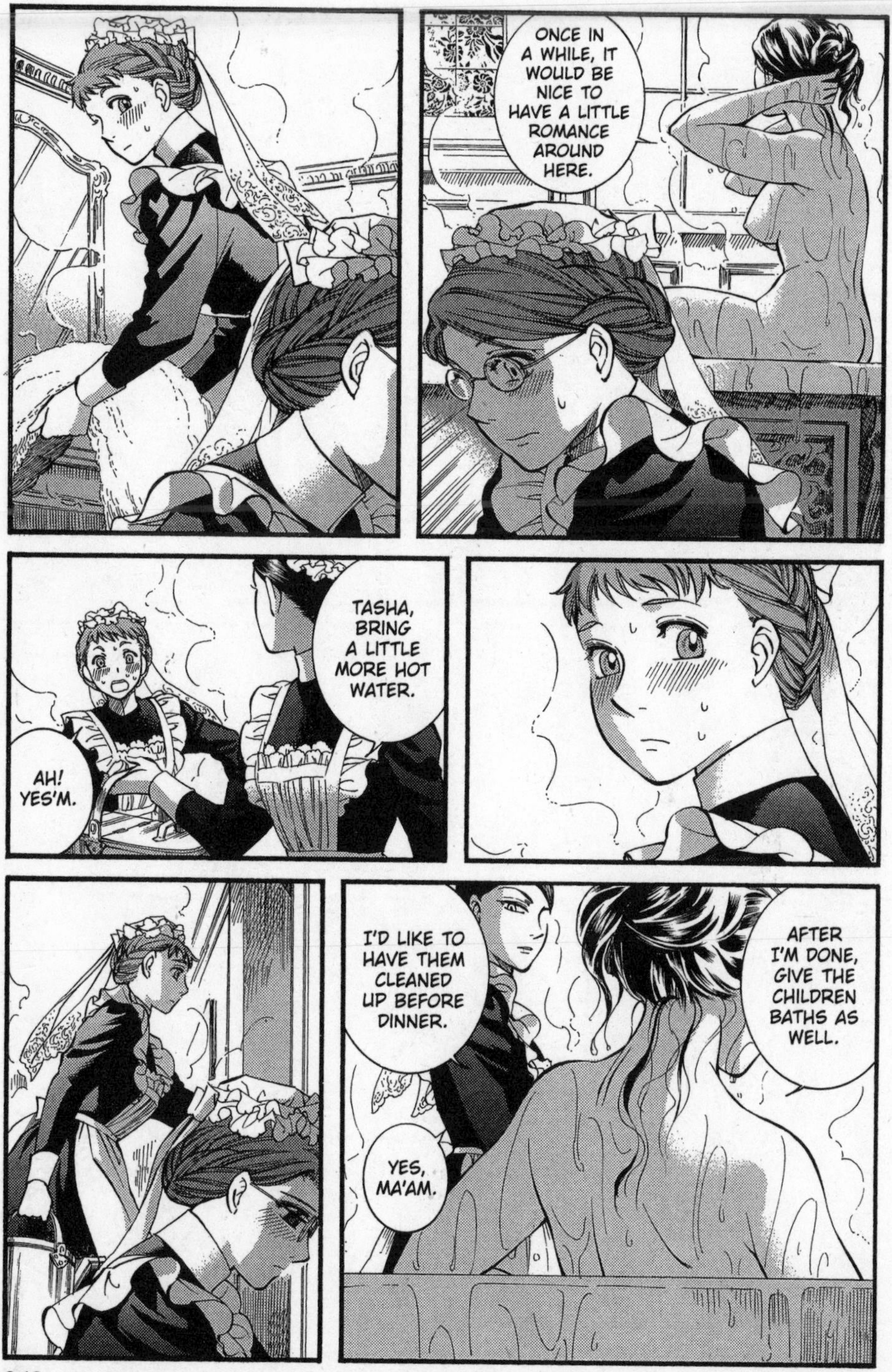
ONCE IN A WHILE, IT WOULD BE NICE TO HAVE A LITTLE ROMANCE AROUND HERE.
TASHA, BRING A LITTLE MORE HOT WATER.
AH! YES'M.
AFTER I'M DONE, GIVE THE CHILDREN BATHS AS WELL.
I'D LIKE TO HAVE THEM CLEANED UP BEFORE DINNER.
YES, MA'AM.

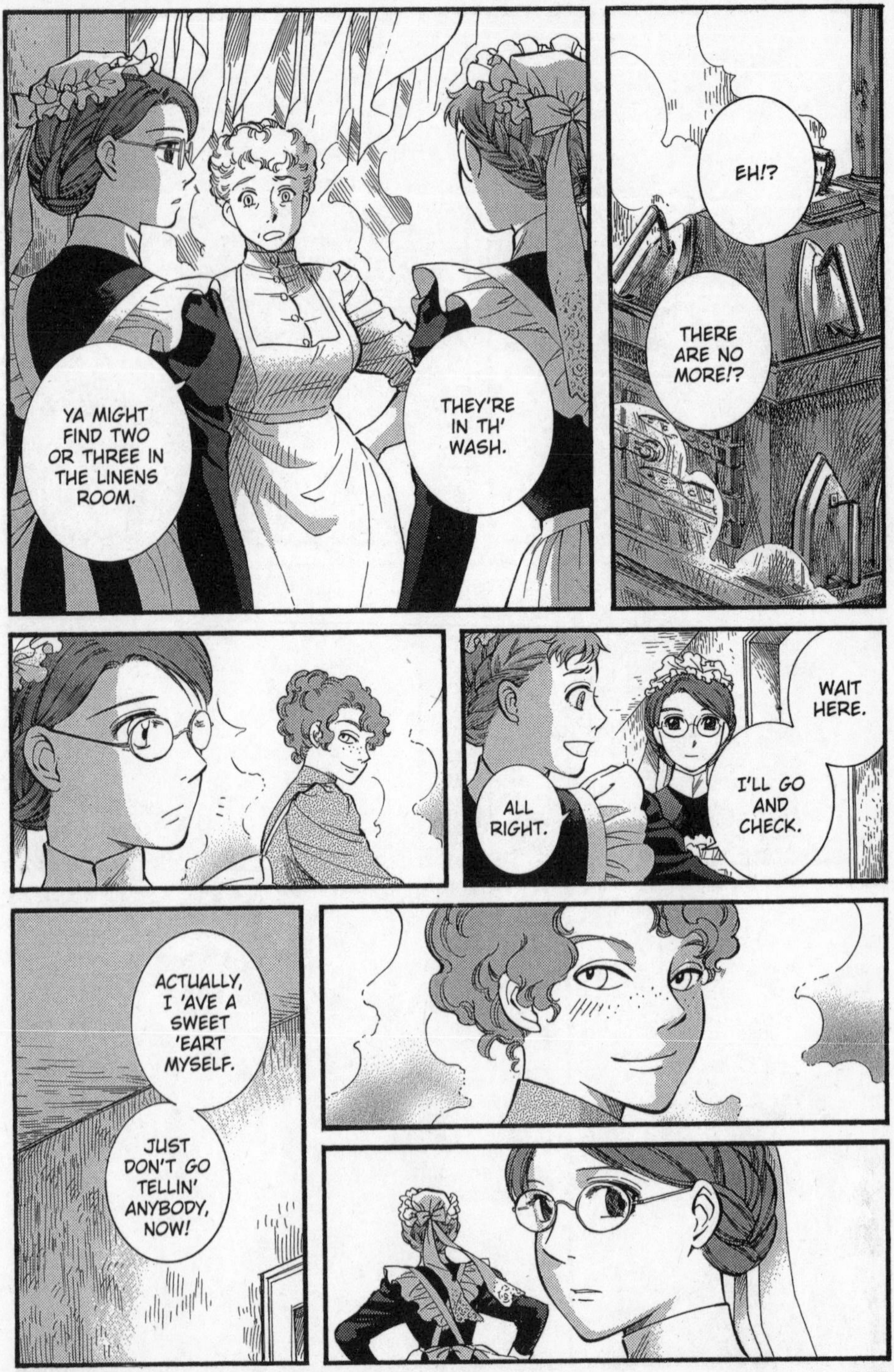
EH!?
THERE ARE NO MORE!?
THEY'RE IN TH' WASH.
YA MIGHT FIND TWO OR THREE IN THE LINENS ROOM.
WAIT HERE.
I'LL GO AND CHECK.
ALL RIGHT.
ACTUALLY, I 'AVE A SWEET 'EART MYSELF.
JUST DON'T GO TELLIN' ANYBODY, NOW!

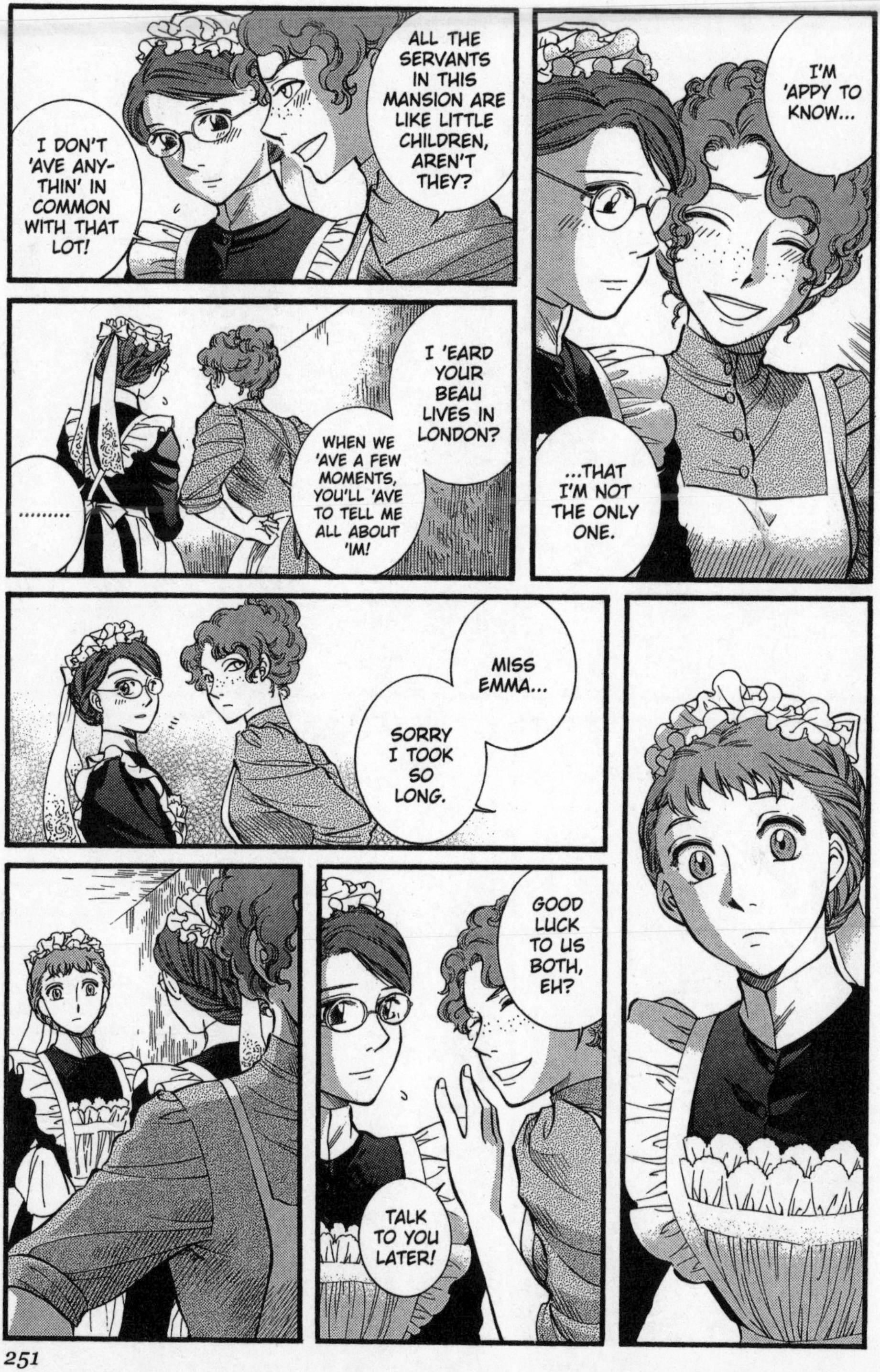
I'M 'APPY TO KNOW...
...THAT I'M NOT THE ONLY ONE.
ALL THE SERVANTS IN THIS MANSION ARE LIKE LITTLE CHILDREN, AREN'T THEY?
I DON'T 'AVE ANYTHIN' IN COMMON WITH THAT LOT!
I 'EARD YOUR BEAU LIVES IN LONDON?
WHEN WE 'AVE A FEW MOMENTS, YOU'LL 'AVE TO TELL ME ALL ABOUT 'IM!
....
MISS EMMA...
SORRY I TOOK SO LONG.
GOOD LUCK TO US BOTH, EH?
TALK TO YOU LATER!

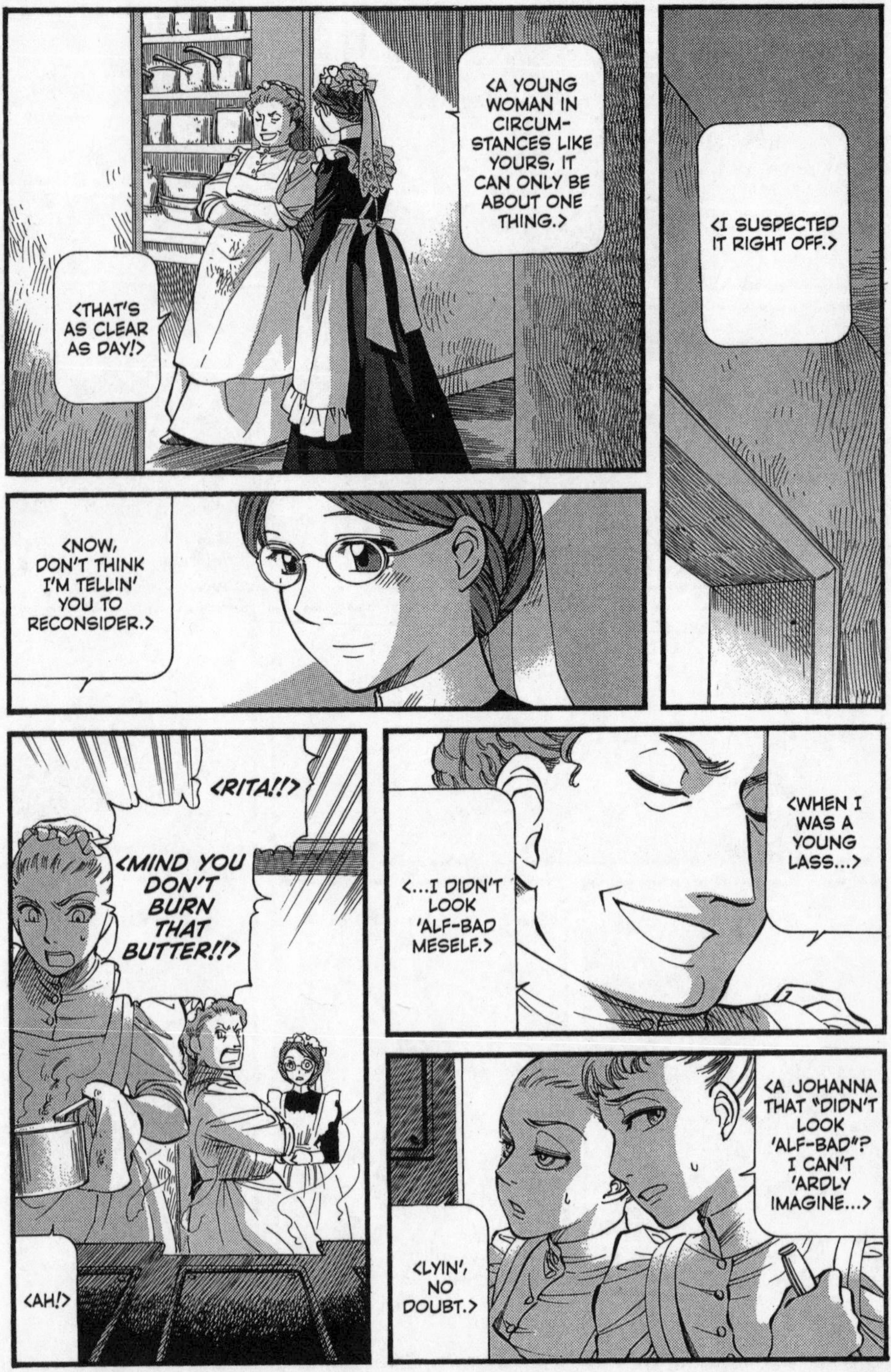
<I SUSPECTED IT RIGHT OFF.>
<A YOUNG WOMAN IN CIRCUM-STANCES LIKE YOURS, IT CAN ONLY BE ABOUT ONE THING.>
<THAT'S AS CLEAR AS DAY!>
<NOW, DON'T THINK I'M TELLIN' YOU TO RECONSIDER.>
<WHEN I WAS A YOUNG LASS...>
<...I DIDN'T LOOK 'ALF-BAD MESELF.>
<A JOHANNA THAT "DIDN'T LOOK 'ALF-BAD"? I CAN'T 'ARDLY IMAGINE...>
<LYIN', NO DOUBT.>
<RITA!!>
<MIND YOU DON'T BURN THAT BUTTER!!>
<AH!>

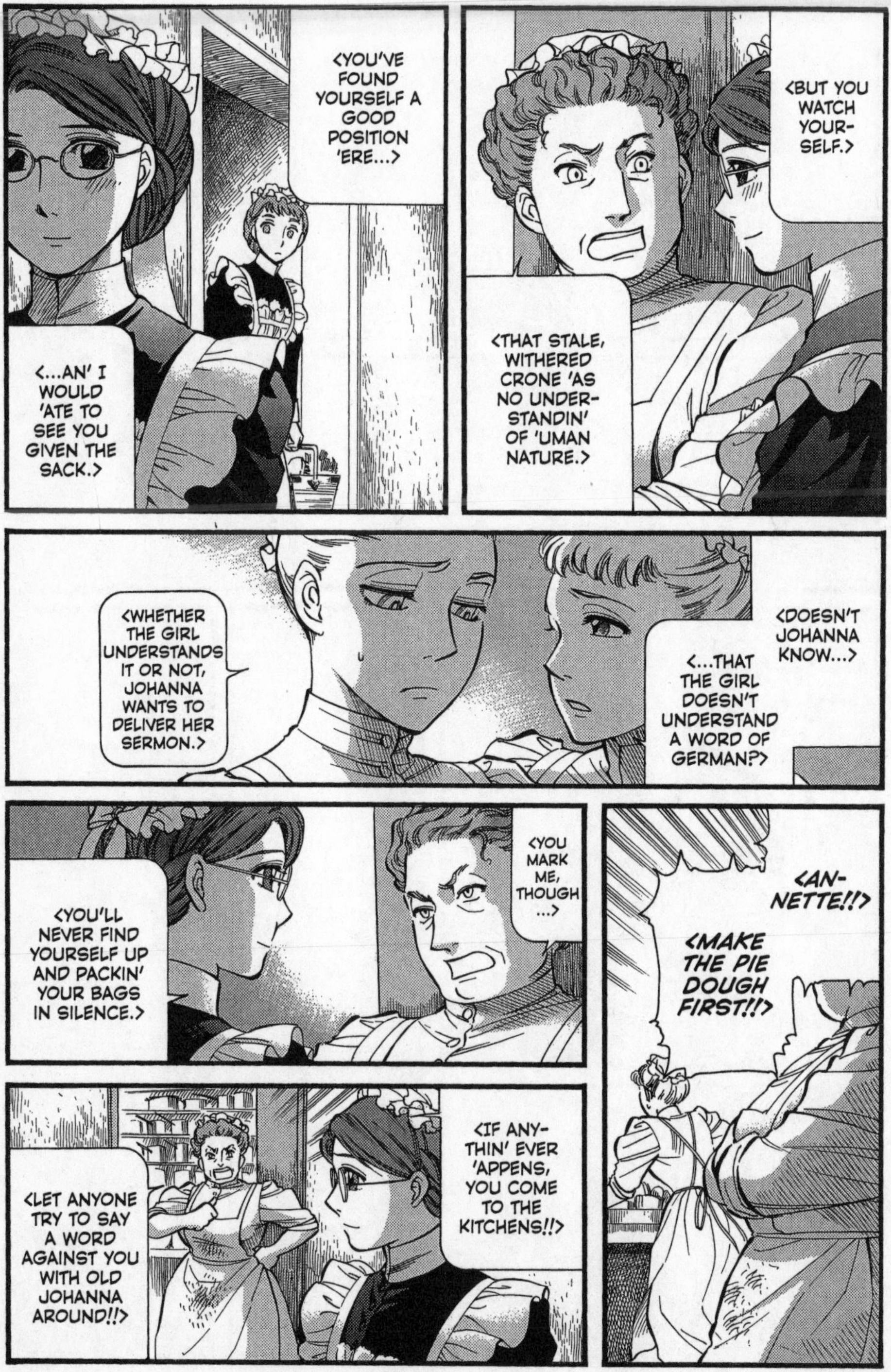

<BUT YOU WATCH YOUR-SELF.>
<THAT STALE, WITHERED CRONE 'AS NO UNDER-STANDIN' OF 'UMAN NATURE.>
<YOU'VE FOUND YOURSELF A GOOD POSITION 'ERE...>
<...AN' I WOULD 'ATE TO SEE YOU GIVEN THE SACK.>
<DOESN'T JOHANNA KNOW...>
<...THAT THE GIRL DOESN'T UNDERSTAND A WORD OF GERMAN?>
<WHETHER THE GIRL UNDERSTANDS IT OR NOT, JOHANNA WANTS TO DELIVER HER SERMON.>
<AN-NETTE!!>
<MAKE THE PIE DOUGH FIRST!!>
<YOU MARK ME, THOUGH ...>
<YOU'LL NEVER FIND YOURSELF UP AND PACKIN' YOUR BAGS IN SILENCE.>
<IF ANY-THIN' EVER 'APPENS, YOU COME TO THE KITCHENS!!>
<LET ANYONE TRY TO SAY A WORD AGAINST YOU WITH OLD JOHANNA AROUND!!>

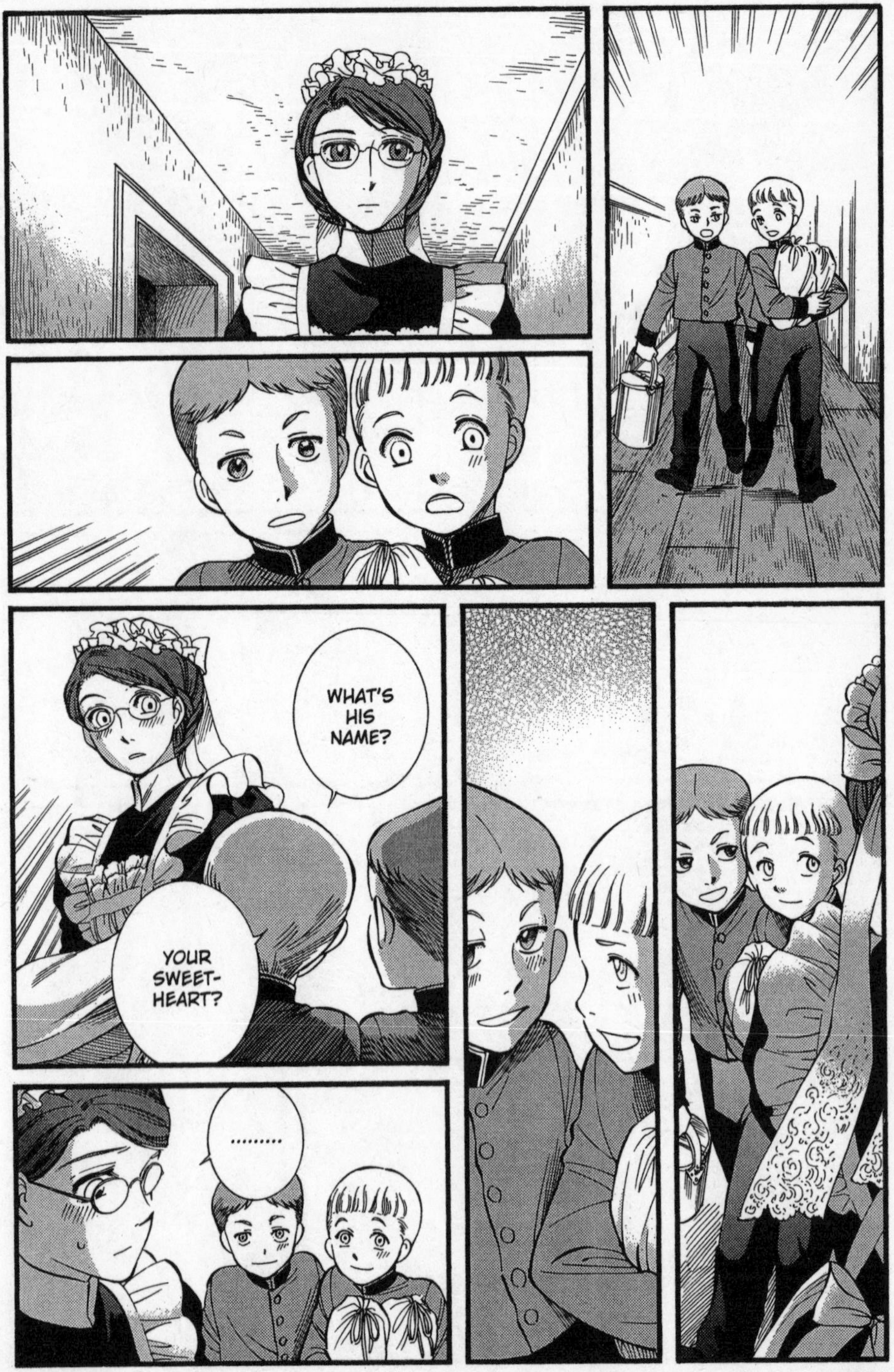
WHAT'S HIS NAME?
YOUR SWEET-HEART?
....

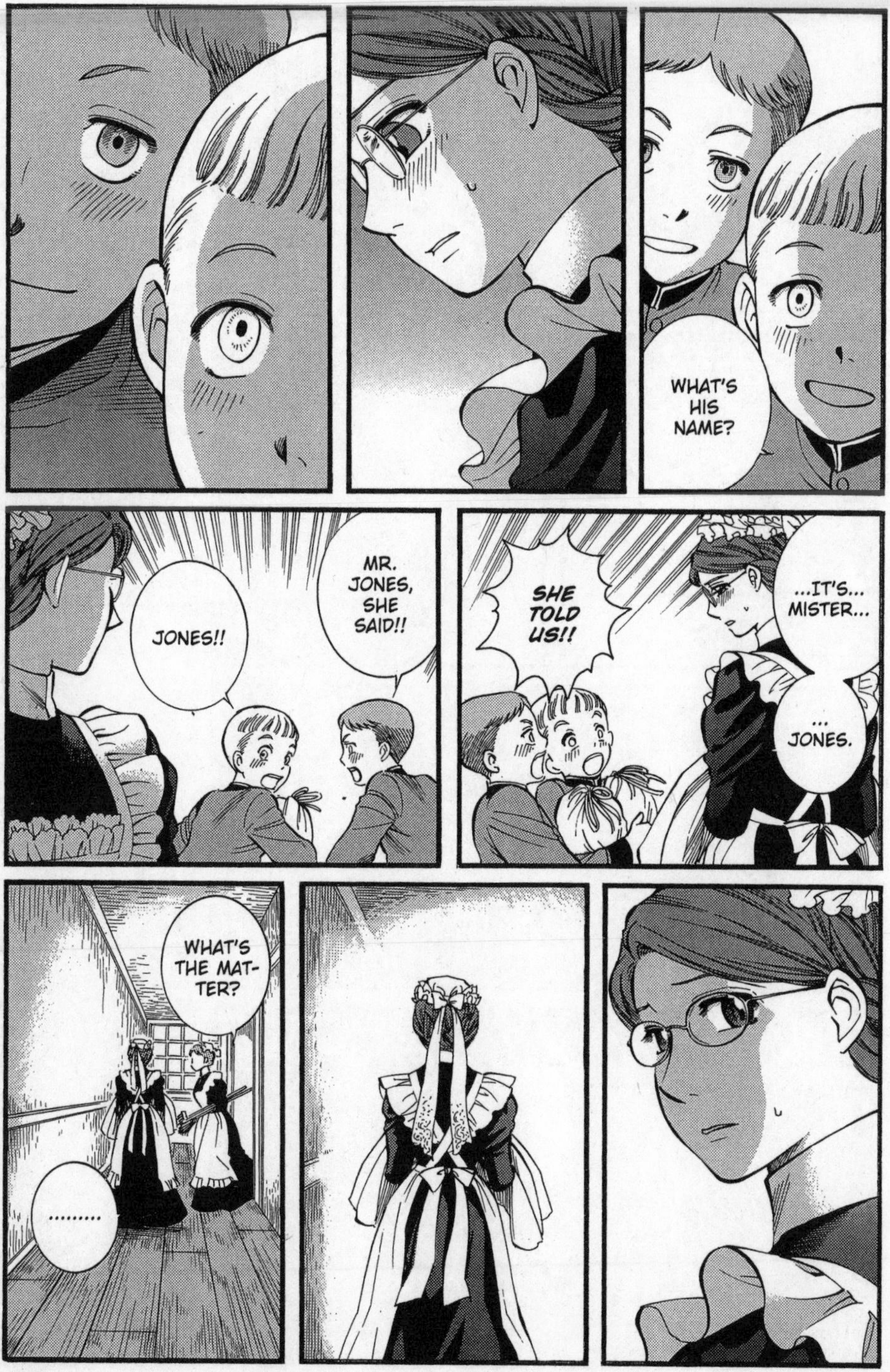
WHAT'S HIS NAME?
...IT'S... MISTER...
... JONES.
SHE TOLD US!!
MR. JONES, SHE SAID!!
JONES!!
WHAT'S THE MAT-TER?
....

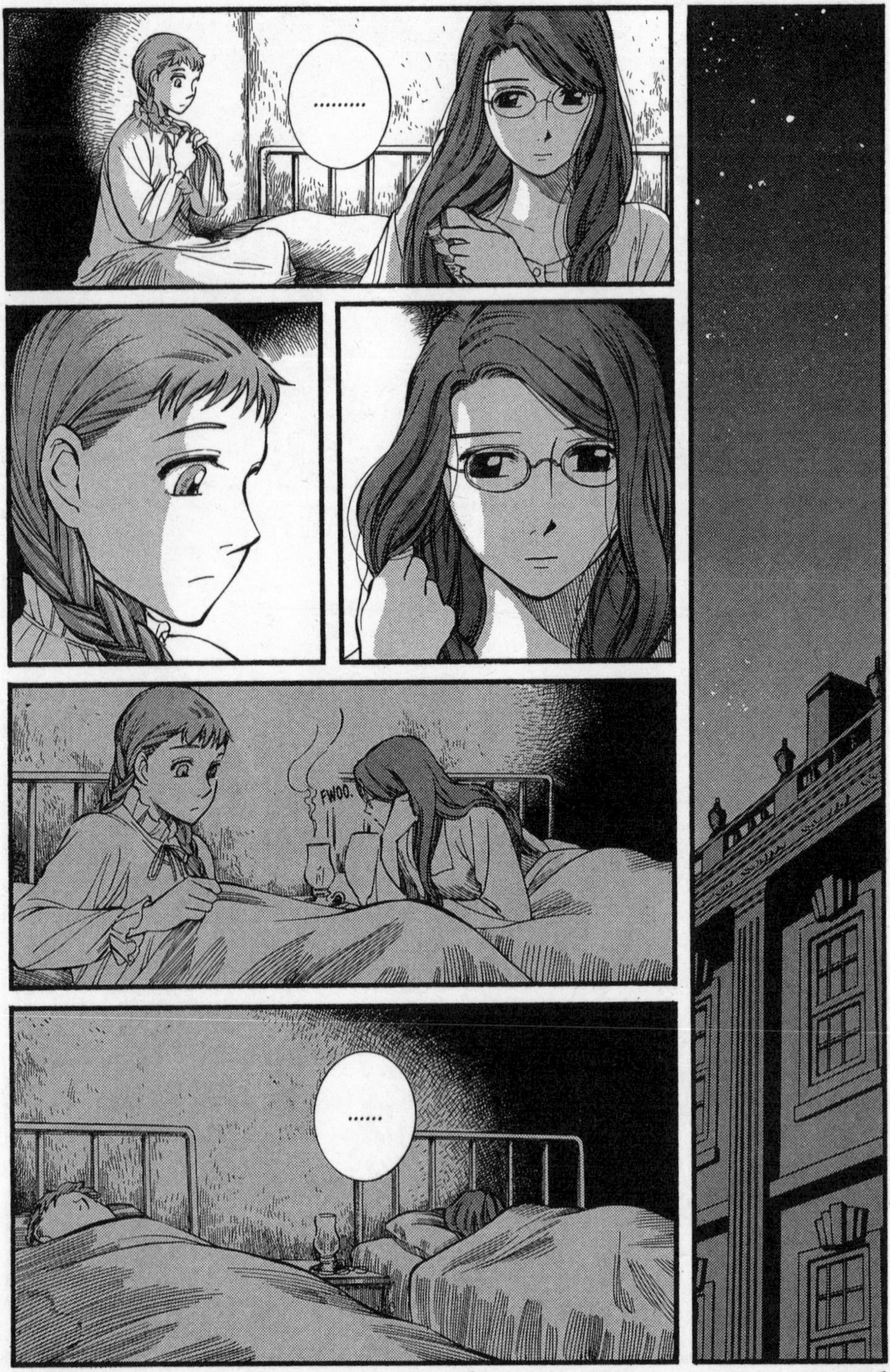
....
FWOO.
......

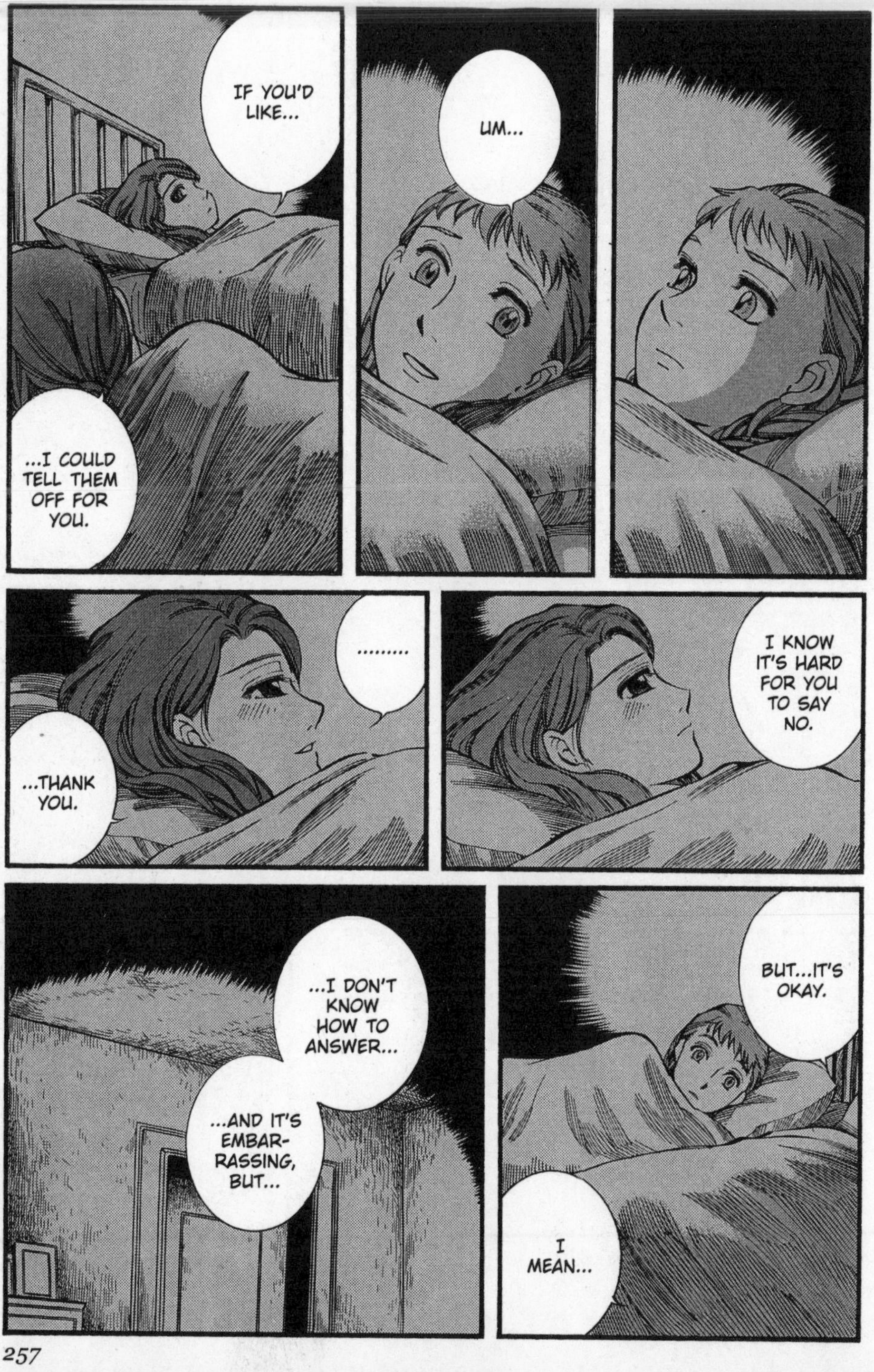
UM...
IF YOU'D LIKE...
...I COULD TELL THEM OFF FOR YOU.
I KNOW IT'S HARD FOR YOU TO SAY NO.
....
...THANK YOU.
BUT...IT'S OKAY.
I MEAN...
...I DON'T KNOW HOW TO ANSWER...
...AND IT'S EMBARRASSING, BUT...

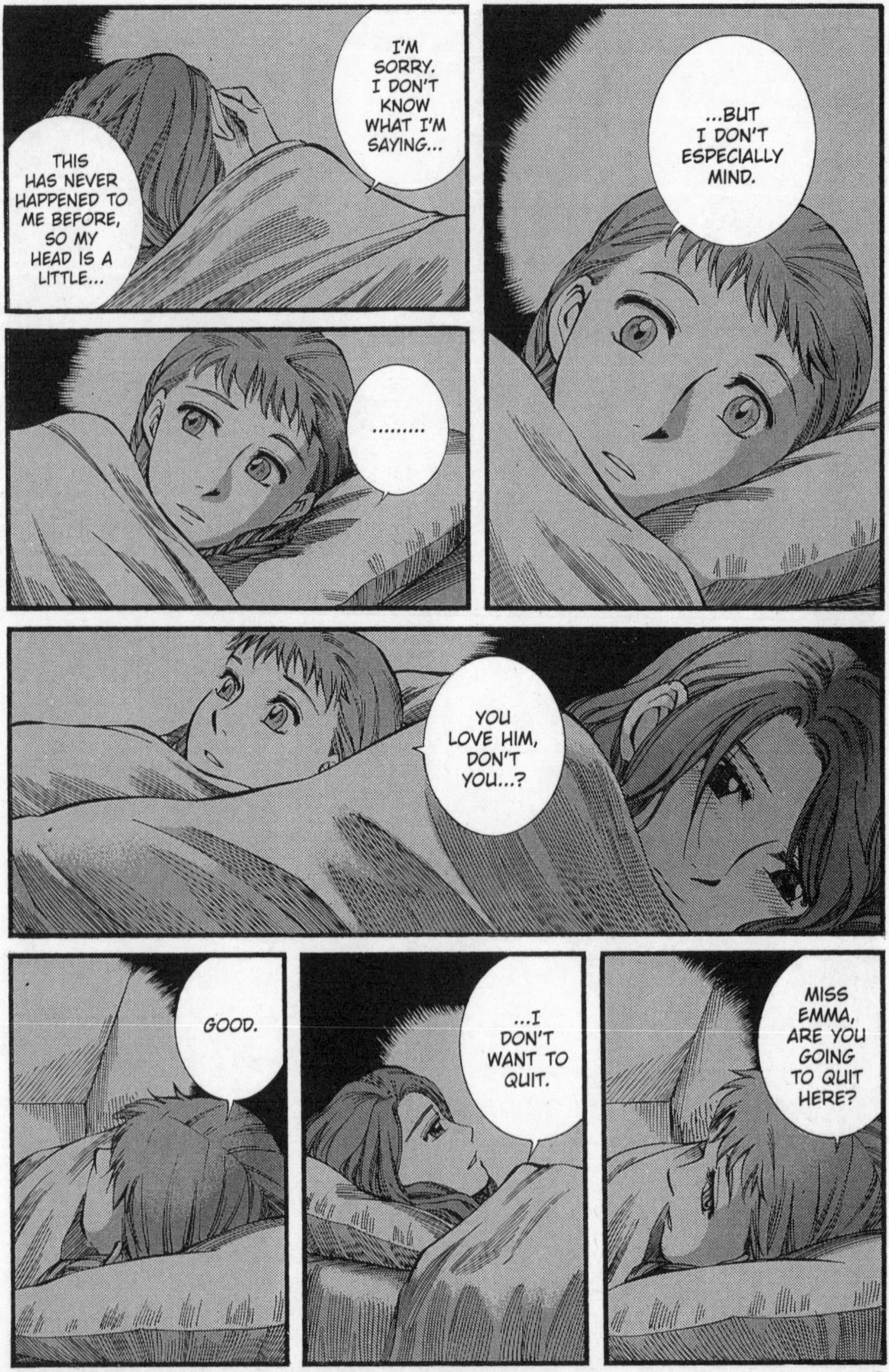
...BUT I DON'T ESPECIALLY MIND.
I'M SORRY. I DON'T KNOW WHAT I'M SAYING...
THIS HAS NEVER HAPPENED TO ME BEFORE, SO MY HEAD IS A LITTLE...
....
YOU LOVE HIM, DON'T YOU...?
MISS EMMA, ARE YOU GOING TO QUIT HERE?
...I DON'T WANT TO QUIT.
GOOD.

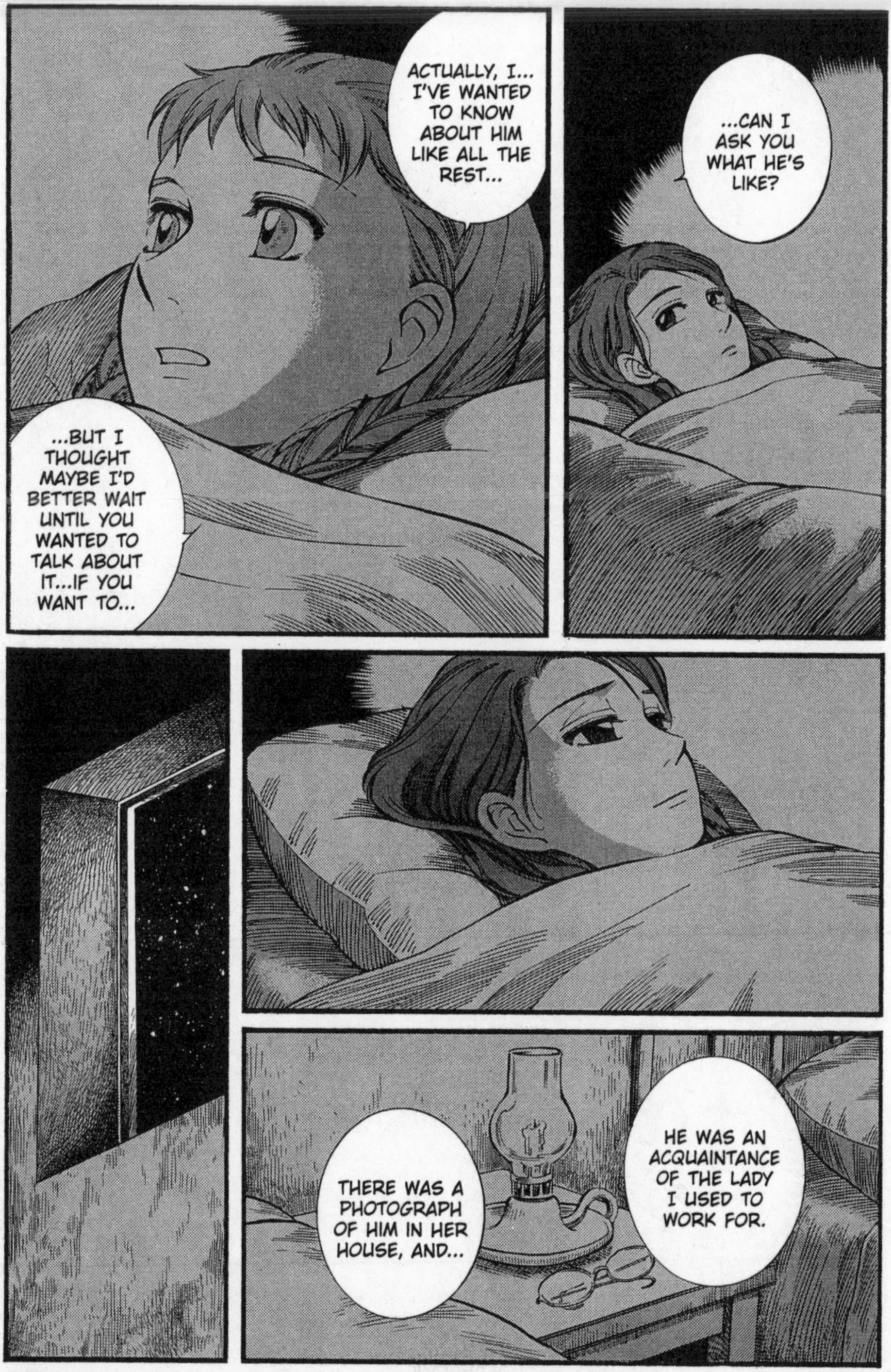
...CAN I ASK YOU WHAT HE'S LIKE?
ACTUALLY, I... I'VE WANTED TO KNOW ABOUT HIM LIKE ALL THE REST...
...BUT I THOUGHT MAYBE I'D BETTER WAIT UNTIL YOU WANTED TO TALK ABOUT IT...IF YOU WANT TO...
HE WAS AN ACQUAINTANCE OF THE LADY I USED TO WORK FOR.
THERE WAS A PHOTOGRAPH OF HIM IN HER HOUSE, AND...

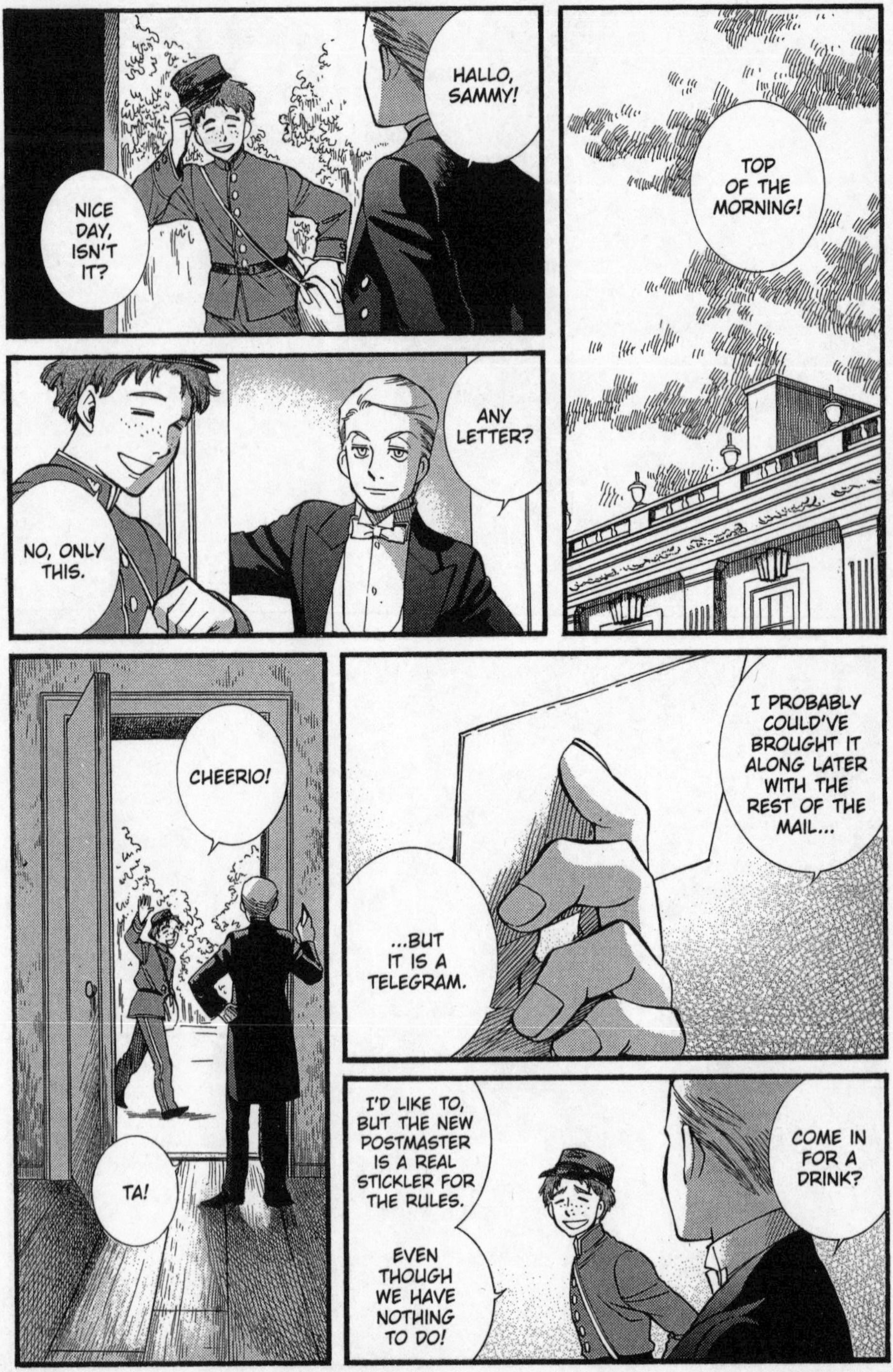
TOP OF THE MORNING!
HALLO, SAMMY!
NICE DAY, ISN'T IT?
ANY LETTER?
NO, ONLY THIS.
I PROBABLY COULD'VE BROUGHT IT ALONG LATER WITH THE REST OF THE MAIL...
...BUT IT IS A TELEGRAM.
COME IN FOR A DRINK?
I'D LIKE TO, BUT THE NEW POSTMASTER IS A REAL STICKLER FOR THE RULES.
EVEN THOUGH WE HAVE NOTHING TO DO!
CHEERIO!
TA!

Chapter 39: End

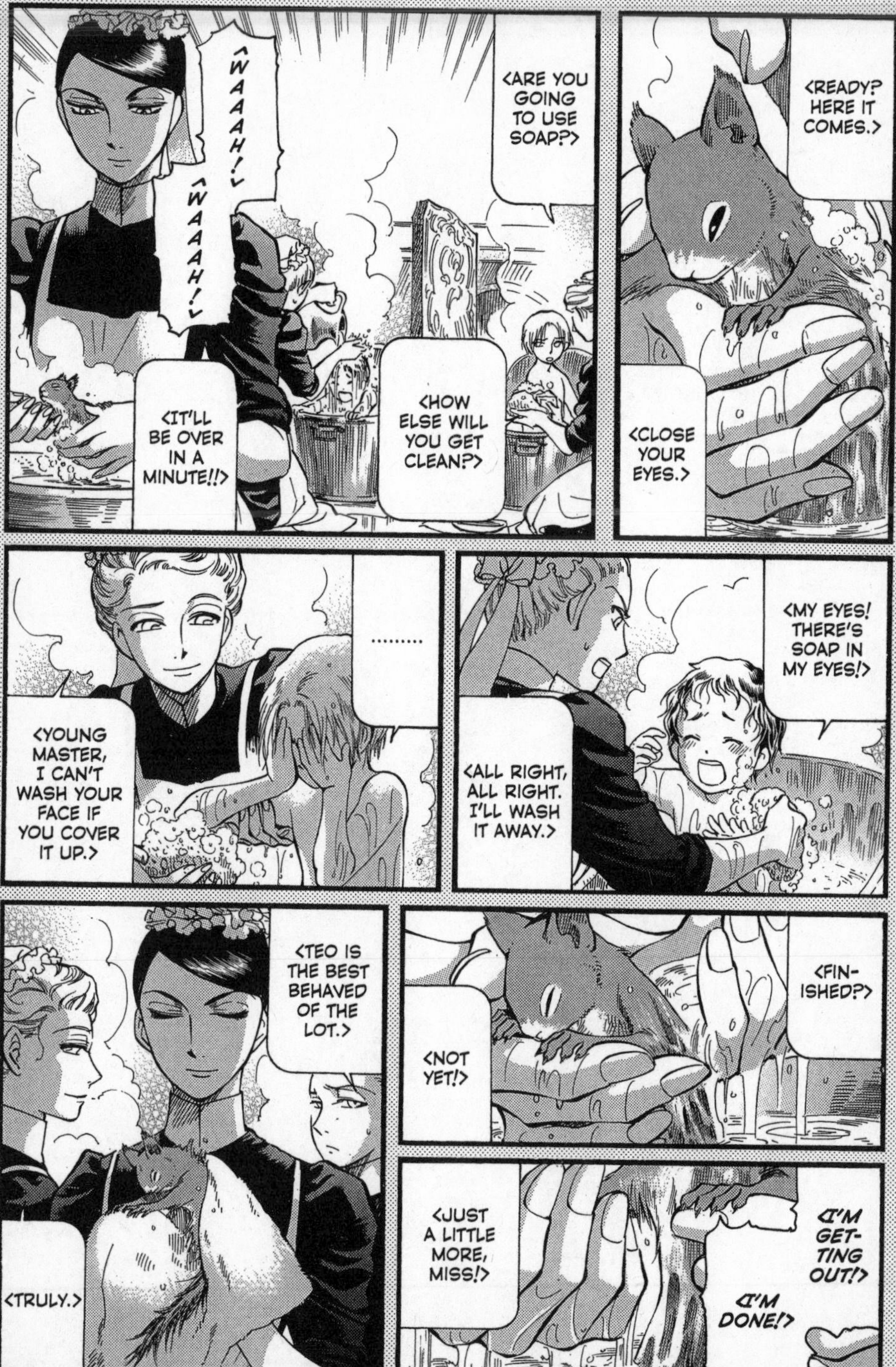
<READY? HERE IT COMES.>
<CLOSE YOUR EYES.>
<ARE YOU GOING TO USE SOAP?>
<WAAAAH!>
<WAAAAH!>
<HOW ELSE WILL YOU GET CLEAN?>
<IT'LL BE OVER IN A MINUTE!!>
<MY EYES! THERE'S SOAP IN MY EYES!>
<ALL RIGHT, ALL RIGHT. I'LL WASH IT AWAY.>
....
<YOUNG MASTER, I CAN'T WASH YOUR FACE IF YOU COVER IT UP.>
<FIN-ISHED?>
<NOT YET!>
<I'M GET-TING OUT!>
<I'M DONE!>
<JUST A LITTLE MORE, MISS!>
<TEO IS THE BEST BEHAVED OF THE LOT.>
<TRULY.>

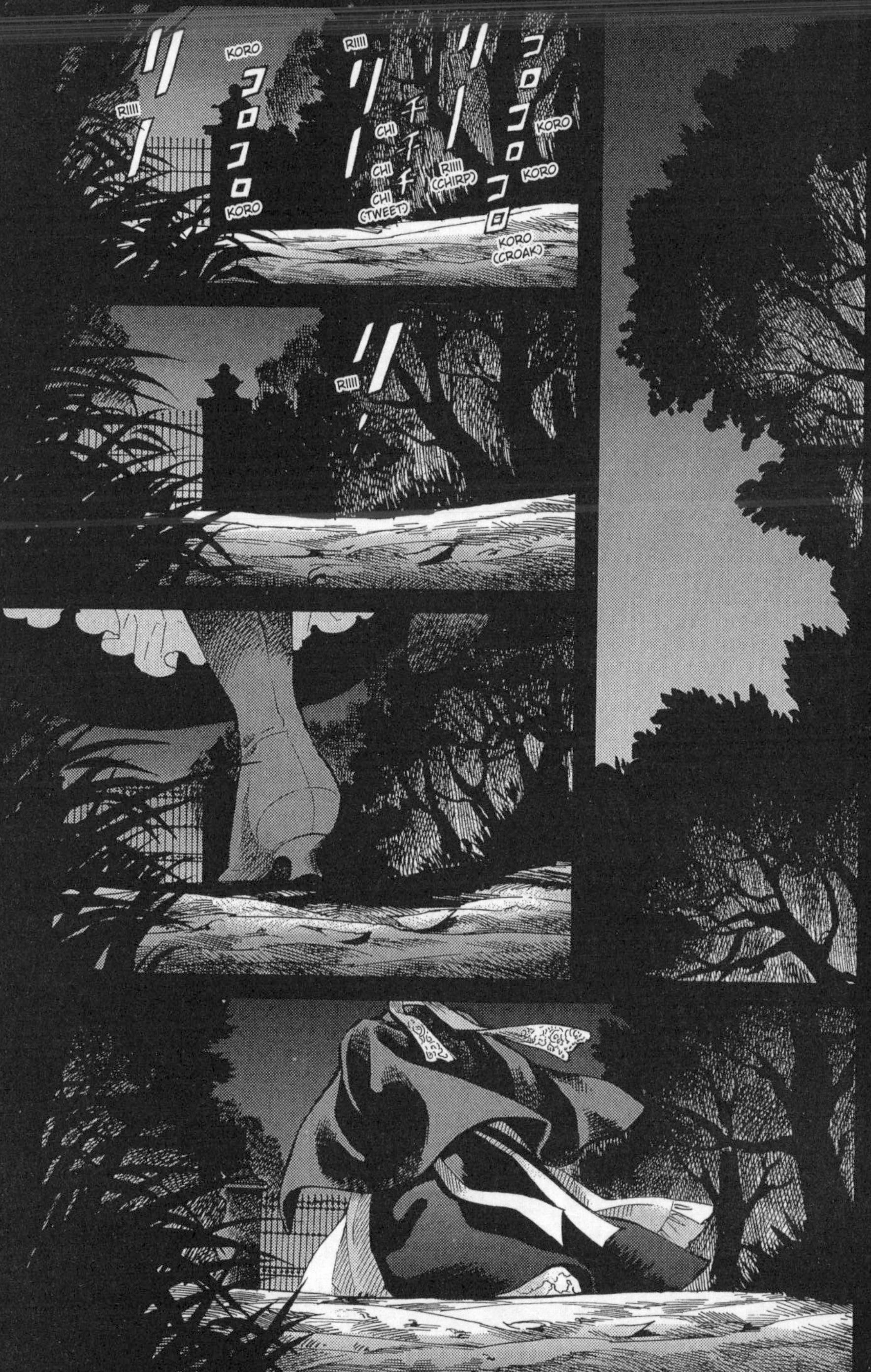
コロコロコロ
KORO
KORO
KORO (CROAK)
リー
RIIII (CHIRP)
チチチ
CHI
CHI
CHI (TWEET)
リー
RIIII
コロコロ
KORO
KORO
リー
RIIII
リ
RIIII

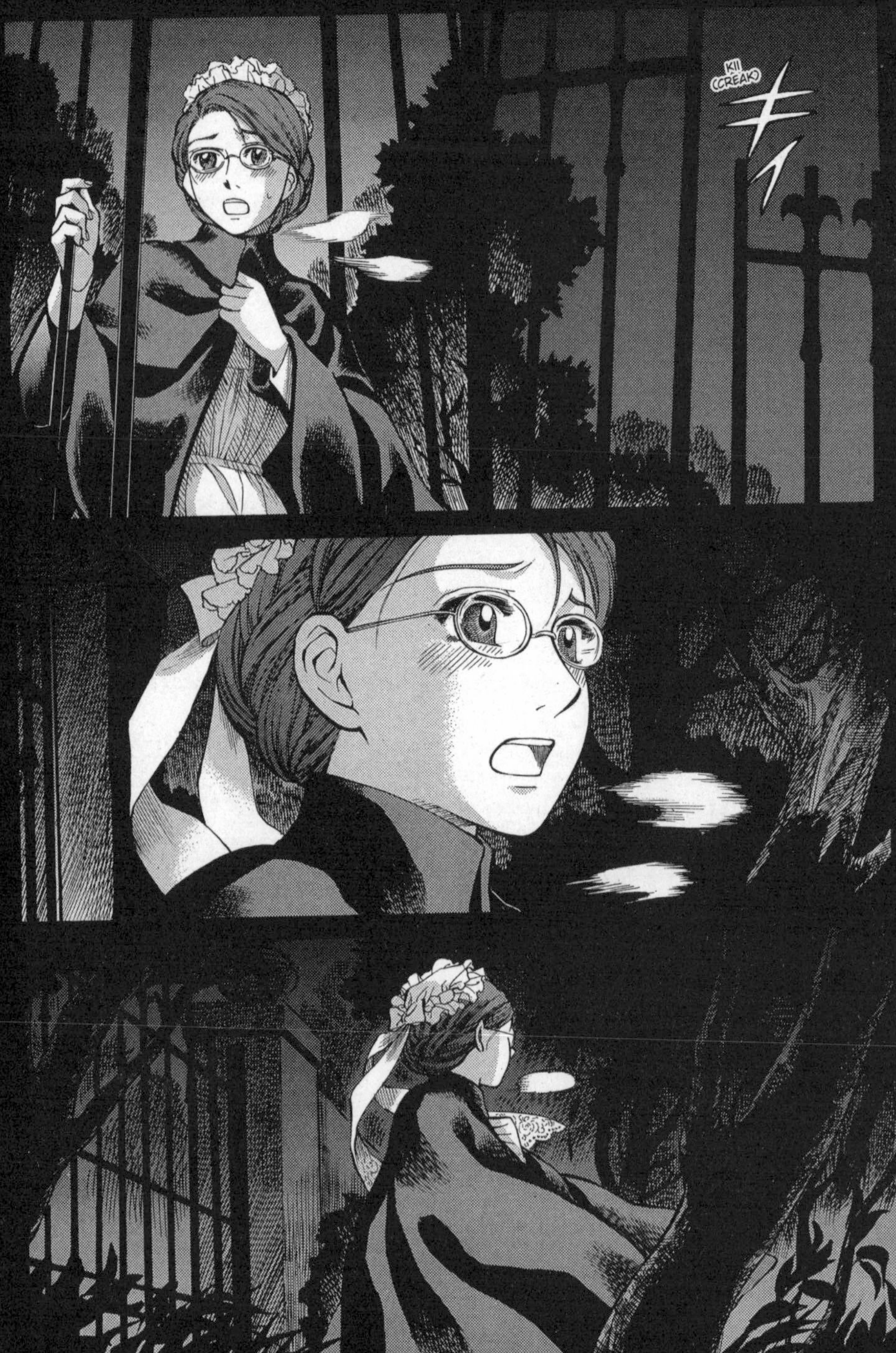
KII (CREAK)
キィ

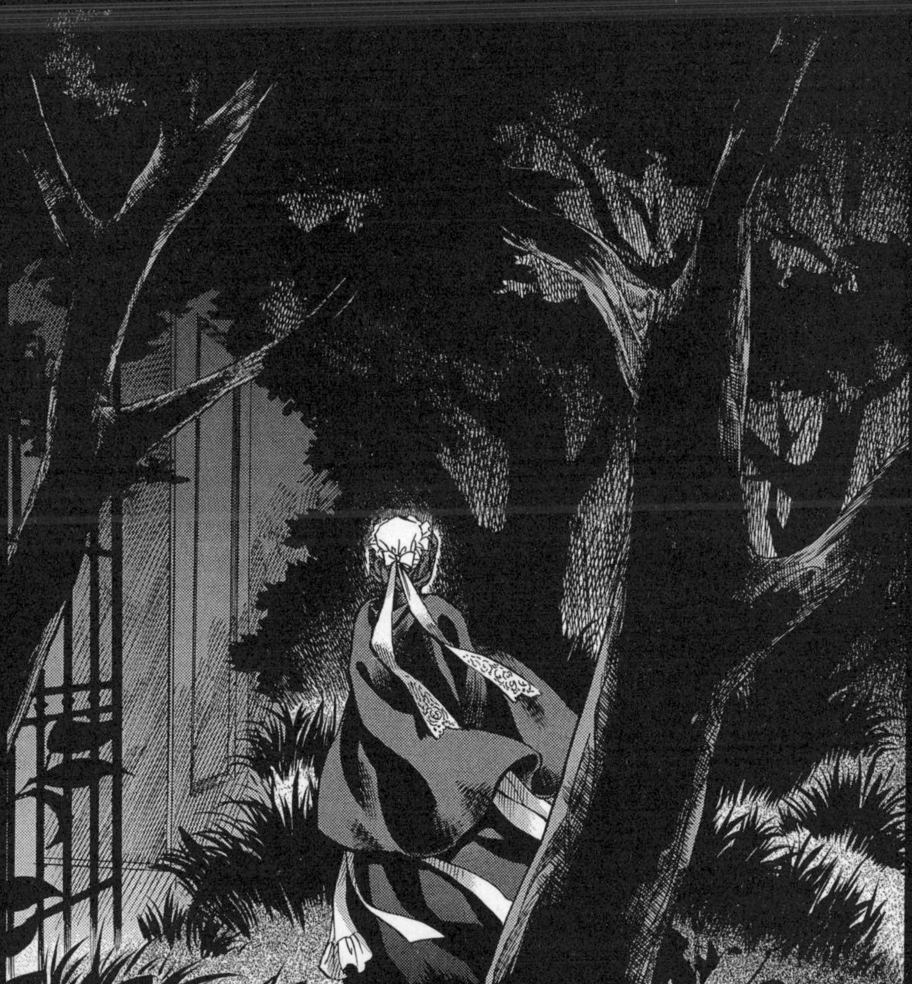

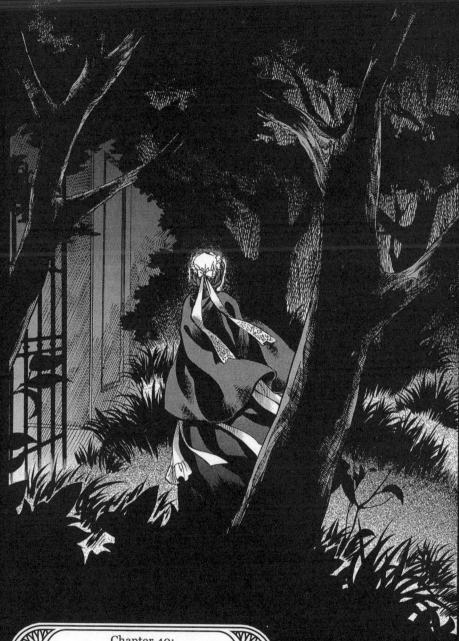

Chapter 40:
The Worst State of Affairs
(Part 3)

THERE'S A TELE- GRAM...

...FOR YOU.

...THANK YOU.

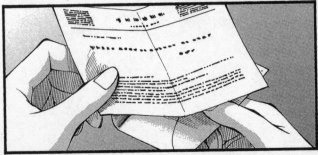

266

....

ELEVEN
P.M...

THE
21ST...

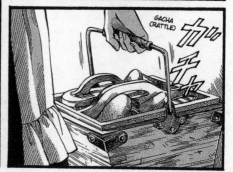

GACHA
(RATTLE)

267

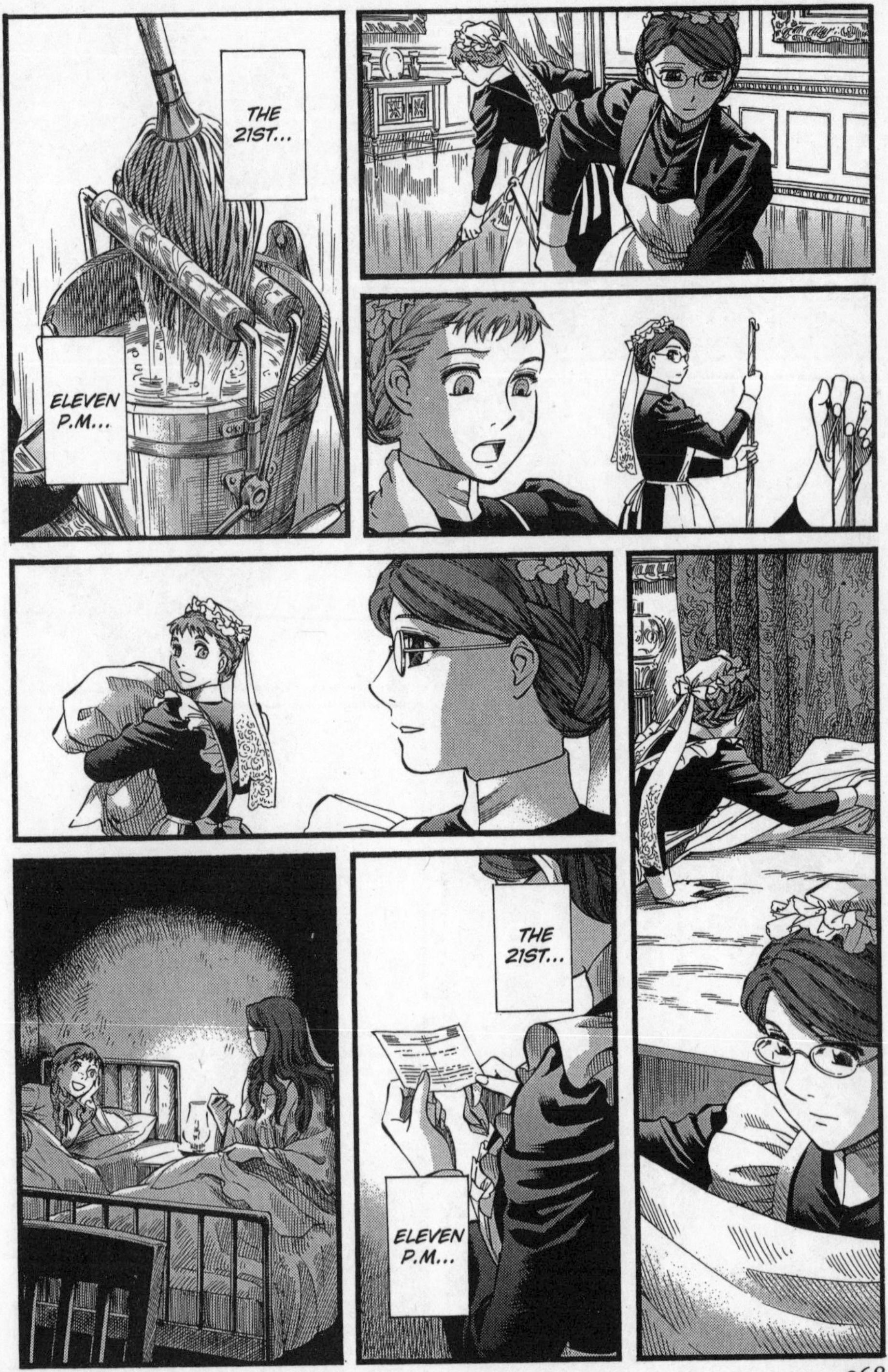
THE 21ST...
ELEVEN P.M...
THE 21ST...
ELEVEN P.M...

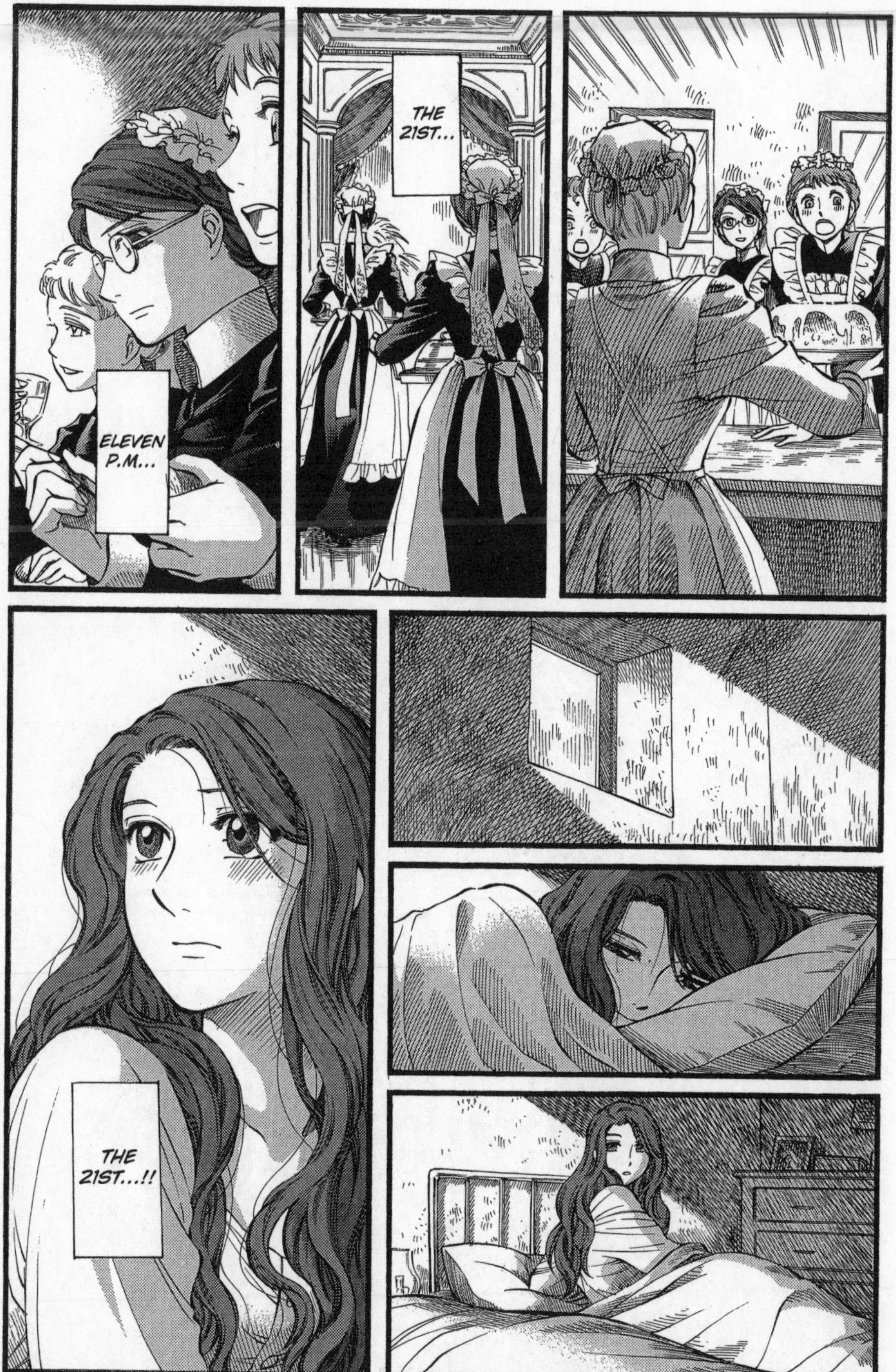
THE 21ST...
ELEVEN P.M...
THE 21ST...!!

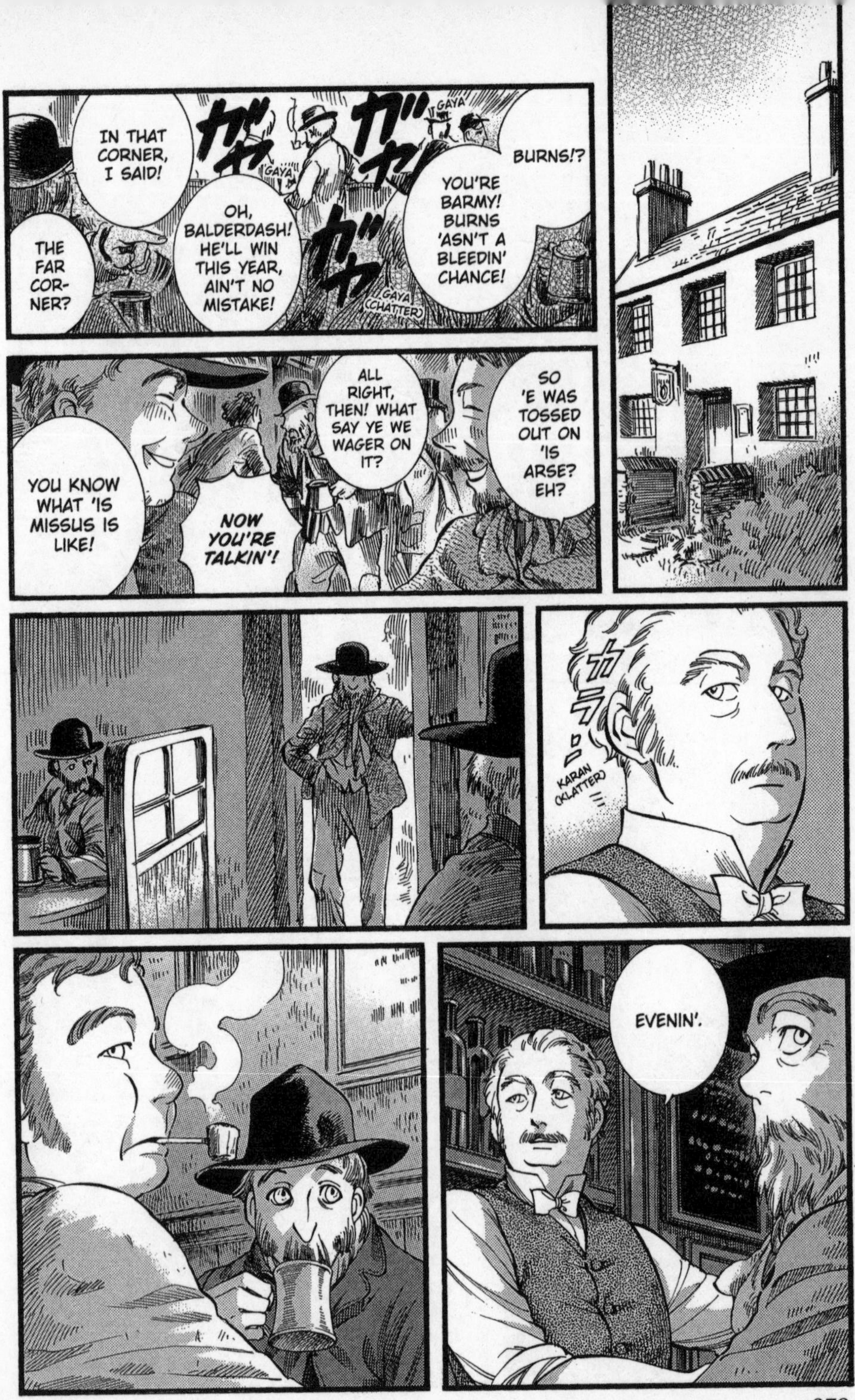

BURNS!?
YOU'RE BARMY! BURNS 'ASN'T A BLEEDIN' CHANCE!
GAYA
OH, BALDERDASH! HE'LL WIN THIS YEAR, AIN'T NO MISTAKE!
GAYA
IN THAT CORNER, I SAID!
THE FAR CORNER?
GAYA (CHATTER)
SO 'E WAS TOSSED OUT ON 'IS ARSE? EH?
ALL RIGHT, THEN! WHAT SAY YE WE WAGER ON IT?
NOW YOU'RE TALKIN'!
YOU KNOW WHAT 'IS MISSUS IS LIKE!
KARAN (KLATTER)
EVENIN'.

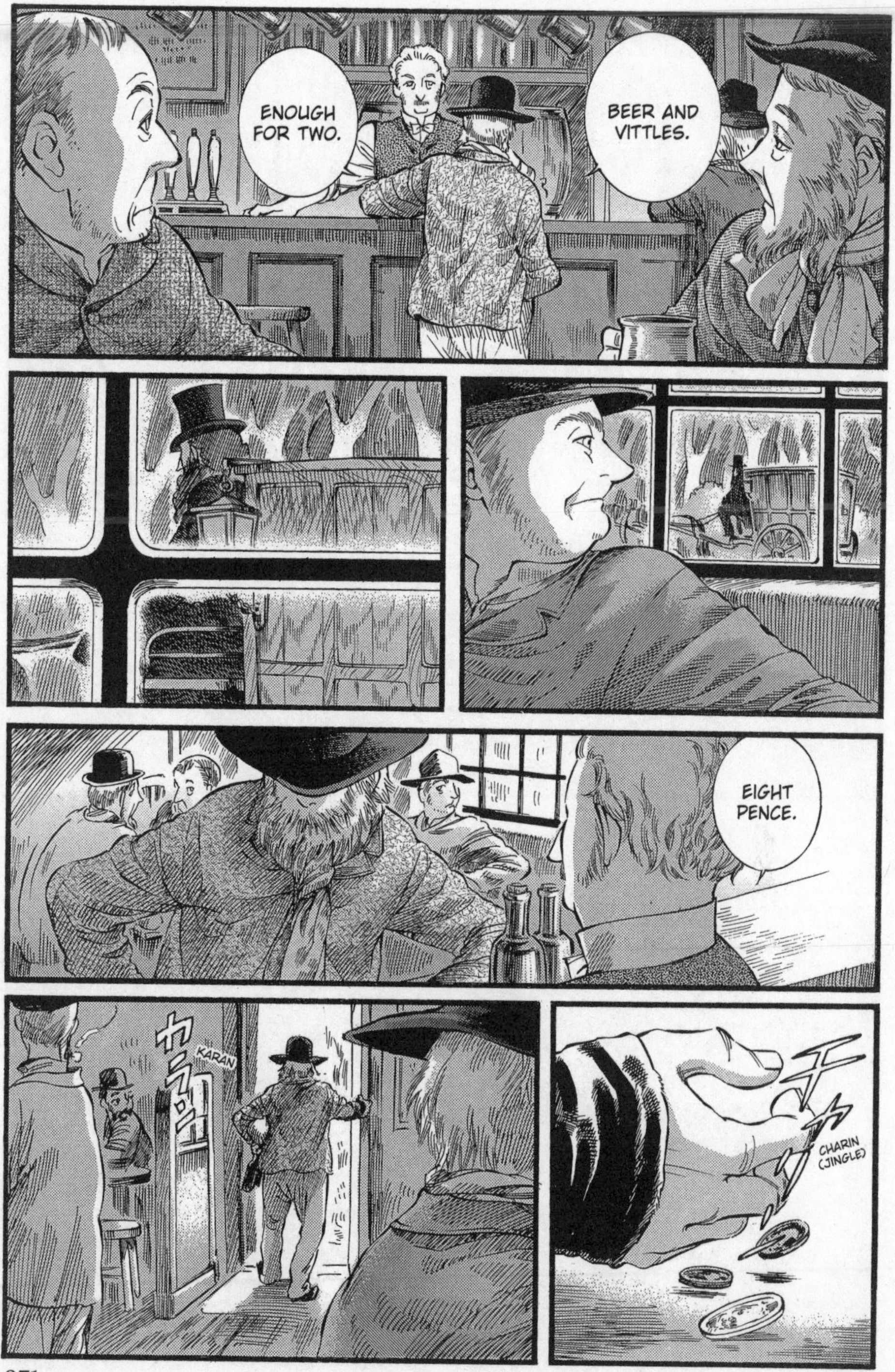
BEER AND VITTLES.
ENOUGH FOR TWO.
EIGHT PENCE.
CHARIN (JINGLE)
KARAN

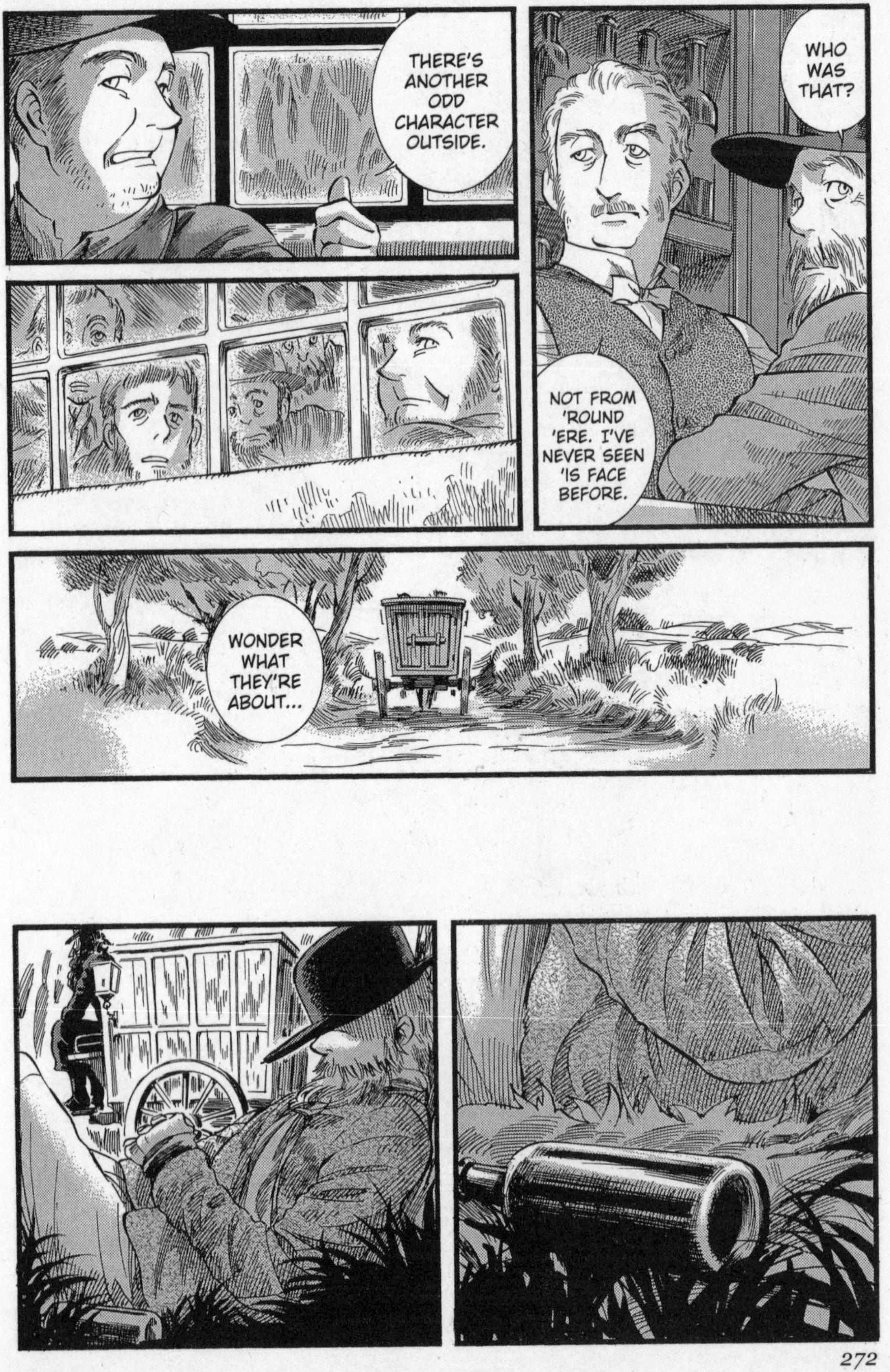
WHO WAS THAT?
NOT FROM 'ROUND 'ERE. I'VE NEVER SEEN 'IS FACE BEFORE.
THERE'S ANOTHER ODD CHARACTER OUTSIDE.
WONDER WHAT THEY'RE ABOUT...

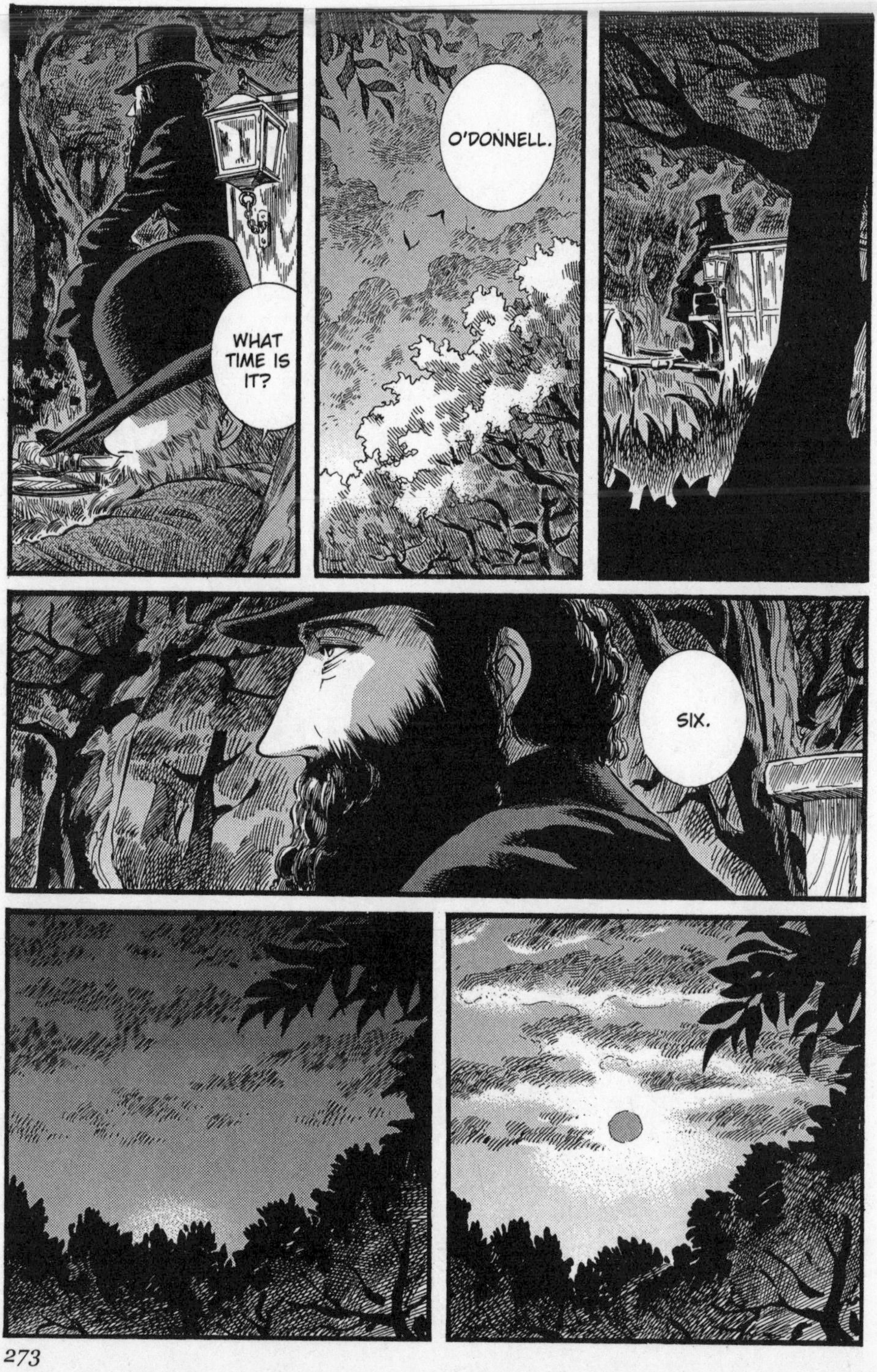
O'DONNELL.
WHAT TIME IS IT?
SIX.

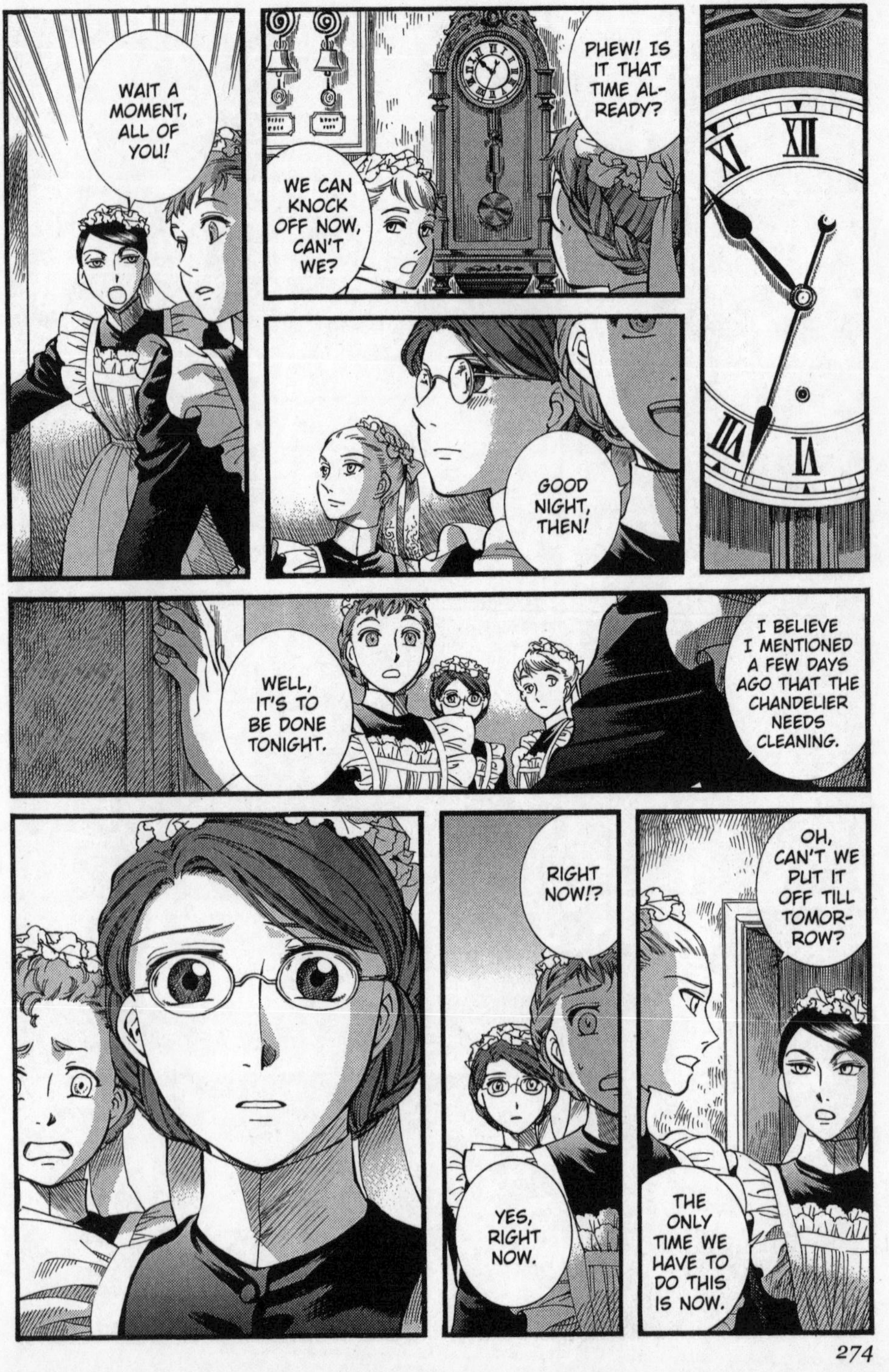
PHEW! IS IT THAT TIME AL-READY?
WE CAN KNOCK OFF NOW, CAN'T WE?
GOOD NIGHT, THEN!
WAIT A MOMENT, ALL OF YOU!
I BELIEVE I MENTIONED A FEW DAYS AGO THAT THE CHANDELIER NEEDS CLEANING.
WELL, IT'S TO BE DONE TONIGHT.
OH, CAN'T WE PUT IT OFF TILL TOMOR-ROW?
THE ONLY TIME WE HAVE TO DO THIS IS NOW.
RIGHT NOW!?
YES, RIGHT NOW.

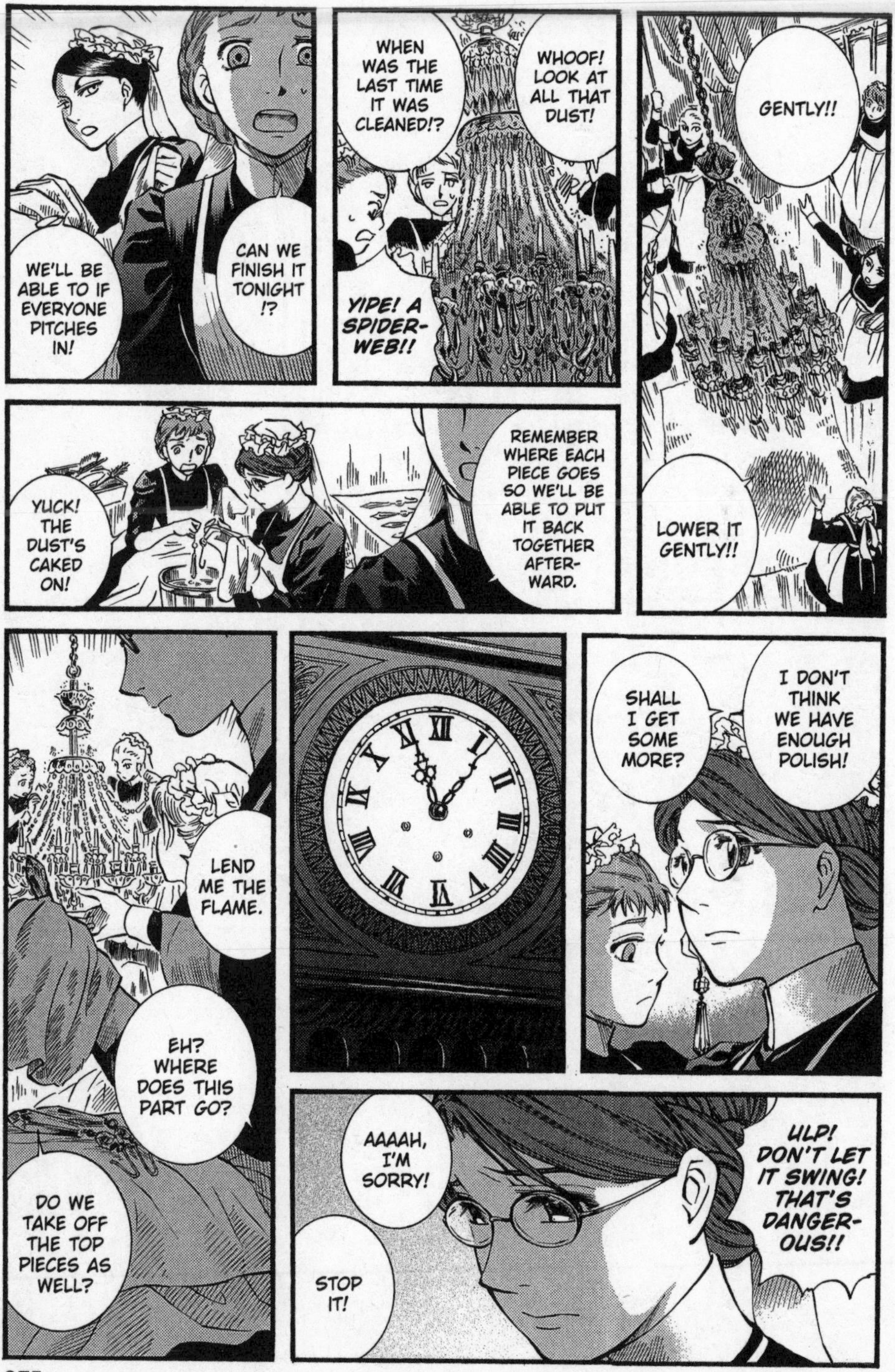
GENTLY!!
LOWER IT GENTLY!!
WHOOF! LOOK AT ALL THAT DUST!
WHEN WAS THE LAST TIME IT WAS CLEANED!?
YIPE! A SPIDER-WEB!!
CAN WE FINISH IT TONIGHT!?
WE'LL BE ABLE TO IF EVERYONE PITCHES IN!
REMEMBER WHERE EACH PIECE GOES SO WE'LL BE ABLE TO PUT IT BACK TOGETHER AFTERWARD.
YUCK! THE DUST'S CAKED ON!
I DON'T THINK WE HAVE ENOUGH POLISH!
SHALL I GET SOME MORE?
ULP! DON'T LET IT SWING! THAT'S DANGEROUS!!
AAAAH, I'M SORRY!
STOP IT!
LEND ME THE FLAME.
EH? WHERE DOES THIS PART GO?
DO WE TAKE OFF THE TOP PIECES AS WELL?

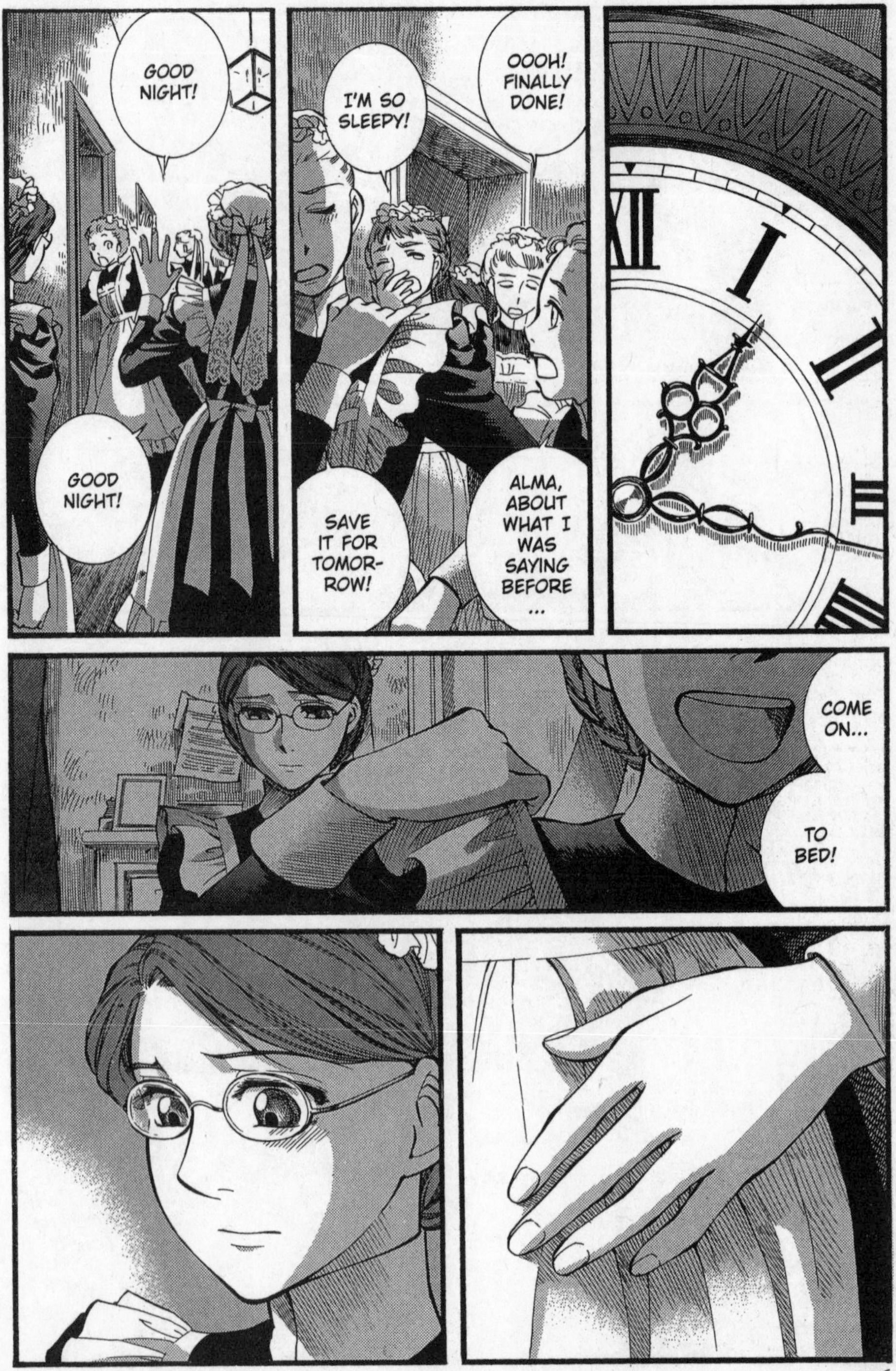

OOOH! FINALLY DONE!
I'M SO SLEEPY!
ALMA, ABOUT WHAT I WAS SAYING BEFORE ...
SAVE IT FOR TOMOR-ROW!
GOOD NIGHT!
GOOD NIGHT!
COME ON...
TO BED!

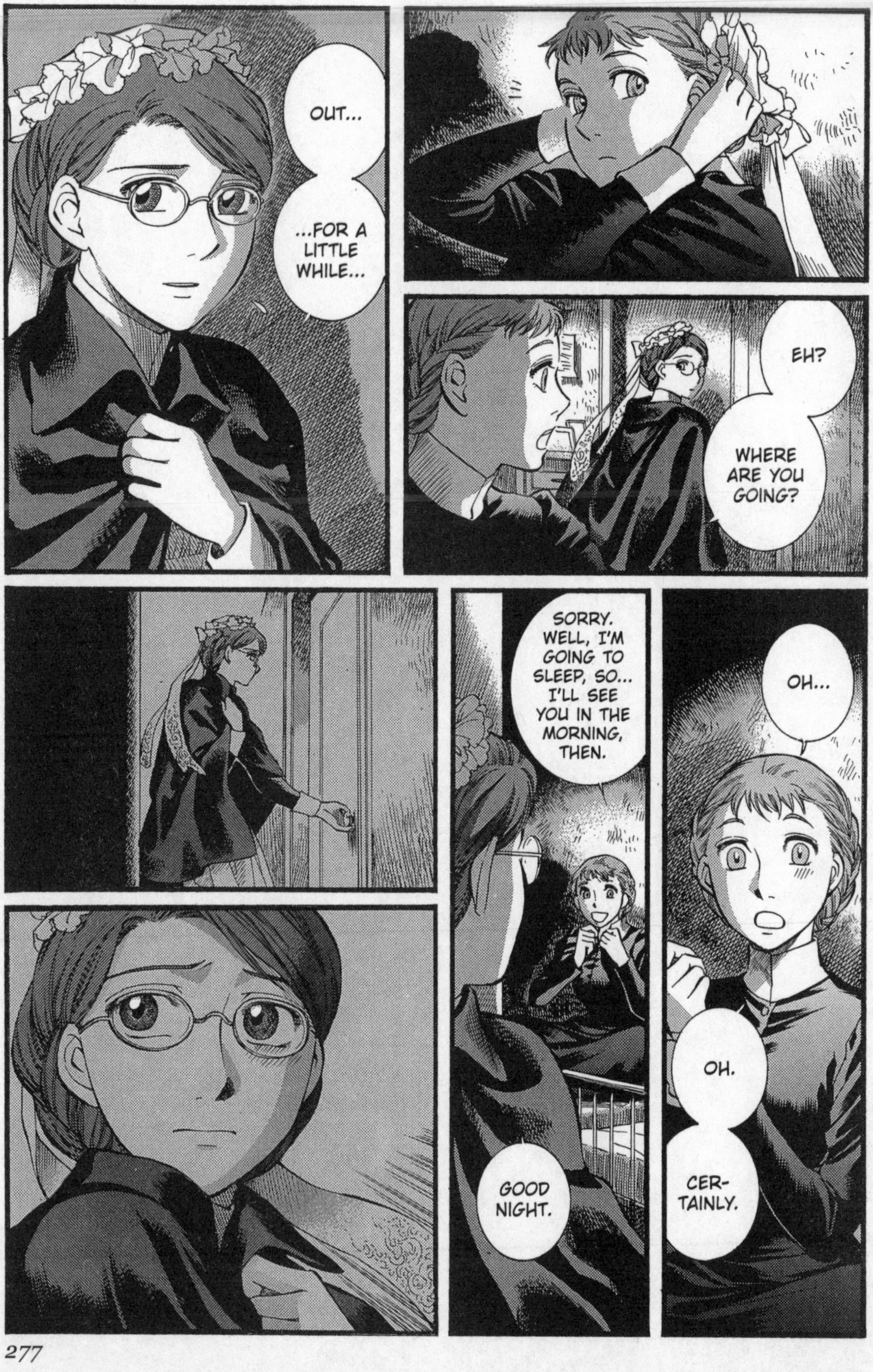
EH?
WHERE ARE YOU GOING?
OUT...
...FOR A LITTLE WHILE...
OH...
OH.
CER-TAINLY.
SORRY. WELL, I'M GOING TO SLEEP, SO... I'LL SEE YOU IN THE MORNING, THEN.
GOOD NIGHT.

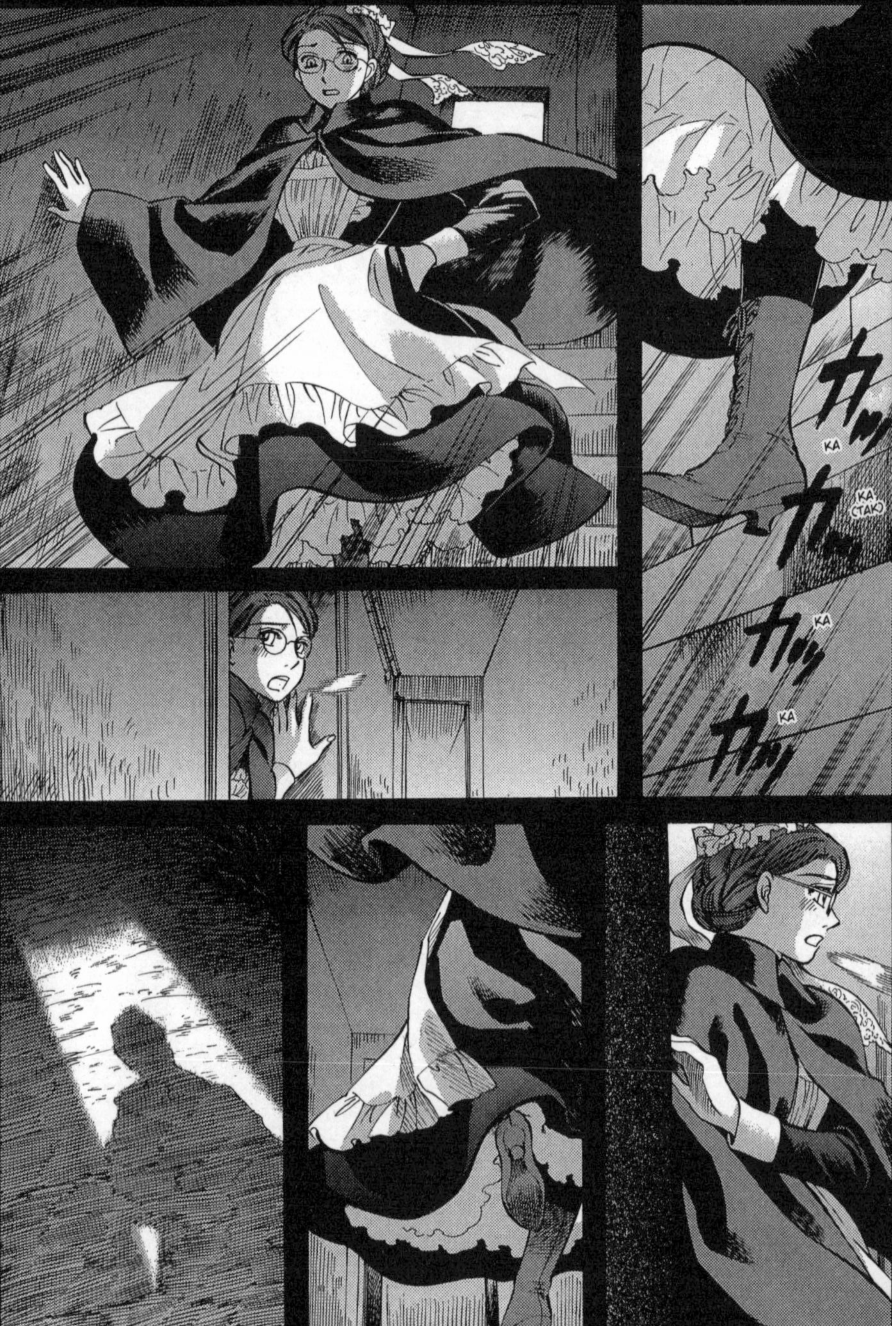
KA
KA (TAK)
KA
KA

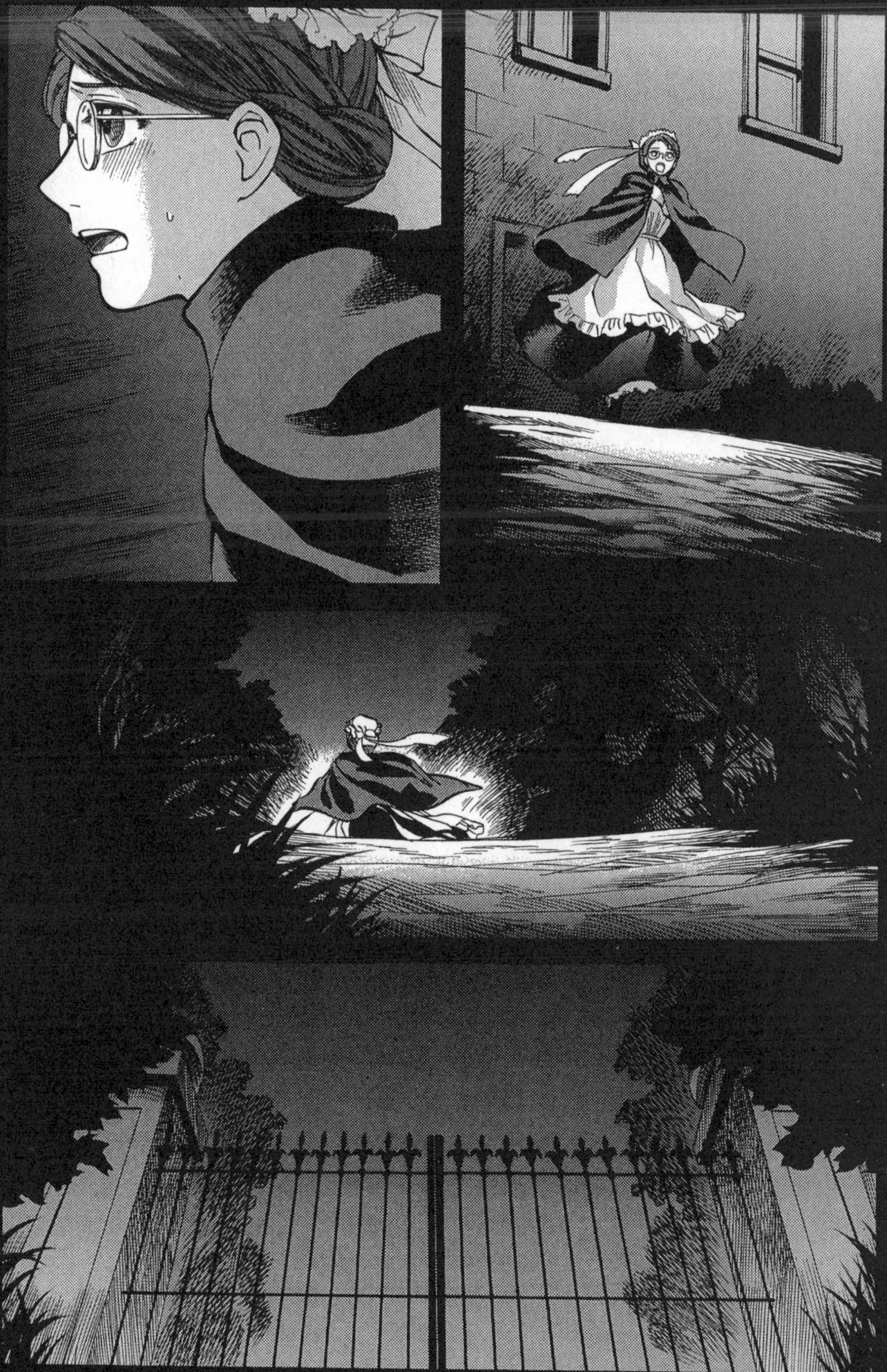

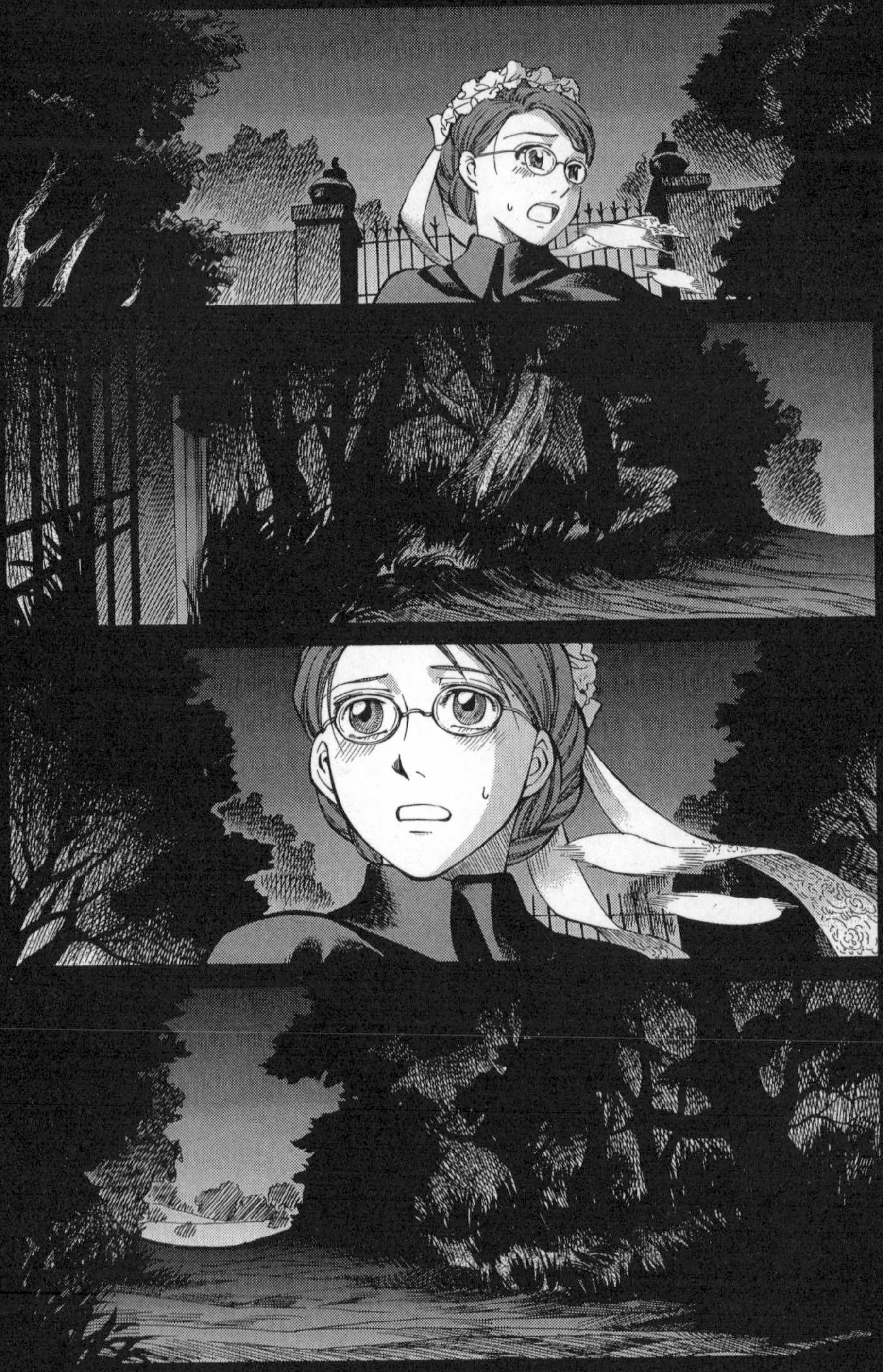

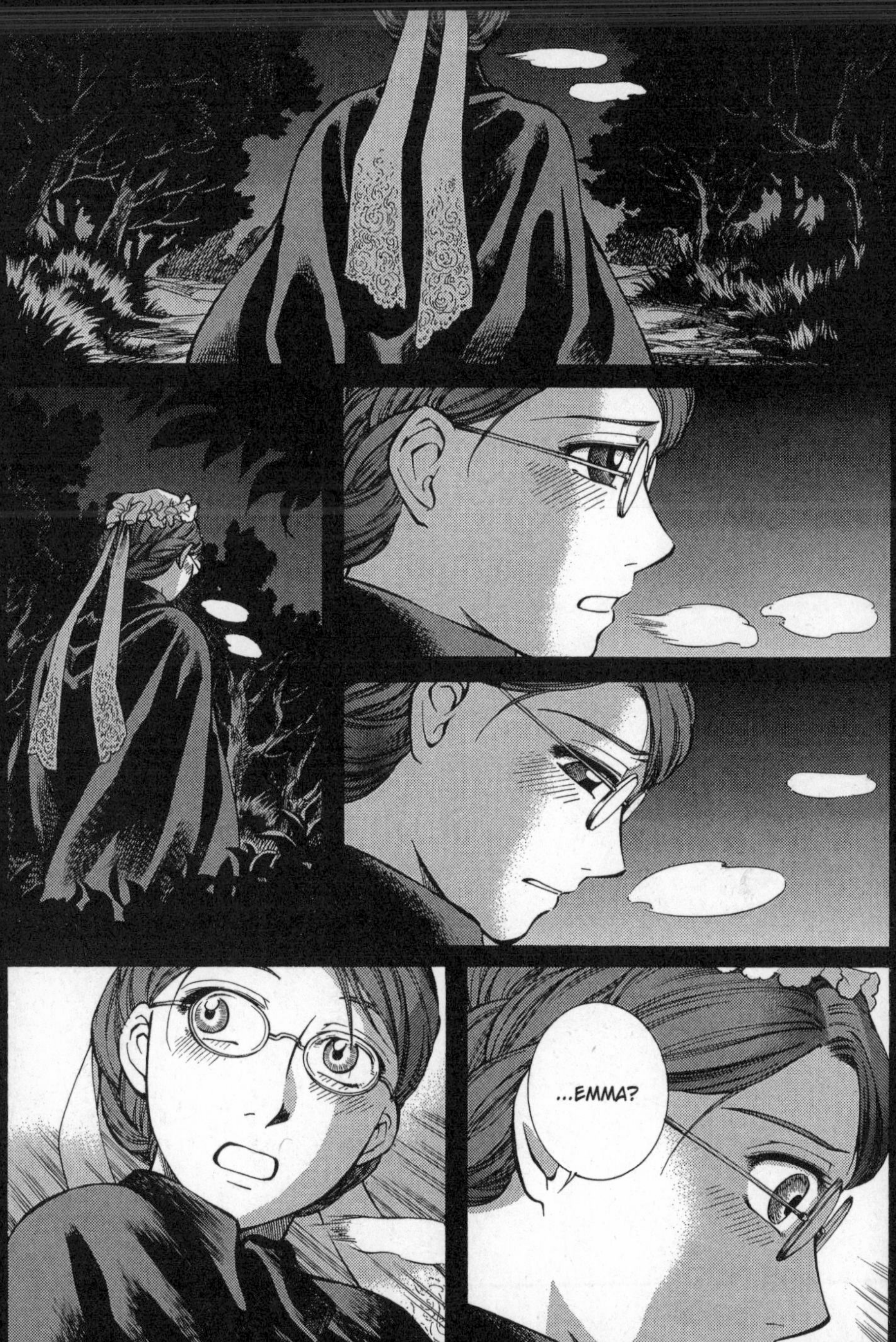
...EMMA?

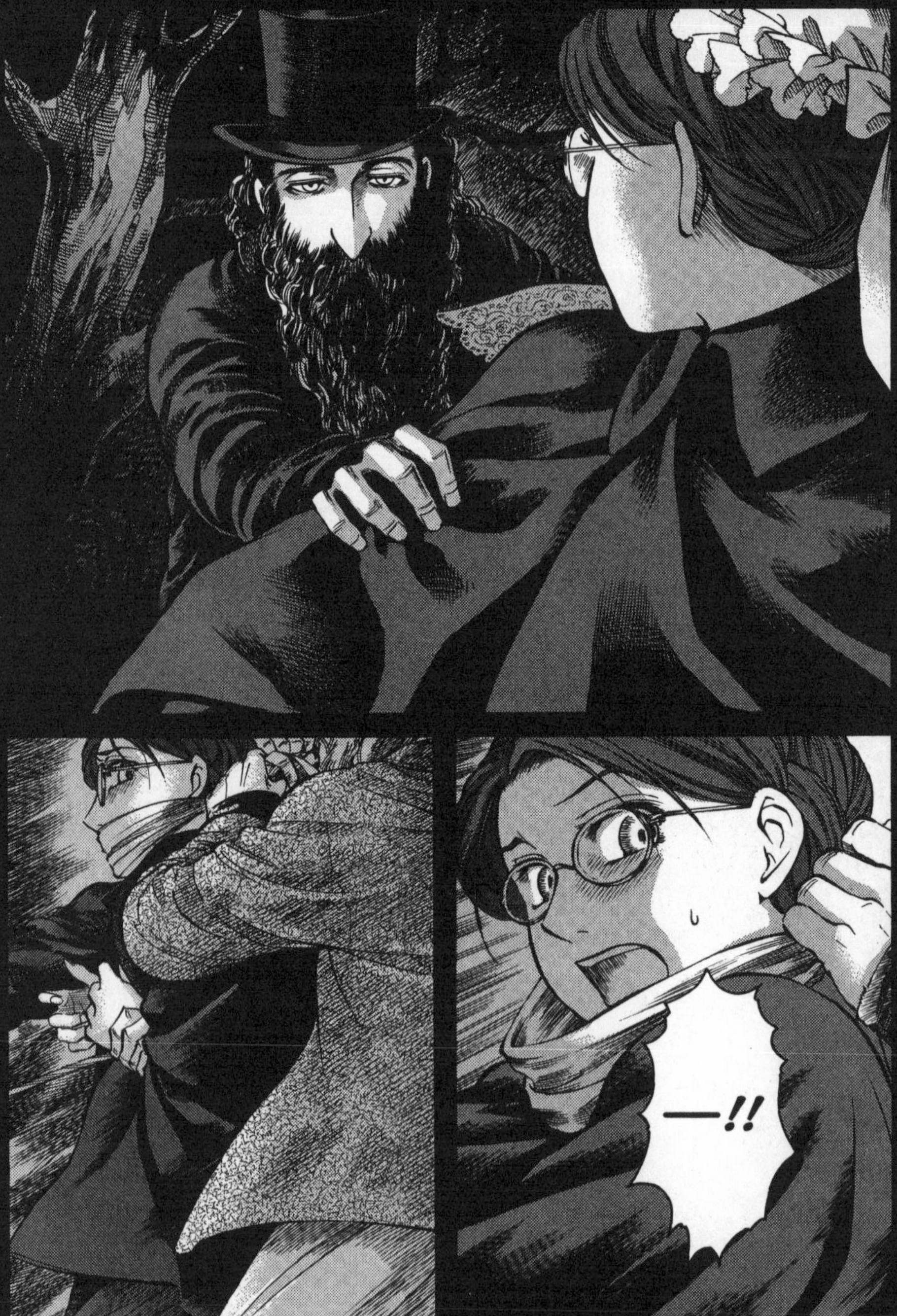
—!!

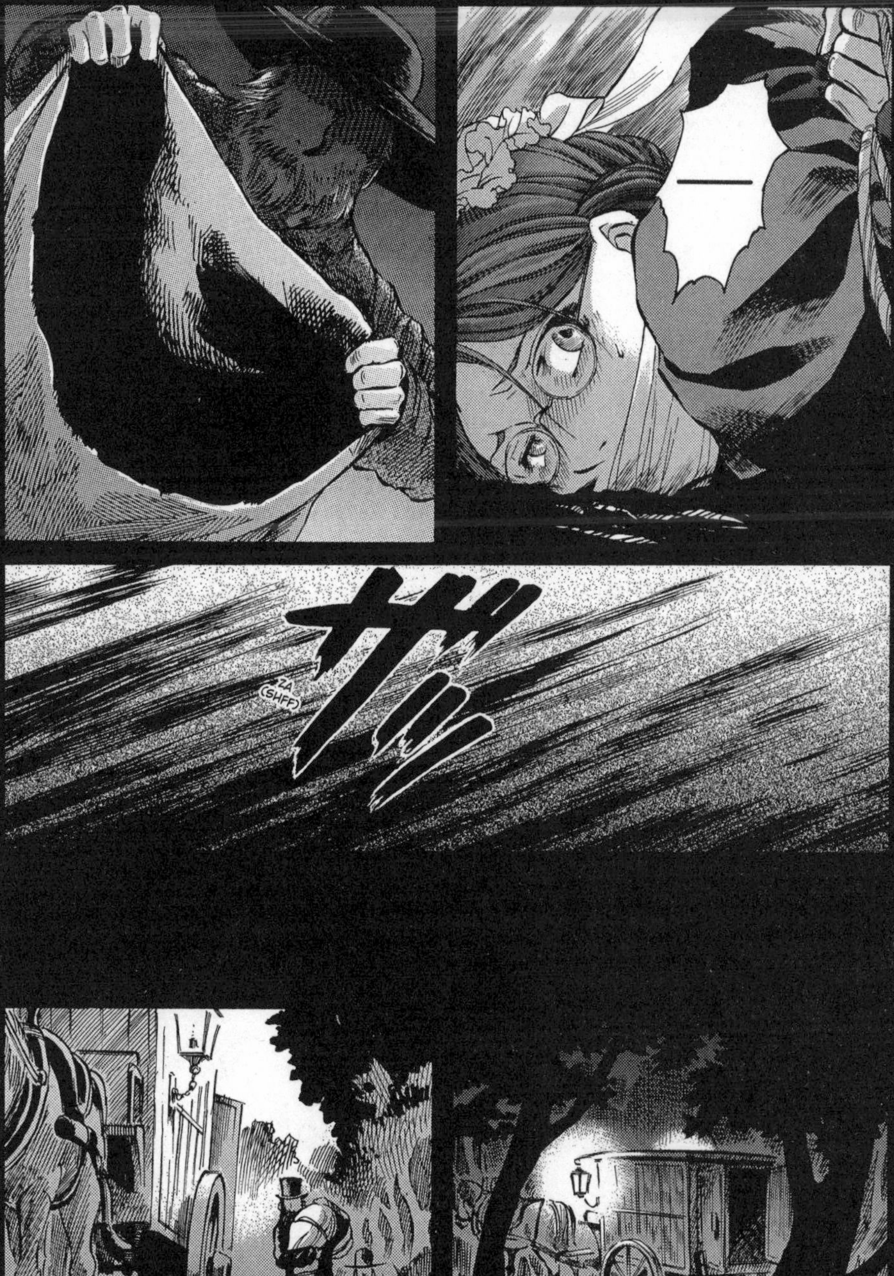
—
ザッ
ZA (SHFF)

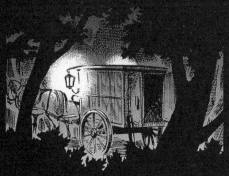

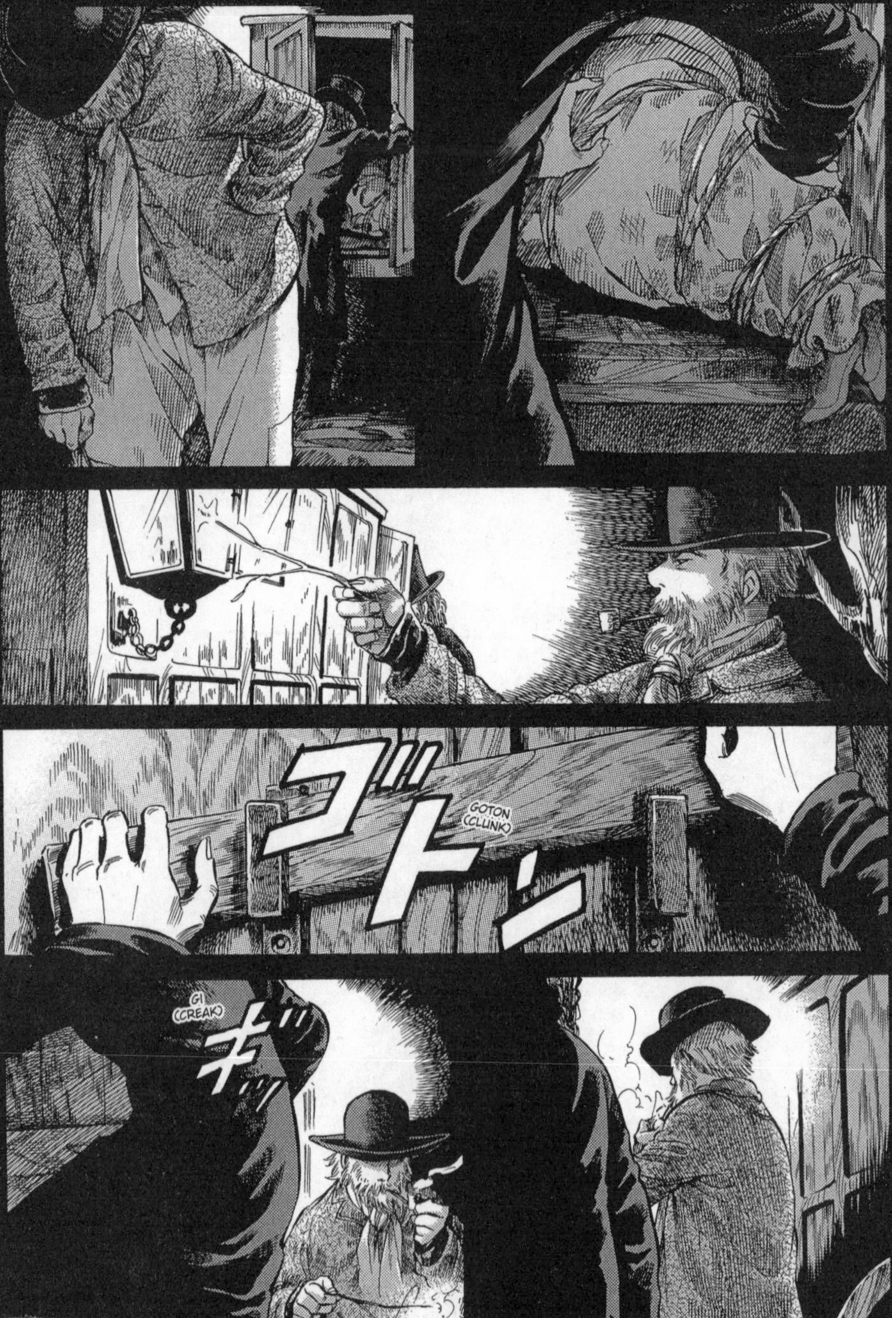
GOTON
(CLUNK)
GI
(CREAK)

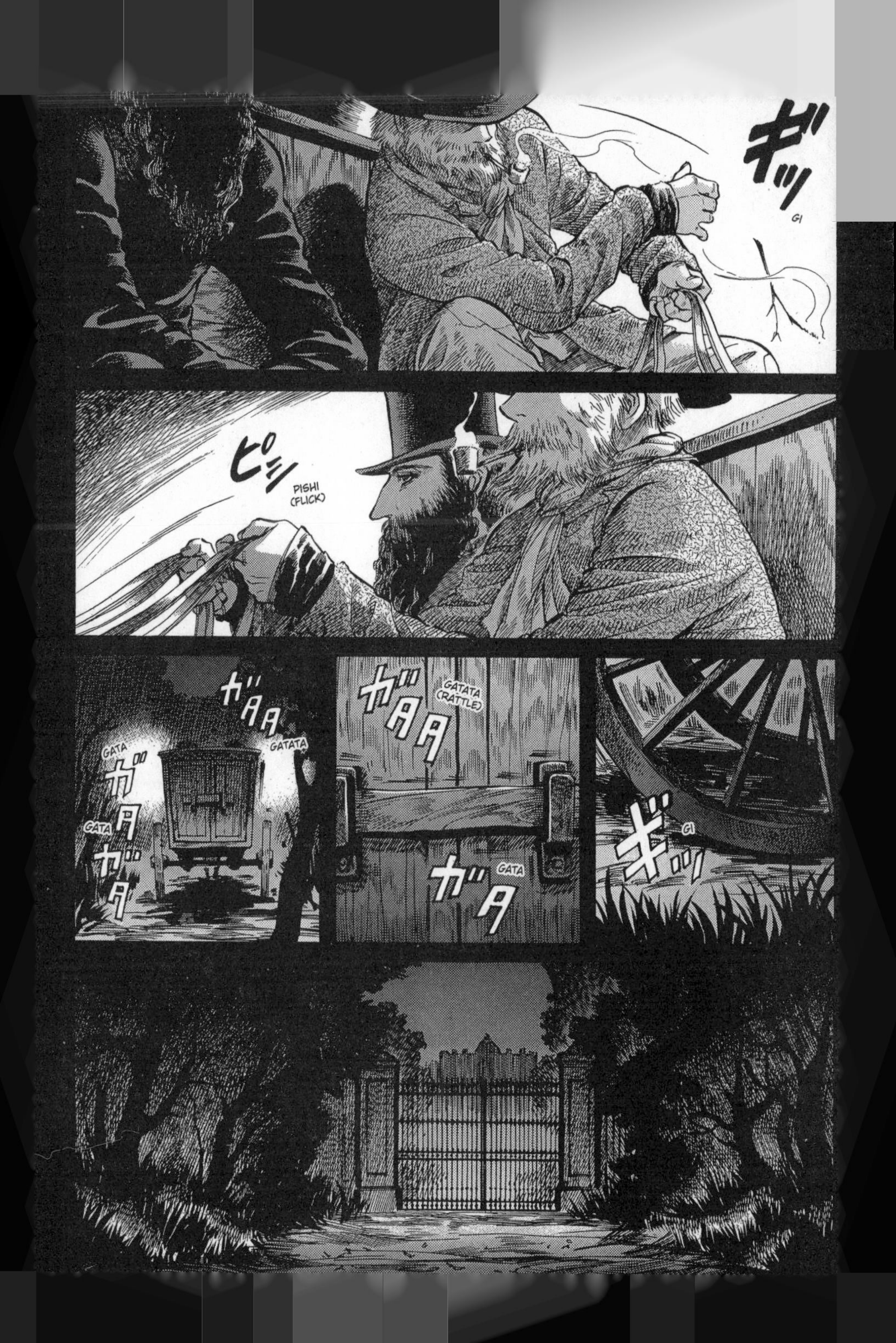
ギッ
GI
ピシ
PISHI (FLICK)
ギッ
GI
ガタタ
GATATA (RATTLE)
ガタ
GATA
ガタタ
GATATA
ガタ
GATA
ガタ
GATA

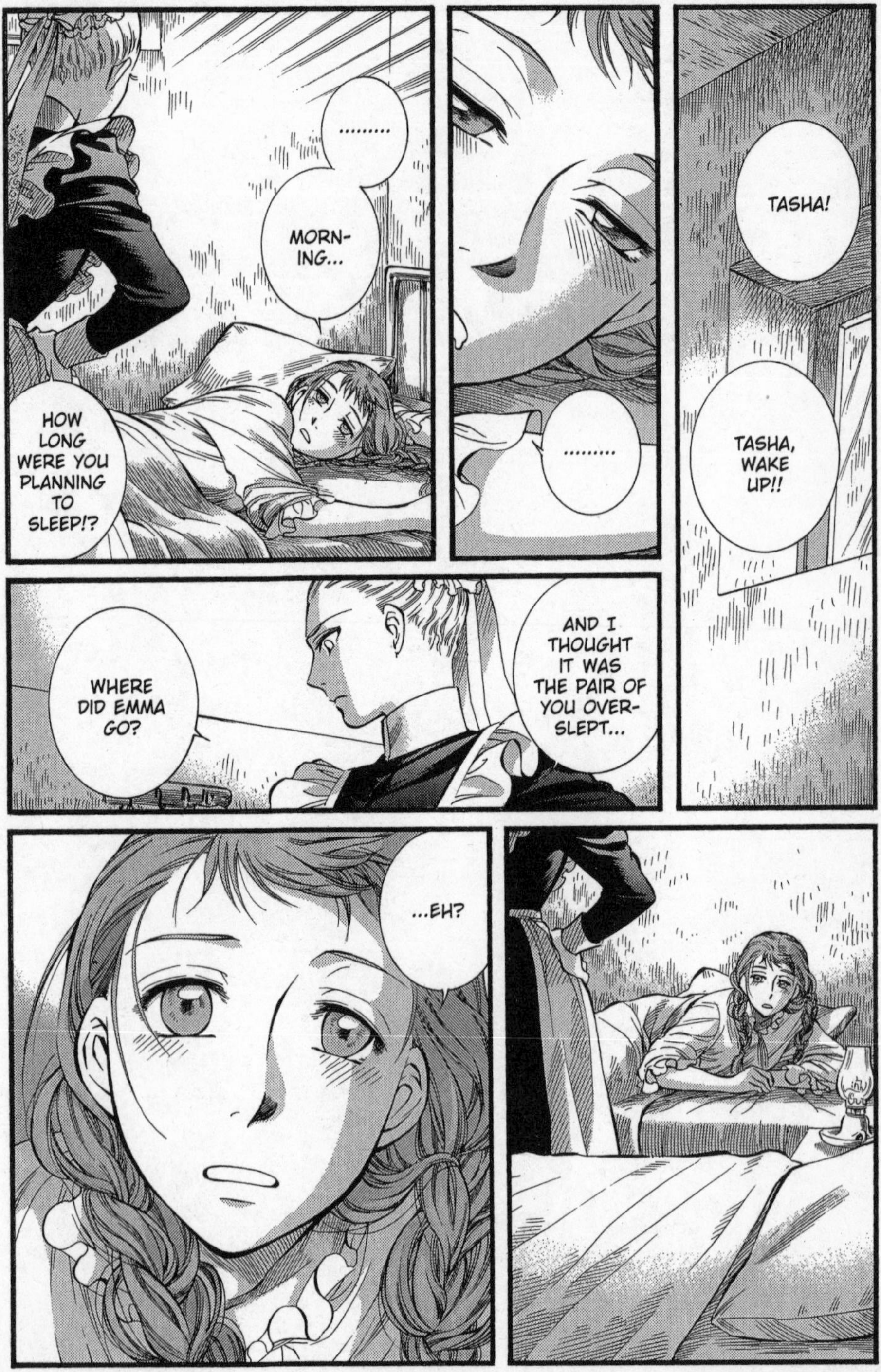
TASHA!
TASHA, WAKE UP!!
....
....
MORNING...
HOW LONG WERE YOU PLANNING TO SLEEP!?
AND I THOUGHT IT WAS THE PAIR OF YOU OVER-SLEPT...
WHERE DID EMMA GO?
...EH?

Chapter 40: End

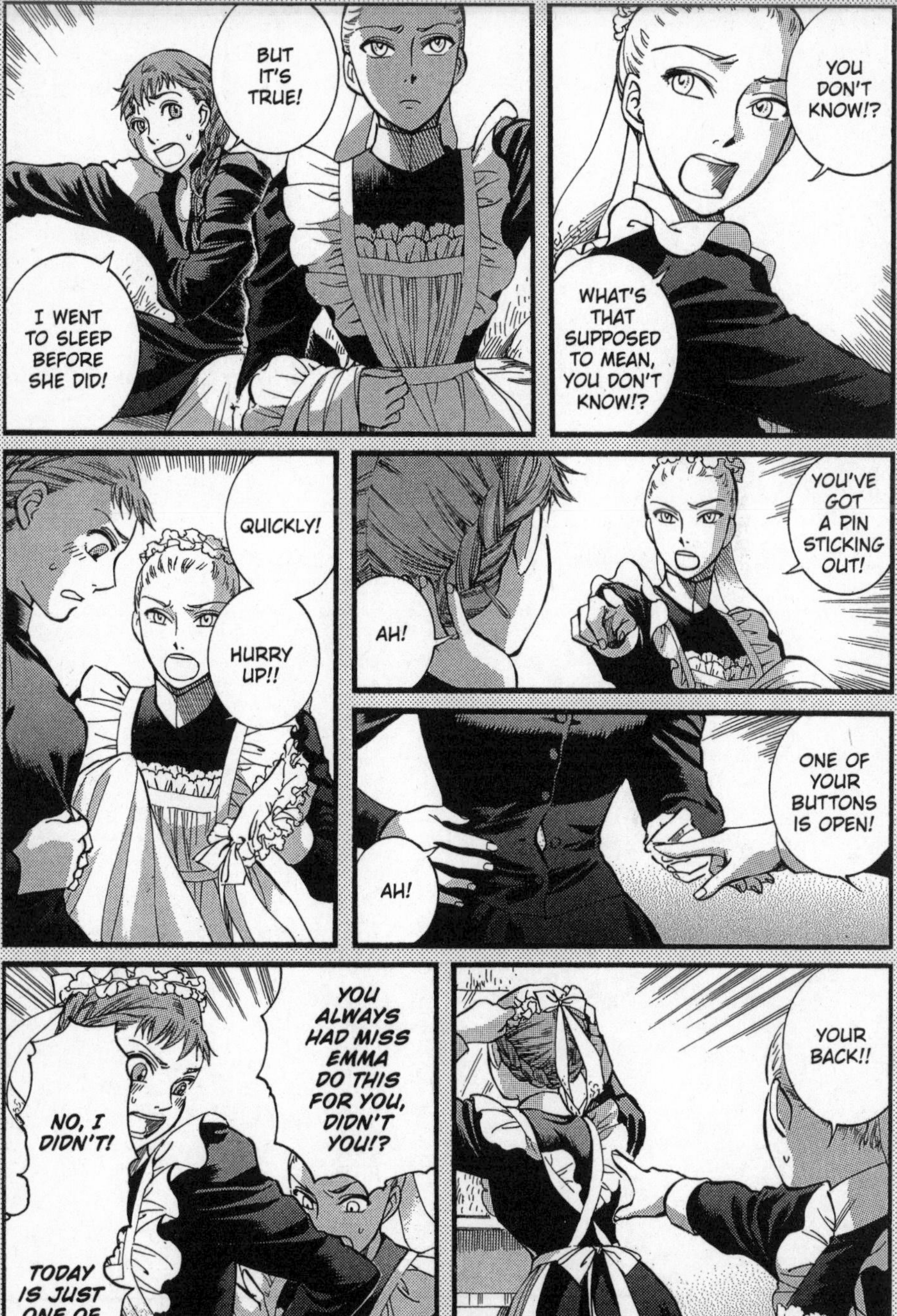
YOU DON'T KNOW!?
WHAT'S THAT SUPPOSED TO MEAN, YOU DON'T KNOW!?
BUT IT'S TRUE!
I WENT TO SLEEP BEFORE SHE DID!
YOU'VE GOT A PIN STICKING OUT!
AH!
ONE OF YOUR BUTTONS IS OPEN!
AH!
QUICKLY!
HURRY UP!!
YOUR BACK!!
YOU ALWAYS HAD MISS EMMA DO THIS FOR YOU, DIDN'T YOU!?
NO, I DIDN'T!
TODAY IS JUST ONE OF THOSE DAYS!!

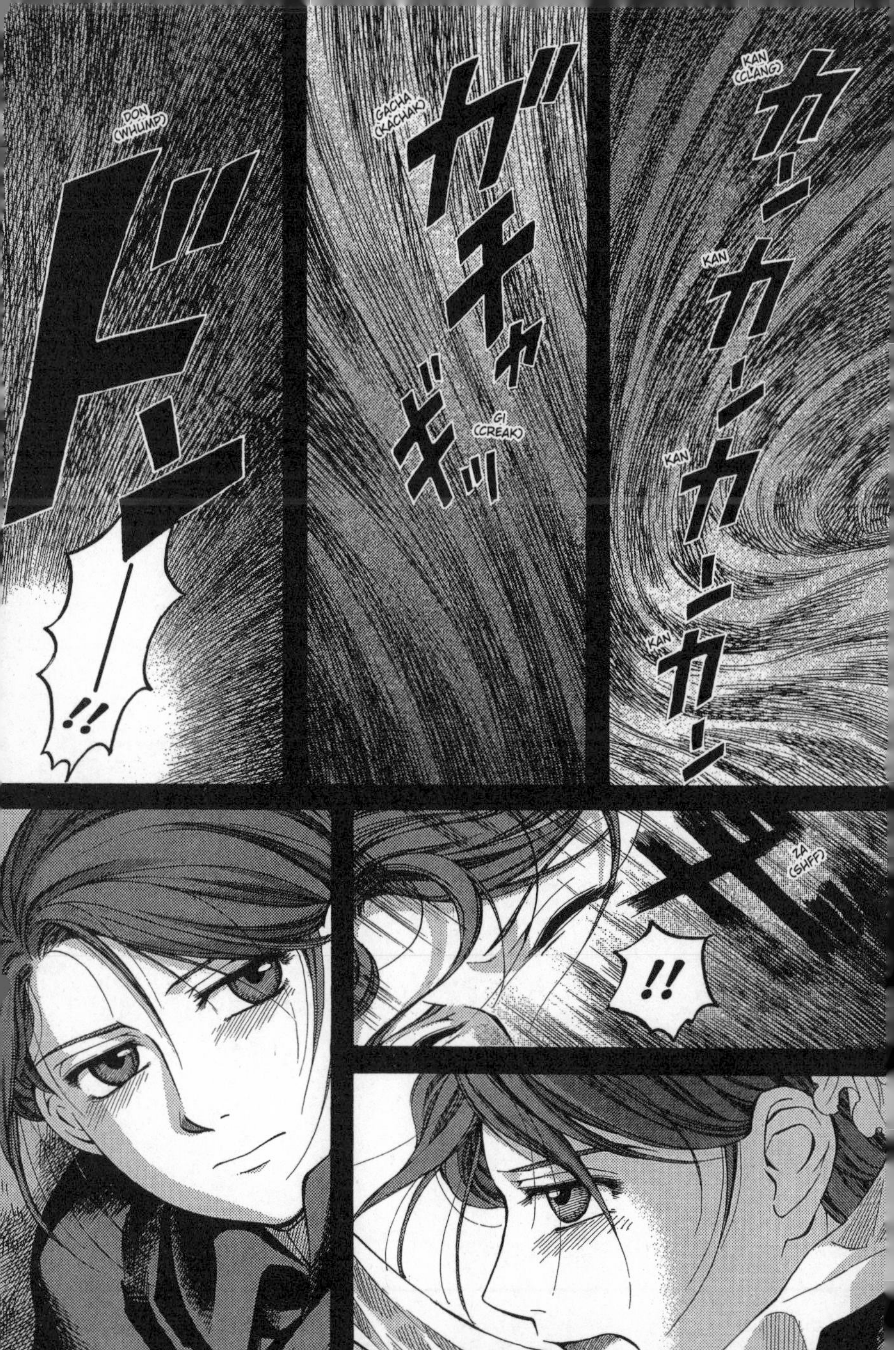
KAN (CLANG)
KAN
KAN
KAN
GACHA (KACHAK)
GI (CREAK)
DON (WHUMP)
!!
ZA (SHFF)
!!

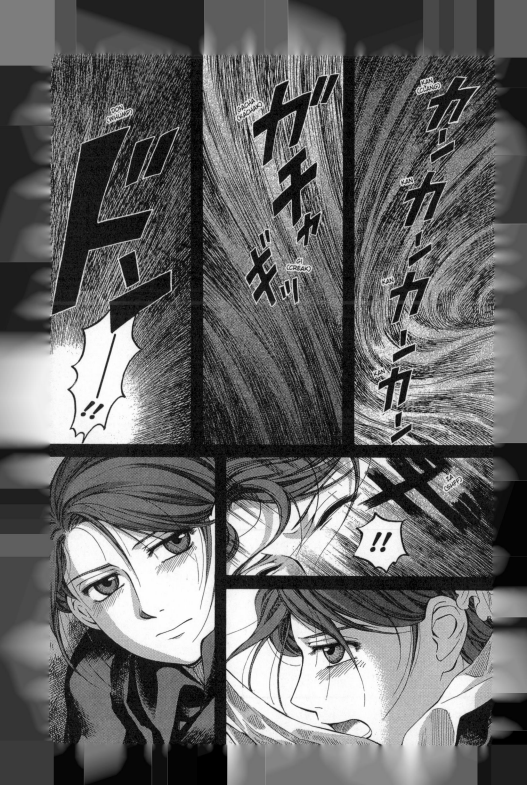

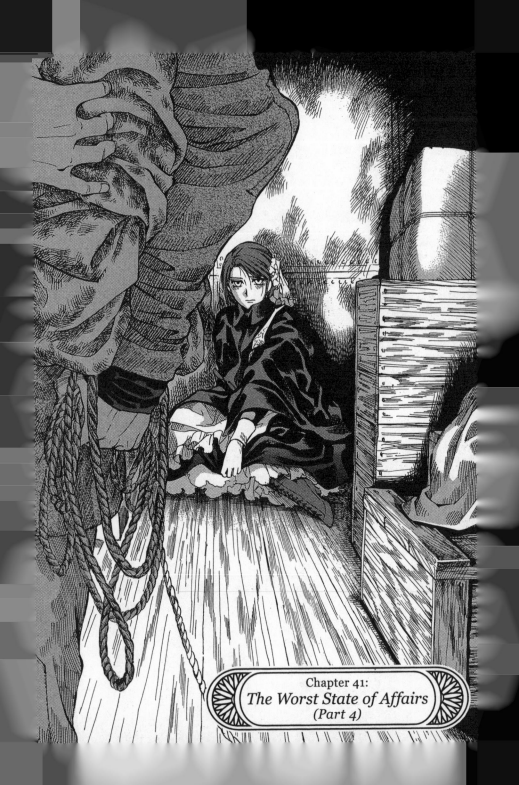

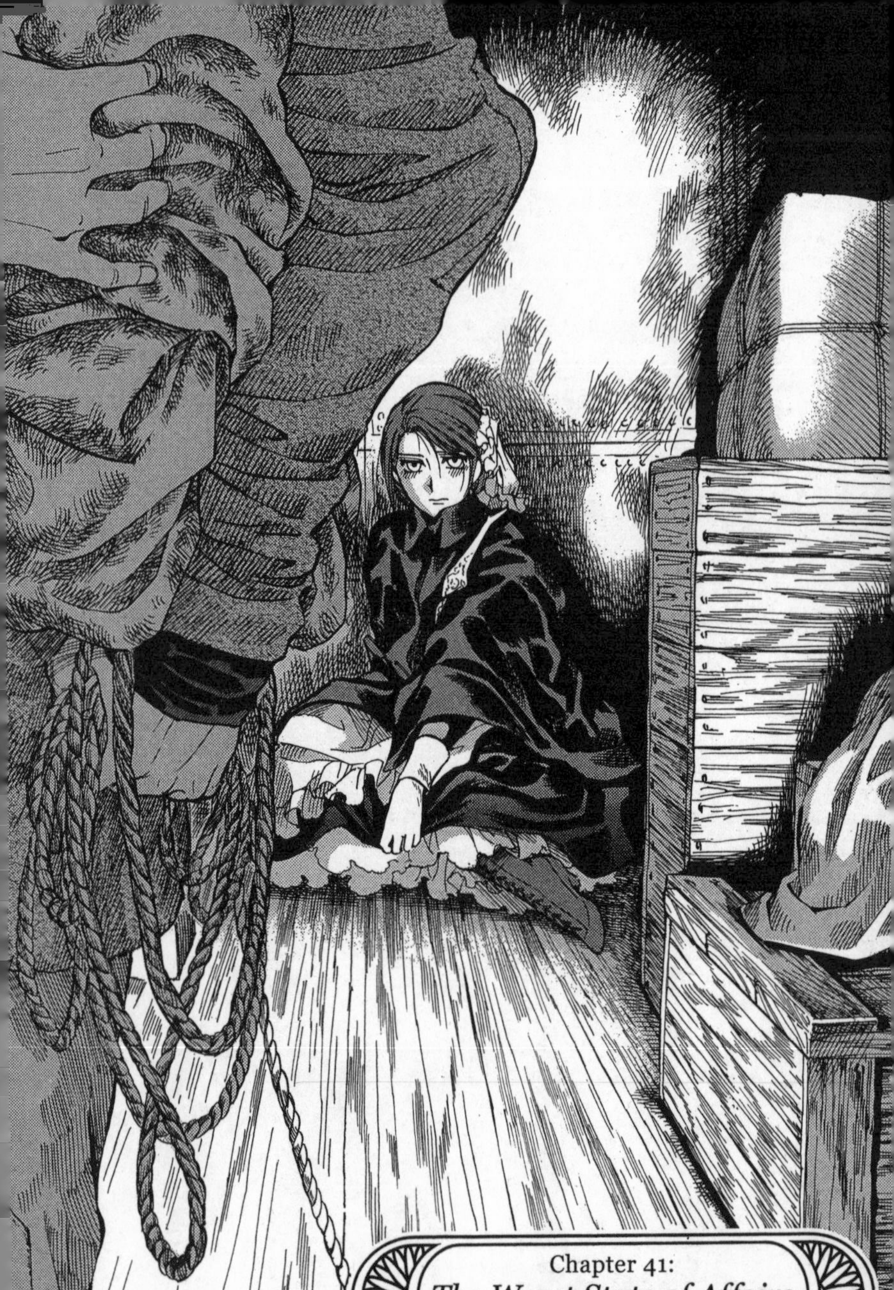
Chapter 41:
The Worst State of Affairs
(Part 4)

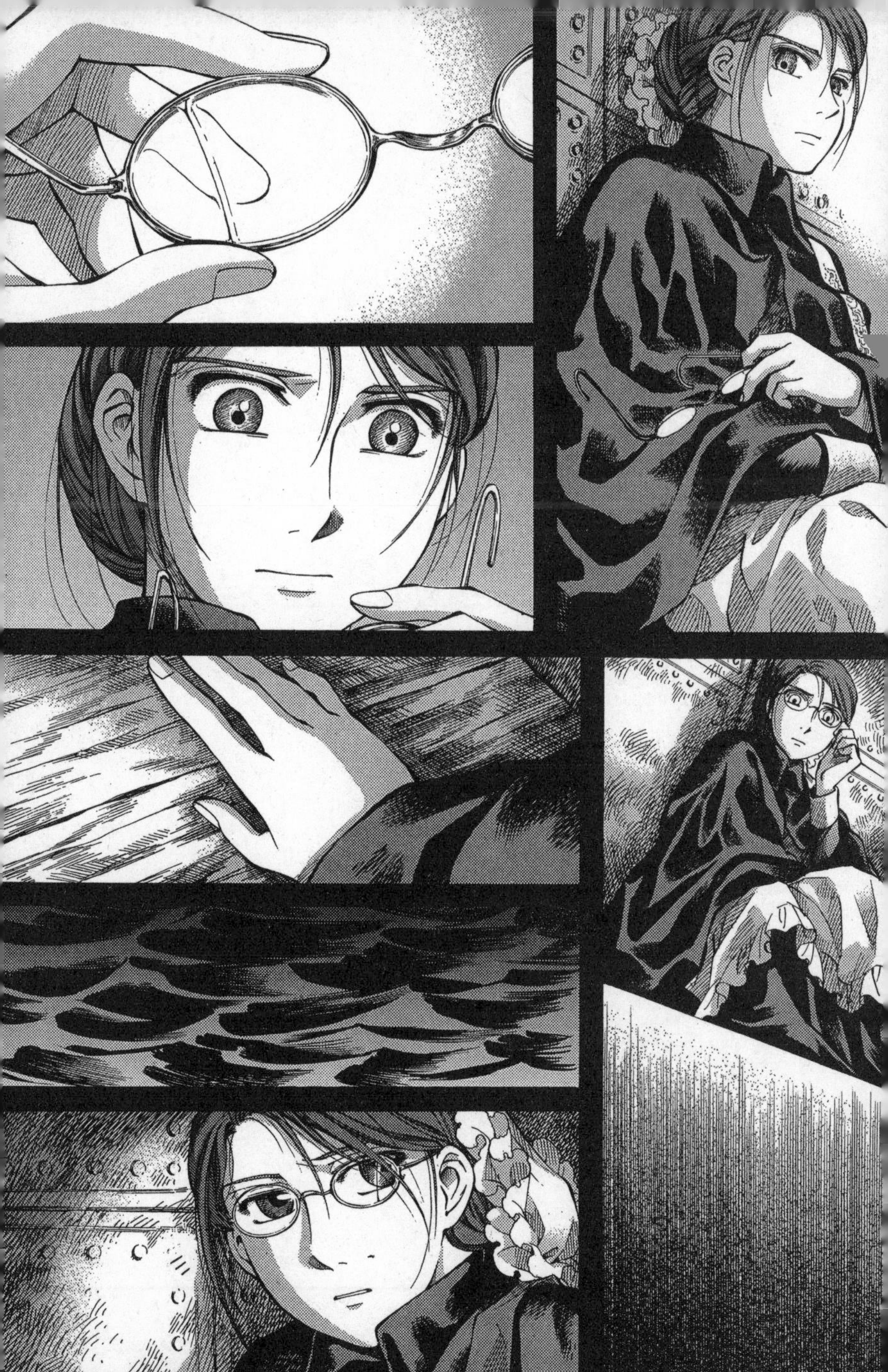

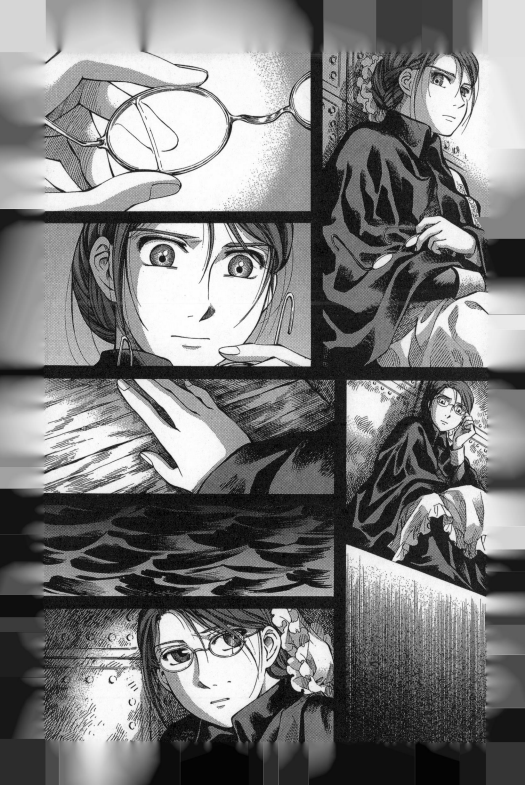

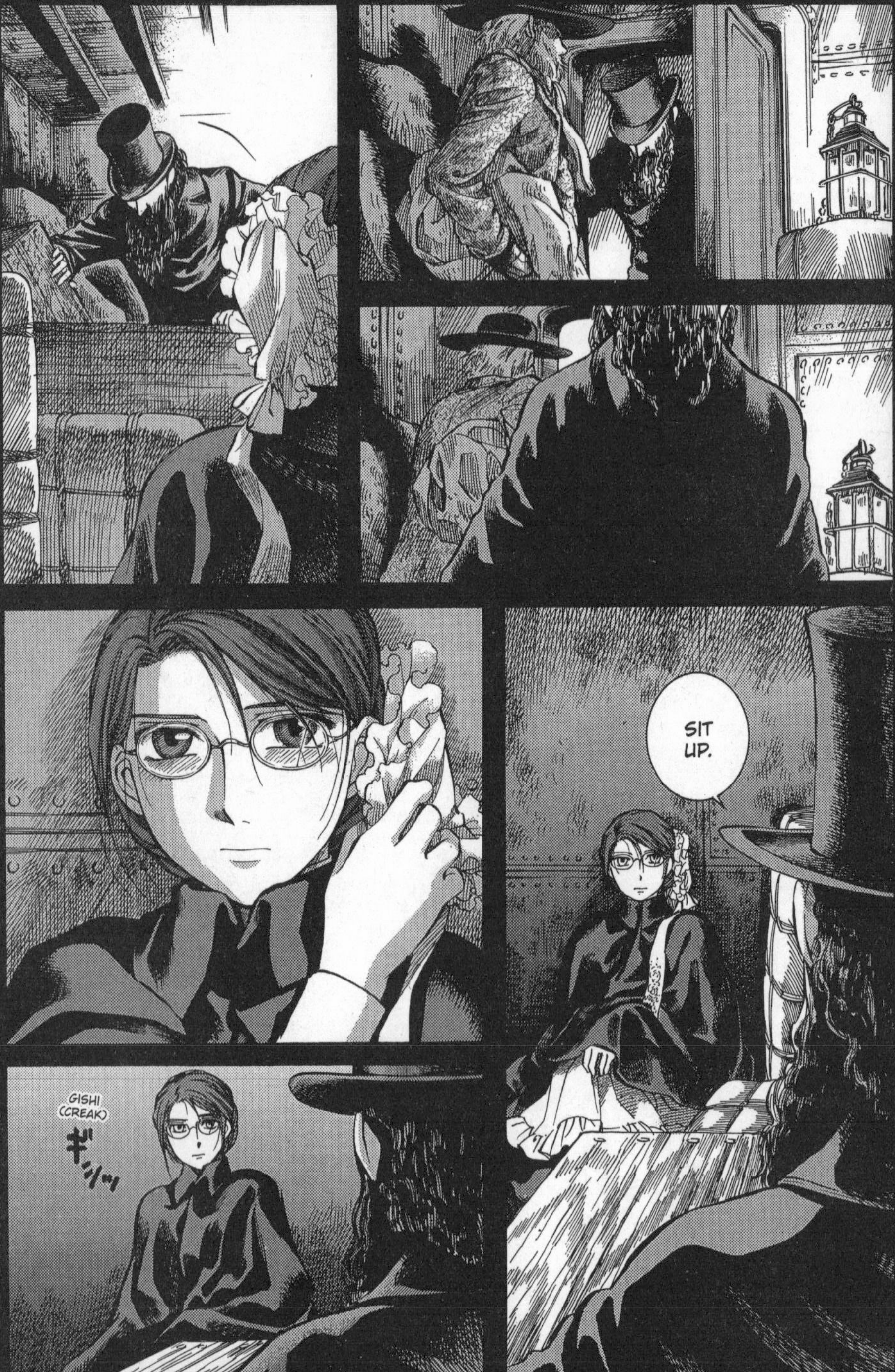
SIT UP.
GISHI (CREAK)

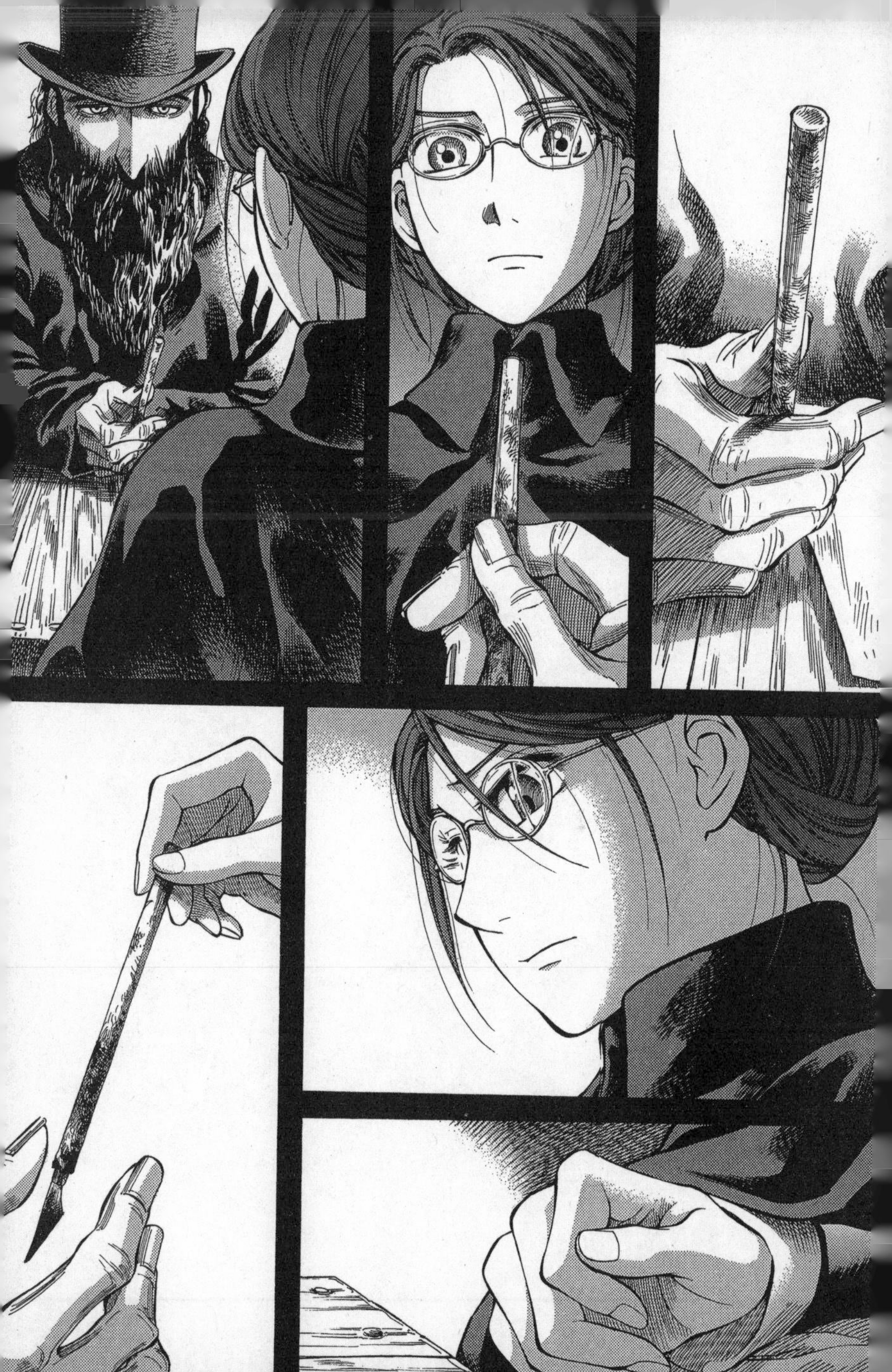

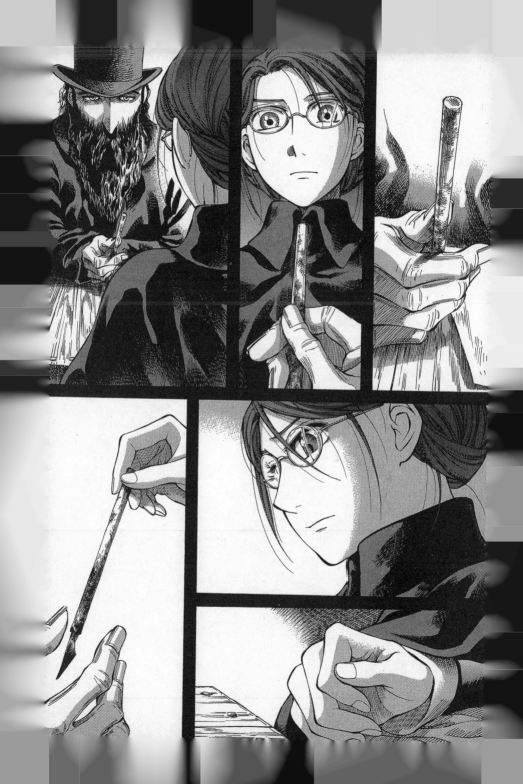

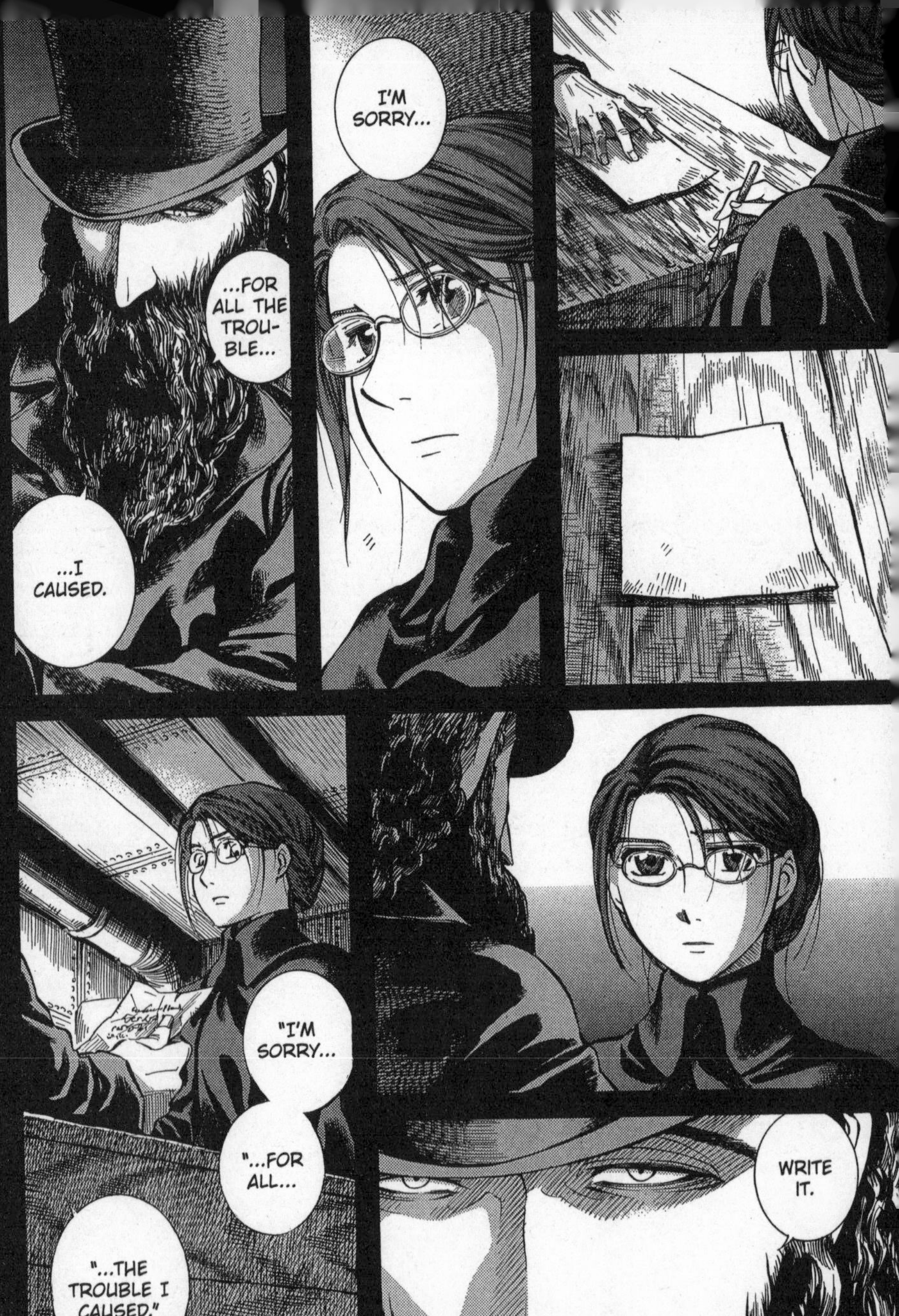
I'M SORRY...
...FOR ALL THE TROU-BLE...
...I CAUSED.
WRITE IT.
"I'M SORRY...
"...FOR ALL...
"...THE TROUBLE I CAUSED."

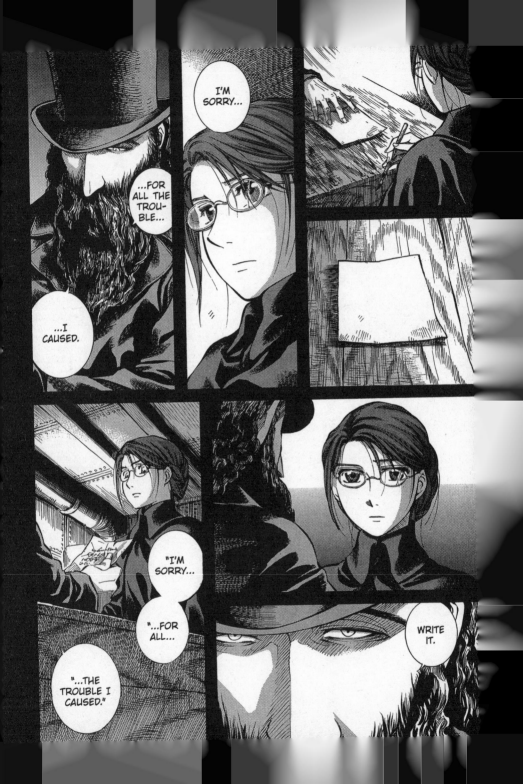

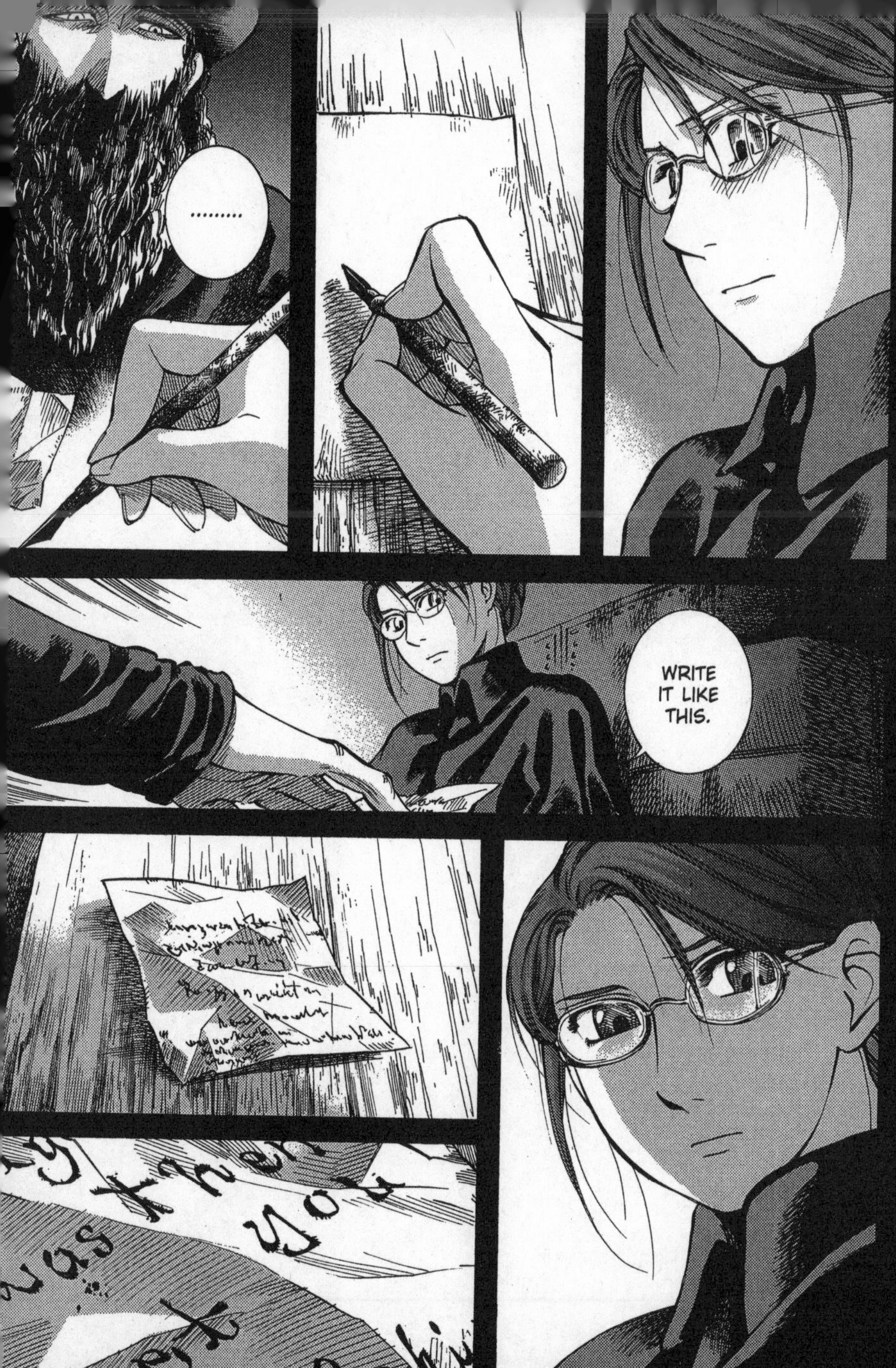
....
WRITE IT LIKE THIS.

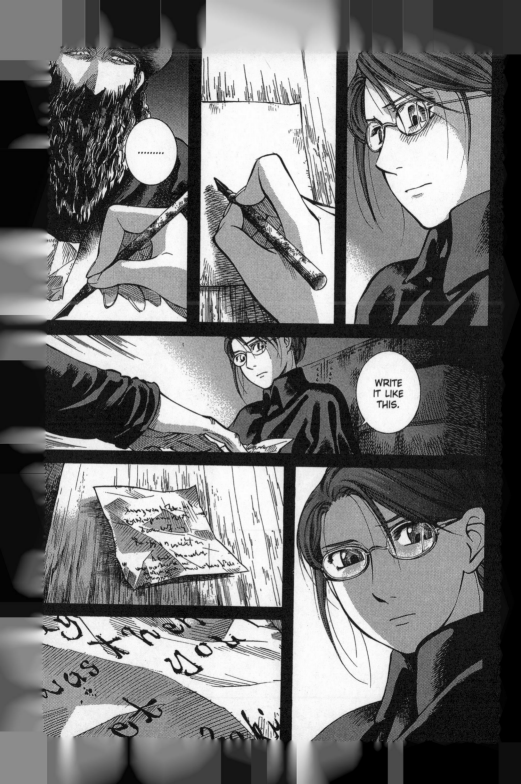

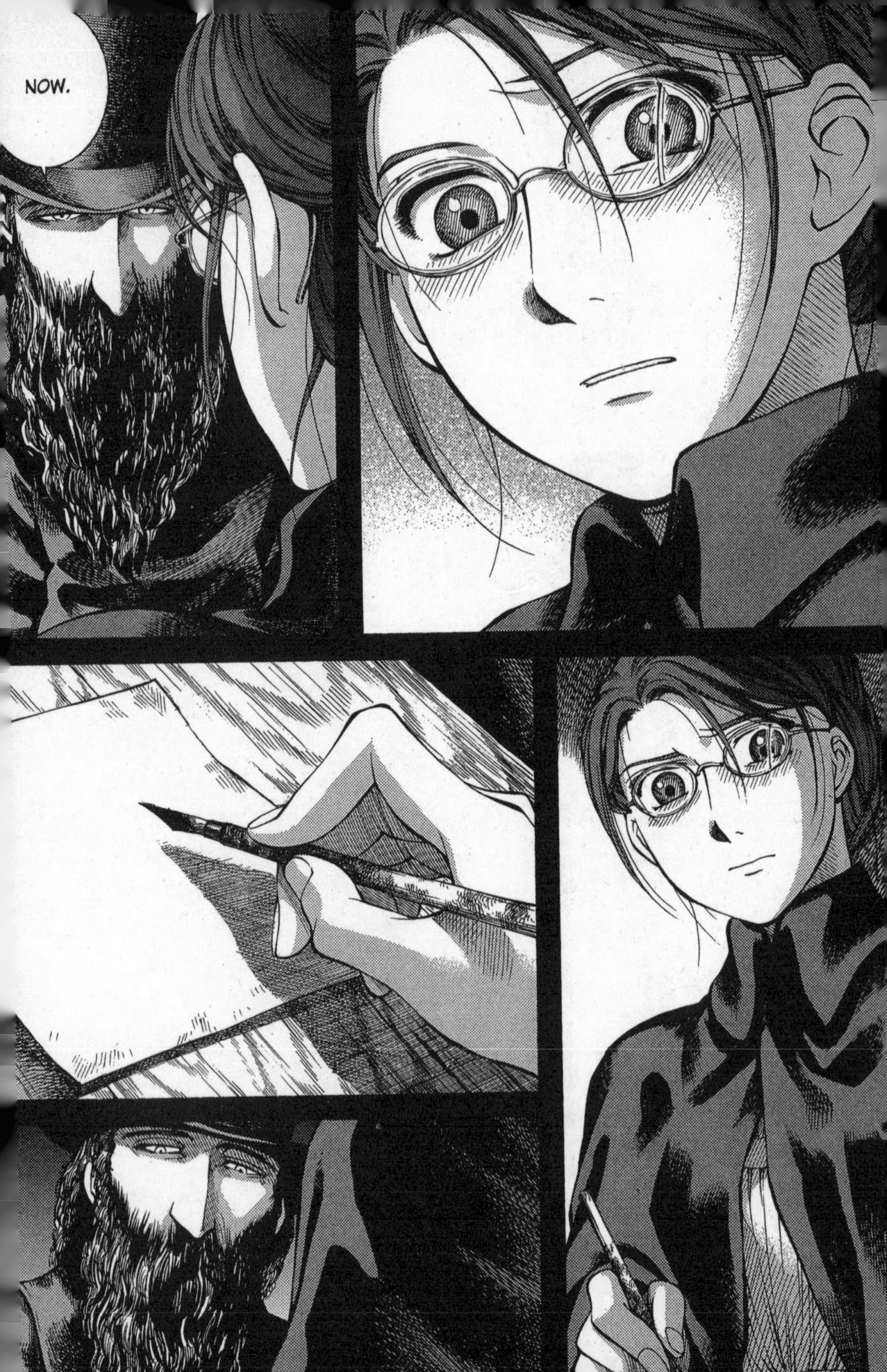
NOW.

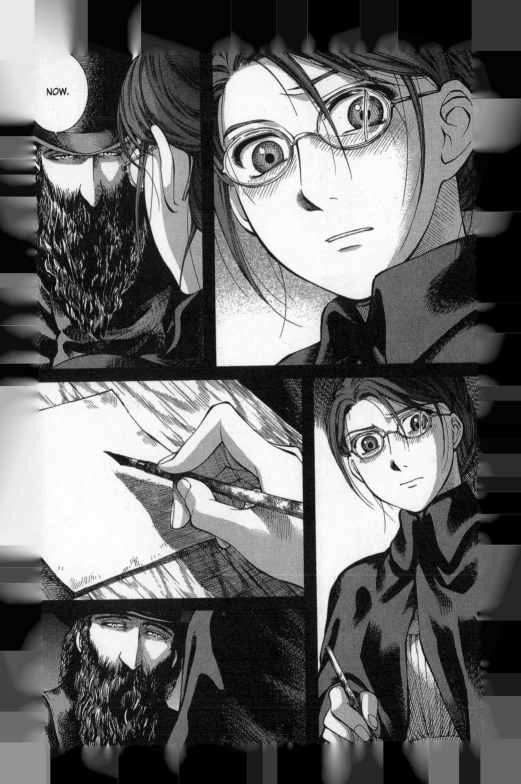

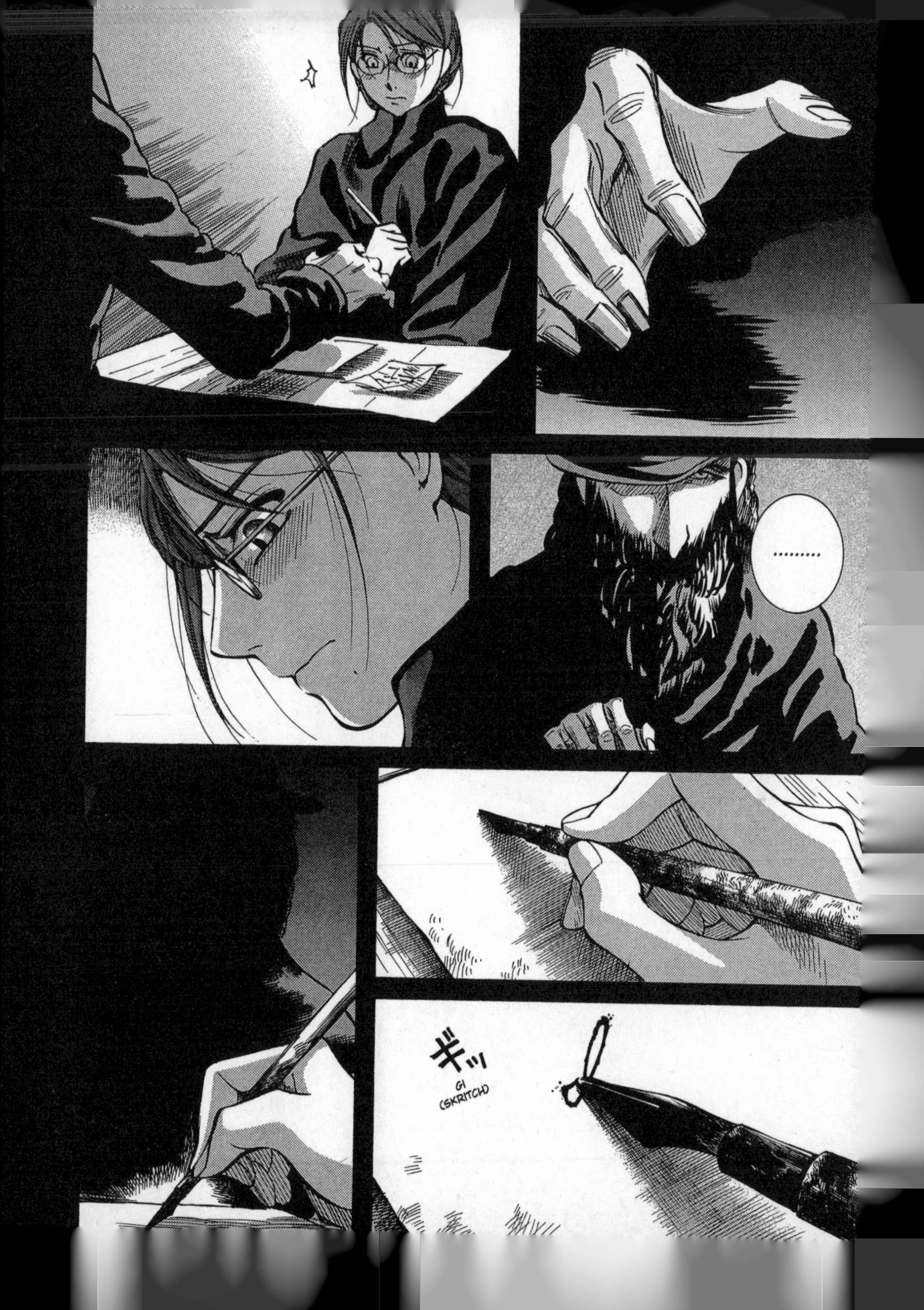
....
ギッ
GI
(SKRITCH)

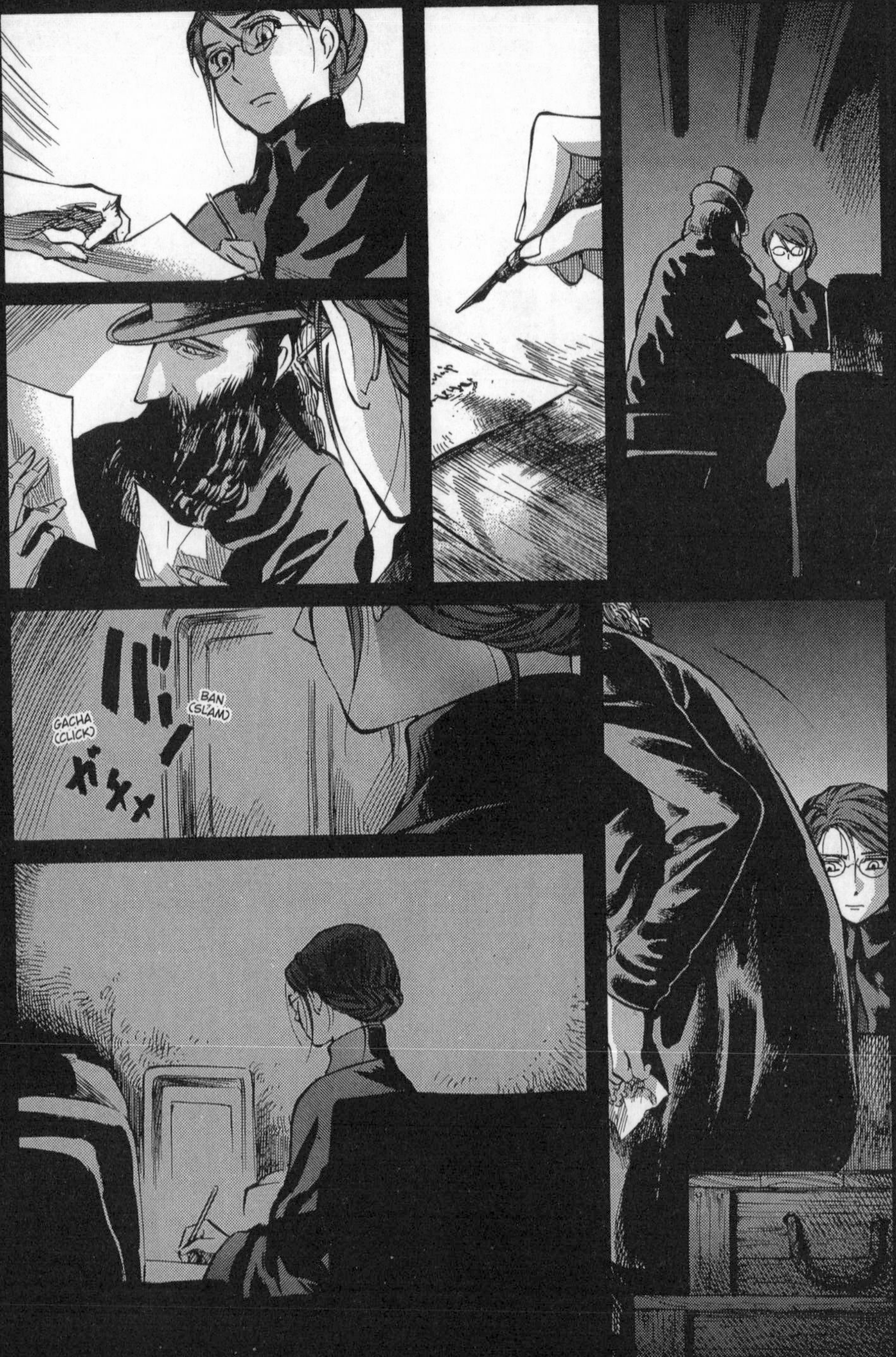
BAN (SLAM)
GACHA (CLICK)

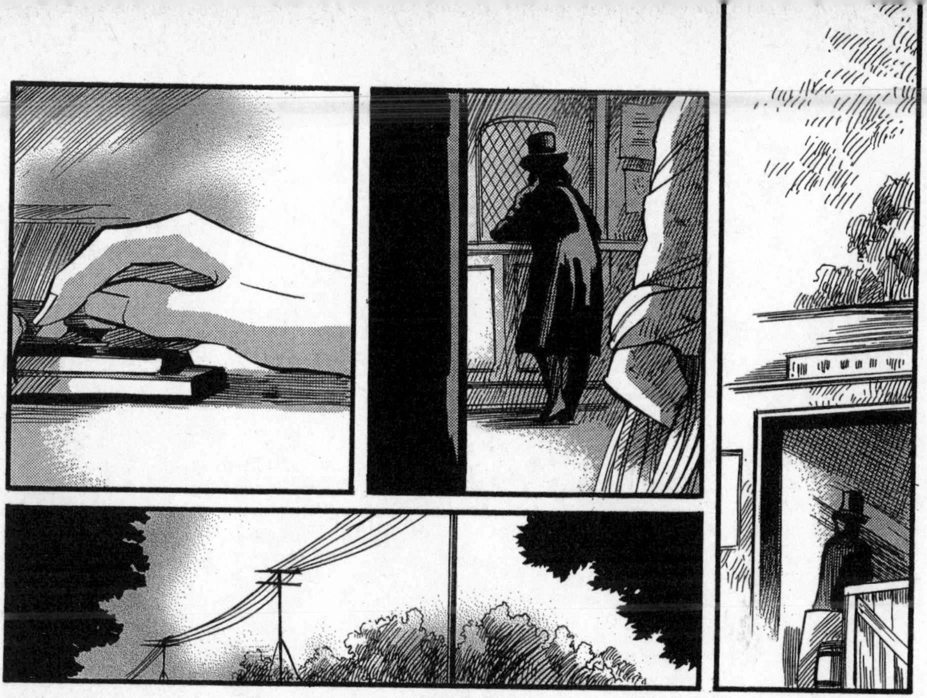

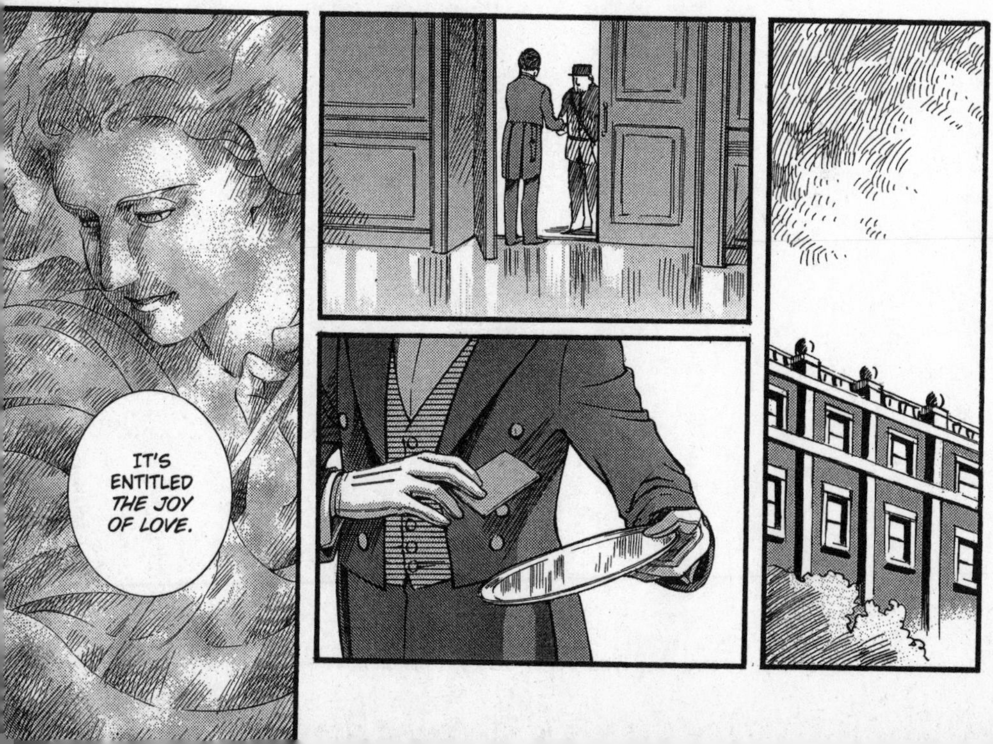
IT'S ENTITLED *THE JOY OF LOVE.*

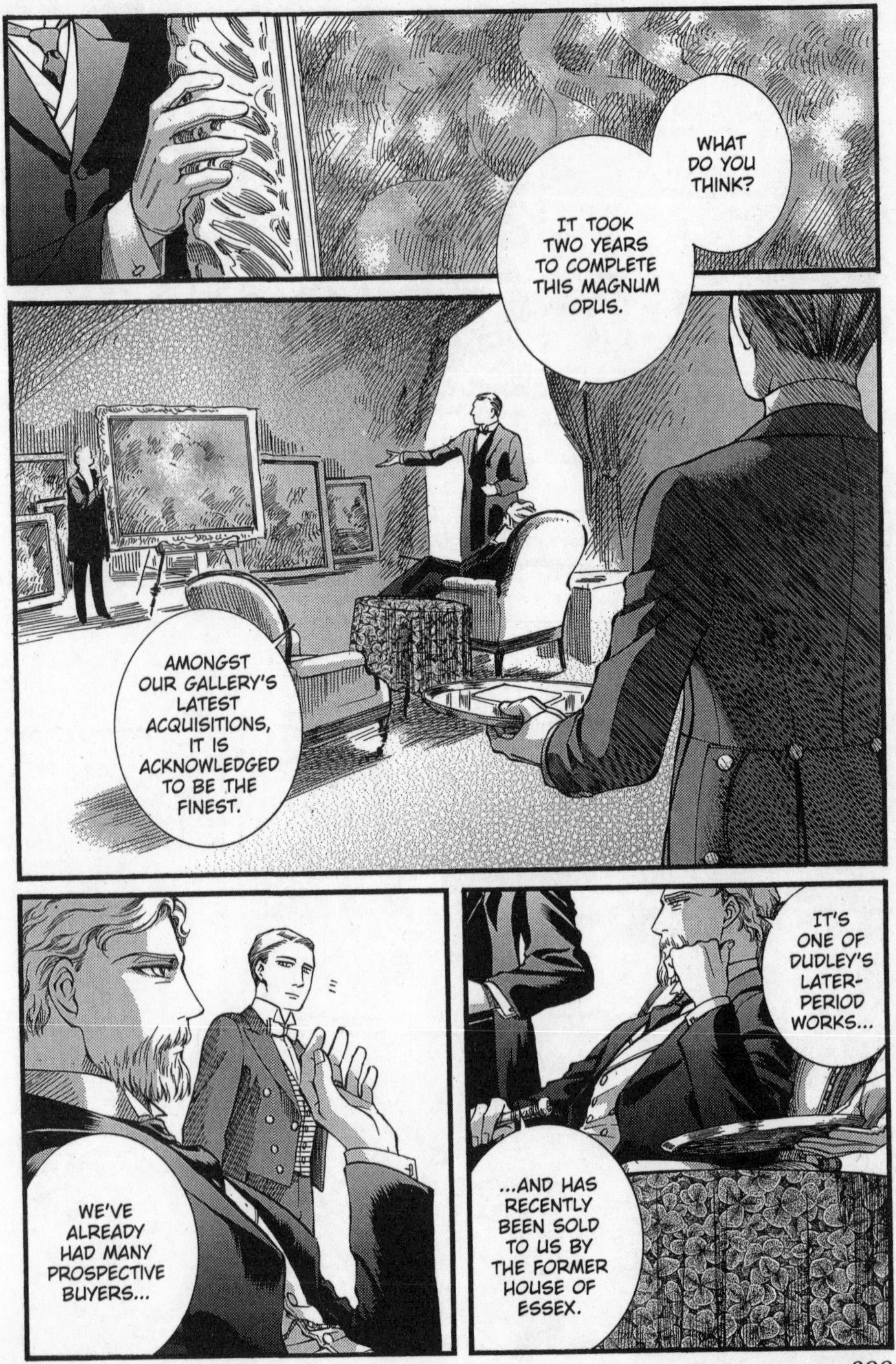
WHAT DO YOU THINK?
IT TOOK TWO YEARS TO COMPLETE THIS MAGNUM OPUS.
AMONGST OUR GALLERY'S LATEST ACQUISITIONS, IT IS ACKNOWLEDGED TO BE THE FINEST.
IT'S ONE OF DUDLEY'S LATER-PERIOD WORKS...
...AND HAS RECENTLY BEEN SOLD TO US BY THE FORMER HOUSE OF ESSEX.
WE'VE ALREADY HAD MANY PROSPECTIVE BUYERS...

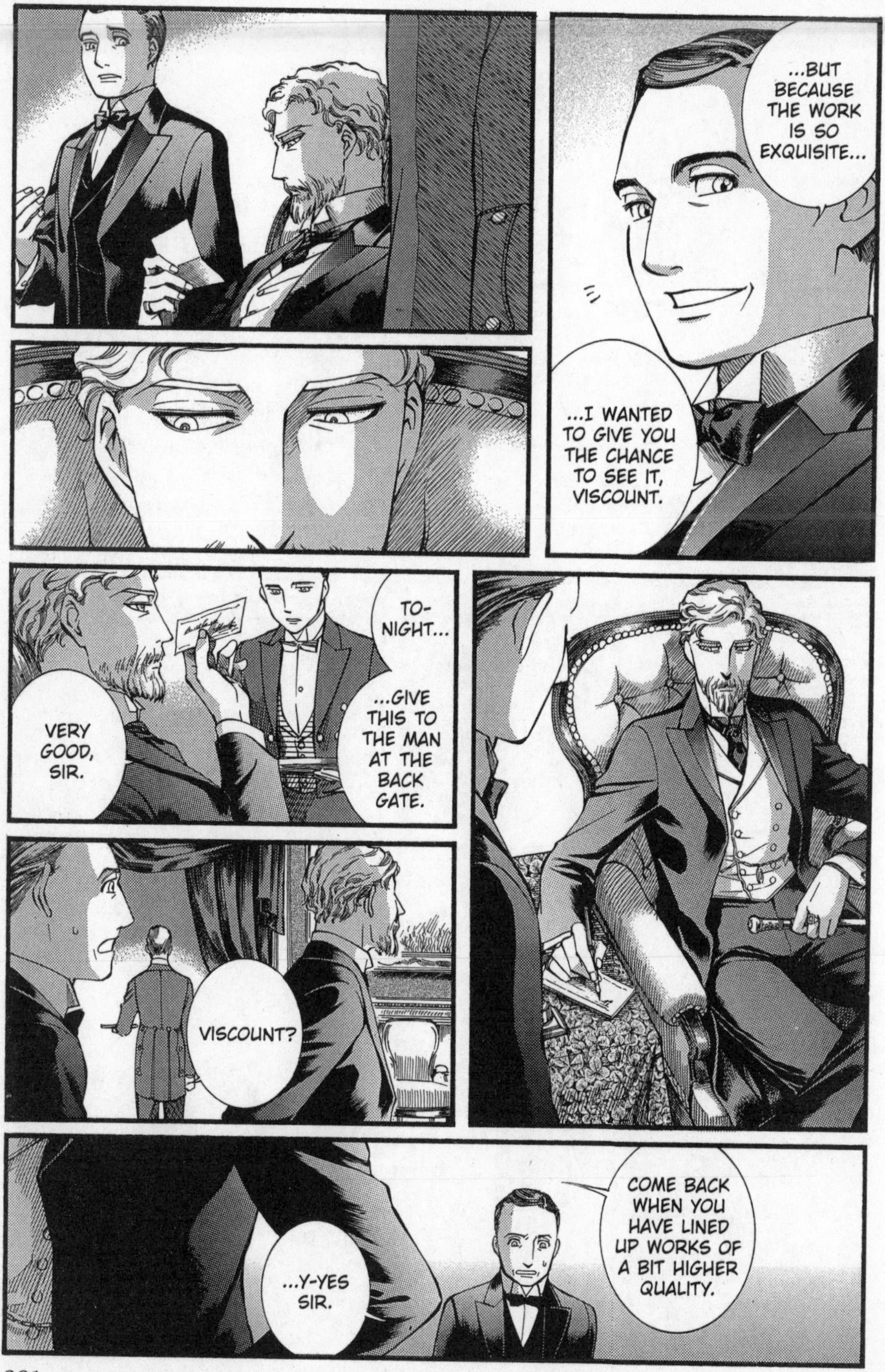
...BUT BECAUSE THE WORK IS SO EXQUISITE...
...I WANTED TO GIVE YOU THE CHANCE TO SEE IT, VISCOUNT.
TO-NIGHT...
...GIVE THIS TO THE MAN AT THE BACK GATE.
VERY GOOD, SIR.
VISCOUNT?
COME BACK WHEN YOU HAVE LINED UP WORKS OF A BIT HIGHER QUALITY.
...Y-YES SIR.

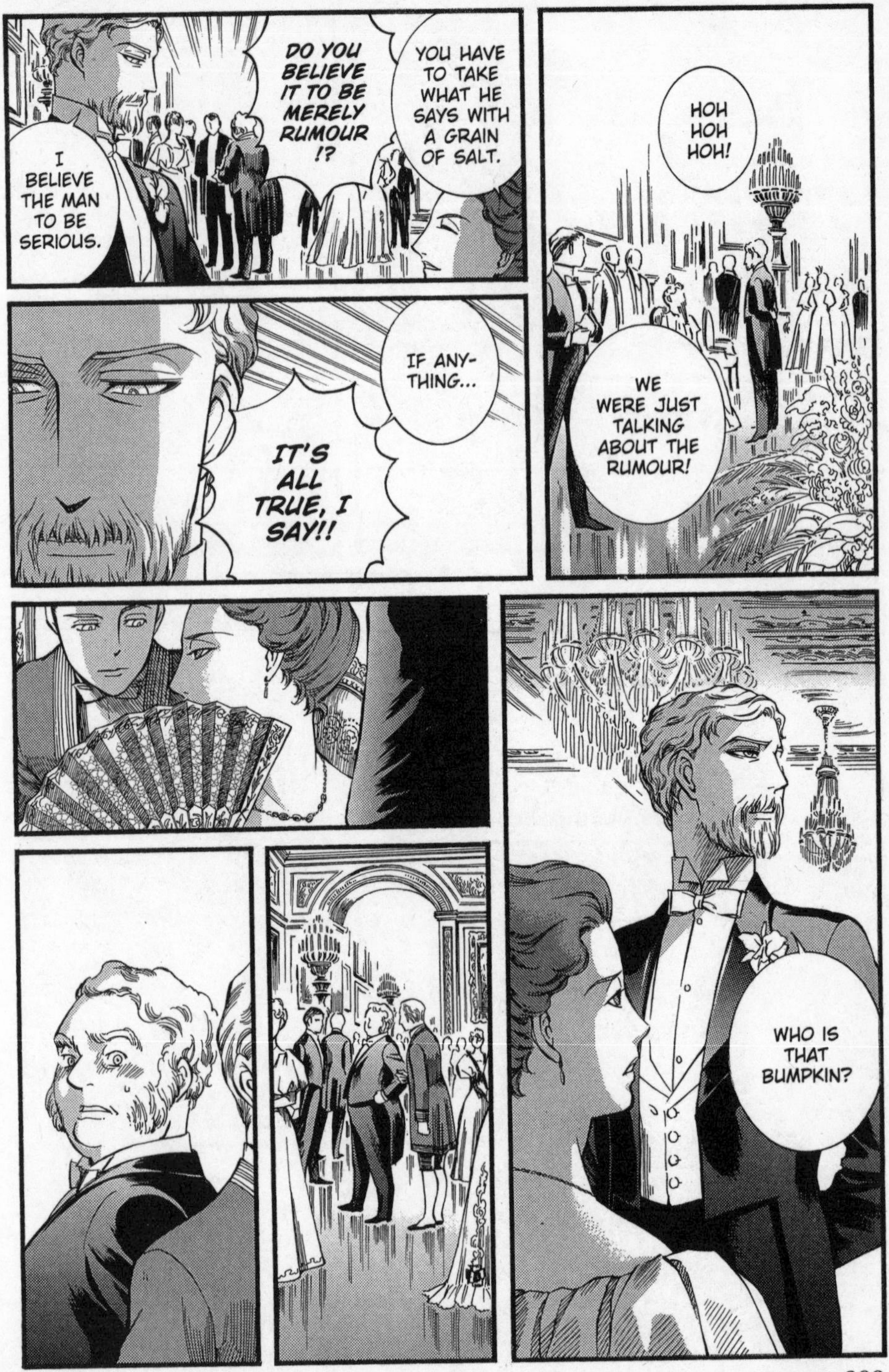
HOH HOH HOH!
WE WERE JUST TALKING ABOUT THE RUMOUR!
YOU HAVE TO TAKE WHAT HE SAYS WITH A GRAIN OF SALT.
DO YOU BELIEVE IT TO BE MERELY RUMOUR!?
I BELIEVE THE MAN TO BE SERIOUS.
IF ANYTHING...
IT'S ALL TRUE, I SAY!!
WHO IS THAT BUMPKIN?

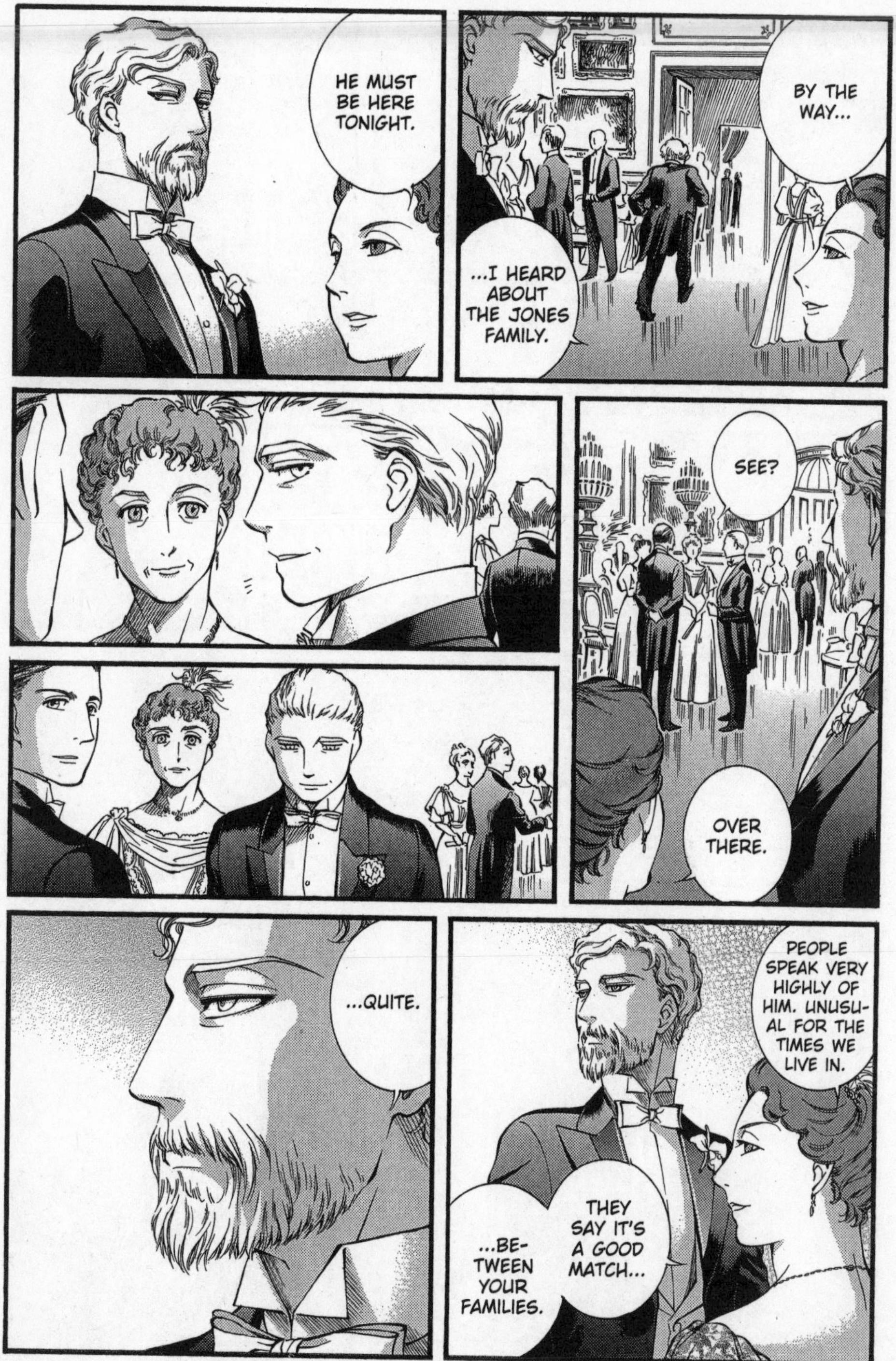
BY THE WAY...
...I HEARD ABOUT THE JONES FAMILY.
HE MUST BE HERE TONIGHT.
SEE?
OVER THERE.
PEOPLE SPEAK VERY HIGHLY OF HIM. UNUSU-AL FOR THE TIMES WE LIVE IN.
THEY SAY IT'S A GOOD MATCH...
...BE-TWEEN YOUR FAMILIES.
...QUITE.

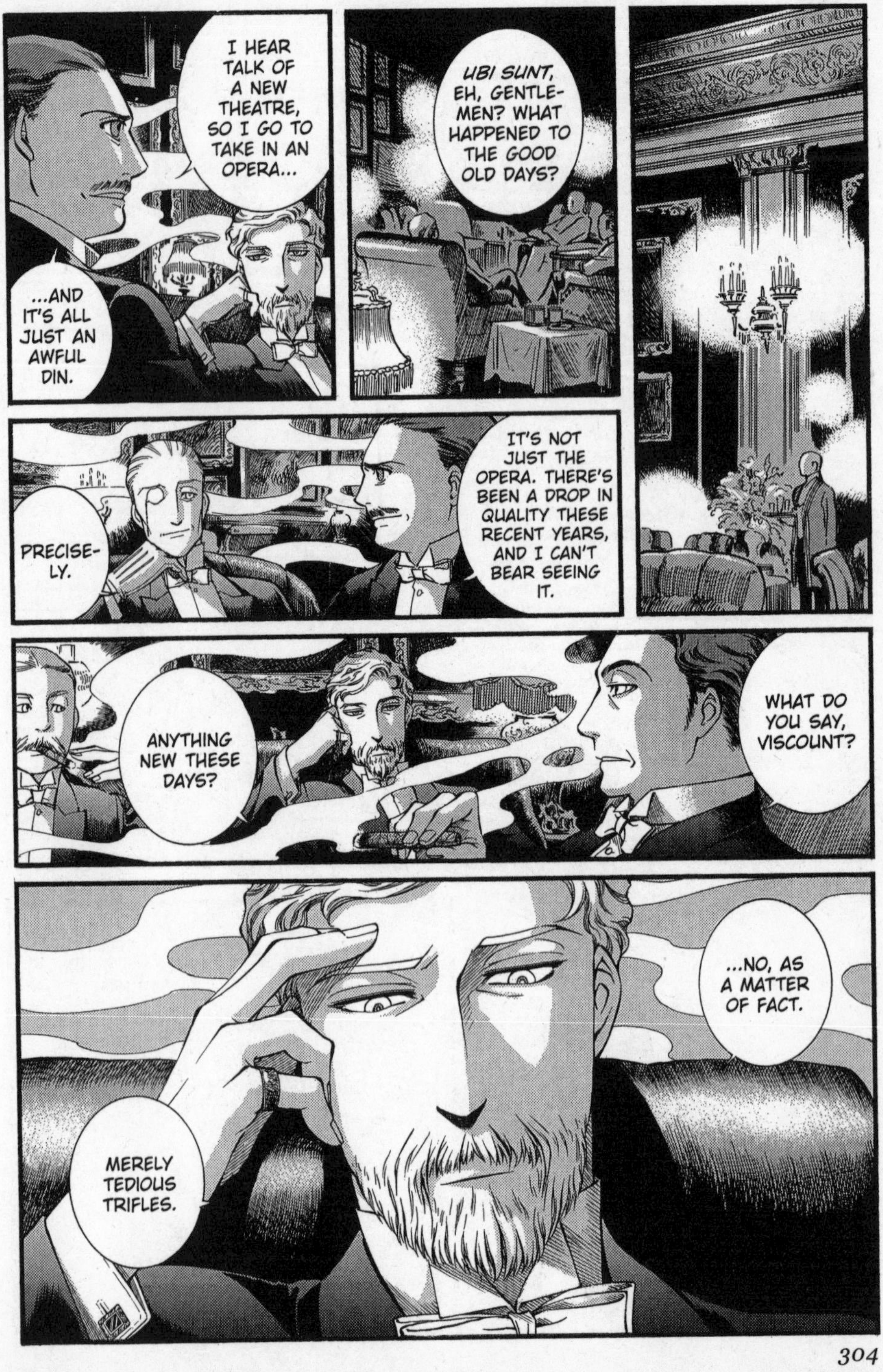
UBI SUNT, EH, GENTLEMEN? WHAT HAPPENED TO THE GOOD OLD DAYS?
I HEAR TALK OF A NEW THEATRE, SO I GO TO TAKE IN AN OPERA...
...AND IT'S ALL JUST AN AWFUL DIN.
IT'S NOT JUST THE OPERA. THERE'S BEEN A DROP IN QUALITY THESE RECENT YEARS, AND I CAN'T BEAR SEEING IT.
PRECISELY.
WHAT DO YOU SAY, VISCOUNT?
ANYTHING NEW THESE DAYS?
...NO, AS A MATTER OF FACT.
MERELY TEDIOUS TRIFLES.

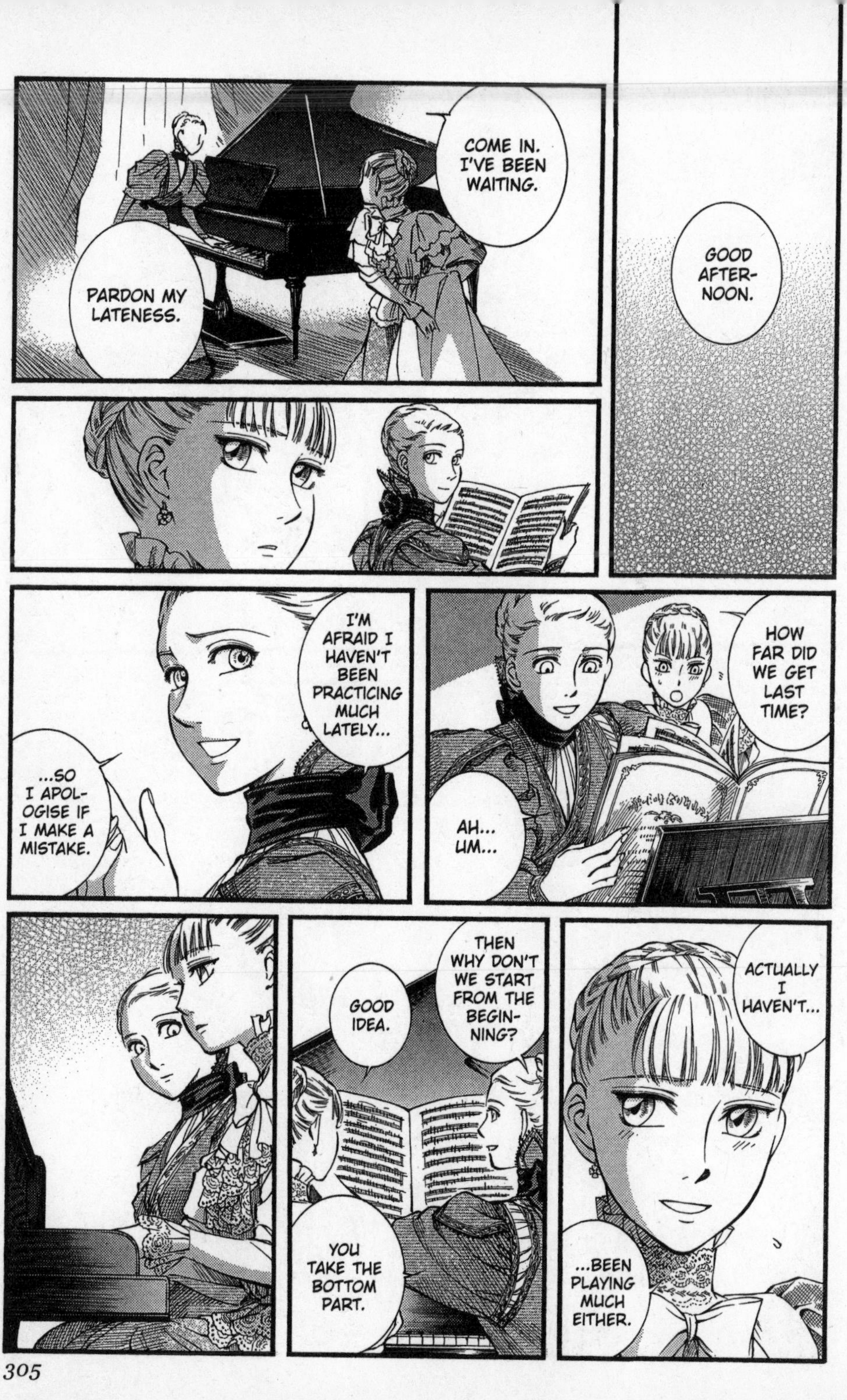
GOOD AFTERNOON.
COME IN. I'VE BEEN WAITING.
PARDON MY LATENESS.
HOW FAR DID WE GET LAST TIME?
AH... UM...
I'M AFRAID I HAVEN'T BEEN PRACTICING MUCH LATELY...
...SO I APOLOGISE IF I MAKE A MISTAKE.
ACTUALLY I HAVEN'T...
...BEEN PLAYING MUCH EITHER.
THEN WHY DON'T WE START FROM THE BEGINNING?
GOOD IDEA.
YOU TAKE THE BOTTOM PART.

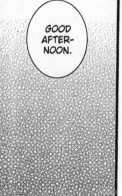

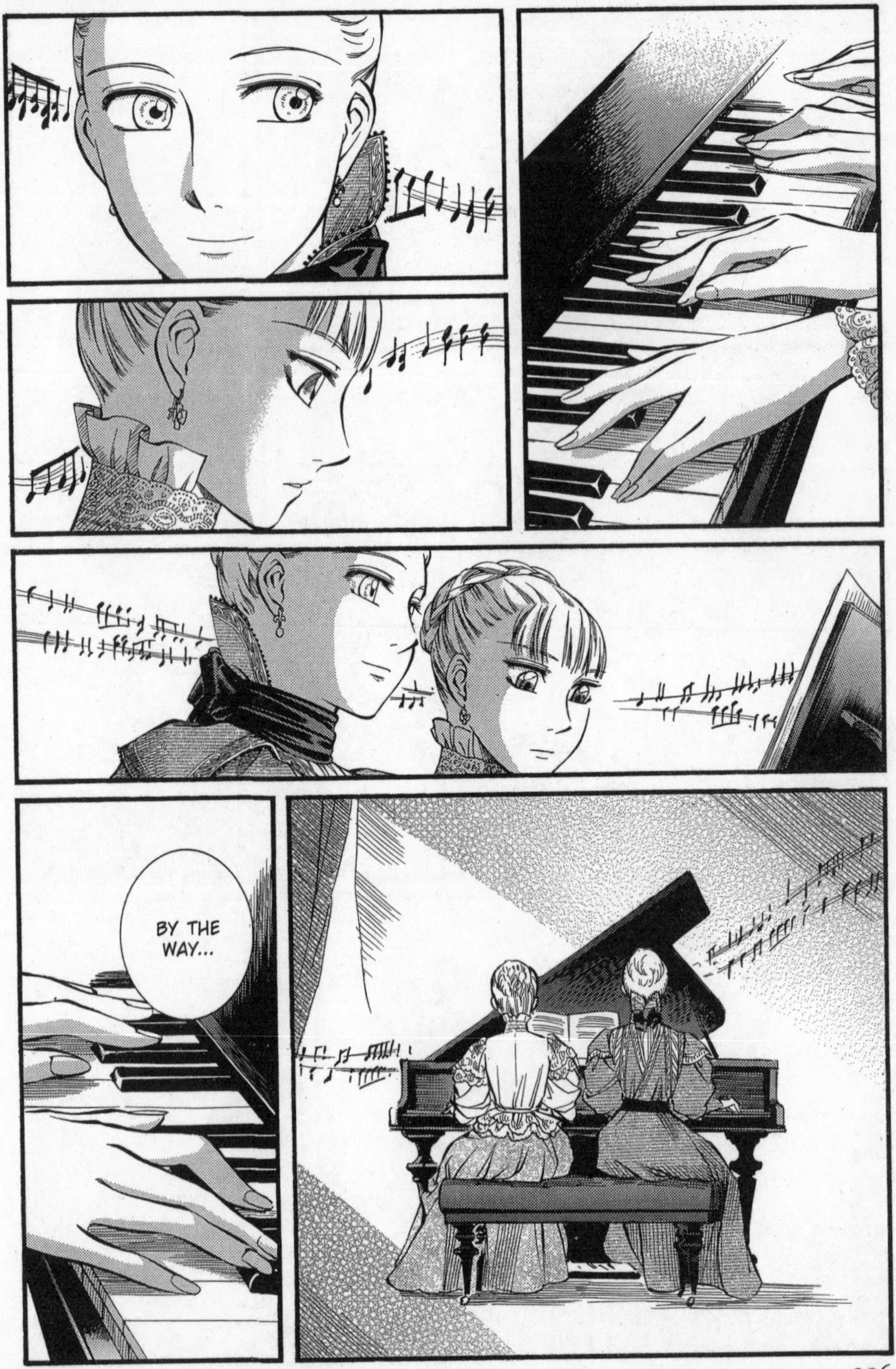
BY THE WAY...

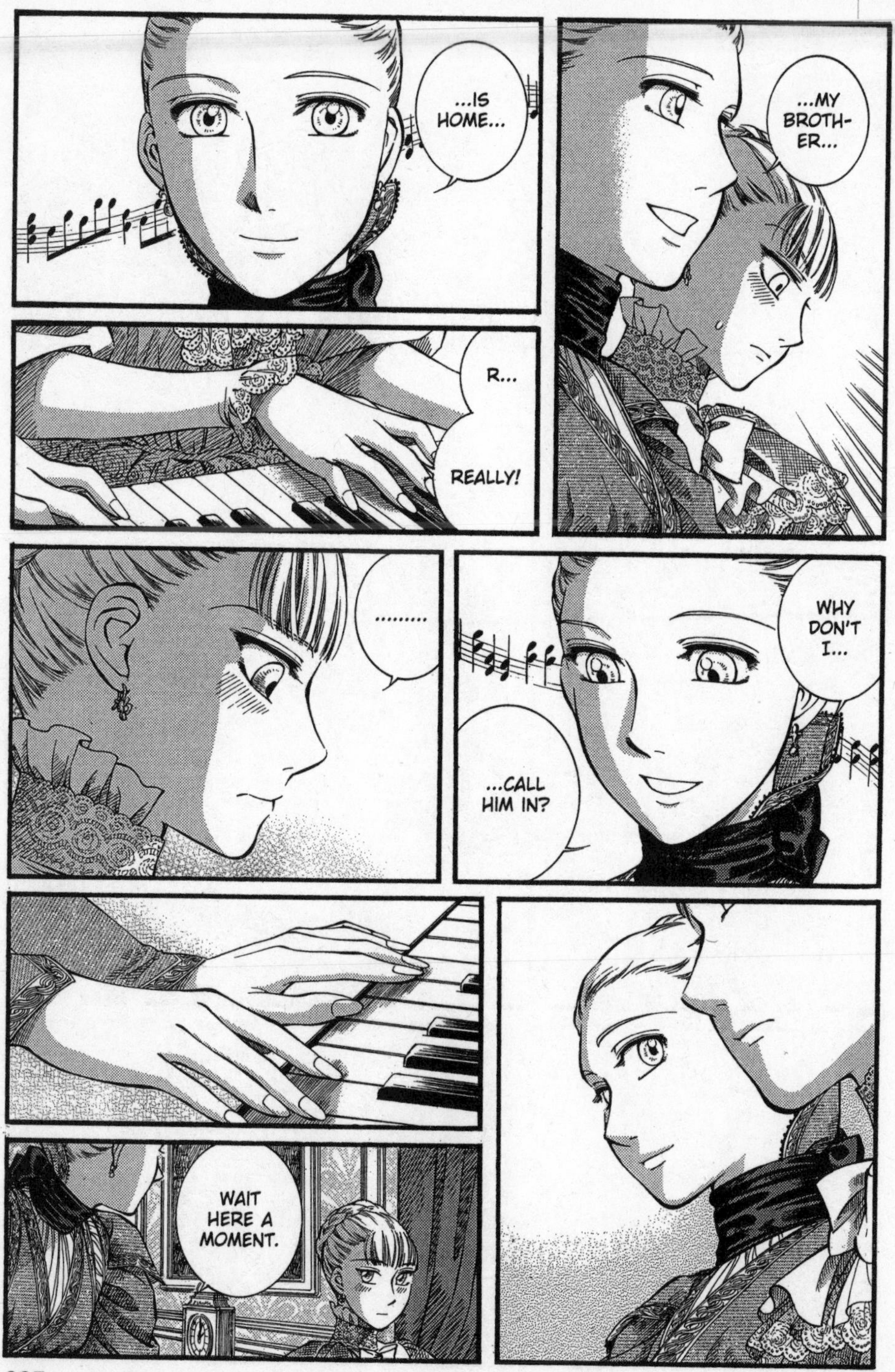
...MY BROTH-ER...
...IS HOME...
R...
REALLY!
WHY DON'T I...
...CALL HIM IN?
....
WAIT HERE A MOMENT.

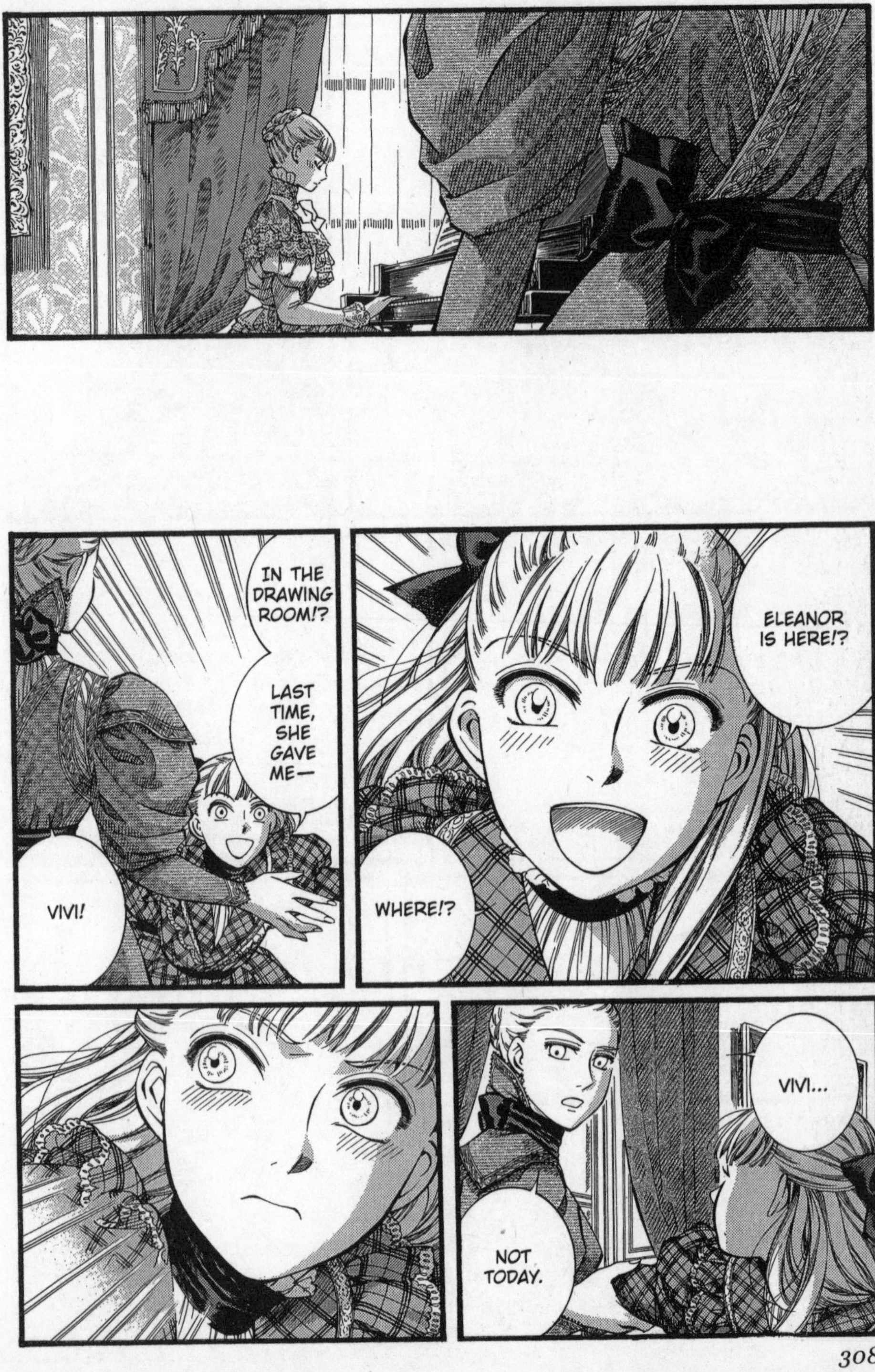
ELEANOR IS HERE!?
WHERE!?
IN THE DRAWING ROOM!?
LAST TIME, SHE GAVE ME—
VIVI!
VIVI...
NOT TODAY.

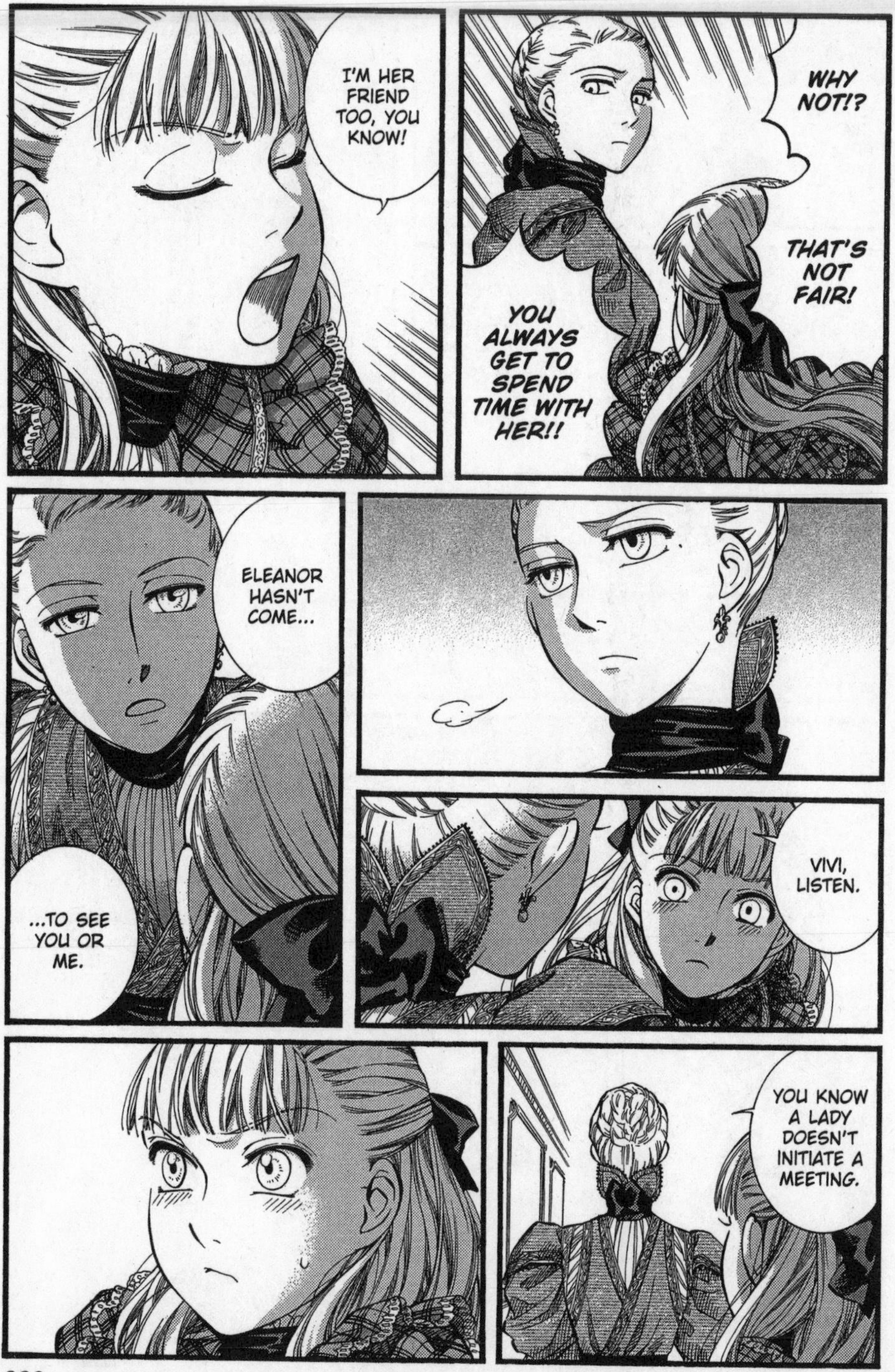
WHY NOT!?
THAT'S NOT FAIR!
YOU ALWAYS GET TO SPEND TIME WITH HER!!
I'M HER FRIEND TOO, YOU KNOW!
VIVI, LISTEN.
ELEANOR HASN'T COME...
...TO SEE YOU OR ME.
YOU KNOW A LADY DOESN'T INITIATE A MEETING.

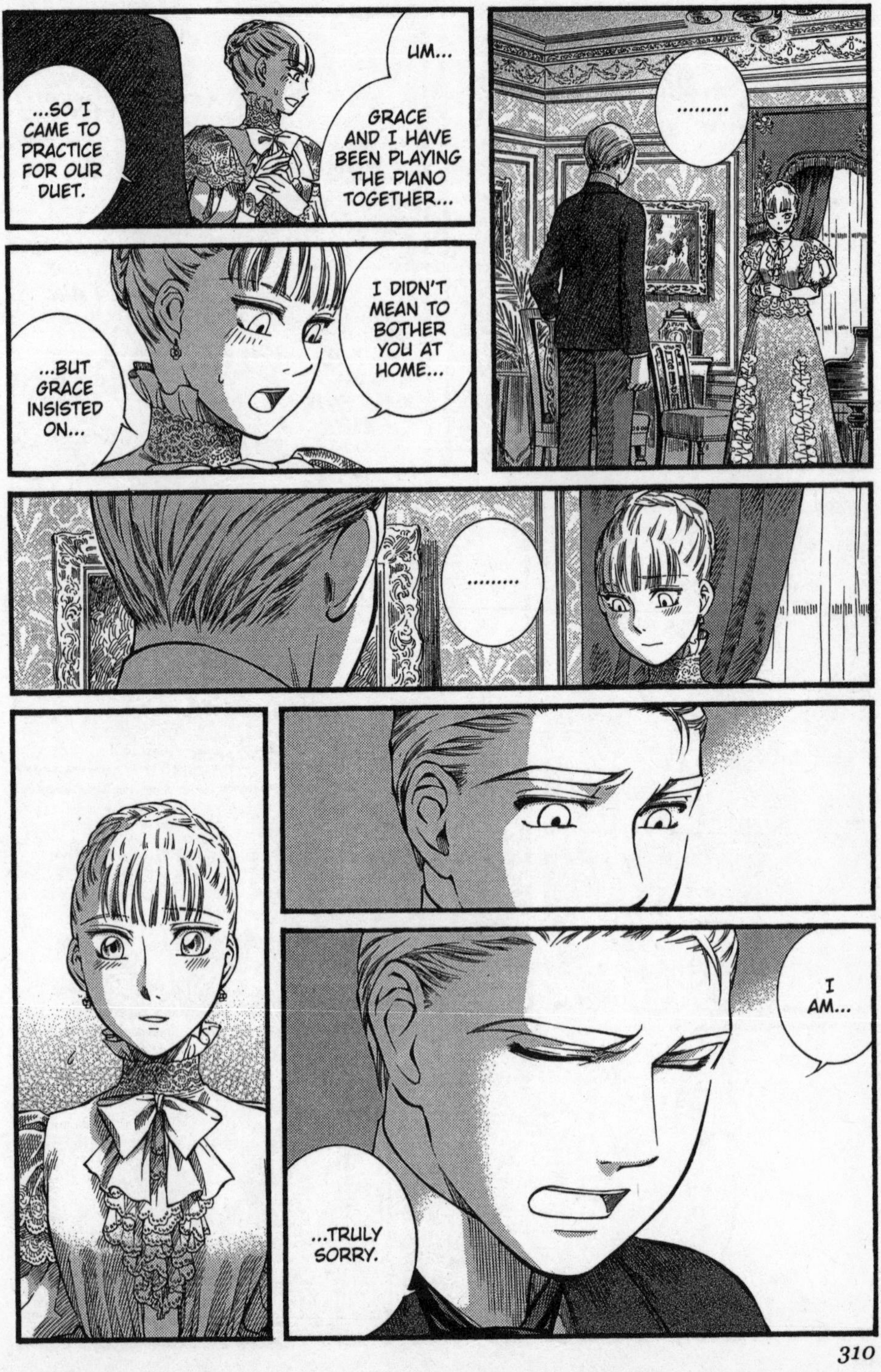
....
UM...
GRACE AND I HAVE BEEN PLAYING THE PIANO TOGETHER...
...SO I CAME TO PRACTICE FOR OUR DUET.
I DIDN'T MEAN TO BOTHER YOU AT HOME...
...BUT GRACE INSISTED ON...
....
I AM...
...TRULY SORRY.

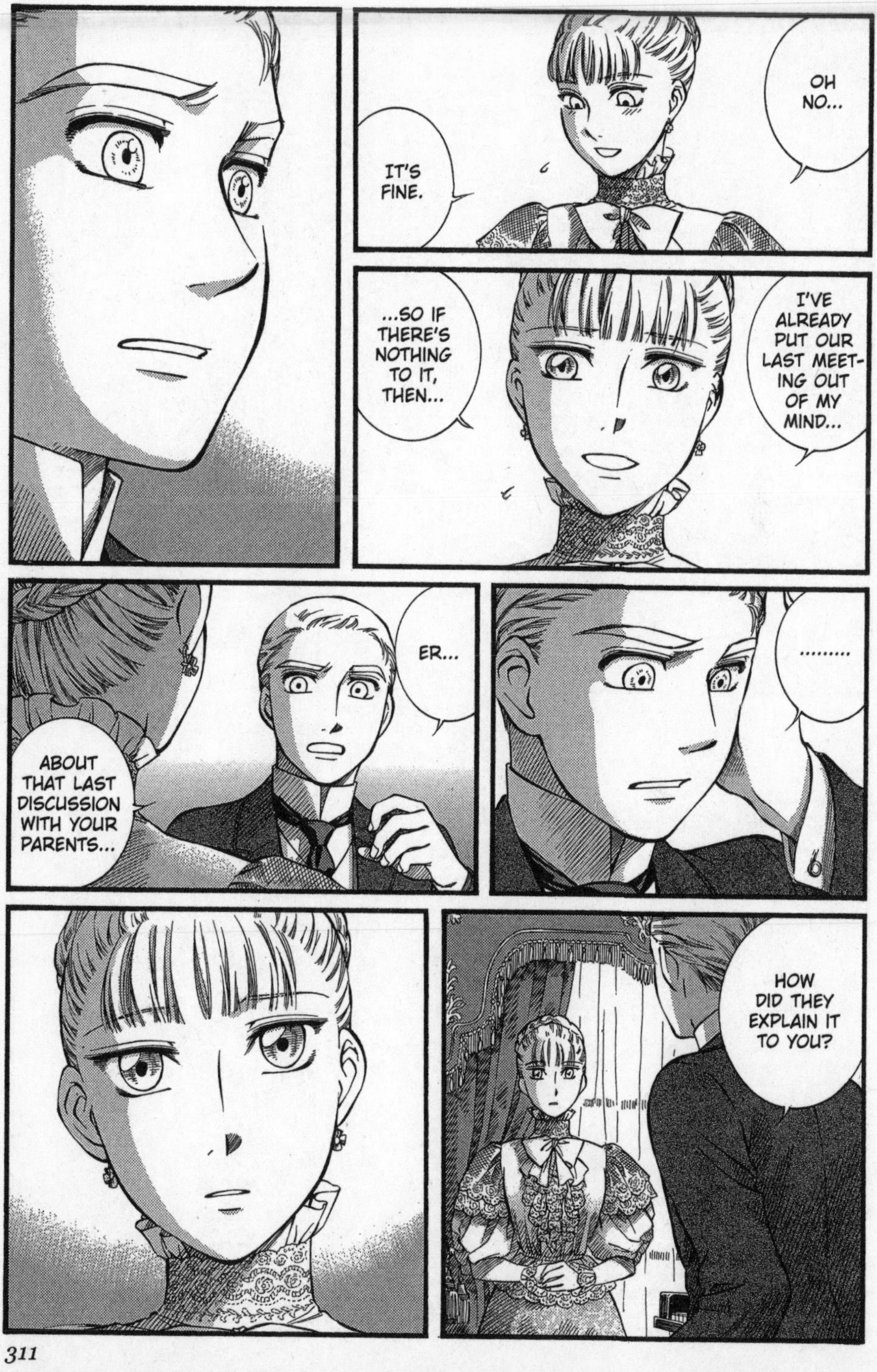
OH NO...
IT'S FINE.
I'VE ALREADY PUT OUR LAST MEETING OUT OF MY MIND...
...SO IF THERE'S NOTHING TO IT, THEN...
....
ER...
ABOUT THAT LAST DISCUSSION WITH YOUR PARENTS...
HOW DID THEY EXPLAIN IT TO YOU?

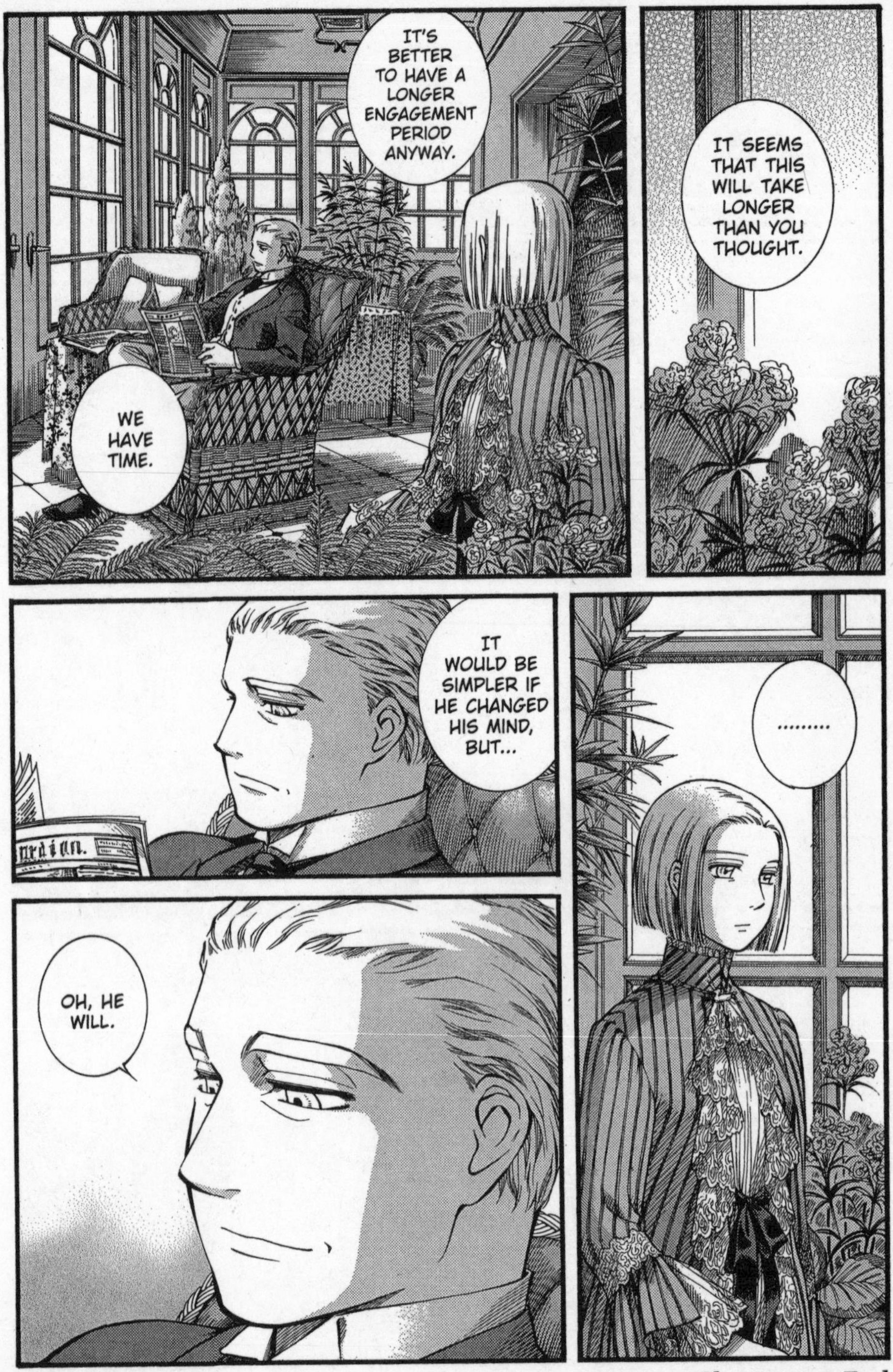
IT SEEMS THAT THIS WILL TAKE LONGER THAN YOU THOUGHT.
IT'S BETTER TO HAVE A LONGER ENGAGEMENT PERIOD ANYWAY.
WE HAVE TIME.
....
IT WOULD BE SIMPLER IF HE CHANGED HIS MIND, BUT...
OH, HE WILL.

Chapter 41: End

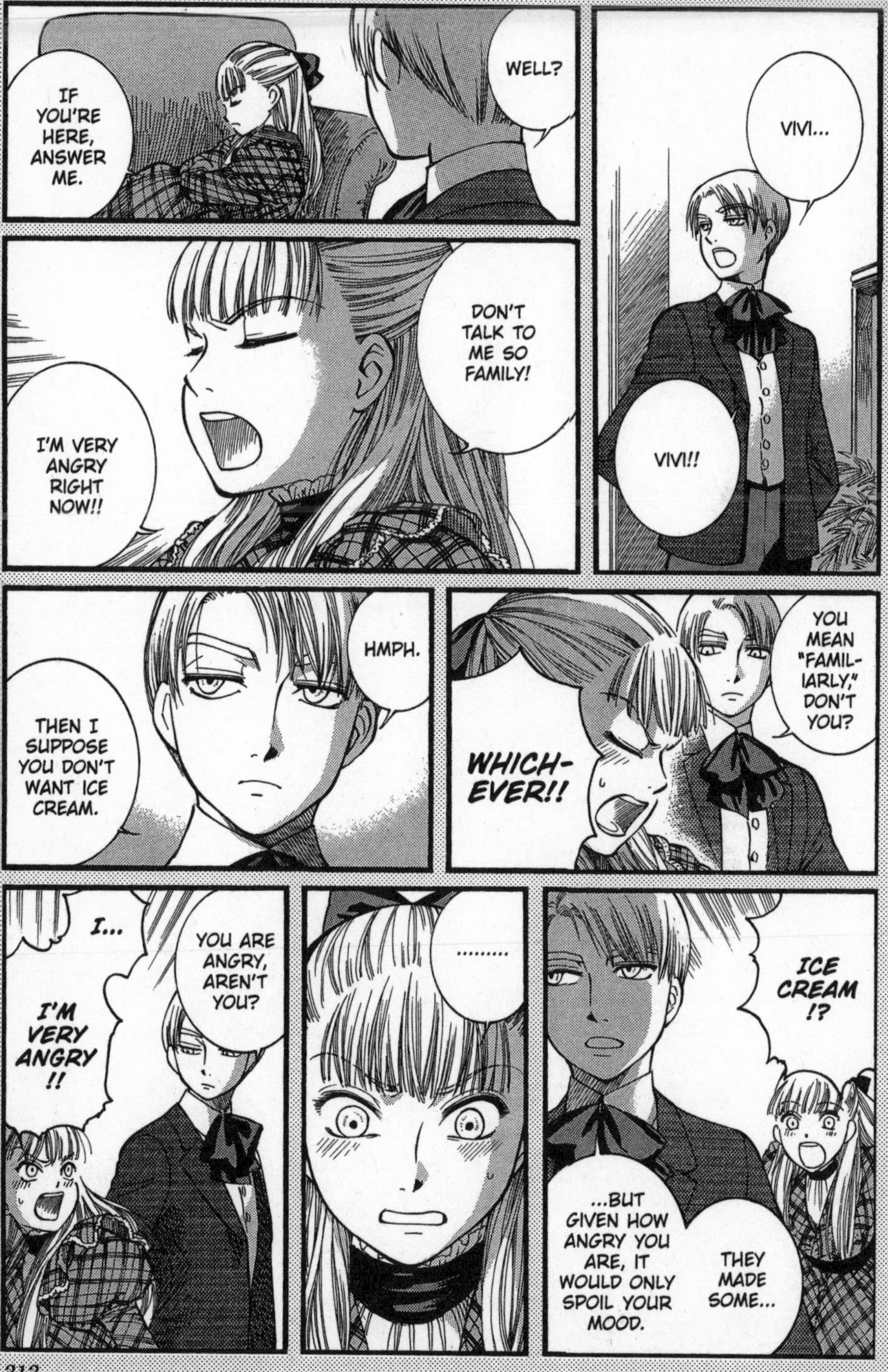
VIVI...
VIVI!!
WELL?
IF YOU'RE HERE, ANSWER ME.
DON'T TALK TO ME SO FAMILY!
I'M VERY ANGRY RIGHT NOW!!
YOU MEAN "FAMILIARLY," DON'T YOU?
WHICHEVER!!
HMPH.
THEN I SUPPOSE YOU DON'T WANT ICE CREAM.
ICE CREAM!?
THEY MADE SOME...
...BUT GIVEN HOW ANGRY YOU ARE, IT WOULD ONLY SPOIL YOUR MOOD.
....
YOU ARE ANGRY, AREN'T YOU?
I...
I'M VERY ANGRY!!

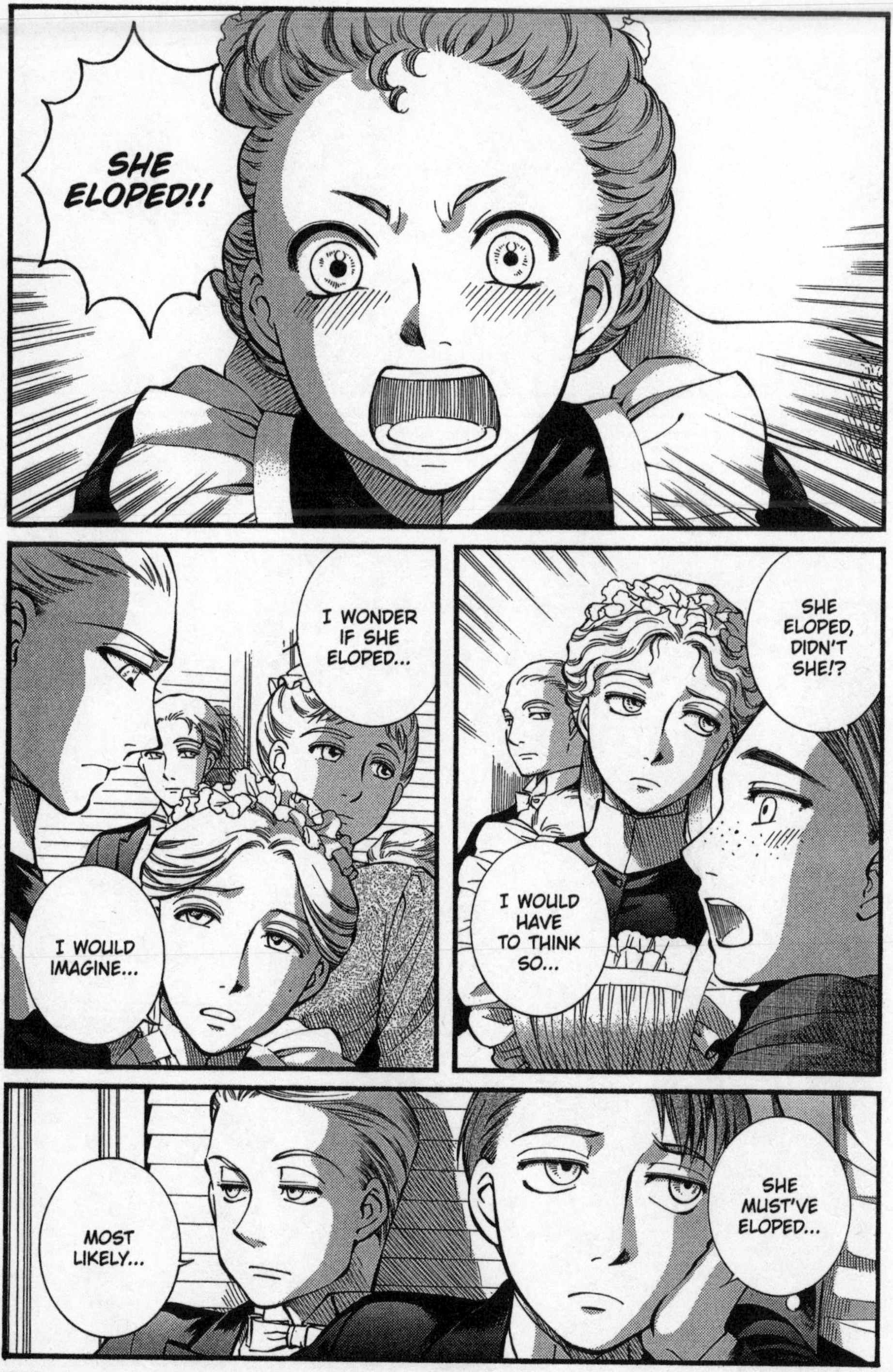
SHE ELOPED!!
SHE ELOPED, DIDN'T SHE!?
I WOULD HAVE TO THINK SO...
I WONDER IF SHE ELOPED...
I WOULD IMAGINE...
SHE MUST'VE ELOPED...
MOST LIKELY...

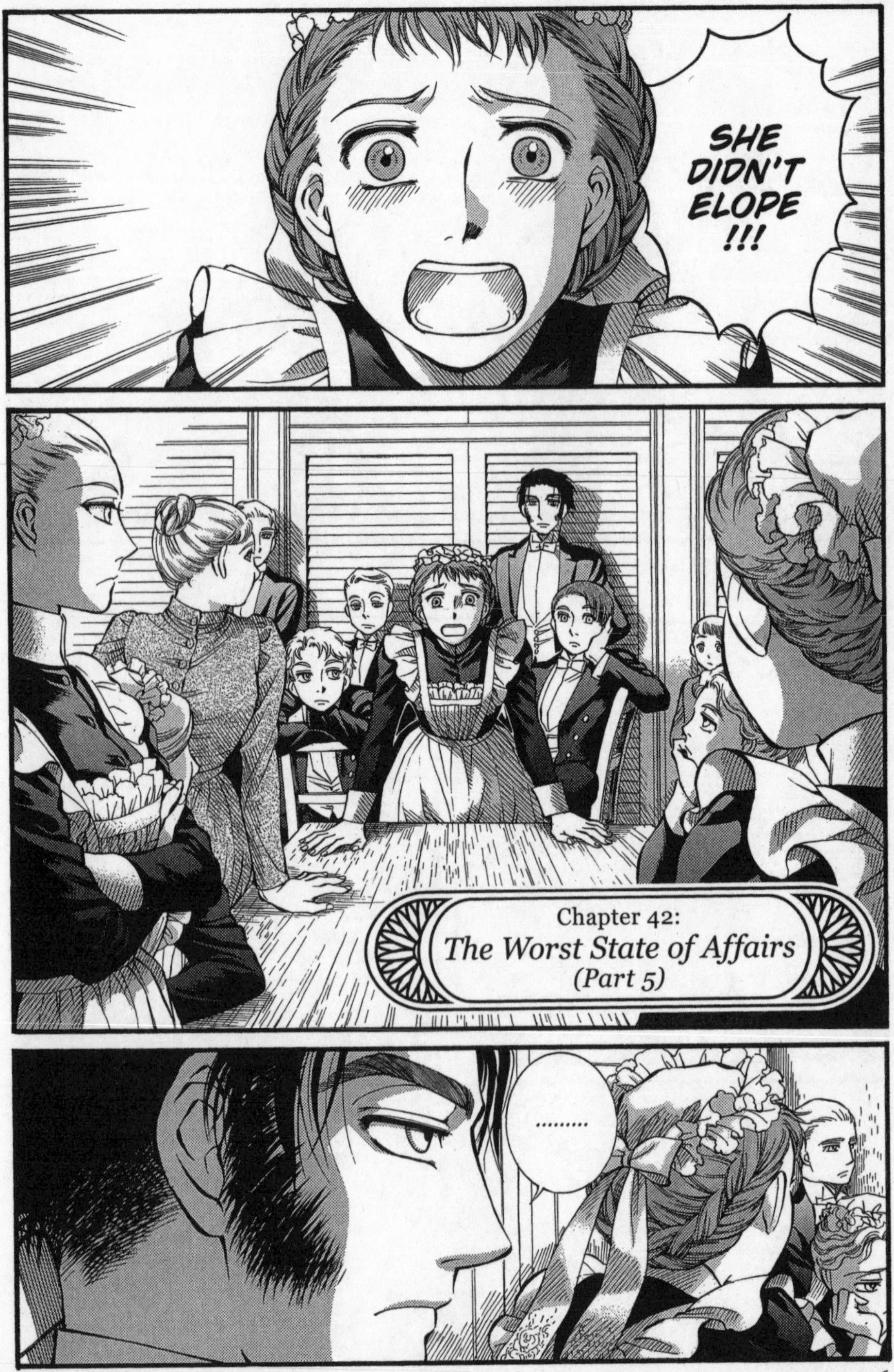
SHE DIDN'T ELOPE !!!
Chapter 42:
The Worst State of Affairs
(Part 5)
....

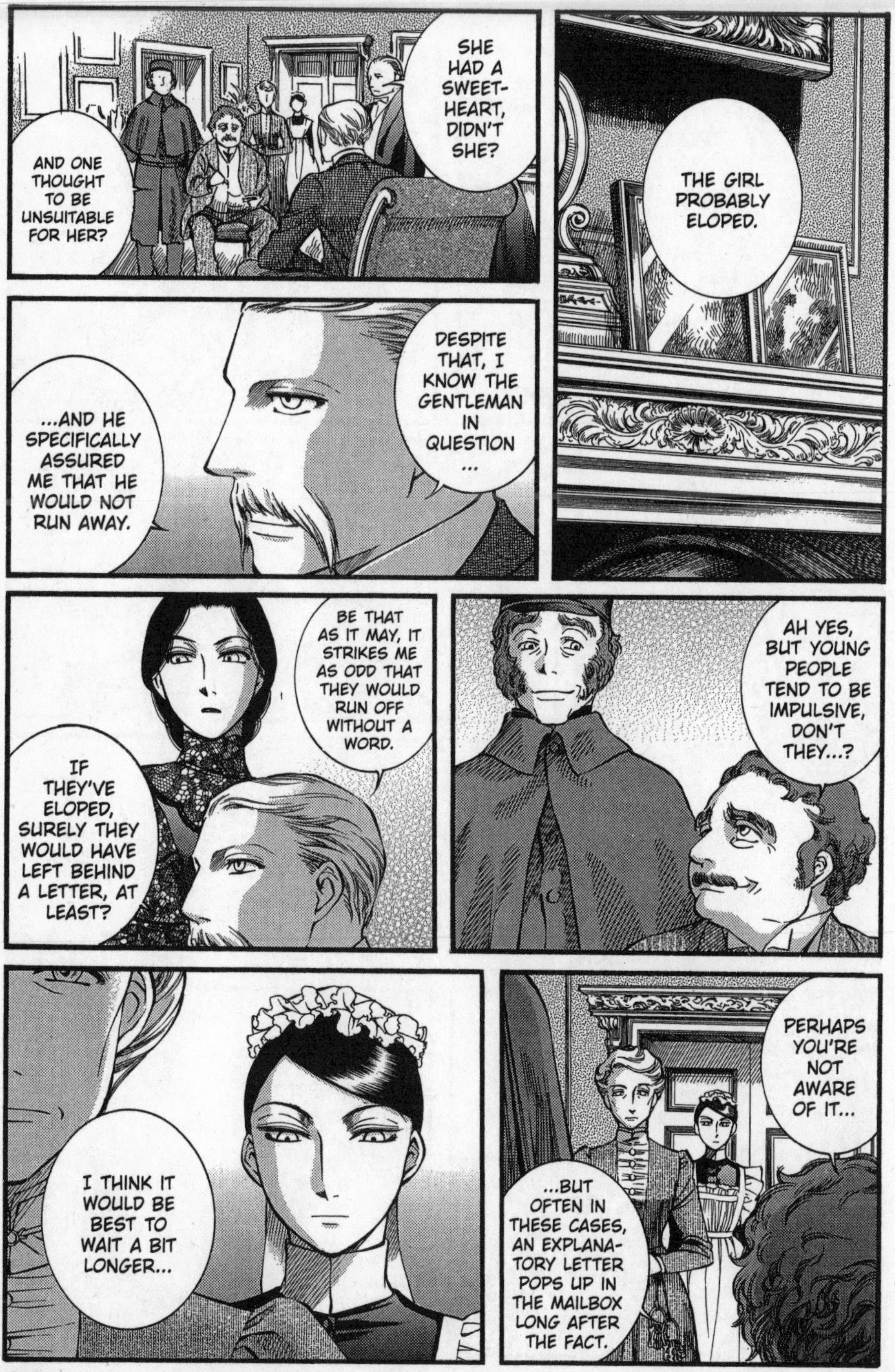
THE GIRL PROBABLY ELOPED.
SHE HAD A SWEET-HEART, DIDN'T SHE?
AND ONE THOUGHT TO BE UNSUITABLE FOR HER?
DESPITE THAT, I KNOW THE GENTLEMAN IN QUESTION ...
...AND HE SPECIFICALLY ASSURED ME THAT HE WOULD NOT RUN AWAY.
AH YES, BUT YOUNG PEOPLE TEND TO BE IMPULSIVE, DON'T THEY...?
BE THAT AS IT MAY, IT STRIKES ME AS ODD THAT THEY WOULD RUN OFF WITHOUT A WORD.
IF THEY'VE ELOPED, SURELY THEY WOULD HAVE LEFT BEHIND A LETTER, AT LEAST?
PERHAPS YOU'RE NOT AWARE OF IT...
...BUT OFTEN IN THESE CASES, AN EXPLANATORY LETTER POPS UP IN THE MAILBOX LONG AFTER THE FACT.
I THINK IT WOULD BE BEST TO WAIT A BIT LONGER...

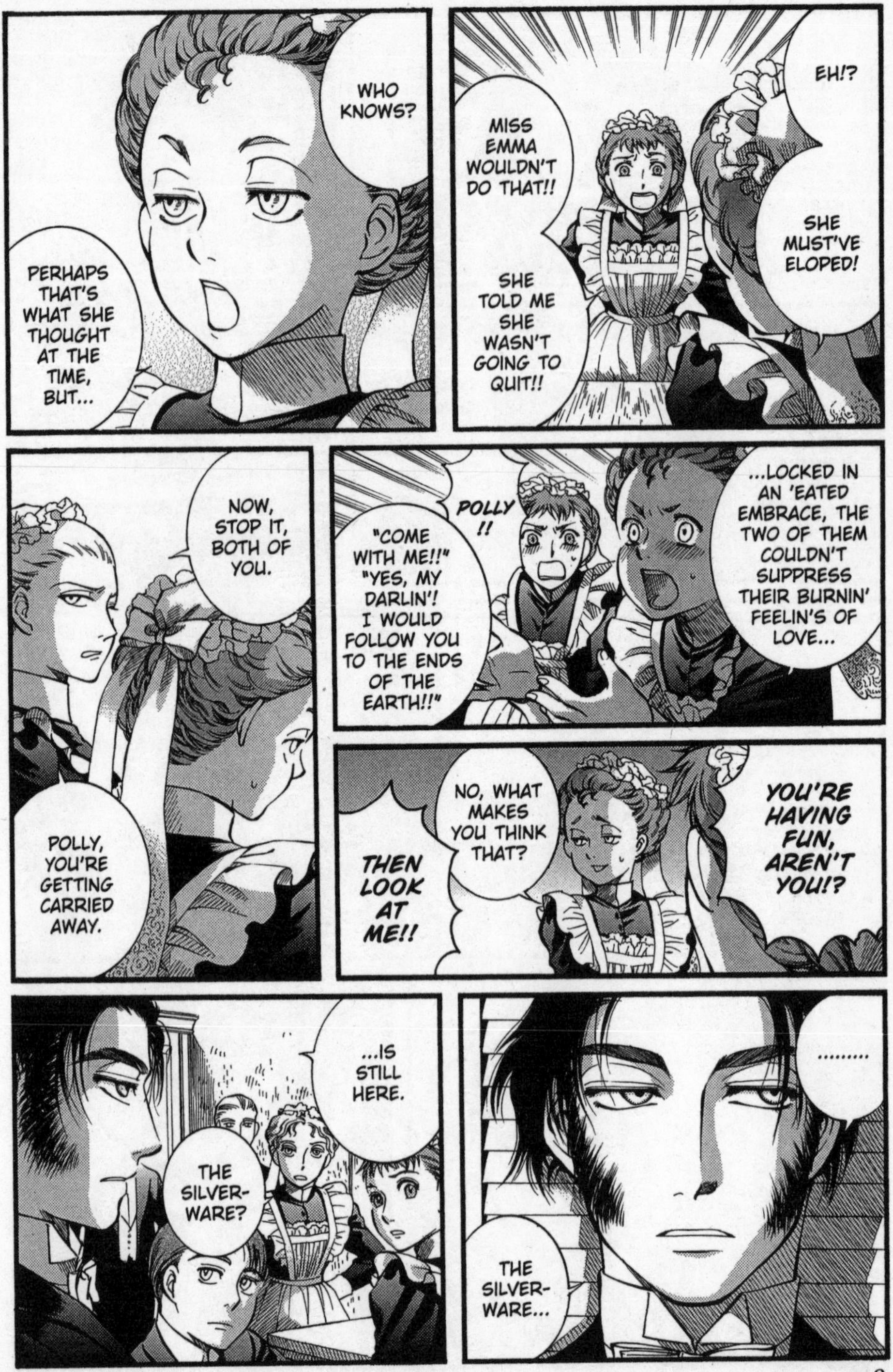
EH!?
SHE MUST'VE ELOPED!
MISS EMMA WOULDN'T DO THAT!!
SHE TOLD ME SHE WASN'T GOING TO QUIT!!
WHO KNOWS?
PERHAPS THAT'S WHAT SHE THOUGHT AT THE TIME, BUT...
...LOCKED IN AN 'EATED EMBRACE, THE TWO OF THEM COULDN'T SUPPRESS THEIR BURNIN' FEELIN'S OF LOVE...
POLLY!!
"COME WITH ME!!" "YES, MY DARLIN'! I WOULD FOLLOW YOU TO THE ENDS OF THE EARTH!!"
YOU'RE HAVING FUN, AREN'T YOU!?
NO, WHAT MAKES YOU THINK THAT?
THEN LOOK AT ME!!
NOW, STOP IT, BOTH OF YOU.
POLLY, YOU'RE GETTING CARRIED AWAY.
....
THE SILVER-WARE...
...IS STILL HERE.
THE SILVER-WARE?

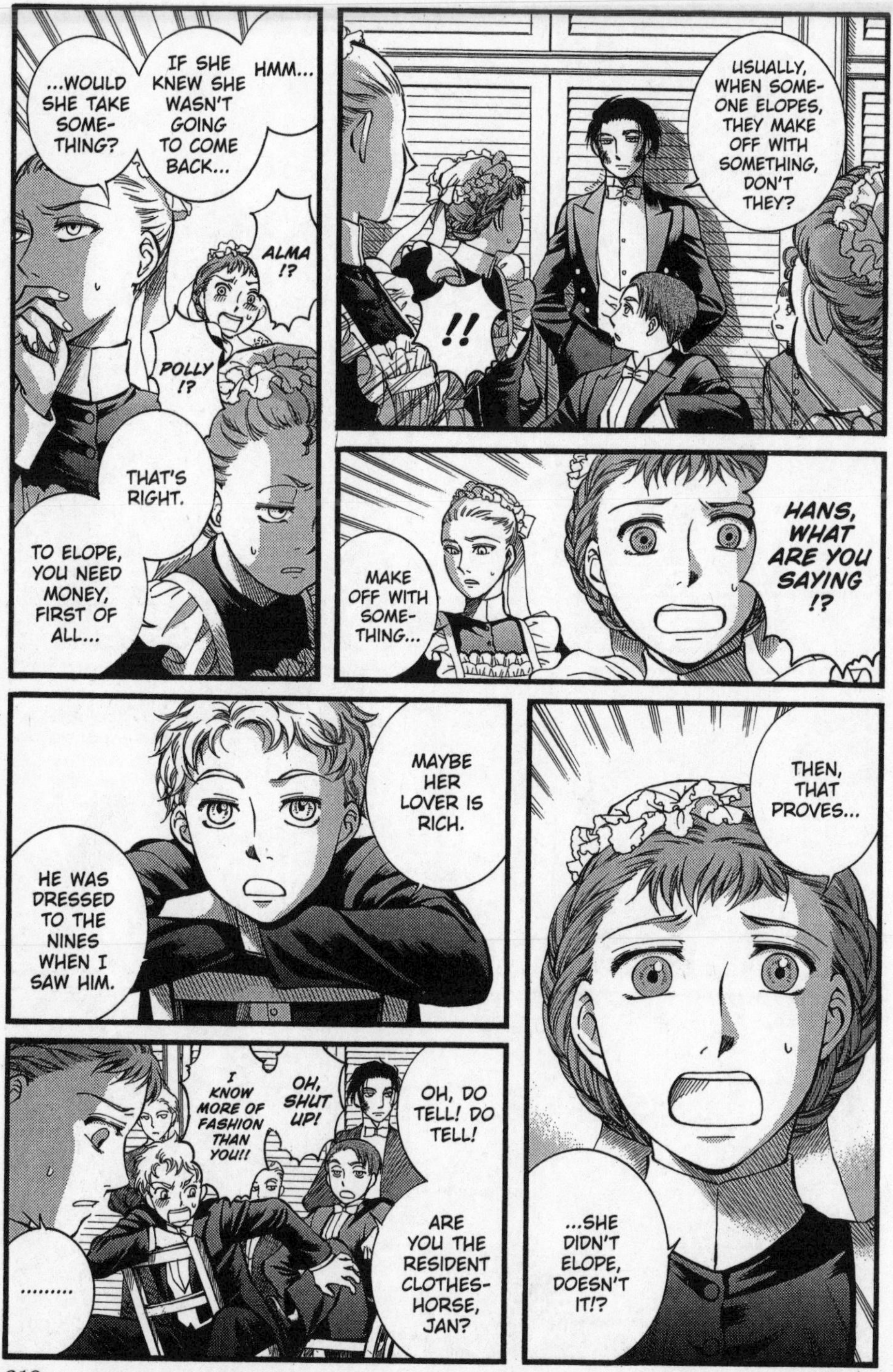
USUALLY, WHEN SOME-ONE ELOPES, THEY MAKE OFF WITH SOMETHING, DON'T THEY?
!!
HANS, WHAT ARE YOU SAYING !?
MAKE OFF WITH SOME-THING...
HMM...
IF SHE KNEW SHE WASN'T GOING TO COME BACK...
...WOULD SHE TAKE SOME-THING?
ALMA !?
POLLY !?
THAT'S RIGHT.
TO ELOPE, YOU NEED MONEY, FIRST OF ALL...
THEN, THAT PROVES...
...SHE DIDN'T ELOPE, DOESN'T IT!?
MAYBE HER LOVER IS RICH.
HE WAS DRESSED TO THE NINES WHEN I SAW HIM.
OH, DO TELL! DO TELL!
ARE YOU THE RESIDENT CLOTHES-HORSE, JAN?
OH, SHUT UP!
I KNOW MORE OF FASHION THAN YOU!!
....

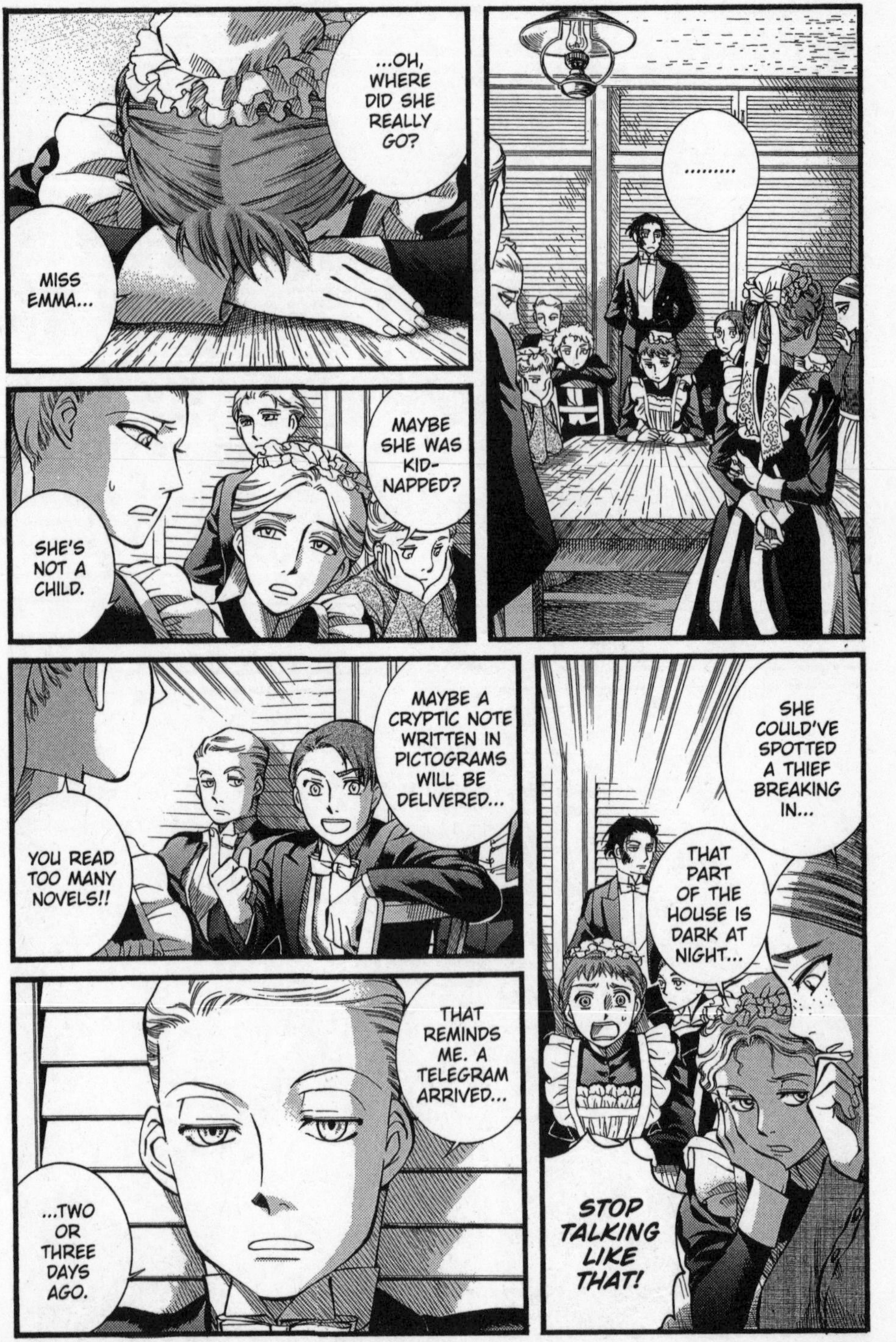
....
...OH, WHERE DID SHE REALLY GO?
MISS EMMA...
MAYBE SHE WAS KID-NAPPED?
SHE'S NOT A CHILD.
SHE COULD'VE SPOTTED A THIEF BREAKING IN...
THAT PART OF THE HOUSE IS DARK AT NIGHT...
STOP TALKING LIKE THAT!
MAYBE A CRYPTIC NOTE WRITTEN IN PICTOGRAMS WILL BE DELIVERED...
YOU READ TOO MANY NOVELS!!
THAT REMINDS ME. A TELEGRAM ARRIVED...
...TWO OR THREE DAYS AGO.

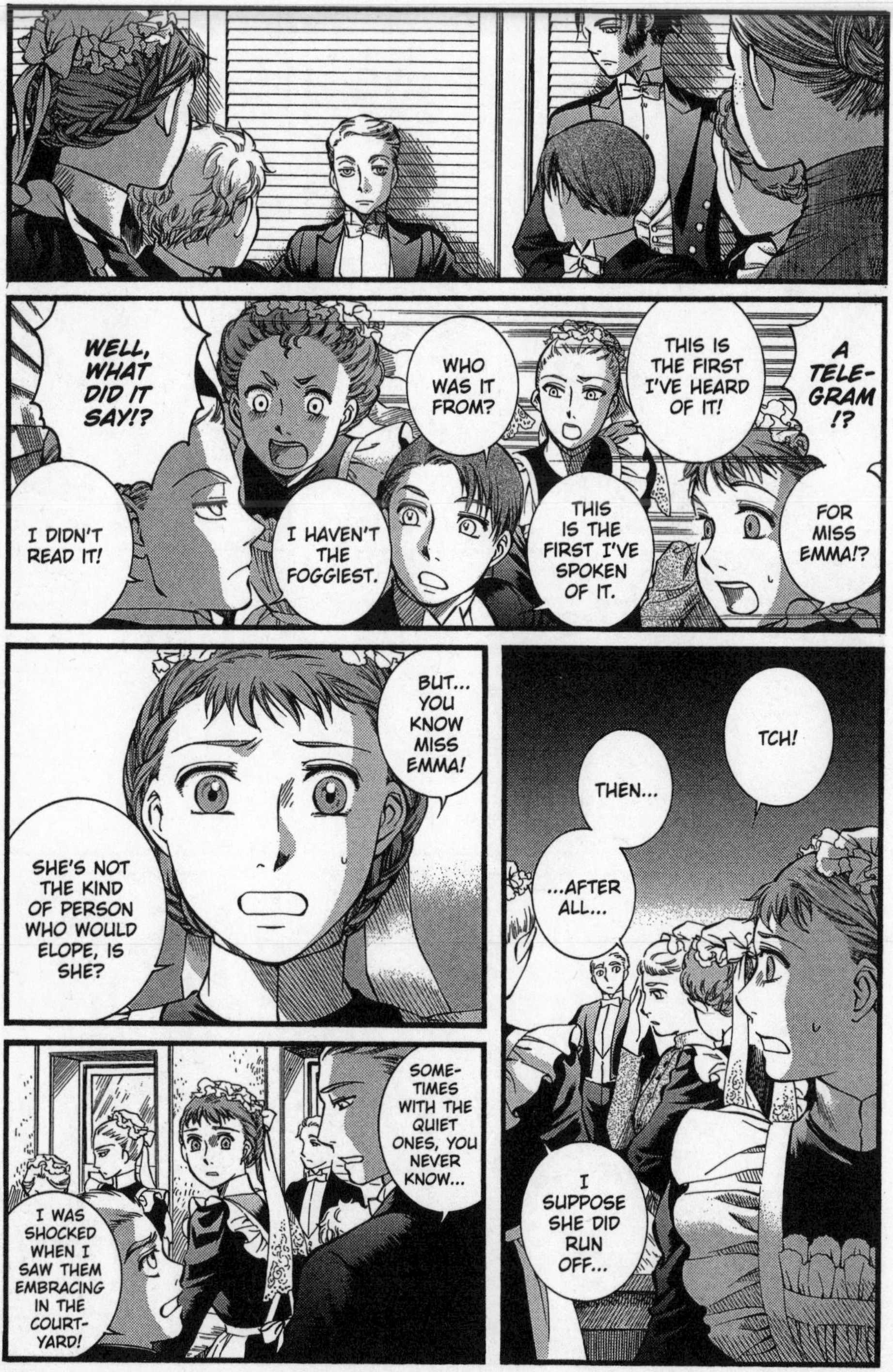
A TELEGRAM!?
FOR MISS EMMA!?
THIS IS THE FIRST I'VE HEARD OF IT!
THIS IS THE FIRST I'VE SPOKEN OF IT.
WHO WAS IT FROM?
I HAVEN'T THE FOGGIEST.
WELL, WHAT DID IT SAY!?
I DIDN'T READ IT!
TCH!
THEN...
...AFTER ALL...
I SUPPOSE SHE DID RUN OFF...
BUT... YOU KNOW MISS EMMA!
SHE'S NOT THE KIND OF PERSON WHO WOULD ELOPE, IS SHE?
SOME-TIMES WITH THE QUIET ONES, YOU NEVER KNOW...
I WAS SHOCKED WHEN I SAW THEM EMBRACING IN THE COURT-YARD!

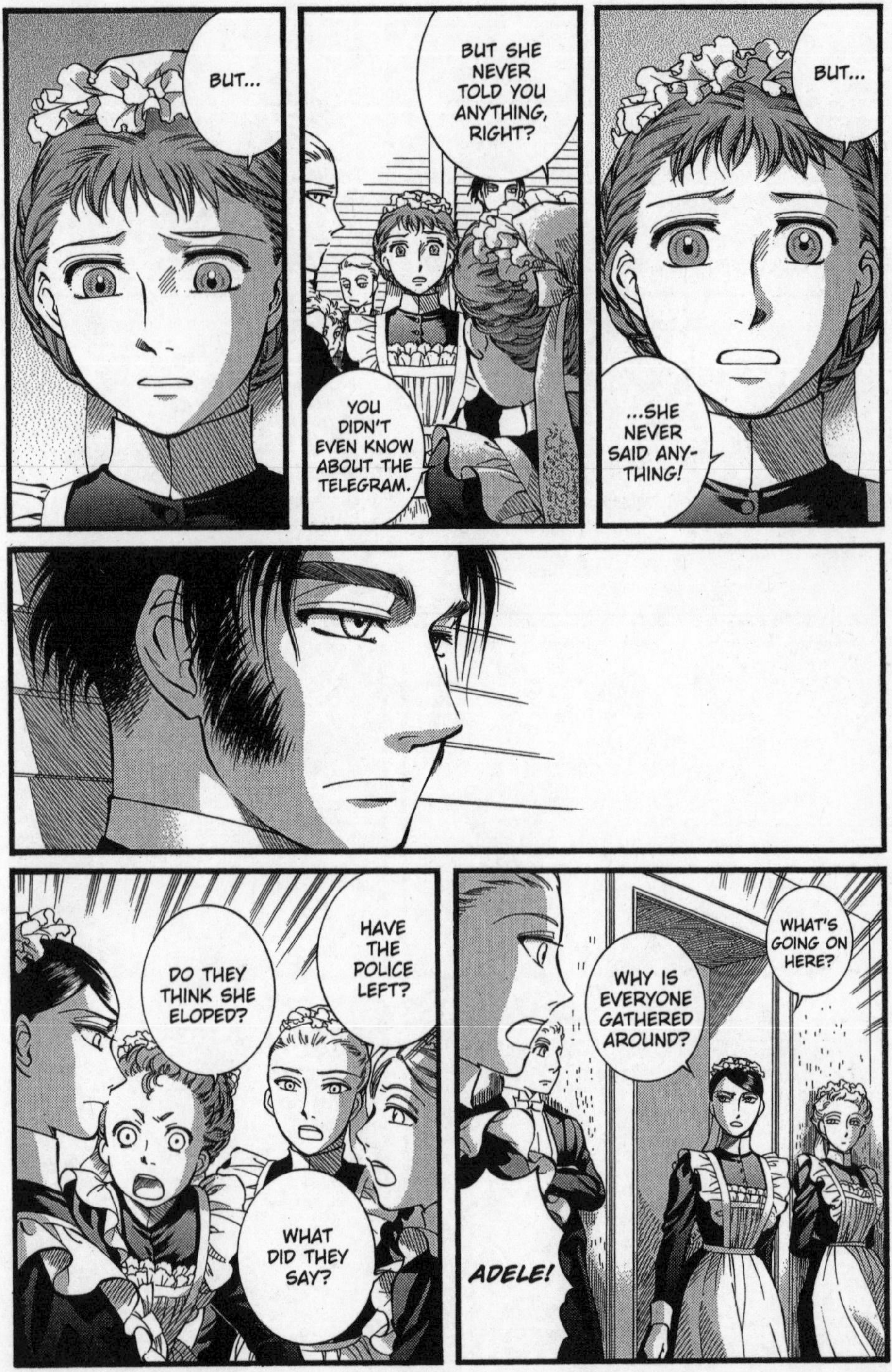
BUT...
...SHE NEVER SAID ANYTHING!
BUT SHE NEVER TOLD YOU ANYTHING, RIGHT?
YOU DIDN'T EVEN KNOW ABOUT THE TELEGRAM.
BUT...
WHAT'S GOING ON HERE?
WHY IS EVERYONE GATHERED AROUND?
ADELE!
HAVE THE POLICE LEFT?
DO THEY THINK SHE ELOPED?
WHAT DID THEY SAY?

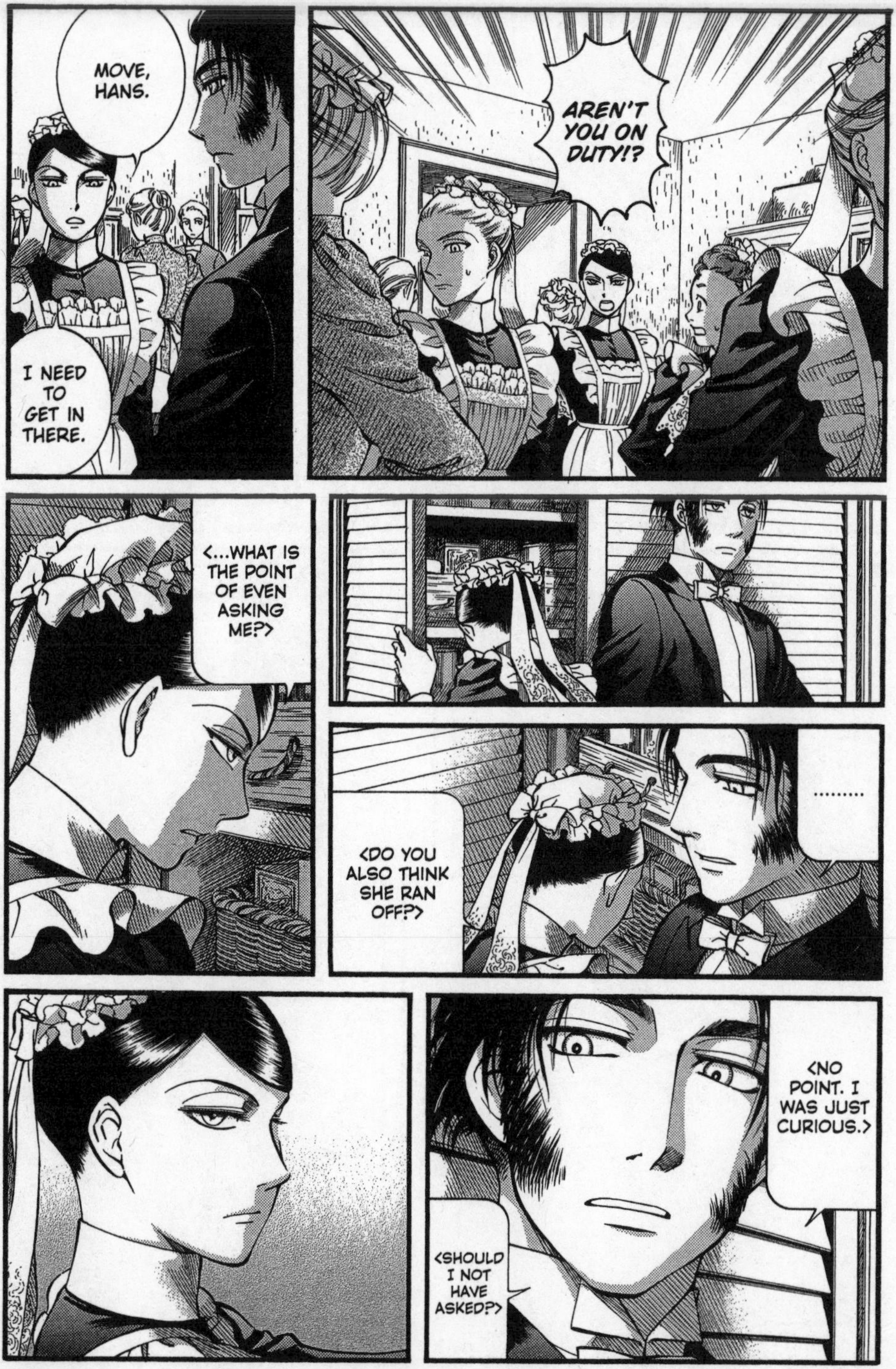
AREN'T YOU ON DUTY!?
MOVE, HANS.
I NEED TO GET IN THERE.
....
<DO YOU ALSO THINK SHE RAN OFF?>
<...WHAT IS THE POINT OF EVEN ASKING ME?>
<NO POINT. I WAS JUST CURIOUS.>
<SHOULD I NOT HAVE ASKED?>

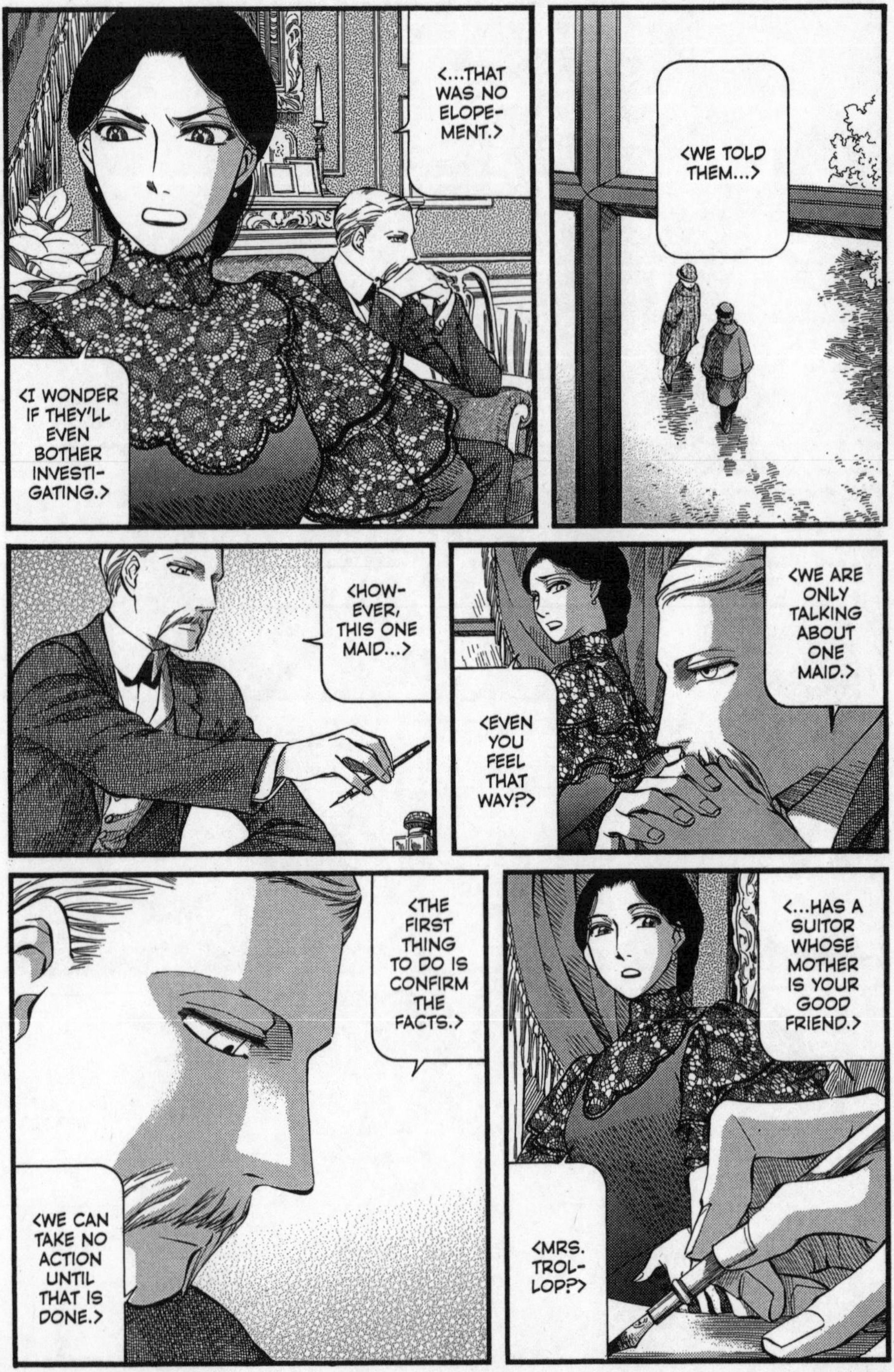
<WE TOLD THEM...>
<...THAT WAS NO ELOPEMENT.>
<I WONDER IF THEY'LL EVEN BOTHER INVESTIGATING.>
<WE ARE ONLY TALKING ABOUT ONE MAID.>
<EVEN YOU FEEL THAT WAY?>
<HOWEVER, THIS ONE MAID...>
<...HAS A SUITOR WHOSE MOTHER IS YOUR GOOD FRIEND.>
<MRS. TROLLOP?>
<THE FIRST THING TO DO IS CONFIRM THE FACTS.>
<WE CAN TAKE NO ACTION UNTIL THAT IS DONE.>

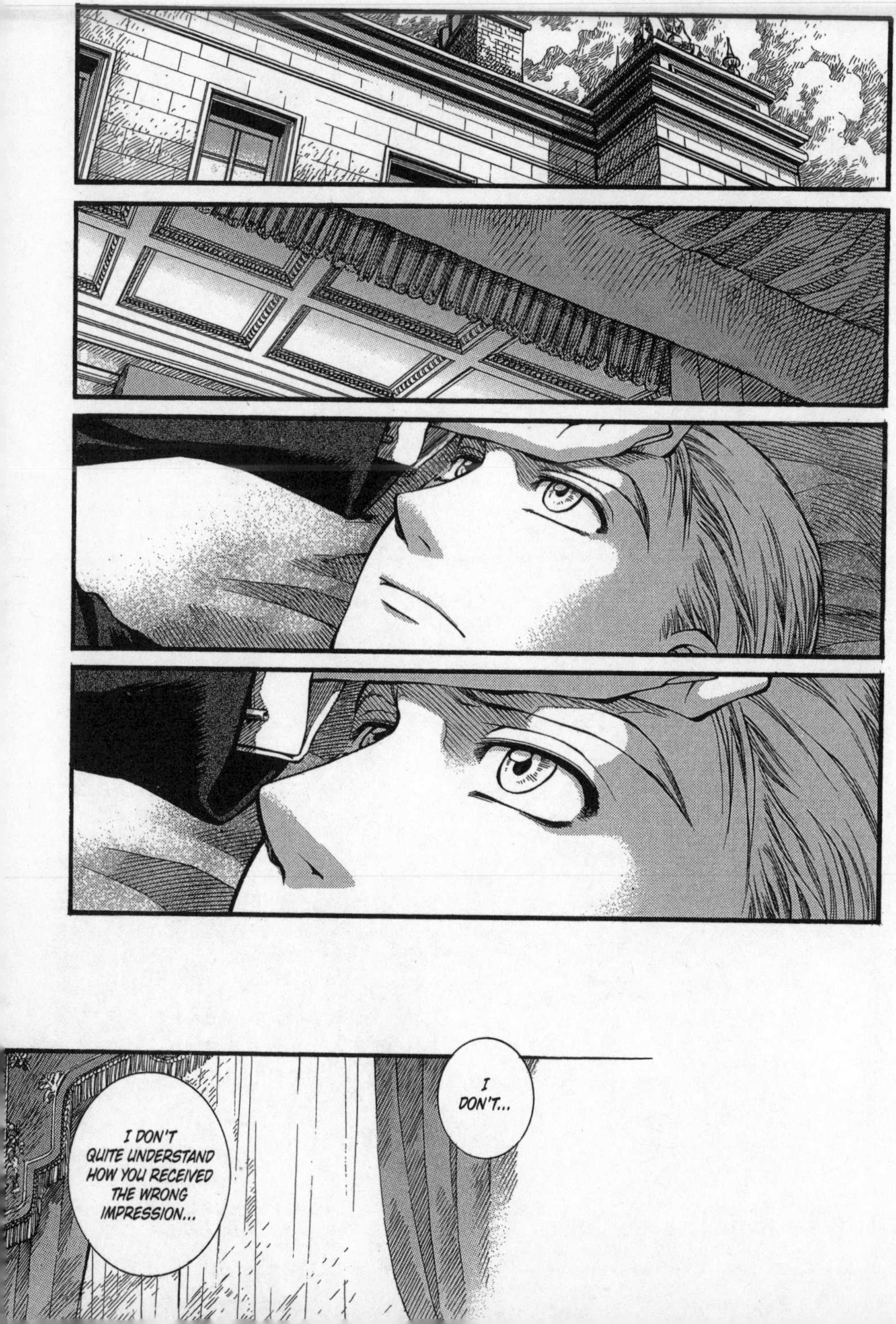
I DON'T...
I DON'T QUITE UNDERSTAND HOW YOU RECEIVED THE WRONG IMPRESSION...

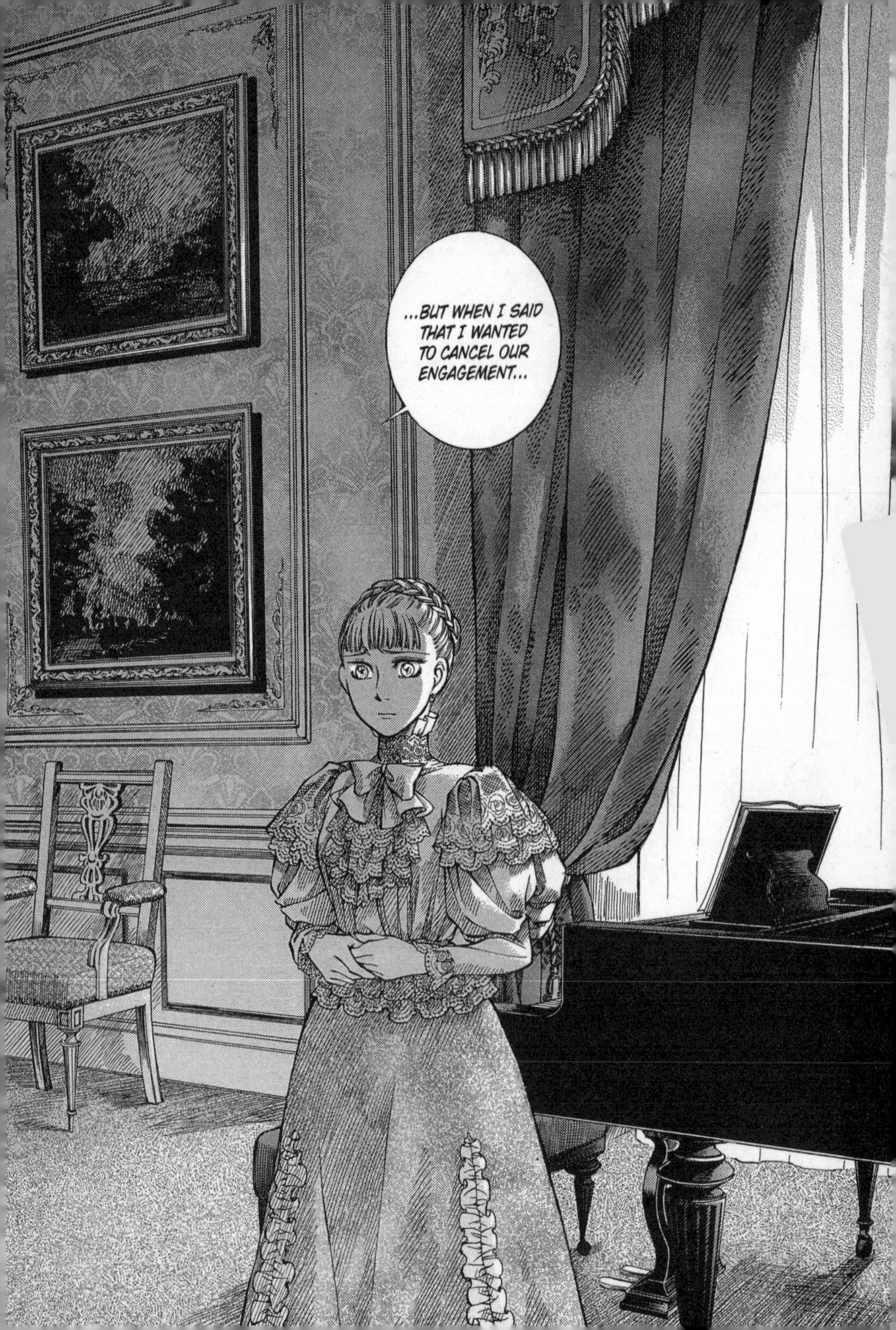
...BUT WHEN I SAID THAT I WANTED TO CANCEL OUR ENGAGEMENT...

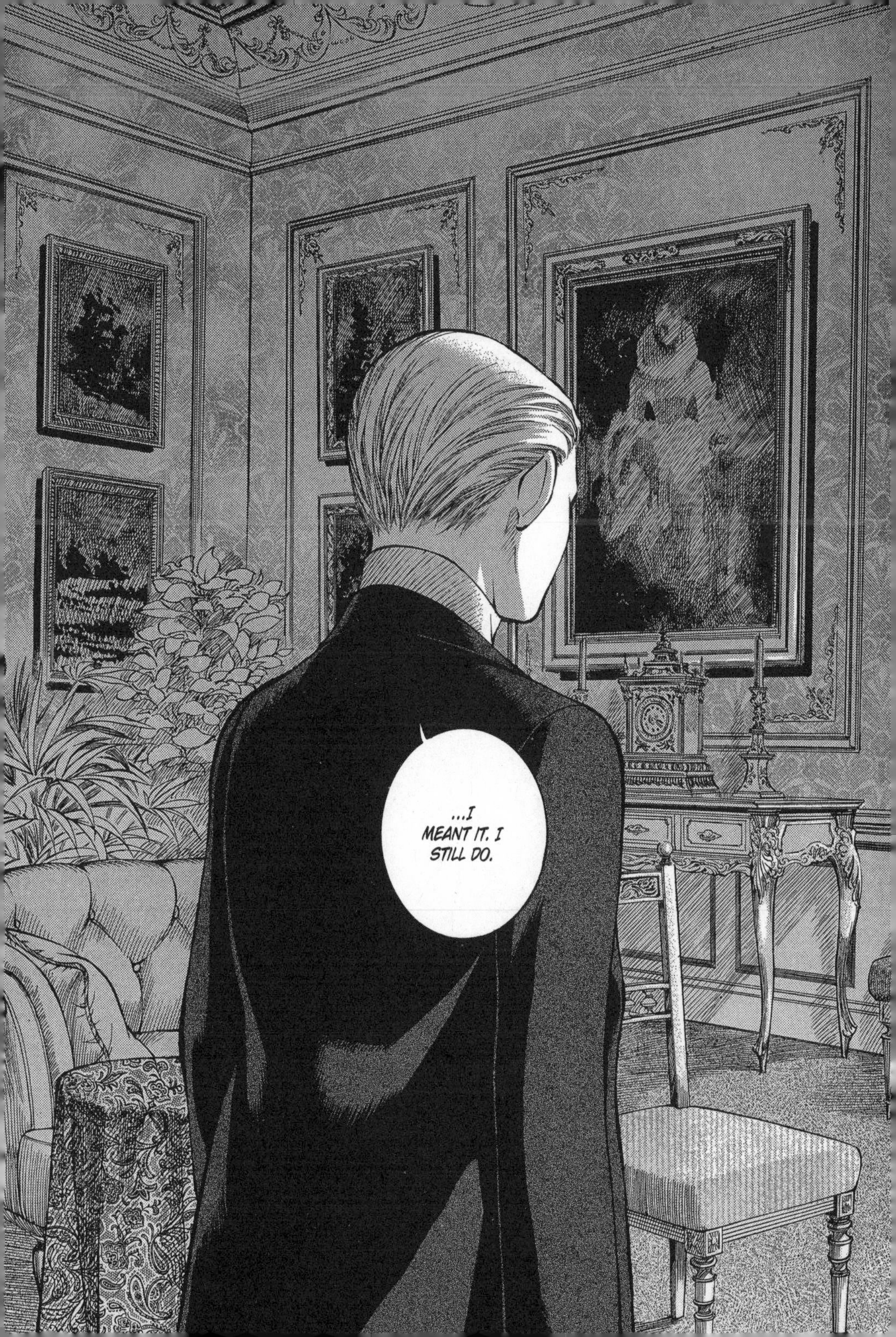
...I MEANT IT. I STILL DO.

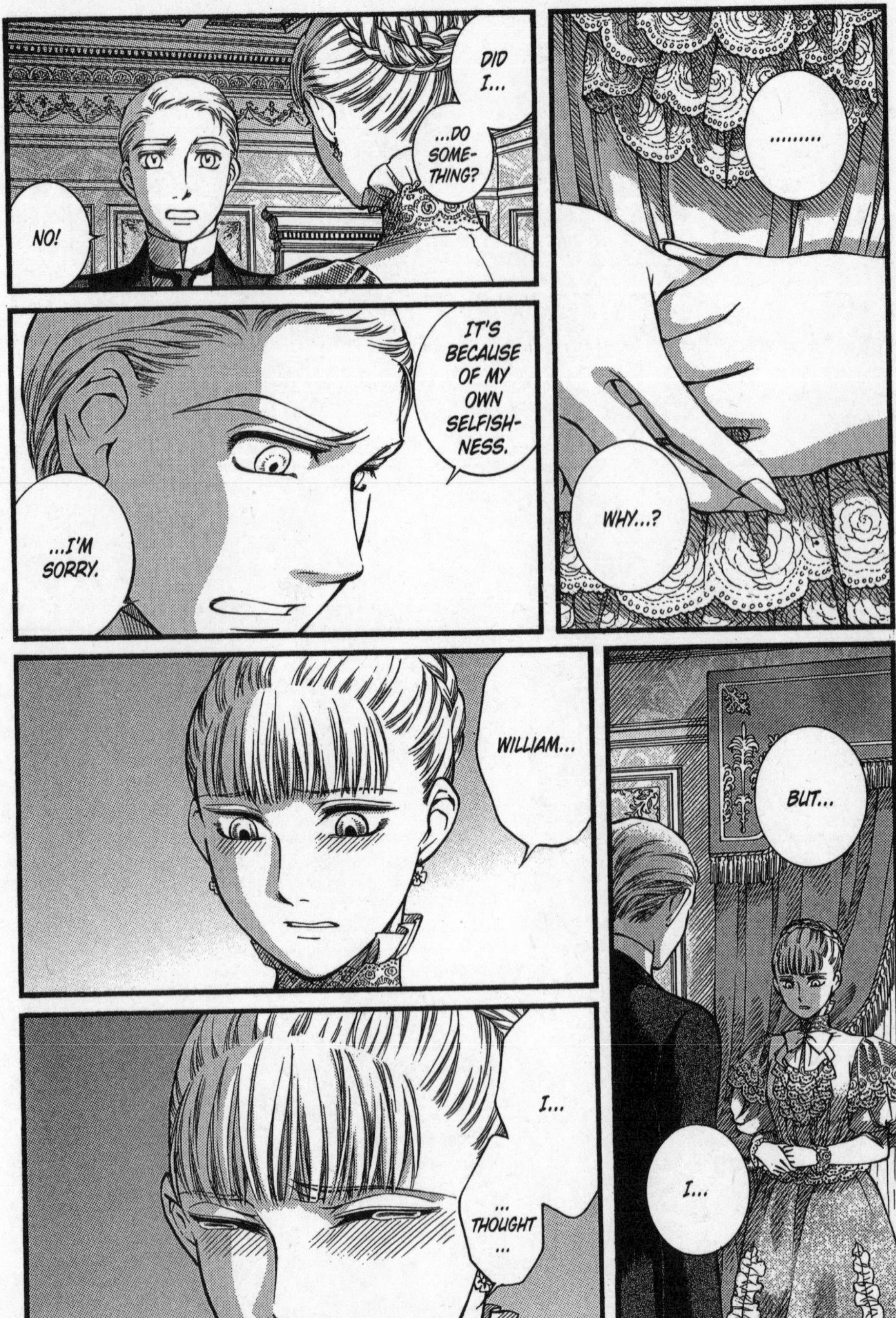
....
WHY...?
DID I...
...DO SOMETHING?
NO!
IT'S BECAUSE OF MY OWN SELFISHNESS.
...I'M SORRY.
BUT...
I...
WILLIAM...
I...
...THOUGHT...

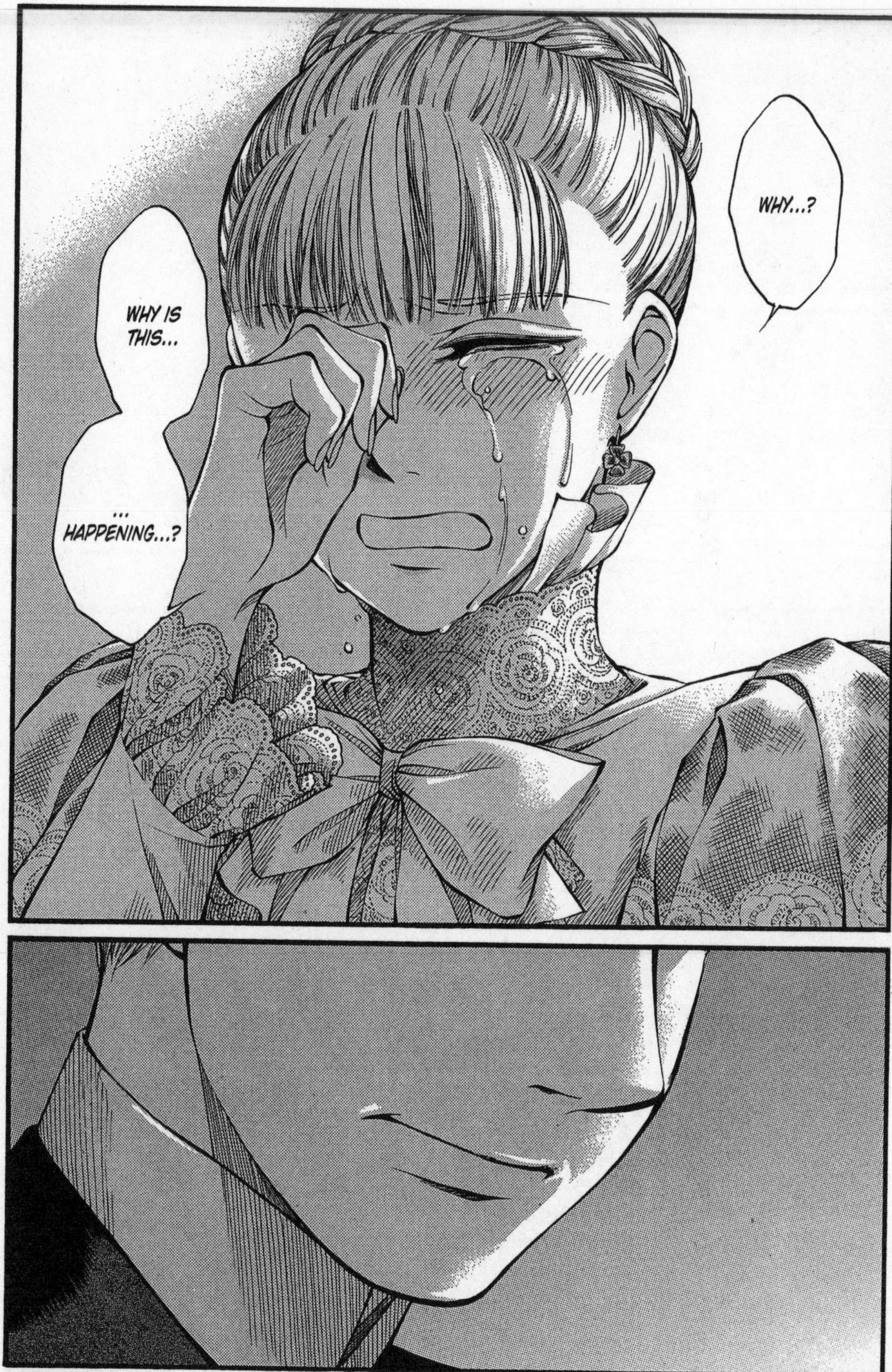
WHY...?
WHY IS THIS...
... HAPPENING...?

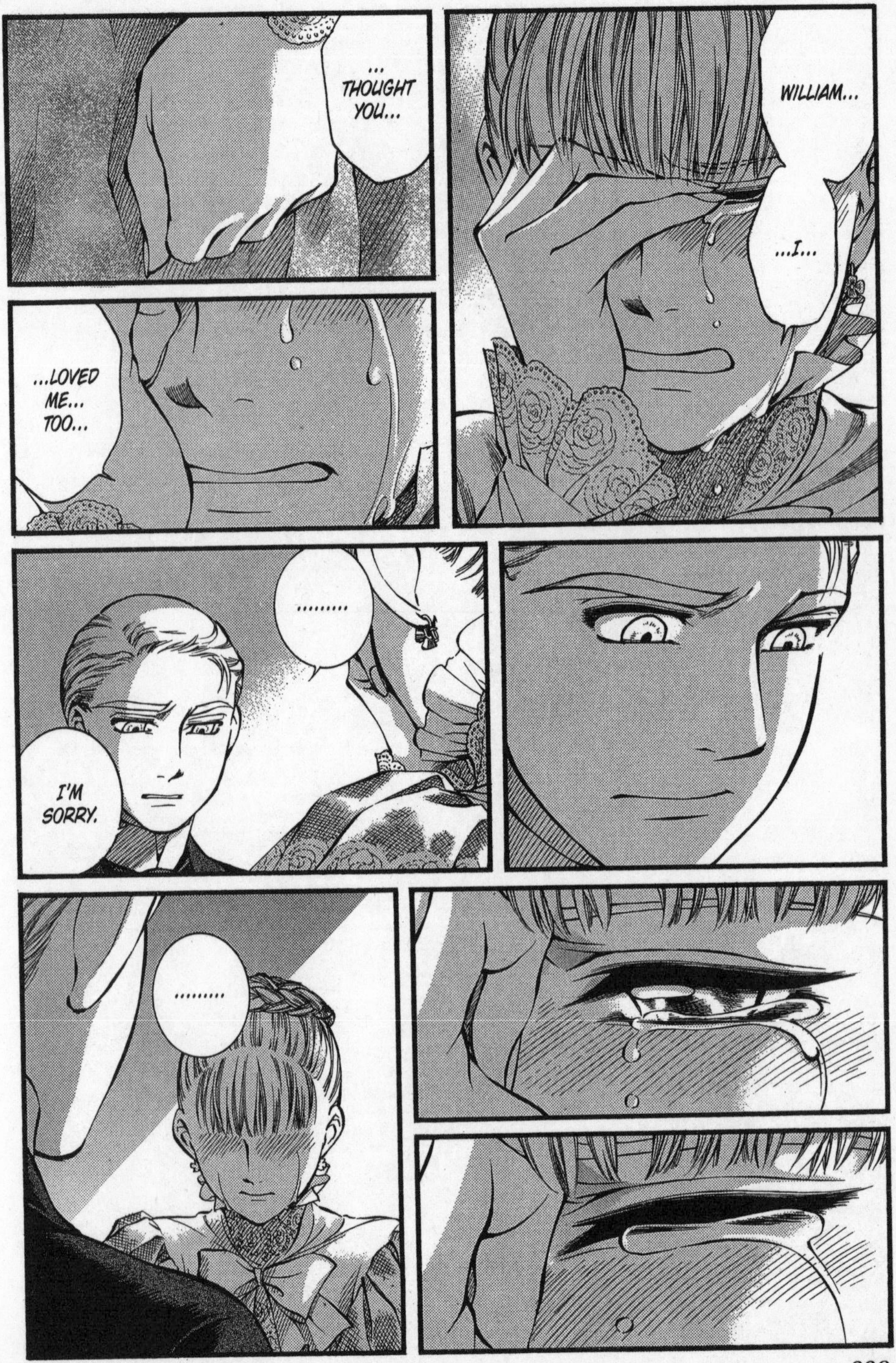
WILLIAM...
...I...
...THOUGHT YOU...
...LOVED ME... TOO...
....
I'M SORRY.
....

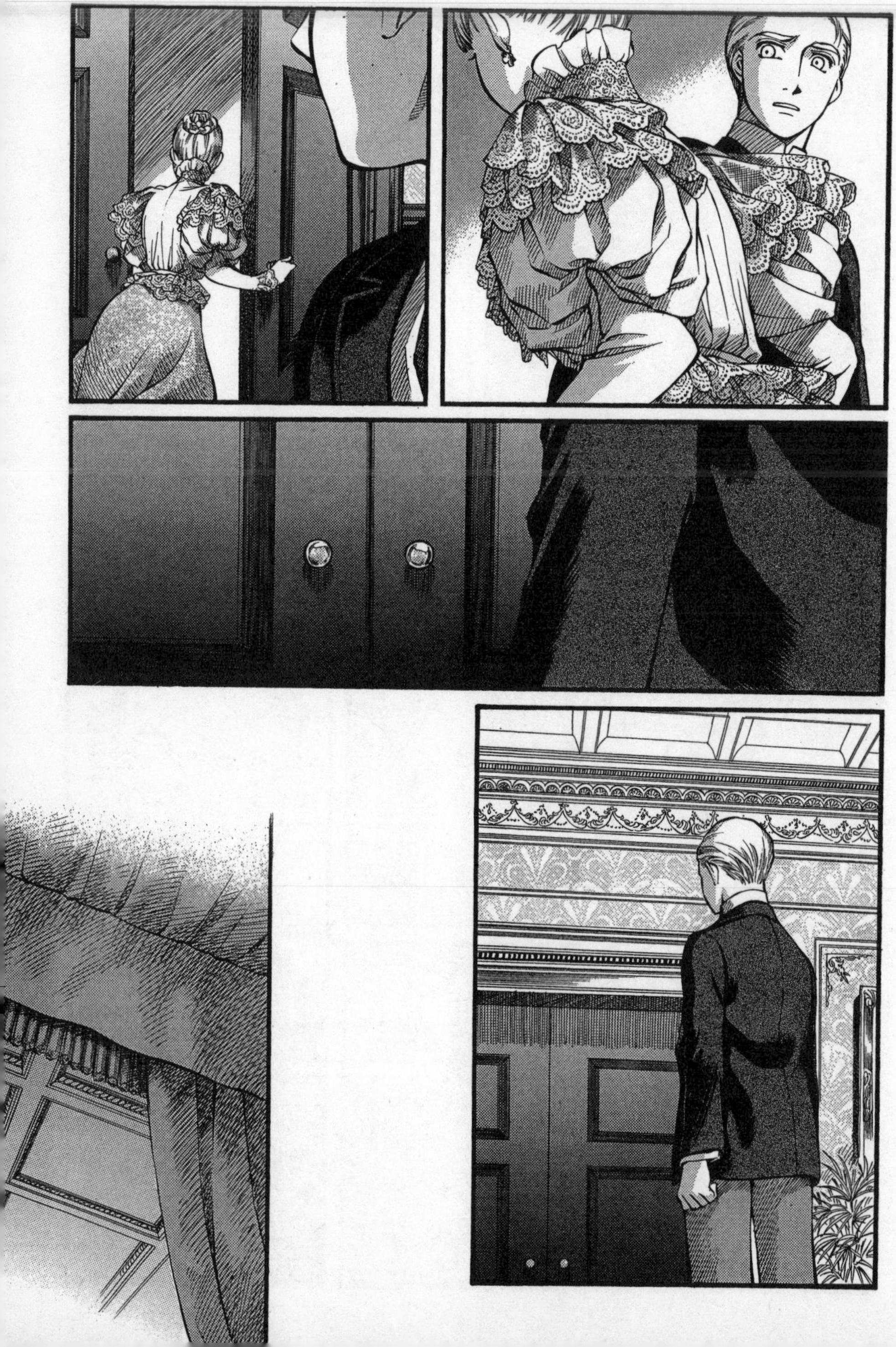

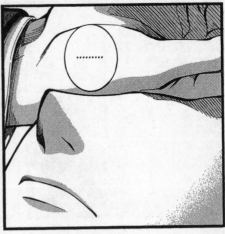

....

WILLIAM?

EH?

WHERE'S ELEANOR?

SHE LEFT A LITTLE WHILE AGO.

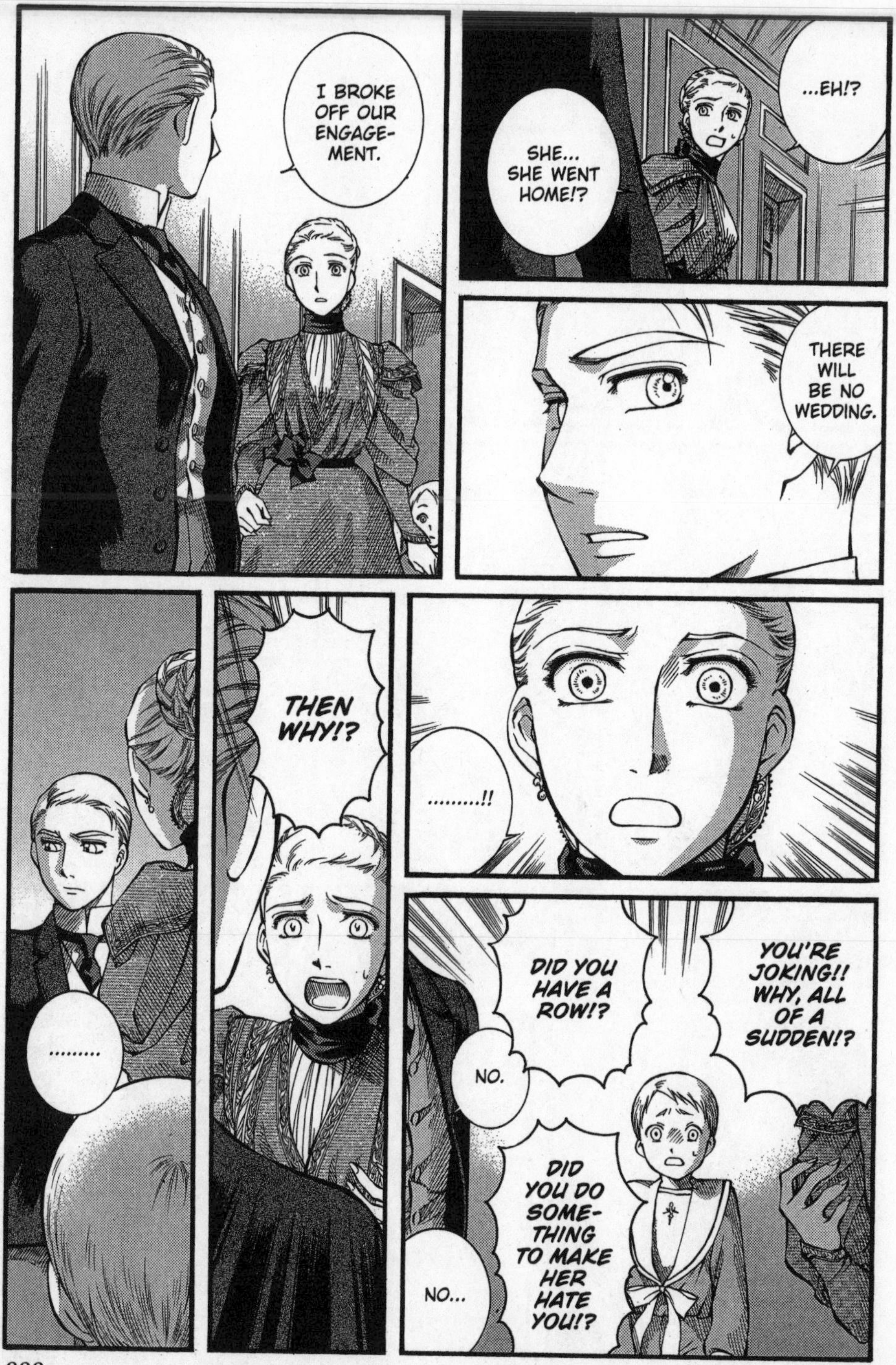

...EH!?
SHE... SHE WENT HOME!?
THERE WILL BE NO WEDDING.
I BROKE OFF OUR ENGAGE-MENT.
.........!!
YOU'RE JOKING!! WHY, ALL OF A SUDDEN!?
DID YOU HAVE A ROW!?
NO.
DID YOU DO SOME-THING TO MAKE HER HATE YOU!?
NO...
THEN WHY!?
....

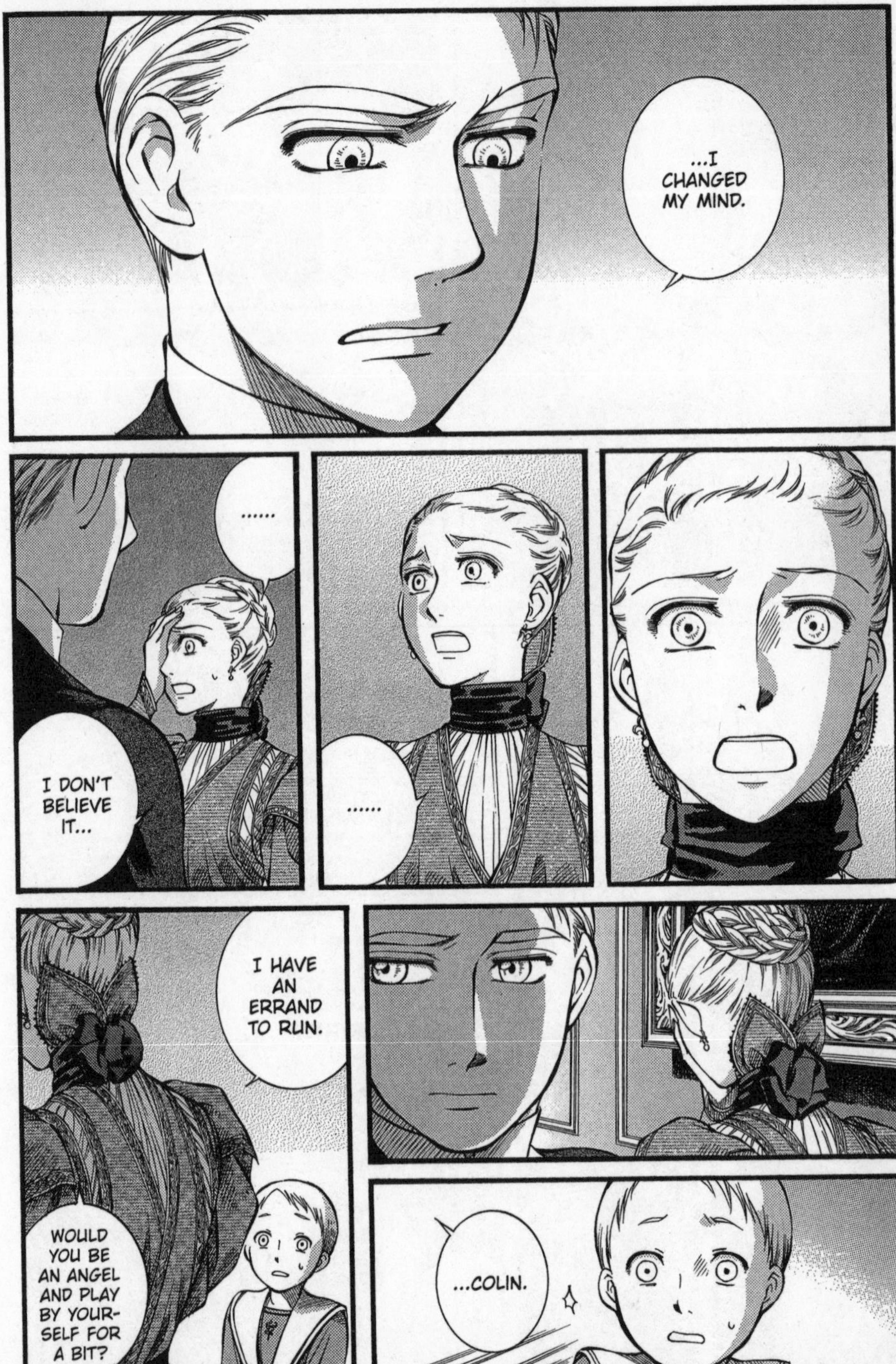
...I CHANGED MY MIND.
......
......
I DON'T BELIEVE IT...
...COLIN.
I HAVE AN ERRAND TO RUN.
WOULD YOU BE AN ANGEL AND PLAY BY YOUR-SELF FOR A BIT?

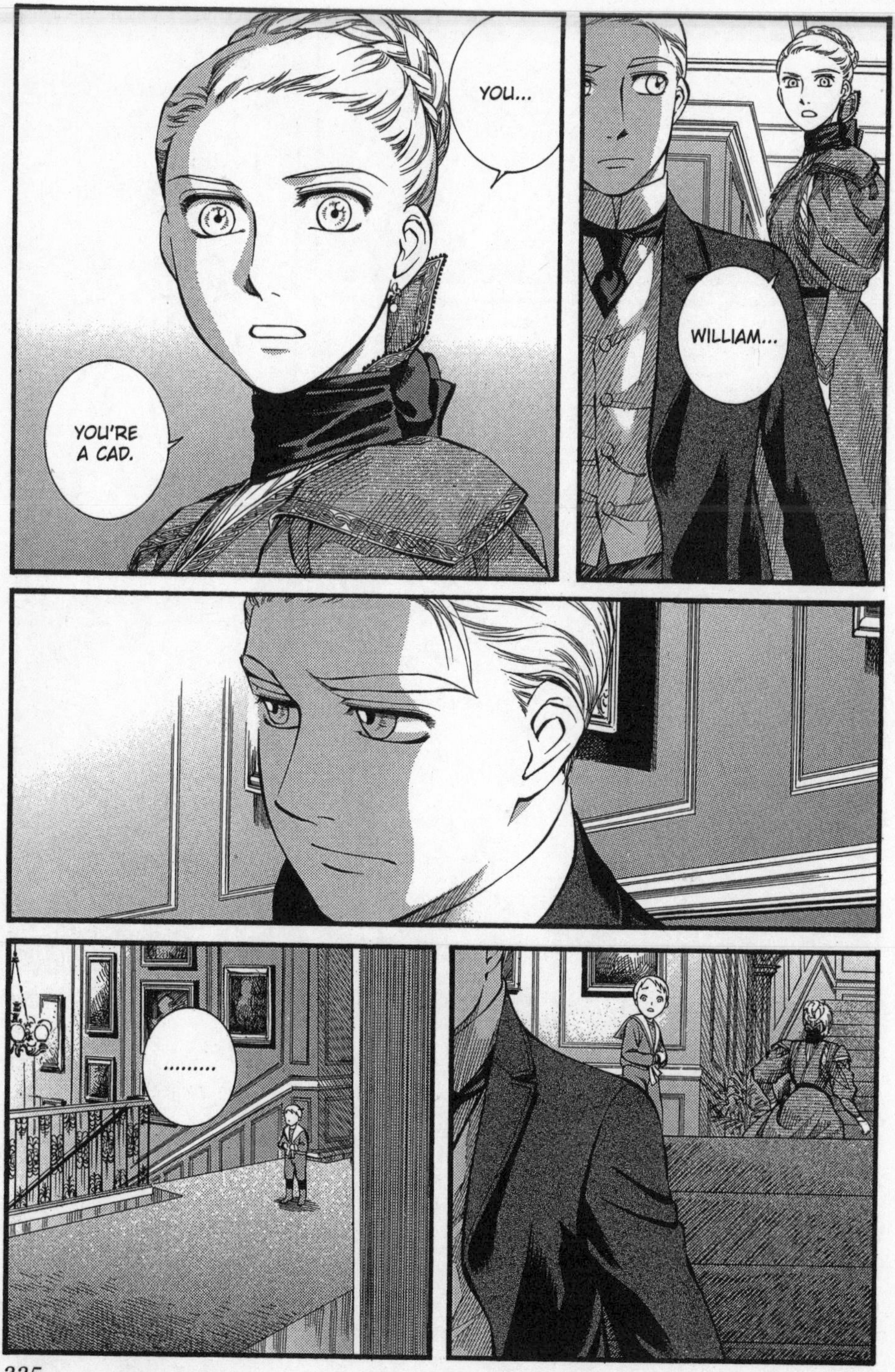
WILLIAM...
YOU...
YOU'RE A CAD.
....

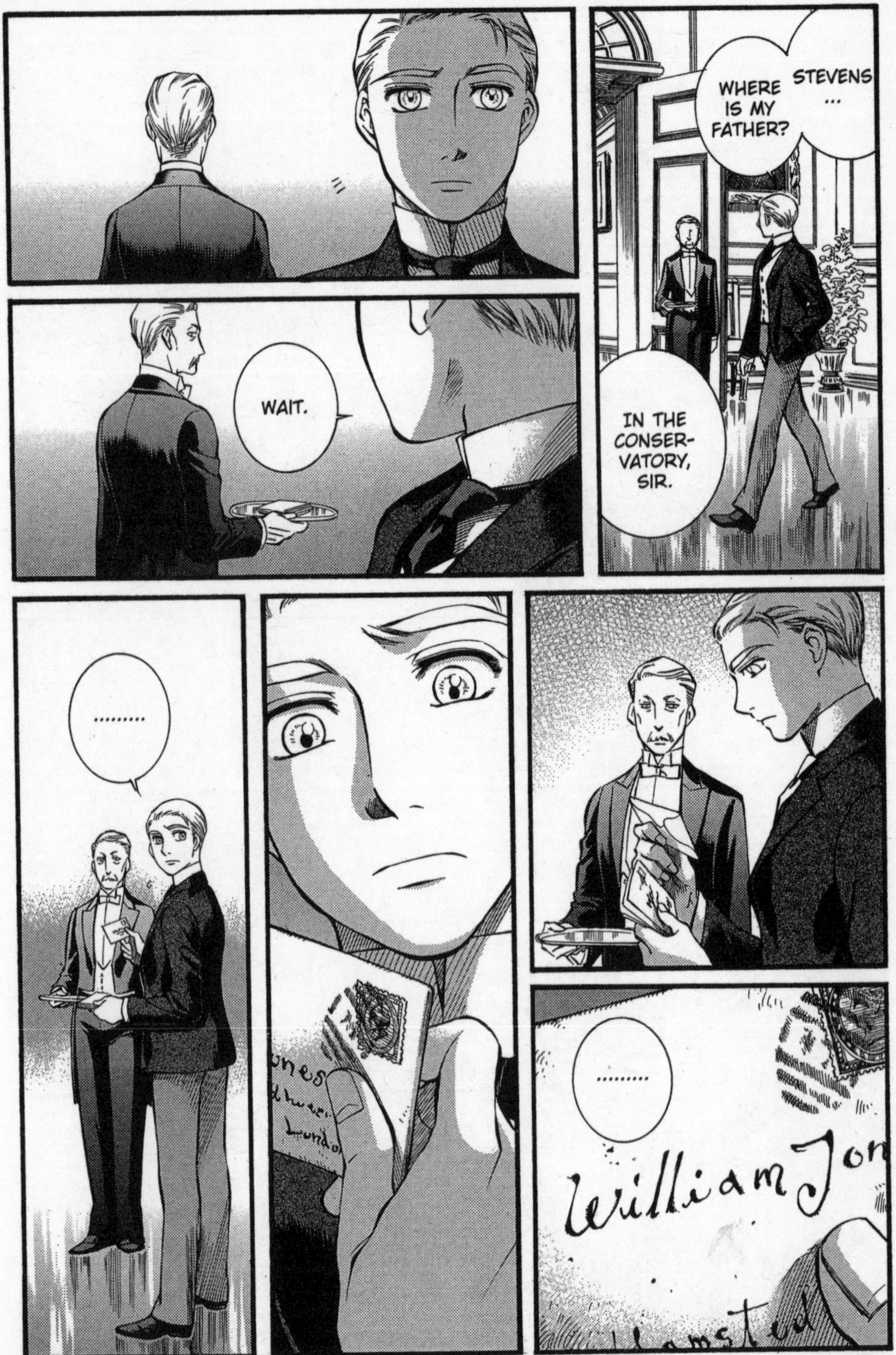
STEVENS ...
WHERE IS MY FATHER?
IN THE CONSERVATORY, SIR.
WAIT.
....
....
....

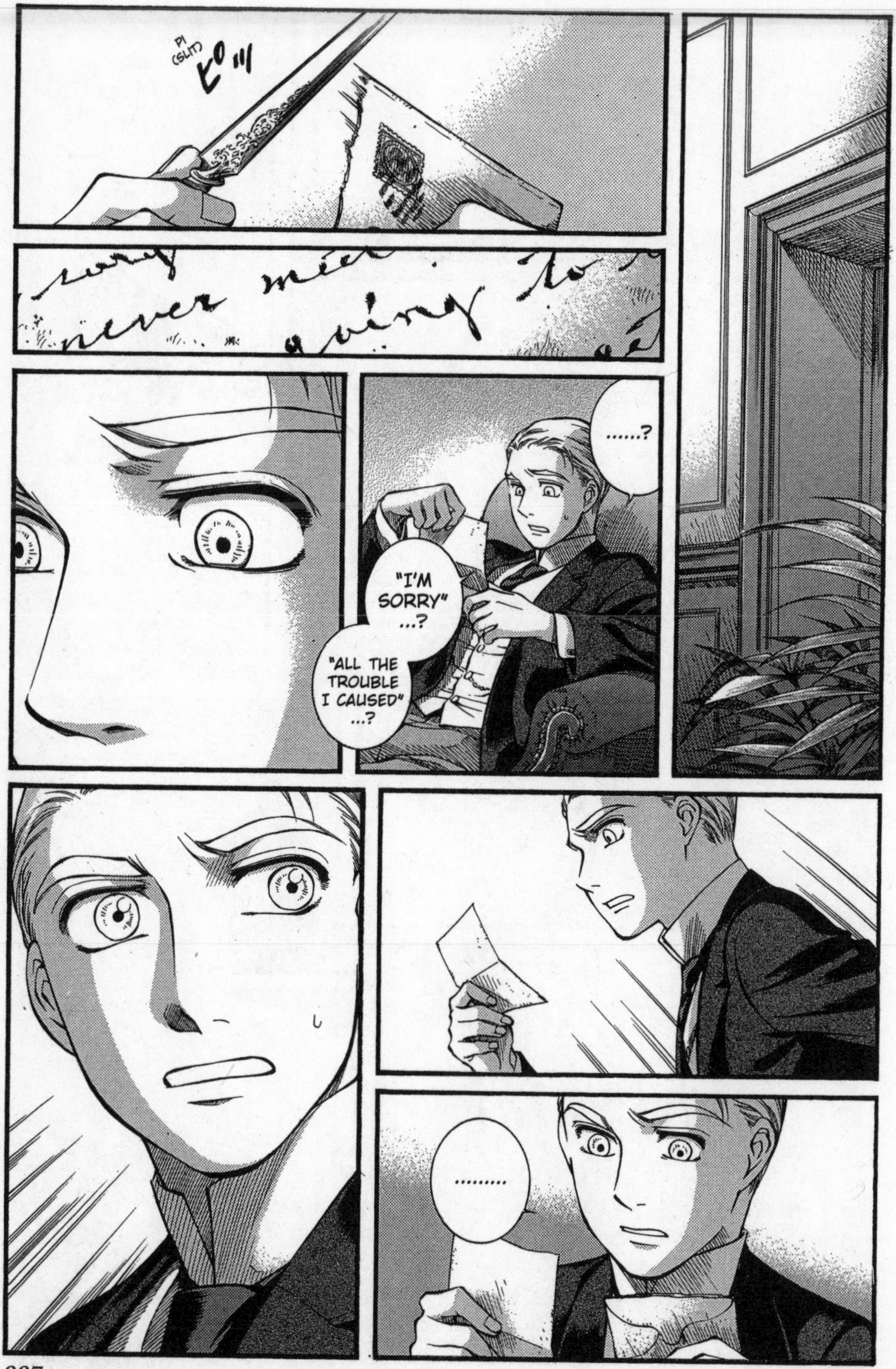
PI (SLIT) ピッ
......?
"I'M SORRY" ...?
"ALL THE TROUBLE I CAUSED" ...?
....

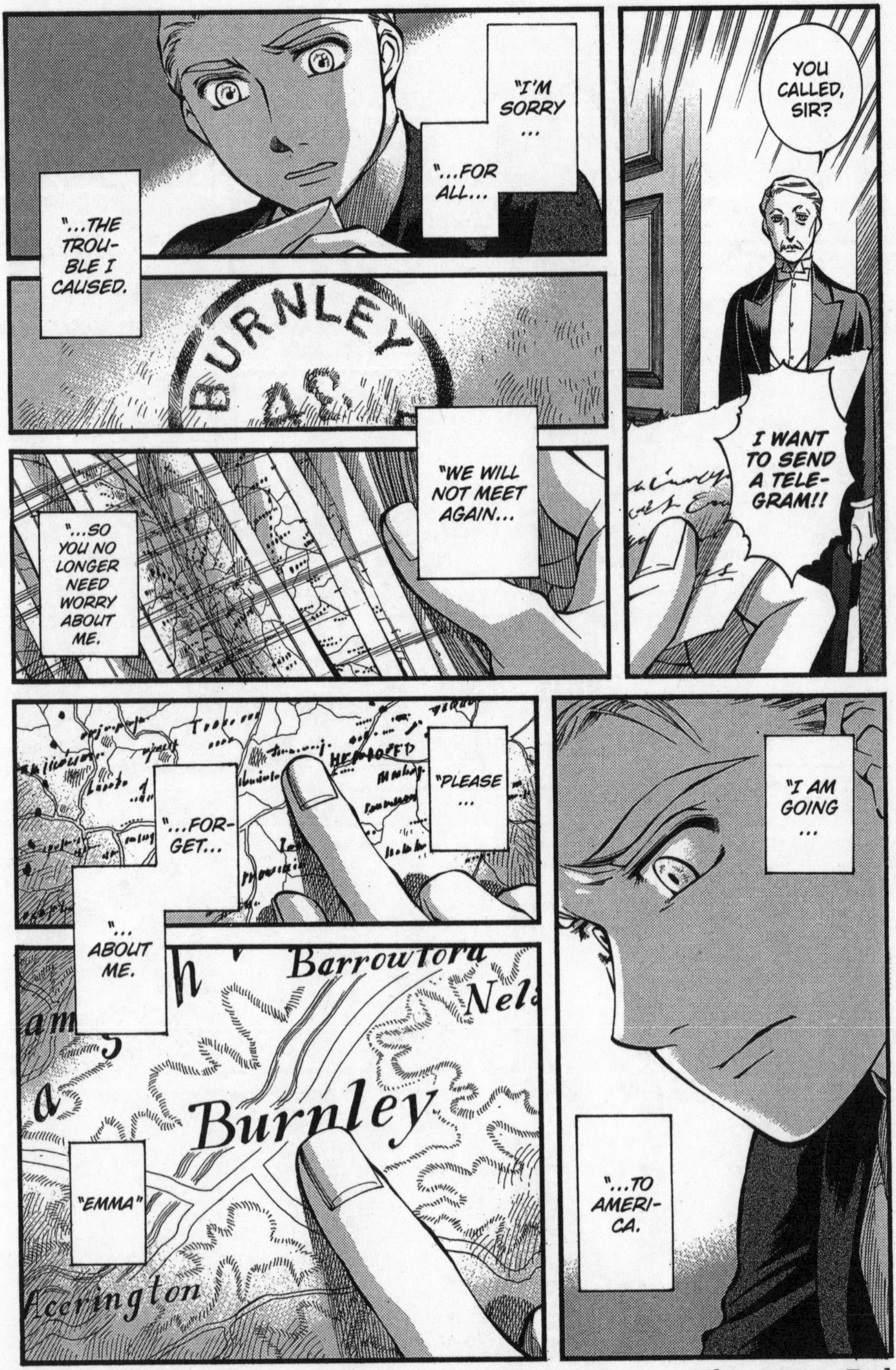
YOU CALLED, SIR?
I WANT TO SEND A TELE-GRAM!!
"I'M SORRY ...
"...FOR ALL...
"...THE TROU-BLE I CAUSED.
BURNLEY
"WE WILL NOT MEET AGAIN...
"...SO YOU NO LONGER NEED WORRY ABOUT ME.
"I AM GOING ...
"...TO AMERI-CA.
"PLEASE ...
"...FOR-GET...
"... ABOUT ME.
Barrowford
Burnley
Accrington
"EMMA"

Chapter 42: End

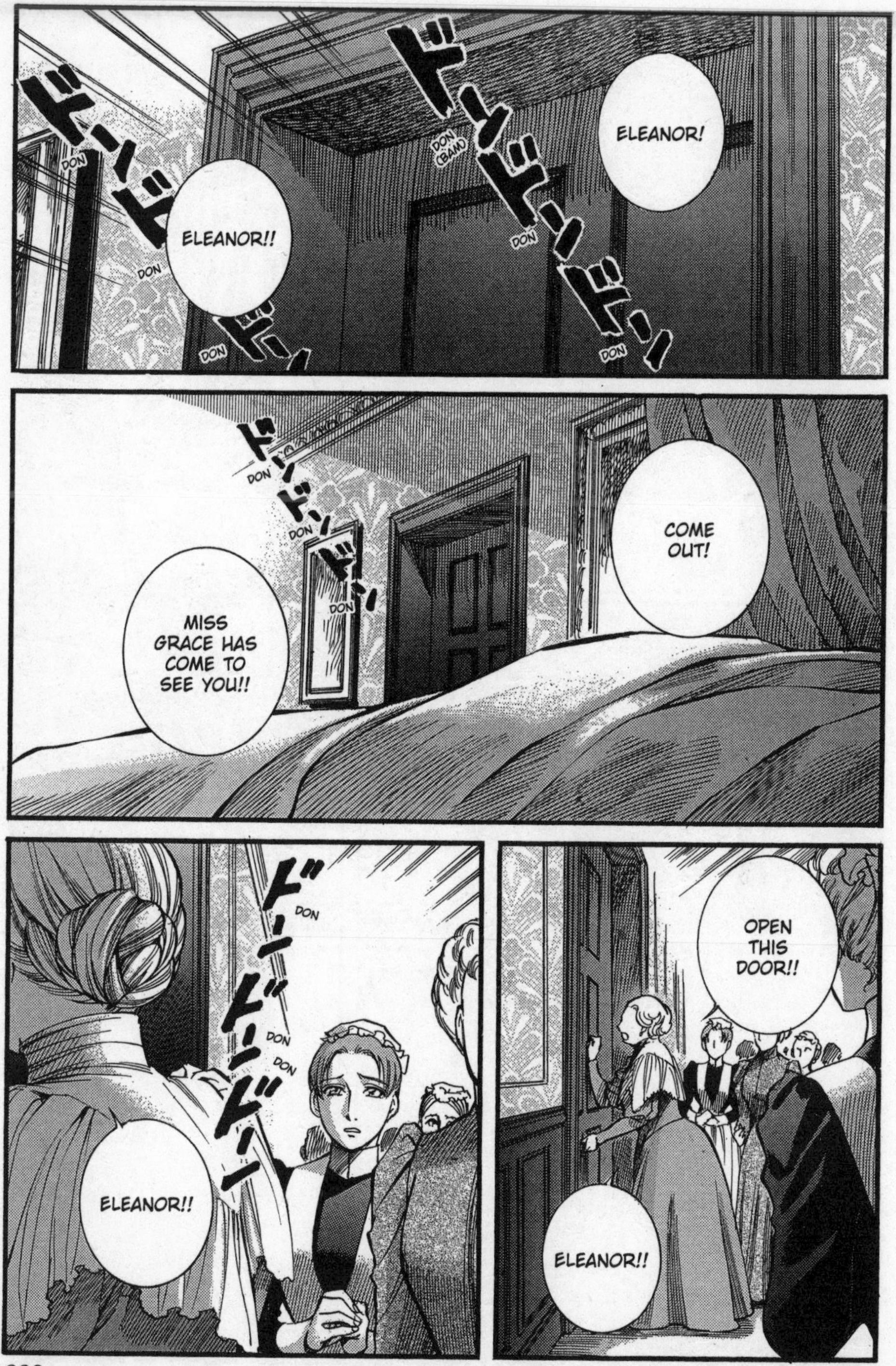
ELEANOR!
DON (BAM)
DON
DON
ELEANOR!!
DON
DON
DON
COME OUT!
DON
DON
DON
MISS GRACE HAS COME TO SEE YOU!!
OPEN THIS DOOR!!
ELEANOR!!
DON
DON
DON
ELEANOR!!

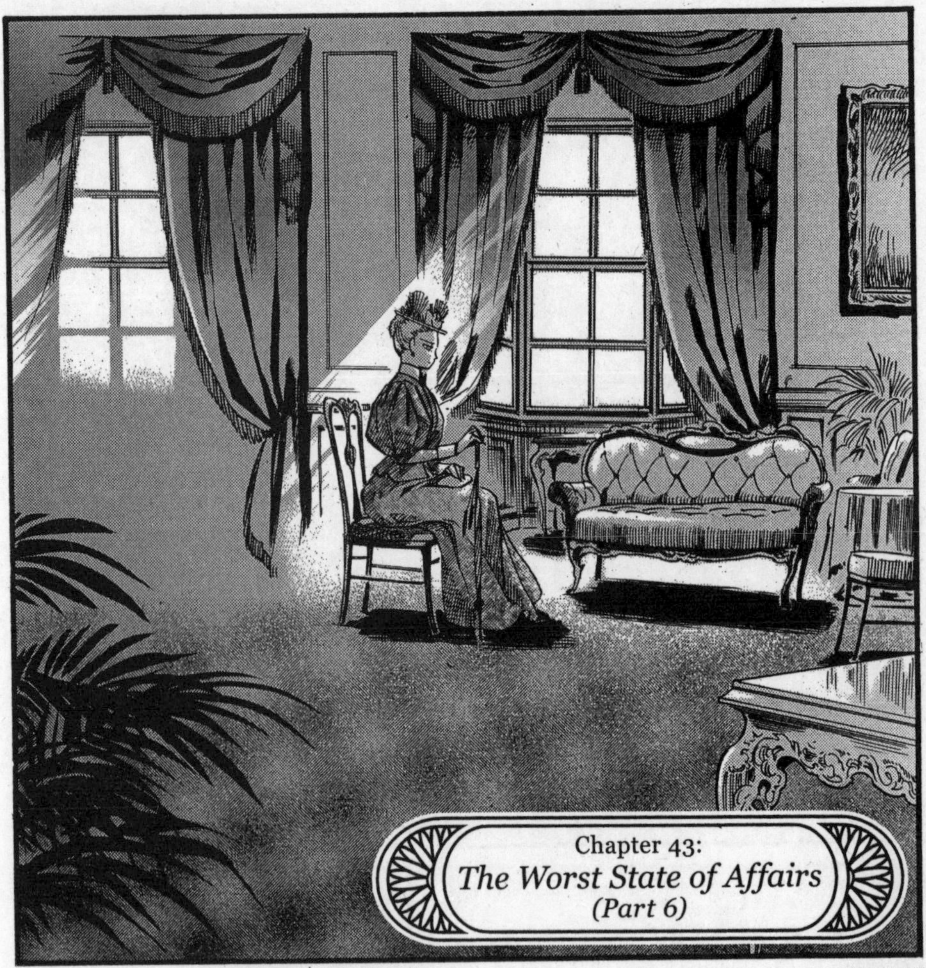
Chapter 43:
The Worst State of Affairs
(Part 6)
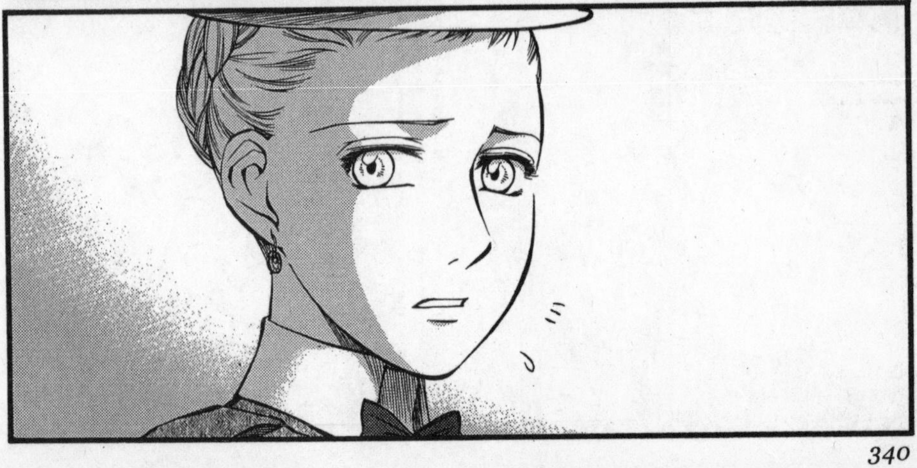

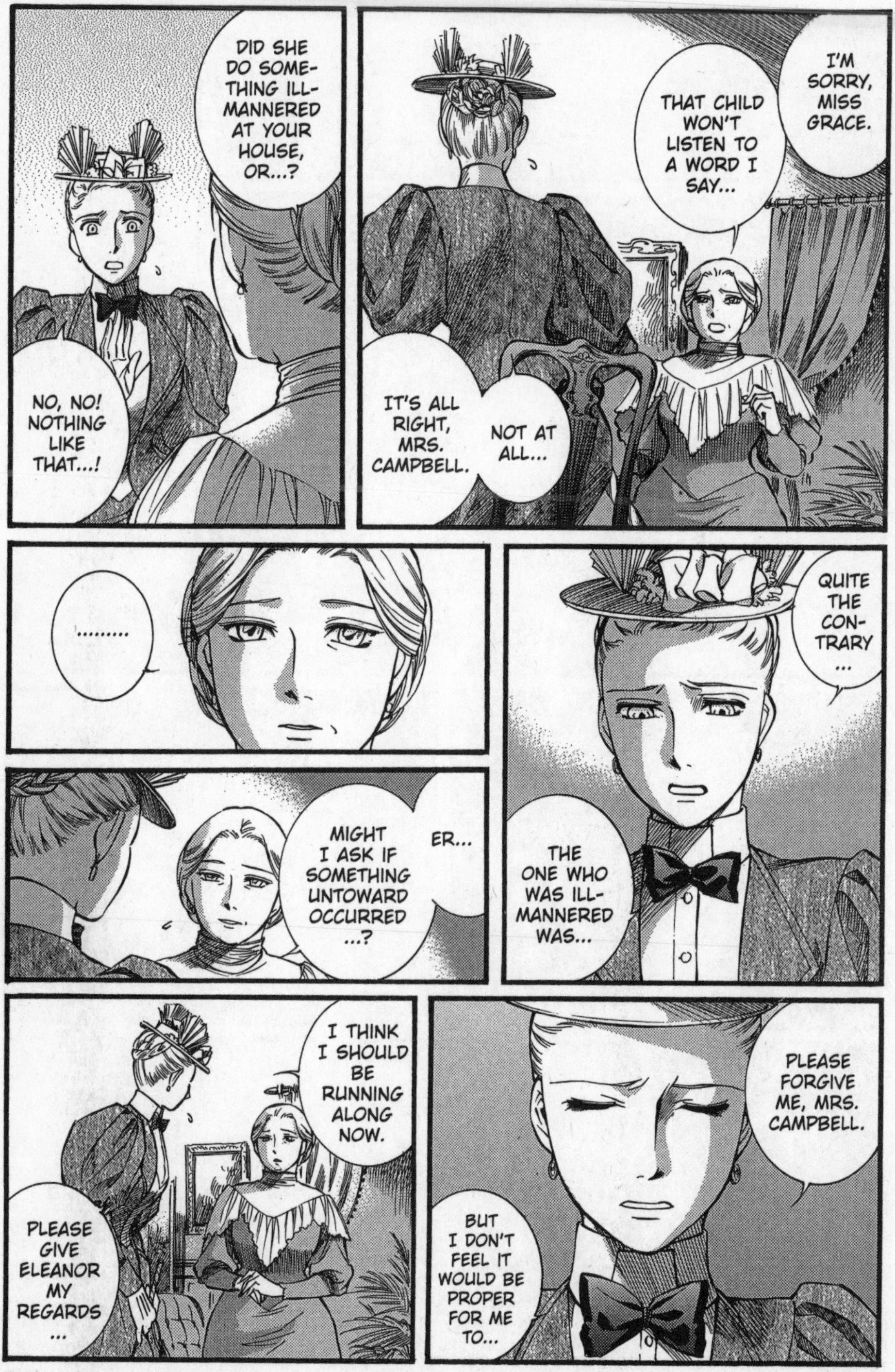
I'M SORRY, MISS GRACE.
THAT CHILD WON'T LISTEN TO A WORD I SAY...
NOT AT ALL...
IT'S ALL RIGHT, MRS. CAMPBELL.
DID SHE DO SOMETHING ILL-MANNERED AT YOUR HOUSE, OR...?
NO, NO! NOTHING LIKE THAT...!
QUITE THE CONTRARY...
THE ONE WHO WAS ILL-MANNERED WAS...
....
ER...
MIGHT I ASK IF SOMETHING UNTOWARD OCCURRED...?
PLEASE FORGIVE ME, MRS. CAMPBELL.
BUT I DON'T FEEL IT WOULD BE PROPER FOR ME TO...
I THINK I SHOULD BE RUNNING ALONG NOW.
PLEASE GIVE ELEANOR MY REGARDS...

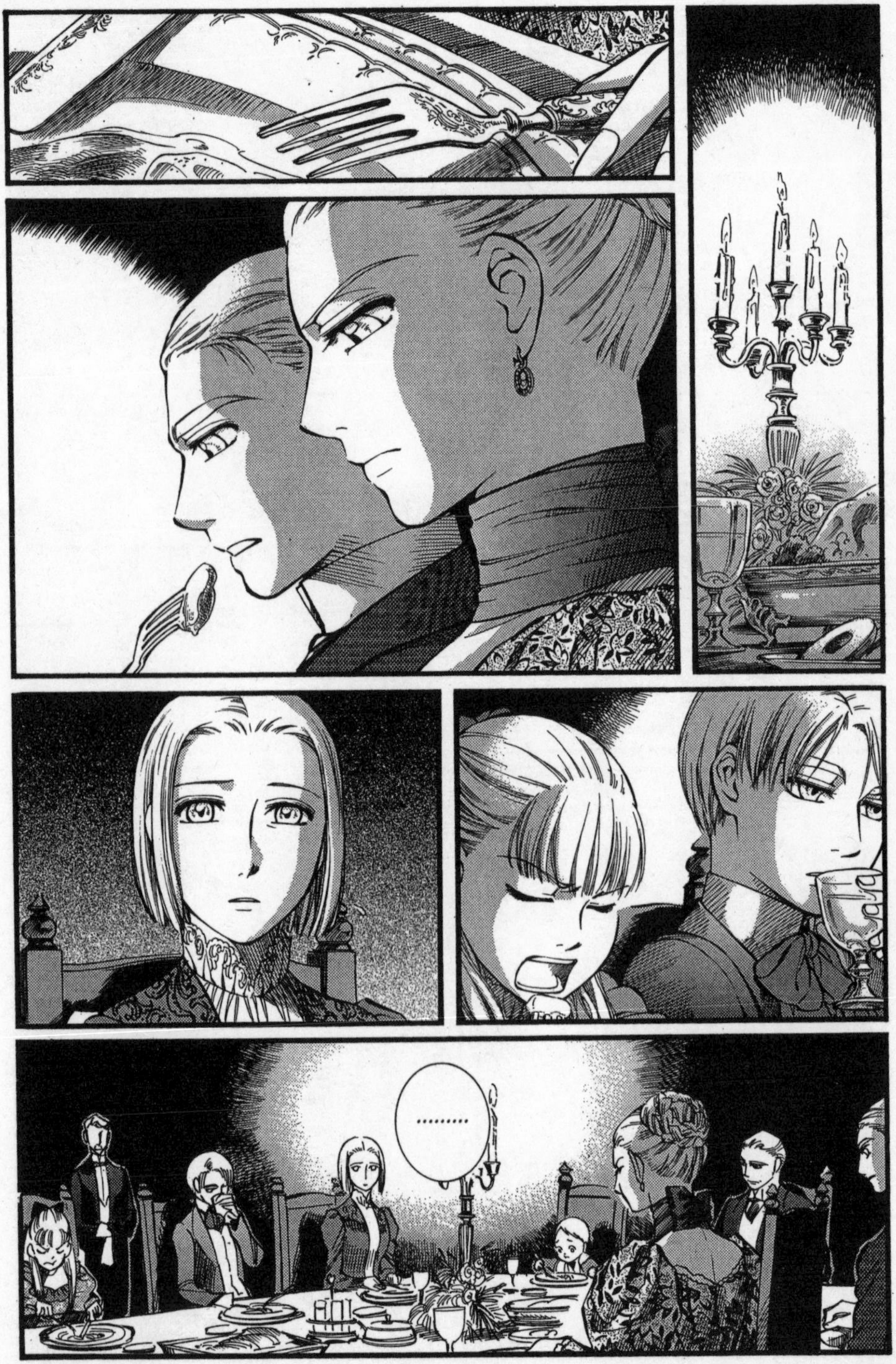
....

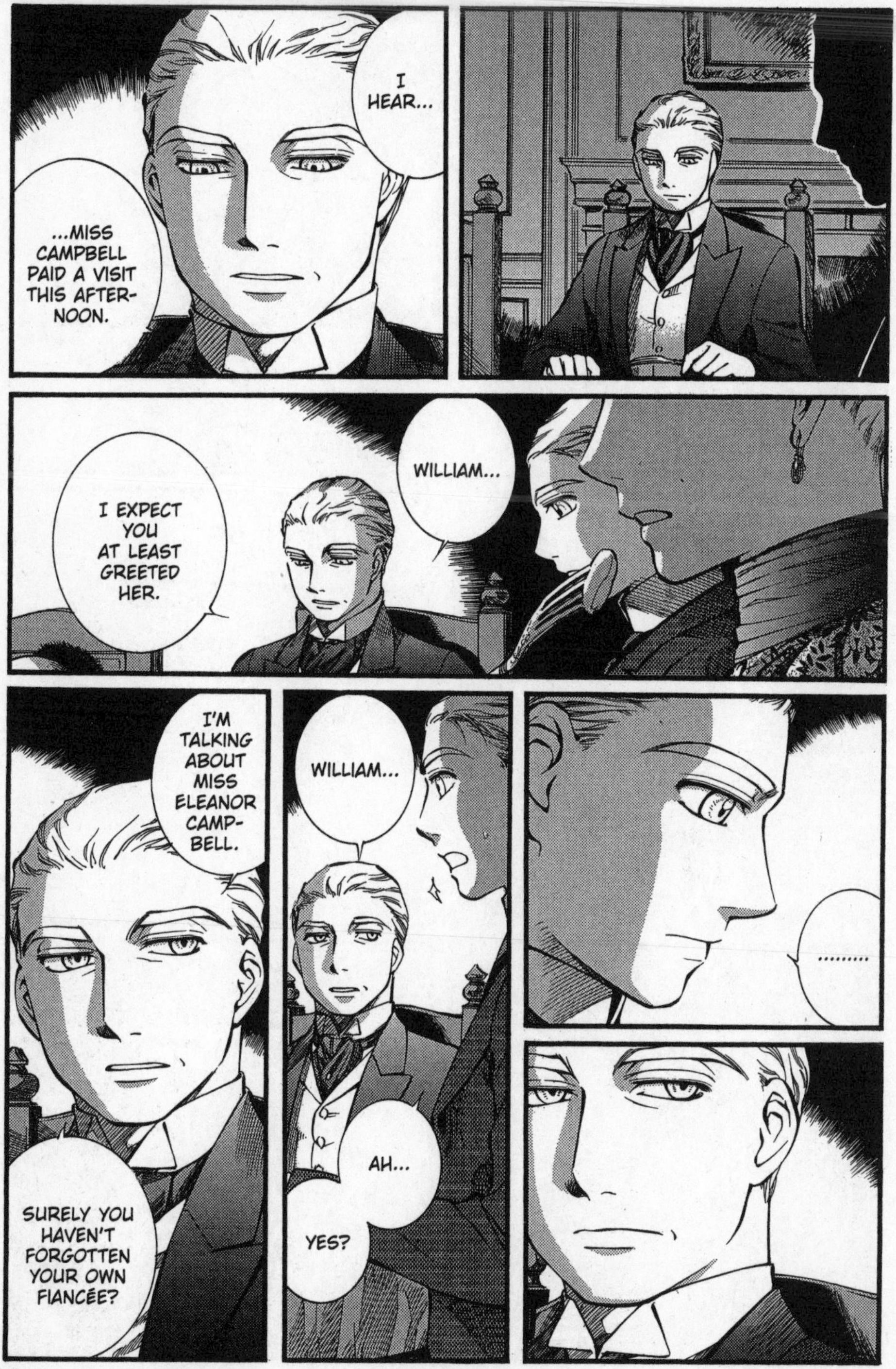
I HEAR...
...MISS CAMPBELL PAID A VISIT THIS AFTERNOON.
WILLIAM...
I EXPECT YOU AT LEAST GREETED HER.
....
WILLIAM...
AH...
YES?
I'M TALKING ABOUT MISS ELEANOR CAMPBELL.
SURELY YOU HAVEN'T FORGOTTEN YOUR OWN FIANCÉE?

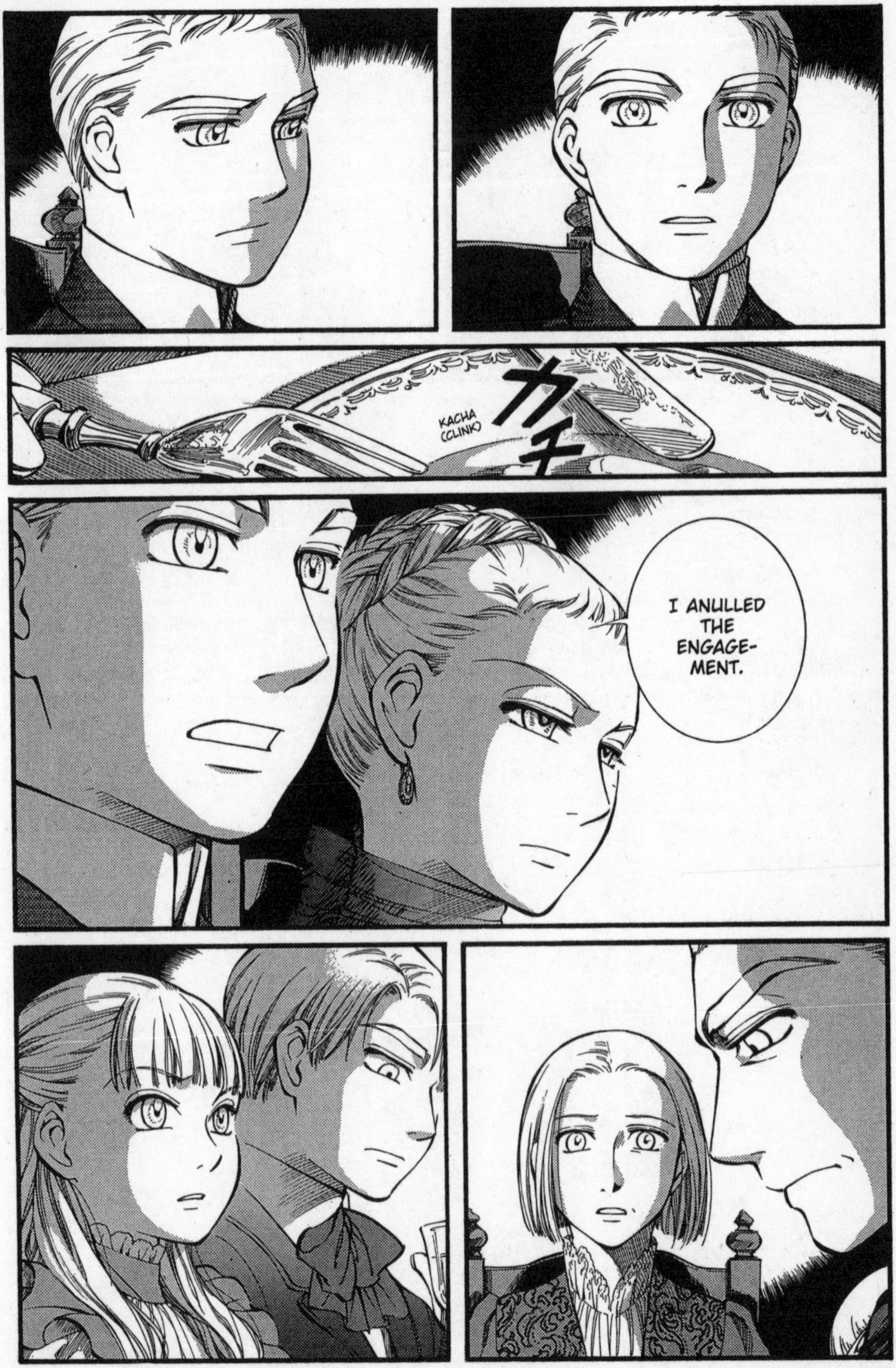
カチ
KACHA (CLINK)
I ANULLED THE ENGAGE-MENT.

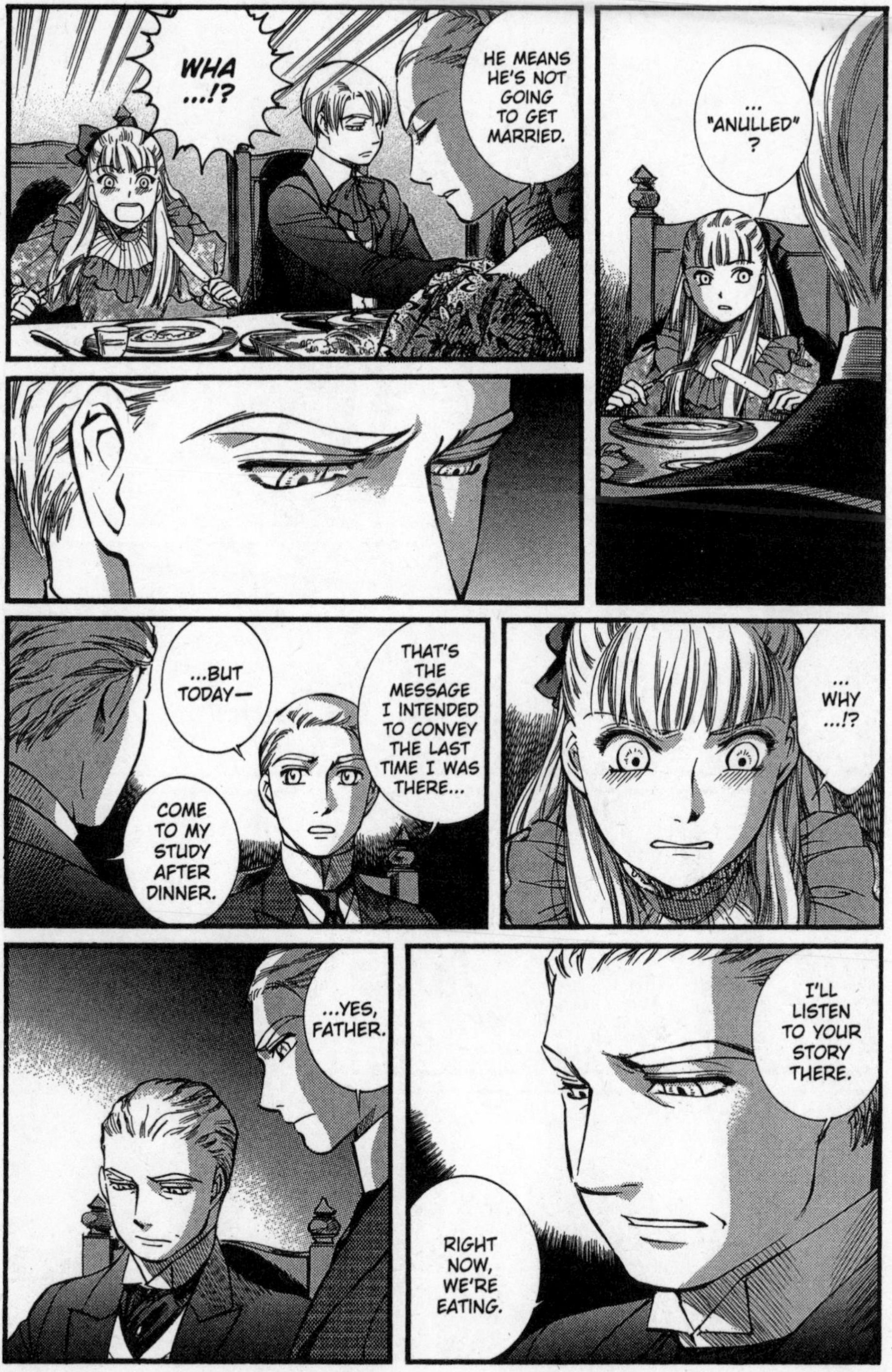
... "ANULLED" ?
HE MEANS HE'S NOT GOING TO GET MARRIED.
WHA ...!?
... WHY ...!?
THAT'S THE MESSAGE I INTENDED TO CONVEY THE LAST TIME I WAS THERE...
...BUT TODAY—
COME TO MY STUDY AFTER DINNER.
I'LL LISTEN TO YOUR STORY THERE.
RIGHT NOW, WE'RE EATING.
...YES, FATHER.

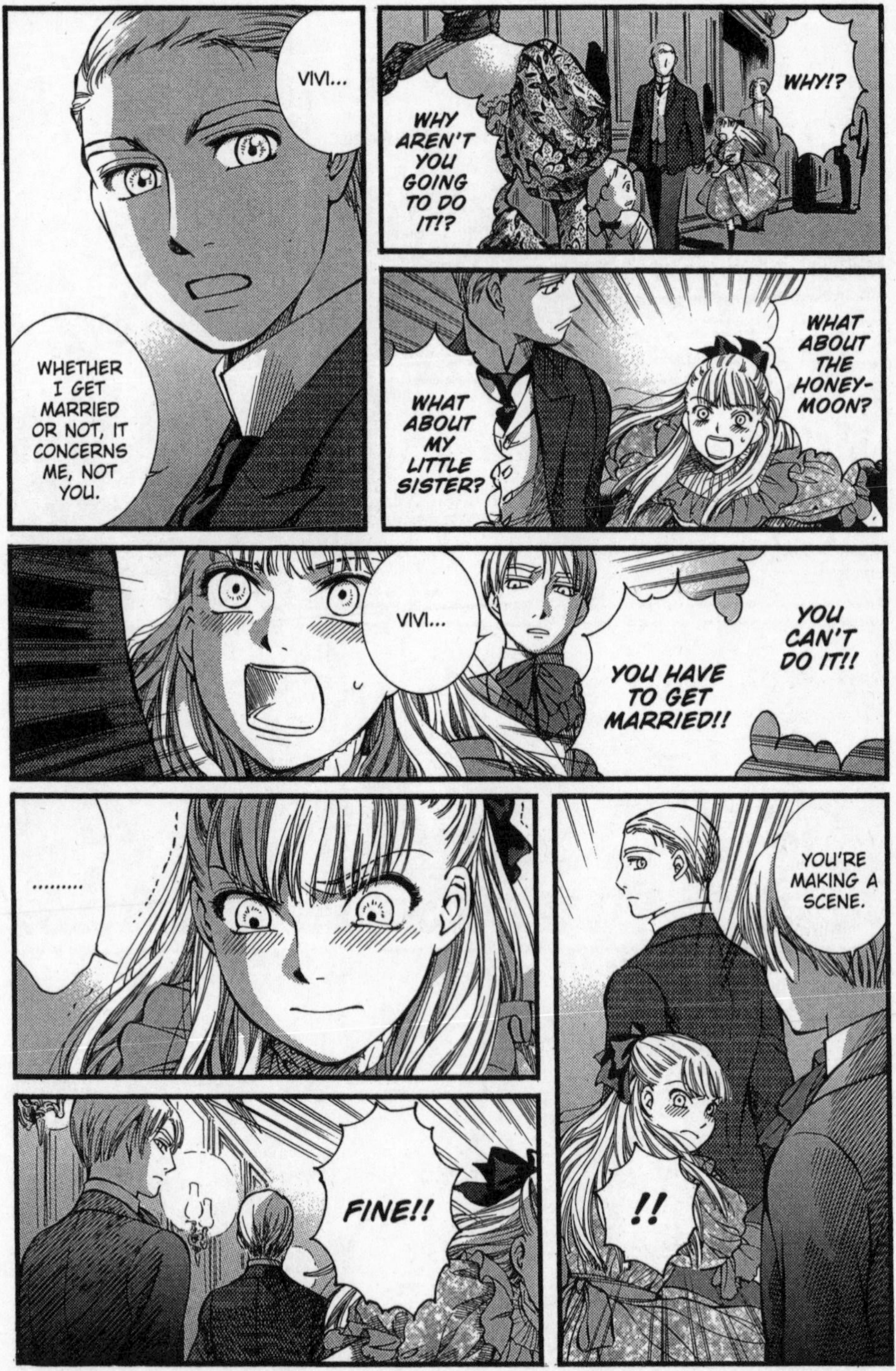
WHY!?
WHY AREN'T YOU GOING TO DO IT!?
WHAT ABOUT THE HONEY-MOON?
WHAT ABOUT MY LITTLE SISTER?
VIVI...
WHETHER I GET MARRIED OR NOT, IT CONCERNS ME, NOT YOU.
YOU CAN'T DO IT!!
YOU HAVE TO GET MARRIED!!
VIVI...
YOU'RE MAKING A SCENE.
!!
....
FINE!!

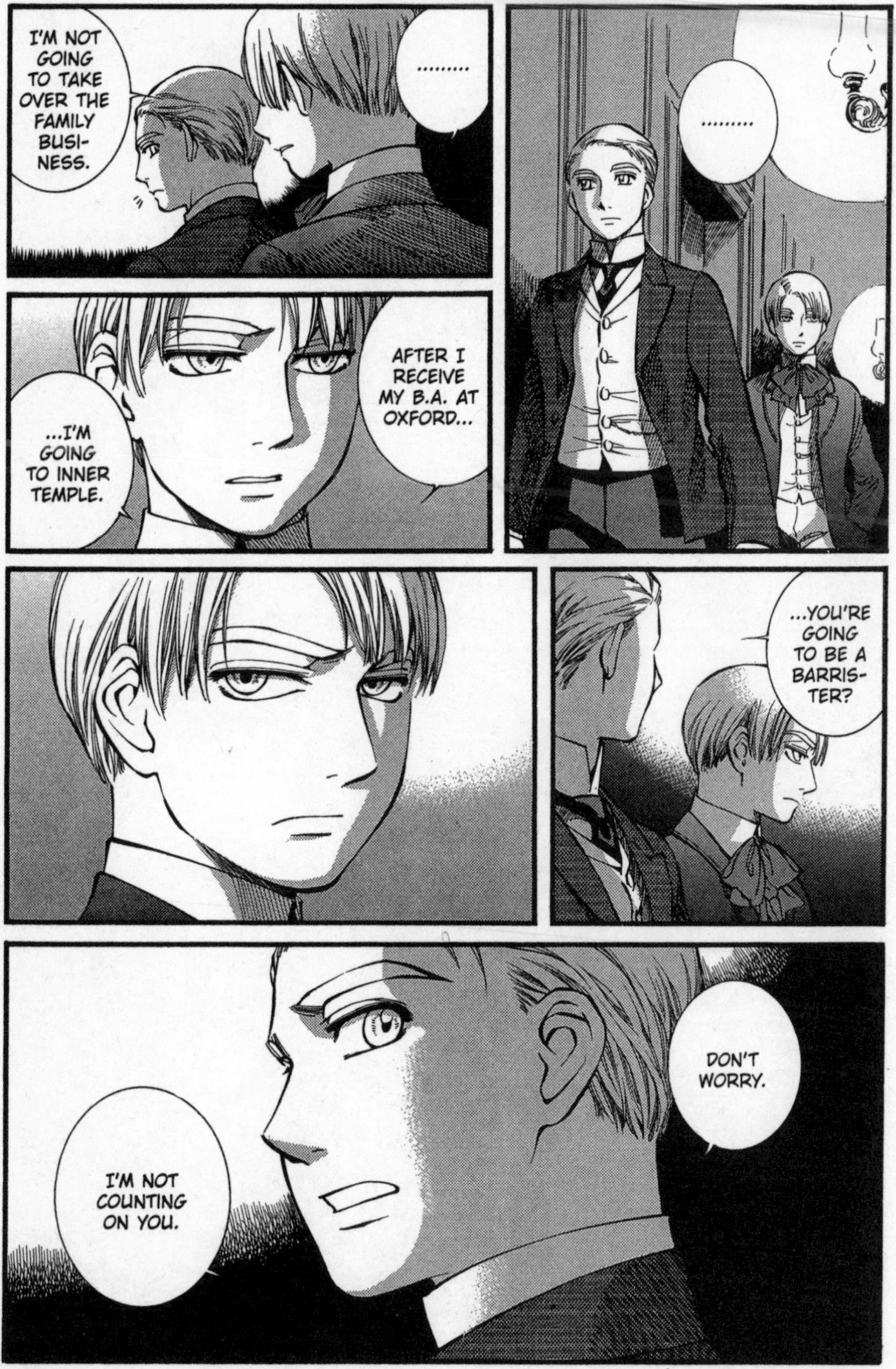
....
....
I'M NOT GOING TO TAKE OVER THE FAMILY BUSINESS.
AFTER I RECEIVE MY B.A. AT OXFORD...
...I'M GOING TO INNER TEMPLE.
...YOU'RE GOING TO BE A BARRISTER?
DON'T WORRY.
I'M NOT COUNTING ON YOU.

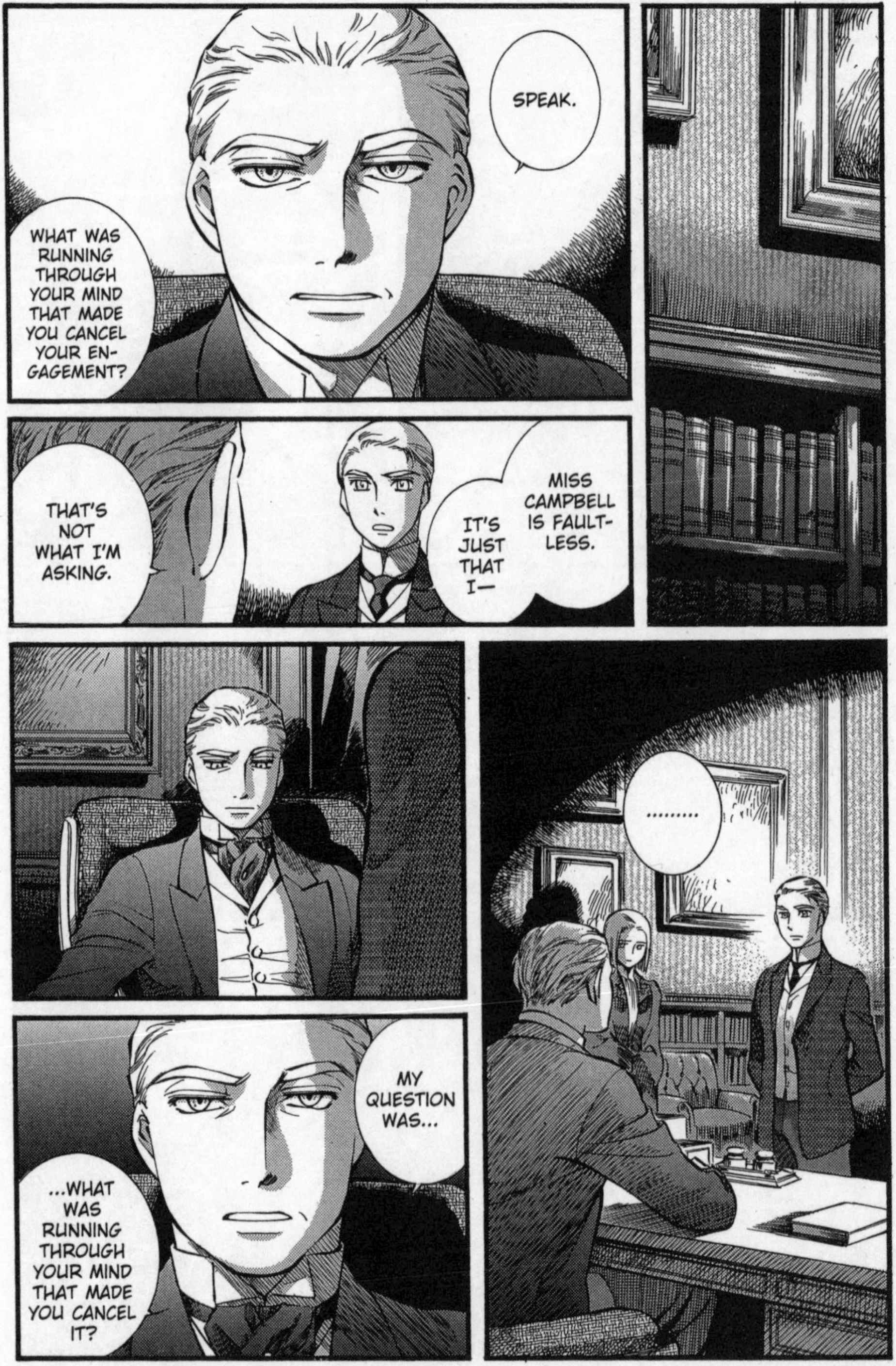
SPEAK.
WHAT WAS RUNNING THROUGH YOUR MIND THAT MADE YOU CANCEL YOUR ENGAGEMENT?
MISS CAMPBELL IS FAULTLESS.
IT'S JUST THAT I—
THAT'S NOT WHAT I'M ASKING.
....
MY QUESTION WAS...
...WHAT WAS RUNNING THROUGH YOUR MIND THAT MADE YOU CANCEL IT?

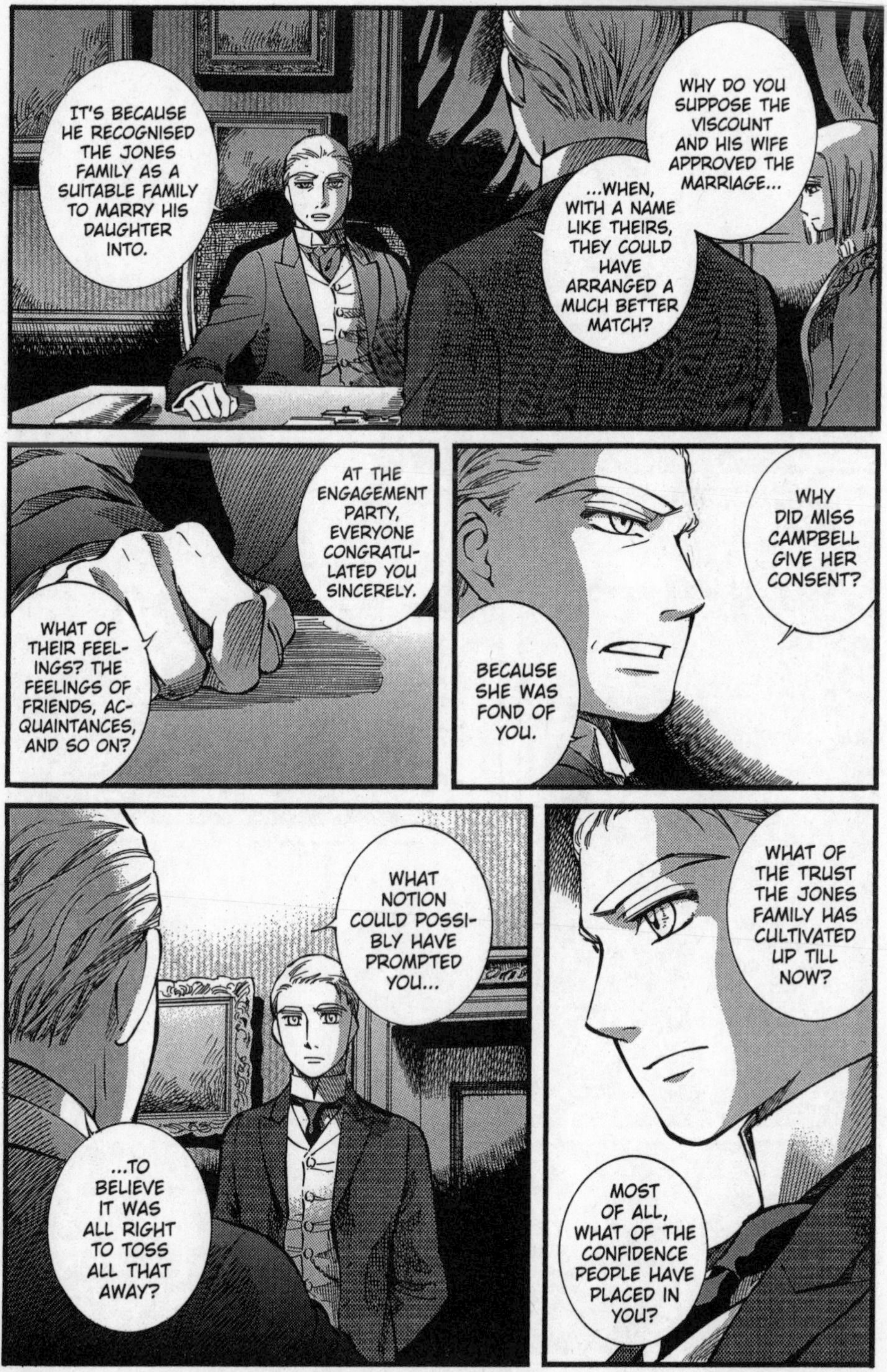
WHY DO YOU SUPPOSE THE VISCOUNT AND HIS WIFE APPROVED THE MARRIAGE...
...WHEN, WITH A NAME LIKE THEIRS, THEY COULD HAVE ARRANGED A MUCH BETTER MATCH?
IT'S BECAUSE HE RECOGNISED THE JONES FAMILY AS A SUITABLE FAMILY TO MARRY HIS DAUGHTER INTO.
WHY DID MISS CAMPBELL GIVE HER CONSENT?
BECAUSE SHE WAS FOND OF YOU.
AT THE ENGAGEMENT PARTY, EVERYONE CONGRATU-LATED YOU SINCERELY.
WHAT OF THEIR FEEL-INGS? THE FEELINGS OF FRIENDS, AC-QUAINTANCES, AND SO ON?
WHAT OF THE TRUST THE JONES FAMILY HAS CULTIVATED UP TILL NOW?
MOST OF ALL, WHAT OF THE CONFIDENCE PEOPLE HAVE PLACED IN YOU?
WHAT NOTION COULD POSSI-BLY HAVE PROMPTED YOU...
...TO BELIEVE IT WAS ALL RIGHT TO TOSS ALL THAT AWAY?

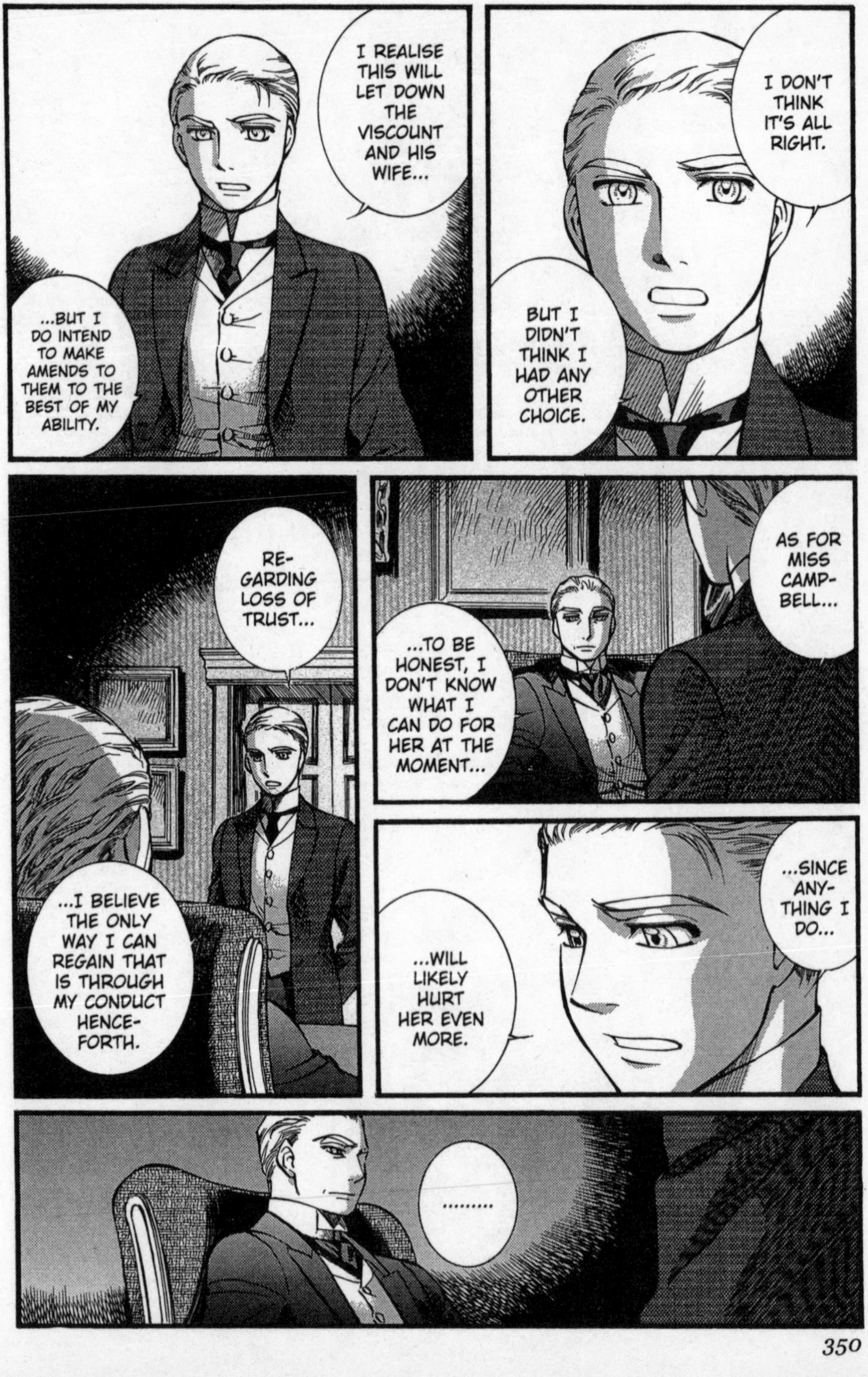
I DON'T THINK IT'S ALL RIGHT.
BUT I DIDN'T THINK I HAD ANY OTHER CHOICE.
I REALISE THIS WILL LET DOWN THE VISCOUNT AND HIS WIFE...
...BUT I DO INTEND TO MAKE AMENDS TO THEM TO THE BEST OF MY ABILITY.
AS FOR MISS CAMPBELL...
...TO BE HONEST, I DON'T KNOW WHAT I CAN DO FOR HER AT THE MOMENT...
...SINCE ANYTHING I DO...
...WILL LIKELY HURT HER EVEN MORE.
RE-GARDING LOSS OF TRUST...
...I BELIEVE THE ONLY WAY I CAN REGAIN THAT IS THROUGH MY CONDUCT HENCE-FORTH.
....

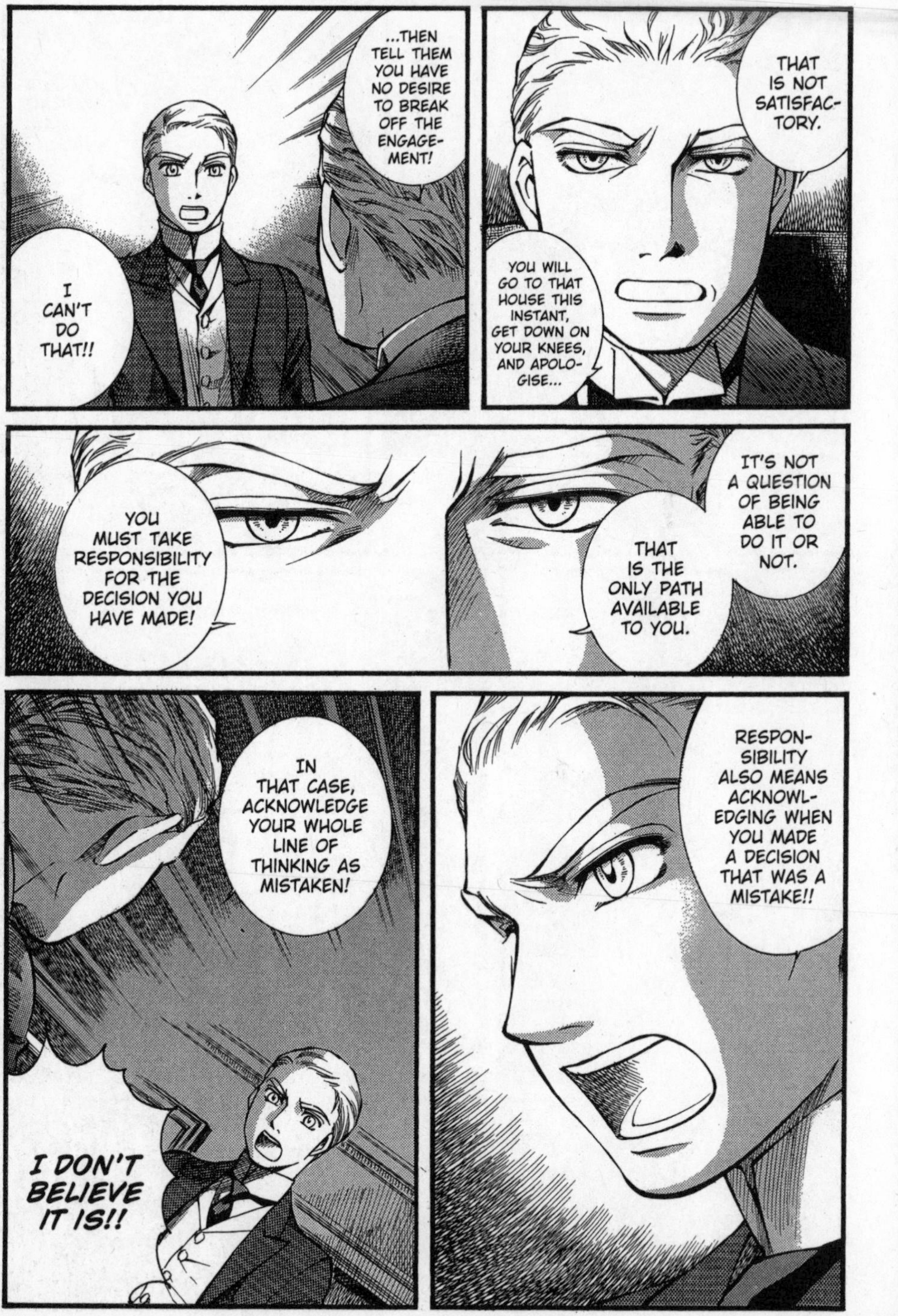
THAT IS NOT SATISFACTORY.
YOU WILL GO TO THAT HOUSE THIS INSTANT, GET DOWN ON YOUR KNEES, AND APOLOGISE...
...THEN TELL THEM YOU HAVE NO DESIRE TO BREAK OFF THE ENGAGEMENT!
I CAN'T DO THAT!!
IT'S NOT A QUESTION OF BEING ABLE TO DO IT OR NOT.
THAT IS THE ONLY PATH AVAILABLE TO YOU.
YOU MUST TAKE RESPONSIBILITY FOR THE DECISION YOU HAVE MADE!
RESPONSIBILITY ALSO MEANS ACKNOWLEDGING WHEN YOU MADE A DECISION THAT WAS A MISTAKE!!
IN THAT CASE, ACKNOWLEDGE YOUR WHOLE LINE OF THINKING AS MISTAKEN!
I DON'T BELIEVE IT IS!!

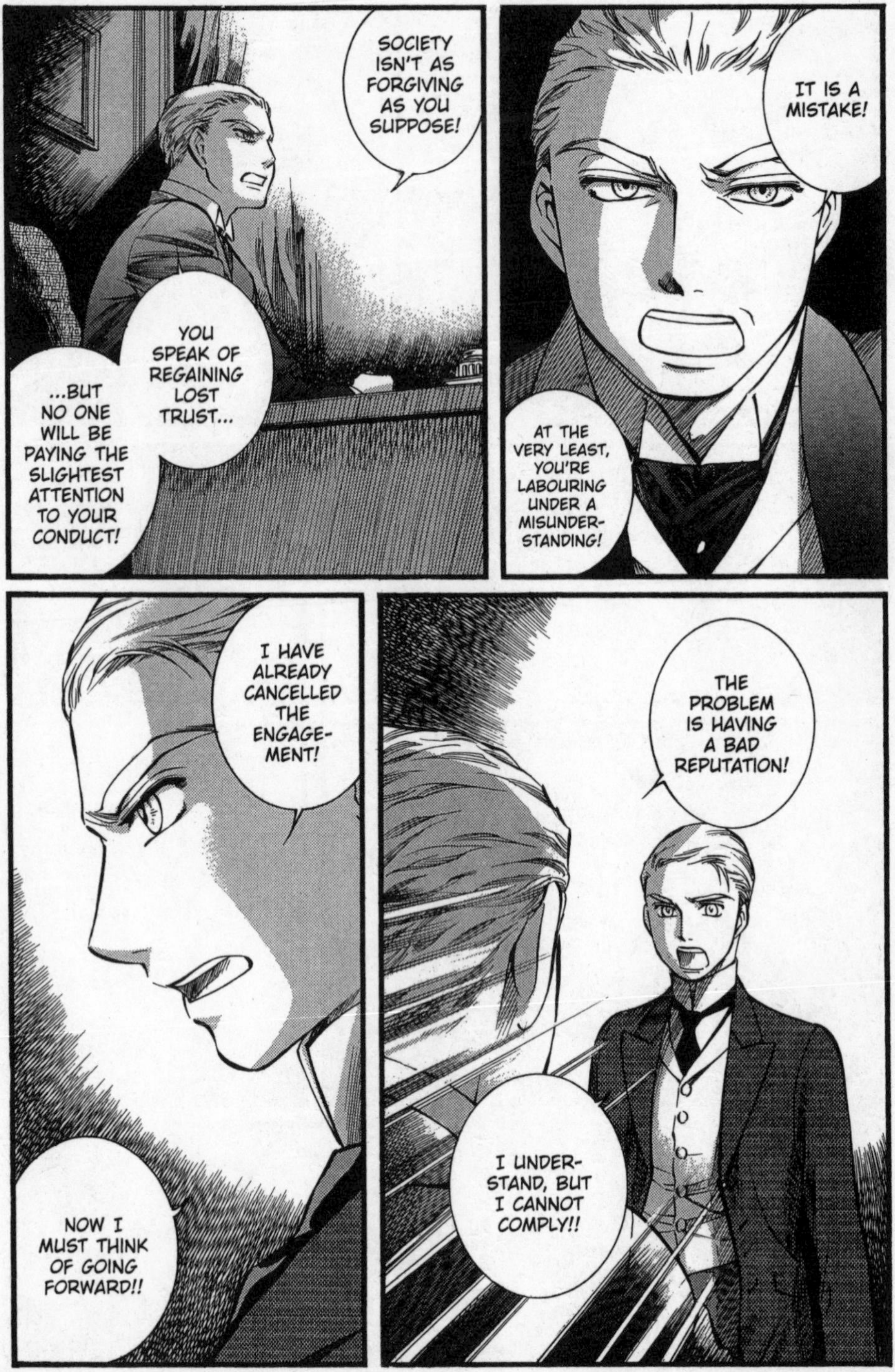
IT IS A MISTAKE!
AT THE VERY LEAST, YOU'RE LABOURING UNDER A MISUNDER-STANDING!
SOCIETY ISN'T AS FORGIVING AS YOU SUPPOSE!
YOU SPEAK OF REGAINING LOST TRUST...
...BUT NO ONE WILL BE PAYING THE SLIGHTEST ATTENTION TO YOUR CONDUCT!
THE PROBLEM IS HAVING A BAD REPUTATION!
I UNDER-STAND, BUT I CANNOT COMPLY!!
I HAVE ALREADY CANCELLED THE ENGAGE-MENT!
NOW I MUST THINK OF GOING FORWARD!!

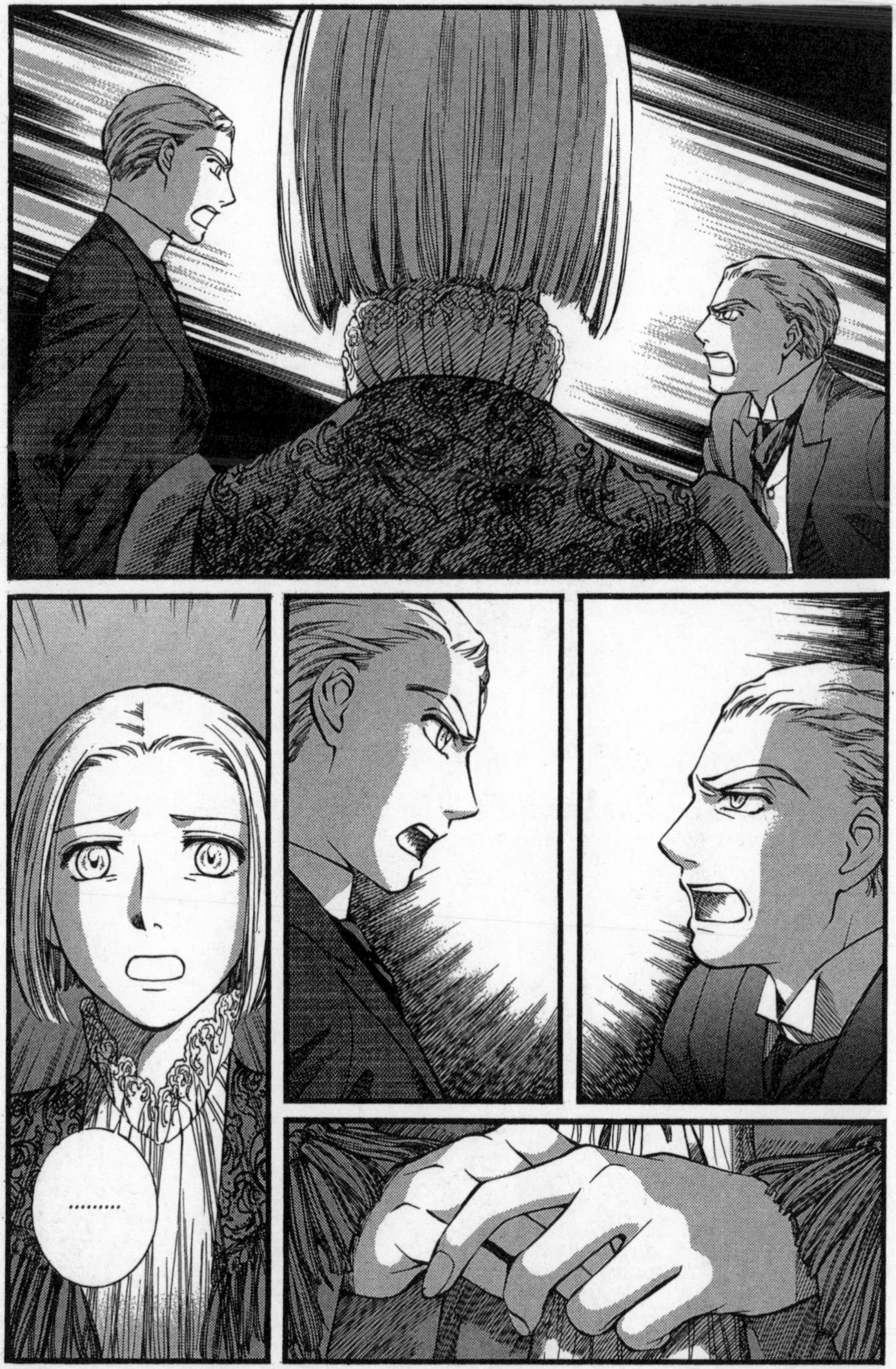
....

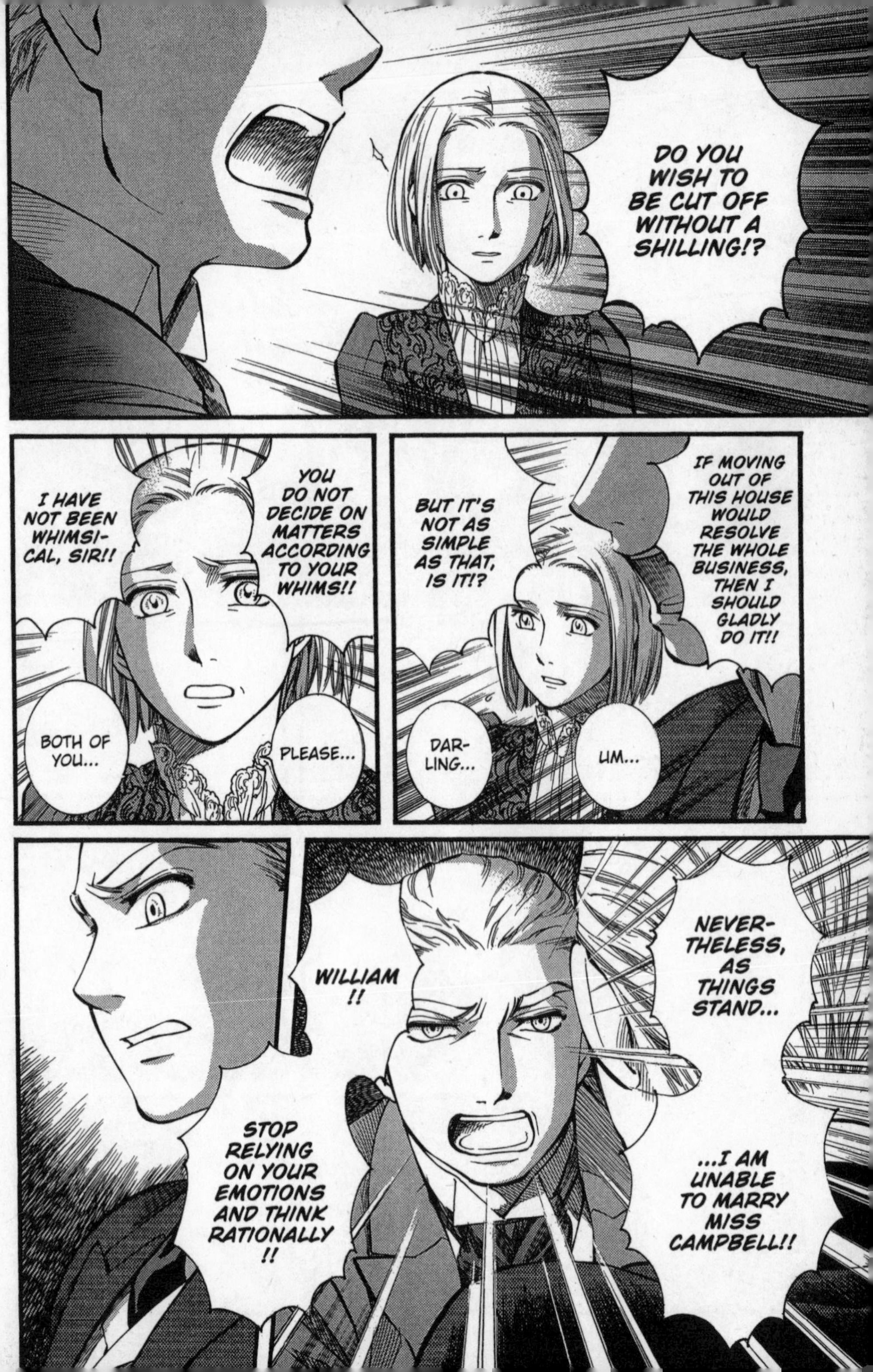
DO YOU WISH TO BE CUT OFF WITHOUT A SHILLING!?
IF MOVING OUT OF THIS HOUSE WOULD RESOLVE THE WHOLE BUSINESS, THEN I SHOULD GLADLY DO IT!!
BUT IT'S NOT AS SIMPLE AS THAT, IS IT!?
UM...
DAR-LING...
YOU DO NOT DECIDE ON MATTERS ACCORDING TO YOUR WHIMS!!
I HAVE NOT BEEN WHIMSI-CAL, SIR!!
PLEASE...
BOTH OF YOU...
NEVER-THELESS, AS THINGS STAND...
...I AM UNABLE TO MARRY MISS CAMPBELL!!
WILLIAM !!
STOP RELYING ON YOUR EMOTIONS AND THINK RATIONALLY !!

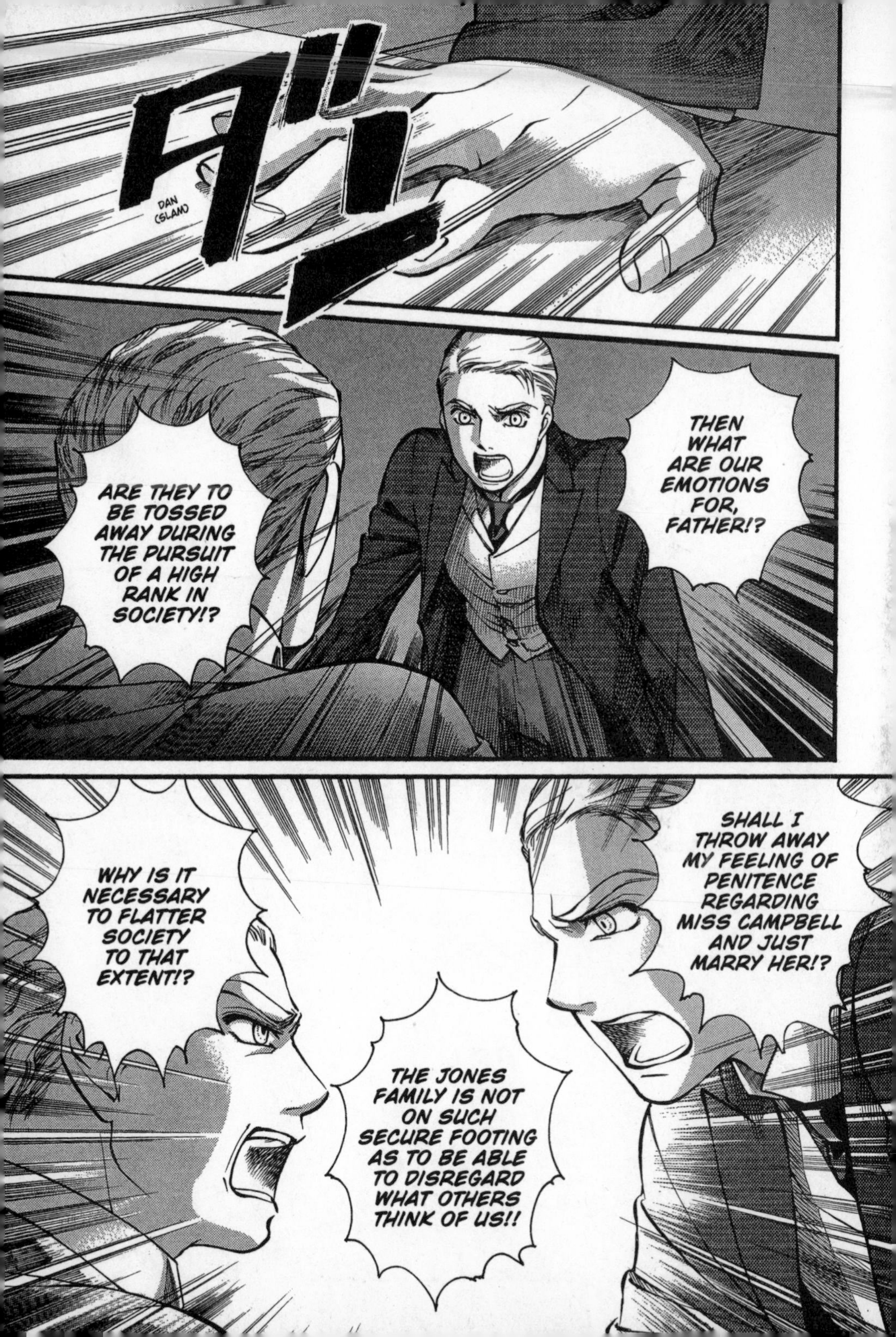
ダン
DAN (SLAM)
THEN WHAT ARE OUR EMOTIONS FOR, FATHER!?
ARE THEY TO BE TOSSED AWAY DURING THE PURSUIT OF A HIGH RANK IN SOCIETY!?
SHALL I THROW AWAY MY FEELING OF PENITENCE REGARDING MISS CAMPBELL AND JUST MARRY HER!?
WHY IS IT NECESSARY TO FLATTER SOCIETY TO THAT EXTENT!?
THE JONES FAMILY IS NOT ON SUCH SECURE FOOTING AS TO BE ABLE TO DISREGARD WHAT OTHERS THINK OF US!!

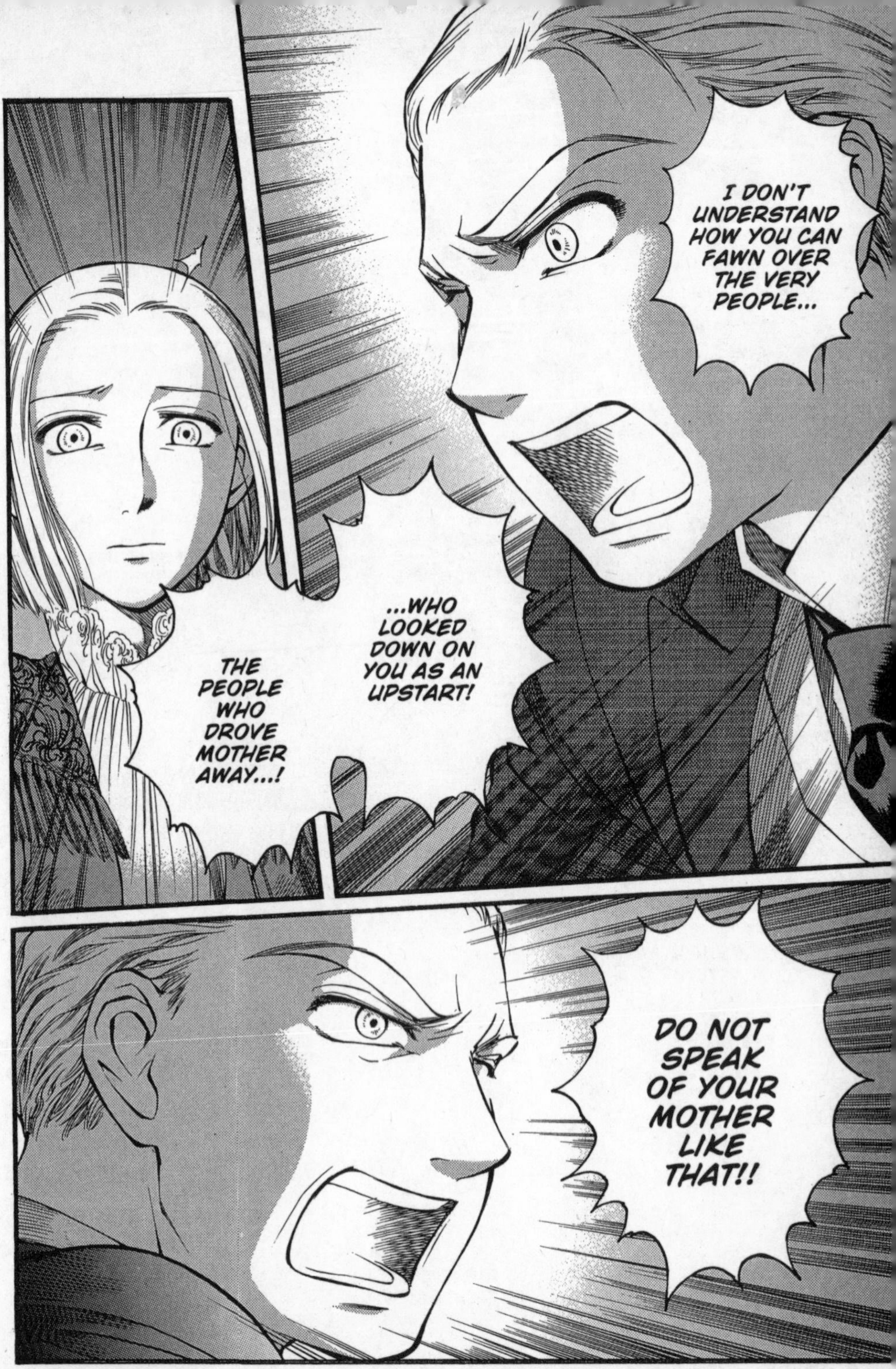
I DON'T UNDERSTAND HOW YOU CAN FAWN OVER THE VERY PEOPLE...
...WHO LOOKED DOWN ON YOU AS AN UPSTART!
THE PEOPLE WHO DROVE MOTHER AWAY...!
DO NOT SPEAK OF YOUR MOTHER LIKE THAT!!

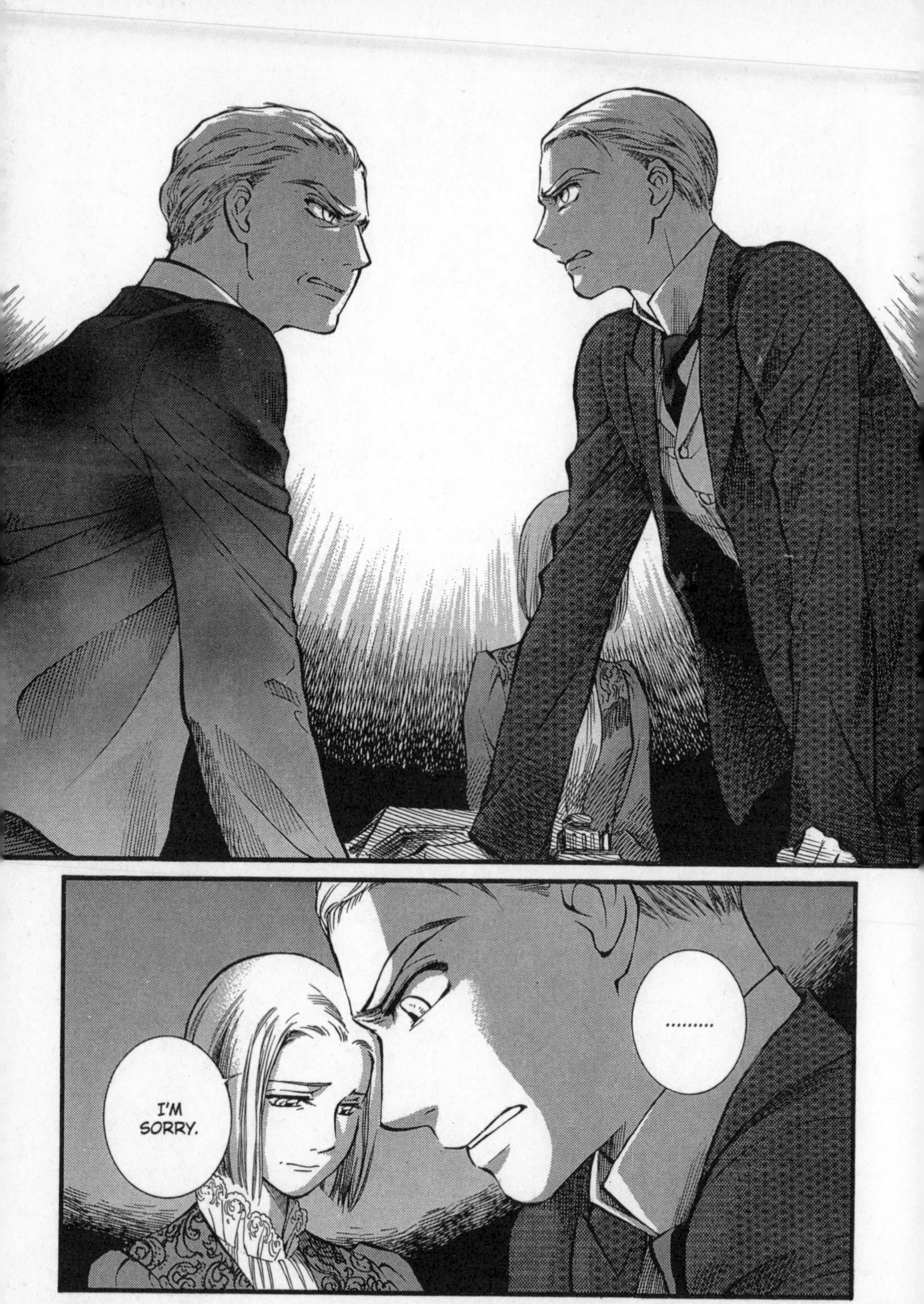
....
I'M SORRY.

....

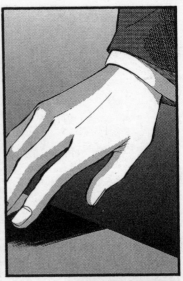

IF YOU ARE DONE AS WELL, FATHER...

...THEN I SHALL...

THAT'S ALL...

...I HAVE TO SAY.

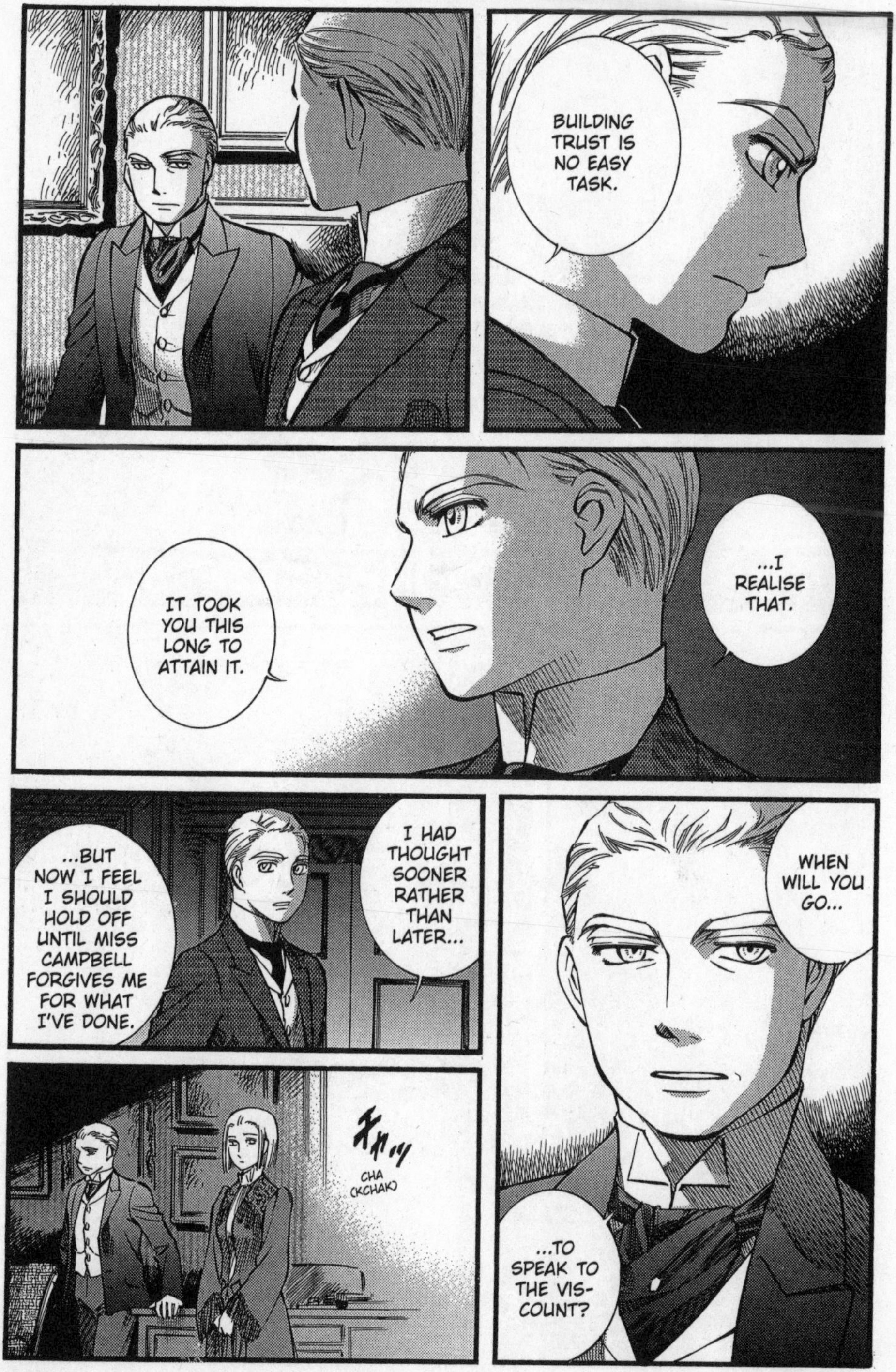
BUILDING TRUST IS NO EASY TASK.
...I REALISE THAT.
IT TOOK YOU THIS LONG TO ATTAIN IT.
WHEN WILL YOU GO...
...TO SPEAK TO THE VIS-COUNT?
I HAD THOUGHT SOONER RATHER THAN LATER...
...BUT NOW I FEEL I SHOULD HOLD OFF UNTIL MISS CAMPBELL FORGIVES ME FOR WHAT I'VE DONE.
CHA (KCHAK)

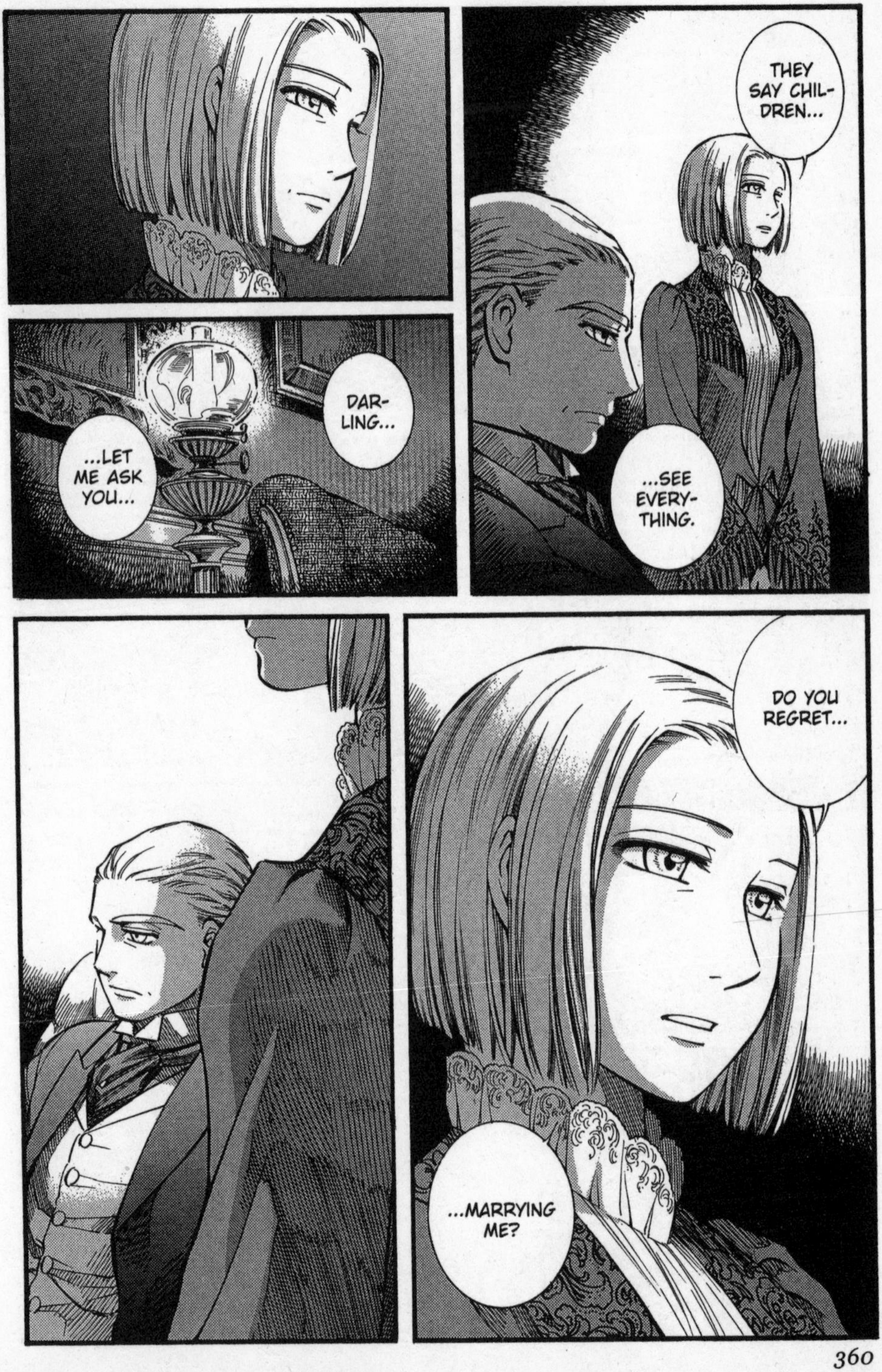
THEY SAY CHIL-DREN...
...SEE EVERY-THING.
DAR-LING...
...LET ME ASK YOU...
DO YOU REGRET...
...MARRYING ME?

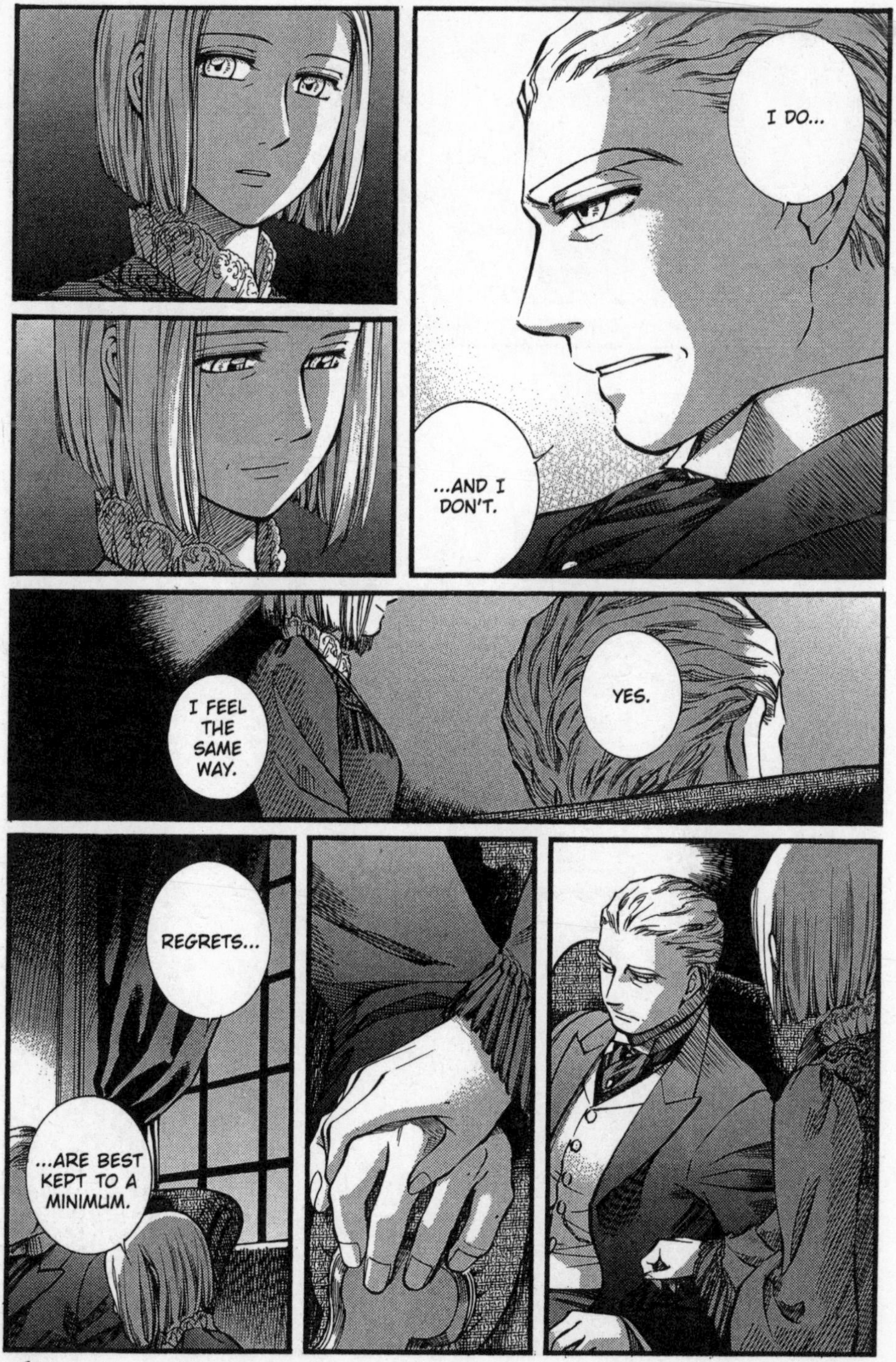
I DO...
...AND I DON'T.
YES.
I FEEL THE SAME WAY.
REGRETS...
...ARE BEST KEPT TO A MINIMUM.

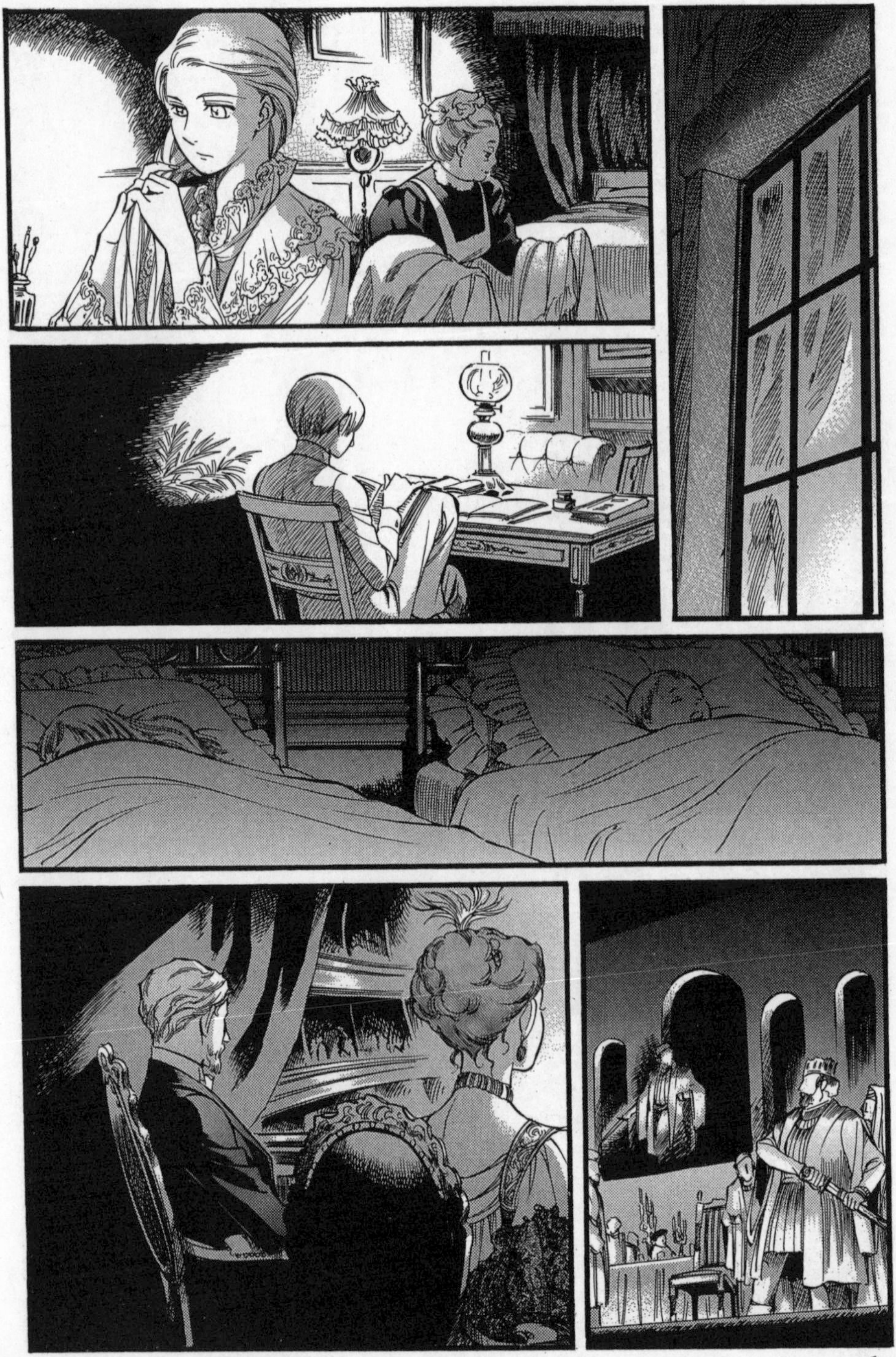

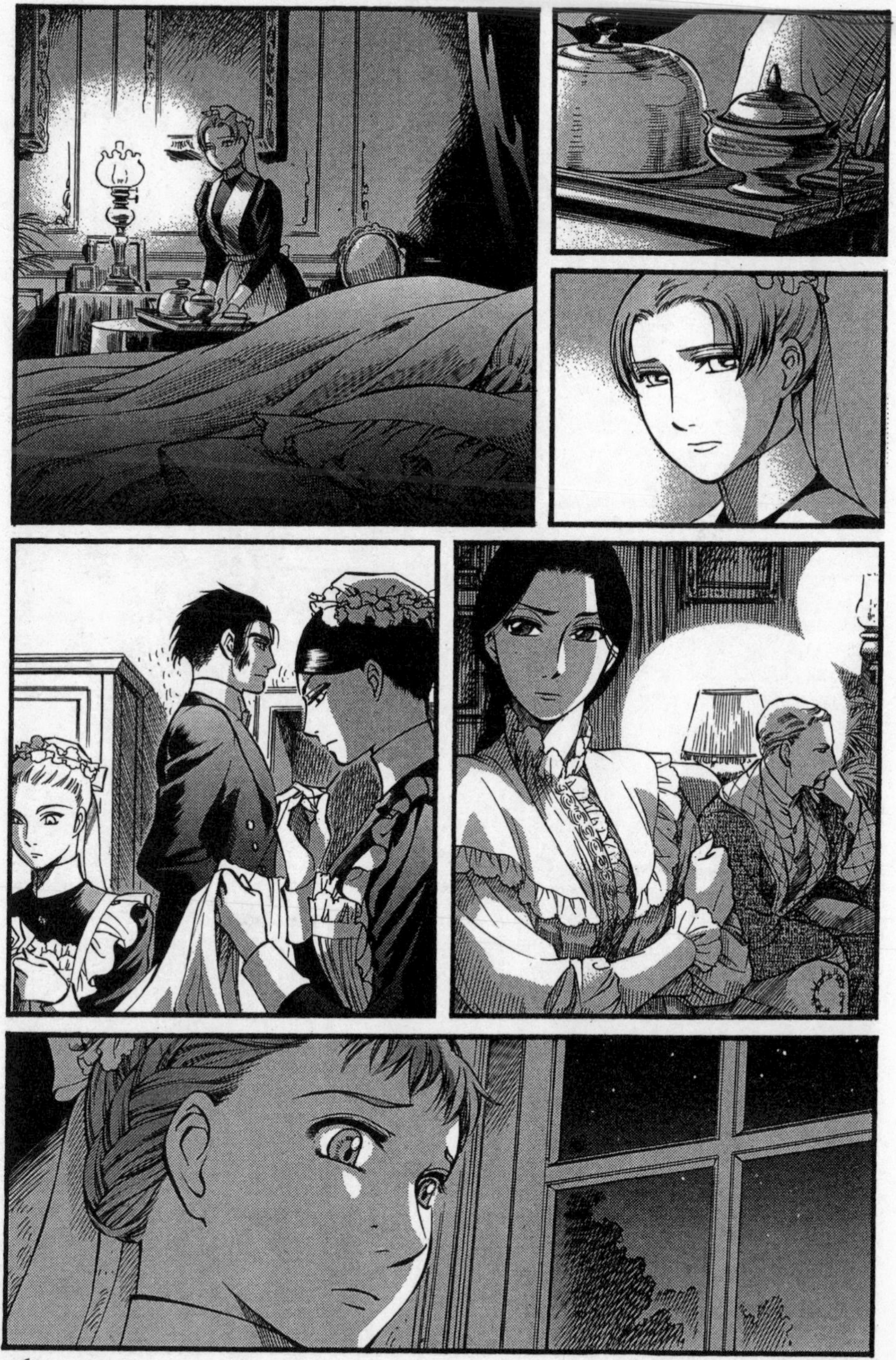

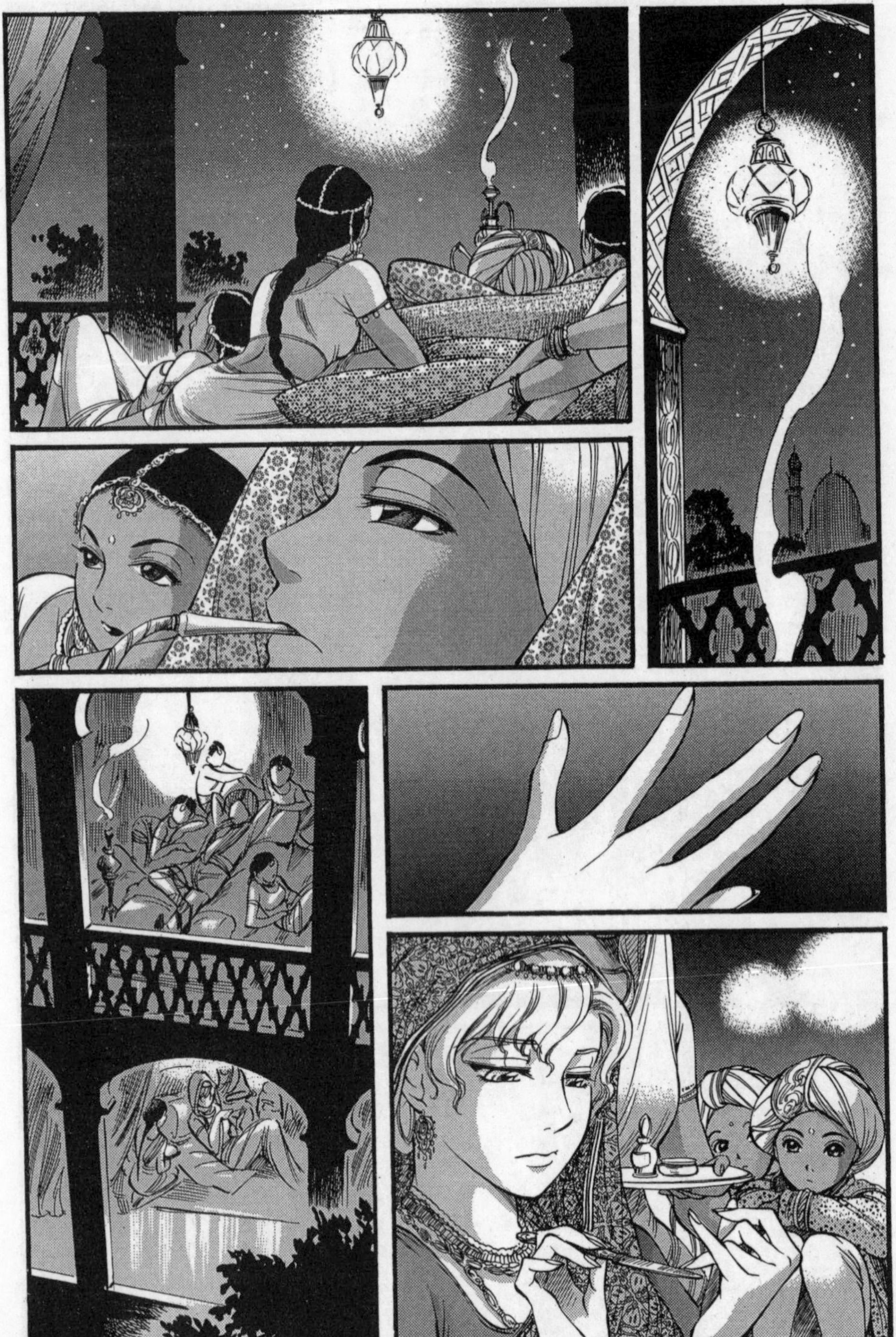

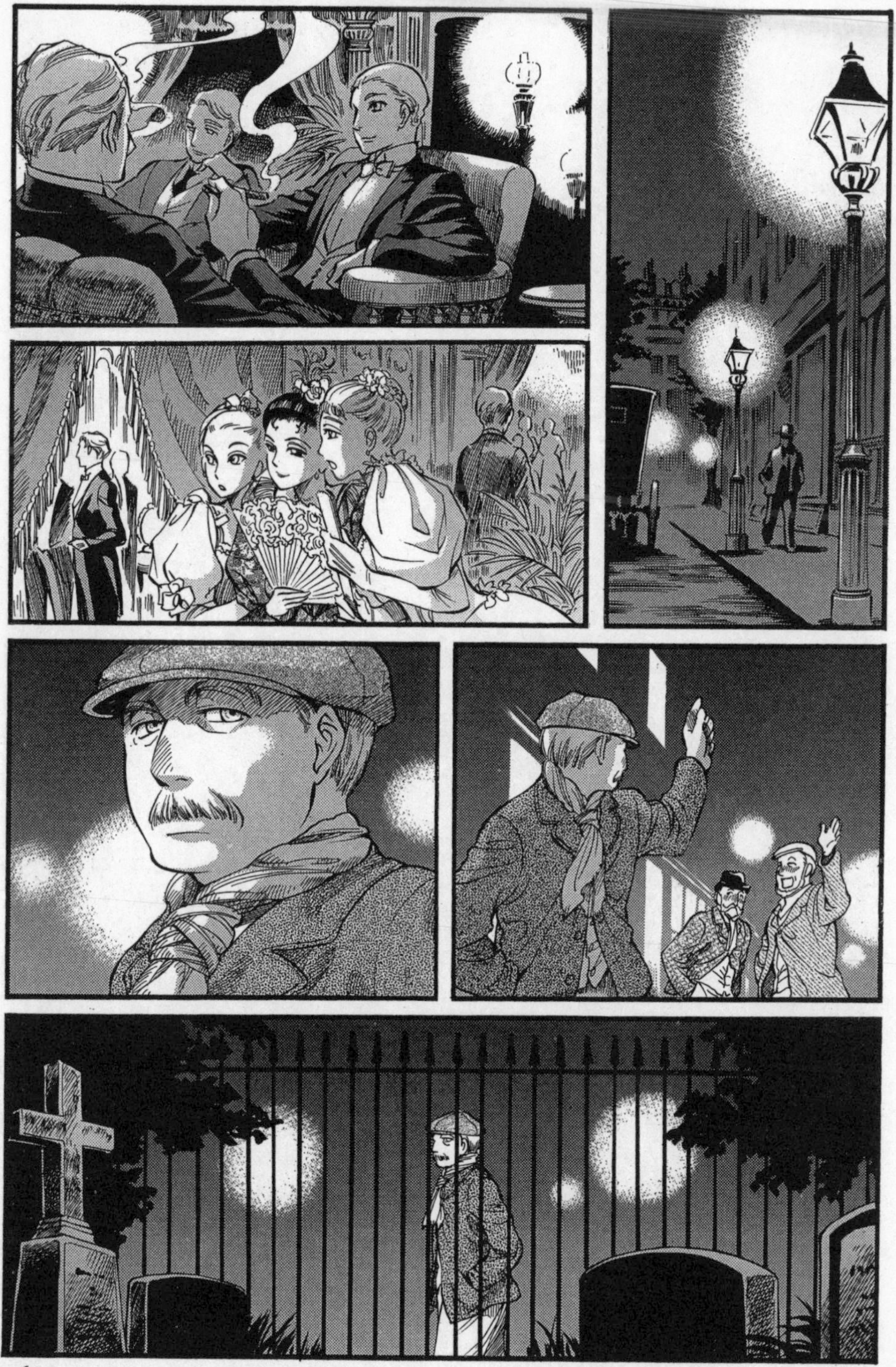

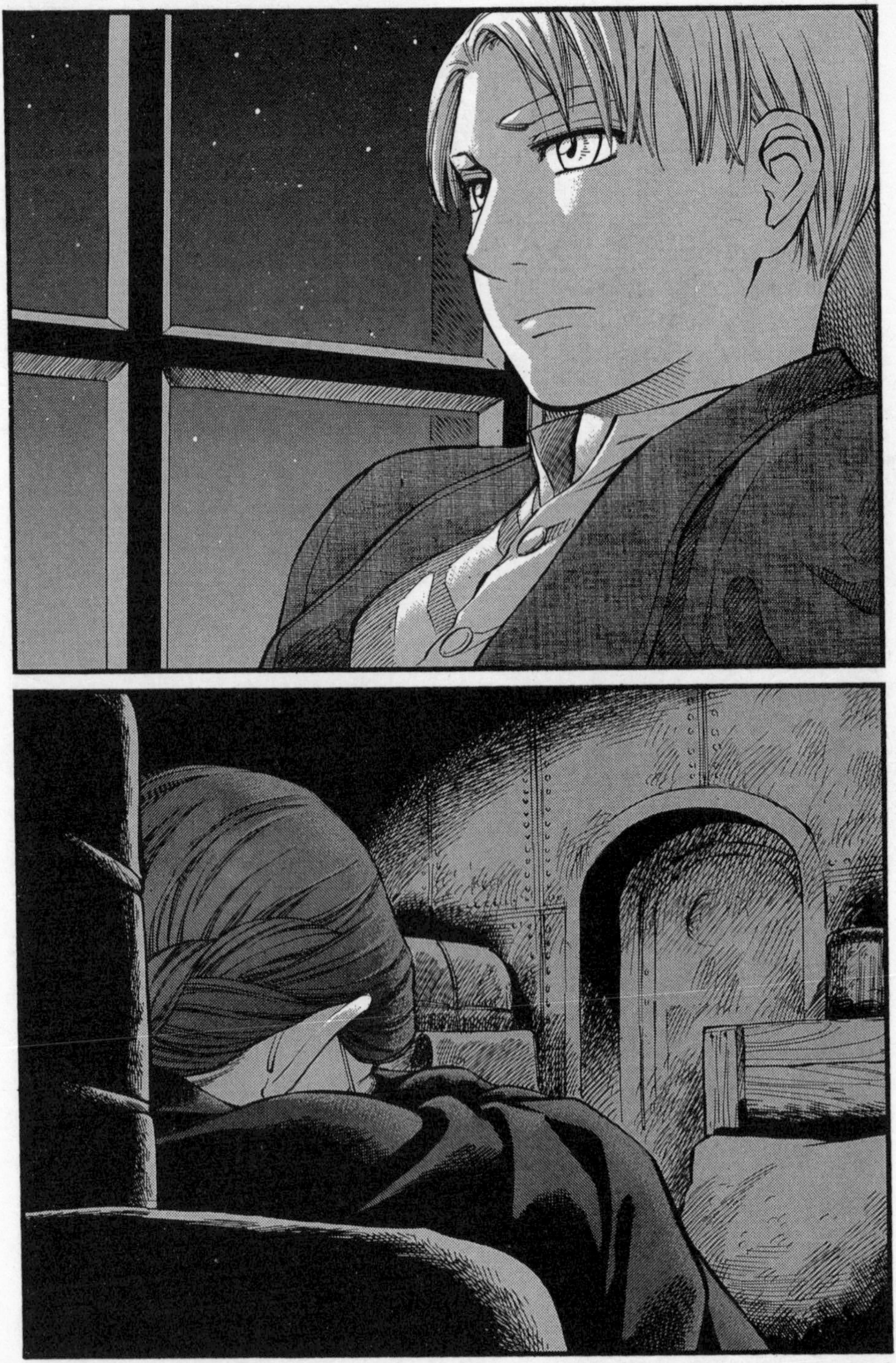

Chapter 43: End

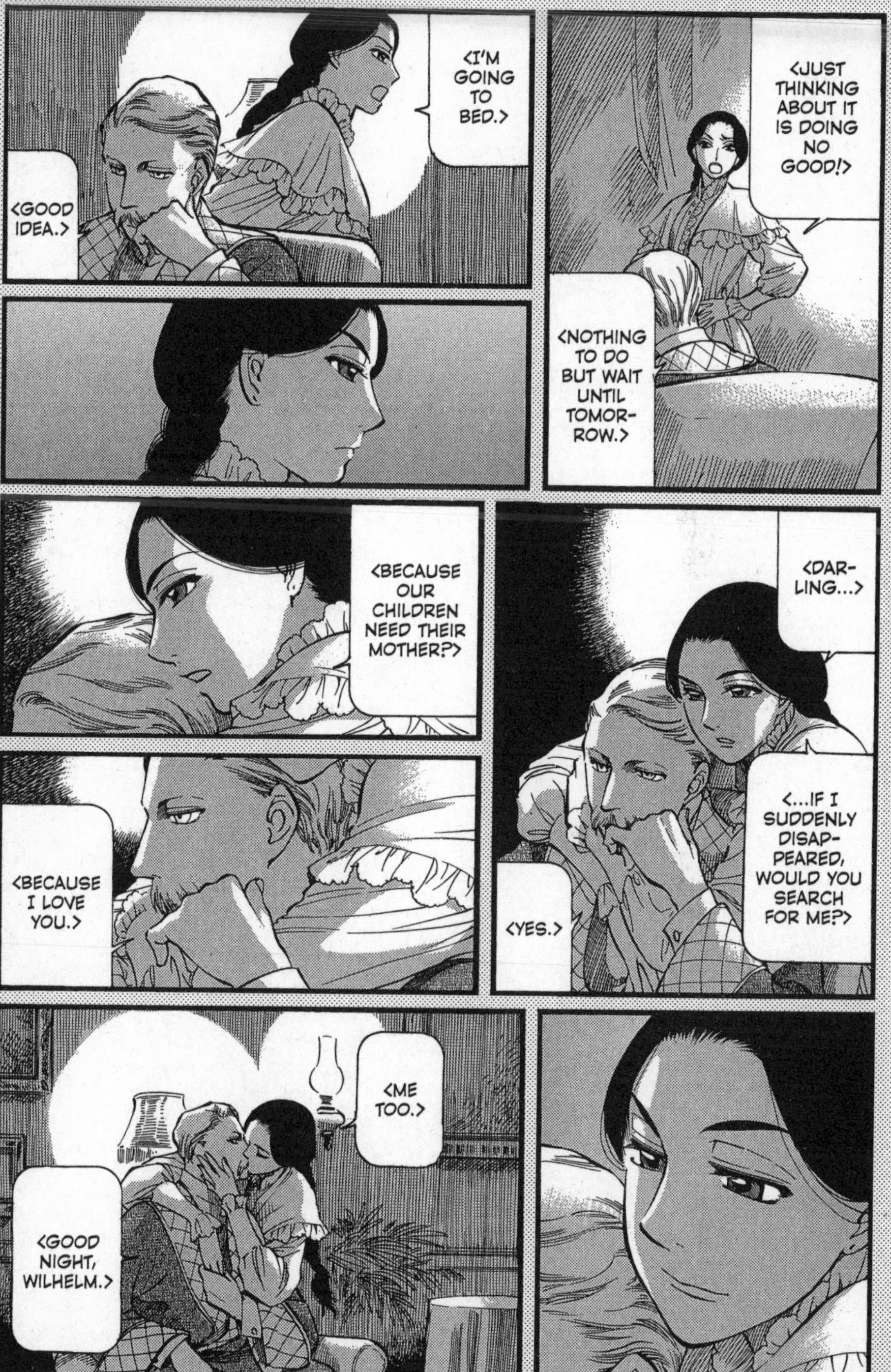

<JUST THINKING ABOUT IT IS DOING NO GOOD!>
<NOTHING TO DO BUT WAIT UNTIL TOMOR-ROW.>
<I'M GOING TO BED.>
<GOOD IDEA.>
<DAR-LING...>
<...IF I SUDDENLY DISAP-PEARED, WOULD YOU SEARCH FOR ME?>
<YES.>
<BECAUSE OUR CHILDREN NEED THEIR MOTHER?>
<BECAUSE I LOVE YOU.>
<ME TOO.>
<GOOD NIGHT, WILHELM.>

EMMA ③

Kaoru Mori

Translation: Sheldon Drzka

Lettering: Abigail Blackman

EMMA Volume 5, 6
© 2005 Kaoru Mori.
All rights reserved.
First published in Japan in 2005 by KADOKAWA CORPORATION ENTERBRAIN
English translation rights arranged with KADOKAWA CORPORATION ENTERBRAIN
through Tuttle-Mori Agency, Inc., Tokyo.

Translation © 2015 by Hachette Book Group

Yen Press
Hachette Book Group
1290 Avenue of the Americas
New York, NY 10104

www.hachettebookgroup.com
www.yenpress.com

Yen Press is an imprint of Hachette Book Group, Inc. The Yen Press name and logo are trademarks of Hachette Book Group, Inc.

The publisher is not responsible for websites (or their content) not owned by the publisher.

First Yen Press Edition: December 2015

ISBN: 978-0-316-30445-0

10 9 8 7 6 5 4 3 2 1

BVG

Printed in the
United States of America

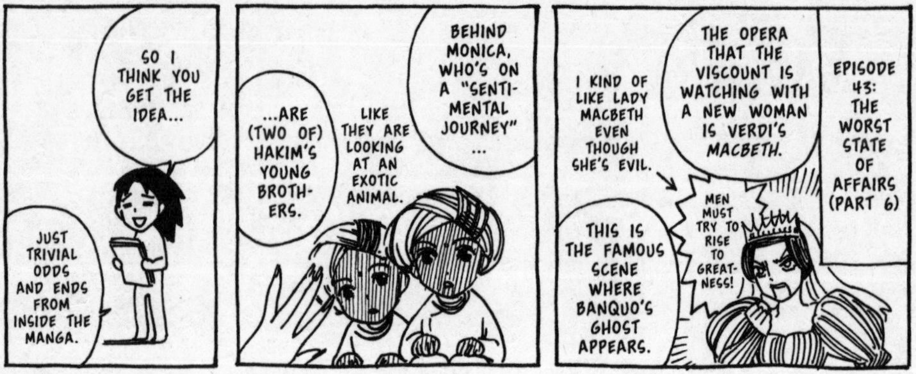
EPISODE 43: THE WORST STATE OF AFFAIRS (PART 6)
THE OPERA THAT THE VISCOUNT IS WATCHING WITH A NEW WOMAN IS VERDI'S MACBETH.
I KIND OF LIKE LADY MACBETH EVEN THOUGH SHE'S EVIL.
MEN MUST TRY TO RISE TO GREATNESS!
THIS IS THE FAMOUS SCENE WHERE BANQUO'S GHOST APPEARS.
BEHIND MONICA, WHO'S ON A "SENTIMENTAL JOURNEY"...
LIKE THEY ARE LOOKING AT AN EXOTIC ANIMAL.
...ARE (TWO OF) HAKIM'S YOUNG BROTHERS.
SO I THINK YOU GET THE IDEA...
JUST TRIVIAL ODDS AND ENDS FROM INSIDE THE MANGA.

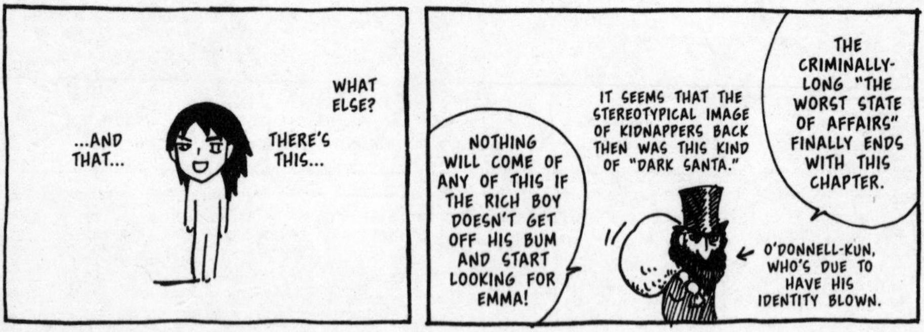
THE CRIMINALLY-LONG "THE WORST STATE OF AFFAIRS" FINALLY ENDS WITH THIS CHAPTER.
IT SEEMS THAT THE STEREOTYPICAL IMAGE OF KIDNAPPERS BACK THEN WAS THIS KIND OF "DARK SANTA."
O'DONNELL-KUN, WHO'S DUE TO HAVE HIS IDENTITY BLOWN.
NOTHING WILL COME OF ANY OF THIS IF THE RICH BOY DOESN'T GET OFF HIS BUM AND START LOOKING FOR EMMA!
WHAT ELSE?
THERE'S THIS...
...AND THAT...

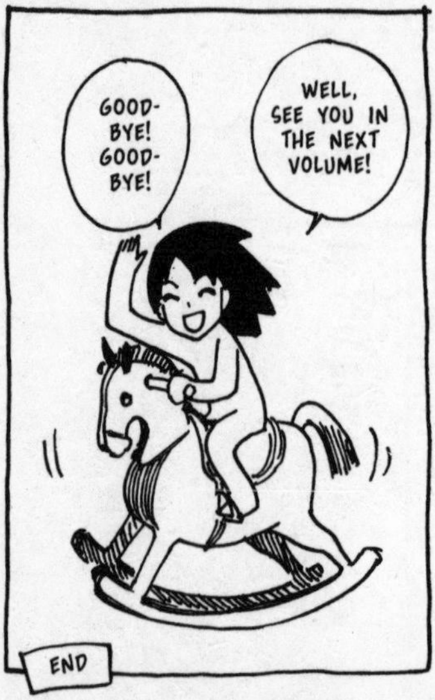
WELL, SEE YOU IN THE NEXT VOLUME!
GOOD-BYE! GOOD-BYE!
END

TO EVERYONE WHO'S SENT ME LETTERS OR MATERIALS OR PHOTOS, ETC., THANK YOU VERY MUCH.

IT LOOKS LIKE I'M NOT GOING TO BE ABLE TO REPLY, BUT I REALLY APPRECIATE EVERYTHING.

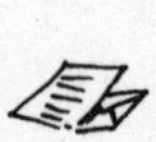

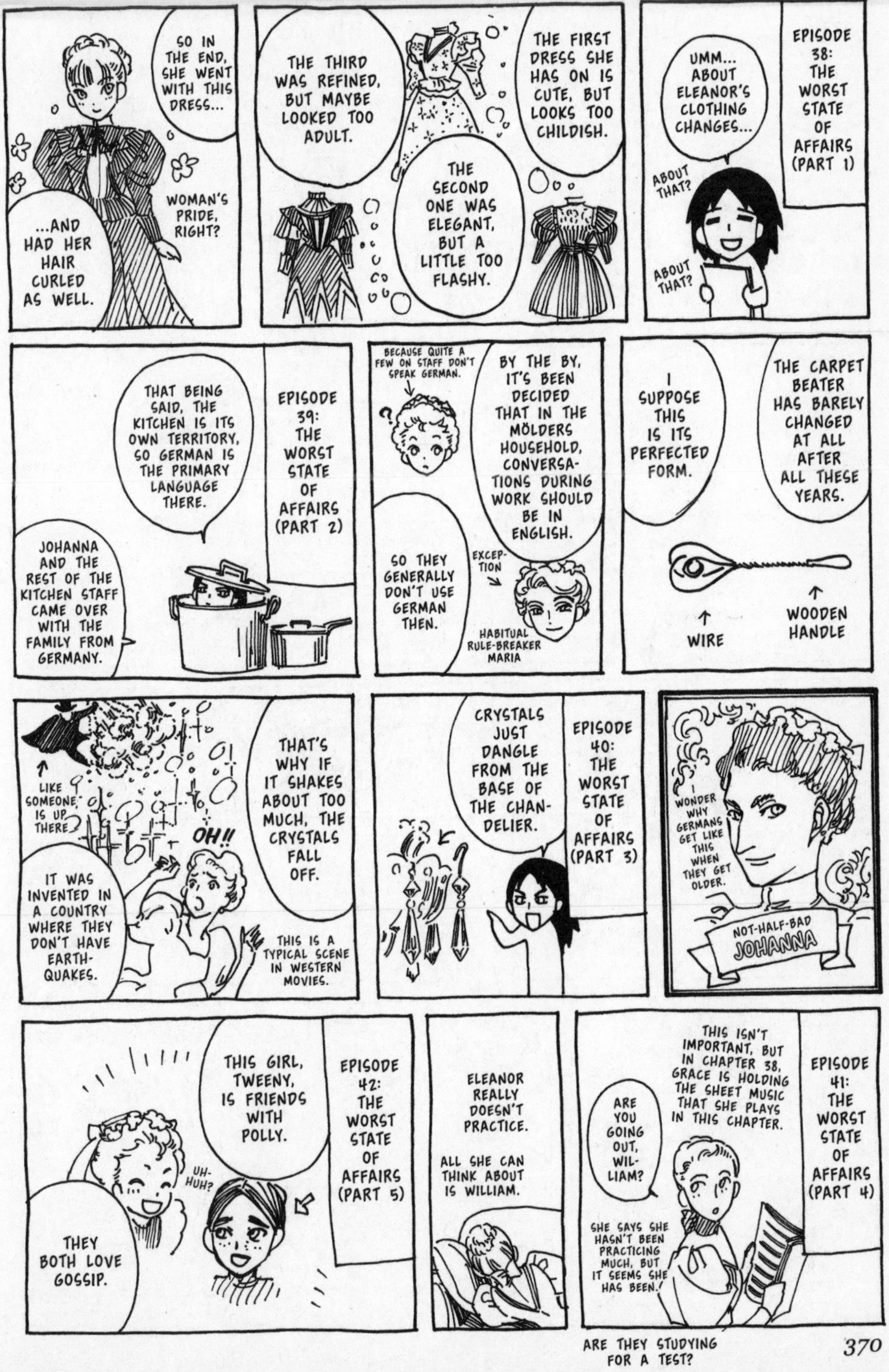
EPISODE 38: THE WORST STATE OF AFFAIRS (PART 1)
UMM... ABOUT ELEANOR'S CLOTHING CHANGES...
ABOUT THAT?
ABOUT THAT?
THE FIRST DRESS SHE HAS ON IS CUTE, BUT LOOKS TOO CHILDISH.
THE THIRD WAS REFINED, BUT MAYBE LOOKED TOO ADULT.
THE SECOND ONE WAS ELEGANT, BUT A LITTLE TOO FLASHY.
SO IN THE END, SHE WENT WITH THIS DRESS...
WOMAN'S PRIDE, RIGHT?
...AND HAD HER HAIR CURLED AS WELL.
THE CARPET BEATER HAS BARELY CHANGED AT ALL AFTER ALL THESE YEARS.
I SUPPOSE THIS IS ITS PERFECTED FORM.
WOODEN HANDLE
WIRE
BY THE BY, IT'S BEEN DECIDED THAT IN THE MÖLDERS HOUSEHOLD, CONVERSATIONS DURING WORK SHOULD BE IN ENGLISH.
BECAUSE QUITE A FEW ON STAFF DON'T SPEAK GERMAN.
EXCEPTION
HABITUAL RULE-BREAKER MARIA
SO THEY GENERALLY DON'T USE GERMAN THEN.
EPISODE 39: THE WORST STATE OF AFFAIRS (PART 2)
THAT BEING SAID, THE KITCHEN IS ITS OWN TERRITORY, SO GERMAN IS THE PRIMARY LANGUAGE THERE.
JOHANNA AND THE REST OF THE KITCHEN STAFF CAME OVER WITH THE FAMILY FROM GERMANY.
I WONDER WHY GERMANS GET LIKE THIS WHEN THEY GET OLDER.
NOT-HALF-BAD JOHANNA
EPISODE 40: THE WORST STATE OF AFFAIRS (PART 3)
CRYSTALS JUST DANGLE FROM THE BASE OF THE CHANDELIER.
THAT'S WHY IF IT SHAKES ABOUT TOO MUCH, THE CRYSTALS FALL OFF.
THIS IS A TYPICAL SCENE IN WESTERN MOVIES.
LIKE SOMEONE IS UP THERE
OH!!
IT WAS INVENTED IN A COUNTRY WHERE THEY DON'T HAVE EARTHQUAKES.
EPISODE 41: THE WORST STATE OF AFFAIRS (PART 4)
THIS ISN'T IMPORTANT, BUT IN CHAPTER 38, GRACE IS HOLDING THE SHEET MUSIC THAT SHE PLAYS IN THIS CHAPTER.
ARE YOU GOING OUT, WILLIAM?
SHE SAYS SHE HASN'T BEEN PRACTICING MUCH, BUT IT SEEMS SHE HAS BEEN.
ELEANOR REALLY DOESN'T PRACTICE.
ALL SHE CAN THINK ABOUT IS WILLIAM.
EPISODE 42: THE WORST STATE OF AFFAIRS (PART 5)
THIS GIRL, TWEENY, IS FRIENDS WITH POLLY.
UH-HUH?
THEY BOTH LOVE GOSSIP.

ARE THEY STUDYING FOR A TEST?

AFTERWORD TAN-TA-DAHH! MANGA!!

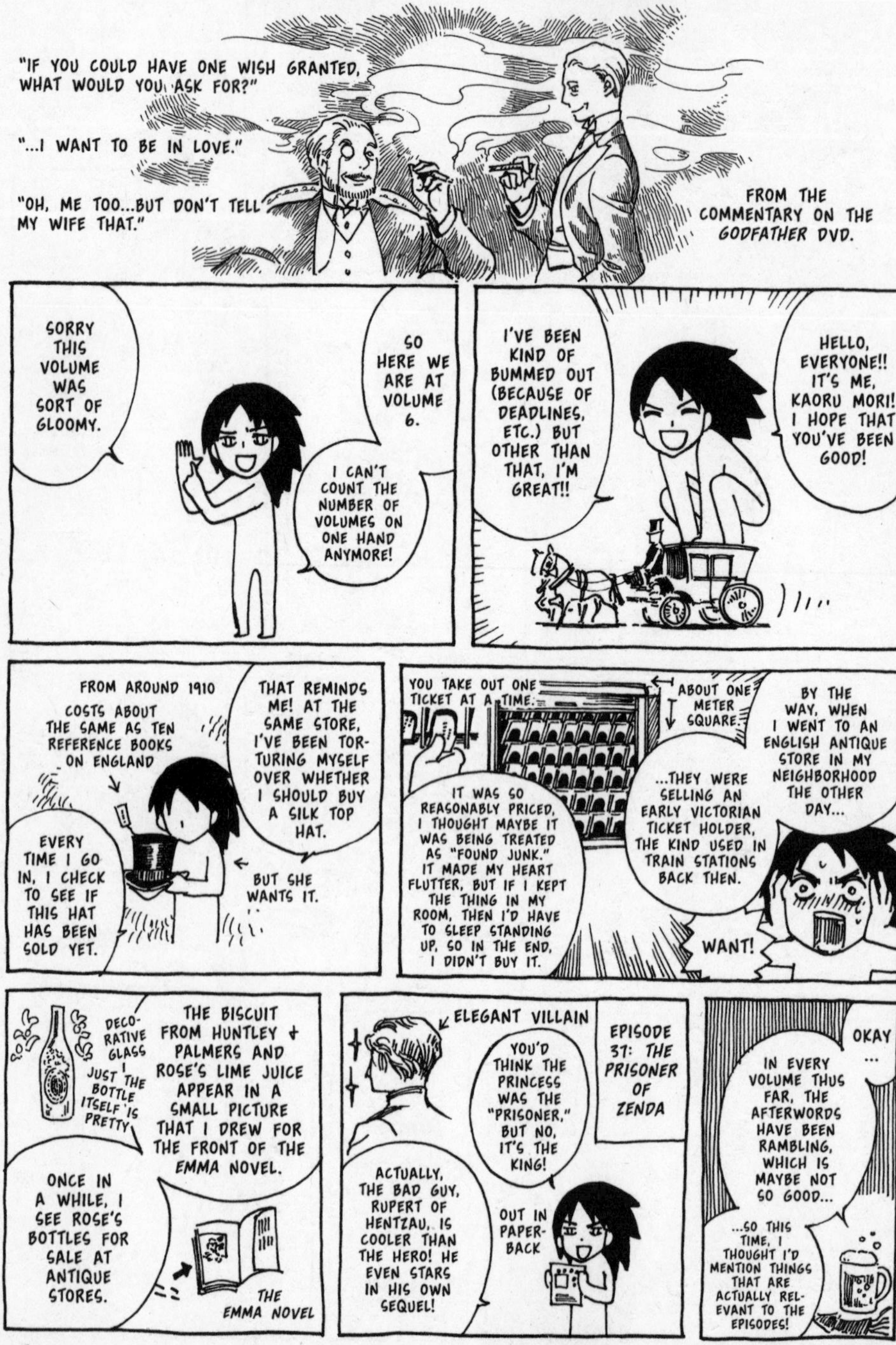
"IF YOU COULD HAVE ONE WISH GRANTED, WHAT WOULD YOU ASK FOR?"
"...I WANT TO BE IN LOVE."
"OH, ME TOO...BUT DON'T TELL MY WIFE THAT."
FROM THE COMMENTARY ON THE GODFATHER DVD.
HELLO, EVERYONE!! IT'S ME, KAORU MORI! I HOPE THAT YOU'VE BEEN GOOD!
I'VE BEEN KIND OF BUMMED OUT (BECAUSE OF DEADLINES, ETC.) BUT OTHER THAN THAT, I'M GREAT!!
SO HERE WE ARE AT VOLUME 6.
SORRY THIS VOLUME WAS SORT OF GLOOMY.
I CAN'T COUNT THE NUMBER OF VOLUMES ON ONE HAND ANYMORE!
BY THE WAY, WHEN I WENT TO AN ENGLISH ANTIQUE STORE IN MY NEIGHBORHOOD THE OTHER DAY...
ABOUT ONE METER SQUARE.
YOU TAKE OUT ONE TICKET AT A TIME.
...THEY WERE SELLING AN EARLY VICTORIAN TICKET HOLDER, THE KIND USED IN TRAIN STATIONS BACK THEN.
IT WAS SO REASONABLY PRICED, I THOUGHT MAYBE IT WAS BEING TREATED AS "FOUND JUNK." IT MADE MY HEART FLUTTER, BUT IF I KEPT THE THING IN MY ROOM, THEN I'D HAVE TO SLEEP STANDING UP, SO IN THE END, I DIDN'T BUY IT.
WANT!
THAT REMINDS ME! AT THE SAME STORE, I'VE BEEN TORTURING MYSELF OVER WHETHER I SHOULD BUY A SILK TOP HAT.
FROM AROUND 1910
COSTS ABOUT THE SAME AS TEN REFERENCE BOOKS ON ENGLAND
EVERY TIME I GO IN, I CHECK TO SEE IF THIS HAT HAS BEEN SOLD YET.
BUT SHE WANTS IT.
OKAY...
IN EVERY VOLUME THUS FAR, THE AFTERWORDS HAVE BEEN RAMBLING, WHICH IS MAYBE NOT SO GOOD...
...SO THIS TIME, I THOUGHT I'D MENTION THINGS THAT ARE ACTUALLY RELEVANT TO THE EPISODES!
EPISODE 37: THE PRISONER OF ZENDA
ELEGANT VILLAIN
YOU'D THINK THE PRINCESS WAS THE "PRISONER," BUT NO, IT'S THE KING!
ACTUALLY, THE BAD GUY, RUPERT OF HENTZAU, IS COOLER THAN THE HERO! HE EVEN STARS IN HIS OWN SEQUEL!
OUT IN PAPER-BACK
THE BISCUIT FROM HUNTLEY & PALMERS AND ROSE'S LIME JUICE APPEAR IN A SMALL PICTURE THAT I DREW FOR THE FRONT OF THE EMMA NOVEL.
DECORATIVE GLASS
JUST THE BOTTLE ITSELF IS PRETTY
ONCE IN A WHILE, I SEE ROSE'S BOTTLES FOR SALE AT ANTIQUE STORES.
THE EMMA NOVEL